## Online Statistics Workshops

www.thomsonedu.com/psychology/workshops/

One-Way ANOVA? Scatter Plots? *t* Tests? *z* Scores? It's no wonder that many students experience anxiety at the prospect of taking statistics—even its terminology can sound intimidating to the novice! And, in addition to learning a whole new language, they're learning a whole new set of skills.

Thomson Wadsworth's online statistics workshops can help by giving your students hands-on experience with statistical topics. Interactive examples, graphs, straightforward explanations, and exercises walk students through concepts that they need to understand in your course and throughout their professional career. They can visit the site any time, 24/7, for extra support and practical advice that reinforces what they cover in this text and in your class. It couldn't be more convenient!

*Note: Screens shown on these pages in one color appear in full color when you visit the websites.*

### Our statistics workshops are continually being updated and expanded. Current topics include

Scale of Measurement
Central Limit Theorem
Tests of Means
Bivariate Scatter Plots
Factorial ANOVA
Choosing the Correct Statistical Test
Sampling Distribution
Statistical Power
Central Tendency and Variability

*z* Scores
Standard Error
Hypothesis Testing
Single-Sample *t* Test
Independent versus Repeated *t* Tests
One-Way ANOVA
Two-Way ANOVA
Correlation
Chi-Square

In addition, we offer 20 workshops on research methods.
Visit www.thomsonedu.com/psychology/workshops/ today!

For a listing of symbols, see the inside back cover.

# Based on 30 years of successful teaching experience, this text puts your students on the inside track to understanding descriptive and inferential statistics.

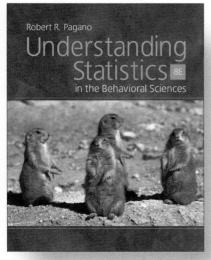

*Understanding Statistics in the Behavioral Sciences*
Eighth Edition
Robert R. Pagano

Robert R. Pagano's intuitive, concept-based approach to statistics focuses on *ideas* rather than just numbers, ensuring that your students never lose sight of the concepts that lie at the heart of sound statistical reasoning.

Pagano's presentation of descriptive material is at a level that serves as a foundation for the inference chapters while also teaching students to adequately describe data for its own sake. Next, he introduces inferential statistics using the sign test, having found that this sequence of topics promotes optimal learning among his students.

Even students who are not mathematically inclined have praised this text for its clarity, detail, interesting examples, and use of humor. It's a combination that has worked for thousands of students who are taking their first statistics course in the behavioral sciences.

## Highlights of the Eighth Edition

- **A more manageable, 18-chapter format** combines the previous chapters on "Introduction to the Analysis of Variance" and "Multiple Comparisons."
- **A new section on eta squared** appears in Chapter 15, "Introduction to the Analysis of Variance."
- **Increased coverage of confidence intervals** is included in Chapter 14, "Student's *t* Test for Correlated and Independent Groups."
- **Thorough explanations and illustrative examples** precede the introduction of every formula—and are followed by fully solved practice problems. *See pages P-2 through P-4.*
- **WebTutor™ Advantage on WebCT® or Blackboard®** combines course management capabilities with text-specific resources; for instance, students learn how to use Microsoft® Excel® to solve illustrative and practice problems using conceptual equations. Also includes material previously found on the book companion CD-ROM. *See page P-6.*
- **The expanded Book Companion Website** gives students an opportunity to learn how to solve text problems using SPSS®.

*From teaching from this text for a number of years, it is very apparent that Pagano is extremely talented in the field of statistics. His expertise really shows.*
Mary Hooten
Troy State University, Alabama

*Students have told me that the text is surprisingly easy to read. I think the introductory sections of each chapter are very well written and encourage further reading. The examples are good and usually highly relevant to the psychology student.*
Laurence Nolan
Wagner College, New York

*Turn the page to begin your preview of the text and its accompanying resources.* ▶

# Detailed explanations and clear examples . . .

Pagano describes concepts and formulas in detail in a theoretically oriented presentation that requires only high school algebra for understanding. His exposition includes varied and interesting illustrative examples, which are immediately followed by practice problems. Graphs, cartoons, and other visual aids help clarify difficult concepts while making them easier to remember.

table 10.1  Results of the marijuana experiment

| Patient No. | Experimental Condition THC Pill Food Eaten (calories) | Control Condition Placebo Pill Food Eaten (calories) | Difference Score (calories) |
|---|---|---|---|
| 1 | 1325 | 1012 | +313 |
| 2 | 1350 | 1275 | + 75 |
| 3 | 1248 | 950 | +298 |
| 4 | 1087 | 840 | +247 |
| 5 | 1047 | 942 | +105 |
| 6 | 943 | 860 | + 83 |
| 7 | 1118 | 1154 | − 36 |
| 8 | 908 | 763 | +145 |
| 9 | 1084 | 920 | +164 |
| 10 | 1088 | 876 | +212 |

Pagano introduces inferential statistics using the sign test to help students master important concepts involved in understanding hypothesis testing before they encounter more complicated inference tests. He begins by describing an interesting experiment, "Marijuana and the Treatment of AIDS Patients." Next, he shows a summary of the data, and the derived positive and negative difference scores that become the basis of analysis.

Pagano then walks through the process of evaluating the data using the sign test. He explains such key concepts as null hypothesis, alternative hypothesis, Type I and Type II errors, and others.

Note the definitions—shaded and set apart to make them readily visible to the reader. Important terms, with page references, are also summarized at the end of each chapter.

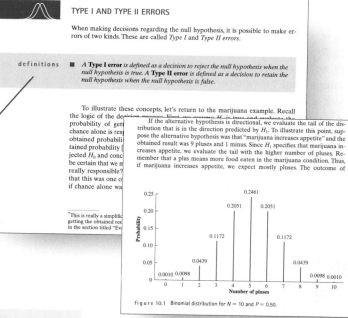

**TYPE I AND TYPE II ERRORS**

When making decisions regarding the null hypothesis, it is possible to make errors of two kinds. These are called *Type I* and *Type II* errors.

definitions ■ *A* **Type I error** *is defined as a decision to reject the null hypothesis when the null hypothesis is true. A* **Type II error** *is defined as a decision to retain the null hypothesis when the null hypothesis is false.*

To illustrate these concepts, let's return to the marijuana example. Recall the logic of the decision process. First, we assume $H_0$ is true and evaluate the probability of getting [...] chance alone is res[...] obtained probabili[...] tained probability [...] jected $H_0$ and conc[...] be certain that we n[...] really responsible?[...] that this was one of[...] if chance alone wa[...]

If the alternative hypothesis is directional, we evaluate the tail of the distribution that is in the direction predicted by $H_1$. To illustrate this point, suppose the alternative hypothesis was that "marijuana increases appetite" and the obtained result was 9 pluses and 1 minus. Since $H_1$ specifies that marijuana increases appetite, we evaluate the tail with the higher number of pluses. Remember that a plus means more food eaten in the marijuana condition. Thus, if marijuana increases appetite, we expect mostly pluses. The outcome of

*This is really a simplific[...] getting the obtained res[...] in the section titled "Ev[...]

figure 10.1  Binomial distribution for $N = 10$ and $P = 0.50$.

*The writing is perhaps the key strength of this text. I found the writing consistently engaging, very clear, and concise.*
Dennis Goff
Randolph-Macon Woman's College, Virginia

# . . . work hand-in-hand with fully solved practice problems.

Throughout the text, at least two fully solved practice problems follow the analysis of each illustrative example. This gives students immediate practice in solving problems as well as a step-by-step model against which to compare their work.

Several interesting practice problems with detailed solutions show students how to apply the concepts—and allow them to practice using the sign test to evaluate data.

sume that the appropriate criterion has been met and it is proper to use a directional $H_1$.

We are now ready to do a complete problem in exactly the same way any scientist would if he or she were using the sign test to evaluate the data.

### Practice Problem 10.1

Assume we have conducted an experiment to test the hypothesis that marijuana affects the appetites of AIDS patients. The procedure and population are the same as we described previously, except this time we have sampled 12 AIDS patients. The results are shown here (the scores are in calories):

| Condition | Patient | | | | | | | | | | | |
| --- | --- | --- | --- | --- | --- | --- | --- | --- | --- | --- | --- | --- |
| | 1 | 2 | 3 | 4 | 5 | 6 | 7 | 8 | 9 | 10 | 11 | 12 |
| THC | 1051 | 1066 | 963 | 1179 | 1144 | 912 | 1093 | 1113 | 985 | 1271 | 978 | 951 |
| Placebo | 872 | 943 | 912 | 1213 | 1034 | 854 | 1125 | 1042 | 922 | 1136 | 886 | 902 |

a. What is the nondirectional alternative hypothesis?
b. What is the null hypothesis?
c. Using $\alpha = 0.05_{2\,\text{tail}}$, what do you conclude?
d. What error may you be making by your conclusion in part **c**?
e. To what population does your conclusion apply?

The solution follows.

### SOLUTION

a. Nondirectional alternative hypothesis:  Marijuana affects appetites of AIDS patients who are being treated at your hospital.
b. Null hypothesis:  Marijuana has no effect on appetites of AIDS patients who are being treated at your hospital.
c. Conclusion, using $\alpha = 0.05_{2\,\text{tail}}$:

   **STEP 1: Calculate the number of pluses and minuses.**  The first step is to calculate the number of pluses and minuses in the sample. We have subtracted the "placebo" scores from the corresponding "THC" scores. The reverse could also have been done. There are 10 pluses and 2 minuses.

   **STEP 2: Evaluate the number of pluses and minuses.**  Once we have calculated the obtained number of pluses and minuses, we must determine the probability of getting this outcome or any

   *(continued)*

esting Using the Sign Test

ven more extreme in both directions because this is a two-ailed evaluation. The binomial distribution is appropriate for his determination. $N$ = the number of difference scores pluses and minuses) = 12. We can let $P$ = the probability of a lus with any subject. If marijuana has no effect on appetite, hance alone accounts for whether any subject scores a plus or minus. Therefore, $P = 0.50$. The obtained result was 10 luses and 2 minuses, so the number of $P$ events = 10. The robability of getting an outcome as extreme as or more ex-eme than 10 pluses (two-tailed) equals the probability of 0, , 2, 10, 11, or 12 pluses. Since the distribution is symmetrical, (0, 1, 2, 10, 11, or 12 pluses) equals $p(10, 11, \text{or } 12 \text{ pluses}) \times 2$. hus, from Table B:

Table B entry

| N | No. of $P$ Events | $P$ 0.50 |
| --- | --- | --- |
| 12 | 10 | 0.0161 |
| | 11 | 0.0029 |
| | 12 | 0.0002 |

2, 10, 11 or 12 pluses)
= $p(10, 11, \text{or } 12 \text{ pluses}) \times 2$
= $[p(10) + p(11) + p(12)] \times 2$
= $(0.0161 + 0.0029 + 0.0002) \times 2$
= $0.0384$

value would have been obtained if we had added the six prob-ogether rather than finding the one-tailed probability and mul-y 2. Since $0.0384 < 0.05$, we reject the null hypothesis. It is not ble explanation of the results. Therefore, we conclude that mar-fects appetite. It appears to increase it.

error:  By rejecting the null hypothesis, you might be making error. In reality, the null hypothesis may be true and you have t.

on:  These results apply to the population of AIDS patients ch the sample was taken.

### Practice Problem 10.2

You have good reason to believe a particular TV program is causing in-creased violence in teenagers. To test this hypothesis, you conduct an ex-periment in which 15 individuals are randomly sampled from the teenagers attending your neighborhood high school. Each subject is run in an experi-mental and a control condition. In the experimental condition, the teenagers watch the TV program for 3 months during which you record the number of violent acts committed. The control condition also lasts for

# A complete chapter on power helps bring hypothesis testing into focus.

Immediately following the chapter on the sign test, Pagano presents the concept of power in detail—simplifying the discussion by using the sign test as the vehicle for power analysis. Once the basic hypothesis testing concepts are mastered, Pagano moves on to the more complicated inference tests such as the $z$ test, $t$ test, and ANOVA.

To ease students into the topic, Pagano returns to the familiar example on the use of marijuana in treating AIDS patients. A simple graphic explains how $P_{real}$ values are a measure of the size of the real effect of the IV. Table 11.2 then shows the effect of $N$, size of real effect, and alpha level on power.

table 11.2   Calculation of power and beta

| $N$ | $H_0$ | $\alpha$ | Sample Outcomes[*] | Size of Marijuana Effect | Power | $\beta$ |
|---|---|---|---|---|---|---|
| 5 | $P_{null} = 0.50$ | $0.05_{2\,tail}$ | None | For all $P_{real}$ values | 0 | 1.0000 |
| 10 | $P_{null} = 0.50$ | $0.05_{2\,tail}$ | 0, 1, 9, or 10 pluses | $P_{real} = 1.00$ | 1.0000 | 0.0000 |
| | | | | $P_{real} = 0.90$ | 0.7361 | 0.2639 |
| | | | | $P_{real} = 0.70$ | 0.1494 | 0.8506 |
| | | | | $P_{null} = 0.50$ | [†] | |
| | | | | $P_{real} = 0.30$ | 0.1494 | 0.8506 |
| | | | | $P_{real} = 0.10$ | 0.7361 | 0.2639 |
| | | | | $P_{real} = 0.00$ | 1.0000 | 0.0000 |
| 20 | $P_{null} = 0.50$ | $0.05_{2\,tail}$ | 0–5 or 15–20 pluses | $P_{real} = 0.30$ | 0.4163 | 0.5837 |
| 20 | $P_{null} = 0.50$ | $0.01_{2\,tail}$ | 0–3 or 17–20 pluses | $P_{real} = 0.30$ | 0.1070 | 0.8930 |

[*]Sample outcomes that would result in rejecting $H_0$.
[†]See Note 11.1.

$H_0$ is false;
has real effect.
a increases appetite.
$P_{real} > 0.50$

| 0+ 10,000− | 1,000+ 9,000− | 3,000+ 7,000− | 5,000+ 5,000− | 7,000+ 3,000− | 9,000+ 1,000− | 10,000+ 0− |

| 0.00 | 0.10 | 0.30 | 0.50 | 0. |

$P_{real}$ and $P_{null}$ values

figure 11.1   Relationship among null hypothesis, size of marijuana effect, and P v

The discussion on power culminates with a section on interpreting nonsignificant results. This discussion is followed by practice problems that walk students through the use of simple mathematics in conjunction with the sign test to apply the concepts they've just learned.

## INTERPRETING NONSIGNIFICANT RESULTS

Although power aids in designing an experiment, it is much more often used when interpreting the results of an experiment that has already been conducted and that has yielded nonsignificant results. Failure to reject $H_0$ may occur because (1) $H_0$ is in fact true or (2) $H_0$ is false, but the experiment was of low power. It is due to the second possible reason that we can *never accept* $H_0$ as being correct when an experiment fails to yield significance. Instead, we say the experiment has failed to allow the null hypothesis to be rejected. It is possible that $H_0$ is indeed false, but the experiment was insensitive; that is, it didn't give $H_0$ much of a chance to be rejected. A case in point is the example we presented before with $N = 5$. In that experiment, whatever results we obtained, they would not reach significance. We could not reject $H_0$ no matter how strong the real effect actually was. It would be a gross error to accept $H_0$ as a result of doing that experiment. The experiment did not give $H_0$ any chance of being rejected. *From this viewpoint, we can see that every experiment exists to give $H_0$ a chance to be rejected. The higher the power, the more the experiment allows $H_0$ to be rejected if it is false.*

Perhaps an analogy will help in understanding this point. We can liken the power of an experiment to the use of a microscope. Physiological psychologists

## Additional Content Highlights

- Correlation (Chapter 6) is introduced before regression (Chapter 7); both are introduced early in the descriptive statistics part of the book.

- Explanations are integrated with equations when discussing inference tests. Empirically derived sampling distributions promote understanding of each inference test.

- A summary chapter ties all of inference testing together, and gives students practice in determining the correct inference test to use across a wide variety of experiments. A decision-tree diagram helps determine the correct test.

*Some students are conversant in algebra. . . . Many students who find mathematics difficult prefer to have statistics taught through graphs, charts, and diagrams. This text strikes a good balance, explaining statistical concepts with both algebraic equations and with well-designed charts and graphs.*
Kirk McClure
University of Kansas

# Applications offer insight into the use of statistics in the real world.

## What Is the Truth?

*What Is the Truth?* sections—typically based on an advertisement or news article—appear in most chapters. Beginning with a brief introduction that focuses students' attention and sparks deeper thought, these interesting and often amusing segments illustrate the practical applications of statistics while helping students become more discerning in evaluating data. For instance, "Data, Data, Where Are the Data?" reviews an ad that offers no experimental data to back up its claims.

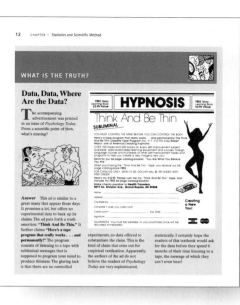

# Problems can be solved with calculators, Microsoft® Excel,® or SPSS.®

## Coded End-of-Chapter Problems

End-of-chapter problems are coded with keywords to identify a specific area within psychology and related fields where the problem is applied. (Specific areas include cognitive, social, developmental, biological, clinical, industrial/organizational, and health psychology, education, and other fields.) This identification is useful to instructors who wish to assign problems by area, as well as to students who want to see how broadly statistical concepts can be applied.

## Assistance with Excel and SPSS

Through **WebTutor Advantage,** students can learn to use Microsoft Excel (rather than computational equations and hand calculators) to solve problems as they work with conceptual equations and raw scores. In addition to these methods of solving illustrative, practice, and homework problems, students are taught to use SPSS in conjunction with solving homework problems in each relevant chapter of the text.

*The book is very well written and it has a lot of examples and practice problems.*
Robert Heredia
Texas A&M International University

# Combine course management with extensive self-help features for students!

## WebTutor™ Advantage on WebCT® and Blackboard®

www.thomsonedu.com/webtutor

*Screens appear in full color on the website.*

Creating an engaging e-learning environment is easier than ever with **WebTutor Advantage**. You'll save time building or web-enhancing your course, posting course materials, incorporating multimedia, tracking progress, and more with this customizable, engaging course management tool.

**WebTutor Advantage** also enhances your students' learning with text-specific learning tools. Material previously found on the book companion CD-ROM has been completely revised and, along with newly added material, provides extensive self-help features for students. And because WebTutor Advantage is available on WebCT® or Blackboard,® students' quiz results can flow directly into these platforms' online gradebooks.

For each chapter, as appropriate, **WebTutor Advantage** includes
- a detailed chapter outline
- learning objectives
- a drag-and-drop game for review of equations, concepts, and other material
- auditory flashcards (with MP3 downloads)
- symbols review chart
- text illustrative problems and text practice problems solved using raw scores with Microsoft Excel
- SPSS problems and solutions
- additional problems solved using computational equations
- a chapter quiz

## Ordering Information

WebTutor Advantage on WebCT packaged with each student text: 0-495-26211-0
WebTutor Advantage on Blackboard packaged with each student text: 0-495-26212-9

# Other Teaching and Learning Resources

## For Instructors

### Instructor's Manual with Test Bank

0-495-09641-5

Written by Robert R. Pagano, the **Instructor's Manual with Test Bank** contains teaching advice; chapter outlines; and approximately 50 multiple-choice, seven short answer, and 15 true/false test questions for every text chapter. It also includes answers to selected textbook problems.

### ExamView® Computerized Testing

0-495-09642-3

**ExamView®** contains all **Test Bank** questions in electronic format, allowing you to create, deliver, and customize tests and study guides (both print and online) in minutes. **ExamView** offers both a Quick Test Wizard and an Online Test Wizard that guide you step-by-step through the process of creating tests, while the unique "WYSIWYG" capability allows you to see the test you are creating on the screen exactly as it will look when printed or displayed online.

### Electronic Transparencies on the Web

0-495-09644-X

Figures and tables from the text are available to you in Microsoft® PowerPoint® format.

### JoinIn™ on TurningPoint®

0-495-09646-6

**JoinIn™ on TurningPoint®** content and software for student classroom response systems tailored to this text allows you to transform your classroom and assess your students' progress with instant in-class quizzes and polls. Pose book-specific questions and display students' answers seamlessly within the Microsoft® PowerPoint® slides of your own lecture, in conjunction with the "clicker" hardware of your choice.

## For Both Students and Instructors

### Book Companion Website

www.thomsonedu.com/psychology/pagano

Here's a great way to make teaching and learning more interactive. Expanded and updated, this site gives students a great opportunity to learn how to solve textbook problems using SPSS. It also contains chapter quizzes and an extended discussion of the Mann-Whitney *U* Test. As students read the text, they'll see references to these materials at the end of each chapter as appropriate.

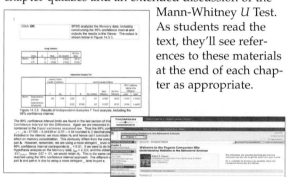

### Online Statistics Workshops

www.thomsonedu.com/psychology/workshops/

Thomson Wadsworth's online workshops give students hands-on experience with statistical topics. Interactive examples, graphs, explanations, and exercises guide students toward a better understanding of a variety of concepts—even the most difficult ones. Topics include statistical power, sampling distribution, one-way ANOVA, two-way ANOVA, and the single-sample *t* test.

### InfoTrac® College Edition

Packaged with each student text: 0-495-26214-5

Catch up on the news and save time by doing research right from your desktop! This searchable online university library contains more than 18 million reliable, full-length articles from 5,000 academic and popular periodicals (including *Psychology Today*, *The New York Times*, *Newsweek*, *Science*, *Forbes*, and *USA Today*). You and your students also have access to InfoMarks®—stable URLs that you can link to articles, journals, and searches to save time when doing research. In addition, students can visit the InfoWrite online resource center for guides to writing research papers, grammar help, critical thinking tips, and more.

# Student Resources

## Study Guide

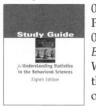

0-495-09643-1
Packaged with the text:
0-495-26213-7
*By William C. Follette and Robert Pagano*
Written to work hand in hand with this text, this comprehensive review of each chapter's material includes an outline, programmed learning concept review, exercises with answers, true/false questions with answers, and a self-quiz in multiple-choice format with answers.

## A Simple Guide to SPSS® for Windows for Versions 12.0 and 13.0

0-495-09036-0
Packaged with the text:
0-495-25888-1
*By Lee A. Kirkpatrick, College of William and Mary; and Brooke C. Feeney, Carnegie Mellon University*
This no-nonsense, streamlined guide provides a thorough introduction to Versions 12.0 and 13.0 of the powerful SPSS software. With this guide, your students can learn how to use SPSS to perform all of the statistical procedures covered by a typical introductory statistics text—from histograms and descriptive statistics through correlation, regression, *t* tests, and analysis of variance. This book will help you to use SPSS to complete home-work problems or to conduct statistical analysis for a research project.

## The Video Guide for SPSS® Version 13.0

0-534-59204-X
Packaged with the text:
0-495-25890-3
*Created by Mark S. Saviano, Brandeis University*
This unique media package provides students with an on-screen SPSS tutor with hours of video files on CD-ROM that lead your students through how to use SPSS. Students can watch the video files on their computer with SPSS open at the same time, allowing for direct and immediate answers.

## The Excel Statistics Companion CD-ROM and Manual, Version 2.0

0-495-18695-3
Packaged with the text:
0-495-25889-X
*By Kenneth M. Rosenberg, State University of New York, Oswego*
This collection of demonstrations, sampling experiments, and interactive exercises dovetails with traditional textbook coverage of descriptive and inferential statistics. The materials give students the hands-on experience they need to master abstract statistical concepts and computational procedures. Microsoft Excel's spreadsheet capabilities for data generation and instant dynamic response to user input provide a platform for learning statistics that goes beyond the usual verbal and visual text-book explanations. All the workbooks on this CD-ROM contain detailed on-screen instructions. For students who are novices in Microsoft® Windows® and/or Microsoft Excel, additional documentation (with extensive use of screen captures) appears in the companion **User's Manual**.

# Understanding Statistics
# in the Behavioral Sciences

# Understanding Statistics in the Behavioral Sciences

EDITION **8**

## Robert R. Pagano

*University of Pittsburgh*

**THOMSON** ™

**WADSWORTH**

Australia • Canada • Mexico • Singapore • Spain
United Kingdom • United States

# THOMSON

✦
TM

## WADSWORTH

*Understanding Statistics in the Behavioral Sciences,* **Eighth Edition**

*Robert R. Pagano*

Publisher: Vicki Knight
Assistant Editor: Jennifer Alexander
Editorial Assistant: Sheila Walsh
Technology Project Manager: Adrian Paz
Marketing Manager: Caroline Croley
Marketing Assistant: Natasha Coats
Marketing Communications Manager: Kelley McAllister
Project Manager, Editorial Production: Catherine Morris
Creative Director: Rob Hugel
Senior Art Director: Vernon Boes
Print Buyer: Doreen Suruki

Permissions Editor: Roberta Broyer
Production Service: Graphic World Publishing Services
Compositor: Graphic World Inc.
Text Designer: E. Kelly Shoemaker
Copy Editor: Graphic World Publishing Services
Illustrator: Graphic World Illustration Studio
Cover Designer: Irene Morris
Cover Image: Acclaim Images
Text and Cover Printer: Transcontinental Printing/
 Louiseville

**Thomson Higher Education**
**10 Davis Drive**
**Belmont, CA 94002-3098**
**USA**

For more information about our products, contact us at:
**Thomson Learning Academic Resource Center**
**1-800-423-0563**

For permission to use material from this text or product, submit a request online at
**http://www.thomsonrights.com.**
Any additional questions about permissions can be submitted by e-mail to **thomsonrights@thomson.com.**

Library of Congress Control Number: 2006925809

Student Edition: ISBN 0-495-09638-5

*I dedicate this eighth edition to those who seek to lead the good life.
May you come to understand how important data-based decision making
and, hence, statistics are to your quest.*

## ABOUT THE AUTHOR

Robert R. Pagano received a Bachelor of Electrical Engineering degree from Rensselaer Polytechnic Institute in 1956 and a Ph.D. in Biological Psychology from Yale University in 1965. He was Assistant Professor and Associate Professor in the Department of Psychology at the University of Washington, Seattle, Washington, from 1965 to 1989. He was Associate Chairman of the Department of Neuroscience at the University of Pittsburgh, Pittsburgh, Pennsylvania, from 1990 to June 2000. While at the Department of Neuroscience, in addition to his other duties, he served as Director of Undergraduate Studies, was the departmental adviser for undergraduate majors, taught both undergraduate and graduate statistics courses, and served as a statistical consultant for departmental faculty. Bob was also Director of the Statistical Cores for two NIH center grants in schizophrenia and Parkinson's disease. He retired from the University of Pittsburgh in June 2000. Bob's research interests are in the psychobiology of learning and memory, and the physiology of consciousness. He has taught courses in introductory statistics at the University of Washington and at the University of Pittsburgh for over thirty years. He has been a finalist for the outstanding teaching award at the University of Washington for his teaching of introductory statistics.

Bob is married to Carol A. Eikleberry and they have a 16-year-old son, Robby. In addition, Bob has five grown daughters, Renee, Laura, Maria, Elizabeth, and Christina, and one granddaughter, Mikaela. Retirement presents new opportunities for him that complement his interests in teaching and writing. Bob loves tennis and is presently training for a shot at the U.S. Open (although thus far he is having difficulty besting his daughter Laura). He also loves the outdoors, especially hiking, and his morning coffee. His favorite cities to visit are Santa Fe, Santa Barbara, and San Diego.

BRIEF CONTENTS

CONTENTS

CHAPTER 15     **Introduction to the Analysis of Variance   358**

**PREFACE**

I have been teaching a course in introductory statistics for more than 30 years, first within the Department of Psychology at the University of Washington, and most recently within the Department of Neuroscience at the University of Pittsburgh. This textbook is the mainstay of the course. Most of my students have been psychology majors, but many have also come from biology, business, education, neuroscience, nursing, and other fields. Because most of these students do not have high aptitude for mathematics and are not well grounded in mathematical skills, I have used an informal rather than strictly mathematical approach. This approach assumes only high school algebra for background knowledge. It relies on clarity of presentation, a particularly effective sequencing of the inferential material, detailed verbal description, interesting illustrative examples, and many fully solved practice problems to help students understand the material.

My statistics course has been quite successful. Students are able to grasp the material, even the more complicated topics like "power," and at the same time, many even enjoy learning it. Student ratings of this course have been quite high. They rate the textbook even higher, saying among other things that it is very clear; they like the touches of humor and state that it helps them to have the material presented in such great detail.

In preparing this eighth edition, I have again been guided by advice and feedback from students and professors. I am very pleased that this feedback has been quite positive. Even so, there were three recommended changes that I have adopted. The first change has been made in Chapter 14, "Student's $t$ Test for Correlated and Independent Groups." At the end of this chapter, I added a section on how to evaluate the effect of the independent variable using a confidence interval approach. Second, in Chapter 15, "Introduction to the Analysis of Variance," I have included a new section on eta squared ($\eta^2$), a second measure of the size of effect. The third change made in the eighth edition doesn't involve new material. Instead, it combines two chapters of the textbook that had already existed in the seventh edition. Chapter 15, "Introduction to the Analysis of Variance," and Chapter 16, "Multiple Comparisons," from the seventh edition have been combined into one chapter, Chapter 15.

In addition to these changes, I have made two other more minor changes. In Chapter 14, in the section on "Size of Effect," I have added Cohen's size of effect criteria so that students will have a yardstick to judge whether the IV effect is small, medium, or large. The other change was made to prevent Chapters 14 and 15 from becoming too long. To prevent this from happening, I have moved Practice Problem 14.2, Practice Problem 14.3, and the demonstration that $F = t^2$ to the Web.

In addition to these changes in the textbook, there have been extensive changes made in the auxiliary material. The CD that accompanied the seventh edition has been eliminated and most of the material it contained has been moved to the Web. The new auxiliary Web material is as follows: First, there are SPSS problems and solutions for each chapter in the textbook as appropriate. This material teaches students to solve problems using SPSS. It replaces the SPSS problems that were contained on the CD. This material also contains SPSS data files for downloading directly into the SPSS Data Editor. Second, a lot of new material, plus some of the CD material, is now available over the Internet via WebTutor. WebTutor is an online course management system for presenting educational material to students and communicating results to instructors. It uses the Blackboard and Web-CT platforms. WebTutor contains the following material for each chapter as appropriate: a detailed chapter outline; a section on what the student should know and be able to do; a drag-and-drop game for review of equations, concepts, and other material; flash cards for review of terms; auditory flash cards for MP3 players to review terms; problems solved using Microsoft Excel; problems solved using SPSS; more practice problems solved using computational equations; and a chapter quiz. The last change is that the extended discussion of the Mann–Whitney $U$ Test that was contained on the CD is now available online via the Web.

Thus the eighth edition of the textbook, plus the auxiliary material, gives students three options for solving problems, plus extensive self-help material. Students can solve problems using computational equations and hand calculators, using conceptual equations and Excel, and via SPSS. One suggested procedure for each chapter, if time and resources permit, is to have students solve illustrative, practice, and one or two end-of-chapter problems using hand calculators or Excel and one or two end-of-chapter problems using SPSS.

## Textbook Rationale

This is an introductory textbook that covers both descriptive and inferential statistics. It is intended for students majoring in the behavioral sciences. For many of these students, statistics is a subject that elicits considerable anxiety and that is avoided for as long as possible. Moreover, I think it is fair to say that when the usual undergraduate course is completed, many students have not understood much of the inferential statistics material. This is partly because the material is inherently difficult and the students themselves are not proficient in mathematics. However, in my opinion, this situation also exists because most textbooks do a poor job of explaining inferential statistics to this group of students. These texts usually err in one or more of the following ways: (1) They are not clearly written; (2) they are not sufficiently detailed; (3) they present the material too mathematically; (4) they present the material at too low a level; (5) they do not give a sufficient number of fully solved problems for the student to practice on; and (6) in inferential statistics, they use an inappropriate sequence of topics, beginning with the sampling distribution of the mean.

In this and the previous seven editions, I have tried to correct such deficiencies by using an informal writing style; using a clearly written, detailed, and theoretically oriented presentation that requires only high school algebra for understanding; including many interesting, fully solved practice problems that are located immediately following the relevant expository material; and using a better sequencing of the inferential material.

I believe a key to understanding inferential statistics is the material presented in the beginning inferential chapters and its sequencing. In my opinion, optimal learning of the material occurs by using the sign test as the first inference test encountered by the student and by using the following sequence of topics: random sampling and probability, binomial distribution, introduction to hypothesis testing using the sign test, power, sampling distributions (including their empirical generation), sampling distribution of the mean, $z$ test for single samples, $t$ test for single samples, confidence intervals, $t$ test for correlated and independent groups, introduction to analysis of variance (including multiple companions), two-way ANOVA, nonparametric tests, and finally, a review of all of inferential statistics.

At the heart of statistical inference lies the concept of "sampling distribution." The first sampling distribution discussed by most texts is the sampling distribution of the mean. The problem with this approach is that the sampling distribution of the mean cannot be generated from simple probability considerations, which makes it hard for students to understand. This problem is compounded by the fact that most texts do not attempt to generate the sampling distribution of the mean in a concrete way. Rather, they define it theoretically, as a probability distribution that would result if an infinite number of random samples of size $N$ were taken from the population and the mean of each sample were calculated. This definition is far too abstract for students, especially when this is their initial contact the *idea* of sampling distributions. *When students fail to grasp the concept of sampling distributions, they fail to grasp the rest of inferential statistics.* What appears to happen is that since students do not understand the material conceptually, they are forced to memorize the equations and to solve problems rotely. Thus, students are often able to solve the problems without genuinely understanding what they are doing, all because they fail to comprehend the essence of sampling distributions.

To impart a basic understanding of sampling distributions, I believe it is far better to begin with the sign test (Chapter 10), a simple inference test for which the binomial distribution is the appropriate sampling distribution. The binomial distribution is very easy to understand, and it can be derived from the basic probability rules developed in an earlier chapter (Chapter 8, "Random Sampling and Probability"). It is entirely dependent on simple, logical considerations. Hence, students can easily follow its generation. Moreover, it can also be generated by the same empirical process that is used later in the text for generating the sampling distribution of the mean. It therefore serves as an important bridge to understanding all the sampling distributions discussed later in the textbook. Introducing hypothesis testing with the sign test has other advantages. All of the important concepts involving hypothesis testing can be illustrated; for example, null hypothesis, alternative hypothesis, alpha level, Type I and Type II errors, size of effect, and power. The sign test also provides an illustration of the before-after (repeated measures) design, which is a superior way to begin, as most students are familiar with this type of experiment and the logic of the design is quite easy to follow.

Chapter 11 discusses power. Many texts do not discuss power at all or, if they do, leave it until near the end of the book. Power is a complicated topic. Using the sign test as the vehicle for a power analysis simplifies matters. Understanding power is necessary if one is to grasp the methodology of scientific investigation itself. When students gain insight into power, they can see why we bother discussing Type II errors. Furthermore, they see for the first time why we conclude by "retaining $H_0$" as a reasonable explanation of the data rather than by "accepting $H_0$ as true" (a most important distinction). In this same vein, students also appreciate the error involved when one concludes that two conditions are equal from data that are not statistically significant. Thus, power is a topic that brings the whole hypothesis testing methodology into sharp focus.

At this state of the exposition, a diligent student can grasp the idea that data analysis basically involves two steps: (1) calculating the appropriate statistic and (2) evaluating the statistic based on its sampling distribution. The time is ripe for a formal discussion of sampling distributions and how they can be generated (Chapter 12). After this, the sampling distribution of the mean is introduced. Rather than depending on an abstract theoretical definition of the sampling distribution of the mean, the text discusses how this sampling distribution can be generated empirically. This gives a much more concrete understanding of the sampling distribution of the mean.

Due to previous experience with one easily understood sampling distribution, the binomial distribution, and using the empirical approach for the sampling distribution of the mean, most conscientious students have a good grasp of what sampling distributions are and why they are essential for inferential statistics. Since the sampling distributions underlying Student's $t$ test and the analysis of variance are also explained in terms of their empirical generation, students can understand the use of these tests rather than just rotely solving problems. With this background, students can comprehend that all of the concepts of hypothesis testing are the same as we go from statistic to statistic. What varies from experiment to experiment is the statistic used and its accompanying sampling distribution. The stage is set for moving through the remaining inference tests.

Chapters 12, 13, 14, and 17 discuss, in a fairly conventional way, the $z$ test and $t$ test for single samples, the $t$ test for correlated and independent groups, and nonparametric statistics. However, these chapters differ from those in other textbooks in the clarity of presentation, the number and interest value of fully solved problems, and the use of empirically derived sampling distributions. In addition, there are differences that are specific to each test. For example, (1) the $t$ test for correlated groups is introduced directly after the $t$ test for single samples and is developed as a special case of the $t$ test for single samples, only this time using difference scores rather than raw scores; (2) the sign test and the $t$ test for correlated groups are compared to illustrate the difference in power that results from using one or the other; (3) there is a discussion of the factors influencing the power of experiments using Student's t test; and (4) the correlated and independent groups designs are compared with regard to utility.

Chapters 15 and 16 deal with the analysis of variance. In these chapters, single rather than double subscript notation is deliberately used. The more complex double subscript notation serves to confuse students. In my view, the single subscript notation and resulting single summations work better for the undergraduate major in psychology and related fields because they are simpler, and for this audience, they promote understanding of this reasonably complicated material. In using single subscript notation I have followed in part the notation used by E. Minium, *Sta-*

*tistical Reasoning in Psychology and Education*, 2nd edition, John Wiley & Sons, New York, 1978. I am indebted to Professor Minium for this contribution.

Other features of this textbook are worth noting. Chapter 8, on probability, does not delve deeply into probability theory. This is not necessary because the proper mathematical foundation for all of the inference tests contained in this textbook can be built by the use of basic probability definitions, in conjunction with the addition and multiplication rules, as has been done in Chapter 8. Chapter 15, covering both planned and *post hoc* comparisons, discusses two *post hoc* tests, the Tukey HSD test and the Newman–Keuls test. Chapter 16 is a separate chapter on two-way ANOVA for instructors wishing to cover this topic in depth. For instructors with insufficient time for in-depth handling of two-way ANOVA, at the beginning of Chapter 16 I have qualitatively described the two-way ANOVA technique, emphasizing the concepts of main effects and interactions. Chapter 18 is a review chapter that brings together all of the inference tests and provides practice in determining which test to use when analyzing data from different experimental designs and data of different levels of scaling. Students especially like the tree diagram in this chapter for helping them determine the appropriate test. Finally, at various places throughout the text, there are sections titled "What Is the Truth?" These sections show students practical applications of statistics.

Some comments about the descriptive statistics part of this book are in order. The descriptive material is written at a level that (1) serves as a foundation for the inference chapters and (2) enables students to adequately describe the data for its own sake. For the most part, material on descriptive statistics follows a traditional format, because this works well. Chapter 1 is an exception. It discusses approaches for determining truth and establishes statistics as part of the scientific method, which is rather unusual for a statistics textbook.

## Eighth Edition Changes

New Material   As mentioned earlier, because of positive feedback from reviewers of the seventh edition, changes for the eighth edition are few. Thus there are only three major and two minor changes in the textbook itself. However, there have been major changes made in the ancillaries.

- ◆ **A New Section Titled "Evaluating the Effect of the Independent Variable Using Confidence Intervals–Independent Groups Design" (in Chapter 14).** The first change has been made in Chapter 14, "Student's *t* Test for Correlated and Independent Groups." At the end of this chapter, I added a section on how to evaluate the effect of the independent variable using a confidence interval approach. In recent years there has been a bit of a trend toward analyzing the data of experiments using the confidence interval approach instead of the null-hypothesis testing approach. Two reviewers felt this trend has reached a level that I should include a discussion of it. After surveying the research literature, and in light of these reviewers' recommendations, I decided not to include extensive coverage of this topic at this time. This because it is a complicated topic and because, in my opinion, usage to date doesn't warrant extensive coverage in an introductory statistics textbook. However, I do think that it deserves some discussion, hence this new section at the end of Chapter 14.

- ◆ **A New Section Titled "Eta Squared ($\eta^2$)" (in Chapter 15).** This section discusses eta squared ($\eta^2$), a measure of the size of effect. This is the second measure of the size of effect discussed in Chapter 15. One reviewer recommended this change. Accordingly, I did a survey of the research literature, which revealed that even though $\eta^2$ gives a biased estimate of the size of effect, it is currently used much more often than $\hat{\omega}^2$ (the first measure discussed) for reporting size of effect in ANOVA designs. For this reason I thought students should be aware of $\eta^2$ and know how to compute it. Hence, a new section on this topic was added.

- **Chapter 15 and Chapter 16 Combined into One Chapter, Chapter 15.** The third change made in the eight edition doesn't involve new material. Instead it combines two chapters of the textbook that already existed in the seventh edition, Chapter 15 and Chapter 16. Chapter 15 in the seventh edition discussed doing an overall $F$ test in conjunction with one-way ANOVA. Chapter 16 in the seventh edition discussed the multiple comparisons that ordinarily would be done following an analysis resulting in a significant $F_{obt}$ value. Since in practice, after finding a significant $F_{obt}$ value, one almost always conducts multiple comparisons to determine which groups differ from each other as part of the ANOVA analysis, it makes sense to have both discussed in the same chapter. Therefore I have combined both chapters into Chapter 15 in the eighth edition.

- **Cohen's Size of Effect Criteria Have Been Added to the Section Titled "Size of Effect" (in Chapter 14).** This gives students a yardstick to judge whether the effect of the independent variable is small, medium, or large.

- **Practice Problem 14.2, Practice Problem 14.3, and the demonstration that $F = t^2$ have been moved to the Web.** This has been done to keep Chapter 14 and Chapter 15 from becoming too long.

Ancillary Package   The supplements consist of:

- A **student's study guide** that is intended for review and consolidation of the material contained in each chapter of the textbook. Each chapter of the study guide has a chapter outline, a programmed learning concept review, exercises and answers to exercises, true/false questions and answers, and an end-of-chapter self-quiz with answers. Many students have commented on the helpfulness of this study guide. (0-495-09643-1)

- An **instructor's manual with test bank** that contains teaching advice, chapter outlines for the textbook material, test questions for each chapter, and answers to selected end-of-chapter problems contained in the textbook. The test questions for each chapter are short answer, multiple-choice, and true/false questions. The answers to the multiple-choice and true/false questions are given in bold type to the left of the question. Because of requests from instructors, I have not included answers to *all* the computational end-of-chapter problems found in the text; instead, I have omitted answers from at least one problem in each chapter. These answers are found at the end of the instructor's manual. (0-495-09641-5)

- **SPSS Problems and Solutions.** This material, available via the Web, teaches students to solve problems for each chapter in the textbook as appropriate, using SPSS. It replaces the SPSS problems that were contained on the CD. This material also contains SPSS data files for downloading directly into the SPSS Data Editor. The SPSS problems and solutions are available on the Book Companion Website at www.thomsonedu.com/psychology/ pagano. For more training in SPSS than is offered in this material, I recommend L. A. Kirkpatrick and B. C. Feeney, *A Simple Guide for SPSS for Windows for Version 12.0 & 13.0,* Wadsworth, Belmont, CA, 2006. It comes with or without the Student Software disc. The manual is available from Wadsworth, alone (ISBN 0-495-09036-0) or bundled with a disc containing the student version of SPSS. Either may be bundled with the textbook if so desired.

- ◆ **Chapter Quiz.** Each chapter has a quiz that students can use to test their understanding of the chapter. These quizzes are available on the Book Companion Website at www.thomsonedu.com/psychology/pagano.

- ◆ **Mann–Whitney *U* Test Chapter.** The extended discussion of the Mann–Whitney *U* Test that was contained on the CD is now available on the Book Companion Website at www.thomsonedu.com/psychology/pagano.

- ◆ **WebTutor.** In the eighth edition, some of the CD material plus extensive new material is presented over the Internet via WebTutor. WebTutor is an online course management system for presenting educational material to students and communicating results to instructors. It uses the Blackboard and WebCT platforms. For the eighth edition of this textbook, WebTutor contains the following sections for each chapter as appropriate:

  - ▪ **Detailed Chapter Outline.**
  - ▪ **What the Student Should Know and Be Able to Do.**
  - ▪ **Drag & Drop Game for Review of Equations, Concepts, and Other Material.** This is essentially a matching game that aids students in applying and memorizing equations and in reviewing other conceptual material.
  - ▪ **Flash Cards for Review of Terms.** This is comprised of online flash cards to help students memorize the definitions of important terms.
  - ▪ **Auditory Flash Cards for MP3 Players.** Allows students to download from the Web auditory flash cards of terms and definitions to help them memorize the definitions of important terms.
  - ▪ **Flash Cards for Review of Symbols.** Helps students memorize symbols and the concepts for which they stand.
  - ▪ **Problems Solved Using Excel.** Students are taught to solve illustrative and practice problems for each chapter in the textbook as appropriate, using Excel, conceptual equations, and raw scores. This allows instructors who would prefer to use conceptual equations rather than computational equations to do so. It also gives students training in using Excel, which is superior to using a hand calculator. For extensive training in using Excel to learn statistics, I recommend K. M. Rosenberg, *The Excel Statistics Companion CD-ROM and Manual, Version 2,* Wadsworth, Belmont, CA, 2004 (ISBN 0-495-18695-3). This companion can be bundled with the textbook if so desired.
  - ▪ **Problems Solved Using SPSS.** This section contains the same material as mentioned previously under "SPSS Problems and Solutions." It teaches students to solve problems for each chapter in the textbook as appropriate, using SPSS. This section also contains SPSS data files for downloading directly into the SPSS Data Editor.
  - ▪ **More Problems Solved Using Computational Equations.** Additional practice problems are completely solved using computational equations. These are essentially the same additional practice problems and solutions that were contained on the CD that accompanied the seventh edition.
  - ▪ **Chapter Quiz.** This is the same chapter quiz that was mentioned previously in connection with the Book Companion Website.

## Acknowledgments

Many individuals have been helpful in the development and production of this edition. First I would like to acknowledge the excellent work of the Wadsworth staff. While all deserve my thanks, two individuals stand out especially. First and foremost is Vicki Knight, my editor. I want to thank her for her very high standards, her availability to me despite a very heavy workload, her developmental skills and her willingness to go the extra mile to produce a high-quality product. Next, I would like to thank Adrian Paz, Technology Project Manager. Without his technical skills, tireless efforts, high energy, and willingness to implement new ideas, none of the Web material would have been possible. I give him very high praise. The remaining Wadsworth staff that I would like to thank are Jennifer Alexander, Assistant Editor; Sheila Walsh, Editorial Assistant; Catherine Morris, Content Project Manager; Vernon Boes, Senior Art Director; Roberta Broyer, Permissions Editor; Dory Schaeffer and Caroline Croley, Marketing Managers; Kelley McAllister, Marketing Communications; and Natasha Coats, Marketing Assistant.

I am grateful to Marlene Veach, Marlene Veach Marketing Communications, for the fine work she did on the Visual Preface. I am very thankful to Mike Ederer, Production Editor, Graphic World Publishing Services, who made the book production go smoothly.

I wish to thank the following reviewers for their valuable comments regarding past editions:

Bryan Auday, Gordon College
David Bennett, Simmons College
Michael Biderman, University of Tennessee at Chattanooga
Michael Brown, University of Washington
James Diefendorff, Louisiana State University
Virginia Diehl, Western Illinois University
Jean Doerr, SUNY Fredonia
Dennis Doverspike, University of Akron
Thomas Eissenbert, Virginia Commonwealth University
David Falcone, LaSalle University
Penny Fidler, California State University, Long Beach
Michael Gardner, California State University, Northridge
William Gibson, Northern Arizona University
Roderick Gillis, University of Miami
Tim Goldsmith, University of New Mexico
James Ha, University of Washington

Richard Hagen, Florida State University
Steve Hall, Embry-Riddle Aeronautical University
Le Xuan Hy, Seattle University
George P. Knight, Arizona State University
Daniel Langmeyer, University of Cincinnati (special thanks)
Deana Liddy, University of Nebraska
Jae Myung, Ohio State University
Susan Nolan, Seton Hall University
Nona Phillips, University of Washington
Ladonna Rush, College of Wooster
Erwin Segal, SUNY Buffalo
Anna Smith, Troy State University
Paul Smith, Alverno College
Eva Szeli, University of Miami
Mary Tallent-Runnels, Texas Tech University
Evangeline Wheeler, Towson State University
Todd Zakrajsek, Southern Oregon State College

I am especially grateful to the reviewers of the eighth edition:

Bryan Auday, Gordon College
Vern Bacharach, Appalachian State University
Dennis Goff, Randolph-Macon Women's College
Roberto Heredia, Texas A&M International University
Mary Hooten, Troy State University
Kirk McClure, University of Kansas
Timothy Murphy, Brock University
Laurence Nolan, Wagner College
Alexander Wilson, University of New Brunswick

I am grateful to the Literary Executor of the Late Sir Ronald A. Fisher, F.R.S.; to Dr. Frank Yates, F.R.S.; and to the Longman Group Ltd., London, for permission to reprint Tables III, IV, and VII from their book *Statistical Tables for Biological, Agricultural and Medical Research* (sixth edition, 1974).

The material covered in this textbook, study guide, and instructor's manual, and the Web-based material are appropriate for undergraduate students with a major in psychology or related behavioral science discipline. I believe the approach I have followed helps considerably to impart this subject matter with understanding. I am grateful to receive any comments that will improve the quality of these materials.

*Robert R. Pagano*

# OVERVIEW

PART **one**

**1** Statistics and Scientific Method

# Statistics and Scientific Method

## INTRODUCTION

Have you ever wondered how we come to know truth? Most college students would agree that finding out what is true about the world, ourselves, and others constitutes a very important activity. A little reflection reveals that much of our time is spent in precisely this way. If we are studying geography, we want to know what is *true* about the geography of a particular region. Is the region mountainous or flat, agricultural or industrial? If our interest is in studying human beings, we want to know what is *true* about humans. Do we *truly* possess a spiritual nature, or are we *truly* reducible solely to atoms and molecules, as the reductionists would have it? How do humans think? What happens in the body to produce a sensation or a movement? When I get angry, is it *true* that there is a unique underlying physiological pattern? What is the pattern? Is my *true* purpose in life to become a teacher? Is it *true* that animals think? We could go on indefinitely with examples because so much of our lives is spent seeking and acquiring truth.

## METHODS OF KNOWING

Historically, humankind has employed four methods to acquire knowledge. They are authority, rationalism, intuition, and the scientific method.

**Authority**   When using the method of authority, something is considered true because of tradition or because some person of distinction says it is true. Thus, we may believe in the theory of evolution because our distinguished professors tell us it is true, or we may believe that God truly exists because our parents say so. Although this method of knowing is currently in disfavor and does sometimes lead to error, it is used a lot in living our daily lives. We frequently accept a large amount of information on the basis of authority, if for no other reason than we do not have the time or the expertise to check it out firsthand. For example, I believe, on the basis of physics authorities, that electrons exist, but I have never seen one; or perhaps closer to home, if the surgeon general tells me that smoking causes cancer, I stop smoking because I have faith in the surgeon general and do not have the time or means to investigate the matter personally.

**Rationalism**   The method of rationalism uses reasoning alone to arrive at knowledge. It assumes that if the premises are sound and the reasoning is carried out correctly according to the rules of logic, then the conclusions will yield truth. We are very familiar with reason because we use it so much. As an example, consider the following syllogism:

> All statistics professors are interesting people.
> Mr. X is a statistics professor.
> Therefore, Mr. X is an interesting person.

Assuming the first statement is true (who could doubt it?), then it follows that if the second statement is true, the conclusion must be true. Joking aside, hardly anyone would question the importance of the reasoning process in yielding truth. However, there are a great number of situations in which reason alone is inadequate in determining the truth.

To illustrate, let's suppose you notice that John, a friend of yours, has been depressed for a couple of months. As a psychology major, you know that psychological problems can produce depression. Therefore, it is reasonable to believe John may have psychological problems that are producing his depression. On the other hand, you also know that an inadequate diet can result in depression, and it is reasonable to believe that this may be at the root of his trouble. In this situation, there are two reasonable explanations of the phenomenon. Hence, reason alone is inadequate in distinguishing between them. We must resort to experience. Is John's diet in fact deficient? Will improved eating habits correct the situation? Or does John have serious psychological problems that, when worked through, will lift the depression? Reason alone, then, may be sufficient to yield truth in some situations, but it is clearly inadequate in others. As we shall see, the scientific method also uses reason to arrive at truth, but reasoning alone is only part of the process. Thus, the scientific method incorporates reason but is not synonymous with it.

Intuition   Knowledge is also acquired through intuition. By intuition, we mean that sudden insight, the clarifying idea that springs into consciousness all at once as a whole. It is not arrived at by reason. On the contrary, the idea often seems to occur after conscious reasoning has failed. Beveridge* gives numerous occurrences taken from prominent individuals. Here are a couple of examples:

> Here is Metchnikoff's own account of the origin of the idea of phagocytosis: "One day when the whole family had gone to the circus to see some extraordinary performing apes, I remained alone with my microscope, observing the life in the mobile cells of a transparent starfish larva, when a new thought suddenly flashed across my brain. It struck me that similar cells might serve in the defense of the organism against intruders. Feeling that there was in this something of surpassing interest, I felt so excited that I began striding up and down the room and even went to the seashore to collect my thoughts."

> Hadamard cites an experience of the mathematician Gauss, who wrote concerning a problem he had tried unsuccessfully to prove for years: "Finally two days ago I succeeded . . . like a sudden flash of lightning the riddle happened to be solved. I cannot myself say what was the conducting thread which connected what I previously knew with what made my success possible."

It is interesting to note that the intuitive idea often occurs after conscious reasoning has failed and the individual has put the problem aside for a while. Thus, Beveridge[†] quotes two scientists as follows:

> Freeing my mind of all thoughts of the problem I walked briskly down the street, when suddenly at a definite spot which I could locate today—as if from the clear sky above me—an idea popped into my head as emphatically as if a voice had shouted it.

> I decided to abandon the work and all thoughts relative to it, and then, on the following day, when occupied in work of an entirely different type, an idea came to my mind as suddenly as a flash of lightning and it was the solution . . . the utter simplicity made me wonder why I hadn't thought of it before.

Despite the fact that intuition has probably been used as a source of knowledge for as long as humans have existed, it is still a very mysterious process about which we have only the most rudimentary understanding.

Scientific method   Although the scientific method uses both reasoning and intuition for establishing truth, its reliance on objective assessment is what differentiates this method from the others. At the heart of science lies the *scientific experiment*. The method of science is rather straightforward. By some means, usually by reasoning deductively from existing theory or inductively from existing facts or through intuition, the scientist arrives at a hypothesis about some feature of reality. He or she then designs an experiment to objectively test the hypothesis. The data from the experiment are then analyzed statistically, and the hypothesis is either supported or rejected. The feature of overriding importance in this methodology is that no matter what the scientist believes is true regarding the

---

*W. I. B. Beveridge, *The Art of Scientific Investigation,* Vintage Books/Random House, New York, 1957, pp. 94–95.
[†]Ibid., p. 92.

hypothesis under study, the experiment provides the basis for an *objective* evaluation of the hypothesis. The data from the experiment force a conclusion consonant with reality. Thus, scientific methodology has a built-in safeguard for ensuring that truth assertions of any sort about reality must conform to what is demonstrated to be objectively true about the phenomena before the assertions are given the status of scientific truth.

An important aspect of this methodology is that the experimenter can hold incorrect hunches, and the data will expose them. The hunches can then be revised in light of the data and retested. This methodology, although sometimes painstakingly slow, has a self-correcting feature that, over the long run, has a high probability of yielding truth. Since in this textbook we emphasize statistical analysis rather than experimental design, we cannot spend a great deal of time discussing the design of experiments. Nevertheless, some experimental design will be covered because it is so intertwined with statistical analysis.

## DEFINITIONS

In discussing this and other material throughout the book, we shall be using certain technical terms. The terms and their definitions follow:

- ◆ **Population** *A population is the complete set of individuals, objects, or scores that the investigator is interested in studying.* In an actual experiment, the population is the larger group of individuals from which the subjects run in the experiment have been taken.
- ◆ **Sample** *A sample is a subset of the population.* In an experiment, for economical reasons, the investigator usually collects data on a smaller group of subjects than the entire population. This smaller group is called the sample.
- ◆ **Variable** *A variable is any property or characteristic of some event, object, or person that may have different values at different times depending on the conditions.* Height, weight, reaction time, and drug dosage are examples of variables. A variable should be contrasted with a *constant,* which, of course, does not have different values at different times. An example is the mathematical constant $\pi$; it always has the same value (3.14 to two-decimal-place accuracy).
- ◆ **Independent variable** *The independent variable in an experiment is the variable that is systematically manipulated by the investigator.* In most experiments, the investigator is interested in determining the effect that one variable, say, variable $A$, has on one or more other variables. To do so, the investigator manipulates the levels of variable $A$ and measures the effect on the other variables. Variable $A$ is called the *independent* variable because its levels are controlled by the experimenter, independent of any change in the other variables. To illustrate, an investigator might be interested in the effect of alcohol on social behavior. To investigate this, he or she would probably vary the amount of alcohol consumed by the subjects and measure its effect on their social behavior. In this example, the experimenter is manipulating the amount of alcohol and measuring its consequences on social behavior. Alcohol amount is the independent variable. In another experiment, the effect of sleep deprivation on aggressive behavior is studied. Subjects are deprived of various amounts of sleep, and the consequences on aggressiveness are observed. Here, the amount of sleep deprivation is being manipulated. Hence, it is the independent variable.

- **Dependent variable** *The dependent variable in an experiment is the variable that the investigator measures to determine the effect of the independent variable.* For example, in the experiment studying the effects of alcohol on social behavior, the amount of alcohol is the independent variable. The social behavior of the subjects is measured to see whether it is affected by the amount of alcohol consumed. Thus, social behavior is the dependent variable. It is called *dependent* because it may depend on the amount of alcohol consumed. In the investigation of sleep deprivation and aggressive behavior, the amount of sleep deprivation is being manipulated and the subjects' aggressive behavior is being measured. The amount of sleep deprivation is the independent variable, and aggressive behavior is the dependent variable.
- **Data** *The measurements that are made on the subjects of an experiment are called data.* Usually data consist of the measurements of the dependent variable or of other subject characteristics, such as age, gender, number of subjects, and so on. The data as originally measured are often referred to as *raw* or *original* scores.
- **Statistic** *A statistic is a number calculated on sample data that quantifies a characteristic of the sample.* Thus, the average value of a sample set of scores would be called a statistic.
- **Parameter** *A parameter is a number calculated on population data that quantifies a characteristic of the population.* For example, the average value of a population set of scores is called a parameter. It should be noted that a statistic and a parameter are very similar concepts. The only difference is that a statistic is calculated on a sample and a parameter is calculated on a population.

## An Overall Example: Mode of Presentation and Retention

Let's now consider an illustrative experiment and apply the previously discussed terms to it.

*An educator conducts an experiment to determine whether the mode of presentation affects how well prose material is remembered. For this experiment, the educator uses several prose passages that are presented visually or auditorily. Fifty students are selected from the undergraduates attending the university at which the educator works. The students are divided into two groups of 25 students per group. The first group receives a visual presentation of the prose passages, and the second group hears the passages through an auditory presentation. At the end of their respective presentations, the subjects are asked to write down as much of the material as they can remember. The average number of words remembered by each group is calculated, and the two group averages are compared to see whether the mode of presentation had an effect.*

In this experiment, the independent variable is the mode of presentation of the prose passages (i.e., auditory or visual). The dependent variable is the number of words remembered. The sample is the 50 students who participated in the experiment. The population is the larger group of individuals from which the sample was taken, namely, the undergraduates attending the university. The data are the number of words recalled by each student in the sample. The average number of words recalled by each group is a statistic because it quantifies a characteristic of the sample scores. Since there was no measurement made of any population characteristic, there was no parameter calculated in this experiment. However, for illustrative purposes, suppose the entire population had been given a visual presentation of the passages. If we calculate the average number of words remembered by the population, the average number would be called a parameter because it quantifies a characteristic of the population scores.

Now, let's do a problem to practice identifying these terms.

## Practice Problem 1.1

For the experiment described below, specify the following: the independent variable, the dependent variable(s), the sample, the population, the data, the statistic(s), and the parameter(s).

A professor of gynecology at a prominent medical school wants to determine whether an experimental birth control implant has side effects on body weight and depression. A group of 5000 adult women living in a nearby city volunteers for the experiment. The gynecologist selects 100 of these women to participate in the study. Fifty of the women are assigned to group 1 and the other fifty to group 2 such that the mean body weight and the mean depression scores of each group are equal at the beginning of the experiment. Treatment conditions are the same for both groups, except that the women in group 1 are surgically implanted with the experimental birth control device, whereas the women in group 2 receive a placebo implant. Body weight and depressed mood state are measured at the beginning and end of the experiment. A standardized questionnaire designed to measure degree of depression is used for the mood state measurement. The higher the score on this questionnaire is, the more depressed the individual is. The mean body weight and the mean depression scores of each group at the end of the experiment are compared to determine whether the experimental birth control implant had an effect on these variables. To safeguard the women from unwanted pregnancy, another method of birth control that does not interact with the implant is used for the duration of the experiment.

### SOLUTION

*Independent variable:* The experimental birth control implant versus the placebo.

*Dependent variables:* Body weight and depressed mood state.

*Sample:* 100 women who participated in the experiment.

*Population:* 5000 women who volunteered for the experiment.

*Data:* The individual body weight and depression scores of the 100 women at the beginning and end of the experiment.

*Statistics:* Mean body weight of group 1 at the beginning of the experiment, mean body weight of group 1 at the end of the experiment, mean depression score of group 1 at the beginning of the experiment, mean depression score of group 1 at the end of the experiment, plus the same four statistics for group 2.

*Parameter:* No parameters were given or computed in this experiment. If the gynecologist had measured the body weights of all 5000 volunteers at the beginning of the experiment, the mean of these 5000 weights would be a parameter.

## SCIENTIFIC RESEARCH AND STATISTICS

Scientific research may be divided into two categories: observational studies and true experiments. Statistical techniques are important in both kinds of research.

**Observational studies**    In this type of research, no variables are actively manipulated by the investigator. Included within this category of research are (1) naturalistic observation, (2) parameter estimation, and (3) correlational studies. With naturalistic observation research, a major goal is to obtain an accurate description of the situation being studied. Much anthropological and etiological research is of this type. Parameter estimation research is conducted on samples to estimate the level of one or more population characteristics (e.g., the population average or percentage). Surveys, public opinion polls, and much market research fall into this category. In correlational research, the investigator focuses attention on two or more variables to determine whether they are related. For example, to determine whether obesity and high blood pressure are related in adults older than 30 years, an investigator might measure the fat level and blood pressure of individuals in a sample of adults older than 30. The investigator would then analyze the results to see whether a relationship exists between these variables; that is, do individuals with low fat levels also have low blood pressure, do individuals with moderate fat levels have moderate blood pressure, and do individuals with high fat levels have high blood pressure?

**True experiments**    In this type of research, an attempt is made to determine whether changes in one variable produce changes in another variable. In a true experiment, an independent variable is manipulated and its effect on some dependent variable is studied. If desired, there can be more than one independent variable and more than one dependent variable. In the simplest case, there is only one independent and one dependent variable. One example of this case is the experiment mentioned previously that investigated the effect of alcohol on social behavior. In this experiment, you will recall, alcohol level was manipulated by the experimenter and its effect on social behavior was measured.

## RANDOM SAMPLING

In all of the research described previously, data are usually collected on a sample of subjects rather than on the entire population to which the results are intended to apply. Ideally, of course, the experiment would be performed on the whole population, but usually it is far too costly, so a sample is taken. Note that not just any sample will do. The sample should be a *random* sample. Random sampling is discussed in Chapter 8. For now, it is sufficient to know that random sampling allows the laws of probability, also discussed in Chapter 8, to apply to the data and at the same time helps achieve a sample that is representative of the population. Thus, the results obtained from the sample should also apply to the population. Once the data are collected, they are statistically analyzed and the appropriate conclusions about the population are drawn.

## DESCRIPTIVE AND INFERENTIAL STATISTICS

Statistical analysis, of course, is the main theme of this textbook. It has been divided into two areas: (1) *descriptive statistics* and (2) *inferential statistics*. Both involve analyzing data. If an analysis is done for the purpose of describing or characterizing the data, then we are in the area of descriptive statistics. To illustrate, suppose your biology professor has just recorded the scores from an exam he has recently given you. He hands back the tests and now wants to describe the scores. He might decide to calculate the average of the distribution to describe its *central tendency*. Perhaps he will also determine its range to characterize its *variability*. He might also plot the scores on a graph to show the *shape* of the distribution. Since all of these procedures are for the purpose of describing or characterizing the data already collected, they fall within the realm of descriptive statistics.

Inferential statistics, on the other hand, is not concerned with just describing the obtained data. Rather, it embraces techniques that allow one to use obtained sample data to make inferences or draw conclusions about populations. This is the more complicated part of statistical analysis. It involves probability and various inference tests, such as *Student's* t *test* and the *analysis of variance*.

To illustrate the difference between descriptive and inferential statistics, suppose we were interested in determining the average IQ of the entire freshman class at your university. It would be too costly and time-consuming to measure the IQ of every student in the population, so we would take a random sample of, say, 200 students and give each an IQ test. We would then have 200 *sample* IQ scores, which we want to use to determine the average IQ in the *population*. Although we can't determine the exact value of the population average, we can estimate it using the sample data in conjunction with an inference test called Student's *t* test. The results would allow us to make a statement such as, "We are 95% confident that the interval of 115–120 contains the mean IQ of the population." Here, we are not just describing the obtained scores, as was the case with the biology exam. Rather, we are using the sample scores to infer to a population value. We are therefore in the domain of inferential statistics. *Descriptive* and *inferential statistics* can be defined as follows:

definitions   ■ **Descriptive statistics** *is concerned with techniques that are used to describe or characterize the obtained data.*

■ **Inferential statistics** *involves techniques that use the obtained sample data to infer to populations.*

## USING COMPUTERS IN STATISTICS

The use of computers in statistics has increased greatly over the past decade. In fact, today almost all research data in the behavioral sciences are analyzed using statistical computer programs rather than by "hand" with a calculator. This is good news for students, who often like the ideas, concepts, and results of statistics but hate the drudgery of hand computation. The fact is that researchers hate computational drudgery too and therefore almost always use a computer to analyze data sets of any appreciable size. Computers have the advantages of saving time and labor, minimizing the chances of computational error, allowing easy graphical display of the data, and providing better management of large data sets. As useful as computers are, there is often not enough time in a basic statistics course to include them. Therefore, I have written this edition so that you can learn the statistical content with or without the computer material.

Several computer programs are available to do statistical analysis. The most popular are Statistical Package for the Social Sciences (SPSS), Biomedical Computer Programs-P series (BMDP), Statistical Analysis System (SAS), SYSTAT, MINITAB, and Excel. Versions of SPSS, SAS, SYSTAT, and MINITAB are available for both mainframes and microcomputers. It is worth taking the extra time to learn one or more of these programs.

As you begin solving problems using computers, I believe you will begin to experience the fun and power that statistical software can bring to your study and use of statistics. In fact, once you have used software like SPSS to analyze data, you will probably wonder, "Why do I have to do any of these complicated calculations by hand?" Unfortunately, when you are using statistical software to calculate the value of a statistic, it does not help you understand that statistic. Understanding the statistic and its proper use is best achieved by doing hand calculations or step-by-step calculations using Excel. Of course, once you have learned everything you can from these calculations, using statistical software like SPSS to grind out correct values of the statistic seems eminently reasonable.

## STATISTICS AND THE "REAL WORLD"

As I mentioned previously, one major purpose of statistics is to aid in the scientific evaluation of truth assertions. Although you may view this as rather esoteric and far removed from everyday life, I believe you will be convinced, by the time you have finished this text, that understanding statistics has very important practical aspects that can contribute to your satisfaction with and success in life. As you go through this text, I hope you will become increasingly aware of how frequently in ordinary life we are bombarded with "authorities" telling us, based on "truth assertions," what we should do, how we should live, what we should buy, what we should value, and so on. In areas of real importance to you, I hope you will begin to ask questions such as: "Are these truth assertions supported by data?" "How good are the data?" "Is chance a reasonable explanation of the data?" If there are no data presented, or if the data presented are of the form "My experience is that . . ." rather than from well-controlled experiments, I hope that you will begin to question how seriously you should take the authority's advice.

To help develop this aspect of your statistical decision making, I have included, at the end of certain chapters, applications taken from everyday life. These are titled, "What Is the Truth?" To begin, let's consider the following material.

## WHAT IS THE TRUTH?

### Data, Data, Where Are the Data?

The accompanying advertisement was printed in an issue of *Psychology Today*. From a scientific point of view, what's missing?

***Answer*** This ad is similar to a great many that appear these days. It promises a lot, but offers no experimental data to back up its claims. The ad puts forth a truth assertion: **"Think And Be Thin."** It further claims **"Here's a tape program that really works . . . and permanently!"** The program consists of listening to a tape with subliminal messages that is supposed to program your mind to produce thinness. The glaring lack is that there are no controlled experiments, no data offered to substantiate the claim. This is the kind of claim that cries out for empirical verification. Apparently, the authors of the ad do not believe the readers of *Psychology Today* are very sophisticated, statistically. I certainly hope the readers of this textbook would ask for the data before they spend 6 months of their time listening to a tape, the message of which they can't even hear!

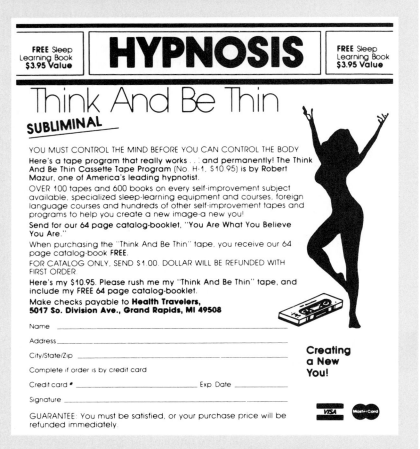

## WHAT IS THE TRUTH?

### Authorities Are Nice, But ...

**A**n advertisement promoting Anacin-3 appeared in an issue of *Cosmopolitan.* The heading of the advertisement was "3 Good Reasons to Try Anacin-3." The advertisement pictured a doctor, a nurse, and a pharmacist making the following three statements:

1. "*Doctors* are recommending acetaminophen, the aspirin-free pain reliever in Anacin-3, more than any other aspirin-free pain reliever."
2. "*Hospitals* use acetaminophen, the aspirin-free pain reliever in Anacin-3, more than any other aspirin-free pain reliever."
3. "*Pharmacists* recommend acetaminophen, the aspirin-free pain reliever in Anacin-3, more than any other aspirin-free pain reliever."

From a scientific point of view, is anything missing?

*Answer*   This is somewhat better than the previous ad. At least relevant authorities are invoked in support of the product. However, the ad is misleading and again fails to present the appropriate data. Much better than the "3 Good Reasons to Try Anacin-3" given in the ad would be reason 4, data from well-conducted experiments showing that (a) acetaminophen is a better pain reliever than any other aspirin-free pain reliever and (b) Anacin-3 relieves pain better than any competitor. Any guesses about why these data haven't been presented? As a budding statistician, are you satisfied with the case made by this ad?

2 GOOD REASONS TO TRY PYRO-Z

1. Doctors are recommending PYRO-Z for pain relief over other products.

2. Hospitals use PYRO-Z, the pain reliever, more than any other pain reliever.

## WHAT IS THE TRUTH?

# Data, Data, What Are the Data?—1

In the previous "What is the Truth?" sections, no data were presented to justify the authors' claims, a cardinal error in science. A little less grievous, but nonetheless questionable, is when data are presented in a study or experiment but the conclusions drawn by the authors seem to stray far from the actual data. A study reported in a recent newspaper article illustrates this point. The article is shown below.

### Cavemen Were Pretty Nice Guys

**By VIRGINIA FENTON**
The Associated Press
*PARIS—Neanderthals might not have been as savage as we think. A 200,000-year-old jawbone discovered in France suggests the primitive hominids took care of each other, in this case feeding a toothless peer, an international team of experts said Friday.*

*A damaged jawbone, discovered last year in southern France, shows that its owner survived without teeth for up to several years—impossible without a helping hand from his or her peers, said Canadian paleontologist Serge Lebel.*

*Lebel directed an international team of experts who discovered the fossil in July 2000. Also on the team was the noted specialist of the*

*Neanderthal period Erik Trinkaus of Washington University in St. Louis and colleagues from Germany, Portugal and France.*

*"This individual must have been quite weak and needed preparation of his or her food, and the social group probably took care of him or her," Lebel said at a news conference.*

*"We mustn't dehumanize these beings. They show an entirely human kind of behavior," said Lebel, who works at the University of Quebec.*

*Others in the group may have gone as far as chewing the food for their sick peer, as well as cutting and cooking it, he said.*

*The discovery may push back ideas of the beginning of social care by 150,000 years, Lebel said. A similar infection that caused a hominid to lose his teeth had previously only been found in fossils*

*dating back 50,000 years, he said.*

*The team's findings were published in the Sept. 25 issue of the U.S. periodical* Proceedings of the National Academy of Sciences.

*However, University of Pittsburgh anthropologist Jeffrey Schwartz was skeptical.*

*"You can eat a lot without your teeth. There is no reason to think the individual couldn't have been chewing soft food—snails, mollusks, even worms."*

Reprinted with permission of The Associated Press.

Do you think the finding of a 200,000-year-old, damaged jawbone by the international team of experts is an adequate database for the conclusions put forth by Dr. Lebel? Or, like Dr. Schwartz, are you skeptical? You can probably guess into which camp I fall.

# WHAT IS THE TRUTH?

## Data, Data, What Are the Data?—2

As discussed in this chapter, using data as the basis for truth assertions is an important part of the scientific process. Sometimes, however, data are reported in a manner that is distorted, leading to false conclusions rather than truth. This point is illustrated in the following article that recently appeared in a local newspaper.

### *Pundits Twist Facts into Urban Legend*

**By TIM RUTTEN**

*Urban legends are anecdotes so engaging, entertaining, anxiety-affirming or prejudice-confirming that people repeat them as true, even when they are not.*

*Their journalistic equivalent is the pithy "poll result" or "study finding" that so neatly encapsulates a social ill or point of partisan contention that no talk-show host or stump orator can resist it.*

*Ronald Reagan, for example, was so notoriously fond of dubious anecdotes that some of his close associates speculated that his years as an actor had rendered him utterly incapable of passing up a good line.*

*That provenance-be-damned attitude hardly ended with the Great Communicator's retirement.*

*CNN political analyst William Schneider, an authority on opinion polling, believes that highly charged*
*political issues or campaigns are particularly prone to spin off fictional study results, which then take on a life of their own.*

*"Social Security is a classic case," Schneider said. "There is a political legend that a 'recent' poll, which is never specified, showed that more young Americans believe Elvis is alive than expect to collect a Social Security check when they retire. Over the past few years, every conservative on Earth and every Republican politician in Washington, including President Bush, has referred to this finding. They all just say, 'Polls or studies show this,' but none ever has. Republicans go on citing this bogus finding because—whether it's true or not—it has great value as political currency."*

*Recently, it was possible to watch another such journalistic legend being born. The* Wall Street Journal's *Leisure & Arts page published an article excerpted from*
*a speech delivered a week before by Bruce Cole, chairman of the National Endowment for the Humanities. In it, he decried the fact "that Americans do not know their history" and reflected on this collective amnesia's particular perils in the wake of Sept. 11, whose memory he fears might even now be fading.*

*All fair points. However, in their support, Cole cited "a nationwide survey recently commissioned by Columbia Law School," which, he said, "found that almost two-thirds of all Americans think Karl Marx's socialist dogma, 'From each according to his ability, to each according to his needs,' was or may have been written by the Founding Fathers and was included in the Constitution."*

*Clear; helpful; alarming. Plausible, even, given the popular taste for altruistic banality. Everything, in other words, that a good rhetorical point should be.*

(continued)

## WHAT IS THE TRUTH?

# Data, Data, What Are the Data?—2

## (*continued*)

*The problem is that is not what the Columbia poll found.*

*It is, however, what the May 29 press release announcing the poll's findings said. In fact, its first paragraph read: "Almost two-thirds of Americans think Karl Marx's maxim, 'From each according to his ability, to each according to his needs' was or could have been written by the framers and included in the Constitution."*

*Note the subtle shift from the release's "could have been written" to Cole's—or his speech writer's— "may have been written."*

*The announcement's second paragraph quotes Columbia Law School professor Michael Dorf on the troubling implications of the Marx "finding" and points the reader to a column the professor has written for a legal Web site, Findlaw.com. In that column, Dorf wrote that "The survey found that 69 percent of respondents either thought that the United States Constitution contained Marx's maxim, or did not know whether or not it did."*

*That is further still from Cole's recitation of the finding.*

*What of the actual poll, which asked a national sample of 1,000 respondents five yes-or-no questions about the Constitution?*

*In response to the query about whether the Marxist maxim is*

*contained the document, 35 percent said yes; 31 percent said no; and 34 percent said "they did not know."*

*Was Dorf entitled to conflate the yes and don't-know respondents into a single, alarming two-thirds? No, Schneider said. "That is a total misinterpretation of what people mean when they tell a pollster they don't know. When people say that, they mean 'I have no idea.' Choosing to interpret it as meaning 'I think it may be true or could be true' simply is misleading on the writer's part."*

*What it does do is add pungency to a finding Schneider described as "wholly unremarkable. It's not at all surprising that about a third of respondents thought that is in the Constitution. Most people, for example, think the right to privacy exists in the Constitution, when no such right is enumerated anywhere in it."*

*In fact, what is remarkable—and far more relevant at the moment— about the Columbia poll is what it shows Americans do know about their Constitution: Fully 83 percent of the respondents recognized the first sentence of the 14th Amendment as part of the national charter, while 60 percent correctly understood that the president may not suspend the Bill of Rights in time of war.*

*More than two-thirds of those asked were aware that Supreme Court justices serve for life.*

*The only other question the respondents flubbed was whether the court's overturning of Roe vs. Wade would make abortion "illegal throughout the United States."*

*Fewer than a third of those polled correctly said it would not, because state statutes guaranteeing choice would remain on the books.*

*These facts notwithstanding, it is a safe bet that radio and television talk-show hosts, editorial writers and all the rest of the usually suspect soon will be sighing, groaning, sneering and raging about Americans' inability to distinguish the thought of James Madison from that of Karl Marx. How long will it be before public education, the liberal media, humanism and single-parent families are blamed?*

*Commentary pages are the soft underbelly of American journalism. Their writers, however self-interested, are held to a different, which is to say lower, standard of proof because of their presumed expertise.*

*In fact, they are responsible for regularly injecting false information of this sort into our public discourse. In the marketplace of ideas, as on the used car lot, caveat emptor still is the best policy.*

The Los Angeles Times, June 14, 2002. Reprinted by permission of Tribune Media Services.

Do you think William Schneider is too cynical, or do you agree with the article's conclusion, "In fact, they are responsible for regularly injecting false information of this sort into our public discourse. In the marketplace of ideas, as on the used car lot, caveat emptor still is the best policy"?

## SUMMARY

In this chapter, I have discussed how truth is established. Traditionally, four methods have been used: authority, reason, intuition, and science. At the heart of science is the scientific experiment. By reasoning or through intuition, the scientist forms a hypothesis about some feature of reality. He or she designs an experiment to objectively test the hypothesis. The data from the experiment are then analyzed statistically, and the hypothesis is either confirmed or rejected.

Most scientific research falls into two categories: observational studies and true experiments. Natural observation, parameter estimation, and correlational studies are included within the observational category. Their major goal is to give an accurate description of the situation, estimate population parameters, or determine whether two or more of the variables are related. Since there is no systematic manipulation of any variable by the experimenter when doing an observational study, this type of research cannot determine whether changes in one variable will produce changes in another variable. This kind of result can be determined only from true experiments.

In true experiments, the investigator systematically manipulates the independent variable and observes its effect on one or more dependent variables. Due to practical considerations, data are collected on only a sample of subjects rather than on the whole population. It is important that the sample be a random sample. The obtained data are then analyzed statistically.

The statistical analysis may be descriptive or inferential. If the analysis just describes or characterizes the obtained data, we are in the domain of descriptive statistics. If the analysis uses the obtained data to infer to populations, we are in the domain of inferential statistics. Understanding statistical analysis has important practical consequences in life.

## IMPORTANT TERMS

Constant (p. 6)
Correlational studies (p. 9)
Data (p. 7)
Dependent variable (p. 7)
Descriptive statistics (p. 10)
Independent variable (p. 6)
Inferential statistics (p. 10)
Intuition (p. 5)

Method of authority (p. 4)
Naturalistic observation research (p. 9)
Observational studies (p. 9)
Parameter (p. 7)
Parameter estimation research (p. 9)
Population (p. 6)

Rationalism (p. 4)
Sample (p. 6)
Scientific method (p. 5)
SPSS (p. 11)
Statistic (p. 7)
True experiment (p. 9)
Variable (p. 6)

## QUESTIONS AND PROBLEMS

*Note to the student:* You will notice that at the end of specific problems in this and all other chapters except Chapter 2, I have identified, in color, a specific area within psychology and related fields where the problem is applied. For example, Problem 6 part **b**, page 18, is a problem in the area of biological psychology. It has been labeled "biological" at the end of the problem, leaving off "psychology" for brevity. The specific areas identified are cognitive psychology, social psychology, developmental psychology, biological psychology, clinical psychology, industrial/organizational (I/O) psychology, health psychology, education, and other. As indicated previously, in the actual labeling I have left off "psychology" for brevity. I hope this labeling will be useful to your instructor in selecting assigned homework problems and to you in seeing the broad application of this material as well as in helping you select additional problems you might enjoy solving beyond the assigned ones.

1. Define each of the following terms:
   Population                Dependent variable
   Sample                    Constant
   Data                      Statistic
   Variable                  Parameter
   Independent variable

2. What are four methods of acquiring knowledge? Write a short paragraph describing the essential characteristics of each.

3. How does the scientific method differ from each of the methods listed here?
   a. Method of authority
   b. Method of rationalism
   c. Method of intuition

4. Write a short paragraph comparing naturalistic observation and true experiments.

5. Distinguish between descriptive and inferential statistics. Use examples to illustrate the points you make.

6. In each of the experiments described here, specify (1) the independent variable, (2) the dependent variable, (3) the sample, (4) the population, (5) the data, and (6) the statistic:

   a. A health psychologist is interested in whether fear motivation is effective in reducing the incidence of smoking. Forty adult smokers are selected from individuals residing in the city in which the psychologist works. Twenty are asked to smoke a cigarette, after which they see a gruesome film about how smoking causes cancer. Vivid pictures of the diseased lungs and other internal organs of deceased smokers are shown in an effort to instill fear of smoking in these subjects. The other group receives the same treatment, except they see a neutral film that is unrelated to smoking. For 2 months after showing the film, the experimenter keeps records on the number of cigarettes smoked daily by the participants. A mean for each group is then computed of the number of cigarettes smoked daily since seeing the film, and these means are compared to determine whether the fear-inducing film had an effect on smoking. health

   b. A physiologist wants to know whether a particular region of the brain (the hypothalamus) is involved in the regulation of eating. An experiment is performed in which 30 rats are selected from the university vivarium and divided into two groups. One of the groups receives lesions in the hypothalamus, whereas the other group is lesioned in a neutral area. After recovery from the operations, all animals are given free access to food for 2 weeks, and a record is kept of the daily food intake of each animal. At the end of the 2-week period, the mean daily food intake for each group is determined. Finally, these means are compared to see whether the lesions in the hypothalamus have affected the amount eaten. biological

   c. A clinical psychologist is interested in evaluating three methods of treating depression: medication, cognitive restructuring, and exercise. A fourth treatment condition, a waiting-only treatment group, is included to provide a baseline control group. Sixty depressed students are

recruited from the undergraduate student body at a large state university, and fifteen are assigned to each treatment method. Treatments are administered for 6 months, after which each student is given a questionnaire designed to measure the degree of depression. The questionnaire is scaled from 0 to 100, with higher scores indicating a higher degree of depression. The mean depression values are then computed for the four treatments and compared to determine the relative effectiveness of each treatment. clinical, health

   d. A social psychologist is interested in determining whether individuals who graduate from high school but get no further education earn more money than high school dropouts. A national survey is conducted in a large midwestern city, sampling 100 individuals from each category and asking each their annual salary. The results are tabulated, and mean salary values are calculated for each group. social

   e. A cognitive psychologist is interested in how retention is affected by the spacing of practice sessions. A sample of 30 seventh graders is selected from a local junior high school and divided into three groups of 10 students in each group. All students are asked to memorize a list of 15 words and are given three practice sessions, each 5 minutes long, in which to do so. Practice sessions for group 1 subjects are spaced 10 minutes apart; for group 2, 20 minutes apart; and for group 3, 30 minutes apart. All groups are given a retention test 1 hour after the last practice session. Results are recorded as the number of words correctly recalled in the test period. Mean values are computed for each group and compared. cognitive

   f. A sport psychologist uses visualization in promoting enhanced performance in college athletes. She is interested in evaluating the relative effectiveness of visualization alone versus visualization plus appropriate self-talk. An experiment is conducted with a college basketball team. Ten members of the team are selected. Five are assigned to a visualization alone group, and five are assigned to a visualization plus self-talk group. Both techniques are designed to increase foul shooting accuracy. Each group practices its technique for 1 month. The foul shooting accuracy of each player is measured before and 1 month after beginning practice of the technique. Difference scores are computed for each player, and the means of the difference scores for each group are compared to determine the relative effectiveness of the two techniques. I/O, other

g. A typing teacher believes that a different arrangement of the typing keys will promote faster typing. Twenty secretarial trainees, selected from a large business school, participate in an experiment designed to test this belief. Ten of the trainees learn to type on the conventional keyboard. The other ten are trained using the new arrangement of keys. At the end of the training period, the typing speed in words per minute of each trainee is measured. The mean typing speeds are then calculated for both groups and compared to determine whether the new arrangement has had an effect. education

7. Indicate which of the following represent a variable and which a constant:
   a. The number of letters in the alphabet
   b. The number of hours in a day
   c. The time at which you eat dinner
   d. The number of students who major in psychology at your university each year
   e. The number of centimeters in a meter
   f. The amount of sleep you get each night
   g. The amount you weigh
   h. The volume of a liter

8. Indicate which of the following situations involve descriptive statistics and which involve inferential statistics:
   a. An annual stockholders' report details the assets of the corporation.
   b. A history instructor tells his class the number of students who received an A on a recent exam.
   c. The mean of a sample set of scores is calculated to characterize the sample.
   d. The sample data from a poll are used to estimate the opinion of the population.
   e. A correlational study is conducted on a sample to determine whether educational level and income in the population are related.
   f. A newspaper article reports the average salaries of federal employees from data collected on all federal employees.

9. For each of the following, identify the sample and population scores:
   a. A social psychologist interested in drinking behavior investigates the number of drinks served in bars in a particular city on a Friday during "happy hour." In the city, there are 213 bars. There are too many bars to monitor all of them, so she selects 20 and records the number of drinks served in them. The following are the data:

| 50 | 82 | 47 | 65 |
|----|----|----|----|
| 40 | 76 | 61 | 72 |
| 35 | 43 | 65 | 76 |
| 63 | 66 | 83 | 82 |
| 57 | 72 | 71 | 58 |

social

b. To make a profit from a restaurant that specializes in low-cost quarter-pound hamburgers, it is necessary that each hamburger served weigh very close to 0.25 pound. Accordingly, the manager of the restaurant is interested in the variability among the weights of the hamburgers served each day. On a particular day, there are 450 hamburgers served. It would take too much time to weigh all 450, so the manager decides instead to weigh just 15. The following weights in pounds were obtained:

| 0.25 | 0.27 | 0.25 |
|------|------|------|
| 0.26 | 0.35 | 0.27 |
| 0.22 | 0.32 | 0.38 |
| 0.29 | 0.22 | 0.28 |
| 0.27 | 0.40 | 0.31 |

other

c. A machine that cuts steel blanks (used for making bolts) to their proper length is suspected of being unreliable. The shop supervisor decides to check the output of the machine. On the day of checking, the machine is set to produce 2-centimeter blanks. The acceptable tolerance is ±0.05 centimeter. It would take too much time to measure all 600 blanks produced in 1 day, so a representative group of 25 is selected. The following lengths in centimeters were obtained:

| 2.01 | 1.99 | 2.05 | 1.94 | 2.05 |
|------|------|------|------|------|
| 2.01 | 2.02 | 2.04 | 1.93 | 1.95 |
| 2.03 | 1.97 | 2.00 | 1.98 | 1.96 |
| 2.05 | 1.96 | 2.00 | 2.01 | 1.99 |
| 1.98 | 1.95 | 1.97 | 2.04 | 2.02 |

I/O

d. A physiological psychologist, working at Tacoma University, is interested in the resting, diastolic heart rates of all the female students attending the university. She randomly samples 30 females from the student body and records the following diastolic heart rates while the students are lying on a cot. Scores are in beats/min.

| | | | | | |
|----|----|----|----|----|----|
| 62 | 85 | 92 | 85 | 88 | 71 |
| 73 | 82 | 84 | 89 | 93 | 75 |
| 81 | 72 | 97 | 78 | 90 | 87 |
| 78 | 74 | 61 | 66 | 83 | 68 |
| 67 | 83 | 75 | 70 | 86 | 72 |

biological

## BOOK COMPANION WEBSITE

Go to www.thomsonedu.com/psychology/pagano for:

- Flash cards for review of terms
- Chapter quiz
- Statistical workshops
- And more

## WebTUTOR

Available via WebTutor for this chapter:

- Detailed chapter outline
- *Know and Be Able To Do* section
- Drag & Drop game for equations, concepts, and other material
- Flash cards for review of terms
- Audio flash cards for MP3 player
- More practice problems using computational equations
- Chapter quiz

# DESCRIPTIVE STATISTICS

PART **two**

# Basic Mathematical and Measurement Concepts

## STUDY HINTS FOR THE STUDENT

Statistics is not an easy subject. It requires learning difficult concepts as well as doing mathematics. There is, however, some advice that I would like to pass on, which I believe will help you greatly in learning this material. This advice is based on many years of teaching the subject; I hope you will take it seriously.

Most students in the behavioral sciences have a great deal of anxiety about taking a course on mathematics or statistics. Without minimizing the difficulty of the subject, a good deal of this anxiety is unnecessary. To learn the material contained in this textbook, you do not have to be a whiz in calculus or differential equations. I have tried hard to present the material so that nonmathematically inclined students can understand it. I cannot, however, totally do away with mathematics. To be successful, you must be able to do elementary algebra and a few other mathematical operations. To help you review, I have included Appendix A, which covers prerequisite mathematics. You should study that material and be sure you can do the problems it contains. If you have difficulty with these problems, it will help to review the topic in a basic textbook on elementary algebra.

Another factor of which you should be aware is that a lot of symbols are used in statistics. For example, to designate the mean of a sample set of scores, we shall use the symbol $\overline{X}$ (read "$X$ bar"). Students often make the material more difficult than necessary by failing to thoroughly learn what the symbols stand for. You can save yourself much grief by taking the symbols seriously. Treat them as though they are foreign vocabulary. Memorize them and be able to deal with them conceptually. For example, if the text says $\overline{X}$, the concept "the mean of the sample" should immediately come to mind.

It is also important to realize that the material in statistics is cumulative. Do not let yourself fall behind. If you do, you will not understand the current material either. The situation can then snowball, and before you know it, you may seem hopelessly behind. Remember, do all you can to keep up with the material.

Finally, my experience indicates that a good deal of the understanding of statistics comes from working lots of problems. Very often, one problem is worth a thousand words. Frequently, although the text is clearly worded, the material won't come into focus until you have worked the problems associated with the topic. Therefore, do lots of problems, and afterward, reread the textual material to be sure you understand it.

In sum, I believe that if you can handle elementary algebra, work diligently on learning the symbols and studying the text, keep up with the material, and work lots of problems, you will do quite well. Believe it or not, as you begin to experience the elegance and fun that are inherent in statistics, you may even come to enjoy it.

## MATHEMATICAL NOTATION

In statistics, we usually deal with group data that result from measuring one or more variables. The data are most often derived from samples, occasionally from populations. For mathematical purposes, it is useful to let symbols stand for the variables measured in the study. Throughout this text, we shall use the Roman capital letter $X$, and sometimes $Y$, to stand for the variable(s) measured. Thus, if we were measuring the age of subjects, we would let $X$ stand for the variable "age." When there are many values of the variable, it is important to distinguish among them. We do this by subscripting the symbol $X$. This process is illustrated in Table 2.1.

t a b l e 2.1   Age of six subjects

| Subject Number | Score Symbol | Score Value, Age (yr) |
|:---:|:---:|:---:|
| 1 | $X_1$ | 8 |
| 2 | $X_2$ | 10 |
| 3 | $X_3$ | 7 |
| 4 | $X_4$ | 6 |
| 5 | $X_5$ | 10 |
| 6 | $X_6$ | 12 |

In this example, we are letting the variable "age" be represented by the symbol $X$. We shall also let $N$ represent the number of scores in the distribution. In this example, $N = 6$. Each of the six scores represents a specific value of $X$. We distinguish among the six scores by assigning a subscript to $X$ that corresponds to the number of the subject that had the specific value. Thus, the score symbol $X_1$ corresponds to the score value 8, $X_2$ to the score value 10, $X_3$ to the value 7, $X_4$ to 6, $X_5$ to 10, and $X_6$ to 12. In general, we can refer to a single score in the $X$ distribution as $X_i$, where $i$ can take on any value from 1 to $N$ depending on which score we wish to designate. To summarize,

- $X$ or $Y$ stands for the variable measured.
- $N$ stands for the total number of subjects or scores.
- $X_i$ is the $i$th score, where $i$ can vary from 1 to $N$.

## SUMMATION

One of the most frequent operations performed in statistics is to sum all or part of the scores in the distribution. Since it is awkward to write out "sum of all the scores" each time this operation is required, particularly in equations, a symbolic abbreviation is used instead. The capital Greek letter sigma ($\Sigma$) indicates the operation of summation. The algebraic phrase employed for summation is

$$\sum_{i=1}^{N} X_i$$

This is read as "sum of the $X$ variable from $i = 1$ to $N$." The notations above and below the summation sign designate which scores to include in the summation. The term below the summation sign tells us the first score in the summation, and the term above the summation sign designates the last score. This phrase, then, indicates that we are to add the $X$ scores, beginning with the first score and ending with the $N$th score. Thus,

$$\sum_{i=1}^{N} X_i = X_1 + X_2 + X_3 + \cdots + X_N \qquad summation\ equation$$

Applied to the age data of the previous table,

$$\sum_{i=1}^{N} X_i = X_1 + X_2 + X_3 + X_4 + X_5 + X_6$$

$$= 8 + 10 + 7 + 6 + 10 + 12 = 53$$

When the summation is over all the scores (from 1 to $N$), the summation phrase itself is often abbreviated by omitting the notations above and below the summation sign and by omitting the subscript $i$. Thus,

$$\sum_{i=1}^{N} X_i \text{ is often written as } \Sigma X.$$

In the previous example,

$$\Sigma X = 53$$

This says that the sum of all the $X$ scores is 53.

Note that it is not necessary for the summation to be from 1 to $N$. For example, we might desire to sum only the second, third, fourth, and fifth scores. Remember, the notation below the summation sign tells us where to begin the summation, and the term above the sign tells us where to stop. Thus, to indicate the operation of summing the second, third, fourth, and fifth scores, we would use the symbol $\displaystyle\sum_{i=2}^{5} X_i$. For the preceding age data,

$$\sum_{i=2}^{5} X_i = X_2 + X_3 + X_4 + X_5 = 10 + 7 + 6 + 10 = 33$$

Let's do some practice problems in summation.

## Practice Problem 2.1

**a.** For the following scores, find $\displaystyle\sum_{i=1}^{N} X_i$:

$X$: 6, 8, 13, 15                $\Sigma X = 6 + 8 + 13 + 15 = 42$

$X$: 4, −10, −2, 20, 25, 8        $\Sigma X = 4 - 10 - 2 + 20 + 25 + 8 = 45$

$X$: 1.2, 3.5, 0.8, 4.5, 6.1      $\Sigma X = 1.2 + 3.5 + 0.8 + 4.5 + 6.1 = 16.1$

**b.** For the following scores, find $\displaystyle\sum_{i=1}^{3} X_i$:

$$X_1 = 10, X_2 = 12, X_3 = 13, X_4 = 18$$

$$\sum_{i=1}^{3} X_i = 10 + 12 + 13 = 35$$

**c.** For the following scores, find $\displaystyle\sum_{i=2}^{4} X_i + 3$:

$$X_1 = 20, X_2 = 24, X_3 = 25, X_4 = 28, X_5 = 30, X_6 = 31$$

$$\sum_{i=2}^{4} X_i + 3 = (24 + 25 + 28) + 3 = 80$$

**d.** For the following scores, find $\displaystyle\sum_{i=2}^{4} (X_i + 3)$:

$$X_1 = 20, X_2 = 24, X_3 = 25, X_4 = 28, X_5 = 30, X_6 = 31$$

$$\sum_{i=2}^{4} (X_i + 3) = (24 + 3) + (25 + 3) + (28 + 3) = 86$$

There are two more summations that we shall frequently encounter later in the textbook. They are $\Sigma X^2$ and $(\Sigma X)^2$. Although they look alike, they are different and generally will yield different answers. The symbol $\Sigma X^2$ (sum of the squared $X$ scores) indicates that we are first to square the $X$ scores and then sum them. Thus,

$$\Sigma X^2 = X_1^2 + X_2^2 + X_3^2 + \cdots + X_N^2$$

Given the scores $X_1 = 3$, $X_2 = 5$, $X_3 = 8$, and $X_4 = 9$,

$$\Sigma X^2 = 3^2 + 5^2 + 8^2 + 9^2 = 179$$

The symbol $(\Sigma X)^2$ (sum of the $X$ scores, quantity squared) indicates that we are first to sum the $X$ scores and then square the resulting sum. Thus,

$$(\Sigma X)^2 = (X_1 + X_2 + X_3 + \cdots + X_N)^2$$

For the previous scores, namely, $X_1 = 3$, $X_2 = 5$, $X_3 = 8$, and $X_4 = 9$,

$$(\Sigma X)^2 = (3 + 5 + 8 + 9)^2 = (25)^2 = 625$$

Note that $\Sigma X^2 \neq (\Sigma X)^2 (179 \neq 625)$. Confusing $\Sigma X^2$ and $(\Sigma X^2)$ is a common error made by students, particularly when calculating the standard deviation. We shall return to this point when we take up the standard deviation in Chapter 4.*

## MEASUREMENT SCALES: NOMINAL, ORDINAL, INTERVAL, AND RATIO SCALES

Since statistics deals with data and data are the result of measurement, we need to spend some time discussing measuring scales. This subject is particularly important because the type of measuring scale employed in collecting the data helps determine which statistical inference test is used to analyze the data. Theoretically, a measuring scale can have one or more of the following mathematical attributes: magnitude, an equal interval between adjacent units, and an absolute zero point. Four types of scales are commonly encountered in the behavioral sciences: *nominal, ordinal, interval,* and *ratio.* They differ in the number of mathematical attributes that they possess.

### Nominal Scales

A *nominal scale* is the lowest level of measurement and is most often used with variables that are qualitative in nature rather than quantitative. Examples of qualitative variables are brands of jogging shoes, kinds of fruit, types of music, days of the month, nationality, religious preference, and eye color. When a nominal scale is used, the variable is divided into its several categories. These categories comprise the "units" of the scale, and objects are "measured" by determining the category to which they belong. Thus, measurement with a nominal scale really amounts to classifying the objects and giving them the name (hence, *nominal* scale) of the category to which they belong.

---

*See Note 2.1 at the end of this chapter for additional summation rules, if desired.

To illustrate, if you are a jogger, you are probably interested in the different brands of jogging shoes available for use, such as Brooks, Nike, Adidas, Saucony, and New Balance, to name a few. Jogging shoes are important because, in jogging, each shoe hits the ground about 800 times a mile. In a 5-mile run, that's 4000 times. If you weigh 125 pounds, you have a total impact of 300 tons on each foot during a 5-mile jog. That's quite a pounding. No wonder joggers are extremely careful about selecting shoes.

The variable "brand of jogging shoes" is a qualitative variable. It is measured on a nominal scale. The different brands mentioned here represent some of the possible categories (units) of this scale. If we had a group of jogging shoes and wished to measure them using this scale, we would take each one and determine to which brand it belonged. It is important to note that because the units of a nominal scale are categories, there is no magnitude relationship between the units of a nominal scale. Thus, there is no quantitative relationship between the categories of Nike and Brooks. The Nike is no more or less a brand of jogging shoe than is the Brooks. They are just different brands. The point becomes even clearer if we were to call the categories jogging shoes 1 and jogging shoes 2 instead of Nike and Brooks. Here, the numbers 1 and 2 are really just names and bear no magnitude relationship to each other.

A fundamental property of nominal scales is that of *equivalence*. By this we mean that all members of a given class are the same from the standpoint of the classification variable. Thus, all pairs of Nike jogging shoes are considered the same from the standpoint of "brand of jogging shoes"—this despite the fact that there may be different types of Nike jogging shoes present.

An operation often performed in conjunction with nominal measurement is that of counting the instances within each class. For example, if we had a bunch of jogging shoes and we determined the brand of each shoe, we would be doing nominal measurement. In addition, we might want to count the number of shoes in each category. Thus, we might find that there are 20 Nike, 19 Saucony, and 6 New Balance shoes in the bunch. These frequencies allow us to compare the number of shoes within each category. This quantitative comparison of numbers within each category should not be confused with the statement made earlier that there is no magnitude relationship between the units of a nominal scale. We can compare quantitatively the numbers of Nike with the numbers of Saucony shoes, but Nike is no more or less a brand of jogging shoe than is Saucony. Thus, a nominal scale does not possess any of the mathematical attributes of magnitude, equal interval, or absolute zero point. It merely allows categorization of objects into mutually exclusive categories.

## Ordinal Scales

An *ordinal scale* represents the next higher level of measurement. It possesses a relatively low level of the property of magnitude. With an ordinal scale, we rank-order the objects being measured according to whether they possess more, less, or the same amount of the variable being measured. Thus, an ordinal scale allows determination of whether $A > B, A = B,$ or $A < B$.

An example of an ordinal scale is the rank ordering of the top five contestants in a speech contest according to speaking ability. Among these speakers, the individual ranked 1 was judged a better speaker than the individual ranked 2, who in turn was judged better than the individual ranked 3. The individual ranked 3 was judged a better speaker than the individual ranked 4, who in turn was judged better than the individual ranked 5. It is important to note that although this scale allows better than, equal to, or less than comparisons, it says nothing about the magnitude of the difference between adjacent units on the scale. In the present example, the difference in speaking ability between the individuals ranked 1 and 2 might be large, and the difference between individuals ranked 2 and 3 might be small. Thus, an ordinal scale does not have the property of equal intervals between adjacent units. Furthermore, since all we have is relative rankings, the scale doesn't tell the absolute level of the variable. Thus, all five of the top-ranked speakers could have a very high level of speaking ability or a low level. This information can't be obtained from an ordinal scale.

Other examples of ordinal scaling are the ranking of runners in the Boston Marathon according to their finishing order, the rank ordering of college football teams according to merit by the Associated Press, the rank ordering of teachers according to teaching ability, and the rank ordering of students according to motivation level.

## Interval Scales

The *interval scale* represents a higher level of measurement than the ordinal scale. It possesses the properties of magnitude and equal interval between adjacent units but doesn't have an absolute zero point. Thus, the interval scale possesses the properties of the ordinal scale and has equal intervals between adjacent units. The phrase "equal intervals between adjacent units" means that there are equal amounts of the variable being measured between adjacent units on the scale.

The Celsius scale of temperature measurement is a good example of the interval scale. It has the property of equal intervals between adjacent units but does not have an absolute zero point. The property of equal intervals is shown by the fact that a given change of heat will cause the same change in temperature reading on the scale no matter where on the scale the change occurs. Thus, the additional amount of heat that will cause a temperature reading to change from 2° to 3° Celsius will also cause a reading to change from 51° to 52° or from 105° to 106° Celsius. This illustrates the fact that equal amounts of heat are indicated between adjacent units throughout the scale.

Since with an interval scale there are equal amounts of the variable between adjacent units on the scale, equal differences between the numbers on the scale represent equal differences in the magnitude of the variable. Thus, we can say the difference in heat is the same between 78° and 75° Celsius as between 24° and 21° Celsius. It also follows logically that greater differences between the numbers on the scale represent greater differences in the magnitude of the variable being measured, and smaller differences between the numbers on the scale represent smaller differences in the magnitude of the variable being measured. Thus, the difference in heat between 80° and 65° Celsius is greater than between 18° and 15° Celsius, and the difference in heat between 93° and 91° Celsius is less than between 48° and 40° Celsius. In light of the preceding discussion, we can see that in addition to being able to determine whether $A = B$, $A > B$, or $A < B$, an interval scale allows us to determine whether $A - B = C - D$, $A - B > C - D$, or $A - B < C - D$.

## Ratio Scales

The next, and highest, level of measurement is called a *ratio scale*. It has all the properties of an interval scale and, in addition, has an absolute zero point. Without an absolute zero point, it is not legitimate to compute ratios with the scale readings. Since the ratio scale has an absolute zero point, ratios are permissible (hence the name *ratio* scale).

A good example to illustrate the difference between interval and ratio scales is to compare the Celsius scale of temperature with the Kelvin scale. Zero on the Kelvin scale is absolute zero (the complete absence of heat). Zero on the Celsius scale is the temperature at which water freezes. It is an arbitrary zero point that actually occurs at 273° Kelvin. The Celsius scale is an interval scale, and the Kelvin scale is a ratio scale. The difference in heat between 8° and 9° is the same as between 99° and 100° whether the scale is Celsius or Kelvin. However, we cannot compute ratios with the Celsius scale. A reading of 20° Celsius is not twice as hot as 10° Celsius. This can be seen by converting the Celsius readings to the actual heat they represent. In terms of actual heat, 20° Celsius is really 293° (273° + 20°), and 10° Celsius is really 283° (273° + 10°). It is obvious that 293° is not twice 283°. Since the Kelvin scale has an absolute zero, a reading of 20° on it is twice as hot as 10°. Thus, ratios are permissible with the Kelvin scale.

Other examples of variables measured with ratio scales include reaction time, length, weight, age, and frequency of any event, such as the number of Nike shoes contained in the bunch of jogging shoes discussed previously. With a ratio scale, you can construct ratios and perform all the other mathematical operations usually associated with numbers (e.g., addition, subtraction, multiplication, and division). The four scales of measurement and their characteristics are summarized in Figure 2.1.

**Nominal**

Units of the scale are categories. Objects are measured by determining the category to which they belong. There is no magnitude relationship between the categories.

*Nike*    *New Balance*    *Saucony*

**Ordinal**

Possesses the property of magnitude. Can rank-order the objects according to whether they possess more, less, or the same amount of the variable being measured. Thus, can determine whether $A > B, A = B, A < B$. Cannot determine how much greater or less $A$ is than $B$ in the attribute being measured.

| | | | | | | |
|---|---|---|---|---|---|---|
| Celsius | −273 | 0 | 10 | 20 | 30 | 40 |
| Kelvin | 0 | 273 | 283 | 293 | 303 | 313 |

**Interval and Ratio**

*Interval*: Possesses the properties of magnitude and equal intervals between adjacent units. Can do same determinations as with an ordinal scale, plus can determine whether $A - B = C - D$, $A - B > C - D$, or $A - B < C - D$.

*Ratio*: Possesses the properties of magnitude, equal interval between adjacent units, and an absolute zero point. Can do all the mathematical operations usually associated with numbers, including ratios.

**figure 2.1** Scales of measurement and their characteristics.

## MEASUREMENT SCALES IN THE BEHAVIORAL SCIENCES

In the behavioral sciences, many of the scales used are often treated as though they were of interval scaling without clearly establishing that the scale really does possess equal intervals between adjacent units. Measurement of IQ, emotional variables such as anxiety and depression, personality variables (e.g., self-sufficiency, introversion, extroversion, and dominance), end-of-course proficiency or achievement variables, attitudinal variables, and so forth fall into this category. With all of these variables, it is clear that the scales are not ratio. For example, with IQ, if an individual actually scored a zero on the Wechsler Adult Intelligence Scale (WAIS), we would not say that he had zero intelligence. Presumably, some questions could be found that he could answer which would indicate an IQ over zero. Thus, the WAIS does not have an absolute zero point, and ratios are not appropriate. Hence, it is not correct to say that a person with an IQ of 140 is twice as smart as someone with an IQ of 70.

On the other hand, it seems that we can do more than just specify a rank ordering of individuals. An individual with an IQ of 100 is closer in intelligence to someone with an IQ of 110 than to someone with an IQ of 60. This appears to be interval scaling, but it is difficult to establish that the scale actually possesses *equal* intervals between adjacent units. Many researchers treat those variables as though they were measured on interval scales, particularly when the measuring instrument is well standardized, as is the WAIS. It is more controversial to treat poorly standardized scales measuring psychological variables as interval scales. This issue arises particularly in inferential statistics, where the level of scaling can influence the selection of the test to be used for data analysis. There are two schools of thought. The first claims that certain tests, such as Student's *t* test and the analysis of variance, should be limited in use to data that are interval or ratio in scaling. The second disagrees, claiming that these tests can also be used with nominal and ordinal data. The issue, however, is too complex to be treated here.*

## CONTINUOUS AND DISCRETE VARIABLES

In Chapter 1, we defined a variable as a property or characteristic of something that can take on more than one value. We also distinguished between independent and dependent variables. In addition, variables may be continuous or discrete:

---

*The interested reader should consult N. H. Anderson, "Scales and Statistics: Parametric and Nonparametric," *Psychological Bulletin, 58* (1961), 305–316; F. M. Lord, "On the Statistical Treatment of Football Numbers," *American Psychologist, 8* (1953), 750–751; W. L. Hays, *Statistics for the Social Sciences,* 2nd ed., Holt, Rinehart and Winston, New York, 1973, pp. 87–90; S. Siegel, *Nonparametric Statistics for the Behavioral Sciences,* McGraw-Hill, New York, 1956, pp. 18–20; and S. S. Stevens, "Mathematics, Measurement, and Psychophysics," in *Handbook of Experimental Psychology,* S. S. Stevens, ed., Wiley, New York, 1951, pp. 23–30.

definitions

■ *A **continuous variable** is one that theoretically can have an infinite number of values between adjacent units on the scale.*

■ *A **discrete variable** is one in which there are no possible values between adjacent units on the scale.*

Weight, height, and time are examples of continuous variables. With each of these variables, there are potentially an infinite number of values between adjacent units. If we are measuring time and the smallest unit on the clock that we are using is 1 second, between 1 and 2 seconds there are an infinite number of possible values: 1.1 seconds, 1.01 seconds, 1.001 seconds, and so forth. The same argument could be made for weight and height.

This is not the case with a discrete variable. "Number of children in a family" is an example of a discrete variable. Here the smallest unit is one child, and there are no possible values between one or two children, two or three children, and so on. The characteristic of a discrete variable is that the variable changes in fixed amounts, with no intermediate values possible. Other examples include "number of students in your class," "number of professors at your university," and "number of dates you had last month."

## Real Limits of a Continuous Variable

Since a continuous variable may have an infinite number of values between adjacent units on the scale, all measurements made on a continuous variable are *approximate*. Let's use weight to illustrate this point. Suppose you began dieting yesterday. Assume it is spring, heading into summer, and bathing suit weather is just around the corner. Anyway, you weighed yourself yesterday morning, and your weight was shown by the solid needle in Figure 2.2. Assume that the scale shown in the figure has accuracy only to the nearest pound. The weight you record is 180 pounds. This morning, when you weighed yourself after a day of star-

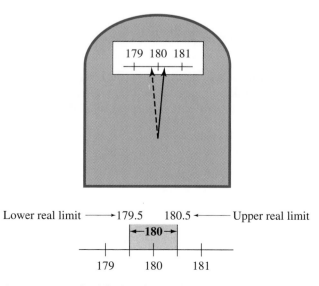

figure 2.2 Real limits of a continuous variable.

vation, the pointer was shown by the dashed needle. What weight do you report this time? We know as a humanist that you would like to record 179 pounds, but as a budding scientist, it is *truth* at all costs. You again record 180 pounds. When would you be justified in reporting 179 pounds? When the needle is below the halfway point between 179 and 180 pounds. Similarly, you would still record 180 pounds if the needle was above 180 but below the halfway point between 180 and 181 pounds. Thus, anytime the weight 180 pounds is recorded, we don't necessarily mean exactly 180 pounds, but rather that the weight was between 180 $\pm$ 0.5 pounds. We don't know the exact value of the weight, but we are sure it is in the range 179.5 to 180.5. This range specifies the *real limits* of the weight 180 pounds. The value 179.5 is called the *lower real limit,* and 180.5 is the *upper real limit.*

definition ■ *The* **real limits of a continuous variable** *are those values that are above and below the recorded value by one-half of the smallest measuring unit of the scale.*

To illustrate, if the variable is weight, the smallest unit is 1 pound, and we record 180 pounds, the real limits are above and below 180 pounds by $\frac{1}{2}$ pound. Thus, the real limits are 179.5 and 180.5 pounds.* If the smallest unit were 0.1 pound rather than 1 pound and we recorded 180.0 pounds, then the real limits would be 180 $\pm \frac{1}{2}(0.1)$, or 179.95 and 180.05.

## Significant Figures

In statistics, we analyze data, and data analysis involves performing mathematical calculations. Very often, we wind up with a decimal remainder (e.g., after doing a division). When this happens, we need to decide to how many decimal places we should carry the remainder.

In the physical sciences, we usually follow the practice of carrying the same number of significant figures as are in the raw data. For example, if we measured the weights of five subjects to three significant figures (173, 156, 162, 165, and 175 pounds) and we were calculating the average of these weights, our answer should also contain only three significant figures. Thus,

$$\overline{X} = \frac{\Sigma X}{N} = \frac{173 + 156 + 162 + 165 + 175}{5} = \frac{831}{5} = 166.2 = 166$$

The answer of 166.2 would be rounded to three significant figures, giving a final answer of 166 pounds. For various reasons, this procedure has not been followed in the behavioral sciences. Instead, a tradition has evolved in which most final values are reported to two or three decimal places regardless of the number of significant figures in the raw data. Since this is a text for use in the behavioral sciences, we have chosen to follow this tradition. Thus, in this text, we shall report most of our final answers to two decimal places. Occasionally there will be exceptions. For example, correlation and regression coefficients have three decimal places, and probability values are often given to four places, as is consistent with tradition. *It is standard practice to carry all intermediate calculations to two or*

---

*Actually, the real limits are 179.500000 . . . and 180.499999 . . . , but it is not necessary to be that accurate here.

*more decimal places than will be reported in the final answer.* Thus, when the final answer is required to have two decimal places, you should carry intermediate calculations to at least four decimal places and round the final answer to two places.

## Rounding

Given that we shall be reporting our final answers to two and sometimes three or four decimal places, we need to decide how we determine what value the last digit should have. Happily, the rules to be followed are rather simple and straightforward:

1. Divide the number you wish to round into two parts: the potential answer and the remainder. The potential answer is the original number extending through the desired number of decimal places. The remainder is the rest of the number.
2. Place a decimal point in front of the first digit of the remainder, creating a decimal remainder.
3. If the decimal remainder is greater than $\frac{1}{2}$, add 1 to the last digit of the answer.
4. If the decimal remainder is less than $\frac{1}{2}$, leave the last digit of the answer unchanged.
5. If the decimal remainder is equal to $\frac{1}{2}$, add 1 to the last digit of the answer if it is an odd digit, but if it is even, leave it unchanged.

Let's try a few examples. Round the numbers in the left-hand column of Table 2.2 to two decimal places.

To accomplish the rounding, the number is divided into two parts: the potential answer and the remainder. Since we are rounding to two decimal places, the potential answer ends at the second decimal place. The rest of the number constitutes the remainder. For the first number, 34.01350, 34.01 constitutes the potential answer and .350 the remainder. Since .350 is below $\frac{1}{2}$, the last digit of the potential answer remains unchanged and the final answer is 34.01. For the second number, 34.01761, the decimal remainder (.761) is above $\frac{1}{2}$. Therefore, we must add 1 to the last digit, making the correct answer 34.02. For the next two numbers, the decimal remainder equals $\frac{1}{2}$. The number 45.04500 becomes 45.04 because the last digit in the potential answer is even. The number 45.05500 becomes 45.06 because the last digit is odd.

table 2.2   Rounding

| Number | Answer; Remainder | Decimal Remainder | Final Answer | Reason |
|---|---|---|---|---|
| 34.01350 | 34.01;350 | .350 | 34.01 | Decimal remainder is below $\frac{1}{2}$. |
| 34.01761 | 34.01;761 | .761 | 34.02 | Decimal remainder is above $\frac{1}{2}$. |
| 45.04500 | 45.04;500 | .500 | 45.04 | Decimal remainder equals $\frac{1}{2}$, and last digit is even. |
| 45.05500 | 45.05;500 | .500 | 45.06 | Decimal remainder equals $\frac{1}{2}$, and last digit is odd. |

## SUMMARY

In this chapter, we have discussed basic mathematical and measurement concepts. The topics covered were notation, summation, measuring scales, discrete and continuous variables, and rounding. In addition, we pointed out that to do well in statistics, you do not need to be a mathematical whiz. If you have a sound knowledge of elementary algebra, do lots of problems, pay special attention to the symbols, and keep up, you should achieve a thorough understanding of the material.

## IMPORTANT TERMS

Continuous variable (p. 31)
Discrete variable (p. 31)
Interval scale (p. 29)

Nominal scale (p. 27)
Ordinal scale (p. 28)
Ratio scale (p. 29)

Real limits of a continuous
   variable (p. 32)
Summation (p. 25)

## QUESTIONS AND PROBLEMS

1. Define and give an example of each of the terms in the Important Terms section.
2. Identify which of the following represent continuous variables and which are discrete variables:
   a. Time of day
   b. Number of females in your class
   c. Number of bar presses by a rat in a Skinner box
   d. Age of subjects in an experiment
   e. Number of words remembered
   f. Weight of food eaten
   g. Percentage of students in your class who are females
   h. Speed of runners in a race
3. Identify the scaling of each of the following variables:
   a. Number of bicycles ridden by students in the freshman class
   b. Types of bicycles ridden by students in the freshman class
   c. The IQ of your teachers (assume equal interval scaling)
   d. Proficiency in mathematics graded in the categories of poor, fair, and good
   e. Anxiety over public speaking scored on a scale of 0–100 (Assume the difference in anxiety between adjacent units throughout the scale is not the same.)
   f. The weight of a group of dieters
   g. The time it takes to react to the sound of a tone
   h. Proficiency in mathematics is scored on a scale of 0–100. The scale is well standardized and can be thought of as having equal intervals between adjacent units.
   i. Ratings of professors by students on a 50-point scale. There is an insufficient basis for assuming equal intervals between adjacent units.

4. A student is measuring assertiveness with an interval scale. Is it correct to say that a score of 30 on the scale represents half as much assertiveness as a score of 60? Explain.
5. For each of the following sets of scores, find
$$\sum_{i=1}^{N} X_i:$$
   a. 2, 4, 5, 7
   b. 2.1, 3.2, 3.6, 5.0, 7.2
   c. 11, 14, 18, 22, 25, 28, 30
   d. 110, 112, 115, 120, 133
6. Round the following numbers to two decimal places:
   a. 14.53670
   b. 25.26231
   c. 37.83500
   d. 46.50499
   e. 52.46500
   f. 25.48501
7. Determine the real limits of the following values:
   a. 10 pounds (assume the smallest unit of measurement is 1 pound)
   b. 2.5 seconds (assume the smallest unit of measurement is 0.1 second)
   c. 100 grams (assume the smallest unit of measurement is 10 grams)
   d. 2.01 centimeters (assume the smallest unit of measurement is 0.01 centimeter)
   e. 5.232 seconds (assume the smallest unit of measurement is 1 millisecond)
8. Find the values of the expressions listed here:
   a. Find $\sum_{i=1}^{4} X_i$ for the scores $X_1 = 3$, $X_2 = 5$, $X_3 = 7$, $X_4 = 10$.
   b. Find $\sum_{i=1}^{6} X_i$ for the scores $X_1 = 2$, $X_2 = 3$, $X_3 = 4$, $X_4 = 6$, $X_5 = 9$, $X_6 = 11$, $X_7 = 14$.

c. Find $\sum_{i=2}^{N} X_i$ for the scores $X_1 = 10, X_2 = 12,$ $X_3 = 13, X_4 = 15, X_5 = 18.$

d. Find $\sum_{i=3}^{N-1} X_i$ for the scores $X_1 = 22, X_2 = 24,$ $X_3 = 28, X_4 = 35, X_5 = 38, X_6 = 40.$

9. In an experiment measuring the reaction times of eight subjects, the following scores in milliseconds were obtained:

| Subject | Reaction Time |
|---------|---------------|
| 1 | 250 |
| 2 | 378 |
| 3 | 451 |
| 4 | 275 |
| 5 | 225 |
| 6 | 430 |
| 7 | 325 |
| 8 | 334 |

   a. If $X$ represents the variable of reaction time, assign each of the scores its appropriate $X_i$ symbol.
   b. Compute $\Sigma X$ for these data.

10. Represent each of the following with summation notation. Assume the total number of scores is 10.
   a. $X_1 + X_2 + X_3 + X_4 + \cdots + X_{10}$
   b. $X_1 + X_2 + X_3$
   c. $X_2 + X_3 + X_4$
   d. $X_2^2 + X_3^2 + X_4^2 + X_5^2$

11. Round the following numbers to one decimal place:
   a. 1.423
   b. 23.250
   c. 100.750
   d. 41.652
   e. 35.348

12. For each of the sets of scores given in Problems 5b and 5c, show that $\Sigma X^2 \neq (\Sigma X)^2$.

13. Given the scores $X_1 = 3, X_2 = 4, X_3 = 7,$ and $X_4 = 12,$ find the values of the following expressions. (This question pertains to Note 2.1.)
   a. $\sum_{i=1}^{N} (X_i + 2)$     b. $\sum_{i=1}^{N} (X_i - 3)$
   c. $\sum_{i=1}^{N} (2X_i)$     d. $\sum_{i=1}^{N} (X_i/4)$

14. Round each of the following numbers to one decimal place and two decimal places.
   a. 4.1482
   b. 4.1501
   c. 4.1650
   d. 4.1950

## NOTES

2.1 Many textbooks present a discussion of additional summation rules, such as the summation of a variable plus a constant, summation of a variable times a constant, and so forth. Since this knowledge is not necessary for understanding any of the material in this textbook, we have not included it in the main body but have presented the material here. Knowledge of summation rules may come in handy as background for statistics courses taught at the graduate level.

**Rule 1**     The sum of the values of a variable plus a constant is equal to the sum of the values of the variable plus $N$ times the constant. In equation form,

$$\sum_{i=1}^{N} (X_i + a) = \sum_{i=1}^{N} X_i + Na$$

The validity of this equation can be seen from the following simple algebraic proof:

$$\sum_{i=1}^{N} (X_i + a) = (X_1 + a) + (X_2 + a) + (X_3 + a)$$
$$+ \cdots + (X_N + a)$$
$$= (X_1 + X_2 + X_3 + \cdots + X_N)$$
$$+ (a + a + a + \cdots + a)$$
$$= \sum_{i=1}^{N} X_i + Na$$

To illustrate the use of this equation, suppose we wish to find the sum of the following scores with a constant of 3 added to each score:

$$X: \quad 4, 6, 8, 9$$

$$\sum_{i=1}^{N} (X_i + 3) = \sum_{i=1}^{N} X_i + Na = 27 + 4(3) = 39$$

**Rule 2**     The sum of the values of a variable minus a constant is equal to the sum of the values of the variable minus $N$ times the constant. In equation form,

$$\sum_{i=1}^{N} (X_i - a) = \sum_{i=1}^{N} X_i - Na$$

The algebraic proof of this equation is as follows:

$$\sum_{i=1}^{N} (X_i - a) = (X_1 - a) + (X_2 - a) + (X_3 - a)$$
$$+ \cdots + (X_N - a)$$
$$= (X_1 + X_2 + X_3 + \cdots + X_N)$$
$$+ (-a - a - a - a - \cdots - a)$$
$$= \sum_{i=1}^{N} X_i - Na$$

To illustrate the use of this equation, suppose we wish to find the sum of the following scores with a constant of 2 subtracted from each score:

$$X: \quad 3, 5, 6, 10$$

$$\sum_{i=1}^{N} (X_i - 2) = \sum_{i=1}^{N} X_i - Na = 24 - 4(2) = 16$$

**Rule 3**   The sum of a constant times the value of a variable is equal to the constant times the sum of the values of the variable. In equation form,

$$\sum_{i=1}^{N} aX_i = a \sum_{i=1}^{N} X_i$$

The validity of this equation is shown here:

$$\sum_{i=1}^{N} aX_i = aX_1 + aX_2 + aX_3 + \cdots + aX_N$$
$$= a(X_1 + X_2 + X_3 + \cdots + X_N)$$
$$= a \sum_{i=1}^{N} X_i$$

To illustrate the use of this equation, suppose we wish to determine the sum of 4 times each of the following scores:

$$X: \quad 2, 5, 7, 8, 12$$
$$\sum_{i=1}^{N} 4X_i = 4 \sum_{i=1}^{N} X_i = 4(34) = 136$$

 **BOOK COMPANION WEBSITE**

Go to www.thomsonedu.com/psychology/pagano for:

- SPSS problems and solutions
- Flash cards for review of terms
- Chapter quiz
- Statistical workshops
- And more

**Rule 4**   The sum of a constant divided into the values of a variable is equal to the constant divided into the sum of the values of the variable. In equation form,

$$\sum_{i=1}^{N} \frac{X_i}{a} = \frac{\sum_{i=1}^{N} X_i}{a}$$

The validity of this equation is shown here:

$$\sum_{i=1}^{N} \frac{X_i}{a} = \frac{X_1}{a} + \frac{X_2}{a} + \frac{X_3}{a} + \cdots + \frac{X_N}{a}$$
$$= \frac{X_1 + X_2 + X_3 + \cdots + X_N}{a}$$
$$= \frac{\sum_{i=1}^{N} X_i}{a}$$

Again, let's do an example to illustrate the use of this equation. Suppose we want to find the sum of 4 divided into the following scores:

$$X: \quad 3, 4, 7, 10, 11$$

$$\sum_{i=1}^{N} \frac{X_i}{4} = \frac{\sum_{i=1}^{N} X_i}{4} = \frac{35}{4} = 8.75$$

# Web**TUTOR**™

Available via WebTutor for this chapter:

- Detailed chapter outline
- *Know and Be Able To Do* section
- Drag & Drop game for equations, concepts, and other material
- Flash cards for review of terms
- Audio flash cards for MP3 player
- Solving problems using Excel
- Solving problems using SPSS
- More practice problems using computational equations
- Chapter quiz

# Frequency Distributions

CHAPTER **3**

## INTRODUCTION: UNGROUPED FREQUENCY DISTRIBUTIONS

Let's suppose you have just been handed back your first exam in statistics. You received an 86. Naturally, you are interested in how well you did relative to the other students. You have lots of questions: How many other students received an 86? Were there many scores higher than yours? How many scores were lower? The raw scores from the exam are presented haphazardly in Table 3.1. Although all the scores are shown, it is difficult to make much sense out of them the way they are arranged in the table. A more efficient arrangement, and one that conveys more meaning, is to list the scores with their frequency of occurrence. This listing is called a *frequency distribution*.

**t a b l e 3.1**   Scores from statistics exam ($N = 70$)

| | | | | | | |
|---|---|---|---|---|---|---|
| 95 | 57 | 76 | 93 | 86 | 80 | 89 |
| 76 | 76 | 63 | 74 | 94 | 96 | 77 |
| 65 | 79 | 60 | 56 | 72 | 82 | 70 |
| 67 | 79 | 71 | 77 | 52 | 76 | 68 |
| 72 | 88 | 84 | 70 | 83 | 93 | 76 |
| 82 | 96 | 87 | 69 | 89 | 77 | 81 |
| 87 | 65 | 77 | 72 | 56 | 78 | 78 |
| 58 | 54 | 82 | 82 | 66 | 73 | 79 |
| 86 | 81 | 63 | 46 | 62 | 99 | 93 |
| 82 | 92 | 75 | 76 | 90 | 74 | 67 |

**definition**   ■   *A **frequency distribution** presents the score values and their frequency of occurrence.* When presented in a table, the score values are listed in rank order, with the lowest score value usually at the bottom of the table.

The scores in Table 3.1 have been arranged into a frequency distribution that is shown in Table 3.2. The data now are more meaningful. First, it is easy to see that there are 2 scores of 86. Furthermore, by summing the appropriate frequencies ($f$), we can determine the number of scores higher and lower than 86. It turns out that there are 15 scores higher and 53 scores lower than your score. It is also quite easy to determine the range of the scores when they are displayed as a frequency distribution. For the statistics test, the scores ranged from 46 to 99. From this illustration, it can be seen that the major purpose of a frequency distribution is to present the scores in such a way to facilitate ease of understanding and interpretation.

**t a b l e 3.2**   Scores from Table 3.1 organized into a frequency distribution

| Score | $f$ | Score | $f$ | Score | $f$ | Score | $f$ |
|---|---|---|---|---|---|---|---|
| 99 | 1 | 85 | 0 | 71 | 1 | 57 | 1 |
| 98 | 0 | 84 | 1 | 70 | 2 | 56 | 2 |
| 97 | 0 | 83 | 1 | 69 | 1 | 55 | 0 |
| 96 | 2 | 82 | 5 | 68 | 1 | 54 | 1 |
| 95 | 1 | 81 | 2 | 67 | 2 | 53 | 0 |
| 94 | 1 | 80 | 1 | 66 | 1 | 52 | 1 |
| 93 | 3 | 79 | 3 | 65 | 2 | 51 | 0 |
| 92 | 1 | 78 | 2 | 64 | 0 | 50 | 0 |
| 91 | 0 | 77 | 4 | 63 | 2 | 49 | 0 |
| 90 | 1 | 76 | 6 | 62 | 1 | 48 | 0 |
| 89 | 2 | 75 | 1 | 61 | 0 | 47 | 0 |
| 88 | 1 | 74 | 2 | 60 | 1 | 46 | 1 |
| 87 | 2 | 73 | 1 | 59 | 0 | | |
| 86 | 2 | 72 | 3 | 58 | 1 | | |

## GROUPING SCORES

When there are many scores and the scores range widely, as they do on the statistics exam we have been considering, listing individual scores results in many values with a frequency of zero and a display from which it is difficult to visualize the shape of the distribution and its central tendency. Under these conditions, the individual scores are usually grouped into class intervals and presented as a *frequency distribution of grouped scores.* Table 3.3 shows the statistics exam scores grouped into two frequency distributions, one with each interval being 2 units wide and the other having intervals 19 units wide.

t a b l e **3.3**   Scores from Table 3.1 grouped into class intervals of different widths

| Class Interval (width = 2) | f | Class Interval (width = 19) | f |
|---|---|---|---|
| 98–99 | 1 | 95–113 | 4 |
| 96–97 | 2 | 76–94 | 38 |
| 94–95 | 2 | 57–75 | 23 |
| 92–93 | 4 | 38–56 | 5 |
| 90–91 | 1 | | $N = \overline{70}$ |
| 88–89 | 3 | | |
| 86–87 | 4 | | |
| 84–85 | 1 | | |
| 82–83 | 6 | | |
| 80–81 | 3 | | |
| 78–79 | 5 | | |
| 76–77 | 10 | | |
| 74–75 | 3 | | |
| 72–73 | 4 | | |
| 70–71 | 3 | | |
| 68–69 | 2 | | |
| 66–67 | 3 | | |
| 64–65 | 2 | | |
| 62–63 | 3 | | |
| 60–61 | 1 | | |
| 58–59 | 1 | | |
| 56–57 | 3 | | |
| 54–55 | 1 | | |
| 52–53 | 1 | | |
| 50–51 | 0 | | |
| 48–49 | 0 | | |
| 46–47 | 1 | | |
| | $N = \overline{70}$ | | |

When you are grouping data, one of the important issues is how wide each interval should be. Whenever data are grouped, some information is lost. The wider the interval, the more information lost. For example, consider the distribution shown in Table 3.3 with intervals 19 units wide. Although an interval this large does result in a smooth display (there are no zero frequencies), a lot of information has been lost. For instance, how are the 38 scores distributed in the interval from 76 to 94? Do they fall at 94? Or at 76? Or are they evenly distributed throughout the interval? The point is that we do not know how they are distributed in the interval. We have lost that information by the grouping. Note that the larger the interval, the greater the ambiguity.

It should be obvious that the narrower the interval, the more faithfully the original data are preserved. The extreme case is where the interval is reduced to 1 unit wide and we are back to the individual scores. Unfortunately, when the interval is made too narrow, we encounter the same problems as with individual scores—namely, values with zero frequency and an unclear display of the shape of the distribution and its central tendency. The frequency distribution with intervals 2 units wide, shown in Table 3.3, is an example where the intervals are too narrow.

From the preceding discussion, we can see that in grouping scores there is a trade-off between losing information and presenting a meaningful visual display. To have the best of both worlds, we must choose an interval width neither too wide nor too narrow. In practice, we usually determine interval width by dividing the distribution into 10 to 20 intervals. Over the years, this range of intervals has been shown to work well with most distributions. Within this range, the specific number of intervals used depends on the number and range of the raw scores. Note that the more intervals used, the narrower each interval becomes.

## Constructing a Frequency Distribution of Grouped Scores

The steps for constructing a frequency distribution of grouped scores are as follows:

1. Find the range of the scores.
2. Determine the width of each class interval ($i$).
3. List the limits of each class interval, placing the interval containing the lowest score value at the bottom.
4. Tally the raw scores into the appropriate class intervals.
5. Add the tallies for each interval to obtain the interval frequency.

Let's apply these steps to the data of Table 3.1.

1. *Finding the range.*

$$\text{Range} = \text{Highest score minus lowest score} = 99 - 46 = 53$$

2. *Determining interval width (i).* Let's assume we wish to group the data into approximately 10 class intervals.

$$i = \frac{\text{Range}}{\text{Number of class intervals}} = \frac{53}{10} = 5.3 \quad \textit{(round to 5)}$$

When $i$ has a decimal remainder, we'll follow the rule of rounding $i$ to the same number of decimal places as in the raw scores. Thus, $i$ rounds to 5.

3. *Listing the intervals.* We begin with the lowest interval. The first step is to determine the lower limit of this interval. There are two requirements:
   a. The lower limit of this interval must be such that the interval contains the lowest score.
   b. It is customary to make the lower limit of this interval evenly divisible by $i$.

   Given these two requirements, the lower limit is assigned the value of the lowest score in the distribution if it is evenly divisible by $i$. If not, then the lower limit is assigned the next lower value that is evenly divisible by $i$. In the present example, the lower limit of the lowest interval begins with 45 because the lowest score (46) is not evenly divisible by 5.

   Once the lower limit of the lowest interval has been found, we can list all of the intervals. Since each interval is 5 units wide, the lowest interval ranges from 45 to 49. Although it may seem as though this interval is only 4 units wide, it really is 5. If in doubt, count the units (45, 46, 47, 48, 49). In listing the other intervals, we must be sure that the intervals are continuous and mutually exclusive. By mutually exclusive, we mean that the intervals must be such that no score can be legitimately included in more than one interval. Following these rules, we wind up with the intervals shown in Table 3.4. Note that, consistent with our discussion of real limits in Chapter 2, the class intervals shown in the first column represent apparent limits. The real limits are shown in the second column. The usual practice is to list just the apparent limits of each interval and omit listing the real limits. We have followed this practice in the remaining examples.

4. *Tallying the scores.* Next, the raw scores are tallied into the appropriate class intervals. Tallying is a procedure whereby one systematically goes through the distribution and for each raw score enters a tally mark next to the interval that contains the score. Thus, for 95 (the first score in Table 3.1), a tally mark is placed in the interval 95–99. This procedure has been followed for all the scores, and the results are shown in Table 3.4.

5. *Summing into frequencies.* Finally, the tally marks are converted into frequencies by adding the tallies within each interval. These frequencies are also shown in Table 3.4.

t a b l e 3.4 Construction of frequency distribution for grouped scores

| Class Interval | Real Limits | Tally | $f$ |
|---|---|---|---|
| 95–99 | 94.5–99.5 | (score of 95) → //// | 4 |
| 90–94 | 89.5–94.5 | /N/ / | 6 |
| 85–89 | 84.5–89.5 | /N/ // | 7 |
| 80–84 | 79.5–84.5 | /N/ /N/ | 10 |
| 75–79 | 74.5–79.5 | /N/ /N/ /N/ / | 16 |
| 70–74 | 69.5–74.5 | /N/ //// | 9 |
| 65–69 | 64.5–69.5 | /N/ // | 7 |
| 60–64 | 59.5–64.5 | //// | 4 |
| 55–59 | 54.5–59.5 | //// | 4 |
| 50–54 | 49.5–54.5 | // | 2 |
| 45–49 | 44.5–49.5 | / | 1 |
| | | | $N = 70$ |

## Practice Problem 3.1

Let's try a practice problem. Given the following 90 scores, construct a frequency distribution of grouped scores having approximately 12 intervals.

| | | | | | | | | |
|-----|-----|-----|-----|-----|-----|-----|-----|-----|
| 112 | 68  | 55  | 33  | 72  | 80  | 35  | 55  | 62  |
| 102 | 65  | 104 | 51  | 100 | 74  | 45  | 60  | 58  |
| 92  | 44  | 122 | 73  | 65  | 78  | 49  | 61  | 65  |
| 83  | 76  | 95  | 55  | 50  | 82  | 51  | 138 | 73  |
| 83  | 72  | 89  | 37  | 63  | 95  | 109 | 93  | 65  |
| 75  | 24  | 60  | 43  | 130 | 107 | 72  | 86  | 71  |
| 128 | 90  | 48  | 22  | 67  | 76  | 57  | 86  | 114 |
| 33  | 54  | 64  | 82  | 47  | 81  | 28  | 79  | 85  |
| 42  | 62  | 86  | 94  | 52  | 106 | 30  | 117 | 98  |
| 58  | 32  | 68  | 77  | 28  | 69  | 46  | 53  | 38  |

### SOLUTION

1. *Find the range.* Range = Highest score − Lowest score = 138 − 22 = 116.
2. *Determine the interval width (i):*

$$i = \frac{\text{Range}}{\text{Number of intervals}} = \frac{116}{12} = 9.7 \qquad i \text{ rounds to } 10$$

3. *List the limits of each class interval.* Because the lowest score in the distribution (22) is not evenly divisible by *i*, the lower limit of the lowest interval is 20. Why 20? Because it is the next lowest scale value evenly divisible by 10. The limits of each class interval have been listed in Table 3.5.
4. *Tally the raw scores into the appropriate class intervals.* This has been done in Table 3.5.
5. *Add the tallies for each interval to obtain the interval frequency.* This has been done in Table 3.5.

**table 3.5** Frequency distribution of grouped scores for Practice Problem 3.1

| Class Interval | Tally | *f* | Class Interval | Tally | *f* |
|----------------|-------|-----|----------------|-------|-----|
| 130–139 | // | 2 | 70–79 | /// /// /// | 13 |
| 120–129 | // | 2 | 60–69 | /// /// /// | 15 |
| 110–119 | /// | 3 | 50–59 | /// /// // | 12 |
| 100–109 | /// / | 6 | 40–49 | /// /// | 8 |
| 90–99 | /// // | 7 | 30–39 | /// // | 7 |
| 80–89 | /// /// / | 11 | 20–29 | //// | 4 |
| | | | | | $N = \overline{90}$ |

## Practice Problem 3.2

Given the 130 scores shown here, construct a frequency distribution of grouped scores having approximately 15 intervals.

| | | | | | | | | | |
|---|---|---|---|---|---|---|---|---|---|
| 1.4 | 2.9 | 3.1 | 3.2 | 2.8 | 3.2 | 3.8 | 1.9 | 2.5 | 4.7 |
| 1.8 | 3.5 | 2.7 | 2.9 | 3.4 | 1.9 | 3.2 | 2.4 | 1.5 | 1.6 |
| 2.5 | 3.5 | 1.8 | 2.2 | 4.2 | 2.4 | 4.0 | 1.3 | 3.9 | 2.7 |
| 2.5 | 3.1 | 3.1 | 4.6 | 3.4 | 2.6 | 4.4 | 1.7 | 4.0 | 3.3 |
| 1.9 | 0.6 | 1.7 | 5.0 | 4.0 | 1.0 | 1.5 | 2.8 | 3.7 | 4.2 |
| 2.8 | 1.3 | 3.6 | 2.2 | 3.5 | 3.5 | 3.1 | 3.2 | 3.5 | 2.7 |
| 3.8 | 2.9 | 3.4 | 0.9 | 0.8 | 1.8 | 2.6 | 3.7 | 1.6 | 4.8 |
| 3.5 | 1.9 | 2.2 | 2.8 | 3.8 | 3.7 | 1.8 | 1.1 | 2.5 | 1.4 |
| 3.7 | 3.5 | 4.0 | 1.9 | 3.3 | 2.2 | 4.6 | 2.5 | 2.1 | 3.4 |
| 1.7 | 4.6 | 3.1 | 2.1 | 4.2 | 4.2 | 1.2 | 4.7 | 4.3 | 3.7 |
| 1.6 | 2.8 | 2.8 | 2.8 | 3.5 | 3.7 | 2.9 | 3.5 | 1.0 | 4.1 |
| 3.0 | 3.1 | 2.7 | 2.2 | 3.1 | 1.4 | 3.0 | 4.4 | 3.3 | 2.9 |
| 3.2 | 0.8 | 3.2 | 3.2 | 2.9 | 2.6 | 2.2 | 3.6 | 4.4 | 2.2 |

**SOLUTION**

1. *Find the range.*   Range = Highest score − Lowest score = 5.0 − 0.6 = 4.4.
2. *Determine the interval width (i):*

$$i = \frac{\text{Range}}{\text{Number of intervals}} = \frac{4.4}{15} = 0.29 \qquad i \text{ rounds to } 0.3$$

3. *List the limits of each class interval.*   Since the lowest score in the distribution (0.6) is evenly divisible by *i*, it becomes the lower limit of the lowest interval. The limits of each class interval are listed in Table 3.6.
4. *Tally the raw scores into the appropriate class intervals.*   This has been done in Table 3.6.
5. *Add the tallies for each interval to obtain the interval frequency.*   This has been done in Table 3.6. Note that since the smallest unit of measurement in the raw scores is 0.1, the real limits for any score are ±0.05 away from the score. Thus, the real limits for the interval 4.8–5.0 are 4.75–5.05.

table **3.6** Frequency distribution of grouped scores for Practice Problem 3.2

| Class Interval | Tally | $f$ | Class Interval | Tally | $f$ |
|---|---|---|---|---|---|
| 4.8–5.0 | // | 2 | 2.4–2.6 | /N/ /N/ | 10 |
| 4.5–4.7 | /N/ | 5 | 2.1–2.3 | /N/ //// | 9 |
| 4.2–4.4 | /N/ /// | 8 | 1.8–2.0 | /N/ //// | 9 |
| 3.9–4.1 | /N/ / | 6 | 1.5–1.7 | /N/ /// | 8 |
| 3.6–3.8 | /N/ /N/ / | 11 | 1.2–1.4 | /N/ / | 6 |
| 3.3–3.5 | /N/ /N/ /N/ / | 16 | 0.9–1.1 | //// | 4 |
| 3.0–3.2 | /N/ /N/ /N/ / | 16 | 0.6–0.8 | /// | 3 |
| 2.7–2.9 | /N/ /N/ /N/ // | 17 | | | $N = 130$ |

## Relative Frequency, Cumulative Frequency, and Cumulative Percentage Distributions

It is often desirable to express the data from a frequency distribution as a relative frequency, a cumulative frequency, or a cumulative percentage distribution.

Table 3.7 shows the frequency distribution of statistics exam scores expressed as relative frequency, cumulative frequency, and cumulative percentage distributions. To convert a frequency distribution into a relative frequency distribution, the frequency for each interval is divided by the total number of scores. Thus,

$$\text{Relative } f = \frac{f}{N}$$

For example, the relative frequency for the interval 45–49 is found by dividing its frequency (1) by the total number of scores (70). Thus, the relative frequency for this interval $= \frac{1}{70} = 0.01$. The relative frequency is useful because it tells us the proportion of scores contained in the interval.

The cumulative frequency for each interval is found by adding the frequency of that interval to the frequencies of all the class intervals below it. Thus, the cumulative frequency for the interval 60–64 $= 4 + 4 + 2 + 1 = 11$.

table **3.7** Relative frequency, cumulative frequency, and cumulative percentage distributions for the grouped scores in Table 3.4

| Class Interval | $f$ | Relative $f$ | Cumulative $f$ | Cumulative % |
|---|---|---|---|---|
| 95–99 | 4 | 0.06 | 70 | 100 |
| 90–94 | 6 | 0.09 | 66 | 94.29 |
| 85–89 | 7 | 0.10 | 60 | 85.71 |
| 80–84 | 10 | 0.14 | 53 | 75.71 |
| 75–79 | 16 | 0.23 | 43 | 61.43 |
| 70–74 | 9 | 0.13 | 27 | 38.57 |
| 65–69 | 7 | 0.10 | 18 | 25.71 |
| 60–64 | 4 | 0.06 | 11 | 15.71 |
| 55–59 | 4 | 0.06 | 7 | 10.00 |
| 50–54 | 2 | 0.03 | 3 | 4.29 |
| 45–49 | 1 | 0.01 | 1 | 1.43 |
|  | 70 | 1.00 |  |  |

The cumulative percentage for each interval is found by converting cumulative frequencies to cumulative percentages. The equation for doing this is:

$$\text{cum\%} = \frac{\text{cum } f}{N} \times 100$$

For the interval 60–64,

$$\text{cum\%} = \frac{\text{cum } f}{N} \times 100 = \frac{11}{70} \times 100 = 15.71\%$$

Cumulative frequency and cumulative percentage distributions are especially useful for finding percentiles and percentile ranks.

## PERCENTILES

Percentiles are measures of relative standing. They are used extensively in education to compare the performance of an individual to that of a reference group.

definition ■ *A **percentile** or **percentile point** is the value on the measurement scale below which a specified percentage of the scores in the distribution fall.*

Thus, the 60th percentile point is the value on the measurement scale below which 60% of the scores in the distribution fall.

## Computation of Percentile Points

Let's assume we are interested in computing the 50th percentile point for the statistics exam scores. The scores have been presented in Table 3.8 as cumulative frequency and cumulative percentage distributions. We shall use the symbol $P_{50}$ to stand for the 50th percentile point. What do we mean by the 50th percentile point? From the definition of percentile point, $P_{50}$ is the scale value below which 50% of the scores fall. Since there are 70 scores in the distribution, $P_{50}$ must be the value below which 35 scores fall (50% of 70 = 35). Looking at the cumulative frequency column and moving up from the bottom, we see that $P_{50}$ falls in the interval 75–79. At this stage, however, we do not know what scale value to assign $P_{50}$. All we know is that it falls somewhere between the real limits of the interval 75–79, which are 74.5 to 79.5. To find where in the interval $P_{50}$ falls, we make the assumption that all the scores in the interval are equally distributed throughout the interval.

Since 27 of the scores fall below a value of 74.5, we need to move into the interval until we acquire 8 more scores (see Figure 3.1). Because there are 16 scores in the interval and the interval is 5 scale units wide, each score in the interval takes up $\frac{5}{16}$ of a unit. To acquire 8 more scores, we need to move into the interval $\frac{5}{16} \times 8 = 2.5$ units. Adding 2.5 to the lower limit of 74.5, we arrive at $P_{50}$. Thus,

$$P_{50} = 74.5 + 2.5 = 77.0$$

To find any percentile point, follow these steps:

1. *Determine the frequency of scores below the percentile point.* We will symbolize this frequency as "cum $f_P$."

$$\text{cum } f_P = (\% \text{ of scores below the percentile point}) \times N$$
$$\text{cum } f_P \text{ for } P_{50} = 50\% \times N = (0.50) \times 70 = 35$$

2. *Determine the lower real limit of the interval containing the percentile point.* We will call the real lower limit $X_L$. Knowing the number of scores

table **3.8** Computation of percentile points for the scores of Table 3.1

| Class Interval | $f$ | Cum $f$ | Cum % | Percentile Computation |
|---|---|---|---|---|
| 95–99 | 4 | 70 | 100 | Percentile point $= X_L + (i/f_i)(\text{cum } f_P - \text{cum } f_L)$ |
| 90–94 | 6 | 66 | 94.29 | |
| 85–89 | 7 | 60 | 85.71 | |
| 80–84 | 10 | 53 | 75.71 | |
| 75–79 | 16 | 43 | 61.43 | $P_{50} = 74.5 + \left(\frac{5}{16}\right)(35 - 27) = 77.00$ |
| 70–74 | 9 | 27 | 38.57 | |
| 65–69 | 7 | 18 | 25.71 | $P_{20} = 64.5 + \left(\frac{5}{7}\right)(14 - 11) = 66.64$ |
| 60–64 | 4 | 11 | 15.71 | |
| 55–59 | 4 | 7 | 10.00 | |
| 50–54 | 2 | 3 | 4.29 | |
| 45–49 | 1 | 1 | 1.43 | |

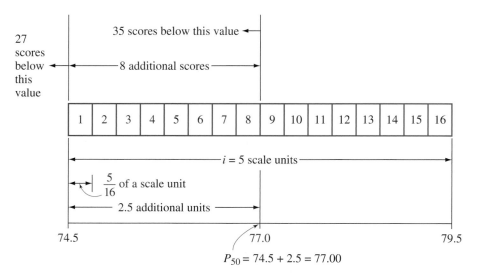

From *Statistical Reasoning in Psychology and Education* by E. W. Minium. Copyright © 1978 John Wiley & Sons, Inc. Adapted by permission.

**f i g u r e  3.1**  Determining the scale value of $P_{50}$ for the statistics exam scores.

below the percentile point, we can locate the interval containing the percentile point by comparing cum $f_P$ with the cumulative frequency for each interval. Once the interval containing the percentile point is located, we can immediately ascertain its lower real limit, $X_L$. For this example, the interval containing $P_{50}$ is 75–79 and its real lower limit, $X_L = 74.5$.

3. *Determine the number of additional scores we must acquire in the interval to reach the percentile point.*

$$\text{Number of additional scores} = \text{cum } f_P - \text{cum } f_L$$

*where*    cum $f_L$ =  frequency of scores below the lower real limit of the interval containing the percentile point.

For the preceding example,

$$
\begin{aligned}
\text{Number of additional scores} &= \text{cum } f_P - \text{cum } f_L \\
&= 35 - 27 \\
&= 8
\end{aligned}
$$

4. *Determine the number of additional units into the interval we must go to acquire the additional number of scores.*

$$
\begin{aligned}
\text{Additional units} &= (\text{Number of units per score}) \times \text{Number of additional scores} \\
&= (i/f_i) \times \text{Number of additional scores} \\
&= \left(\tfrac{5}{16}\right) \times 8 \\
&= 2.5
\end{aligned}
$$

Note that

  $f_i$ *is the number of scores in the interval and*
  $i/f_i$ *gives us the number of units per score for the interval*

5. *Determine the percentile point.* This is accomplished by adding the additional units to the lower real limit of the interval containing the percentile point.

$$\text{Percentile point} = X_L + \text{Additional units}$$
$$P_{50} = 74.5 + 2.5 = 77.00$$

These steps can be put into equation form. Thus,

$$\text{Percentile point} = X_L + (i/f_i)(\text{cum } f_P - \text{cum } f_L)^*$$

*equation for computing percentile point*

where

$X_L$ = value of the lower real limit of the interval containing the percentile point

cum $f_P$ = frequency of scores below the percentile point

cum $f_L$ = frequency of scores below the lower real limit of the interval containing the percentile point

$f_i$ = frequency of the interval containing the percentile point

$i$ = width of the interval

Using this equation to calculate $P_{50}$, we obtain

$$\text{Percentile point} = X_L + (i/f_i)(\text{cum } f_P - \text{cum } f_L)$$
$$P_{50} = 74.5 + (\tfrac{5}{16})(35 - 27)$$
$$= 74.5 + 2.5 = 77.00$$

## Practice Problem 3.3

Let's try another problem. This time we'll calculate $P_{20}$, the value below which 20% of the scores fall.

In terms of cumulative frequency, $P_{20}$ is the value below which 14 scores fall (20% of 70 = 14). From Table 3.8 (p. 47), we see that $P_{20}$ lies in the interval 65–69. Since 11 scores fall below a value of 64.5, we need 3 more scores. Given there are 7 scores in the interval and the interval is 5 units wide, we must move $\tfrac{5}{7} \times 3 = 2.14$ units into the interval. Thus,

$$P_{20} = 64.5 + 2.14 = 66.64$$

$P_{20}$ could also have been found directly by using the equation for percentile point. Thus,

$$\text{Percentile point} = X_L + (i/f_i)(\text{cum } f_P - \text{cum } f_L)$$
$$P_{20} = 64.5 + (\tfrac{5}{7})(14 - 11)$$
$$= 64.5 + 2.14 = 66.64$$

---

*I am indebted to LeAnn Wilson for suggesting this form of the equation.

## Practice Problem 3.4

Let's try one more problem. This time let's compute $P_{75}$. $P_{75}$ is the scale value below which 75% of the scores fall.

In terms of cumulative frequency, $P_{75}$ is the scale value below which 52.5 scores fall (cum $f_P$ = 75% of 70 = 52.5). From Table 3.8 (p. 47), we see that $P_{75}$ falls in the interval 80–84. Since 43 scores fall below this interval's lower limit of 79.5, we need to add to 79.5 the number of scale units appropriate for 52.5 − 43 = 9.5 more scores. Since there are 10 scores in this interval and the interval is 5 units wide, we need to move into the interval $\frac{5}{10} \times 9.5 = 4.75$ units. Thus,

$$P_{75} = 79.5 + 4.75 = 84.25$$

$P_{75}$ also could have been found directly by using the equation for percentile point. Thus,

$$\text{Percentile point} = X_L + (i/f_i)(\text{cum } f_P - \text{cum } f_L)$$
$$P_{75} = 79.5 + (\tfrac{5}{10})(52.5 - 43)$$
$$= 79.5 + 4.75$$
$$= 84.25$$

## PERCENTILE RANK

Sometimes we want to know the percentile rank of a raw score. For example, since your score on the statistics exam was 86, it would be useful to you to know the percentile rank of 86.

definition ■ *The **percentile rank** of a score is the percentage of scores with values lower than the score in question.*

### Computation of Percentile Rank

This situation is just the reverse of calculating a percentile point. Now, we are given the score and must calculate the percentage of scores below it. Again, we must assume that the scores within any interval are evenly distributed throughout the interval. From the class interval column of Table 3.9, we see that the score of 86 falls in the interval 85–89. There are 53 scores below 84.5, the lower limit of this interval. Since there are 7 scores in the interval and the interval is 5 scale units wide, there are $\frac{7}{5}$ scores per scale unit. Between a score of 86 and 84.5, there are $(\frac{7}{5})(86 - 84.5) = 2.1$ additional scores. There are, therefore, a total of $53 + 2.1 = 55.1$ scores below 86. Since there are 70 scores in the distribution, the percentile rank of $86 = (\frac{55.1}{70}) \times 100 = 78.71$.

These operations are summarized in the following equation:

$$\text{Percentile rank} = \frac{\text{cum } f_L + (f_i/i)(X - X_L)}{N} \times 100$$

*equation for computing percentile rank*

where
$\text{cum } f_L =$ frequency of scores below the lower real limit of the interval containing the score $X$

$X =$ score whose percentile rank is being determined

$X_L =$ scale value of the lower real limit of the interval containing the score $X$

$i =$ interval width

$f_i =$ frequency of the interval containing the score $X$

$N =$ total number of raw scores

Using this equation to find the percentile rank of 86, we obtain

$$\text{Percentile rank} = \frac{\text{cum } f_L + (f_i/i)(X - X_L)}{N} \times 100$$

$$= \frac{53 + (\frac{7}{5})(86 - 84.5)}{70} \times 100$$

$$= \frac{53 + 2.1}{70} \times 100$$

$$= \frac{55.1}{70} \times 100$$

$$= 78.71$$

## Practice Problem 3.5

Let's do another problem for practice. Find the percentile rank of 59.

The score of 59 falls in the interval 55–59. There are 3 scores below 54.5. Since there are 4 scores within the interval, there are $(\frac{4}{5})(59 - 54.5) = 3.6$ scores within the interval below 59. In all, there are $3 + 3.6 = 6.6$ scores below 59. Thus, the percentile rank of $59 = (\frac{6.6}{70}) \times 100 = 9.43$.

*(continued)*

The solution is presented in equation form in Table 3.9.

table 3.9   Computation of percentile rank for the scores of Table 3.1

| Class Interval | $f$ | Cum $f$ | Cum % | Percentile Rank Computation |
|---|---|---|---|---|
| 95–99 | 4 | 70 | 100 | Percentile rank $= \dfrac{\text{cum } f_L + (f_i/i)(X - X_L)}{N} \times 100$ |
| 90–94 | 6 | 66 | 94.29 | |
| 85–89 | 7 | 60 | 85.71 | |
| 80–84 | 10 | 53 | 75.71 | |
| 75–79 | 16 | 43 | 61.43 | |
| 70–74 | 9 | 27 | 38.57 | |
| 65–69 | 7 | 18 | 25.71 | |
| 60–64 | 4 | 11 | 15.71 | |
| 55–59 | 4 | 7 | 10.00 | Percentile rank of 59 $= \dfrac{3 + (\frac{4}{5})(59 - 54.5)}{70} \times 100$ |
| 50–54 | 2 | 3 | 4.29 | |
| 45–49 | 1 | 1 | 1.43 | $= 9.43$ |

## Practice Problem 3.6

Let's do one more practice problem. Using the frequency distribution of grouped scores shown in Table 3.5 (p. 43), determine the percentile rank of a score of 117.

The score of 117 falls in the interval 110–119. The lower limit of this interval is 109.5. There are $6 + 7 + 11 + 13 + 15 + 12 + 8 + 7 + 4 = 83$ scores below 109.5. Since there are 3 scores within the interval and the interval is 10 units wide, there are $(\frac{3}{10})(117 - 109.5) = 2.25$ scores within the interval that are below a score of 117. In all, there are $83 + 2.25 = 85.25$ scores below a score of 117. Thus, the percentile rank of $117 = (\frac{85.25}{90}) \times 100 = 94.72$.

This problem could also have been solved by using the equation for percentile rank. Thus,

$$\text{Percentile rank} = \frac{\text{cum } f_L + (f_i/i)(X - X_L)}{N} \times 100$$

$$= \frac{83 + (\frac{3}{10})(117 - 109.5)}{90} \times 100$$

$$= 94.72$$

## GRAPHING FREQUENCY DISTRIBUTIONS

Frequency distributions are often displayed as graphs rather than tables. Since a graph is based completely on the tabled scores, the graph does not contain any new information. However, a graph presents the data pictorially, which often makes it easier to see important features of the data. I have assumed, in writing this section, that you are already familiar with constructing graphs. Even so, it is worthwhile to review a few of the important points.

1. A graph has two axes: vertical and horizontal. The vertical axis is called the *ordinate,* or *Y* axis, and the horizontal axis is the *abscissa,* or *X* axis.
2. Very often the independent variable is plotted on the *X* axis and the dependent variable on the *Y* axis. In graphing a frequency distribution, the score values are usually plotted on the *X* axis and the frequency of the score values is plotted on the *Y* axis.
3. Suitable units for plotting scores should be chosen along the axes.
4. To avoid distorting the data, it is customary to set the intersection of the two axes at zero and then choose scales for the axes such that the height of the graphed data is about three-fourths of the width. Figure 3.2 shows how violation of this rule can bias the impression conveyed by the graph. The figure shows two graphs plotted from the same data, namely, enrollment at a large university during the years 1993–2005. Part (a) follows the rule we have just elaborated. In part (b), the scale on the ordinate does not begin at zero and is greatly expanded from that of part (a). The impressions conveyed by the two graphs are very different. Part (a) gives the correct impression of a very stable enrollment, whereas part (b) greatly distorts the data, making them seem as though there were large enrollment fluctuations.
5. Ordinarily, the intersection of the two axes is at zero for both scales. When it is not, this is indicated by breaking the relevant axis near the intersection. For example, in Figure 3.4, the horizontal axis is broken to indicate that a part of the scale has been left off.
6. Each axis should be labeled, and the title of the graph should be both short and explicit.

Four main types of graphs are used to graph frequency distributions: the *bar graph,* the *histogram,* the *frequency polygon,* and the *cumulative percentage curve.*

### The Bar Graph

Frequency distributions of nominal or ordinal data are customarily plotted using a bar graph. This type of graph is shown in Figure 3.3. A bar is drawn for each category, where the height of the bar represents the frequency or number of members of that category. Since there is no numerical relationship between the categories in nominal data, the various groups can be arranged along the horizontal axis in any order. In Figure 3.3, they are arranged from left to right according to the magnitude of frequency in each category. Note that the bars for each category in a bar graph do not touch each other. This further emphasizes the lack of a quantitative relationship between the categories.

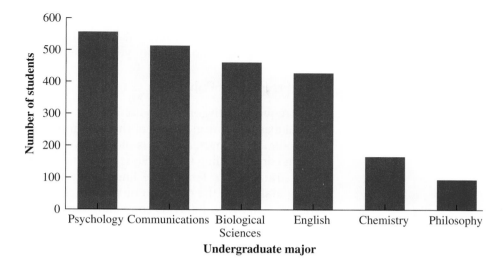

figure 3.3   Bar graph: Students enrolled in various undergraduate majors in a college of arts and sciences.

## The Histogram

The histogram is used to represent frequency distributions composed of interval or ratio data. It resembles the bar graph, but with the histogram, a bar is drawn for each class interval. The class intervals are plotted on the horizontal axis such that each class bar begins and terminates at the real limits of the interval. The height of the bar corresponds to the frequency of the class interval. Since the intervals are continuous, the vertical bars must touch each other rather than be spaced apart as is done with the bar graph. Figure 3.4 shows the statistics exam

| Class interval | f |
|---|---|
| 95–99 | 4 |
| 90–94 | 6 |
| 85–89 | 7 |
| 80–84 | 10 |
| 75–79 | 16 |
| 70–74 | 9 |
| 65–69 | 7 |
| 60–64 | 4 |
| 55–59 | 4 |
| 50–54 | 2 |
| 45–49 | 1 |

figure 3.4   Histogram: Statistics exam scores of Table 3.4.

scores (Table 3.4, p. 42) displayed as a histogram. Note that it is customary to plot the midpoint of each class interval on the abscissa. The grouped scores have been presented again in the figure for your convenience.

## The Frequency Polygon

The frequency polygon is also used to represent interval or ratio data. The horizontal axis is identical to that of the histogram. However, for this type of graph, instead of using bars, a point is plotted over the midpoint of each interval at a height corresponding to the frequency of the interval. The points are then joined with straight lines. Finally, the line joining the points is extended to meet the horizontal axis at the midpoint of the two class intervals falling immediately beyond the end class intervals containing scores. This closing of the line with the horizontal axis forms a polygon from which the name of this graph is taken. Figure 3.5 displays the scores listed in Table 3.4 as a frequency polygon. The major difference between a histogram and a frequency polygon is the following: The histogram displays the scores as though they were equally distributed over the interval, whereas the frequency polygon displays the scores as though they were all concentrated at the midpoint of the interval. Some investigators prefer to use the frequency polygon when they are comparing the shapes of two or more distributions. The frequency polygon also has the effect of displaying the scores as though they were continuously distributed, which in many instances is actually the case.

figure 3.5   Frequency polygon: Statistics exam scores of Table 3.4.

## The Cumulative Percentage Curve

Cumulative frequency and cumulative percentage distributions may also be presented in graphical form. We shall illustrate only the latter because the graphs are basically the same and cumulative percentage distributions are more often encountered. You will recall that the cumulative percentage for a class interval indicates the percentage of scores that fall below the upper real limit of the interval. Thus, the vertical axis for the cumulative percentage curve is plotted in cumulative percentage units. On the horizontal axis, instead of plotting points at the midpoint of each class interval, we plot them at the upper real limit of the interval. Figure 3.6 shows the scores of Table 3.7 (p. 46) displayed as a cumulative percentage curve. It should be obvious that the cumulative frequency curve would have the same shape, the only difference being that the vertical axis would be plotted in cumulative frequency rather than in cumulative percentage units. Both percentiles and percentile ranks can be read directly off the cumulative percentage curve. The cumulative percentage curve is also called an *ogive*, implying an S shape.

## Shapes of Frequency Curves

Frequency distributions can take many different shapes. Some of the more commonly encountered shapes are shown in Figure 3.7. Curves are generally classified as *symmetrical* or *skewed*.

definition ■ *A curve is* **symmetrical** *if when folded in half the two sides coincide. If a curve is not symmetrical, it is* **skewed.**

The curves shown in Figure 3.7(a), (b), and (c) are symmetrical. The curves shown in parts (d), (e), and (f) are skewed. If a curve is skewed, it may be *positively* or *negatively skewed*.

| Class interval | Cum f | Cum % |
|---|---|---|
| 95–99 | 70 | 100 |
| 90–94 | 66 | 94.3 |
| 85–89 | 60 | 85.7 |
| 80–84 | 53 | 75.7 |
| 75–79 | 43 | 61.4 |
| 70–74 | 27 | 38.6 |
| 65–69 | 18 | 25.7 |
| 60–64 | 11 | 15.7 |
| 55–59 | 7 | 10.0 |
| 50–54 | 3 | 4.3 |
| 45–49 | 1 | 1.4 |

Score of 59: 9.43%

$P_{50} = 77.00$

figure 3.6 Cumulative percentage curve: Statistics exam scores of Table 3.7.

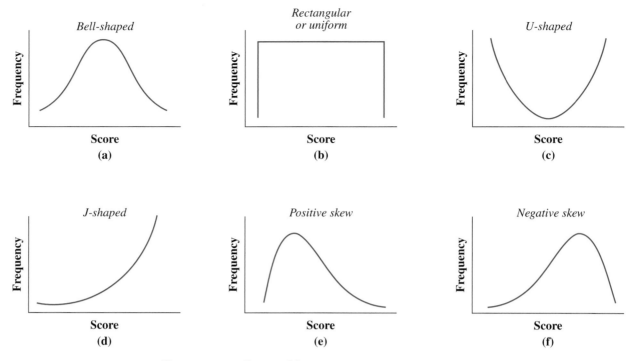

figure 3.7 Shapes of frequency curves.

■ *When a curve is **positively skewed,** most of the scores occur at the lower values of the horizontal axis and the curve tails off toward the higher end. When a curve is **negatively skewed,** most of the scores occur at the higher values of the horizontal axis and the curve tails off toward the lower end.*

The curve in part (e) is positively skewed, and the curve in part (f) is negatively skewed.

Frequency curves are often referred to according to their shape. Thus, the curves shown in parts (a), (b), (c), and (d) are, respectively, called bell-shaped, rectangular or uniform, U-shaped, and J-shaped curves.

## EXPLORATORY DATA ANALYSIS

Exploratory data analysis is a recently developed procedure. It employs easy-to-construct diagrams that are quite useful in summarizing and describing sample data. One of the most popular of these is the *stem and leaf diagram.*

### Stem and Leaf Diagrams

Stem and leaf diagrams were first developed in 1977 by John Tukey, working at Princeton University. They are a simple alternative to the histogram and are most useful for summarizing and describing data when the data set includes less than

100 scores. Unlike what happens with a histogram, however, a stem and leaf diagram does not lose any of the original data. A stem and leaf diagram for the statistics exam scores of Table 3.1 is shown in Figure 3.8.

In constructing a stem and leaf diagram, each score is represented by a *stem* and a *leaf.* The stem is placed to the left of the vertical line and the leaf to the right. For example, the stems and leafs for the first and last original scores are:

| stem | leaf | | stem | leaf |
|------|------|---|------|------|
| 9 | 5 | | 6 | 7 |

In a stem and leaf diagram, stems are placed in order vertically down the page, and the leafs are placed in order horizontally across the page. The leaf for each score is usually the last digit, and the stem is the remaining digits. Occasionally, the leaf is the last two digits depending on the range of the scores.

Note that in stem and leaf diagrams, stem values can be repeated. In Figure 3.8, the stem values are repeated twice. This has the effect of stretching the

**Original Scores**

| 95 | 57 | 76 | 93 | 86 | 80 | 89 |
|----|----|----|----|----|----|----|
| 76 | 76 | 63 | 74 | 94 | 96 | 77 |
| 65 | 79 | 60 | 56 | 72 | 82 | 70 |
| 67 | 79 | 71 | 77 | 52 | 76 | 68 |
| 72 | 88 | 84 | 70 | 83 | 93 | 76 |
| 82 | 96 | 87 | 69 | 89 | 77 | 81 |
| 87 | 65 | 77 | 72 | 56 | 78 | 78 |
| 58 | 54 | 82 | 82 | 66 | 73 | 79 |
| 86 | 81 | 63 | 46 | 62 | 99 | 93 |
| 82 | 92 | 75 | 76 | 90 | 74 | 67 |

**Stem and Leaf Diagram**

| | |
|---|---|
| 4 | 6 |
| 5 | 2 4 |
| 5 | 6 6 7 8 |
| 6 | 0 2 3 3 |
| 6 | 5 5 6 7 7 8 9 |
| 7 | 0 0 1 2 2 2 3 4 4 |
| 7 | 5 6 6 6 6 6 6 7 7 7 7 8 8 9 9 9 |
| 8 | 0 1 1 2 2 2 2 2 3 4 |
| 8 | 6 6 7 7 8 9 9 |
| 9 | 0 2 3 3 3 4 |
| 9 | 5 6 6 9 |

figure 3.8 Stem and leaf diagram: Statistics exam scores of Table 3.1.

stem—that is, creating more intervals and spreading the scores out. A stem and leaf diagram for the statistics scores with stem values listed only once is shown here.

| | |
|---|---|
| 4 | 6 |
| 5 | 2 4 6 6 7 8 |
| 6 | 0 2 3 3 5 5 6 7 7 8 9 |
| 7 | 0 0 1 2 2 2 3 4 4 5 6 6 6 6 6 6 7 7 7 7 8 8 9 9 9 |
| 8 | 0 1 1 2 2 2 2 2 3 4 6 6 7 7 8 9 9 |
| 9 | 0 2 3 3 3 4 5 6 6 9 |

Listing stem values only once results in fewer, wider intervals, with each interval generally containing more scores. This makes the display appear more crowded. Whether stem values should be listed once, twice, or even more than twice depends on the range of the scores.

You should observe that rotating the stem and leaf diagram of Figure 3.8 counterclockwise 90°, such that the stems are at the bottom, results in a diagram very similar to the histogram shown in Figure 3.4. With the histogram, however, we have lost the original scores; with the stem and leaf diagram, the original scores are preserved.

## WHAT IS THE TRUTH?

### Stretch the Scale, Change the Tale

An article appeared in the business section of a newspaper discussing the rate increases of Puget Power & Light Company. The company was in poor financial condition and had proposed still another rate increase in 1984 to try to help it get out of trouble. The issue was particularly sensitive because rate increases had plagued the region recently to pay for huge losses in nuclear power plant construction. The graph on the following page appeared in the article along with the caption "Puget Power rates have climbed steadily during the past 14 years." Do you notice anything peculiar about the graph?

# WHAT IS THE TRUTH?

## Stretch the Scale, Change the Tale

### (*continued*)

***Answer*** Take a close look at the *X* axis. From 1970 to 1980, the scale is calibrated in 2-year intervals. After 1980, the same distance on the *X* axis represents 1 year rather than 2 years. Given the data, stretching this part of the scale gives the false impression that costs have risen "steadily." When plotted properly, as is done in the bottom graph, you can see that rates have not risen steadily, but instead have greatly accelerated over the last 3 years (including the proposed rate increase). Labeling the rise as a "steady" rise rather than a greatly accelerating increase obviously is in the company's interest. It is unclear whether the company furnished the graph or whether the newspaper constructed its own. In any case, when the axes of graphs are not uniform, reader beware!

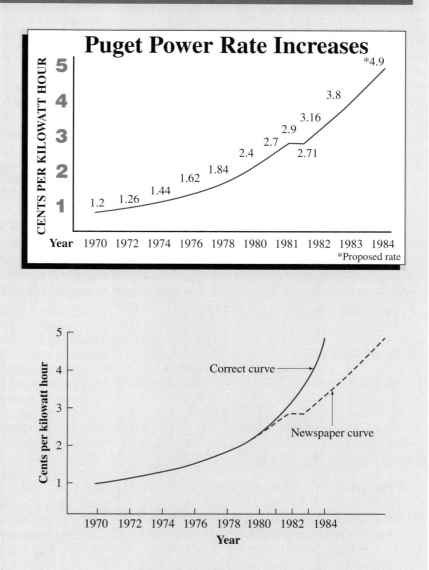

**Puget Power Rate Increases**

CENTS PER KILOWATT HOUR

5
4
3
2
1

1.2   1.26   1.44   1.62   1.84   2.4   2.7   2.9   3.16   3.8   *4.9
2.71

Year   1970   1972   1974   1976   1978   1980   1981   1982   1983   1984
*Proposed rate

Cents per kilowatt hour

5
4
3
2
1

Correct curve

Newspaper curve

1970   1972   1974   1976   1978   1980   1982   1984
Year

## SUMMARY

In this chapter, I have discussed frequency distributions and how to present them in tables and graphs. In descriptive statistics, we are interested in characterizing a set of scores in the most meaningful manner. When faced with a large number of scores, it is easier to understand, interpret, and discuss the scores when they are presented as a frequency distribution. A frequency distribution is a listing of the score values in rank order along with their frequency of occurrence. If there are many scores existing over a wide range, the scores are usually grouped together in equal intervals to allow a more meaningful interpretation. The scores can be presented as an ordinary frequency distribution, a relative frequency distribution, a cumulative frequency distribution, or a cumulative percentage distribution. I discussed each of these and how to construct them. I also presented the concepts of percentile point and percentile rank and discussed how to compute each.

When frequency distributions are graphed, frequency is plotted on the vertical axis and the score value on the horizontal axis. Four main types of graphs are used: the bar graph, the histogram, the frequency polygon, and the cumulative percentage curve. I discussed the use of each type and how to construct them.

Frequency curves can also take on various shapes. I illustrated some of the common shapes encountered (e.g., bell-shaped, U-shaped, and J-shaped) and discussed the difference between symmetrical and skewed curves. Finally, I discussed the use of an exploratory data analysis technique: stem and leaf diagrams.

## IMPORTANT TERMS

Bar graph (p. 53)
Bell-shaped curve (p. 58)
Cumulative frequency distribution (p. 45)
Cumulative percentage distribution (p. 45)
Exploratory data analysis (p. 58)
Frequency distribution (p. 39)

Frequency distribution of grouped scores (p. 40)
Frequency polygon (p. 56)
Histogram (p. 55)
J-shaped curve (p. 58)
Negatively skewed curve (p. 58)
Percentile point (p. 46)
Percentile rank (p. 50)
Positively skewed curve (p. 58)

Relative frequency distribution (p. 45)
Skewed curve (p. 58)
Stem and leaf diagrams (p. 58)
Symmetrical curve (p. 57)
U-shaped curve (p. 58)
$X$ axis (abscissa) (p. 53)
$Y$ axis (ordinate) (p. 53)

## QUESTIONS AND PROBLEMS

1. Define each of the terms in the Important Terms section.
2. How do bar graphs, histograms, and frequency polygons differ in construction? What type of scaling is appropriate for each?
3. The following table gives the 2002 median annual salaries of various categories of scientists in the United States holding PhDs. Construct a bar graph for these data with "Annual Salary" on the $Y$ axis and "Category of Scientist" on the $X$ axis. Arrange the categories so that the salaries decrease from left to right.

| Category of Scientist | Annual Salary ($) |
| --- | --- |
| Biological and Health Sciences | 70,100 |
| Chemistry | 79,100 |
| Computer and Math Sciences | 75,000 |
| Psychology | 66,700 |
| Sociology and Anthropology | 63,100 |

4. A graduate student has collected data involving 66 scores. Based on these data, he has constructed

two frequency distributions of grouped scores. These are shown here. Do you see anything wrong with these distributions? Explain.

a.

| Class Interval | f |
|---|---|
| 48–63 | 17 |
| 29–47 | 28 |
| 10–28 | 21 |

b.

| Class Interval | f | Class Interval | f |
|---|---|---|---|
| 62–63 | 2 | 34–35 | 2 |
| 60–61 | 4 | 32–33 | 0 |
| 58–59 | 3 | 30–31 | 5 |
| 56–57 | 1 | 28–29 | 3 |
| 54–55 | 0 | 26–27 | 0 |
| 52–53 | 4 | 24–25 | 4 |
| 50–51 | 5 | 22–23 | 5 |
| 48–49 | 2 | 20–21 | 2 |
| 46–47 | 0 | 18–19 | 0 |
| 44–45 | 5 | 16–17 | 3 |
| 42–43 | 4 | 14–15 | 1 |
| 40–41 | 3 | 12–13 | 0 |
| 38–39 | 0 | 10–11 | 2 |
| 36–37 | 6 | | |

5. The following scores were obtained by a college sophomore class on an English exam:

| | | | | | | | | | | |
|---|---|---|---|---|---|---|---|---|---|---|
| 60 | 94 | 75 | 82 | 72 | 57 | 92 | 75 | 85 | 77 | 91 |
| 72 | 85 | 64 | 78 | 75 | 62 | 49 | 70 | 94 | 72 | 84 |
| 55 | 90 | 88 | 81 | 64 | 91 | 79 | 66 | 68 | 67 | 74 |
| 45 | 76 | 73 | 68 | 85 | 73 | 83 | 85 | 71 | 87 | 57 |
| 82 | 78 | 68 | 70 | 71 | 78 | 69 | 98 | 65 | 61 | 83 |
| 84 | 69 | 77 | 81 | 87 | 79 | 64 | 72 | 55 | 76 | 68 |
| 93 | 56 | 67 | 71 | 83 | 72 | 82 | 78 | 62 | 82 | 49 |
| 63 | 73 | 89 | 78 | 81 | 93 | 72 | 76 | 73 | 90 | 76 |

a. Construct a frequency distribution of the ungrouped scores ($i = 1$).
b. Construct a frequency distribution of grouped scores having approximately 15 intervals. List both the apparent and real limits of each interval.

c. Construct a histogram of the frequency distribution constructed in part **b**.
d. Is the distribution skewed or symmetrical? If it is skewed, is it skewed positively or negatively?
e. Construct a stem and leaf diagram with the last digit being a leaf and the first digit a stem. Repeat stem values twice.
f. Which diagram do you like better, the histogram of part **c** or the stem and leaf diagram of part **e**? Explain. education

6. Express the grouped frequency distribution of part **b** of Problem 5 as a relative frequency, a cumulative frequency, and a cumulative percentage distribution. education

7. Using the cumulative frequency arrived at in Problem 6, determine
   a. $P_{75}$
   b. $P_{40}$ education

8. Again, using the cumulative distribution and grouped scores arrived at in Problem 6, determine
   a. The percentile rank of a score of 81
   b. The percentile rank of a score of 66
   c. The percentile rank of a score of 87 education

9. Construct a histogram of the distribution of grouped English exam scores determined in Problem 5, part **b**. education

10. The following scores show the amount of weight lost (in pounds) by each client of a weight control clinic during the last year:

| | | | | | | | | | |
|---|---|---|---|---|---|---|---|---|---|
| 10 | 13 | 22 | 26 | 16 | 23 | 35 | 53 | 17 | 32 |
| 41 | 35 | 24 | 23 | 27 | 16 | 20 | 60 | 48 | 43 |
| 52 | 31 | 17 | 20 | 33 | 18 | 23 | 8 | 24 | 15 |
| 26 | 46 | 30 | 19 | 22 | 13 | 22 | 14 | 21 | 39 |
| 28 | 43 | 37 | 15 | 20 | 11 | 25 | 9 | 15 | 21 |
| 21 | 25 | 34 | 10 | 23 | 29 | 28 | 18 | 17 | 24 |
| 16 | 26 | 7 | 12 | 28 | 20 | 36 | 16 | 14 | |
| 18 | 16 | 57 | 31 | 34 | 28 | 42 | 19 | 26 | |

a. Construct a frequency distribution of grouped scores with approximately 10 intervals.
b. Construct a histogram of the frequency distribution constructed in part **a**.
c. Is the distribution skewed or symmetrical? If it is skewed, is it skewed positively or negatively?

d. Construct a stem and leaf diagram with the last digit being a leaf and the first digit a stem. Repeat stem values twice.

e. Which diagram do you like better, the histogram of part **b** or the stem and leaf diagram of part **d**? Explain. clinical, health

11. Convert the grouped frequency distribution of weight losses determined in Problem 10 to a relative frequency and a cumulative frequency distribution. clinical, health

12. Using the cumulative frequency distribution arrived at in Problem 11, determine
a. $P_{50}$
b. $P_{25}$ clinical, health

13. Again using the cumulative frequency distribution of Problem 11, determine
a. The percentile rank of a score of 41
b. The percentile rank of a score of 28 clinical, health

14. Construct a frequency polygon using the grouped frequency distribution determined in Problem 10. Is the curve symmetrical? If not, is it positively or negatively skewed? clinical, health

15. A small eastern college uses the grading system of 0–4.0, with 4.0 being the highest possible grade. The scores shown here are the grade point averages of the students currently enrolled as psychology majors at the college.

| | | | | | | | |
|---|---|---|---|---|---|---|---|
| 2.7 | 1.9 | 1.0 | 3.3 | 1.3 | 1.8 | 2.6 | 3.7 |
| 3.1 | 2.2 | 3.0 | 3.4 | 3.1 | 2.2 | 1.9 | 3.1 |
| 3.4 | 3.0 | 3.5 | 3.0 | 2.4 | 3.0 | 3.4 | 2.4 |
| 2.4 | 3.2 | 3.3 | 2.7 | 3.5 | 3.2 | 3.1 | 3.3 |
| 2.1 | 1.5 | 2.7 | 2.4 | 3.4 | 3.3 | 3.0 | 3.8 |
| 1.4 | 2.6 | 2.9 | 2.1 | 2.6 | 1.5 | 2.8 | 2.3 |
| 3.3 | 3.1 | 1.6 | 2.8 | 2.3 | 2.8 | 3.2 | 2.8 |
| 2.8 | 3.8 | 1.4 | 1.9 | 3.3 | 2.9 | 2.0 | 3.2 |

a. Construct a frequency distribution of grouped scores with approximately 10 intervals.
b. Construct a histogram of the frequency distribution constructed in part **a**.
c. Is the distribution skewed or symmetrical? If skewed, is it skewed positively or negatively?
d. Construct a stem and leaf diagram with the last digit being a leaf and the first digit a stem. Repeat stem values five times.

e. Which diagram do you like better, the histogram of part **b** or the stem and leaf diagram of part **d**? Explain. education

16. For the grouped scores in Problem 15, determine
a. $P_{80}$
b. $P_{20}$ education

17. Sarah's grade point average is 3.1. Based on the frequency distribution of grouped scores constructed in Problem 15, part **a**, what is the percentile rank of Sarah's grade point average? education

18. The policy of the school in Problem 15 is that to graduate with a major in psychology, a student must have a grade point average of 2.5 or higher.
a. Based on the ungrouped scores shown in Problem 15, what percentage of current psychology majors needs to raise its grades?
b. Based on the frequency distribution of grouped scores, what percentage needs to raise its grades?
c. Explain the difference between the answers to parts **a** and **b**. education

19. Construct a frequency polygon using the distribution of grouped scores constructed in Problem 15. Is the curve symmetrical or positively or negatively skewed?

20. The psychology department of a large university maintains its own vivarium of rats for research purposes. A recent sampling of 50 rats from the vivarium revealed the following rat weights:

| | | | | | | | | | |
|---|---|---|---|---|---|---|---|---|---|
| 320 | 282 | 341 | 324 | 340 | 302 | 336 | 265 | 313 | 317 |
| 310 | 335 | 353 | 318 | 296 | 309 | 308 | 310 | 277 | 288 |
| 314 | 298 | 315 | 360 | 275 | 315 | 297 | 330 | 296 | 274 |
| 250 | 274 | 318 | 287 | 284 | 267 | 292 | 348 | 302 | 297 |
| 270 | 263 | 269 | 292 | 298 | 343 | 284 | 352 | 345 | 325 |

a. Construct a frequency distribution of grouped scores with approximately 11 intervals.
b. Construct a histogram of the frequency distribution constructed in part **a**.
c. Is the distribution symmetrical or skewed?
d. Construct a stem and leaf diagram with the last digit being a leaf and the first two digits a stem. Do not repeat stem values.
e. Which diagram do you like better, the histogram or the stem and leaf diagram? Why? biological

21. Convert the grouped frequency distribution of rat weights determined in Problem 20 to a relative frequency, cumulative frequency, and cumulative percentage distribution. biological

22. Using the cumulative frequency distribution arrived at in Problem 21, determine
    a. $P_{50}$
    b. $P_{75}$ biological

23. Again using the cumulative frequency distribution arrived at in Problem 21, determine
    a. The percentile rank of a score of 275
    b. The percentile rank of a score of 318 biological

24. A professor is doing research on individual differences in the ability of students to become hypnotized. As part of the experiment, she administers a portion of the Stanford Hypnotic Susceptibility Scale to 85 students who volunteered for the experiment. The results are scored from 0–12, with 12 indicating the highest degree of hypnotic susceptibility and 0 the lowest. The scores are shown here.

| 9  | 7 | 11 | 4 | 9  | 7 | 8  | 8  | 10 | 6 |
|----|---|----|---|----|---|----|----|----|---|
| 6  | 4 | 3  | 5 | 5  | 4 | 6  | 2  | 6  | 8 |
| 10 | 8 | 6  | 7 | 3  | 7 | 1  | 6  | 5  | 3 |
| 2  | 7 | 6  | 2 | 6  | 9 | 4  | 7  | 9  | 6 |
| 5  | 9 | 5  | 0 | 5  | 6 | 3  | 6  | 7  | 9 |
| 7  | 5 | 4  | 2 | 9  | 8 | 11 | 7  | 12 | 3 |
| 8  | 6 | 5  | 4 | 10 | 7 | 4  | 10 | 8  | 7 |
| 6  | 2 | 7  | 5 | 3  | 4 | 8  | 6  | 4  | 5 |
| 4  | 6 | 5  | 8 | 7  |   |    |    |    |   |

a. Construct a frequency distribution of the scores.
b. Construct a histogram of the frequency distribution constructed in part **a**.
c. Is the distribution symmetrical or skewed?
d. Determine the percentile rank of a score of 5 and a score of 10. clinical, cognitive, health

## BOOK COMPANION WEBSITE

Go to www.thomsonedu.com/psychology/pagano for:

- SPSS problems and solutions
- Flash cards for review of terms
- Chapter quiz
- Statistical workshops
- And more

## Web**TUTOR**

Available via WebTutor for this chapter:

- Detailed chapter outline
- *Know and Be Able To Do* section
- Drag & Drop game for review of equations, concepts, and other material
- Flash cards for review of terms
- Audio flash cards for MP3 player
- Solving problems using SPSS
- More practice problems using computational equations
- Chapter quiz

# Measures of Central Tendency and Variability

## INTRODUCTION

In Chapter 3, we discussed how to organize and present data in meaningful ways. The frequency distribution and its many derivatives are useful in this regard, but by themselves, they do not allow quantitative statements that characterize the distribution as a whole to be made, nor do they allow quantitative comparisons to be made between two or more distributions. It is often desirable to describe the characteristics of distributions quantitatively. For example, suppose a psychologist has conducted an experiment to determine whether men and women differ in mathematical aptitude. She has two sets of scores, one from the men and one from the women in the experiment. How can she compare the distributions? To do so, she needs to quantify them. This is most often done by computing the average score for each group and then comparing the averages. The measure computed is a measure of the *central tendency* of each distribution.

A second characteristic of distributions that is very useful to quantify is the *variability* of the distribution. Variability specifies the extent to which scores are different from each other, are dispersed, or are spread out. It is important for two reasons. First, determining the variability of the data is required by many of the statistical inference tests that we shall be discussing later in this book. In addition, the variability of a distribution can be useful in its own right. For example, suppose you were hired to design and evaluate an educational program for disadvantaged youngsters. When evaluating the program, you would be interested not only in the average value of the end-of-program scores but also in how variable the scores were. The variability of the scores is important because you need to know whether the effect of the program is uniform or varies over the youngsters. If it varies, as it almost assuredly will, how large is the variability? Is the program doing a good job with some students and a poor job with others? If so, the program may need to be redesigned to do a better job with those youngsters who have not been adequately benefiting from it.

Central tendency and variability are the two characteristics of distributions that are most often quantified. In this chapter, we shall discuss the most important measures of these two characteristics.

## MEASURES OF CENTRAL TENDENCY: ARITHMETIC MEAN, MEDIAN, AND MODE

The three most often used measures of central tendency are the arithmetic mean, the median, and the mode.

### The Arithmetic Mean

You are probably already familiar with the arithmetic mean. It is the value you ordinarily calculate when you average something. For example, if you wanted to know the average number of hours you studied per day for the past 5 days, you would add the hours you studied each day and divide by 5. In so doing, you would be calculating the arithmetic mean.

definition    ■ *The* **arithmetic mean** *is defined as the sum of the scores divided by the number of scores. In equation form,*

$$\overline{X} = \frac{\Sigma X_i}{N} = \frac{X_1 + X_2 + X_3 + \cdots + X_N}{N} \qquad \textit{mean of a sample}$$

*or*

$$\mu = \frac{\Sigma X_i}{N} = \frac{X_1 + X_2 + X_3 + \cdots + X_N}{N} \qquad \textit{mean of a population set of scores}$$

*where*
$$X_1, \ldots, X_N = \text{raw scores}$$
$$\overline{X} \ (\text{read ``X bar''}) = \text{mean of a sample set of scores}$$
$$\mu \ (\text{read ``mew''}) = \text{mean of a population set of scores}$$
$$\Sigma \ (\text{read ``sigma''}) = \text{summation sign}$$
$$N = \text{number of scores}$$

Note that we use two symbols for the mean: $\overline{X}$ if the scores are sample scores and $\mu$ (the Greek letter mu) if the scores are population scores. The computations, however, are the same regardless of whether the scores are sample or population scores. We shall use $\mu$ without any subscript to indicate that this is the mean of a population of raw scores. Later on in the text, we shall calculate population means of other kinds of scores for which we shall add the appropriate subscript.

Let's try a few problems for practice.

## Practice Problem 4.1

Calculate the mean for each of the following sample sets of scores:

**a.** $X$:  3, 5, 6, 8, 14

$$\overline{X} = \frac{\Sigma X_i}{N} = \frac{3 + 5 + 6 + 8 + 14}{5}$$
$$= \frac{36}{5} = 7.20$$

**b.** $X$:  20, 22, 28, 30, 37, 38

$$\overline{X} = \frac{\Sigma X_i}{N} = \frac{20 + 22 + 28 + 30 + 37 + 38}{6}$$
$$= \frac{175}{6} = 29.17$$

**c.** $X$:  2.2, 2.4, 3.1, 3.1

$$\overline{X} = \frac{\Sigma X_i}{N} = \frac{2.2 + 2.4 + 3.1 + 3.1}{4}$$
$$= \frac{10.8}{4} = 2.70$$

**Properties of the mean**    The mean has many important properties or characteristics. First,

*The mean is sensitive to the exact value of all the scores in the distribution.*

To calculate the mean you have to add *all* the scores, so a change in any of the scores will cause a change in the mean. This is not true of the median or the mode.

A second property is the following:

*The sum of the deviations about the mean equals zero. Written algebraically, this property becomes $\Sigma (X_i - \overline{X}) = 0$.*

This property says that if the mean is subtracted from each score, the sum of the differences will equal zero. The algebraic proof is presented in Note 4.1 at the end of this chapter. A demonstration of its validity is shown in Table 4.1. This property results from the fact that the mean is the balance point of the distribution. The mean can be thought of as the fulcrum of a seesaw, to use a mechanical analogy. The analogy is shown in Figure 4.1, using the scores of Table 4.1. When the scores are distributed along the seesaw according to their values, the mean of the distribution occupies the position where the scores are in balance.

t a b l e  4.1   Demonstration that $\Sigma\,(X_i - \bar{X}) = 0$

| $X_i$ | $X_i - \bar{X}$ | Calculation of $\bar{X}$ |
|---|---|---|
| 2 | $-4$ | |
| 4 | $-2$ | $\bar{X} = \dfrac{\Sigma\,X_i}{N} = \dfrac{30}{5}$ |
| 6 | $0$ | |
| 8 | $+2$ | $= 6.00$ |
| $\underline{10}$ | $\underline{+4}$ | |
| $\Sigma\,X_i = 30$ | $\Sigma\,(X_i - \bar{X}) = 0$ | |

A third property of the mean also derives from the fact that the mean is the balance point of the distribution:

*The mean is very sensitive to extreme scores.*

A glance at Figure 4.1 should convince you that, if we added an extreme score (one far from the mean), it would greatly disrupt the balance. The mean would have to shift a considerable distance to reestablish balance. The mean is more sensitive to extreme scores than is the median or the mode. We shall discuss this more fully when we take up the median.

A fourth property of the mean has to do with the variability of the scores about the mean. This property states the following:

*The sum of the squared deviations of all the scores about their mean is a minimum. Stated algebraically, $\Sigma\,(X_i - \bar{X})^2$ is a minimum.*

This is an important characteristic used in many areas of statistics, particularly in regression. Elaborated a little more fully, this property states that although the sum of the squared deviations about the mean does not usually equal zero, it is smaller than if the squared deviations were taken about any other value. The validity of this property is demonstrated in Table 4.2. The scores of the distribution are given in the first column. Their mean equals 5.00. The fourth column shows the squared deviations of the $X_i$ scores about their mean $(X_i - 5)^2$. The sum of these squared deviations is 20. The other columns show the squared deviations of the $X_i$ scores about values other than the mean. In the third column, the value is 4 $(X_i - 4)^2$, the second column 3, the fifth column 6, and the sixth column 7. Note that the sum of the squared deviations about each of these values is larger than the sum of the squared deviations about the

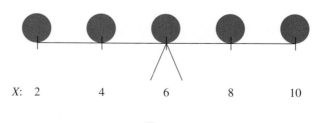

$X:$   2        4        6        8        10

$\bar{X} = 6.00$

f i g u r e  4.1   The mean as the balance point in the distribution.

t a b l e  4.2  Demonstration that $\Sigma (X_i - \bar{X})^2$ is a minimum

| $X_i$ | $(X_i - 3)^2$ | $(X_i - 4)^2$ | $(X_i - \bar{X})^2$ $(X_i - 5)^2$ | $(X_i - 6)^2$ | $(X_i - 7)^2$ | Calculation of $\bar{X}$ |
|---|---|---|---|---|---|---|
| 2 | 1 | 4 | 9 | 16 | 25 | $\bar{X} = \dfrac{\Sigma X_i}{N}$ |
| 4 | 1 | 0 | 1 | 4 | 9 | |
| 6 | 9 | 4 | 1 | 0 | 1 | $= \dfrac{20}{4}$ |
| 8 | $\underline{25}$ | $\underline{16}$ | $\underline{9}$ | $\underline{4}$ | $\underline{1}$ | |
| | 36 | 24 | 20 | 24 | 36 | $= 5.00$ |

mean of the distribution. Not only is the sum larger, but the farther the value gets from the mean, the larger the sum becomes. This implies that although we've compared only four other values, it holds true for all other values. Thus, although the sum of the squared deviations about the mean does not usually equal zero, it is smaller than if the squared deviations are taken about any other value.

The last property has to do with the use of the mean for statistical inference. This property states the following:

*Under most circumstances, of the measures used for central tendency, the mean is least subject to sampling variation.*

If we were repeatedly to take samples from a population on a random basis, the mean would vary from sample to sample. The same is true for the median and the mode. However, the mean varies less than these other measures of central tendency. This is very important in inferential statistics and is a major reason why the mean is used in inferential statistics whenever possible.

### The Overall Mean

Occasionally, the situation arises where we know the mean of several groups of scores and we want to calculate the mean of all the scores combined. Of course, we could start from the beginning again and just sum all the raw scores and divide by the total number of scores. However, there is a shortcut available if we already know the mean of the groups and the number of scores in each group. The equation for this method derives from the basic definition of the mean. Suppose we have several groups of scores that we wish to combine to calculate the overall mean. We'll let $k$ equal the number of groups. Then,

$$\bar{X}_{\text{overall}} = \frac{\text{Sum of all scores}}{N}$$

$$= \frac{\Sigma X_i(\text{first group}) + \Sigma X_i(\text{second group}) + \cdots + \Sigma X_i(\text{last group})}{n_1 + n_2 + \cdots + n_k}$$

*where*  $N$ = total number of scores
$n_1$ = number of scores in the first group
$n_2$ = number of scores in the second group
$n_k$ = number of scores in the last group

Since $\overline{X}_1 = \Sigma\, X_i$ (first group)$/n_1$, multiplying by $n_1$, we have $\Sigma\, X_i$ (first group) $= n_1\overline{X}_1$. Similarly, $\Sigma\, X_i$ (second group) $= n_2\overline{X}_2$, and $\Sigma\, X_i$ (last group) $= n_k\overline{X}_k$, where $\overline{X}_k$ is the mean of the last group. Substituting these values in the numerator of the preceding equation, we arrive at

$$\overline{X}_{overall} = \frac{n_1\overline{X}_1 + n_2\overline{X}_2 + \cdots + n_k\overline{X}_k}{n_1 + n_2 + \cdots + n_k} \qquad overall\ mean\ of\ several\ groups$$

In words, this equation states that the overall mean is equal to the sum of the mean of each group times the number of scores in the group, divided by the sum of the number of scores in each group.

To illustrate how this equation is used, suppose a sociology professor gave a final exam to two classes. The mean of one of the classes was 90, and the number of scores was 20. The mean of the other class was 70, and 40 students took the exam. Calculate the mean of the two classes combined.

The solution is as follows: Given that $\overline{X}_1 = 90$ and $n_1 = 20$ and that $\overline{X}_2 = 70$ and $n_2 = 40$,

$$\overline{X}_{overall} = \frac{n_1\overline{X}_1 + n_2\overline{X}_2}{n_1 + n_2} = \frac{20(90) + 40(70)}{20 + 40} = 76.67$$

The overall mean is much closer to the average of the class with 40 scores than the class with 20 scores. In this context, we can see that each of the means is being *weighted* by its number of scores. We are counting the mean of 70 forty times and the mean of 90 only twenty times. Thus, the overall mean really is a weighted mean, where the weights are the number of scores used in determining each mean. Let's do one more problem for practice.

## Practice Problem 4.2

A researcher conducted an experiment involving three groups of subjects. The mean of the first group was 75, and there were 50 subjects in the group. The mean of the second group was 80, and there were 40 subjects. The third group had a mean of 70 and 25 subjects. Calculate the overall mean of the three groups combined.

### SOLUTION

The solution is as follows: Given that $\overline{X}_1 = 75$, $n_1 = 50$; $\overline{X}_2 = 80$, $n_2 = 40$; and $\overline{X}_3 = 70$, $n_3 = 25$,

$$\overline{X}_{overall} = \frac{n_1\overline{X}_1 + n_2\overline{X}_2 + n_3\overline{X}_3}{n_1 + n_2 + n_3} = \frac{50(75) + 40(80) + 25(70)}{50 + 40 + 25}$$

$$= \frac{8700}{115} = 75.65$$

## The Median

The second most frequently encountered measure of central tendency is the median.

*The **median** (symbol Mdn) is defined as the scale value below which 50% of the scores fall.* It is therefore the same thing as $P_{50}$.

In Chapter 3, we discussed how to calculate $P_{50}$; therefore, you already know how to calculate the median for grouped scores. For practice, however, Practice Problem 4.3 contains another problem and its solution. You should try this problem and be sure you can solve it before going on.

### Practice Problem 4.3

Calculate the median of the grouped scores listed in Table 4.3.

**table 4.3**   Calculating the median from grouped scores

| Class Interval | $f$ | Cum $f$ | Cum % | Calculation of Median |
|---|---|---|---|---|
| 3.6–4.0 | 4 | 52 | 100.00 | |
| 3.1–3.5 | 6 | 48 | 92.31 | |
| 2.6–3.0 | 8 | 42 | 80.77 | |
| 2.1–2.5 | 10 | 34 | 65.38 | Mdn $= P_{50}$ |
| 1.6–2.0 | 9 | 24 | 46.15 | $= X_L + (i l f_i)(\text{cum } f_P - \text{cum } f_L)$ |
| 1.1–1.5 | 7 | 15 | 28.85 | $= 2.05 + (0.5/10)(26 - 24)$ |
| 0.6–1.0 | 5 | 8 | 15.38 | $= 2.05 + 0.10 = 2.15$ |
| 0.1–0.5 | 3 | 3 | 5.77 | |

**SOLUTION**

The median is the value below which 50% of the scores fall. Since $N = 52$, the median is the value below which 26 of the scores fall (50% of 52 = 26). From Table 4.3, we see that the median lies in the interval 2.1–2.5. Since 24 scores fall below a value of 2.05, we need two more scores to make up the 26. Given there are 10 scores in the interval and the interval is 0.5 unit wide, we must move $0.5/10 \times 2 = 0.10$ unit into the interval. Thus,

$$\text{Median} = 2.05 + 0.10 = 2.15$$

The median could also have been found by using the equation for percentile point. This solution is shown in Table 4.3.

When dealing with raw (ungrouped) scores, it is quite easy to find the median. First, arrange the scores in rank order.

*The median is the centermost score if the number of scores is odd. If the number is even, the median is taken as the average of the two centermost scores.*

To illustrate, suppose we have the scores 5, 2, 3, 7, and 8 and want to determine their median. First, we rank-order the scores: 2, 3, 5, 7, 8. Since the number of scores is odd, the median is the centermost score. In this example, the median is 5. It may seem that 5 is not really $P_{50}$ for the set of scores. However, consider the score of 5 to be evenly distributed over the interval 4.5–5.5. Now it becomes obvious that half of the scores fall below 5.0. Thus, 5.0 is $P_{50}$.

Let's try another example, this time with an even number of scores. Given the scores 2, 8, 6, 4, 12, and 10, determine their median. First, we rank-order the scores: 2, 4, 6, 8, 10, 12. Since the number of scores is even, the median is the average of the two centermost scores. The median for this example is $(6 + 8)/2 = 7$. For additional practice, Practice Problem 4.4 presents a few problems dealing with raw scores.

## Practice Problem 4.4

Calculate the median for the following sets of scores:

**a.** 8, 10, 4, 3, 1, 15        Rank order: 1, 3, 4, 8, 10, 15        Mdn = $(4 + 8)/2 = 6$
**b.** 100, 102, 108, 104, 112        Rank order: 100, 102, 104, 108, 112        Mdn = 104
**c.** 2.5, 1.8, 1.2, 2.4, 2.0        Rank order: 1.2, 1.8, 2.0, 2.4, 2.5        Mdn = 2.0
**d.** 10, 11, 14, 14, 16, 14, 12        Rank order: 10, 11, 12, 14, 14, 14, 16        Mdn = 14

In the last set of scores in Practice Problem 4.4, the median occurs at 14, where there are three scores. Technically, we should consider the three scores equally spread out over the interval 13.5–14.5. Then we would find the median by using the equation shown in Table 4.3 (p. 72), with $i = 1$ (Mdn = 13.67). However, when raw scores are being used, this refinement is often not made. Rather, the median is taken at 14. We shall follow this procedure. Thus, if the median occurs at a value where there are tied scores, we shall use the tied score as the median.

**Properties of the median**    There are two properties of the median worth noting. First,

*The median is less sensitive than the mean to extreme scores.*

To illustrate this property, consider the scores shown in the first column of Table 4.4. The three distributions shown are the same except for the last score. In the second distribution, the score of 100 is very different in value from the other scores. In the third distribution, the score of 1000 is even more extreme. Note t a b l e 4.4  Effect of extreme scores on the mean and median

| Scores | Mean | Median |
|--------|------|--------|
| 3, 4, 6, 7, 10 | 6 | 6 |
| 3, 4, 6, 7, 100 | 24 | 6 |
| 3, 4, 6, 7, 1000 | 204 | 6 |

what happens to the mean in the second and third distributions. Since the mean is sensitive to extreme scores, it changes considerably with the extreme scores. How about the median? Does it change too? As we see from the third column, the answer is no! The median stays the same. Since the median is not responsive to each individual score but rather divides the distribution in half, it is not as sensitive to extreme scores as is the mean. For this reason, when the distribution is strongly skewed, it is probably better to represent the central tendency with the median rather than the mean. Certainly, in the third distribution of Table 4.4, the median of 6 does a better job representing most of the scores than does the mean of 204.

The second property of the median involves its sampling stability. It states that

*Under usual circumstances, the median is more subject to sampling variability than the mean but less subject to sampling variability than the mode.*

Because the median is usually less stable than the mean from sample to sample, it is not as useful in inferential statistics.

## The Mode

The third and last measure of central tendency that we shall discuss is the mode.

definition  ■  *The **mode** is defined as the most frequent score in the distribution.*[*]

Clearly, this is the easiest of the three measures to determine. The mode is found by inspection of the scores; there isn't any calculation necessary. For instance, to find the mode of the data in Table 3.2 (p. 39), all we need to do is search the frequency column. The mode for these data is 76. With grouped scores, the mode is designated as the midpoint of the interval with the highest frequency. The mode of the grouped scores in Table 3.4 (p. 42) is 77.

Usually, distributions are *unimodal;* that is, they have only one mode. However, it is possible for a distribution to have many modes. When a distribution has two modes, as is the case with the scores 1, 2, 3, 3, 3, 3, 4, 5, 7, 7, 7, 7, 8, 9, the distribution is called *bimodal.* Histograms of a unimodal and bimodal distribution

---

[*]When all the scores in the distribution have the same frequency, it is customary to say that the distribution has no mode.

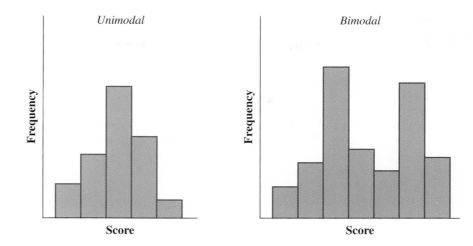

f i g u r e 4.2   Unimodal and bimodal histograms.

are shown in Figure 4.2. Although the mode is the easiest measure of central tendency to determine, it is not used very much in the behavioral sciences because it is not very stable from sample to sample and often there is more than one mode for a given set of scores.

## Measures of Central Tendency and Symmetry

If the distribution is unimodal and symmetrical, the mean, median, and mode will all be equal. An example of this is the bell-shaped curve mentioned in Chapter 3 and shown in Figure 4.3. When the distribution is skewed, the mean and median will not be equal. Since the mean is most affected by extreme scores, it will have a value closer to the extreme scores than will the median. Thus, with a negatively skewed distribution, the mean will be lower than the median. With a positively skewed curve, the mean will be larger than the median. Figure 4.3 shows these relationships.

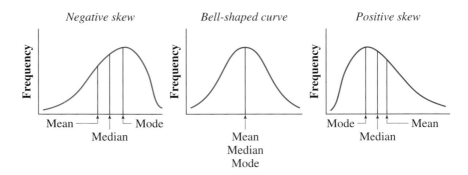

From *Statistical Reasoning in Psychology and Education* by E. W. Minium. Copyright © 1978 John Wiley & Sons, Inc. Adapted by permission of John Wiley & Sons, Inc.

f i g u r e 4.3   Symmetry and measures of central tendency.

## MEASURES OF VARIABILITY: RANGE, STANDARD DEVIATION, AND VARIANCE

Previously in this chapter, we pointed out that variability specifies how far apart the scores are spread. Whereas measures of central tendency are a quantification of the average value of the distribution, measures of variability quantify the extent of dispersion. Three measures of variability are commonly used in the behavioral sciences: the range, the standard deviation, and the variance.

### The Range

We have already used the range when we were constructing frequency distributions of grouped scores.

---

definition ■ *The **range** is defined as the difference between the highest and lowest scores in the distribution. In equation form,*

$$\text{Range} = \text{Highest score} - \text{Lowest score}$$

---

The range is easy to calculate but gives us only a relatively crude measure of dispersion, because the range really measures the spread of only the extreme scores and not the spread of any of the scores in between. Although the range is easy to calculate, we've included some problems for you to practice on. Better to be sure than sorry.

---

### Practice Problem 4.5

Calculate the range for the following distributions:

**a.** 2, 3, 5, 8, 10            Range = 10 − 2 = 8
**b.** 18, 12, 28, 15, 20        Range = 28 − 12 = 16
**c.** 115, 107, 105, 109, 101   Range = 115 − 101 = 14
**d.** 1.2, 1.3, 1.5, 1.8, 2.3   Range = 2.3 − 1.2 = 1.1

---

### The Standard Deviation

Before discussing the standard deviation, it is necessary to introduce the concept of a deviation score.

Deviation scores    So far, we've been dealing mainly with raw scores. You will recall that a raw score is the score as originally measured. For example, if we are interested in IQ and we measure an IQ of 126, then 126 is a raw score.

| definition | ■ | *A **deviation score** tells how far away the raw score is from the mean of its distribution.* |

In equation form, a deviation score is defined as

$$X - \overline{X} \qquad \textit{deviation score for sample data}$$
$$X - \mu \qquad \textit{deviation score for population data}$$

As an illustration, consider the sample scores in Table 4.5. The raw scores are shown in the first column, and their transformed deviation scores are in the second column. The deviation score tells how far the raw score lies above or below the mean. Thus, the raw score of 2 ($X = 2$) lies 4 units below the mean ($X - \overline{X} = -4$). The raw scores and their deviation scores are also shown pictorially in Figure 4.4.

Let's suppose that you are a budding mathematician (use your imagination if necessary). You have been assigned the task of deriving a measure of dispersion that gives the average deviation of the scores about the mean. After some reflection, you say, "That's easy. Just calculate the deviation from the mean of each score and average the deviation scores." Your logic is impeccable. There is only one stumbling block. Consider the scores in Table 4.6. For the sake of this example, we will assume this is a population set of scores. The first column contains the population raw scores and the second column the deviation scores. We want to calculate the average deviation of the raw scores about their mean. According to your method, we would first compute the deviation scores (second column) and average them by dividing the sum of the deviation scores [$\Sigma (X - \mu)$] by $N$. The stumbling block is that $\Sigma (X - \mu) = 0$. Remember this is a general property of the mean. The sum of the deviations about the mean always equals zero. Thus, if we follow your suggestion, the average of the deviations would always equal zero, no matter how dispersed the scores were [$\Sigma (X - \mu)/N = 0/N = 0$].

You are momentarily stunned by this unexpected low blow. However, you don't give up. You look at the deviation scores and you see that the negative scores are canceling the positive ones. Suddenly, you have a flash of insight. Why not square each deviation score? Then all the scores would be positive, and their sum would no longer be zero. Eureka! You have solved the problem. Now you can divide the sum of the squared scores by $N$ to get the average value [$\Sigma (X - \mu)^2/N$], and the average won't equal zero. You should note that the numerator of this formula [$\Sigma (X - \mu)^2$] is called the *sum of squares* or, more accurately, *sum of squared deviations,* and is symbolized as $SS_{pop}$. The only trouble at this point is that you have now calculated the average *squared deviation,* not the average deviation. What you need to do is "unsquare" the answer. This is done by taking the square root of $SS_{pop}/N$.

table 4.5   Calculating deviation scores

| $X$ | $X - \overline{X}$ | Calculation of $\overline{X}$ |
|---|---|---|
| 2 | $2 - 6 = -4$ | $\overline{X} = \dfrac{\Sigma X}{N} = \dfrac{30}{5}$ |
| 4 | $4 - 6 = -2$ | |
| 6 | $6 - 6 = \phantom{+}0$ | $= 6.00$ |
| 8 | $8 - 6 = +2$ | |
| 10 | $10 - 6 = +4$ | |

f i g u r e 4.4   Raw scores and their corresponding deviation scores.

Your reputation as a mathematician is vindicated! You have come up with the equation for standard deviation used by many statisticians. The symbol for the standard deviation of population scores is $\sigma$ (the lowercase Greek letter sigma) and for samples is $s$. Your derived equation for population scores is as follows:

$$\sigma = \sqrt{\frac{SS_{pop}}{N}} = \sqrt{\frac{\Sigma\,(X - \mu)^2}{N}} \qquad \textit{standard deviation of a population set of raw scores—deviation method}$$

*where*     $SS_{pop} = \Sigma\,(X - \mu)^2$     *sum of squares—population data*

Calculation of the standard deviation of a population set of scores using the deviation method is shown in Table 4.6.

Technically, the equation is the same for calculating the standard deviation of sample scores. However, when we calculate the standard deviation of sample data, we usually want to use our calculation to estimate the population standard deviation. It can be shown algebraically that the equation with $N$ in the denominator gives an estimate that on the average is too small. Dividing by $N - 1$, instead of $N$, gives a more accurate estimate of $\sigma$. Since estimation of the population standard deviation is an important use of the sample standard deviation and since it saves confusion later on in this textbook when we cover Student's $t$ test and the $F$ test, we have chosen to adopt the equation with $N - 1$ in the denominator for calculating the standard deviation of sample scores. Thus,

$$s = \text{Estimated } \sigma = \sqrt{\frac{SS}{N - 1}} = \sqrt{\frac{\Sigma\,(X - \overline{X})^2}{N - 1}} \qquad \textit{standard deviation of a sample set of raw scores— deviation method}$$

*where*     $SS = \Sigma\,(X - \overline{X})^2$     *sum of squares—sample data*

t a b l e 4.6   Calculation of the standard deviation of a population set of scores using the deviation method

| $X$ | $X - \mu$ | $(X - \mu)^2$ | Calculation of $\mu$ and $\sigma$ |
|---|---|---|---|
| 3 | $-2$ | 4 | $\mu = \dfrac{\Sigma\,X}{N} = \dfrac{25}{5} = 5.00$ |
| 4 | $-1$ | 1 | |
| 5 | $0$ | 0 | |
| 6 | $+1$ | 1 | $\sigma = \sqrt{\dfrac{SS_{pop}}{N}} = \sqrt{\dfrac{\Sigma\,(X - \mu)^2}{N}} = \sqrt{\dfrac{10}{5}} = 1.41$ |
| 7 | $+2$ | 4 | |
| | $\Sigma\,(X - \mu) = 0$ | $\Sigma\,(X - \mu)^2 = 10$ | |

**t a b l e  4.7**    Calculation of the standard deviation of sample scores using the deviation method

| $X$ | $X - \bar{X}$ | $(X - \bar{X})^2$ | Calculation of $\bar{X}$ and $s$ |
|---|---|---|---|
| 2 | $-4$ | 16 | $\bar{X} = \dfrac{\Sigma X}{N} = \dfrac{30}{5} = 6.00$ |
| 4 | $-2$ | 4 | |
| 6 | 0 | 0 | |
| 8 | $+2$ | 4 | $s = \sqrt{\dfrac{SS}{N-1}} = \sqrt{\dfrac{\Sigma (X - \bar{X})^2}{N-1}} = \sqrt{\dfrac{40}{5-1}}$ |
| 10 | $+4$ | 16 | |
| | $\Sigma (X - \bar{X}) = 0$ | $SS = 40$ | $= \sqrt{10} = 3.16$ |

In most practical situations, the data are from samples rather than populations. Calculation of the standard deviation of a sample using the preceding equation for samples is shown in Table 4.7. Although this equation gives the best conceptual understanding of the standard deviation and it does yield the correct answer, it is quite cumbersome to use in practice. This is especially true if the mean is not a whole number. Table 4.8 shows an illustration, using the previous equation with a mean that has a decimal remainder. Note that each deviation score has a decimal remainder that must be squared to get $(X - \bar{X})^2$. A great deal of rounding is necessary, which may contribute to inaccuracy. In addition, we are dealing with adding five-digit numbers, which increases the possibility of error. You can see how cumbersome using this equation becomes when the mean is not an integer, and in most practical problems, the mean is not an integer!

**Calculating the standard deviation of a sample using the raw scores method**
It can be shown algebraically that

$$SS = \Sigma X^2 - \frac{(\Sigma X)^2}{N} \qquad sum \; of \; squares$$

**t a b l e  4.8**    Calculation of the standard deviation using deviation scores when the mean is not a whole number

| $X$ | $X - \bar{X}$ | $(X - \bar{X})^2$ | Calculation of $\bar{X}$ and $s$ |
|---|---|---|---|
| 10 | $-6.875$ | 47.2656 | $\bar{X} = \dfrac{\Sigma X}{N} = \dfrac{135}{8} = 16.875$ |
| 12 | $-4.875$ | 23.7656 | |
| 13 | $-3.875$ | 15.0156 | |
| 15 | $-1.875$ | 3.5156 | $s = \sqrt{\dfrac{SS}{N-1}} = \sqrt{\dfrac{\Sigma (X - \bar{X})^2}{N-1}}$ |
| 18 | 1.125 | 1.2656 | |
| 20 | 3.125 | 9.7656 | $= \sqrt{\dfrac{192.8748}{7}}$ |
| 22 | 5.125 | 26.2656 | |
| 25 | 8.125 | 66.0156 | $= \sqrt{27.5535}$ |
| $\Sigma X = 135$ | $\Sigma (X - \bar{X}) = 0.000$ | $SS = 192.8748$ | |
| $N = 8$ | | | $= 5.25$ |

The derivation is presented in Note 4.2. Using this equation to find *SS* allows us to use the raw scores without the necessity of calculating deviation scores. This, in turn, avoids the decimal remainder difficulties described previously. We shall call this method of computing *SS* "the raw score method" to distinguish it from the "deviation method." Since the raw score method is generally easier to use and avoids potential errors, it is the method of choice in computing *SS* and will be used throughout the remainder of this text. When using the raw score method, *you must be sure not to confuse* $\Sigma X^2$ *and* $(\Sigma X)^2$. $\Sigma X^2$ is read "sum X square," or "sum of the squared X scores," and $(\Sigma X)^2$ is read "sum X quantity squared," or "sum of the X scores, squared." To find $\Sigma X^2$, we square each score and then sum the squares. To find $(\Sigma X)^2$, we sum the scores and then square the sum. The result is different for the two procedures. In addition, *SS* must be positive. If your calculation turns out negative, you have probably confused $\Sigma X^2$ and $(\Sigma X)^2$.

Table 4.9 shows the calculation of the standard deviation, using the raw score method, of the data presented in Table 4.8. When using this method, we first calculate *SS* from the raw score equation and then substitute the obtained value in the equation for the standard deviation.

**Properties of the standard deviation**   The standard deviation has many important characteristics. First, the *standard deviation gives us a measure of dispersion relative to the mean.* This differs from the range, which gives us an absolute measure of the spread between the two most extreme scores. Second, *the standard deviation is sensitive to each score in the distribution.* If a score is moved closer to the mean, then the standard deviation will become smaller. Conversely, if a score shifts away from the mean, then the standard deviation will increase. Third, *like the mean, the standard deviation is stable with regard to sampling fluctuations.* If samples were taken repeatedly from populations of the type usually encountered in the behavioral sciences, the standard deviation of the samples would vary much less from sample to sample than the range. This property is one of the main reasons why the standard deviation is used so much more often than the range for reporting variability. Finally, both the mean and the standard deviation can be manipulated algebraically. This allows mathematics to be done with them for use in inferential statistics.

Now let's do Practice Problems 4.6 and 4.7.

**table 4.9**   Calculation of the standard deviation using the raw score method

| $X$ | $X^2$ | Calculation of *SS* | Calculation of *s* |
|---|---|---|---|
| 10 | 100 | $SS = \Sigma X^2 - \dfrac{(\Sigma X)^2}{N}$ | $s = \sqrt{\dfrac{SS}{N-1}}$ |
| 12 | 144 | | |
| 13 | 169 | | |
| 15 | 225 | $= 2471 - \dfrac{(135)^2}{8}$ | $= \sqrt{\dfrac{192.875}{7}}$ |
| 18 | 324 | | |
| 20 | 400 | $= 2471 - 2278.125$ | $= \sqrt{27.5536}$ |
| 22 | 484 | | |
| 25 | 625 | $= 192.875$ | $= 5.25$ |
| $\Sigma X = 135$ | $\Sigma X^2 = 2471$ | | |
| $N = 8$ | | | |

## Practice Problem 4.6

Calculate the standard deviation of the scores contained in the first column of the following table:

| X | $X^2$ | Calculation of SS | Calculation of s |
|---|---|---|---|
| 25 | 625 | $SS = \Sigma X^2 - \dfrac{(\Sigma X)^2}{N}$ | $s = \sqrt{\dfrac{SS}{N-1}}$ |
| 28 | 784 | | |
| 35 | 1,225 | | |
| 37 | 1,369 | $= 15,545 - \dfrac{(387)^2}{10}$ | $= \sqrt{\dfrac{568.1}{9}}$ |
| 38 | 1,444 | | |
| 40 | 1,600 | | |
| 42 | 1,764 | $= 15,545 - 14,976.9$ | $= \sqrt{63.1222}$ |
| 45 | 2,025 | | |
| 47 | 2,209 | $= 568.1$ | $= 7.94$ |
| 50 | 2,500 | | |
| $\Sigma X = 387$ | $\Sigma X^2 = 15,545$ | | |
| $N = 10$ | | | |

## Practice Problem 4.7

Calculate the standard deviation of the scores contained in the first column of the following table:

| X | $X^2$ | Calculation of SS | Calculation of s |
|---|---|---|---|
| 1.2 | 1.44 | $SS = \Sigma X^2 - \dfrac{(\Sigma X)^2}{N}$ | $s = \sqrt{\dfrac{SS}{N-1}}$ |
| 1.4 | 1.96 | | |
| 1.5 | 2.25 | | |
| 1.7 | 2.89 | $= 60.73 - \dfrac{(25.9)^2}{12}$ | $= \sqrt{\dfrac{4.8292}{11}}$ |
| 1.9 | 3.61 | | |
| 2.0 | 4.00 | $= 60.73 - 55.9008$ | $= \sqrt{0.4390}$ |
| 2.2 | 4.84 | | |
| 2.4 | 5.76 | $= 4.8292$ | $= 0.66$ |
| 2.5 | 6.25 | | |
| 2.8 | 7.84 | | |
| 3.0 | 9.00 | | |
| 3.3 | 10.89 | | |
| $\Sigma X = 25.9$ | $\Sigma X^2 = 60.73$ | | |
| $N = 12$ | | | |

## The Variance

The variance of a set of scores is just the square of the standard deviation. For sample scores, the variance equals

$$s^2 = \text{Estimated } \sigma^2 = \frac{SS}{N-1} \qquad \textit{variance of a sample}$$

For population scores, the variance equals

$$\sigma^2 = \frac{SS_{\text{pop}}}{N} \qquad \textit{variance of a population}$$

The variance is not used much in descriptive statistics because it gives us squared units of measurement. However, it is used quite frequently in inferential statistics.

## SUMMARY

In this chapter, we have discussed the central tendency and variability of distributions. The most common measures of central tendency are the arithmetic mean, the median, and the mode. The arithmetic mean gives the average of the scores and is computed by summing the scores and dividing by $N$. The median divides the distribution in half and, hence, is the scale value that is at the 50th percentile point of the distribution. The mode is the most frequent score in the distribution. The mean possesses special properties that make it by far the most commonly used measure of central tendency. However, if the distribution is quite skewed, the median should be used instead of the mean because it is less affected by extreme scores. In addition to presenting these measures, we showed how to calculate each and elaborated their most important properties. We also showed how to obtain the overall mean when the average of several means is desired. Finally, we discussed the relationship between the mean, median, and mode of a distribution and its symmetry.

The most common measures of variability are the range, the standard deviation, and the variance. The range is a crude measure that tells the dispersion between the two most extreme scores. The standard deviation is the most frequently encountered measure of variability. It gives the average dispersion about the mean of the distribution. The variance is just the square of the standard deviation. As with the measures of central tendency, our discussion of variability included how to calculate each measure. Finally, since the standard deviation is the most important measure of variability, we also presented its properties.

## IMPORTANT TERMS

Arithmetic mean  (p. 67)
Central tendency  (p. 67)
Deviation score  (p. 76)
Dispersion  (p. 76)

Median  (p. 72)
Mode  (p. 74)
Overall mean  (p. 70)
Range  (p. 76)

Standard deviation  (p. 76)
Sum of squares  (p. 78)
Variability  (p. 66)
Variance  (p. 82)

## QUESTIONS AND PROBLEMS

1. Define or identify the terms in the Important Terms section.
2. State four properties of the mean and illustrate each with an example.
3. Under what condition might you prefer to use the median rather than the mean as the best measure of central tendency? Explain why.
4. Why is the mode not used very much as a measure of central tendency?
5. The overall mean ($\overline{X}_{\text{overall}}$) is a weighted mean. Is this statement correct? Explain.
6. Discuss the relationship between the mean and median for distributions that are symmetrical and skewed.
7. Why is the range not as useful a measure of dispersion as the standard deviation?
8. The standard deviation is a relative measure of average dispersion. Is this statement correct? Explain.
9. Why do we use $N - 1$ in the denominator for computing $s$ but use $N$ in the denominator for determining $\sigma$?

10. What is the raw score equation for *SS*? When is it useful?
11. Give three properties of the standard deviation.
12. How are the variance and standard deviation related?
13. If $s = 0$, what must be true about the scores in the distribution? Verify your answer using an example.
14. Can the value of the range, standard deviation, or variance of a set of scores be negative? Explain.
15. Give the symbol for each of the following:
    a. Mean of a sample
    b. Mean of a population
    c. Standard deviation of a sample
    d. Standard deviation of a population
    e. A raw score
    f. Variance of a sample
    g. Variance of a population
16. Calculate the mean, median, and mode for the following scores:
    a. 5, 2, 8, 2, 3, 2, 4, 0, 6
    b. 30, 20, 17, 12, 30, 30, 14, 29
    c. 1.5, 4.5, 3.2, 1.8, 5.0, 2.2
17. Calculate the mean of the following set of sample scores: 1, 3, 4, 6, 6.
    a. Add a constant of 2 to each score. Calculate the mean for the new values. Generalize to answer the question, "What is the effect on the mean of adding a constant to each score?"
    b. Subtract a constant of 2 from each score. Calculate the mean for the new values. Generalize to answer the question, "What is the effect on the mean of subtracting a constant from each score?"
    c. Multiply each score by a constant of 2. Calculate the mean for the new values. Generalize to answer the question, "What is the effect on the mean of multiplying each score by a constant?"
    d. Divide each score by a constant of 2. Calculate the mean for the new values. Generalize to answer the question, "What is the effect on the mean of dividing each score by a constant?"
18. The following scores resulted from a biology exam:

| Scores | *f* | Scores | *f* |
|--------|-----|--------|-----|
| 95–99 | 3 | 65–69 | 7 |
| 90–94 | 3 | 60–64 | 6 |
| 85–89 | 5 | 55–59 | 5 |
| 80–84 | 6 | 50–54 | 3 |
| 75–79 | 6 | 45–49 | 2 |
| 70–74 | 8 | | |

   a. What is the median for this exam?
   b. What is the mode? education

19. Using the scores shown in Table 3.5 (p. 43),
    a. Determine the median.
    b. Determine the mode.
20. Using the scores shown in Table 3.6 (p. 46),
    a. Determine the median.
    b. Determine the mode.
21. For the following distributions, state whether you would use the mean or the median to represent the central tendency of the distribution. Explain why.
    a. 2, 3, 8, 5, 7, 8
    b. 10, 12, 15, 13, 19, 22
    c. 1.2, 0.8, 1.1, 0.6, 25
22. Given the following values of central tendency for each distribution, determine whether the distribution is symmetrical, positively skewed, or negatively skewed:
    a. Mean = 14, median = 12, mode = 10
    b. Mean = 14, median = 16, mode = 18
    c. Mean = 14, median = 14, mode = 14
23. A student kept track of the number of hours she studied each day for a 2-week period. The following daily scores were recorded (scores are in hours): 2.5, 3.2, 3.8, 1.3, 1.4, 0, 0, 2.6, 5.2, 4.8, 0, 4.6, 2.8, 3.3. Calculate
    a. The mean number of hours studied per day
    b. The median number of hours studied per day
    c. The modal number of hours studied per day education
24. Two salesmen working for the same company are having an argument. Each claims that the average number of items he sold, averaged over the last month, was the highest in the company. Can they both be right? Explain. I/O, other
25. An ornithologist studying the glaucous-winged gull on Puget Sound counts the number of aggressive interactions per minute among a group of sea gulls during 9 consecutive minutes. The following scores resulted: 24, 9, 12, 15, 10, 13, 22, 20, 14. Calculate
    a. The mean number of aggressive interactions per minute
    b. The median number of aggressive interactions per minute
    c. The model number of aggressive interactions per minute biological
26. A reading specialist tests the reading speed of children in four ninth-grade English classes. There are 42 students in class A, 35 in class B, 33 in class C, and 39 in class D. The mean reading speed in words per minute for the classes were as follows: class A, 220; class B, 185; class C, 212; and class D, 172. What is the mean reading speed for all classes combined? education

27. For the following sample sets of scores, calculate the range, the standard deviation, and the variance:
    a. 6, 2, 8, 5, 4, 4, 7
    b. 24, 32, 27, 45, 48
    c. 2.1, 2.5, 6.6, 0.2, 7.8, 9.3
28. In a particular statistics course, three exams were given. Each student's grade was based on a weighted average of his or her exam scores. The first test had a weight of 1, the second test had a weight of 2, and the third test had a weight of 2. The exam scores for one student are listed here. What was the student's overall average?

| Exam | 1 | 2 | 3 |
|------|-----|-----|-----|
| Score | 83 | 97 | 92 |

29. The timekeeper for a particular mile race uses a stopwatch to determine the finishing times of the racers. He then calculates that the mean time for the first three finishers was 4.25 minutes. After checking his stopwatch, he notices to his horror that the stopwatch begins timing at 15 seconds rather than at 0, resulting in scores each of which is 15 seconds too long. What is the correct mean time for the first three finishers? I/O, other
30. The manufacturer of brand A jogging shoes wants to determine how long the shoes last before resoling is necessary. She randomly samples from users in Chicago, New York, and Seattle. In Chicago, the sample size was 28, and the mean duration before resoling was 7.2 months. In New York, the sample size was 35, and the mean duration before resoling was 6.3 months. In Seattle, the sample size was 22, and the mean duration before resoling was 8.5 months. What is the overall mean duration before resoling is necessary for brand A jogging shoes? I/O, other
31. Calculate the standard deviation of the following set of sample scores: 1, 3, 4, 6, 6.
    a. Add a constant of 2 to each score. Calculate the standard deviation for the new values. Generalize to answer the question, "What is the effect on the standard deviation of adding a constant to each score?"
    b. Subtract a constant of 2 from each score. Calculate the standard deviation for the new values. Generalize to answer the question, "What is the effect on the standard deviation of subtracting a constant from each score?"
    c. Multiply each score by a constant of 2. Calculate the standard deviation for the new values. Generalize to answer the question, "What is the effect on the standard deviation of multiplying each score by a constant?"
    d. Divide each score by a constant of 2. Calculate the standard deviation for the new val-

ues. Generalize to answer the question, "What is the effect on the standard deviation of dividing each score by a constant?"
32. An industrial psychologist observed eight drill-press operators for 3 working days. She recorded the number of times each operator pressed the "faster" button instead of the "stop" button to determine whether the design of the control panel was contributing to the high rate of accidents in the plant. Given the scores 4, 7, 0, 2, 7, 3, 6, 7, compute the following:
    a. Mean                b. Median
    c. Mode                d. Range
    e. Standard deviation  f. Variance I/O
33. Without actually calculating the variability, study the following sample distributions:
    Distribution a: 21, 24, 28, 22, 20
    Distribution b: 21, 32, 38, 15, 11
    Distribution c: 22, 22, 22, 22, 22
    a. Rank-order them according to your best guess of their relative variability.
    b. Calculate the standard deviation of each to verify your rank ordering.
34. Compute the standard deviation for the following sample scores. Why is *s* so high in part **b**, relative to part **a**?
    a. 6, 8, 7, 3, 6, 4
    b. 6, 8, 7, 3, 6, 35
35. A social psychologist interested in the dating habits of college undergraduates samples 10 students and determines the number of dates they have had in the last month. Given the scores 1, 8, 12, 3, 8, 14, 4, 5, 8, 16, compute the following:
    a. Mean                b. Median
    c. Mode                d. Range
    e. Standard deviation  f. Variance social
36. A cognitive psychologist measures the reaction times of 6 subjects to emotionally laden words. The following scores in milliseconds are recorded: 250, 310, 360, 470, 425, 270. Compute the following:
    a. Mean                b. Median
    c. Mode                d. Range
    e. Standard deviation  f. Variance cognitive
37. A biological psychologist records the number of cells in a particular brain region of cats that respond to a tactile stimulus. Nine cats are used. The following cell counts/animal are recorded: 15, 28, 33, 19, 24, 17, 21, 34, 12. Compute the following:
    a. Mean                b. Median
    c. Mode                d. Range
    e. Standard deviation  f. Variance biological
38. What happens to the mean of a set of scores if
    a. A constant *a* is added to each score in the set?
    b. A constant *a* is subtracted from each score in the set?

c. Each score is multiplied by a constant $a$?

d. Each score is divided by a constant $a$?

Illustrate each of these with a numerical example.

39. What happens to the standard deviation of a set of scores if

a. A constant $a$ is added to each score in the set?

b. A constant $a$ is subtracted from each score in the set?

c. Each score is multiplied by a constant $a$?

d. Each score is divided by a constant $a$?

Illustrate each of these with a numerical example.

40. Suppose that, as is done in some lotteries, we sample balls from a big vessel. The vessel contains a large number of balls, each labeled with a single number, 0–9. There are an equal number of balls for each number, and the balls are continually being mixed. For this example, let's collect 10 samples of three balls each. Each sample is formed by selecting balls one at a time and replacing each ball back in the vessel before selecting the next ball. The selection process used ensures that every ball in the vessel has an equal chance of being chosen on each selection. Assume the following samples are collected.

1, 3, 4    2, 2, 6    3, 8, 8    1, 6, 7    5, 6, 9

3, 4, 7    1, 2, 6    2, 3, 7    6, 8, 9    4, 7, 9

a. Calculate the mean of each sample.

b. Calculate the median of each sample.

c. Based on the properties of the mean and median discussed previously in the chapter, do you expect more variability in the means or medians? Verify this by calculating the standard deviation of the means and medians. other

## NOTES

4.1 To show that $\Sigma (X_i - \bar{X}) = 0$,

$$
\begin{aligned}
\Sigma (X_i - \bar{X}) &= \Sigma X_i - \Sigma \bar{X} \\
&= \Sigma X_i - N\bar{X} \\
&= \Sigma X_i - N\left(\frac{\Sigma X_i}{N}\right) \\
&= \Sigma X_i - \Sigma X_i \\
&= 0
\end{aligned}
$$

4.2 To show that $SS = \Sigma X^2 - [(\Sigma X)^2/N]$,

$$
\begin{aligned}
SS &= \Sigma (X - \bar{X})^2 \\
&= \Sigma (X^2 - 2X\bar{X} + \bar{X}^2) \\
&= \Sigma X^2 - \Sigma 2X\bar{X} + \Sigma \bar{X}^2 \\
&= \Sigma X^2 - 2\bar{X}\,\Sigma X + N\bar{X}^2 \\
&= \Sigma X^2 - 2\left(\frac{\Sigma X}{N}\right)\Sigma X + \frac{N(\Sigma X)^2}{N^2} \\
&= \Sigma X^2 - \frac{2(\Sigma X)^2}{N} + \frac{(\Sigma X)^2}{N} \\
&= \Sigma X^2 - \frac{(\Sigma X)^2}{N}
\end{aligned}
$$

 **BOOK COMPANION WEBSITE**

Go to www.thomsonedu.com/psychology/pagano for:

• SPSS problems and solutions

• Flash cards for review of terms

• Chapter quiz

• Statistical workshops

• And more

## WebTUTOR™

Available via WebTutor for this chapter:

• Detailed chapter outline

• *Know and Be Able To Do* section

• Drag & Drop game for review of equations, concepts, and other material

• Flash cards for review of terms

• Audio flash cards for MP3 player

• Solving problems using Excel

• Solving problems using SPSS

• More practice problems using computational equations

• Chapter quiz

# The Normal Curve and Standard Scores

CHAPTER **5**

## INTRODUCTION

The normal curve is a very important distribution in the behavioral sciences. There are three principal reasons why. First, many of the variables measured in behavioral science research have distributions that quite closely approximate the normal curve. Height, weight, intelligence, and achievement are a few examples. Second, many of the inference tests used in analyzing experiments have sampling distributions that become normally distributed with increasing sample size. The sign test and Mann–Whitney *U* test are two such tests, which we shall cover later in the text. Finally, many inference tests require sampling distributions that are normally distributed (we shall discuss sampling distributions in Chapter 12). The *z* test, Student's *t* test, and the *F* test are examples of inference tests that depend on this point. Thus, much of the importance of the normal curve occurs in conjunction with inferential statistics.

## THE NORMAL CURVE

The normal curve is a theoretical distribution of population scores. It is a bell-shaped curve that is described by the following equation:

$$Y = \frac{N}{\sqrt{2\pi}\,\sigma}\, e^{-(X-\mu)^2/2\sigma^2} \qquad \textit{equation of the normal curve}$$

*where*  $Y$ = frequency of a given value of $X$*
$X$ = any score in the distribution
$\mu$ = mean of the distribution
$\sigma$ = standard deviation of the distribution
$N$ = total frequency of the distribution
$\pi$ = a constant of 3.1416
$e$ = a constant of 2.7183

Most of us will never need to know the exact equation for the normal curve. It has been given here primarily to make the point that the normal curve is a theoretical curve that is mathematically generated. An example of the normal curve is shown in Figure 5.1.

Note that the curve has two inflection points, one on each side of the mean. Inflection points are located where the curvature changes direction. In Figure 5.1, the inflection points are located where the curve changes from being convex downward to being convex upward. If the bell-shaped curve is a normal curve, the inflection points are at 1 standard deviation from the mean ($\mu + 1\sigma$ and $\mu - 1\sigma$). Note also that as the curve approaches the horizontal axis, it is slowly changing its $Y$ value. Theoretically, the curve never quite reaches the axis. It approaches the horizontal axis and gets closer and closer to it, but it never quite touches it. The curve is said to be *asymptotic* to the horizontal axis.

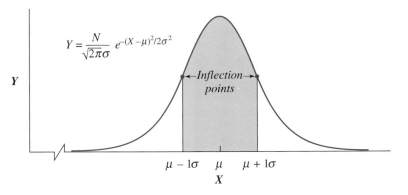

figure 5.1 Normal curve.

---

*The labeling of $Y$ as "frequency" is a slight simplification. I believe this simplification aids considerably in understanding and applying the material that follows. Strictly speaking, it is the area under the curve, between any two $X$ values, that is properly referred to as "frequency." For a discussion of this point, see E. Minium, B. King, and G. Bear, *Statistical Reasoning in Psychology and Education*, 3rd ed., John Wiley and Sons, New York, 1993, pp. 123–124.

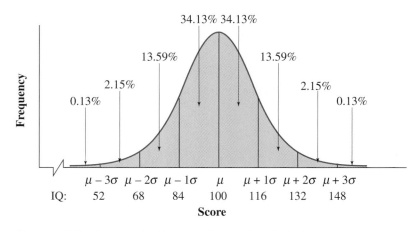

**figure 5.2** Areas under the normal curve for selected scores.

## Area Contained Under the Normal Curve

In distributions that are normally shaped, there is a special relationship between the mean and the standard deviation with regard to the area contained under the curve. When a set of scores is normally distributed, 34.13% of the area under the curve is contained between the mean ($\mu$) and a score that is equal to $\mu + 1\sigma$; 13.59% of the area is contained between a score equal to $\mu + 1\sigma$ and a score of $\mu + 2\sigma$; 2.15% of the area is contained between scores of $\mu + 2\sigma$ and $\mu + 3\sigma$; and 0.13% of the area exists beyond $\mu + 3\sigma$. This accounts for 50% of the area. Since the curve is symmetrical, the same percentages hold for scores below the mean. These relationships are shown in Figure 5.2. Since frequency is plotted on the vertical axis, these percentages represent the *percentage of scores* contained within the area.

To illustrate, suppose we have a population of 10,000 IQ scores. The distribution is normally shaped, with $\mu = 100$ and $\sigma = 16$. Since the scores are normally distributed, 34.13% of the scores are contained between scores of 100 and 116 ($\mu + 1\sigma = 100 + 16 = 116$), 13.59% between 116 and 132 ($\mu + 2\sigma = 100 + 32 = 132$), 2.15% between 132 and 148, and 0.13% above 148. Similarly, 34.13% of the scores fall between 84 and 100, 13.59% between 68 and 84, 2.15% between 52 and 68, and 0.13% below 52. These relationships are also shown in Figure 5.2.

To calculate the number of scores in each area, all we must do is multiply the relevant percentage by the total number of scores. Thus, there are 34.13% $\times$ 10,000 = 3413 scores between 100 and 116, 13.59% $\times$ 10,000 = 1359 scores between 116 and 132, and 215 scores between 132 and 148; 13 scores are greater than 148. For the other half of the distribution, there are 3413 scores between 84 and 100, 1359 scores between 68 and 84, and 215 scores between 52 and 68; there are 13 scores below 52. Note that these frequencies would be true only if the distribution is exactly normally distributed. In actual practice, the frequencies would vary slightly depending on how close the distribution is to this theoretical model.

## STANDARD SCORES (*z* SCORES)

Suppose someone told you your IQ was 132. Would you be happy or sad? In the absence of additional information, it is difficult to say. An IQ of 132 is meaningless unless you have a reference group to compare against. Without such a group, you can't tell whether the score is high, average, or low. For the sake of this illustration, let's assume your score is one of the 10,000 scores of the distribution just described. Now we can begin to give your IQ score of 132 some meaning. For example, we can determine the percentage of scores in the distribution that are lower than 132. You will recognize this as determining the percentile rank of the score of 132. (As you no doubt recall, the percentile rank of a score is defined as the percentage of scores that is below the score in question.) Referring to Figure 5.2, we can see that 132 is 2 standard deviations above the mean. In a normal curve, there are 34.13 + 13.59 = 47.72% of the scores between the mean and a score that is 2 standard deviations above the mean. To find the percentile rank of 132, we need to add to this percentage the 50.00% that lie below the mean. Thus, 97.72% (47.72 + 50.00) of the scores fall below your IQ score of 132. You should be quite happy to be so intelligent. The solution is shown in Figure 5.3.

To solve this problem, we had to determine how many standard deviations the raw score of 132 was above or below the mean. In so doing, we transformed the raw score into a *standard score,* also called a *z score.*

---

**definition**    ■   *A **z score** is a transformed score that designates how many standard deviation units the corresponding raw score is above or below the mean.*

---

In equation form,

$$z = \frac{X - \mu}{\sigma} \qquad z \text{ score for population data}$$

$$z = \frac{X - \overline{X}}{s} \qquad z \text{ score for sample data}$$

For the previous example,

$$z = \frac{X - \mu}{\sigma} = \frac{132 - 100}{16} = 2.00$$

The process by which the raw score is altered is called a *score transformation.* We shall see later that the *z* transformation results in a distribution having a mean of 0 and a standard deviation of 1. The reason *z* scores are called standard scores is that they are expressed relative to a distribution mean of 0 and a standard deviation of 1.

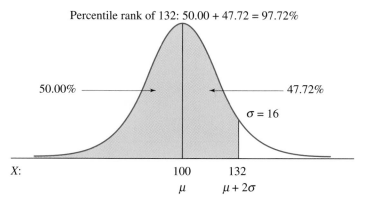

figure 5.3   Percentile rank of an IQ of 132.

In conjunction with a normal curve, $z$ scores allow us to determine the number or percentage of scores that fall above or below any score in the distribution. In addition, $z$ scores allow comparison between scores in different distributions, even when the units of the distributions are different. To illustrate this point, let's consider another population set of scores that are normally distributed. Suppose that the weights of all the rats housed in a university vivarium are normally distributed, with $\mu = 300$ and $\sigma = 20$ grams. What is the percentile rank of a rat weighing 340 grams?

The solution is shown in Figure 5.4. First, we need to convert the raw score of 340 grams to its corresponding $z$ score:

$$z = \frac{X - \mu}{\sigma} = \frac{340 - 300}{20} = 2.00$$

Since the scores are normally distributed, $34.13 + 13.59 = 47.72\%$ of the scores are between the score and the mean. Adding the remaining 50.00% that lie below the mean, we arrive at a percentile rank of $47.72 + 50.00 = 97.72\%$ for the weight of 340 grams. Thus, the IQ score of 132 and the rat's weight of 340 grams have something in common. They both occupy the same relative position in their respective distributions. The rat is as heavy as you are smart.

This example, although somewhat facetious, illustrates an important use of $z$ scores—namely, to compare scores that are not otherwise directly comparable. Ordinarily, we would not be able to compare intelligence and weight. They are measured on different scales and have different units. But by converting the scores to their $z$-transformed scores, we eliminate the original units and replace them with a universal unit, the standard deviation. Thus, your score of 132 IQ units becomes a score of 2 standard deviation units above the mean, and the rat's weight of 340 grams also becomes a score of 2 standard deviation units above the mean. In this way, it is possible to compare "anything with anything" as long as the measuring scales allow computation of the mean and standard deviation. The ability to compare scores that are measured on different scales is of fundamental importance to the topic of correlation. We shall discuss this in more detail when we take up that topic in Chapter 6.

So far, the examples we've been considering have dealt with populations. It might be useful to practice computing $z$ scores using sample data. Let's do this in the next practice problem.

f i g u r e 5.4 Percentile rank of a rat weighing 340 grams.

## Practice Problem 5.1

For the set of sample raw scores $X = 1, 4, 5, 7, 8$, determine the $z$ score for each raw score.

STEP 1: **Determine the mean of the raw scores.**

$$\bar{X} = \frac{\Sigma X_i}{N} = \frac{25}{5} = 5.00$$

STEP 2: **Determine the standard deviation of the scores.**

$$s = \sqrt{\frac{SS}{N-1}} \qquad SS = \Sigma X^2 - \frac{(\Sigma X)^2}{N}$$

$$= \sqrt{\frac{30}{4}} \qquad\qquad = 155 - \frac{(25)^2}{5}$$

$$= 2.7386 \qquad\qquad = 30$$

STEP 3: **Compute the $z$ score for each raw score.**

| $X$ | $z$ |
|-----|-----|
| 1 | $z = \dfrac{X - \bar{X}}{s} = \dfrac{1-5}{2.7386} = -1.46$ |
| 4 | $z = \dfrac{X - \bar{X}}{s} = \dfrac{4-5}{2.7386} = -0.37$ |
| 5 | $z = \dfrac{X - \bar{X}}{s} = \dfrac{5-5}{2.7386} = 0.00$ |
| 7 | $z = \dfrac{X - \bar{X}}{s} = \dfrac{7-5}{2.7386} = 0.73$ |
| 8 | $z = \dfrac{X - \bar{X}}{s} = \dfrac{8-5}{2.7386} = 1.10$ |

## Characteristics of $z$ Scores

There are three characteristics of $z$ scores worth noting. First, *the z scores have the same shape as the set of raw scores.* Transforming the raw scores into their corresponding $z$ scores does not change the shape of the distribution. Nor do the scores change their relative positions. All that is changed are the score values. Figure 5.5 illustrates this point by showing the IQ scores and their corresponding $z$ scores. You should note that although we have used $z$ scores in conjunction with the normal distribution, all $z$ distributions are not normally shaped. If we use the $z$ equation given previously, $z$ scores can be calculated for distributions of any shape. The resulting $z$ scores will take on the shape of the raw scores.

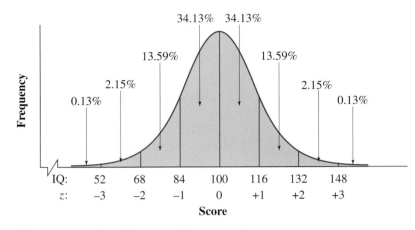

**figure 5.5** Raw IQ scores and corresponding *z* scores.

Second, *the mean of the z scores always equals zero* ($\mu_z = 0$). This follows from the observation that the scores located at the mean of the raw scores will also be at the mean of the *z* scores (see Figure 5.5). The *z* value for raw scores at the mean equals zero. For example, the *z* transformation for a score at the mean of the IQ distribution is given by $z = (X - \mu)/\sigma = (100 - 100)/16 = 0$. Thus, the mean of the *z* distribution equals zero. The last characteristic of importance is that the *standard deviation of z scores always equals 1* ($\sigma_z = 1$). This follows because a raw score that is 1 standard deviation above the mean has a *z* score of +1:

$$z = \frac{(\mu + 1\sigma) - \mu}{\sigma} = 1$$

## Finding Areas Corresponding to Any Raw Score

In the previous examples with IQ and weight, the *z* score was carefully chosen so that the solution could be found from Figure 5.2. However, suppose instead of an IQ of 132, we desire to find the percentile rank of an IQ of 142. Assume the same population parameters. The solution is shown in Figure 5.6. First, draw a curve showing the population and locate the relevant area by entering the score 142 on the horizontal axis. Then shade in the area desired. Next, calculate *z*:

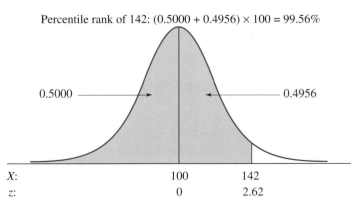

**figure 5.6** Percentile rank of an IQ of 142 in a normal distribution with $\mu = 100$ and $\sigma = 16$.

$$z = \frac{X - \mu}{\sigma} = \frac{142 - 100}{16} = \frac{42}{16} = 2.62$$

Since neither Figure 5.2 nor Figure 5.5 shows a percentage corresponding to a $z$ score of 2.62, we cannot use these figures to solve the problem. Fortunately, the areas under the normal curve for various $z$ scores have been computed, and the resulting values are shown in Table A of Appendix D.

*The first column of the table (column A) contains the z score. Column B lists the proportion of the total area between a given z score and the mean. Column C lists the proportion of the total area that exists beyond the z score.*

We can use Table A to find the percentile rank of 142. First, we locate the $z$ score of 2.62 in column A. Next, we determine from column B the proportion of the total area between the $z$ score and the mean. For a $z$ score of 2.62, this area equals 0.4956. To this value we must add 0.5000 to take into account the scores lying below the mean (the picture helps remind us to do this). Thus, the proportion of scores that lie below an IQ of 142 is $0.4956 + 0.5000 = 0.9956$. To convert this proportion to a percentage, we must multiply by 100. Thus, the percentile rank of 142 is 99.56. Table A can be used to find the area for any $z$ score provided the scores are normally distributed. When using Table A, it is usually sufficient to round $z$ values to two-decimal-place accuracy. Let's do a few more illustrative problems for practice.

## Practice Problem 5.2

The scores on a nationwide mathematics aptitude exam are normally distributed, with $\mu = 80$ and $\sigma = 12$. What is the percentile rank of a score of 84?

**SOLUTION**

*In solving problems involving areas under the normal curve, it is wise, at the outset, to draw a picture of the curve and locate the relevant areas on it.* The accompanying figure shows such a picture. The shaded area contains all the scores lower than 84. To find the percentile rank of 84, we must first convert 84 to its corresponding $z$ score:

$$z = \frac{X - \mu}{\sigma} = \frac{84 - 80}{12} = \frac{4}{12} = 0.33$$

To find the area between the mean and a $z$ score of 0.33, we enter Table A, locate the $z$ value in column A, and read off the corresponding entry in column B. This value is 0.1293. Thus, the proportion of the total area between the mean and a $z$ score of 0.33 is 0.1293. From the accompanying figure, we can see that the remaining scores below the mean occupy 0.5000 proportion of the total area. If we add these two areas together, we shall have the proportion of scores lower than 84. Thus, the proportion of scores lower than 84 is $0.1293 + 0.5000 = 0.6293$. The percentile rank of 84 is then $0.6293 \times 100 = 62.93$. *(continued)*

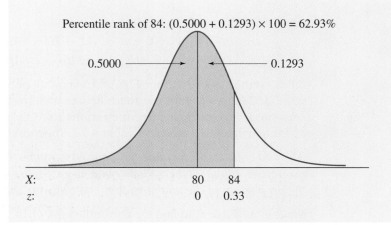

Percentile rank of 84: $(0.5000 + 0.1293) \times 100 = 62.93\%$

0.5000    →    ←    0.1293

| X: | 80 | 84 |
|---|---|---|
| z: | 0 | 0.33 |

## Practice Problem 5.3

What percentage of aptitude scores are below a score of 66?

**SOLUTION**

Again, the first step is to draw the appropriate diagram. This is shown in the accompanying figure. From this diagram, we can see that the relevant area (shaded) lies beyond the score of 66. To find the percentage of scores contained in this area, we must first convert 66 to its corresponding $z$ score. Thus,

$$z = \frac{X - \mu}{\sigma} = \frac{66 - 80}{12} = \frac{-14}{12} = -1.17$$

From Table A, column C, we find that the area beyond a $z$ score of 1.17 is 0.1210. Thus, the percentage of scores below 66 is $0.1210 \times 100 = 12.10\%$. Table A does not show any negative $z$ scores. However, this does not cause a problem because the normal curve is symmetrical and negative $z$ scores have the same proportion of area as positive $z$ scores of the same magnitude. Thus, the proportion of total area lying beyond a $z$ score of $+1.17$ is the same as the proportion lying beyond a $z$ score of $-1.17$.

Percentage below 66 = 12.10%

0.1210

| X: | 66 | 80 |
|---|---|---|
| z: | −1.17 | 0 |

## Practice Problem 5.4

Using the same population as in Practice Problem 5.3, what percentage of scores fall between 64 and 90?

### SOLUTION

The relevant diagram is shown at the end of the practice problem. This time, the shaded areas are on either side of the mean. To solve this problem, we must find the area between 64 and 80 and add it to the area between 80 and 90. As before, to determine area, we must calculate the appropriate *z* score. This time, however, we must compute two *z* scores. For the area to the left of the mean,

$$z = \frac{64 - 80}{12} = \frac{-16}{12} = -1.33$$

For the area to the right of the mean,

$$z = \frac{90 - 80}{12} = \frac{10}{12} = 0.83$$

Since the areas we want to determine are between the mean and the *z* score, we shall use column B of Table A. The area corresponding to a *z* score of $-1.33$ is 0.4082, and the area corresponding to a *z* score of 0.83 is 0.2967. The total area equals the sum of these two areas. Thus, the proportion of scores falling between 64 and 90 is $0.4082 + 0.2967 = 0.7049$. The percentage of scores between 64 and 90 is $0.7049 \times 100 = 70.49\%$. Note that in this problem we cannot just subtract 64 from 90 and divide by 12. The areas in Table A are designated with the mean as a reference point. Therefore, to solve this problem, we must relate the scores of 64 and 90 to the mean of the distribution. You should also note that you cannot just subtract one *z* value from the other because the curve is not rectangular; rather, it has differing amounts of area under various points of the curve.

Percentage between 64 and 90: $(0.4082 + 0.2967) \times 100 = 70.49\%$

## Practice Problem 5.5

Another type of problem arises when we want to determine the area between two scores and both scores are either above or below the mean. Let's try a problem of this sort. Find the percentage of aptitude scores falling between the scores of 95 and 110.

**SOLUTION**

The accompanying figure shows the distribution and the relevant area. As in Practice Problem 5.4, we can't just subtract 95 from 110 and divide by 12 to find the appropriate $z$ score. Rather we must use the mean as our reference point. In this problem, we must find (1) the area between 110 and the mean and (2) the area between 95 and the mean. By subtracting these two areas, we shall arrive at the area between 95 and 110. As before, we must calculate two $z$ scores:

$$z = \frac{110 - 80}{12} = \frac{30}{12} = 2.50 \quad \textit{z transformation of 110}$$

$$z = \frac{95 - 80}{12} = \frac{15}{12} = 1.25 \quad \textit{z transformation of 95}$$

From column B of Table A,

$$\text{Area } (z = 2.50) = 0.4938$$

and

$$\text{Area } (z = 1.25) = 0.3944$$

Thus, the proportion of scores falling between 95 and 110 is 0.4938 − 0.3944 = 0.0994. The percentage of scores is 0.0994 × 100 = 9.94%.

Percentage between 95 and 110: (0.4938 − 0.3944) × 100 = 9.94%

| $X$: | 80 | 95 | 110 |
| --- | --- | --- | --- |
| $z$: | 0 | 1.25 | 2.50 |

## Finding the Raw Score Corresponding to a Given Area

Sometimes we know the area and want to determine the corresponding score. The following problem is of this kind. Find the raw score that divides the distribution of aptitude scores such that 70% of the scores are below it.

This problem is just the reverse of the previous one. Here, we are given the area and need to determine the score. Figure 5.7 shows the appropriate diagram. Although we don't know what the raw score value is, we can determine its corresponding z score from Table A. Once we know the z score, we can solve for the raw score using the z equation. If 70% of the scores lie below the raw score, then 30% must lie above it. We can find the z score by searching in Table A, column C, until we locate the area closest to 0.3000 (30%) and then noting that the z score corresponding to this area is 0.52. To find the raw score, all we need to do is substitute the relevant values in the z equation and solve for X. Thus,

$$z = \frac{X - \mu}{\sigma}$$

Substituting and solving for X,

$$0.52 = \frac{X - 80}{12}$$

$$X = 80 + 12(0.52) = 86.24$$

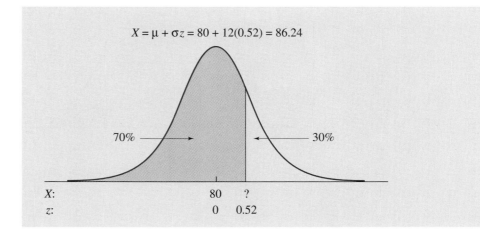

$$X = \mu + \sigma z = 80 + 12(0.52) = 86.24$$

70% ⟶          ⟵ 30%

X:                80    ?
z:                 0   0.52

**f i g u r e 5.7**  Determining the score below which 70% of the distribution falls in a normal distribution with $\mu = 80$ and $\sigma = 12$.

## Practice Problem 5.6

Let's try another problem of this type. What is the score that divides the distribution such that 99% of the area is below it?

### SOLUTION

The diagram is shown below. If 99% of the area is below the score, 1% must be above it. To solve this problem, we locate the area in column C of Table A that is closest to 0.0100 (1%) and note that $z = 2.33$. We convert the $z$ score to its corresponding raw score by substituting the relevant values in the $z$ equation and solving for $X$. Thus,

$$z = \frac{X - \mu}{\sigma}$$

$$2.33 = \frac{X - 80}{12}$$

$$X = 80 + 12(2.33) = 107.96$$

**Practice  Problem  5.7**

Let's do one more problem. What are the scores that bound the middle 95% of the distribution?

**SOLUTION**

The diagram is shown below. There is an area of 2.5% above and below the middle 95%. To determine the scores that bound the middle 95% of the distribution, we must first find the *z* values and then convert these values to raw scores. The *z* scores are found in Table A by locating the area in column C closest to 0.0250 (2.5%) and reading the associated *z* score in column A. In this case, $z = \pm 1.96$. The raw scores are found by substituting the relevant values in the *z* equation and solving for *X*. Thus,

$$z = \frac{X - \mu}{\sigma}$$

$$-1.96 = \frac{X - 80}{12}$$
$$X = 80 + 12(-1.96)$$
$$= 56.48$$

$$+1.96 = \frac{X - 80}{12}$$
$$X = 80 + 12(1.96)$$
$$= 103.52$$

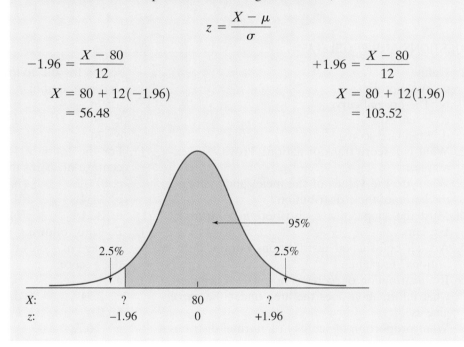

## SUMMARY

In this chapter, we have discussed the normal curve and standard scores. We pointed out that the normal curve is a bell-shaped curve and gave the equation describing it. Next, we discussed the area contained under the normal curve and its relation to $z$ scores. A $z$ score is a transformation of a raw score. It designates how many standard deviation units the corresponding raw score is above or below the mean. A $z$ distribution has the following characteristics: (1) The $z$ scores have the same shape as the set of raw scores, (2) the mean of $z$ scores always equals 0, and (3) the standard deviation of $z$ scores always equals 1. Finally, we showed how to use $z$ scores in conjunction with a normal distribution to find (1) the percentage or frequency of scores corresponding to any raw score in the distribution and (2) the raw score corresponding to any frequency or percentage of scores in the distribution.

## IMPORTANT TERMS

Asymptotic (p. 87)                  Normal curve  (p. 87)                  Standard scores ($z$ scores)  (p. 88)

## QUESTIONS AND PROBLEMS

1. Define
   a. Asymptotic
   b. The normal curve
   c. $z$ scores
   d. Standard scores
2. What is a score transformation? Provide an example.
3. What are the values of the mean and standard deviation of the $z$ distribution?
4. Must the shape of a $z$ distribution be normal? Explain.
5. Are all bell-shaped distributions normal distributions? Explain.
6. If a distribution of scores is normally distributed, what information does the area under the curve give us?
7. What proportion of scores in a normal distribution will have values lower than $z = 0$? What proportion will have values greater than $z = 0$?
8. Given the set of sample raw scores 10, 12, 16, 18, 19, 21,
   a. Convert each raw score to its $z$-transformed value.
   b. Compute the mean and standard deviation of the $z$ scores.
9. Assume the raw scores in Problem 8 are population scores and perform the calculations called for in parts **a** and **b**.
10. A population of raw scores is normally distributed with $\mu = 60$ and $\sigma = 14$. Determine the $z$ scores for the following raw scores taken from that population:
    a. 76                 b. 48
    c. 86                 d. 60
    e. 74                 f. 46
11. For the following $z$ scores, determine the percentage of scores that lie beyond $z$:
    a. 0                  b. 1
    c. 1.54              d. −2.05
    e. 3.21              f. −0.45
12. For the following $z$ scores, determine the percentage of scores that lie between the mean and the $z$ score:
    a. 1                  b. −1
    c. 2.34              d. −3.01
    e. 0                  f. 0.68
    g. −0.73
13. For each of the following, determine the $z$ score that divides the distribution such that the given percentage of scores lies above the $z$ score (round to two decimal places):
    a. 50%               b. 2.50%
    c. 5%                d. 30%
    e. 80%               f. 90%
14. Given that a population of scores is normally distributed with $\mu = 110$ and $\sigma = 8$, determine the following:
    a. The percentile rank of a score of 120
    b. The percentage of scores that are below a score of 99

c. The percentage of scores that are between a score of 101 and 122
d. The percentage of scores that are between a score of 114 and 124
e. The score in the population above which 5% of the scores lie

15. At the end of a particular quarter, Carol took four final exams. The mean and standard deviation for each exam along with Carol's grade on each exam are listed here. Assume that the grades on each exam are normally distributed.

| Exam | Mean | Standard Deviation | Carol's Grade |
|---|---|---|---|
| French | 75.4 | 6.3 | 78.2 |
| History | 85.6 | 4.1 | 83.4 |
| Psychology | 88.2 | 3.5 | 89.2 |
| Statistics | 70.4 | 8.6 | 82.5 |

a. On which exam did Carol do best relative to the other students taking the exam?
b. What was her percentile rank on this exam? education

16. A hospital in a large city records the weight of every infant born at the hospital. The distribution of weights is normally shaped, has a mean $\mu = 2.9$ kilograms, and has a standard deviation $\sigma = 0.45$. Determine the following:
a. The percentage of infants who weighed less than 2.1 kilograms
b. The percentile rank of a weight of 4.2 kilograms
c. The percentage of infants who weighed between 1.8 and 4.0 kilograms
d. The percentage of infants who weighed between 3.4 and 4.1 kilograms
e. The weight that divides the distribution such that 1% of the weights are above it
f. Beyond what weights do the most extreme 5% of the scores lie?
g. If 15,000 infants have been born at the hospital, how many weighed less than 3.5 kilograms? health, I/O

17. A statistician studied the records of monthly rainfall for a particular geographic locale. She found that the average monthly rainfall was normally distributed with a mean $\mu = 8.2$ centimeters and a standard deviation $\sigma = 2.4$. What is the percentile rank of the following scores?
a. 12.4
b. 14.3

c. 5.8
d. 4.1
e. 8.2 I/O, other

18. Using the same population parameters as in Problem 17, what percentage of scores are above the following scores?
a. 10.5
b. 13.8
c. 7.6
d. 3.5
e. 8.2 I/O, other

19. Using the same population parameters as in Problem 17, what percentage of scores are between the following scores?
a. 6.8 and 10.2
b. 5.4 and 8.0
c. 8.8 and 10.5 I/O, other

20. A jogging enthusiast keeps track of how many miles he jogs each week. The following scores are sampled from his year 2005 records:

| Week | Distance* | Week | Distance |
|---|---|---|---|
| 5 | 32 | 30 | 36 |
| 8 | 35 | 32 | 38 |
| 10 | 30 | 38 | 35 |
| 14 | 38 | 43 | 31 |
| 15 | 37 | 48 | 33 |
| 19 | 36 | 49 | 34 |
| 24 | 38 | 52 | 37 |

*Scores are miles run.

a. Determine the $z$ scores for the distances shown in the table. Note that the distances are sample scores.
b. Plot a frequency polygon for the raw scores.
c. On the same graph, plot a frequency polygon for the $z$ scores.
d. Is the $z$ distribution normally shaped? If not, explain why.
e. Compute the mean and standard deviation of the $z$ distribution. I/O, other

21. A stock market analyst has kept records for the past several years of the daily selling price of a particular blue-chip stock. The resulting distribution of scores is normally shaped with a mean $\mu = \$84.10$ and a standard deviation $\sigma = \$7.62$.
a. Determine the percentage of selling prices that were below a price of $95.00.
b. What percentage of selling prices were between $76.00 and $88.00?
c. What percentage of selling prices were above $70.00?

d. What selling price divides the distribution such that 2.5% of the scores are above it? I/O

22. Anthony is deciding whether to go to graduate school in business or law. He has taken nationally administered aptitude tests for both fields. Anthony's scores along with the national norms are shown here. Based solely on Anthony's relative standing on these tests, which field should he enter? Assume that the scores on both tests are normally distributed.

| Field | National Norms μ | National Norms σ | Anthony's Scores |
|---|---|---|---|
| Business | 68 | 4.2 | 80.4 |
| Law | 85 | 3.6 | 89.8 |

education

23. On which of the following exams did Rebecca do better? How about Maurice? Assume the scores on each exam are normally distributed.

| | μ | σ | Rebecca's Scores | Maurice's Scores |
|---|---|---|---|---|
| Exam 1 | 120 | 6.8 | 130 | 132 |
| Exam 2 | 50 | 2.4 | 56 | 52 |

education

24. A psychologist interested in the intelligence of children develops a standardized test for selecting "gifted" children. The test scores are normally distributed, with $\mu = 75$ and $\sigma = 8$. Assume a gifted child is defined as one who scores in the upper 1% of the distribution. What is the minimum score needed to be selected as gifted?

cognitive, developmental

## BOOK COMPANION WEBSITE

Go to www.thomsonedu.com/psychology/pagano for:

- SPSS problems and solutions
- Flash cards for review of terms
- Chapter quiz
- Statistical workshops
- And more

## WebTUTOR

Available via WebTutor for this chapter:

- Detailed chapter outline
- *Know and Be Able To Do* section
- Drag & Drop game for equations, concepts, and other material
- Flash cards for review of terms
- Audio flash cards for MP3 player
- Solving problems using Excel
- Solving problems using SPSS
- More practice problems using computational equations
- Chapter quiz

# Correlation

## INTRODUCTION

In the previous chapters, we were mainly concerned with single distributions and how to best characterize them. In addition to describing individual distributions, it is often desirable to determine whether the scores of one distribution are related to the scores of another distribution. For example, the person in charge of hiring employees for a large corporation might be very interested in knowing whether there was a relationship between the college grades that were earned by their employees and their success in the company. If a strong relationship between these two variables did exist, college grades could be used to predict success in the company and hence would be very useful in screening prospective employees.

Aside from the practical utility of using a relationship for prediction, why would anyone be interested in determining whether two variables are related? One important reason is that if the variables are related, it is possible that one of them is the cause[*] of the other. As we shall see later in this chapter, the fact that two variables are related is not sufficient basis for proving causality. Nevertheless, because correlational studies are among the easiest to carry out, showing that a correlation exists between the variables is often the first step toward proving that they are causally related. Conversely, if a correlation does not exist between the two variables, a causal relationship can be ruled out.

Another very important use of correlation is to assess the "test–retest reliability" of testing instruments. Test–retest reliability means consistency in scores over repeated administrations of the test. For example, assuming an individual's IQ is stable from month to month, we would expect a good test of IQ to show a strong relationship between the scores of two administrations of the test 1 month apart to the same people. Correlational techniques allow us to measure the relationship between the scores derived on the two administrations and, hence, to measure the test–retest reliability of the instrument.

Correlation and regression are very much related. They both involve the relationship between two or more variables. Correlation is primarily concerned with finding out whether a relationship exists and with determining its magnitude and direction, whereas regression is primarily concerned with using the relationship for prediction. In this chapter, we discuss correlation, and in Chapter 7, we will take up the topic of linear regression.

## RELATIONSHIPS

Correlation is a topic that deals primarily with the magnitude and direction of relationships. Before delving into these special aspects of relationships, we will discuss some general features of relationships. With these in hand, we can better understand the material specific to correlation.

### Linear Relationships

To begin our discussion of relationships, let's illustrate a linear relationship between two variables. Table 6.1 shows one month's salary for five salespeople and the dollar value of the merchandise each sold that month.

The relationship between these variables can best be seen by plotting a graph using the paired $X$ and $Y$ values for each salesman as the points on the graph. Such a graph is called a *scatter plot.*

definition  ■  *A* **scatter plot** *is a graph of paired X and Y values.*

---

[*]We recognize that the topic of cause and effect has engendered much philosophical debate. However, we cannot consider the intricacies of this topic here. When we use the term *cause,* we mean it in the common-sense way it is used by nonphilosophers. That is, when we say that *A* caused *B,* we mean that a variation in *A* produced a variation in *B* with all other variables appropriately controlled.

t a b l e  **6.1**   Salary and merchandise sold

| Salesperson | *X* Variable Merchandise Sold ($) | *Y* Variable Salary ($) |
|:-----------:|:---------------------------------:|:-----------------------:|
| 1 | 0 | 500 |
| 2 | 1000 | 900 |
| 3 | 2000 | 1300 |
| 4 | 3000 | 1700 |
| 5 | 4000 | 2100 |

The scatter plot for the salesperson data is shown in Figure 6.1. Referring to this figure, we see that all of the points fall on a straight line. When a straight line describes the relationship between two variables, the relationship is called *linear*.

d e f i n i t i o n    ■   *A* **linear relationship** *between two variables is one in which the relationship can be most accurately represented by a straight line.*

Note that not all relationships are linear. Some relationships are *curvilinear.* In these cases, when a scatter plot of the *X* and *Y* variables is drawn, a *curved* line fits the points better than a straight line.

**Deriving the equation of the straight line**   The relationship between "salary" and "merchandise sold" shown in Figure 6.1 can be described with an equation.

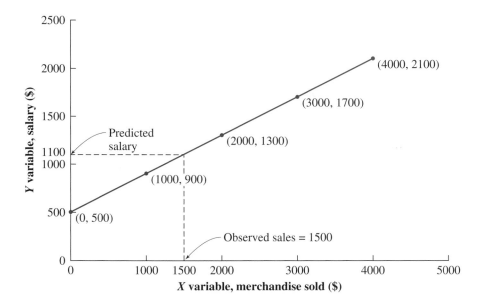

f i g u r e  **6.1**   Scatter plot of the relationship between salary and merchandise sold.

Of course, this equation is the equation of the line joining all of the points. The general form of the equation is given by

$$Y = bX + a \qquad \textit{equation of a straight line}$$

*where*  $a = Y$ intercept (value of $Y$ when $X = 0$)
$b =$ slope of the line

**Finding the $Y$ intercept $a$**  The $Y$ intercept is the value of $Y$ where the line intersects the $Y$ axis. Thus, it is the $Y$ value when $X = 0$. In this problem, we can see from Figure 6.1 that

$$a = Y \text{ intercept} = 500$$

**Finding the slope $b$**  The slope of a line is a measure of its rate of change. It tells us how much the $Y$ score changes for each unit change in the $X$ score. In equation form,

$$b = \text{slope} = \frac{\Delta Y}{\Delta X} = \frac{Y_2 - Y_1}{X_2 - X_1} \qquad \textit{slope of a straight line}$$

Since we are dealing with a straight line, its slope is constant. This means it doesn't matter what values we pick for $X_2$ and $X_1$; the corresponding $Y_2$ and $Y_1$ scores will yield the same value of slope. To calculate the slope, let's vary $X$ from 2000 to 3000. If $X_1 = 2000$, then $Y_1 = 1300$. If $X_2 = 3000$, then $Y_2 = 1700$. Substituting these values into the slope equation,

$$b = \text{slope} = \frac{\Delta Y}{\Delta X} = \frac{Y_2 - Y_1}{X_2 - X_1} = \frac{1700 - 1300}{3000 - 2000} = \frac{400}{1000} = 0.40$$

Thus, the slope is 0.40. This means that the $Y$ value increases 0.40 unit for every 1-unit increase in $X$. The slope and $Y$ intercept determinations are also shown in Figure 6.2. Note that the same slope would occur if we had chosen other values for

**figure  6.2**  Graph of salary and amount of merchandise sold.

$X_1$ and $X_2$. For example, if $X_1 = 1000$ and $X_2 = 4000$, then $Y_1 = 900$ and $Y_2 = 2100$. Solving for the slope,

$$b = \text{slope} = \frac{\Delta Y}{\Delta X} = \frac{Y_2 - Y_1}{X_2 - X_1} = \frac{2100 - 900}{4000 - 1000} = \frac{1200}{3000} = 0.40$$

Again, the slope is 0.40.

The full equation for the linear relationship that exists between salary and merchandise sold can now be written:

$$Y = bX + a$$

Substituting for $a$ and $b$,

$$Y = 0.40X + 500$$

The equation $Y = 0.40X + 500$ describes the relationship between the $Y$ variable (salary) and the $X$ variable (merchandise sold). It tells us that $Y$ increases by 1 unit for every 0.40 increase in $X$. Moreover, as long as the relationship holds, this equation lets us compute an appropriate value for $Y$, given any value of $X$. That makes the equation very useful for prediction.

**Predicting $Y$ given $X$**    When used for prediction, the equation becomes

$$Y' = 0.40X + 500$$

*where*    $Y'$ = the predicted value of the $Y$ variable

With this equation, we can predict any $Y$ value just by knowing the corresponding $X$ value. For example, if $X = 1500$ as in our previous problem, then

$$Y' = 0.40X + 500$$
$$= 0.40(1500) + 500$$
$$= 600 + 500$$
$$= 1100$$

Thus, if a salesperson sells \$1500 worth of merchandise, his or her salary would equal \$1100.

Of course, prediction could also have been done graphically, as shown in Figure 6.1. By vertically projecting the $X$ value of \$1500 until it intersects with the straight line, we can read the predicted $Y$ value from the $Y$ axis. The predicted value is \$1100, which is the same value we arrived at using the equation.

## Positive and Negative Relationships

In addition to being linear or curvilinear, the relationship between two variables may be *positive* or *negative*.

definitions    ■    *A* **positive relationship** *indicates that there is a direct relationship between the variables. A* **negative relationship** *exists when there is an inverse relationship between X and Y.*

The slope of the line tells us whether the relationship is positive or negative. When the relationship is positive, the slope is positive. The previous example had a positive slope; that is, higher values of $X$ were associated with higher values of $Y$, and lower values of $X$ were associated with lower values of $Y$. When the slope is positive, the line runs upward from left to right, indicating that as $X$ increases, $Y$ increases. Thus, a direct relationship exists between the two variables.

When the relationship is negative, there is an inverse relationship between the variables, making the slope negative. An example of a negative relationship is shown in Figure 6.3. Note that with a negative slope, the curve runs downward from left to right. Low values of $X$ are associated with high values of $Y$, and high values of $X$ are associated with low values of $Y$. Another way of saying this is that as $X$ increases, $Y$ decreases.

## Perfect and Imperfect Relationships

In the relationships we have graphed so far, all of the points have fallen on the straight line. When this is the case, the relationship is a *perfect* one. Unfortunately, in the behavioral sciences, perfect relationships are rare. It is much more common to find imperfect relationships.

definitions   ■   *A* **perfect relationship** *is one in which a positive or negative relationship exists and all of the points fall on the line. An* **imperfect relationship** *is one in which a relationship exists, but all of the points do not fall on the line.*

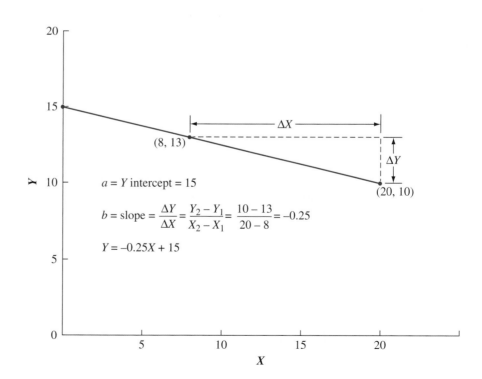

figure 6.3   Example of a negative relationship.

table 6.2   IQ and grade point average of 12 college students

| Student No. | IQ | Grade Point Average |
|:---:|:---:|:---:|
| 1 | 110 | 1.0 |
| 2 | 112 | 1.6 |
| 3 | 118 | 1.2 |
| 4 | 119 | 2.1 |
| 5 | 122 | 2.6 |
| 6 | 125 | 1.8 |
| 7 | 127 | 2.6 |
| 8 | 130 | 2.0 |
| 9 | 132 | 3.2 |
| 10 | 134 | 2.6 |
| 11 | 136 | 3.0 |
| 12 | 138 | 3.6 |

As an example, Table 6.2 shows the IQ scores and grade point averages of a sample of 12 college students. Suppose we wanted to determine the relationship between these hypothetical data. The scatter plot is shown in Figure 6.4. From the scatter plot, it is obvious that the relationship between IQ and college grades is imperfect. The imperfect relationship is positive because lower values of IQ are

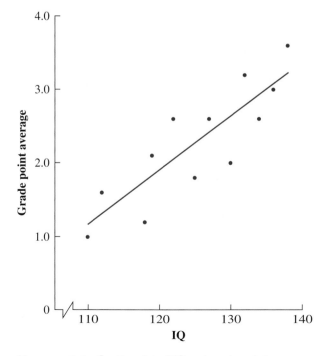

figure 6.4   Scatter plot of IQ and grade point average.

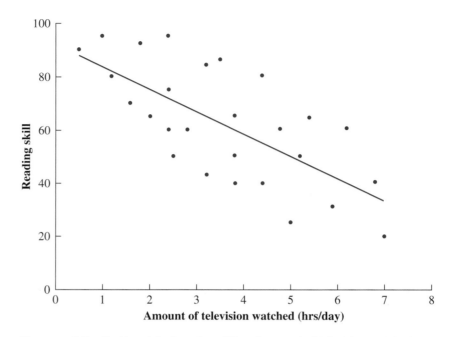

figure 6.5 Scatter plot of reading skill and amount of television watched by sixth graders.

associated with lower values of grade point average, and higher values of IQ are associated with higher values of grade point average. In addition, the relationship appears linear.

To describe this relationship with a straight line, the best we can do is to draw the line that *best* fits the data. Another way of saying this is that, when the relationship is imperfect, we cannot draw a single straight line through all of the points. We can, however, construct a straight line that most accurately fits the data. This line has been drawn in Figure 6.4. This best-fitting line is often used for prediction; when so used, it is called a *regression* line.*

A *USA Today* article reported that there is an inverse relationship between the amount of television watched by primary school students and their reading skills. Suppose the sixth-grade data for the article appeared as shown in Figure 6.5. This is an example of a negative, imperfect, linear relationship. The relationship is negative because higher values of television watching are associated with lower values of reading skill, and lower values of television watching are associated with higher values of reading skill. The linear relationship is imperfect because not all of the points fall on a single straight line. The regression line for these data is also shown in Figure 6.5.

Having completed our background discussion of relationships, we can now move on to the topic of correlation.

---

*The details on how to construct this line will be discussed in Chapter 7.

## CORRELATION

Correlation is a topic that focuses on the *direction* and *degree* of the relationship. The direction of the relationship refers to whether the relationship is positive or negative. The degree of relationship refers to the magnitude or strength of the relationship. The degree of relationship can vary from nonexistent to perfect. When the relationship is perfect, correlation is at its highest and we can exactly predict from one variable to the other. In this situation, as $X$ changes, so does $Y$. Moreover, the same value of $X$ always leads to the same value of $Y$. Alternatively, the same value of $Y$ always leads to the same value of $X$. The points all fall on a straight line, assuming the relationship is linear. When the relationship is nonexistent, correlation is at its lowest and knowing the value of one of the variables doesn't help at all in predicting the other. Imperfect relationships have intermediate levels of correlation, and prediction is approximate. Here, the same value of $X$ doesn't always lead to the same value of $Y$. Nevertheless, on the average, $Y$ changes systematically with $X$, and we can do a better job of predicting $Y$ with knowledge of $X$ than without it.

Although it suffices for some purposes to talk rather loosely about "high" or "low" correlations, it is much more often desirable to know the exact magnitude and direction of the correlation. A *correlation coefficient* gives us this information.

**definition** ■ *A **correlation coefficient** expresses quantitatively the magnitude and direction of the relationship.*

A correlation coefficient can vary from $+1$ to $-1$. The *sign* of the coefficient tells us whether the relationship is *positive* or *negative*. The numerical part of the correlation coefficient describes the magnitude of the correlation. The higher the number, the greater the correlation. Since 1 is the highest number possible, it represents a perfect correlation. A correlation coefficient of $+1$ means the correlation is perfect and the relationship is positive. A correlation coefficient of $-1$ means the correlation is perfect and the relationship is negative. When the relationship is nonexistent, the correlation coefficient equals 0. Imperfect relationships have correlation coefficients varying in magnitude between 0 and 1. They will be plus or minus depending on the direction of the relationship.

Figure 6.6 shows scatter plots of several different linear relationships and the correlation coefficients for each. The Pearson $r$ correlation coefficient has been used because the relationships are linear. We shall discuss Pearson $r$ in the next section. Each scatter plot is made up of paired $X$ and $Y$ values. Note that the closer the points are to the regression line, the higher the magnitude of the correlation coefficient and the more accurate the prediction. Also, when the correlation is zero, there is no relationship between $X$ and $Y$. This means that $Y$ does not increase or decrease systematically with increases or decreases in $X$. Thus, with zero correlation, the regression line for predicting $Y$ is horizontal and knowledge of $X$ does not aid in predicting $Y$.

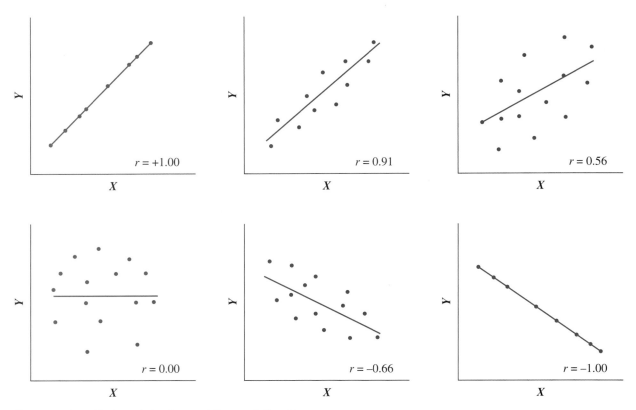

figure 6.6   Scatter plots of several linear relationships.

## The Linear Correlation Coefficient Pearson *r*

You will recall from our discussion in Chapter 5 that a basic problem in measuring the relationship between two variables is that very often the variables are measured on different scales and in different units. For example, if we are interested in measuring the correlation between IQ and grade point average for the data presented in Table 6.2, we are faced with the problem that IQ and grade point average have very different scaling. As was mentioned in Chapter 5, this problem is resolved by converting each score to its $z$-transformed value, in effect putting both variables on the same scale, a $z$ scale.

To appreciate how useful $z$ scores are for determining correlation, consider the following example. Suppose your neighborhood supermarket is having a sale on oranges. The oranges are bagged, and each bag has the total price marked on it. You want to know whether there is a relationship between the weight of the oranges in each bag and their cost. Being a natural-born researcher, you randomly sample six bags and weigh each one. The cost and weight in pounds of the six bags are shown in Table 6.3. A scattergram of the data is plotted in Figure 6.7. Are these two variables related? Yes; in fact, all the points fall on a straight line. There is a perfect positive correlation between the cost and weight of the oranges. Thus, the correlation coefficient must equal +1.

Next, let's see what happens when we convert these raw scores to $z$ scores. The raw scores for weight ($X$) and cost ($Y$) have been expressed as standard scores in the fourth and fifth columns of Table 6.3. Something quite interesting has happened. *The paired raw scores for each bag of oranges have the same z*

**t a b l e  6.3**   Cost and weight in pounds of six bags of oranges

| Bag | Weight (lb) $X$ | Cost ($) $Y$ | $z_X$ | $z_Y$ |
|-----|-----------------|--------------|-------|-------|
| A | 2.25 | 0.75 | −1.34 | −1.34 |
| B | 3.00 | 1.00 | −0.80 | −0.80 |
| C | 3.75 | 1.25 | −0.27 | −0.27 |
| D | 4.50 | 1.50 | 0.27 | 0.27 |
| E | 5.25 | 1.75 | 0.80 | 0.80 |
| F | 6.00 | 2.00 | 1.34 | 1.34 |

*value.* For example, the paired raw scores for bag A are 2.25 and 0.75. However, their respective $z$ scores are both −1.34. The raw score of 2.25 is as many standard deviation units below the mean of the $X$ distribution as the raw score of 0.75 is below the mean of the $Y$ distribution. The same is true for the other paired scores. All of the paired raw scores occupy the same relative position within their own distributions. That is, they have the same $z$ values. When using raw scores, this relationship is obscured because of differences in scaling between the two variables. If the paired scores occupy the same relative position within their own distributions, then the correlation must be perfect ($r = 1$), because knowing one of the paired values will allow us to exactly predict the other value. If prediction is perfect, the relationship must be perfect.

This brings us to the definition of Pearson $r$.

**d e f i n i t i o n     ■   Pearson *r* is a measure of the extent to which paired scores occupy the same or opposite positions within their own distributions.**

Note that this definition also includes the paired scores occupying opposite positions. If the paired $z$ scores have the same magnitude but opposite signs, the correlation would again be perfect and $r$ would equal −1.

This example highlights a very important point. Since correlation is concerned with the relationship between two variables and the variables are often measured

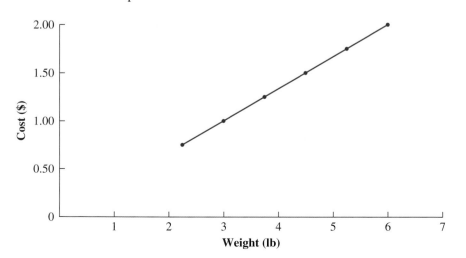

**f i g u r e  6.7**   Cost of oranges versus their weight in pounds.

**t a b l e  6.4**  Cost and weight in kilograms of six bags of oranges

| Bag | Weight (kg) $X$ | Cost ($) $Y$ | $z_X$ | $z_Y$ |
|-----|-----------------|--------------|-------|-------|
| A | 1.02 | 0.75 | −1.34 | −1.34 |
| B | 1.36 | 1.00 | −0.80 | −0.80 |
| C | 1.70 | 1.25 | −0.27 | −0.27 |
| D | 2.04 | 1.50 | 0.27 | 0.27 |
| E | 2.38 | 1.75 | 0.80 | 0.80 |
| F | 2.72 | 2.00 | 1.34 | 1.34 |

in different units and scaling, the magnitude and direction of the correlation coefficient must be independent of the differences in units and scaling that exist between the two variables. Pearson $r$ achieves this by using $z$ scores. Thus, we can correlate such diverse variables as time of day and position of the sun, percent body fat and caloric intake, test anxiety and examination grades, and so forth.

Since this is such an important point, we would like to illustrate it again by taking the previous example one more step. In the example involving the relationship between the cost of oranges and their weight, suppose you weighed the oranges in kilograms rather than in pounds. Should this change the degree of relationship between the cost and weight of the oranges? In light of what we have just presented, the answer is surely no. Correlation must be independent of the units used in measuring the two variables. If the correlation is 1 between the cost of the oranges and their weight in pounds, the correlation should also be 1 between the cost of the oranges and their weight in kilograms. We've converted the weight of each bag of oranges from pounds to kilograms. The data are presented in Table 6.4, and the raw scores are plotted in Figure 6.8. Again, all the scores fall on a straight line, so the correlation equals 1.00. Notice the values of the paired $z$ scores in the fourth and fifth columns of Table 6.4. Once more, they have the same values, and these values are the same as when the oranges were weighed in pounds. Thus, using $z$ scores allows a measurement of the relationship between the two variables that is independent of differences in scaling and of the units used in measuring the variables.

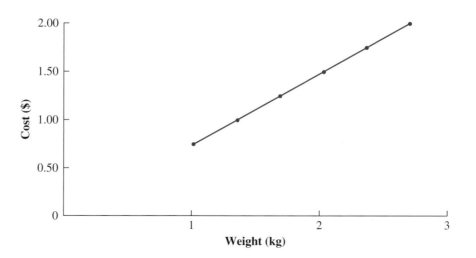

**f i g u r e  6.8**  Cost of oranges versus their weight in kilograms.

**Calculating Pearson *r*** The equation for calculating Pearson *r* using *z* scores is

$$r = \frac{\sum z_X z_Y}{N - 1} \qquad conceptual\ equation$$

*where* $\sum z_X z_Y =$ the sum of the product of each *z* score pair

To use this equation, you must first convert each raw score into its *z*-transformed value. This can take a considerable amount of time and possibly create rounding errors. Using some algebra, this equation can be transformed into a calculation equation that uses the raw scores:

$$r = \frac{\sum XY - \dfrac{(\sum X)(\sum Y)}{N}}{\sqrt{\left[\sum X^2 - \dfrac{(\sum X)^2}{N}\right]\left[\sum Y^2 - \dfrac{(\sum Y)^2}{N}\right]}} \qquad \begin{array}{l} computational\ equation\ for \\ Pearson\ r \end{array}$$

*where* $\sum XY =$ the sum of the product of each *X* and *Y* pair ($\sum XY$ is also called the sum of the cross products.)

Table 6.5 contains some hypothetical data collected from five subjects. Let's use these data to calculate Pearson *r*:

$$r = \frac{\sum XY - \dfrac{(\sum X)(\sum Y)}{N}}{\sqrt{\left[\sum X^2 - \dfrac{(\sum X)^2}{N}\right]\left[\sum Y^2 - \dfrac{(\sum Y)^2}{N}\right]}}$$

**t a b l e  6.5** Hypothetical data for computing Pearson *r*

| Subject | X | Y | X² | Y² | XY |
|---------|---|---|-----|-----|-----|
| A | 1 | 2 | 1 | 4 | 2 |
| B | 3 | 5 | 9 | 25 | 15 |
| C | 4 | 3 | 16 | 9 | 12 |
| D | 6 | 7 | 36 | 49 | 42 |
| E | 7 | 5 | 49 | 25 | 35 |
| *Total* | 21 | 22 | 111 | 112 | 106 |

$$r = \frac{\sum XY - \dfrac{(\sum X)(\sum Y)}{N}}{\sqrt{\left[\sum X^2 - \dfrac{(\sum X)^2}{N}\right]\left[\sum Y^2 - \dfrac{(\sum Y)^2}{N}\right]}}$$

$$= \frac{106 - \dfrac{21(22)}{5}}{\sqrt{\left[111 - \dfrac{(21)^2}{5}\right]\left[112 - \dfrac{(22)^2}{5}\right]}}$$

$$= \frac{13.6}{18.616} = 0.731 = 0.73$$

$\Sigma\ XY$ is called the sum of the cross products. It is found by multiplying the $X$ and $Y$ scores for each subject and then summing the resulting products. Calculation of $\Sigma\ XY$ and the other terms is illustrated in Table 6.5. Substituting these values in the previous equation, we obtain

$$r = \frac{106 - \dfrac{21(22)}{5}}{\sqrt{\left[111 - \dfrac{(21)^2}{5}\right]\left[112 - \dfrac{(22)^2}{5}\right]}} = \frac{13.6}{\sqrt{22.8(15.2)}} = \frac{13.6}{18.616} = 0.731 = 0.73$$

## Practice Problem 6.1

Let's try another problem. This time we shall use data given in Table 6.2. For your convenience, these data are reproduced in the first three columns of the accompanying table. In this example, we have an imperfect linear relationship, and we are interested in computing the magnitude and direction of the relationship using Pearson $r$. The solution is also shown in the following table.

**SOLUTION**

| Student No. | IQ X | Grade Point Average Y | $X^2$ | $Y^2$ | XY |
|:---:|:---:|:---:|:---:|:---:|:---:|
| 1 | 110 | 1.0 | 12,100 | 1.00 | 110.0 |
| 2 | 112 | 1.6 | 12,544 | 2.56 | 179.2 |
| 3 | 118 | 1.2 | 13,924 | 1.44 | 141.6 |
| 4 | 119 | 2.1 | 14,161 | 4.41 | 249.9 |
| 5 | 122 | 2.6 | 14,884 | 6.76 | 317.2 |
| 6 | 125 | 1.8 | 15,625 | 3.24 | 225.0 |
| 7 | 127 | 2.6 | 16,129 | 6.76 | 330.2 |
| 8 | 130 | 2.0 | 16,900 | 4.00 | 260.0 |
| 9 | 132 | 3.2 | 17,424 | 10.24 | 422.4 |
| 10 | 134 | 2.6 | 17,956 | 6.76 | 348.4 |
| 11 | 136 | 3.0 | 18,496 | 9.00 | 408.0 |
| 12 | 138 | 3.6 | 19,044 | 12.96 | 496.8 |
| *Total* | 1503 | 27.3 | 189,187 | 69.13 | 3488.7 |

$$r = \frac{\Sigma\ XY - \dfrac{(\Sigma\ X)(\Sigma\ Y)}{N}}{\sqrt{\left[\Sigma\ X^2 - \dfrac{(\Sigma\ X)^2}{N}\right]\left[\Sigma\ Y^2 - \dfrac{(\Sigma\ Y)^2}{N}\right]}}$$

$$= \frac{3488.7 - \dfrac{1503(27.3)}{12}}{\sqrt{\left[189,187 - \dfrac{(1503)^2}{12}\right]\left[69.13 - \dfrac{(27.3)^2}{12}\right]}} = \frac{69.375}{81.088} = 0.856 \approx 0.86$$

## Practice Problem 6.2

Let's try one more problem. Have you ever wondered whether it is true that opposites attract? We've all been with couples in which the two individuals seem so different from each other. But is this the usual experience? Does similarity or dissimilarity foster attraction?

A social psychologist investigating this problem asked 15 college students to fill out a questionnaire concerning their attitudes toward a variety of topics. Some time later, they were shown the "attitudes" of a stranger to the same items and were asked to rate the stranger as to probable liking for the stranger and probable enjoyment of working with him. The "attitudes" of the stranger were really made up by the experimenter and varied over subjects regarding the proportion of attitudes held by the stranger that were similar to those held by the rater. Thus, for each subject, data were collected concerning his attitudes and the attraction of a stranger based on the stranger's attitudes to the same items. If similarities attract, then there should be a direct relationship between the attraction of the stranger and the proportion of his similar attitudes. The data are presented in the table at the end of this practice problem. The higher the attraction, the higher the score. The maximum possible attraction score is 14. Compute the Pearson $r$ correlation coefficient[*] to determine whether there is a direct relationship between similarity of attitudes and attraction.

### SOLUTION

The solution is shown in the following table.

| Student No. | Proportion of Similar Attitudes $X$ | Attraction $Y$ | $X^2$ | $Y^2$ | $XY$ |
|---|---|---|---|---|---|
| 1 | 0.30 | 8.9 | 0.090 | 79.21 | 2.670 |
| 2 | 0.44 | 9.3 | 0.194 | 86.49 | 4.092 |
| 3 | 0.67 | 9.6 | 0.449 | 92.16 | 6.432 |
| 4 | 0.00 | 6.2 | 0.000 | 38.44 | 0.000 |
| 5 | 0.50 | 8.8 | 0.250 | 77.44 | 4.400 |
| 6 | 0.15 | 8.1 | 0.022 | 65.61 | 1.215 |
| 7 | 0.58 | 9.5 | 0.336 | 90.25 | 5.510 |
| 8 | 0.32 | 7.1 | 0.102 | 50.41 | 2.272 |
| 9 | 0.72 | 11.0 | 0.518 | 121.00 | 7.920 |
| 10 | 1.00 | 11.7 | 1.000 | 136.89 | 11.700 |
| 11 | 0.87 | 11.5 | 0.757 | 132.25 | 10.005 |
| 12 | 0.09 | 7.3 | 0.008 | 53.29 | 0.657 |
| 13 | 0.82 | 10.0 | 0.672 | 100.00 | 8.200 |
| 14 | 0.64 | 10.0 | 0.410 | 100.00 | 6.400 |
| 15 | 0.24 | 7.5 | 0.058 | 56.25 | 1.800 |
| *Total* | 7.34 | 136.5 | 4.866 | 1279.69 | 73.273 |

[*]As will be pointed out later in the chapter, it is legitimate to calculate Pearson $r$ only where the data are of interval or ratio scaling. Therefore, to calculate Pearson $r$ for this problem, we must assume the data are at least of interval scaling.                    (*continued*)

$$r = \frac{\Sigma\, XY - \dfrac{(\Sigma\, X)(\Sigma\, Y)}{N}}{\sqrt{\left[\Sigma\, X^2 - \dfrac{(\Sigma\, X)^2}{N}\right]\left[\Sigma\, Y^2 - \dfrac{(\Sigma\, Y)^2}{N}\right]}}$$

$$= \frac{73.273 - \dfrac{7.34(136.5)}{15}}{\sqrt{\left[4.866 - \dfrac{(7.34)^2}{15}\right]\left[1279.69 - \dfrac{(136.5)^2}{15}\right]}}$$

$$= \frac{6.479}{\sqrt{1.274(37.54)}} = \frac{6.479}{6.916} = 0.936 = 0.94$$

Therefore, based on these students, there is a very strong relationship between similarity and attractiveness.

**A second interpretation for Pearson $r$**    Pearson $r$ can also be interpreted in terms of the variability of $Y$ accounted for by $X$. This approach leads to important additional information about $r$ and the relationship between $X$ and $Y$. Consider Figure 6.9 in which an imperfect relationship is shown between $X$ and $Y$. In this example, the $X$ variable represents spelling competence and the $Y$ variable is writing ability of six students in the third grade. Suppose we are interested in predicting the writing score for Maria, the student whose spelling score is 88. If there were no relationship between writing and spelling, we would predict a score of 50, which is the overall mean of all the writing scores. In the absence of a rela-

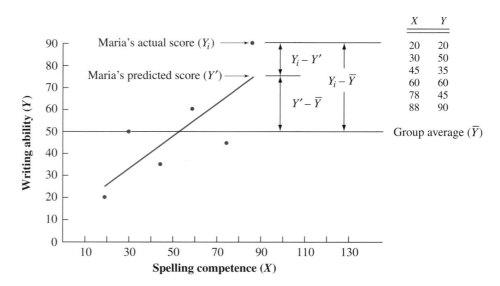

**figure 6.9**  Relationship between spelling and writing.

tionship between $X$ and $Y$, the overall mean is the best predictor. When there is no relationship between $X$ and $Y$, using the mean minimizes prediction errors because the sum of the squared deviations from it is a minimum. You will recognize this as the fourth property of the mean, discussed in Chapter 4. Maria's actual writing score is 90, so our estimate of 50 is in error by 40 points. Thus,

Maria's actual writing score − Group average = $Y_i - \overline{Y}$ = 90 − 50 = 40

However, in this example, the relationship between $X$ and $Y$ is not zero. Although it is not perfect, a relationship greater than zero exists between $X$ and $Y$. Therefore, the overall mean of the writing scores is not the best predictor. Rather, as discussed previously in the chapter, we can use the regression line for these data as the basis of our prediction. The regression line for the writing and spelling scores is shown in Figure 6.9. Using this line, we would predict a writing score of 75 for Maria. Now the error is only 15 points. Thus,

$$\left(\begin{array}{c}\text{Maria's actual} \\ \text{score}\end{array}\right) - \left(\begin{array}{c}\text{Maria's predicted} \\ \text{score using } X\end{array}\right) = Y_i - Y' = 90 - 75 = 15$$

It can be observed in Figure 6.9 that the distance between Maria's score and the mean of the $Y$ scores is divisible into two segments. Thus,

$$Y_i - \overline{Y} \quad = \quad (Y_i - Y') + (Y' - \overline{Y})$$

| *Deviation of $Y_i$* | = | *Error in prediction using the relationship between $X$ and $Y$* | + | *Deviation of $Y_i$ accounted for by the relationship between $X$ and $Y$* |
|---|---|---|---|---|

The segment $Y_i - Y'$ represents the error in prediction. The remaining segment $Y' - \overline{Y}$ represents that part of the deviation of $Y_i$ that is accounted for by the relationship between $X$ and $Y$. You should note that "accounted for by the relationship between $X$ and $Y$" is often abbreviated as "accounted for by $X$."

Suppose we now determine the predicted $Y$ score ($Y'$) for each $X$ score using the regression line. We could then construct $Y_i - \overline{Y}$ for each score. If we squared each $Y_i - \overline{Y}$ and summed over all the scores, we would obtain

$$\Sigma (Y_i - \overline{Y})^2 = \Sigma (Y_i - Y')^2 + \Sigma (Y' - \overline{Y})^2$$

| *Total variability of $Y$* | = | *Variability of prediction errors* | + | *Variability of $Y$ accounted for by $X$* |
|---|---|---|---|---|

Note that $\Sigma (Y_i - \overline{Y})^2$ is the sum of squares of the $Y$ scores. It represents the total variability of the $Y$ scores. Thus, this equation states that the total variability of the $Y$ scores can be divided into two parts: the variability of the prediction errors and the variability of $Y$ accounted for by $X$.

We know that, as the relationship gets stronger, the prediction gets more accurate. In the previous equation, as the relationship gets stronger, the prediction errors get smaller, also causing the variability of prediction errors $\Sigma (Y_i - Y')^2$ to decrease. Since the total variability $\Sigma (Y_i - \overline{Y})^2$ hasn't changed, the variability of

$Y$ accounted for by $X$, namely, $\Sigma (Y' - \overline{Y})^2$, must increase. Thus, the proportion of the total variability of the $Y$ scores that is accounted for by $X$, namely, $\Sigma (Y' - \overline{Y})^2 / \Sigma (Y_i - \overline{Y})^2$, is a measure of the strength of relationship. It turns out that if we take the square root of this ratio and substitute for $Y'$ the appropriate values, we obtain the computational formula for Pearson $r$. We previously defined Pearson $r$ as a measure of the extent to which paired scores occupy the same or opposite positions within their own distributions. From what we have just said, it is also the case that Pearson $r$ equals the square root of the proportion of the variability of $Y$ accounted for by $X$. In equation form,

$$r = \sqrt{\frac{\Sigma(Y' - \overline{Y})^2}{\Sigma(Y_i - \overline{Y})^2}} = \sqrt{\frac{\text{Variability of } Y \text{ that is accounted for by } X}{\text{Total variability of } Y}}$$

$$r = \sqrt{\text{Proportion of the total variability of } Y \text{ that is accounted for by } X}$$

It follows from this equation that the higher $r$ is, the greater the proportion of the variability of $Y$ that is accounted for by $X$.

**Relationship of $r^2$ and explained variability**    If we square the previous equation, we obtain

$$r^2 = \text{Proportion of the total variability of } Y \text{ that is accounted for by } X$$

Thus, $r^2$ is called the *coefficient of determination*. As shown in the equation, $r^2$ equals the proportion of the total variability of $Y$ that is accounted for or explained by $X$. In the problem dealing with grade point average and IQ, the correlation was 0.86. If we square $r$, we obtain

$$r^2 = (0.86)^2 = 0.74$$

This means that 74% of the variability in $Y$ can be accounted for by IQ. If it turns out that IQ is a causal factor in determining grade point average, then $r^2$ tells us that IQ accounts for 74% of the variability in grade point average. What about the remaining 26%? Other factors that can account for the remaining 26% must be influencing grade point average. The important point here is that one can be misled by using $r$ into thinking that $X$ may be a major cause of $Y$ when really it is $r^2$ that tells us how much of the change in $Y$ can be accounted for by $X$. The error isn't so serious when you have a correlation coefficient as high as 0.86. However, in the behavioral sciences, such high correlations are rare. Correlation coefficients of $r = 0.50$ or $0.60$ are considered fairly high, and yet correlations of this magnitude account for only 25 to 36% of the variability in $Y$ ($r^2 = 0.25$ to $0.36$). Table 6.6 shows the relationship between $r$ and the explained variability expressed as a percentage.

## Other Correlation Coefficients

So far, we have discussed correlation and described in some detail the linear correlation coefficient Pearson $r$. We have chosen Pearson $r$ because it is the most frequently encountered correlation coefficient in behavioral science research. However, you should be aware that there are many different correlation coefficients one might employ, each of which is appropriate under different conditions. In deciding which correlation coefficient to calculate, the *shape of the relationship* and the *measuring scale* of the data are the two most important considerations.

t a b l e  **6.6**  Relationship between $r$
and explained variability

| $r$ | Explained Variability, $r^2$ (%) |
|------|------|
| 0.10 | 1 |
| 0.20 | 4 |
| 0.30 | 9 |
| 0.40 | 16 |
| 0.50 | 25 |
| 0.60 | 36 |
| 0.70 | 49 |
| 0.80 | 64 |
| 0.90 | 81 |
| 1.00 | 100 |

**Shape of the relationship**    The choice of which correlation coefficient to calculate depends on whether the relationship is linear or curvilinear. If the data are curvilinear, using a linear correlation coefficient such as Pearson $r$ can seriously underestimate the degree of relationship that exists between $X$ and $Y$. Accordingly, another correlation coefficient $\eta$ (eta) is used for curvilinear relationships. Since $\eta$ is not frequently encountered in behavioral science research, we have not presented a discussion of it.[*] This does, however, emphasize the importance of doing a scatter plot to determine whether the relationship is linear before just routinely going ahead and calculating a linear correlation coefficient.

**Measuring scale**    The choice of correlation coefficient also depends on the type of measuring scale underlying the data. We've already discussed the linear correlation coefficient Pearson $r$. It assumes the data are measured on an interval or ratio scale. Some examples of other linear correlation coefficients are the Spearman rank order correlation coefficient rho ($r_s$), the biserial correlation coefficient ($r_b$), and the phi ($\phi$) coefficient. In actuality, each of these coefficients is the equation for Pearson $r$ simplified to apply to the lower-order scaling. Rho is used when one or both of the variables are of ordinal scaling, $r_b$ is used when one of the variables is at least interval and the other is dichotomous, and phi is used when each of the variables is dichotomous. Although it is beyond the scope of this textbook to present each of these correlation coefficients in detail, the Spearman rank order correlation coefficient rho occurs frequently enough to warrant discussion here.

**The Spearman rank order correlation coefficient rho $(r_s)$**    As mentioned, the Spearman rank order correlation coefficient rho is used when one or both of the variables are only of ordinal scaling. Spearman rho is really the linear correlation coefficient Pearson $r$ applied to data that meet the requirements of ordinal scal-

---

[*]A discussion of $\eta$ as well as the other coefficients presented in this section is contained in N. Downie and R. Heath, *Basic Statistical Methods,* 4th ed., Harper & Row, New York, 1974, pp. 102–114.

ing. The easiest equation for calculating rho when there are no ties or just a few ties relative to the number of paired scores is

$$r_s = 1 - \frac{6\,\Sigma\,D_i^2}{N^3 - N} \quad \textit{computational equation for rho}$$

*where*      $D_i$ = difference between the *i*th pair of ranks = $R(X_i) - R(Y_i)$

$R(X_i)$ = rank of the *i*th $X$ score

$R(Y_i)$ = rank of the *i*th $Y$ score

$N$ = number of pairs of ranks

It can be shown that, with ordinal data having no ties, Pearson *r* reduces algebraically to the previous equation.

To illustrate the use of rho, let's consider an example. Assume that a large corporation is interested in rating a current class of 12 management trainees on their leadership ability. Two psychologists are hired to do the job. As a result of their tests and interviews, the psychologists each independently rank-order the students according to leadership ability. The rankings are from 1 to 12, with 1 representing the highest level of leadership. The data are given in Table 6.7. What is the correlation between the rankings of the two psychologists?

Since the data are of ordinal scaling, we should compute rho. The solution is shown in Table 6.7. Note that subjects 5 and 6 were tied in the rankings of psychologist A. When ties occur, the rule is to give each subject the average of the tied ranks. For example, subjects 5 and 6 were tied for ranks 2 and 3. Therefore, they each received a ranking of 2.5 [(2 + 3)/2 = 2.5]. In giving the two subjects a rank of 2.5, we have effectively used up ranks 2 and 3. The next rank is 4. $D_i$ is the difference between the paired rankings for the *i*th subject. Thus, $D_i = 1$ for

**table 6.7**   Calculation of $r_s$ for leadership example

| Subject | Rank Order of Psychologist A $R(X_i)$ | Rank Order of Psychologist B $R(Y_i)$ | $D_i = R(X_i) - R(Y_i)$ | $D_i^2$ |
|---------|-------------------------------|-------------------------------|-----------------|---------|
| 1 | 6 | 5 | 1 | 1 |
| 2 | 5 | 3 | 2 | 4 |
| 3 | 7 | 4 | 3 | 9 |
| 4 | 10 | 8 | 2 | 4 |
| 5 | 2.5 | 1 | 1.5 | 2.25 |
| 6 | 2.5 | 6 | −3.5 | 12.25 |
| 7 | 9 | 10 | −1 | 1 |
| 8 | 1 | 2 | −1 | 1 |
| 9 | 11 | 9 | 2 | 4 |
| 10 | 4 | 7 | −3 | 9 |
| 11 | 8 | 11 | −3 | 9 |
| 12 | 12 | 12 | 0 | 0 |
| $N=12$ | | | | $\Sigma\,D_i^2 = 56.5$ |

$$r_s = 1 - \frac{6\,\Sigma\,D_i^2}{N^3 - N} = 1 - \frac{6(56.5)}{(12)^3 - 12} = 1 - \frac{339}{1716} = 0.80$$

subject 1. It doesn't matter whether you subtract $R(X_i)$ from $R(Y_i)$ or $R(Y_i)$ from $R(X_i)$ to get $D_i$ because we square each $D_i$ value. The squared $D_i$ values are then summed ($\Sigma D_i^2 = 56.5$). This value is then entered in the equation along with $N$ ($N = 12$), and $r_s$ is computed. For this problem,

$$r_s = 1 - \frac{6\,\Sigma D_i^2}{N^3 - N} = 1 - \frac{6(56.5)}{12^3 - 12} = 1 - \frac{339}{1716} = 0.80$$

## Practice Problem 6.3

To illustrate computation of $r_s$, let's assume that the raters' attitude and attraction scores given in Practice Problem 6.2 were only of ordinal scaling. Given this assumption, determine the value of the linear correlation coefficient rho for these data and compare the value with the value of Pearson $r$ determined in Practice Problem 6.2.

### SOLUTION

The data and solution are shown in the following table.

| Subject | Proportion of Similar Attitudes $X_i$ | Attraction $Y_i$ | Rank of $X_i$ $R(X_i)$ | Rank of $Y_i$ $R(Y_i)$ | $D_i = R(X_i) - R(Y_i)$ | $D_i^2$ |
|---|---|---|---|---|---|---|
| 1 | 0.30 | 8.9 | 5 | 7 | −2 | 4 |
| 2 | 0.44 | 9.3 | 7 | 8 | −1 | 1 |
| 3 | 0.67 | 9.6 | 11 | 10 | 1 | 1 |
| 4 | 0.00 | 6.2 | 1 | 1 | 0 | 0 |
| 5 | 0.50 | 8.8 | 8 | 6 | 2 | 4 |
| 6 | 0.15 | 8.1 | 3 | 5 | −2 | 4 |
| 7 | 0.58 | 9.5 | 9 | 9 | 0 | 0 |
| 8 | 0.32 | 7.1 | 6 | 2 | 4 | 16 |
| 9 | 0.72 | 11.0 | 12 | 13 | −1 | 1 |
| 10 | 1.00 | 11.7 | 15 | 15 | 0 | 0 |
| 11 | 0.87 | 11.5 | 14 | 14 | 0 | 0 |
| 12 | 0.09 | 7.3 | 2 | 3 | −1 | 1 |
| 13 | 0.82 | 10.0 | 13 | 11.5 | 1.5 | 2.25 |
| 14 | 0.64 | 10.0 | 10 | 11.5 | −1.5 | 2.25 |
| 15 | 0.24 | 7.5 | 4 | 4 | 0 | 0 |
| $N = 15$ | | | | | $\Sigma D_i^2 = 36.5$ | |

$$r_s = 1 - \frac{6\,\Sigma D_i^2}{N^3 - N} = 1 - \frac{6(36.5)}{(15)^3 - 15} = 1 - \frac{219}{3360} = 0.93$$

Note that $r_s = 0.93$ and $r = 0.94$. The values are not identical but quite close. In general, when Pearson $r$ is calculated using the interval or ratio properties of data, its values will be close but not exactly the same as when calculated on only the ordinal properties of those data.

## Effect of Range on Correlation

If a correlation exists between *X* and *Y*, restricting the range of either of the variables will have the effect of *lowering* the correlation. This can be seen in Figure 6.10, where we have drawn a scatter plot of freshman grade point average and College Entrance Examination Board (CEEB) scores. The figure has been subdivided into low, medium, and high CEEB scores. Taking the figure as a whole (i.e., considering the full range of the CEEB scores), there is a high correlation between the two variables. However, if we were to consider the three sections separately, the correlation for each section would be much lower. Within each section, the points show much less systematic change in *Y* with changes in *X*. This, of course, indicates a lower correlation between *X* and *Y*. The effect of range restriction on correlation is often encountered in education or industry. For instance, suppose that on the basis of the high correlation between freshman grades and CEEB scores as shown in Figure 6.10, a college decided to admit only high school graduates who have scored in the high range of the CEEB scores. If the subsequent freshman grades of these students were correlated with their CEEB scores, we would expect a much lower correlation because of the range restriction of the CEEB scores for these freshmen. In a similar vein, if one is doing a correlational study and obtains a low correlation coefficient, one should check to be sure that range restriction is not responsible for the low value.

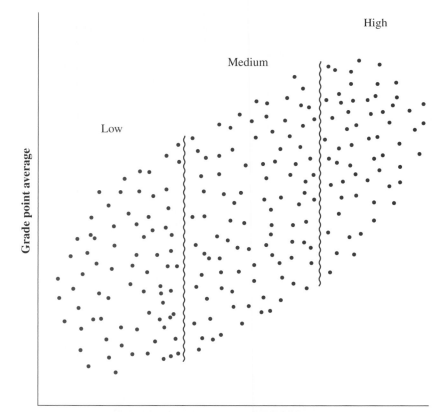

**College Entrance Examination Board (CEEB) scores**

f i g u r e  **6.10**  Freshman grades and CEEB scores.

## Effect of Extreme Score

Consider the effect of an extreme score on the magnitude of the correlation coefficient. Figure 6.11(a) shows a set of scores where all the scores cluster reasonably close together. The value of Pearson $r$ for this set of scores is 0.11. Figure 6.11(b) shows the same set of scores with an extreme score added. The value of Pearson $r$ for this set of scores is 0.94. The magnitude of Pearson $r$ has changed from 0.11 to 0.94. This is a demonstration of the point that *an extreme score can drastically alter the magnitude of the correlation coefficient* and hence change the interpretation of the data. Therefore, it is a good idea to check the scatter plot of the data for extreme scores before computing the correlation coefficient. If an extreme score exists, caution must be exercised in interpreting the relationship. If the sample is a large random sample, an extreme value usually will not greatly alter the size of the correlation. However, if the sample is a small one, as in this example, an extreme score can have a large effect.

## Correlation Does Not Imply Causation

When two variables ($X$ and $Y$) are correlated, it is tempting to conclude that one of them is the cause of the other. However, to do so without further experimentation would be a serious error, because whenever two variables are correlated, there are four possible explanations of the correlation: (1) the correlation between $X$ and $Y$ is spurious, (2) $X$ is the cause of $Y$, (3) $Y$ is the cause of $X$, or (4) a third variable is the cause of the correlation between $X$ and $Y$. The first possibility asserts that it was just due to accidents of sampling unusual people or unusual behavior that the sample showed a correlation; that is, if the experiment were repeated or more samples were taken, the correlation would disappear. If the correlation is really spurious, it is obviously wrong to conclude that there is a causal relation between $X$ and $Y$.

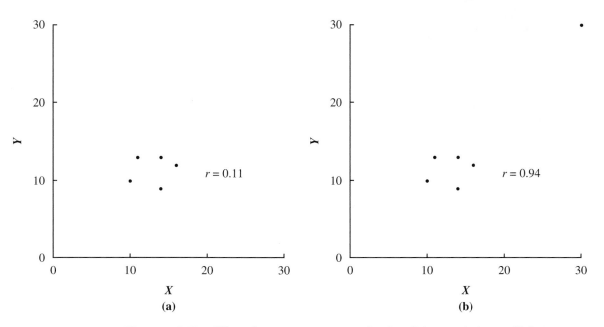

figure  6.11    Effect of an extreme score on the size of the correlation coefficient.

It is also erroneous to assume causality between $X$ and $Y$ if the fourth alternative is correct. Quite often, when $X$ and $Y$ are correlated, they are not causally related to each other but rather a third variable is responsible for the correlation. For example, do you know that there is a close relationship between the salaries of university professors and the price of a fifth of scotch whiskey? Which is the cause and which the effect? Do the salaries of university professors dominate the scotch whiskey market such that when the professors get a raise and thereby can afford to buy more scotch, the price of scotch is raised accordingly? Or perhaps the university professors are paid from the profits of scotch whiskey sales, so when the professors need a raise, the price of a fifth of scotch whiskey goes up? Actually, neither of these explanations is correct. Rather, a third factor is responsible for this correlation. What is that factor? Inflation! Recently, a newspaper article reported a positive correlation between obesity and female crime. Does this mean that if a woman gains 20 pounds, she will become a criminal? Or does it mean that if she is a criminal, she is doomed to being obese? Neither of these explanations seems satisfactory. Frankly, we are not sure how to interpret this correlation. One possibility is that it is a spurious correlation. If not, it could be due to a third factor, namely, socioeconomic status. Both obesity and crime are related to lower socioeconomic status.

The point is that a correlation between two variables is not sufficient to establish causality between them. There are other possible explanations. To establish that one variable is the cause of another, we must conduct an experiment in which we systematically vary *only* the suspected causal variable and measure its effect on the other variable.

## WHAT IS THE TRUTH?

### "Good Principal = Good Elementary School," or Does It?

A major newspaper of a large city carried as a front page headline, printed in large bold letters, **"Equation for success: Good principal = good elementary school."** The article that followed described a study in which elementary school principals were rated by their teachers on a series of questions indicating whether the principals were strong, average, or weak leaders. Students in these schools were evaluated in reading and mathematics on the annual California Achievement Tests. As far as we can tell from the newspaper article, the ratings and test scores were obtained from ongoing principal assignments, with no attempt in the study to randomly assign principals to schools. The results showed that (1) in 11 elementary schools that had strong principals, students were making big academic strides; (2) in 11 schools where principals were weak leaders, students were showing less improvement than average or even falling behind; and (3) in 39 schools where principals were rated as average, the students' test scores were showing just average improvement.

The newspaper reporter interpreted these data as indicated by the headline, "Equation for success: Good principal = good elementary school." In the article, an elementary school principal was quoted, "I've always said 'Show me a good school, and I'll show you a

## WHAT IS THE TRUTH?

### "Good Principal = Good Elementary School," or Does It? (*continued*)

good principal,' but now we have powerful, incontrovertible data that corroborates that." The article further quoted the president of the principals' association as saying: "It's exciting information that carries an enormous responsibility. It shows we can make a real difference in our students' lives." In your view, do the data warrant these conclusions?

***Answer***  Although, personally, I believe that school principals are important to educational quality, the study seems to be strictly a correlational one: paired measurements on two variables, without random assignment to groups. From what we said previously, it is impossible to determine causality from such a

study. The individuals quoted herein have taken a study that shows there is a *correlation* between "strong" leadership by elementary school principals and educational gain and concluded that the principals *caused* the educational gain. The conclusion is too strong. The correlation could be spurious or due to a third variable.

It is truly amazing how often this error is made in real life. Stay on the lookout, and I believe you will be surprised how frequently you encounter individuals concluding causation when the data are only correlational. Of course, now that you are so well informed on this point, you will never make this mistake yourself!

## SUMMARY

In this chapter, we have discussed the topic of correlation. Correlation is a measure of the relationship that exists between two variables. The magnitude and direction of the relationship are given by a correlation coefficient. The correlation coefficient can vary from $+1$ to $-1$. The sign of the coefficient tells us whether the relationship is positive or negative. The numerical part describes the magnitude of the correlation. When the relationship is perfect, the magnitude is 1. If the re-

lationship is nonexistent, the magnitude is 0. Magnitudes between 0 and 1 indicate imperfect relationships.

There are many correlation coefficients that can be computed depending on the scaling of the data and the shape of the relationship. In this chapter, we emphasized Pearson $r$ and Spearman rho. Pearson $r$ is defined as a measure of the extent to which paired scores occupy the same or opposite positions within their own distributions. Using standard scores allows measurement of the relationship that is independent of the differences in scaling and of the units used in measuring the variables. Pearson $r$ is also equal to the square root of the proportion of the total variability in $Y$ that is accounted for by $X$. In addition to these concepts, we presented a computational equation for $r$ and practiced calculating $r$.

Spearman rho is used for linear relationships when one or both of the variables are only of ordinal scaling. The computational equation for rho was presented and several practice problems worked out. Next, we discussed the effect of an extreme score on the size of the correlation. After that, we discussed the effect of range on correlation and pointed out that truncated range will result in a lower correlation coefficient.

As the last topic of correlation, we discussed correlation and causation. We pointed out that if a correlation exists between two variables in an experiment, we cannot conclude they are causally related on the basis of the correlation alone because there are other possible explanations. The correlation may be spurious, or a third variable may be responsible for the correlation between the first two variables. To establish causation, one of the variables must be independently manipulated and its effect on the other variable measured. All other variables should be held constant or vary unsystematically. Even if the two variables are causally related, it is important to keep in mind that $r^2$, rather than $r$, indicates the magnitude of the effect of one variable on the other.

## IMPORTANT TERMS

Biserial coefficient (p. 121)
Coefficient of determination (p. 120)
Correlation (p. 111)
Correlation coefficient (p. 111)
Curvilinear relationship (p. 105)
Direct relationship (p. 107)
Imperfect relationship (p. 108)

Inverse relationship (p. 107)
Linear relationship (p. 104)
Negative relationship (p. 107)
Pearson $r$ (p. 112)
Perfect relationship (p. 108)
Phi coefficient (p. 121)
Positive relationship (p. 107)

Scatter plot (p. 104)
Slope (p. 106)
Spearman rho (p. 121)
Variability accounted for by $X$ (p. 120)
$Y$ intercept (p. 106)

## QUESTIONS AND PROBLEMS

1. Define or identify each of the terms in the Important Terms section.
2. Discuss the different kinds of relationships that are possible between two variables.
3. For each scatter plot in the accompanying figure (parts **a–f**, on page 129), determine whether the relationship is
   a. Linear or curvilinear. If linear, further determine whether it is positive or negative.
   b. Perfect or imperfect
4. Professor Taylor does an experiment and establishes that a correlation exists between variables $A$ and $B$. Based on this correlation, she asserts that $A$ is the cause of $B$. Is this assertion correct? Explain.
5. Give two meanings of Pearson $r$.
6. Why are $z$ scores used as the basis for determining Pearson $r$?
7. What is the range of values that a correlation coefficient may take?

8. A study has shown that the correlation between fatigue and irritability is 0.53. On the basis of this correlation, the author concludes that fatigue is an important factor in producing irritability. Is this conclusion justified? Explain.
9. What factors influence the choice of whether to use a particular correlation coefficient? Give some examples.
10. The Pearson $r$ and Spearman rho correlation coefficients are related. Is this statement correct? Explain.
11. When two variables are correlated, there are four possible explanations of the correlation. What are they?
12. What effect might an extreme score have on the magnitude of relationship between two variables? Discuss.
13. What effect does decreasing the range of the paired scores have on the correlation coefficient?

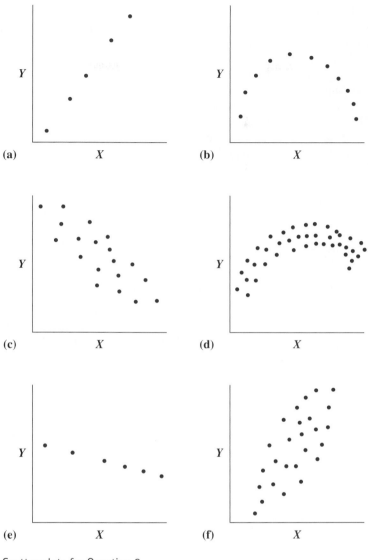

Scatter plots for Question 3

14. Given the following sets of paired sample scores:

| A | | B | | C | |
|---|---|---|---|---|---|
| *X* | *Y* | *X* | *Y* | *X* | *Y* |
| 1 | 1 | 4 | 2 | 1 | 5 |
| 4 | 2 | 5 | 4 | 4 | 4 |
| 7 | 3 | 8 | 5 | 7 | 3 |
| 10 | 4 | 9 | 1 | 10 | 2 |
| 13 | 5 | 10 | 4 | 13 | 1 |

a. Use the equation

$$r = \Sigma \, z_X z_Y / (N - 1)$$

to compute the value of Pearson *r* for each set. Note that in set B, where the correlation is lowest, some of the $z_X z_Y$ values are positive and some are negative. These tend to cancel each other, causing *r* to have a low magnitude. However, in both sets A and C, all the products have the same sign, causing *r* to be large in magnitude. When the paired scores occupy the same or opposite positions within their own distributions, the $z_X z_Y$ products have the same sign, resulting in high magnitudes for r.

b. Compute r for set B, using the raw score equation. Which do you prefer, using the raw score or the z score equation?

c. Add the constant 5 to the X scores in set A and compute r again, using the raw score equation. Has the value changed?

d. Multiply the X scores in set A by 5 and compute r again. Has the value changed?

e. Generalize the results obtained in parts **c** and **d** to subtracting and dividing the scores by a constant. What does this tell you about r?

15. In a large introductory sociology course, a professor gives two exams. The professor wants to determine whether the scores students receive on the second exam are correlated with their scores on the first exam. To make the calculations easier, a sample of eight students is selected. Their scores are shown in the accompanying table.

| Student | Exam 1 | Exam 2 |
|---------|--------|--------|
| 1 | 60 | 60 |
| 2 | 75 | 100 |
| 3 | 70 | 80 |
| 4 | 72 | 68 |
| 5 | 54 | 73 |
| 6 | 83 | 97 |
| 7 | 80 | 85 |
| 8 | 65 | 90 |

a. Construct a scatter plot of the data, using exam 1 score as the X variable. Does the relationship look linear?

b. Assuming a linear relationship exists between scores on the two exams, compute the value for Pearson r.

c. How well does the relationship account for the scores on exam 2? education

16. A graduate student in developmental psychology believes there may be a relationship between birth weight and subsequent IQ. She randomly samples seven psychology majors at her university and gives them an IQ test. Next she obtains the weight at birth of the seven majors from the appropriate hospitals (after obtaining permission from the students, of course). The data are shown in the following table.

| Student | Birth Weight (lbs) | IQ |
|---------|--------------------|-----|
| 1 | 5.8 | 122 |
| 2 | 6.5 | 120 |
| 3 | 8.0 | 129 |
| 4 | 5.9 | 112 |
| 5 | 8.5 | 127 |
| 6 | 7.2 | 116 |
| 7 | 9.0 | 130 |

a. Construct a scatter plot of the data, plotting birth weight on the X axis and IQ on the Y axis. Does the relationship appear to be linear?

b. Assume the relationship is linear and compute the value of Pearson r. developmental

17. A researcher conducts a study to investigate the relationship between cigarette smoking and illness. The number of cigarettes smoked daily and the number of days absent from work in the last year due to illness are determined for 12 individuals employed at the company where the researcher works. The scores are given in the following table.

| Subject | Cigarettes Smoked | Days Absent |
|---------|-------------------|-------------|
| 1 | 0 | 1 |
| 2 | 0 | 3 |
| 3 | 0 | 8 |
| 4 | 10 | 10 |
| 5 | 13 | 4 |
| 6 | 20 | 14 |
| 7 | 27 | 5 |
| 8 | 35 | 6 |
| 9 | 35 | 12 |
| 10 | 44 | 16 |
| 11 | 53 | 10 |
| 12 | 60 | 16 |

a. Construct a scatter plot for these data. Does the relationship look linear?

b. Calculate the value of Pearson r.

c. Eliminate the data from subjects 1, 2, 3, 10, 11, and 12. This decreases the range of both variables. Recalculate $r$ for the remaining subjects. What effect does decreasing the range have on $r$?

    d. Using the full set of scores, what percentage of the variability in the number of days absent is accounted for by the number of cigarettes smoked daily? Of what use is this value? clinical, health

18. An educator has constructed a test for mechanical aptitude. He wants to determine how reliable the test is over two administrations spaced by 1 month. A study is conducted in which 10 students are given two administrations of the test, with the second administration being 1 month after the first. The data are given in the following table.

| Student | Administration 1 | Administration 2 |
|---|---|---|
| 1 | 10 | 10 |
| 2 | 12 | 15 |
| 3 | 20 | 17 |
| 4 | 25 | 25 |
| 5 | 27 | 32 |
| 6 | 35 | 37 |
| 7 | 43 | 40 |
| 8 | 40 | 38 |
| 9 | 32 | 30 |
| 10 | 47 | 49 |

    a. Construct a scatter plot of the paired scores.
    b. Determine the value of $r$.
    c. Would it be fair to say that this is a reliable test? Explain using $r^2$. education

19. A group of researchers has devised a stress questionnaire consisting of 15 life events. They are interested in determining whether there is cross-cultural agreement on the relative amount of adjustment each event entails. The questionnaire is given to 300 Americans and 300 Italians. Each individual is instructed to use the event of "marriage" as the standard and to judge each of the other life events in relation to the adjustment required in marriage. Marriage is arbitrarily given a value of 50 points. If an event is judged to require greater adjustment than marriage, the event should receive more than 50 points. How many more points depends on how much more adjustment is required. After each

subject within each culture has assigned points to the 15 life events, the points for each event are averaged. The results are shown in the following table.

| Life Event | Americans | Italians |
|---|---|---|
| Death of spouse | 100 | 80 |
| Divorce | 73 | 95 |
| Marital separation | 65 | 85 |
| Jail term | 63 | 52 |
| Personal injury | 53 | 72 |
| Marriage | 50 | 50 |
| Fired from work | 47 | 40 |
| Retirement | 45 | 30 |
| Pregnancy | 40 | 28 |
| Sex difficulties | 39 | 42 |
| Business readjustment | 39 | 36 |
| Trouble with in-laws | 29 | 41 |
| Trouble with boss | 23 | 35 |
| Vacation | 13 | 16 |
| Christmas | 12 | 10 |

    a. Assume the data are at least of interval scaling and compute the correlation between the American and Italian ratings.
    b. Assume the data are only of ordinal scaling and compute the correlation between ratings of the two cultures. clinical, health

20. Given the following set of paired scores from five subjects:

| Subject No. | 1 | 2 | 3 | 4 | 5 |
|---|---|---|---|---|---|
| $Y$ | 5 | 6 | 9 | 9 | 11 |
| $X$ | 6 | 8 | 4 | 8 | 7 |

    a. Construct a scatter plot of the data.
    b. Compute the value of Pearson $r$.
    c. Add the following paired scores from a sixth subject to the data: $Y = 26$, $X = 25$.
    d. Construct another scatter plot, this time for the six paired scores.
    e. Compute the value of Pearson $r$ for the six paired scores.

f. Is there much of a difference between your answers for parts **b** and **e**? Explain the difference.

21. The director of an obesity clinic in a large northwestern city believes that drinking soft drinks contributes to obesity in children. To determine whether a relationship exists between these two variables, she conducts the following pilot study. Eight 12-year-old volunteers are randomly selected from children attending a local junior high school. Parents of the children are asked to monitor the number of soft drinks consumed by their child over a 1-week period. The children are weighed at the end of the week and their weights converted into body mass index (BMI) values. The BMI is a common index used to measure obesity and takes into account both height and weight. An individual is considered obese if they have a BMI value $\geq 30$. The following data are collected.

| Child | Number of Soft Drinks Consumed | BMI |
|-------|-------|------|
| 1 | 3 | 20 |
| 2 | 1 | 18 |
| 3 | 14 | 32 |
| 4 | 7 | 24 |
| 5 | 21 | 35 |
| 6 | 5 | 19 |
| 7 | 25 | 38 |
| 8 | 9 | 30 |

a. Graph a scatter plot of the data. Does the relationship appear linear?
b. Assume the relationship is linear and compute Pearson $r$.  health

22. A social psychologist conducts a study to determine the relationship between religion and self-esteem. Ten eighth graders are randomly selected for the study. Each individual receives two tests, one measuring self-esteem and the other religious involvement. For the self-esteem test, the lower the score is, the higher self-esteem is; for the test measuring religious involvement, the higher the score is, the higher religious involvement is. The self-esteem test has a range from 1–10 and the religious involvement test ranges from 0–50. For the purposes of this question, assume both tests are well standardized and of interval scaling. The following data are collected.

| Subject | Religious Involvement | Self-Esteem |
|---------|-------|------|
| 1 | 5 | 8 |
| 2 | 25 | 3 |
| 3 | 45 | 2 |
| 4 | 20 | 7 |
| 5 | 30 | 5 |
| 6 | 40 | 5 |
| 7 | 1 | 4 |
| 8 | 15 | 4 |
| 9 | 10 | 7 |
| 10 | 35 | 3 |

a. If a relationship exists such that the more religiously involved one is, the higher actual self-esteem is, would you expect $r$ computed on the provided values to be negative or positive? Explain.
b. Compute $r$. Were you correct in your answer to part **a**?  social, developmental

23. A psychologist has constructed a paper and pencil test purported to measure depression. To see how the test compares with the ratings of experts, 12 "emotionally disturbed" individuals are given the paper and pencil test. The individuals are also independently rank-ordered by two psychiatrists according to the degree of depression each psychiatrist finds as a result of detailed interviews. The scores are given here. Higher scores represent greater depression.

| Individual | Paper & Pencil Test | Psychiatrist A | Psychiatrist B |
|------------|------|------|------|
| 1 | 48 | 12 | 9 |
| 2 | 37 | 11 | 12 |
| 3 | 30 | 4 | 5 |
| 4 | 45 | 7 | 8 |
| 5 | 31 | 10 | 11 |
| 6 | 24 | 8 | 7 |
| 7 | 28 | 3 | 4 |
| 8 | 18 | 1 | 1 |
| 9 | 35 | 9 | 6 |
| 10 | 15 | 2 | 2 |
| 11 | 42 | 6 | 10 |
| 12 | 22 | 5 | 3 |

a. What is the correlation between the rankings of the two psychiatrists?
b. What is the correlation between the scores on the paper and pencil test and the rankings of each psychiatrist? clinical, health

24. For this problem, let's suppose that you are a psychologist employed in the human resources department of a large corporation. The corporation president has just finished talking with you about the importance of hiring productive personnel in the manufacturing section of the corporation and has asked you to help improve the corporation's ability to do so. There are 300 employees in this section, with each employee making the same item. Until now, the corporation has been depending solely on interviews for selecting these employees. You search the literature and discover two well-standardized paper and pencil performance tests that you think might be related to the performance requirements of this section. To determine whether either might be used as a screening device, you select 10 repre-

sentative employees from the manufacturing section, making sure that a wide range of performance is represented in the sample, and administer the two tests to each employee. The data are shown in the table. The higher the score, the better the performance. The work performance scores are the actual number of items completed by each employee per week, averaged over the past 6 months.

a. Construct a scatter plot of work performance and test 1, using test 1 as the $X$ variable. Does the relationship look linear?
b. Assuming it is linear, compute the value of Pearson $r$.
c. Construct a scatter plot of work performance and test 2, using test 2 as the $X$ variable. Is the relationship linear?
d. Assuming it is linear, compute the value of Pearson $r$.
e. If you could use only one of the two tests for screening prospective employees, would you use either test? If yes, which one? Explain. I/O

| | Employee | | | | | | | | | |
|---|---|---|---|---|---|---|---|---|---|---|
| | *1* | *2* | *3* | *4* | *5* | *6* | *7* | *8* | *9* | *10* |
| Work performance | 50 | 74 | 62 | 90 | 98 | 52 | 68 | 80 | 88 | 76 |
| Test 1 | 10 | 19 | 20 | 20 | 21 | 14 | 10 | 24 | 16 | 14 |
| Test 2 | 25 | 35 | 40 | 49 | 50 | 29 | 32 | 44 | 46 | 35 |

 **BOOK COMPANION WEBSITE**

Go to www.thomsonedu.com/psychology/pagano for:

- SPSS problems and solutions
- Flash cards for review of terms
- Chapter quiz
- Statistical workshops
- And more

**Web**TUTOR™

Available via WebTutor for this chapter:

- Detailed chapter outline
- *Know and Be Able To Do* section
- Drag & Drop game for review of equations, concepts, and other material
- Flash cards for review of terms
- Audio flash cards for MP3 player
- Solving problems using Excel
- Solving problems using SPSS
- More practice problems using computational equations
- Chapter quiz

# Linear Regression

CHAPTER **7**

## INTRODUCTION

Regression and correlation are closely related. At the most basic level, they both involve the relationship between two variables, and they both utilize the same set of basic data: paired scores taken from the same or matched subjects. As we saw in Chapter 6, correlation is concerned with the magnitude and direction of the relationship. Regression focuses on using the relationship for prediction. Prediction is quite easy when the relationship is perfect. If the relationship is perfect, all the points fall on a straight line and all we need do is derive the equation of the straight line and use it for prediction. As you might guess, when the relationship is perfect, so is prediction. All predicted values are exactly equal to the observed values and prediction error equals zero. The situation is more complicated when the relationship is imperfect.

■ **Regression** *is a topic that considers using the relationship between two or more variables for prediction.*

## PREDICTION AND IMPERFECT RELATIONSHIPS

Let's return to the data involving grade point average and IQ that were presented in Chapter 6. For convenience, the data have been reproduced in Table 7.1. Figure 7.1 shows a scatter plot of the data. The relationship is imperfect, positive, and linear. The problem we face for prediction is how to determine the single straight line that best describes the data. The solution most often used is to construct the line that minimizes errors of prediction according to a *least-squares* criterion. Appropriately, this line is called the *least-squares regression line.*

The least-squares regression line for the data in Table 7.1 is shown in Figure 7.2(a). The vertical distance between each point and the line represents the error in prediction. If we let $Y' =$ the predicted $Y$ value and $Y =$ the actual value, then $Y - Y'$ equals the error for each point. It might seem that the total error in prediction should be the simple algebraic sum of $Y - Y'$, summed over all of the points. If this were true, since we are interested in minimizing the error, we would construct the line that minimizes $\Sigma (Y - Y')$. However, the total error in prediction does not equal $\Sigma (Y - Y')$ because some of the $Y'$ values will be greater than $Y$ and some will be less. Thus, there will be both positive and negative error scores, and the simple algebraic sums of these would cancel each other. We encountered a similar situation when considering measures of the average dispersion. In deriving the equation for the standard deviation, we squared $X - \bar{X}$ to overcome the fact that there were positive and negative deviation scores that canceled each other. The same solution works here, too. Instead of just summing

**table 7.1** IQ and grade point average of 12 college students

| Student No. | IQ | Grade Point Average |
|:---:|:---:|:---:|
| 1 | 110 | 1.0 |
| 2 | 112 | 1.6 |
| 3 | 118 | 1.2 |
| 4 | 119 | 2.1 |
| 5 | 122 | 2.6 |
| 6 | 125 | 1.8 |
| 7 | 127 | 2.6 |
| 8 | 130 | 2.0 |
| 9 | 132 | 3.2 |
| 10 | 134 | 2.6 |
| 11 | 136 | 3.0 |
| 12 | 138 | 3.6 |

figure 7.1    Scatter plot of IQ and grade point average.

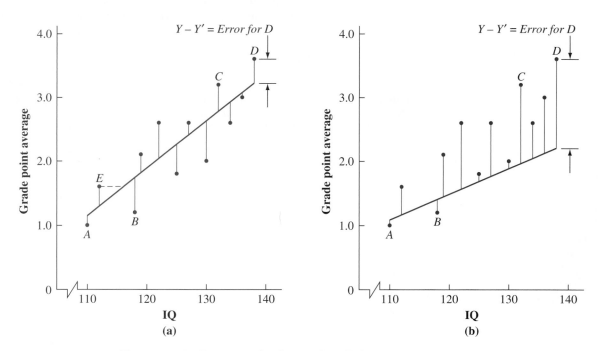

figure 7.2    Two regression lines and prediction error.

$Y - Y'$, we first compute $(Y - Y')^2$ for each score. This removes the negative values and eliminates the cancellation problem. Now, if we minimize $\Sigma (Y - Y')^2$, we minimize the total error of prediction.

**definition**    ■    *The* **least-squares regression line** *is the prediction line that minimizes* $\Sigma (Y - Y')^2$.

For any linear relationship, there is only one line that will minimize $\Sigma (Y - Y')^2$. Thus, there is only one least-squares regression line for each linear relationship.

We said before that there are many "possible" prediction lines we could construct when the relationship is imperfect. Why should we use the least-squares regression line? We use the least-squares regression line because it gives the greatest overall accuracy in prediction. To illustrate this point, another prediction line has been drawn in Figure 7.2(b). This line has been picked arbitrarily and is just one of an infinite number that could have been drawn. How does it compare in prediction accuracy with the least-squares regression line? We can see that it actually does better for some of the points (e.g., points *A* and *B* ). However, it also misses horribly on others (e.g., points *C* and *D*). If we consider all of the points, it is clear that the line of Figure 7.2(a) fits the points better than the line of Figure 7.2(b). The total error in prediction, represented by $\Sigma (Y - Y')^2$, is less for the least-squares regression line than for the line in Figure 7.2(b). In fact, the total error in prediction is less for the least-squares regression line than for any other possible prediction line. Thus, the least-squares regression line is used because it gives greater overall accuracy in prediction than any other possible regression line.

## CONSTRUCTING THE LEAST–SQUARES REGRESSION LINE: REGRESSION OF *Y* ON *X*

The equation for the least-squares regression line for predicting *Y* given *X* is

$$Y' = b_Y X + a_Y \qquad \textit{linear regression equation for predicting Y given X}$$

*where*    $Y'$ = predicted or estimated value of *Y*
$b_Y$ = slope of the line for minimizing errors in predicting *Y*
$a_Y$ = *Y* axis intercept for minimizing errors in predicting *Y*

This is, of course, the general equation for a straight line that we have been using all along. In this context, however, $a_Y$ and $b_Y$ are called *regression constants*. This line is called the regression line of *Y* on *X*, or simply the regression of *Y* on *X*, because we are predicting *Y* given *X*.

The $b_Y$ regression constant is equal to

$$b_Y = \frac{\Sigma XY - \dfrac{(\Sigma X)(\Sigma Y)}{N}}{SS_X}$$

*where*    $SS_X$ = sum of squares of *X* scores  $= \Sigma X^2 - \dfrac{(\Sigma X)^2}{N}$
$N$ = number of *paired* scores

$\Sigma\,XY =$ sum of the product of each $X$ and $Y$ pair (also called the sum of the cross products)

The equation for computing $b_Y$ from the raw scores is

$$b_Y = \frac{\Sigma\,XY - \dfrac{(\Sigma\,X)(\Sigma\,Y)}{N}}{\Sigma\,X^2 - \dfrac{(\Sigma\,X)^2}{N}}$$

*computational equation for determining the* **b** *regression constant for predicting Y given X*

The $a_Y$ regression constant is given by

$$a_Y = \overline{Y} - b_Y\overline{X}$$

*computational equation for determining the* **a** *regression constant for predicting Y given X*

Since we need the $b_Y$ constant to determine the $a_Y$ constant, the procedure is to first find $b_Y$ and then $a_Y$. Once both are found, they are substituted into the regression equation. Let's construct the least-squares regression line for the IQ and grade point data presented previously. For convenience, the data have been presented again in Table 7.2.

**t a b l e  7.2**   IQ and grade point average of 12 college students: Predicting $Y$ from $X$

| Student No. | IQ $X$ | Grade Point Average $Y$ | $XY$ | $X^2$ |
|---|---|---|---|---|
| 1 | 110 | 1.0 | 110.0 | 12,100 |
| 2 | 112 | 1.6 | 179.2 | 12,544 |
| 3 | 118 | 1.2 | 141.6 | 13,924 |
| 4 | 119 | 2.1 | 249.9 | 14,161 |
| 5 | 122 | 2.6 | 317.2 | 14,884 |
| 6 | 125 | 1.8 | 225.0 | 15,625 |
| 7 | 127 | 2.6 | 330.2 | 16,129 |
| 8 | 130 | 2.0 | 260.0 | 16,900 |
| 9 | 132 | 3.2 | 422.4 | 17,424 |
| 10 | 134 | 2.6 | 348.4 | 17,956 |
| 11 | 136 | 3.0 | 408.0 | 18,496 |
| 12 | 138 | 3.6 | 496.8 | 19,044 |
| Total | 1503 | 27.3 | 3488.7 | 189,187 |

$$b_Y = \frac{\Sigma\,XY - \dfrac{(\Sigma\,X)(\Sigma\,Y)}{N}}{\Sigma\,X^2 - \dfrac{(\Sigma\,X)^2}{N}} = \frac{3488.7 - \dfrac{1503(27.3)}{12}}{189,187 - \dfrac{(1503)^2}{12}}$$

$$= \frac{69.375}{936.25} = 0.0741 = 0.074$$

$$a_Y = \overline{Y} - b_Y\overline{X} = 2.275 - 0.0741(125.25) = -7.006$$

$$Y' = b_YX + a_Y = 0.074X - 7.006$$

$$b_Y = \frac{\Sigma XY - \dfrac{(\Sigma X)(\Sigma Y)}{N}}{\Sigma X^2 - \dfrac{(\Sigma X)^2}{N}}$$

$$= \frac{3488.7 - \dfrac{1503(27.3)}{12}}{189,187 - \dfrac{(1503)^2}{12}}$$

$$= \frac{69.375}{936.25} = 0.0741 = 0.074$$

$$a_Y = \overline{Y} - b_Y \overline{X}$$

$$= 2.275 - 0.0741(125.25)$$

$$= -7.006$$

and

$$Y' = 0.074X - 7.006$$

The full solution is also shown in Table 7.2. The regression line has been plotted in Figure 7.3. The equation for $Y'$ can now be used to predict the grade point average knowing only the student's IQ score. For example, suppose a student's IQ score is 124; using this regression line, what is the student's predicted grade point average?

$$Y' = 0.074X - 7.006$$

$$= 0.074(124) - 7.006$$

$$= 2.17$$

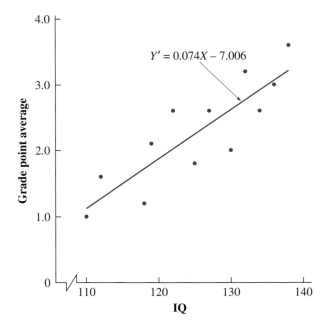

figure  7.3    Regression line for grade point average and IQ.

Let's try a couple of practice problems.

---

## Practice Problem 7.1

A developmental psychologist is interested in determining whether it is possible to use the heights of young boys to predict their eventual height at maturity. To answer this question, she collects the data shown in the following table.

**a.** Draw a scatter plot of the data.

**b.** If the data are linearly related, derive the least-squares regression line.

**c.** Based on these data, what height would you predict for a 20-year-old if at 3 years his height were 42 inches?

| Individual No. | Height at Age 3 $X$ (in.) | Height at Age 20 $Y$ (in.) | $XY$ | $X^2$ |
|---|---|---|---|---|
| 1 | 30 | 59 | 1,770 | 900 |
| 2 | 30 | 63 | 1,890 | 900 |
| 3 | 32 | 62 | 1,984 | 1,024 |
| 4 | 33 | 67 | 2,211 | 1,089 |
| 5 | 34 | 65 | 2,210 | 1,156 |
| 6 | 35 | 61 | 2,135 | 1,225 |
| 7 | 36 | 69 | 2,484 | 1,296 |
| 8 | 38 | 66 | 2,508 | 1,444 |
| 9 | 40 | 68 | 2,720 | 1,600 |
| 10 | 41 | 65 | 2,665 | 1,681 |
| 11 | 41 | 73 | 2,993 | 1,681 |
| 12 | 43 | 68 | 2,924 | 1,849 |
| 13 | 45 | 71 | 3,195 | 2,025 |
| 14 | 45 | 74 | 3,330 | 2,025 |
| 15 | 47 | 71 | 3,337 | 2,209 |
| 16 | 48 | 75 | 3,600 | 2,304 |
| *Total* | 618 | 1077 | 41,956 | 24,408 |

$$b_Y = \frac{\Sigma XY - \dfrac{(\Sigma X)(\Sigma Y)}{N}}{\Sigma X^2 - \dfrac{(\Sigma X)^2}{N}} = \frac{41,956 - \dfrac{618(1077)}{16}}{24,408 - \dfrac{(618)^2}{16}} = 0.6636 = 0.664$$

$$a_Y = \overline{Y} - b_Y\overline{X} = 67.3125 - 0.6636(38.625) = 41.679$$

$$Y' = b_Y X + a_Y = 0.664X + 41.679$$

## SOLUTION

**a.** The scatter plot is shown in the following figure. It is clear that an imperfect relationship that is linear and positive exists between the heights at ages 3 and 20.

**b.** Derive the least-squares regression line.

$$Y' = b_Y X + a_Y$$

$$b_Y = \frac{\Sigma XY - \dfrac{(\Sigma X)(\Sigma Y)}{N}}{\Sigma X^2 - \dfrac{(\Sigma X)^2}{N}} = \frac{41{,}956 - \dfrac{618(1077)}{16}}{24{,}408 - \dfrac{(618)^2}{16}}$$

$$= 0.6636 = 0.664$$

$$a_Y = \overline{Y} - b_Y \overline{X} = 67.3125 - 0.6636(38.625)$$

$$= 41.679$$

Therefore,

$$Y' = b_Y X + a_Y = 0.664X + 41.679$$

This solution is also shown in the previous table. The least-squares regression line is shown on the scatter plot below.

**c.** Predicted height for the 3-year-old of 42 inches:

$$Y' = 0.664X + 41.679$$
$$= 0.664(42) + 41.679$$
$$= 69.55 \text{ inches}$$

## Practice Problem 7.2

A neuroscientist suspects that low levels of the brain neurotransmitter serotonin may be causally related to aggressive behavior. As a first step in investigating this hunch, she decides to do a correlative study involving nine rhesus monkeys. The monkeys are observed daily for 6 months, and the number of aggressive acts are recorded. Serotonin levels in the striatum (a brain region associated with aggressive behavior) are also measured once per day for each animal. The resulting data are shown in the following table. The number of aggressive acts for each animal is the average for the 6 months, given on a per-day basis. Serotonin levels are also average values over the 6-month period.

a. Draw a scatter plot of the data.
b. If the data are linearly related, derive the least-squares regression line for predicting the number of aggressive acts from serotonin level.
c. On the basis of these data, what is the number of aggressive acts per day you would predict if a rhesus monkey had a serotonin level of 0.46 microgm/gm?

| Subject No. | Serotonin Level (microgm/gm) $X$ | Number of Aggressive Acts/day $Y$ | $XY$ | $X^2$ |
|---|---|---|---|---|
| 1 | 0.32 | 6.0 | 1.920 | 0.1024 |
| 2 | 0.35 | 3.8 | 1.330 | 0.1225 |
| 3 | 0.38 | 3.0 | 1.140 | 0.1444 |
| 4 | 0.41 | 5.1 | 2.091 | 0.1681 |
| 5 | 0.43 | 3.0 | 1.290 | 0.1849 |
| 6 | 0.51 | 3.8 | 1.938 | 0.2601 |
| 7 | 0.53 | 2.4 | 1.272 | 0.2809 |
| 8 | 0.60 | 3.5 | 2.100 | 0.3600 |
| 9 | 0.63 | 2.2 | 1.386 | 0.3969 |
| Total | 4.16 | 32.8 | 14.467 | 2.0202 |

$$b_Y = \frac{\Sigma XY - \dfrac{(\Sigma X)(\Sigma Y)}{N}}{\Sigma X^2 - \dfrac{(\Sigma X)^2}{N}} = \frac{14.467 - \dfrac{(4.16)(32.8)}{9}}{2.0202 - \dfrac{(4.16)^2}{9}} = -7.127$$

$$a_Y = \overline{Y} - b_Y\overline{X} = 3.6444 - (-7.1274)(0.4622) = 6.939$$

$$Y' = b_Y X + a_Y = -7.127X + 6.939$$

**SOLUTION**

**a.** The scatter plot follows. It is clear that an imperfect, linear, negative relationship exists between the two variables.

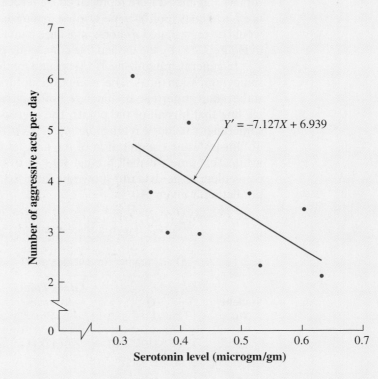

**b.** Derive the least-squares regression line. The solution is shown at the bottom of the previous table and the regression line has been plotted on the scatter plot above.

**c.** Predicted number of aggressive acts:

$$Y' = -7.127X + 6.939$$
$$= -7.127(0.46) + 6.939$$
$$= 3.7 \text{ aggressive acts per day}$$

# REGRESSION OF *X* ON *Y*

So far we have been concerned with predicting *Y* scores from the *X* scores. To do so, we derived a regression line that enabled us to predict *Y* given *X*. As mentioned before, this is sometimes referred to as the *regression line of Y on X*. It is also possible to predict *X* given *Y*. However, to predict *X* given *Y*, we must derive a new regression line. We cannot use the regression equation for predicting *Y* given *X*. For example, in the problem involving IQ (*X*) and grade point average (*Y*), we derived the following regression line:

$$Y' = 0.074X - 7.006$$

This line was appropriate for predicting grade point average given IQ (i.e., for predicting $Y$ given $X$). However, if we want to predict IQ ($X$) given grade point average ($Y$), we cannot use this regression line. We must derive new regression constants because the old regression line was derived to minimize errors in the $Y$ variable. The errors we minimized were represented by vertical lines parallel to the $Y$ axis [see Figure 7.2(a) on p. 136]. Now we want to minimize errors in the $X$ variable. These errors would be represented by horizontal lines parallel to the $X$ axis. An example is shown in Figure 7.2(a) by the dashed line connecting point $E$ to the regression line.

In general, minimizing $Y'$ errors and minimizing $X'$ errors will not lead to the same regression lines. The exception occurs when the relationship is perfect rather than imperfect. In that case, both regression lines coincide, forming the single line that hits all of the points. The regression line for predicting $X$ from $Y$ is sometimes called the *regression line of X on Y* or simply the *regression of X on Y*. To illustrate the computation of the line, let us use the IQ and grade point data again. This time we shall predict IQ ($X$) from the grade point average ($Y$). For convenience, the data are shown in Table 7.3. The linear regression equation for predicting $X$ given $Y$ is

$$X' = b_X Y + a_X \quad \textit{linear regression equation for predicting X given Y}$$

table 7.3 IQ and grade point average of 12 students: Predicting $X$ from $Y$

| Student No. | IQ $X$ | Grade Point Average $Y$ | $XY$ | $Y^2$ |
|---|---|---|---|---|
| 1 | 110 | 1.0 | 110.0 | 1.00 |
| 2 | 112 | 1.6 | 179.2 | 2.56 |
| 3 | 118 | 1.2 | 141.6 | 1.44 |
| 4 | 119 | 2.1 | 249.9 | 4.41 |
| 5 | 122 | 2.6 | 317.2 | 6.76 |
| 6 | 125 | 1.8 | 225.0 | 3.24 |
| 7 | 127 | 2.6 | 330.2 | 6.76 |
| 8 | 130 | 2.0 | 260.0 | 4.00 |
| 9 | 132 | 3.2 | 422.4 | 10.24 |
| 10 | 134 | 2.6 | 348.4 | 6.76 |
| 11 | 136 | 3.0 | 408.0 | 9.00 |
| 12 | 138 | 3.6 | 496.8 | 12.96 |
| *Total* | 1503 | 27.3 | 3488.7 | 69.13 |

$$b_X = \frac{\Sigma XY - \dfrac{(\Sigma X)(\Sigma Y)}{N}}{\Sigma Y^2 - \dfrac{(\Sigma Y)^2}{N}} = \frac{3488.7 - \dfrac{1503(27.3)}{12}}{69.13 - \dfrac{(27.3)^2}{12}}$$

$$= \frac{69.375}{7.0225} = 9.879$$

$$a_X = \overline{X} - b_X \overline{Y} = 125.25 - 9.8790(2.275) = 102.775$$

$$X' = b_X Y + a_X = 9.879Y + 102.775$$

*where*    $X'$ = predicted value of $X$
$b_X$ = slope of the line for minimizing $X'$ errors
$a_X$ = $X$ intercept for minimizing $X'$ errors

The equations for $b_X$ and $a_X$ are

$$b_X = \frac{\Sigma\, XY - \dfrac{(\Sigma\, X)(\Sigma\, Y)}{N}}{SS_Y} = \frac{(\Sigma\, XY) - \dfrac{(\Sigma\, X)(\Sigma\, Y)}{N}}{\Sigma\, Y^2 - \dfrac{(\Sigma\, Y)^2}{N}}$$

*b regression constant for predicting X given Y—computational equation*

*where*    $SS_Y$ = sum of squares of $Y$ scores

$$= \Sigma\, Y^2 - \frac{(\Sigma\, Y)^2}{N}$$

$$a_X = \overline{X} - b_X\overline{Y}$$    *a regression constant for predicting X given Y*

Solving for $b_X$ and $a_X$,

$$b_X = \frac{\Sigma XY - \dfrac{(\Sigma X)(\Sigma Y)}{N}}{\Sigma Y^2 - \dfrac{(\Sigma Y)^2}{N}}$$

$$b_X = \frac{3488.7 - \dfrac{1503(27.3)}{12}}{69.13 - \dfrac{(27.3)^2}{12}} = \frac{69.375}{7.0225} = 9.879$$

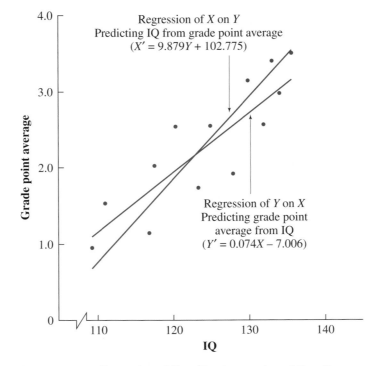

**figure 7.4**   Regression of *X* on *Y* and regression of *Y* on *X*.

$$a_X = \overline{X} - b_X\overline{Y}$$
$$= 125.25 - 9.8790(2.275)$$
$$= 102.775$$

The linear regression equation for predicting $X$ given $Y$ is

$$X' = b_X Y + a_X$$
$$= 9.879Y + 102.775$$

This line, along with the line predicting $Y$ given $X$, is shown in Figure 7.4. Note that the two lines are different, as would be expected when the relationship is imperfect. The solution is summarized in Table 7.3.

*Although different equations do exist for computing the second regression line, they are seldom used. Instead, it is common practice to designate the predicted variable as $Y'$ and the given variable as $X$.* Thus, if we wanted to predict IQ from grade point average, we would designate IQ as the $Y'$ variable and grade point average as the $X$ variable and then use the regression equation for predicting $Y$ given $X$.

## MEASURING PREDICTION ERRORS: THE STANDARD ERROR OF ESTIMATE

The regression line represents our best estimate of the $Y$ scores given their corresponding $X$ values. However, unless the relationship between $X$ and $Y$ is perfect, most of the actual $Y$ values will not fall on the regression line. Thus, when the relationship is imperfect, there will necessarily be prediction errors. It is useful to know the magnitude of the errors. For example, it sounds nice to say that, on the basis of the relationship between IQ and grade point average given previously, we predict that John's grade point average will be 3.2 when he is a senior. However, since the relationship is imperfect, it is unlikely that our prediction is exactly correct. Well, if it is not exactly correct, then how far off is it? If it is likely to be very far off, we can't put much reliance on the prediction. However, if the error is likely to be small, the prediction can be taken seriously and decisions made accordingly.

Quantifying prediction errors involves computing the *standard error of estimate*. The standard error of estimate is much like the standard deviation. You will recall that the standard deviation gave us a measure of the average deviation about the mean. The standard error of estimate gives us a measure of the average deviation of the prediction errors about the regression line. In this context, the regression line can be considered an estimate of the mean of the $Y$ values for each of the $X$ values. It is like a "floating" mean of the $Y$ values, which changes with the $X$ values. With the standard deviation, the sum of the deviations, $\Sigma(X - \overline{X})$, equaled 0. We had to square the deviations to obtain a meaningful average. The situation is the same with the standard error of estimate. Since the sum of the prediction errors, $\Sigma(Y - Y')$, equals 0, we must square them also. The average is then obtained by summing the squared values, dividing by $N - 2$, and taking the square root of the quotient (very much like with the standard deviation). The equation for the standard error of estimate for predicting $Y$ given $X$ is

$$s_{Y|X} = \sqrt{\frac{\Sigma(Y - Y')^2}{N - 2}} \qquad \textit{standard error of estimate when predicting Y given X}$$

Note that we have divided by $N - 2$ rather than $N - 1$, as was done with the sample standard deviation.[*] The calculations involved in using this equation are quite laborious. The computational equation, which is given here, is much easier to use. In determining the $b_Y$ regression coefficient, we have already calculated the values for $SS_X$ and $SS_Y$.

$$s_{Y|X} = \sqrt{\frac{SS_Y - \dfrac{[\Sigma XY - (\Sigma X)(\Sigma Y)/N]^2}{SS_X}}{N - 2}}$$

To illustrate the use of these equations, let's calculate the standard error of estimate for the grade point and IQ data shown in Tables 7.1 and 7.2. As before, we shall let grade point be the $Y$ variable and IQ the $X$ variable, and we shall calculate the standard error of estimate for predicting grade point given IQ. As computed in the tables, $SS_X = 936.25$, $SS_Y = 7.022$, $\Sigma XY - (\Sigma X)(\Sigma Y)/N = 69.375$, and $N = 12$. Substituting these values in the equation for the standard error of estimate for predicting $Y$ given $X$, we obtain

$$s_{Y|X} = \sqrt{\frac{SS_Y - \dfrac{[\Sigma XY - (\Sigma X)(\Sigma Y)/N]^2}{SS_X}}{N - 2}}$$

$$= \sqrt{\frac{7.022 - \dfrac{(69.375)^2}{936.25}}{12 - 2}}$$

$$= \sqrt{0.188} = 0.43$$

Thus, the standard error of estimate = 0.43. This measure has been computed over all the $Y$ scores. For it to be meaningful, we must assume that the variability of $Y$ remains constant as we go from one $X$ score to the next. This assumption is called the assumption of *homoscedasticity*. Figure 7.5(a) shows an illustration where the homoscedasticity assumption is met. Figure 7.5(b) shows an illustration where the

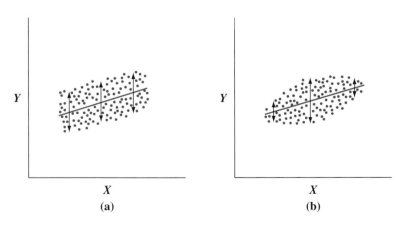

From E. W. Minium, *Statistical Reasoning in Psychology and Education.* Copyright © 1978 by John Wiley & Sons, Inc. Adapted with permission of John Wiley & Sons, Inc.

f i g u r e  7.5  Scatter plots showing the variability of $Y$ as a function of $X$.

---

[*]We divide by $N - 2$ because calculation of the standard error of estimate involves fitting the data to a straight line. To do so requires estimation of two parameters, slope and intercept, leaving the deviations about the line with $N - 2$ degrees of freedom. We shall discuss degrees of freedom in Chapter 13.

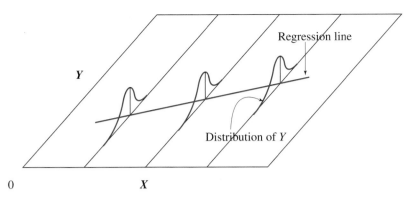

**figure 7.6** Normal distribution of *Y* scores about the regression line.

assumption is violated. The homoscedasticity assumption implies that if we divided the $X$ scores into columns, the variability of $Y$ would not change from column to column. We can see how this is true for Figure 7.5(a) but not for 7.5(b).

What meaning does the standard error of estimate have? Certainly, it is a quantification of the errors of prediction. The larger its value, the less confidence we have in the prediction. Conversely, the smaller its value, the more likely the prediction will be accurate. We can still be more quantitative. We can assume the points are normally distributed about the regression line (Figure 7.6). If the assumption is valid and we were to construct two lines parallel to the regression line at distances of $\pm 1s_{Y|X}$, $\pm 2s_{Y|X}$, and $\pm 3s_{Y|X}$, we would find that approximately 68% of the scores fall between the lines at $\pm 1s_{Y|X}$, approximately 95% lie between $\pm 2s_{Y|X}$, and approximately 99% lie between $\pm 3s_{Y|X}$. To illustrate this point, in Figure 7.7, we have drawn two dashed lines parallel to the regression line

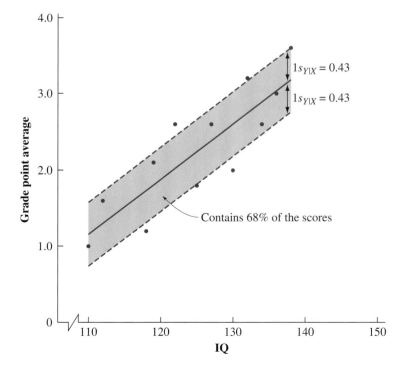

**figure 7.7** Regression line for grade point and IQ data with parallel lines $1s_{Y|X}$ above and below the regression line.

for the grade point and IQ data at a distance of $\pm 1s_{Y|X}$. We have also entered the scores in the figure. According to what we said previously, approximately 68% of the scores should lie between these lines. There are 12 points, so we would expect $0.68(12) = 8$ of the scores to be contained within the lines. In fact, there are 8. The agreement isn't always this good, particularly when there are only 12 scores in the sample. As $N$ increases, the agreement usually increases as well.

## CONSIDERATIONS IN USING LINEAR REGRESSION FOR PREDICTION

The procedures we have described are appropriate for predicting scores based on presumption of a linear relationship existing between the $X$ and $Y$ variables. If the relationship is nonlinear, the prediction will not be very accurate. It follows, then, that the first assumption for successful use of this technique is that *the relationship between X and Y must be linear.* Second, we are not ordinarily interested in using the regression line to predict scores of the individuals who were in the group used for calculating the regression line. After all, why predict their scores when we already know them? Generally, a regression line is determined for use with subjects where one of the variables is unknown. For instance, in the IQ and grade point average problem, a university admissions officer might want to use the regression line to predict the grade point averages of prospective students, knowing their IQ scores. It doesn't make any sense to predict the grade point averages of the 12 students whose data were used in the problem. He already knows their grade point averages. If we are going to use data collected on one group to predict scores of another group, it is important that *the basic computation group be representative*

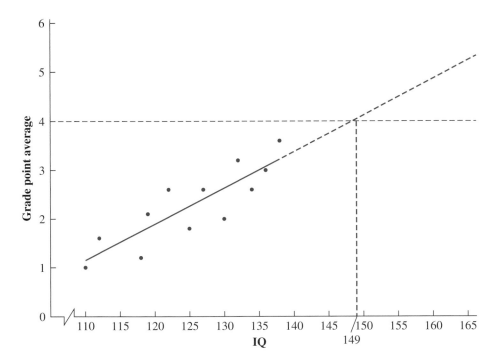

figure **7.8**  Limiting prediction to range of base data.

*of the prediction group.* Often this requirement is handled by randomly sampling from the prediction population and using the sample for deriving the regression equation. Random sampling is discussed in Chapter 8. Finally, the linear regression equation is properly used *just for the range of the variable on which it is based.* For example, when we were predicting grade point average from IQ, we should have limited our predictions to IQ scores ranging from 110 to 138. Since we do not have any data beyond this range, we do not know whether the relationship continues to be linear for more extreme values of IQ.

To illustrate this point, consider Figure 7.8, where we have extended the regression line to include IQ values up to 165. At the university from which these data were sampled, the highest possible grade point average is 4.0. If we used the extended regression line to predict the grade point average for an IQ of 165, we would predict a grade point average of 5.2, a value that is obviously wrong. Prediction for IQs greater than 165 would be even worse. Looking at Figure 7.8, we can see that if the relationship does extend beyond an IQ of 138, it can't extend beyond an IQ of about 149 (the IQ value where the regression line meets a grade point average of 4.0). Of course, there is no reason to believe the relationship exists beyond the base data point of IQ = 138, and hence predictions using this relationship should not be made for IQ values greater than 138.

## RELATION BETWEEN REGRESSION CONSTANTS AND PEARSON $r$

Although we haven't presented this aspect of Pearson $r$ before, it can be shown that Pearson $r$ is the slope of the least-squares regression line when the scores are plotted as $z$ scores. As an example, let's use the data given in Table 6.3 on the weight and cost of six bags of oranges. For convenience, the data have been reproduced in Table 7.4. Figure 7.9(a) shows the scatter plot of the raw scores and the least-squares regression line for these raw scores. This is a perfect, linear relationship, so $r = 1.00$. Figure 7.9(b) shows the scatter plot of the paired $z$ scores and the least-squares regression line for these $z$ scores. The slope of the regression line for the raw scores is $b$, and the slope of the regression line for the $z$ scores is $r$. Note that the slope of this latter regression line is 1.00, as it should be because $r = 1.00$.

t a b l e  7.4   Cost and weight in pounds of six bags of oranges

| Bag | Weight (lb) X | Cost ($) Y | $z_X$ | $z_Y$ |
|-----|---------------|------------|-------|-------|
| A | 2.25 | 0.75 | −1.34 | −1.34 |
| B | 3.00 | 1.00 | −0.80 | −0.80 |
| C | 3.75 | 1.25 | −0.27 | −0.27 |
| D | 4.50 | 1.50 | 0.27 | 0.27 |
| E | 5.25 | 1.75 | 0.80 | 0.80 |
| F | 6.00 | 2.00 | 1.34 | 1.34 |

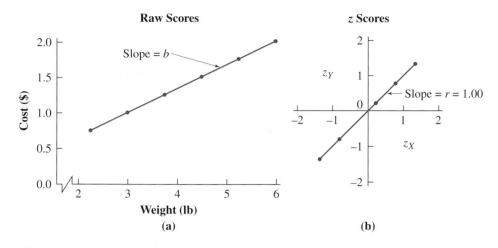

figure 7.9   Relationship between *b* and *r*.

Since Pearson *r* is a slope, it is related to $b_Y$ and $b_X$. It can be shown algebraically that

$$b_Y = r\frac{s_Y}{s_X}$$

and

$$b_X = r\frac{s_X}{s_Y}$$

These equations are useful if we have already calculated $r$, $s_X$, and $s_Y$ and want to determine the least-squares regression line. For example, in the problem involving IQ and grade point average, $r = 0.8556$, $s_Y = 0.7990$, and $s_X = 9.2257$. Suppose we want to find $b_Y$ and $a_Y$, having already calculated $r$, $s_Y$, and $s_X$. The simplest way is to use the equation

$$b_Y = r\frac{s_Y}{s_X} = 0.8556\left(\frac{0.7990}{9.2257}\right) = 0.074$$

Note that this is the same value arrived at previously in the chapter on p. 139 Having found $b_Y$, we would calculate $a_Y$ in the usual way.

## MULTIPLE REGRESSION AND MULTIPLE CORRELATION

Thus far, we have discussed regression and correlation using examples that have involved only two variables. When we were discussing the relationship between grade point average (GPA) and IQ, we determined that $r = 0.856$ and that the equation of the regression line for predicting grade point average from IQ was

$$Y' = 0.74X - 7.006$$

*where*   $Y' = $ predicted value of grade point average
$X = $ IQ score

This equation gave us reasonably accurate prediction. Although we didn't compute it, total prediction error squared $[\Sigma (Y - Y')^2]$ was 1.88, and the amount of variability accounted for was 73.2%. Of course, there are other variables besides IQ that might affect grade point average. The amount of time that students spend studying, motivation to achieve high grades, and interest in the courses taken are a few that come to mind. Even though we have reasonably good prediction accuracy using just IQ alone, we might be able to do better if we also had data relating GPA to one or more of these other variables.

Multiple regression is an extension of simple regression to situations that involve two or more predictor variables. To illustrate, let's assume we had data from the 12 college students that include a second predictor variable called "study time," as well as the original grade point average and IQ scores. The data for these three variables are shown in columns 2, 3, and 4 of Table 7.5. Now we can derive a regression equation for predicting grade point average using the two predictor variables, IQ and study time. The general form of the multiple regression equation for two predictor variables is

$$Y' = b_1 X_1 + b_2 X_2 + a$$

where 
$Y'$ = predicted value of $Y$

$b_1$ = coefficient of the first predictor variable

$X_1$ = first predictor variable

$b$ = coefficient of the second predictor variable

$X_2$ = second predictor variable

$a$ = prediction constant

table 7.5 A comparison of prediction accuracy using one or two predictor variables

| Student No. | IQ ($X_1$) | Study Time (hr/wk) ($X_2$) | Grade Point Average (GPA) ($Y$) | Predicted GPA Using IQ ($Y'$) | Predicted GPA Using IQ + Study Time ($Y'$) | Error Using Only IQ | Error Using IQ + Study Time |
|---|---|---|---|---|---|---|---|
| 1 | 110 | 8 | 1.0 | 1.14 | 1.13 | −0.14 | −0.13 |
| 2 | 112 | 10 | 1.6 | 1.29 | 1.46 | 0.31 | 0.13 |
| 3 | 118 | 6 | 1.2 | 1.74 | 1.29 | −0.54 | −0.09 |
| 4 | 119 | 13 | 2.1 | 1.81 | 2.16 | 0.29 | −0.06 |
| 5 | 122 | 14 | 2.6 | 2.03 | 2.43 | 0.57 | 0.17 |
| 6 | 125 | 6 | 1.8 | 2.26 | 1.63 | −0.46 | 0.17 |
| 7 | 127 | 13 | 2.6 | 2.40 | 2.56 | 0.20 | 0.04 |
| 8 | 130 | 12 | 2.0 | 2.63 | 2.59 | −0.63 | −0.59 |
| 9 | 132 | 13 | 3.2 | 2.77 | 2.81 | 0.42 | 0.39 |
| 10 | 134 | 11 | 2.6 | 2.92 | 2.67 | −0.32 | −0.07 |
| 11 | 136 | 12 | 3.0 | 3.07 | 2.88 | −0.07 | 0.12 |
| 12 | 138 | 18 | 3.6 | 3.21 | 3.69 | 0.38 | 0.09 |

Total error squared = $\Sigma (Y - Y')^2$ = 1.88      = 0.63

This equation is very similar to the one we used in simple regression except that we have added another predictor variable and its coefficient. As before, the coefficient and constant values are determined according to the least-squares criterion that $\Sigma(Y - Y')^2$ is a minimum. However, this time the mathematics is rather formidable and the actual calculations are almost always done on a computer, using statistical software. For the data of our example, the multiple regression equation that minimizes errors in $Y$ is given by

$$Y' = 0.049X_1 + 0.118X_2 - 5.249$$

*where*    $Y' =$ predicted value of grade point average

$b_1 = 0.049$

$X_1 =$ IQ score

$b = 0.118$

$X_2 =$ study time score

$a = 5.249$

To determine whether prediction accuracy is increased by using the multiple regression equation, we have listed in column 5 of Table 7.5 the predicted GPA scores using only IQ for prediction, in column 6 the predicted GPA scores using both IQ and study time as predictor variables, and prediction errors from using each in columns 7 and 8, respectively. We have also plotted in Figure 7.10(a) the actual $Y$ value and the two predicted $Y'$ values for each student. Students have been ordered from left to right on the $X$ axis according to the increased prediction accuracy that results for each by using the multiple regression equation. In Figure 7.10(b), we have plotted the percent improvement in prediction accuracy for each student that results from using IQ + study time rather than just IQ alone. It is clear from Table 7.5 and Figure 7.10 that using the multiple regression equation has greatly improved overall prediction accuracy. For example, prediction accuracy was increased in all students except student number 11, and for student number 3, accuracy was increased by almost 40%. We have also shown $\Sigma(Y - Y')^2$ for each regression line at the bottom of Table 7.5. Adding the second predictor variable reduced the total prediction error squared from 1.88 to 0.63, an improvement of more than 66%.

Since, in the present example, prediction accuracy was increased by using two predictors rather than one, it follows that the proportion of the variability of $Y$ accounted for has also increased. In trying to determine this proportion, you might be tempted, through extension of the concept of $r^2$ from our previous discussion of correlation, to compute $r^2$ between grade point average and each predictor and then simply add the resulting values. Table 7.6 shows a Pearson $r$ correlation matrix involving grade point average, IQ, and study time. If we followed this procedure, the proportion of variability accounted for would be greater than $1.00 \left[(0.856)^2 + (0.829)^2 = 1.42\right]$, which is clearly impossible. One cannot account for more than 100% of the variability. The error occurs because there is overlap in variability accounted for between IQ and study time. Students with higher IQs also tend to study more. Therefore, part of the variability in GPA that is explained by IQ is also explained by study time. To correct for this, we must take the correlation between IQ and study time into account.

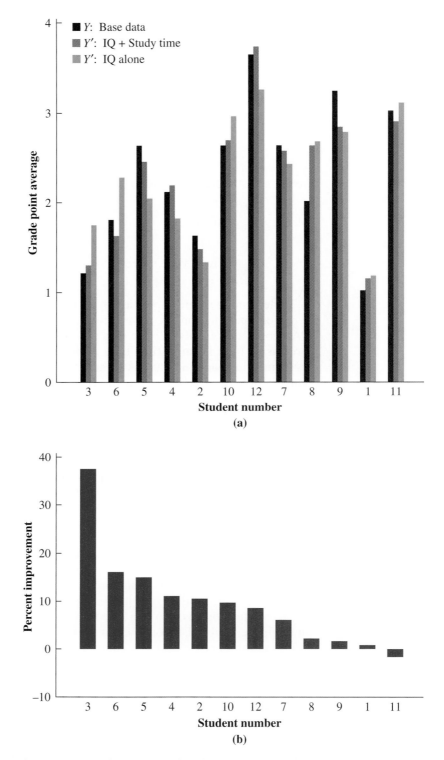

**figure 7.10** Comparison of prediction accuracy using one or two predictor variables.

**t a b l e  7.6**  Pearson correlation matrix between IQ, study time, and grade point average

|  | IQ $(X_1)$ | Study Time $(X_2)$ | Grade Point Average $(Y)$ |
|---|---|---|---|
| IQ $(X_1)$ | 1.000 | | |
| Study time $(X_2)$ | 0.560 | 1.000 | |
| Grade point average $(Y)$ | 0.856 | 0.829 | 1.000 |

The correct equation for computing the proportion of variance accounted for when there are two predictor variables is given by

$$R^2 = \frac{r_{YX_1}^2 + r_{YX_2}^2 - 2r_{YX_1}r_{YX_2}r_{X_1X_2}}{1 - r_{X_1X_2}^2}$$

*where*  $R^2 =$ the multiple coefficient of determination

$r_{YX_1} =$ the correlation between $Y$ and predictor variable $X_1$

$r_{YX_2} =$ the correlation between $Y$ and predictor variable $X_2$

$r_{X_1X_2} =$ the correlation between predictor variables $X_1$ and $X_2$

$R^2$ is also often called the *squared multiple correlation*. Based on the data of the present study, $r_{YX_1} =$ the correlation between grade point average and IQ = 0.856, $r_{YX_2} =$ the correlation between $Y$ and study time = 0.829, and $r_{X_1X_2} =$ the correlation between IQ and study time = 0.560. For these data,

$$R^2 = \frac{(0.856)^2 + (0.829)^2 - 2(0.856)(0.829)(0.560)}{1 - (0.560)^2}$$

$$= 0.910$$

Thus, the proportion of variance accounted for has increased from 0.73 to 0.91 by using IQ and study time.

Of course, just adding another predictor variable per se will not necessarily increase prediction accuracy or the amount of variance accounted for. Whether prediction accuracy and the amount of variance accounted for are increased depends on the strength of the relationship between the variable being predicted and the additional predictor variable and also on the strength of the relationship between the predictor variables themselves. For example, notice what happens to $R^2$ when $r_{X_1X_2} = 0$. This topic is taken up in more detail in advanced textbooks.

## SUMMARY

In this chapter, we have discussed how to use the relationship between two variables for prediction. When the line that best fits the points is used for prediction, it is called a regression line. The regression line most used for linear imperfect relationships fits the points according to a least-squares criterion. Next, we presented the equations for determining the least-squares regression line when predicting $Y$ given $X$ and the regression line when predicting $X$ given $Y$. The two lines are not the same unless the relationship is perfect. We then used these equations to construct regression lines for various sets of data and showed how to use these lines for prediction. Next, we dis-cussed how to quantify the errors in prediction by computing the standard error of estimate. We presented the conditions under which the use of the linear regression line was appropriate: The relationship must be linear, the regression line must have been derived from data representative of the group to which prediction is desired, and prediction must be limited to the range of the base data. Next, we discussed the relationship between $b$ and $r$. Finally, we introduced the topic of multiple regression and multiple correlation; discussed the multiple coefficient of determination, $R^2$; and showed how using two predictor variables can increase the accuracy of prediction.

## IMPORTANT TERMS

Homoscedasticity (p. 147)
Least-squares regression line (p. 137)
Multiple coefficient of determination (p. 155)

Multiple correlation (p. 151)
Multiple regression (p. 151)
Regression (p. 134)
Regression constant (p. 137)

Regression line (p. 135)
Regression of $X$ on $Y$ (p. 143)
Regression of $Y$ on $X$ (p. 137)
Standard error of estimate (p. 146)

## QUESTIONS AND PROBLEMS

1. Define or identify each of the terms in the Important Terms section.
2. List some situations in which it would be useful to have accurate prediction.
3. The least-squares regression line minimizes $\Sigma(Y - Y')^2$ rather than $\Sigma(Y - Y')$. Is this statement correct? Explain.
4. The least-squares regression line is the prediction line that results in the most direct "hits." Is this statement correct? Explain.
5. In general, the regression line of $Y$ on $X$ is not the same as the regression line of $X$ on $Y$. Is this statement correct? Explain.
6. Of what value is it to know the standard error of estimate for a set of paired $X$ and $Y$ scores?
7. Why are there usually two regression lines but only one correlation coefficient for any set of paired scores?
8. What is $R^2$ called? Is it true that conceptually $R^2$ is analogous to $r^2$, except that $R^2$ applies to situations in which there are two or more predictor variables? Explain. Will using a second predictor variable always increase the precision of prediction? Explain.

9. Given the set of paired $X$ and $Y$ scores,

| X | 7 | 10 | 9 | 13 | 7 | 11 | 13 |
|---|---|----|---|----|---|----|----|
| Y | 1 | 2 | 4 | 3 | 3 | 4 | 5 |

   a. Construct a scatter plot of the paired scores. Does the relationship appear linear?
   b. Determine the least-squares regression line for predicting $Y$ given $X$.
   c. Determine the least-squares regression line for predicting $X$ given $Y$. Are they the same? Explain.
   d. Draw both regression lines on the scatter plot.
   e. Using the relationship between $X$ and $Y$, what value would you predict for $Y$ if $X = 12$ (round to two decimal places)?
10. A clinical psychologist is interested in the relationship between testosterone level in married males and the quality of their marital relationship. A study is conducted in which the testosterone levels of eight married men are measured. The eight men also fill out a standardized ques-

tionnaire assessing quality of marital relationship. The questionnaire scale is 0–25, with higher numbers indicating better relationships. Testosterone scores are in nanomoles/liter of serum. The data are shown below.

| Subject Number | 1 | 2 | 3 | 4 | 5 | 6 | 7 | 8 |
|---|---|---|---|---|---|---|---|---|
| Relationship Score | 24 | 15 | 15 | 10 | 19 | 11 | 20 | 19 |
| Testosterone Level | 12 | 13 | 19 | 25 | 9 | 16 | 15 | 21 |

a. On a piece of graph paper, construct a scatter plot of the data. Use testosterone level as the *X* variable.
b. Describe the relationship shown on the graph.
c. Compute the value of Pearson *r*.
d. Determine the least-squares regression line for predicting relationship score from testosterone level. Should $b_Y$ be positive or negative? Why?
e. Draw the least-squares regression line of part **d** on the scatter plot of part **a**.
f. Based on the data of the eight men, what relationship score would you predict for a male who has a testosterone level of 23 nanomoles/liter of serum? clinical, health, biological

11. A popular attraction at a carnival recently arrived in town is the booth where Mr. Clairvoyant (a bright statistics student of somewhat questionable moral character) claims that he can guess the weight of females to within 1 kilogram by merely studying the lines in their hands and fingers. He offers a standing bet that if he guesses incorrectly the woman can pick out any stuffed animal in the booth. However, if he guesses correctly, as a reward for his special powers, she must pay him $2. Unknown to the women who make bets, Mr. Clairvoyant is able to surreptitiously measure the length of their left index fingers while "studying" their hands. Also unknown to the bettors, but known to Mr. Clairvoyant, is the following relationship between the weight of females and the length of their left index fingers:

| Length of Left Index Finger (cm) | 5.6 | 6.2 | 6.0 | 5.4 |
|---|---|---|---|---|
| Weight (kg) | 79.0 | 83.5 | 82.0 | 77.5 |

a. If you were a prospective bettor, having all this information before you, would you make the bet with Mr. Clairvoyant? Explain.

b. Using the data in the accompanying table, what is the least-squares regression line for predicting a woman's weight, given the length of her index finger?
c. Using the least-squares regression line determined in part **b**, if a woman's index finger is 5.7 centimeters, what would be her predicted weight (round to two decimal places)? cognitive

12. A statistics professor conducts a study to investigate the relationship between the performance of his students on exams and their anxiety. Ten students from his class are selected for the experiment. Just before taking the final exam, the 10 students are given an anxiety questionnaire. Here are final exam and anxiety scores for the 10 students:

| Anxiety | 28 | 41 | 35 | 39 | 31 | 42 | 50 | 46 | 45 | 37 |
|---|---|---|---|---|---|---|---|---|---|---|
| Final Exam | 82 | 58 | 63 | 89 | 92 | 64 | 55 | 70 | 51 | 72 |

a. On a piece of graph paper, construct a scatter plot of the paired scores. Use anxiety as the *X* variable.
b. Describe the relationship shown in the graph.
c. Assuming the relationship is linear, compute the value of Pearson *r*.
d. Determine the least-squares regression line for predicting the final exam score given the anxiety level. Should $b_Y$ be positive or negative? Why?
e. Draw the least-squares regression line of part **d** on the scatter plot of part **a**.
f. Based on the data of the 10 students, if a student has an anxiety score of 38, what value would you predict for her final exam score (round to two decimal places)?
g. Calculate the standard error of estimate for predicting final exam scores from anxiety scores. clinical, health, education

13. The sales manager of a large sporting goods store has recently started a national advertising campaign. He has kept a record of the monthly costs of the advertising and the monthly profits. These are shown here. The entries are in thousands of dollars.

| Month | Jan. | Feb. | Mar. | Apr. | May | Jun. | Jul. |
|---|---|---|---|---|---|---|---|
| Monthly Advertising Cost | 10.0 | 14.0 | 11.4 | 15.6 | 16.8 | 11.2 | 13.2 |
| Monthly Profit | 125 | 200 | 160 | 150 | 210 | 110 | 125 |

a. Assuming a linear relationship exists, derive the least-squares regression line for predicting monthly profits from monthly advertising costs.

b. In August, the manager plans to spend $17,000 on advertising. Based on the data, how much profit should he expect that month (round to the nearest $1000)?

c. Given the relationship shown by the paired scores, can you think of a reason why the manager doesn't spend a lot more money on advertising? I/O

14. A newspaper article reported that "there is a strong correlation between continuity and success when it comes to NBA coaches." The article was based on the following data:

| Coach, Team | Tenure as Coach with Same Team (yr) | 1996–1997 Record (% games won) |
|---|---|---|
| Jerry Sloan, Utah | 9 | 79 |
| Phil Jackson, Chicago | 8 | 84 |
| Rudy Tomjanovich, Houston | 6 | 70 |
| George Karl, Seattle | 6 | 70 |
| Lenny Wilkens, Atlanta | 4 | 68 |
| Mike Fratello, Cleveland | 4 | 51 |
| Larry Brown, Indiana | 4 | 48 |

a. Is the article correct in claiming that there is a strong correlation between continuity and success when it comes to NBA coaches?

b. Derive the least-squares regression line for predicting success (% games won) from tenure.

c. Based on your answer to part **b**, what "% games won" would you predict for an NBA coach who had 7 years' "tenure" with the same team? I/O, other

15. During inflationary times, Mr. Chevez has become budget conscious. Since his house is heated electrically, he has kept a record for the past year of his monthly electric bills and of the average monthly outdoor temperature. The data are shown in the following table. Temperature is in degrees Celsius, and the electric bills are in dollars.

a. Assuming there is a linear relationship between the average monthly temperature and the monthly electric bill, determine the least-squares regression line for predicting the monthly electric bill from the average monthly temperature.

b. Based on the almanac forecast for this year, Mr. Chevez expects a colder winter. If February is 8 degrees colder this year, how much should Mr. Chevez allow in his budget for February's electric bill? In calculating your answer, assume that the costs of electricity will rise 10% from last year's costs because of inflation.

c. Calculate the standard error of estimate for predicting the monthly electric bill from average monthly temperature.

| Month | Average Temp. | Elec. Bill |
|---|---|---|
| Jan. | 10 | 120 |
| Feb. | 18 | 90 |
| Mar. | 35 | 118 |
| Apr. | 39 | 60 |
| May | 50 | 81 |
| Jun. | 65 | 64 |
| Jul. | 75 | 26 |
| Aug. | 84 | 38 |
| Sep. | 52 | 50 |
| Oct. | 40 | 80 |
| Nov. | 25 | 100 |
| Dec. | 21 | 124 |

other

16. In Chapter 6, Problem 16, data were presented on the relationship between birth weight and the subsequent IQ of seven randomly selected psychology majors from a particular university. The data are again presented below.

| Student | Birth Weight (lbs) | IQ |
|---|---|---|
| 1 | 5.8 | 122 |
| 2 | 6.5 | 120 |
| 3 | 8.0 | 129 |
| 4 | 5.9 | 112 |
| 5 | 8.5 | 127 |
| 6 | 7.2 | 116 |
| 7 | 9.0 | 130 |

a. Assuming there is a linear relationship, use these data and determine the least-squares regression line for predicting IQ given birth weight.

b. Using this regression line, what IQ would you predict for a birth weight of 7.5? developmental

17. In Chapter 6, Problem 21, data were given on the relationship between the number of soft drinks consumed in a week by eight 12-year-olds and their body mass index (BMI). The 12-year-olds were randomly selected from a junior high school in a large northwestern city. The data are again presented below.

| Child | Number of Soft Drinks Consumed | BMI |
|---|---|---|
| 1 | 3 | 20 |
| 2 | 1 | 18 |
| 3 | 14 | 32 |
| 4 | 7 | 24 |
| 5 | 21 | 35 |
| 6 | 5 | 19 |
| 7 | 25 | 38 |
| 8 | 9 | 30 |

a. Assuming the data show a linear relationship, derive the least-squares regression line for predicting BMI given the number of soft drinks consumed.
b. Using this regression line, what BMI would you predict for a 12-year-old from this school who consumes a weekly average of 17 soft drinks? health

18. In Chapter 6, Problem 22, data were presented from a study conducted to determine the relationship between religious involvement and self-esteem. The data are again presented below.

| Subject | Religious Involvement | Self-Esteem |
|---|---|---|
| 1 | 5 | 8 |
| 2 | 25 | 3 |
| 3 | 45 | 2 |
| 4 | 20 | 7 |
| 5 | 30 | 5 |
| 6 | 40 | 5 |
| 7 | 1 | 4 |
| 8 | 15 | 4 |
| 9 | 10 | 7 |
| 10 | 35 | 3 |

a. Assuming a linear relationship, derive the least-squares regression line for predicting self-esteem from religious involvement.
b. Using this regression line, what value of self-esteem would you predict for an eighth grader who had value of religious involvement of 43? social, developmental

19. In Chapter 6, Problem 24, data were shown on the relationship between the work performance of 10 workers randomly chosen from the manufacturing section of a large corporation and two possible screening tests. The data are again shown below.

In that problem you were asked to recommend which of the two tests should be used as a screening device for prospective employees for that section of the company. Based on the data presented, you recommended using test 2. Now the question is: Would it be better to use both test 1 and test 2, rather than just test 2 alone? Explain your answer, using $R^2$ and $r^2$. Use a computer and statistical software to solve this problem if you have access to them. I/O

| | Employee | | | | | | | | | |
|---|---|---|---|---|---|---|---|---|---|---|
| | 1 | 2 | 3 | 4 | 5 | 6 | 7 | 8 | 9 | 10 |
| Work performance | 50 | 74 | 62 | 90 | 98 | 52 | 68 | 80 | 88 | 76 |
| Test 1 | 10 | 19 | 20 | 20 | 21 | 14 | 10 | 24 | 16 | 14 |
| Test 2 | 25 | 35 | 40 | 49 | 50 | 29 | 32 | 44 | 46 | 35 |

## BOOK COMPANION WEBSITE

Go to www.thomsonedu.com/psychology/pagano for:

- SPSS problems and solutions
- Flash cards for review of terms
- Chapter quiz
- Statistical workshops
- And more

## WebTUTOR

Available via WebTutor for this chapter:

- Detailed chapter outline
- *Know and Be Able To Do* section
- Drag & Drop game for review of equations, concepts, and other material
- Flash cards for review of terms
- Audio flash cards for MP3 player
- Solving problems using Excel
- Solving problems using SPSS
- More practice problems using computational equations
- Chapter quiz

# INFERENTIAL STATISTICS

PART **three**

# Random Sampling and Probability

CHAPTER **8**

## INTRODUCTION

We have now completed our discussion of descriptive statistics and are ready to begin considering the fascinating area of inferential statistics. With descriptive statistics, we were concerned primarily with presenting and describing sets of scores in the most meaningful and efficient way. With inferential statistics, we go beyond mere description of the scores. A basic aim of inferential statistics is to use the sample scores to make a statement about a characteristic of the population. There are two kinds of statements made. One has to do with *hypothesis testing* and the other with *parameter estimation.*

In hypothesis testing, the experimenter is collecting data in an experiment on a sample set of subjects in an attempt to validate some hypothesis involving a population. For example, suppose an educational psychologist believes a new method of teaching mathematics to the third graders in her school district (population) is superior to the usual way of teaching the subject. In her experiment, she employs two samples of third graders, one of which is taught using the new teaching method and the other the old one. Each group is tested on the same final exam. In doing this experiment, the psychologist is not satisfied with just reporting that the mean of the group that received the new method was higher than the mean of the other group. She wants to make a statement such as, "The improvement in final exam scores was due to the new teaching method and not chance factors. Furthermore, the improvement does not apply just to the particular sample tested. Rather, the improvement would be found in the whole population of third graders if they were taught by the new method." The techniques used in inferential statistics make these statements possible.

In parameter estimation experiments, the experimenter is interested in determining the magnitude of a population characteristic. For example, an economist might be interested in determining the average monthly amount of money spent last year on food by single college students. Using sample data, with the techniques of inferential statistics, he can estimate the mean amount spent by the population. He would conclude with a statement such as, "The probability is 0.95 that the interval of \$250–\$300 contains the population mean."

The topics of *random sampling* and *probability* are central to the methodology of inferential statistics. In the next section, we shall consider random sampling. In the remainder of the chapter, we shall be concerned with presenting the basic principles of probability.

## RANDOM SAMPLING

To generalize validly from the sample to the population, both in hypothesis testing and parameter estimation experiments, the sample cannot be *just any subset* of the population. Rather, it is crucial that the sample is a *random* sample.

definition ■ *A* **random sample** *is defined as a sample selected from the population by a process that ensures that* (1) *each possible sample of a given size has an equal chance of being selected and* (2) *all the members of the population have an equal chance of being selected into the sample.*[*]

---

[*]See Note 8.1, p. 198.

To illustrate, consider the situation in which we have a population comprising the scores 2, 3, 4, 5, and 6 and we want to randomly draw a sample of size 2 from the population. Note that normally the population would have a great many more scores in it. We've restricted the population to five scores for ease in understanding the points we wish to make. Let's assume we shall be sampling from the population one score at a time and then placing it back into the population before drawing again. This is called *sampling with replacement* and is discussed later in this chapter. The following comprise all the samples of size 2 we could get from the population using this method of sampling:

| 2, 2 | 3, 2 | 4, 2 | 5, 2 | 6, 2 |
|------|------|------|------|------|
| 2, 3 | 3, 3 | 4, 3 | 5, 3 | 6, 3 |
| 2, 4 | 3, 4 | 4, 4 | 5, 4 | 6, 4 |
| 2, 5 | 3, 5 | 4, 5 | 5, 5 | 6, 5 |
| 2, 6 | 3, 6 | 4, 6 | 5, 6 | 6, 6 |

There are 25 samples of size 2 we might get when sampling one score at a time with replacement. To achieve random sampling, the process must be such that (1) all of the 25 possible samples have an equally likely chance of being selected and (2) all of the population scores (2, 3, 4, 5, and 6) have an equal chance of being selected into the sample.

The sample should be a random sample for two reasons. First, to generalize from a sample to a population, it is necessary to apply the laws of probability to the sample. If the sample has not been generated by a process ensuring that each possible sample of that size has an equal chance of being selected, we can't apply the laws of probability to the sample. The importance of this aspect of randomness and of probability to statistical inference will become apparent when we have covered the chapters on hypothesis testing and sampling distributions (see Chapters 10 and 12, respectively).

The second reason for random sampling is that, to generalize from a sample to a population, it is necessary that the sample be representative of the population. One way to achieve representativeness is to choose the sample by a process that ensures that all the members of the population have an equal chance of being selected into the sample. Thus, requiring the sample to be random allows the laws of probability to be used on the sample and at the same time results in a sample that should be representative of the population.

It is tempting to think that we can achieve representativeness by using methods other than random sampling. Very often, however, the selected procedure results in a biased (unrepresentative) sample. An example of this was the famous *Literary Digest* presidential poll of 1936, which predicted a landslide victory for Landon (57% to 43%). In fact, Roosevelt won, gaining 62% of the ballots. The *Literary Digest* prediction was grossly in error. Why? Later analysis showed that the error occurred because the sample was not representative of the voting population. It was a *biased* sample. The individuals selected were chosen from sources like the telephone book, club lists, and lists of registered automobile owners. These lists systematically excluded the poor, who were unlikely to have telephones or automobiles. It turned out that the poor voted overwhelmingly for Roosevelt. Even if other methods of sampling do on occasion result in a representative sample, the methods would not be useful for inference because we could not apply the laws of probability necessary to go from the sample to the population.

## Techniques for Random Sampling

It is beyond the scope of this textbook to delve deeply into the ways of generating random samples. This topic can be complex, particularly when dealing with surveys. We shall, however, present a few of the more commonly used techniques in conjunction with some simple situations so that you can get a feel for what is involved. Suppose we have a population of 100 people and wish to randomly sample 20 for an experiment. One way to do this would be to number the individuals in the population from 1 to 100, then take 100 slips of paper and write one of the numbers on each slip, and put the slips into a hat, shake them around a lot, and pick out one. We would repeat the shaking and pick out another. Then we would continue this process until 20 slips have been picked. The numbers contained on the slips of paper would identify the individuals to be used in the sample. With this method of random sampling, it is crucial that the population be thoroughly mixed to ensure randomness.

A common way to produce random samples is to use a table of random numbers, such as Table J in Appendix D. These tables are most often constructed by a computer using a program that guarantees that all the digits (0–9) have an equal chance of occurring each time a digit is printed.

The table may be used as successive single digits, as successive two-digit numbers, as successive three-digit numbers, and so forth. For example, in Table J, p. 550, if we begin at row 1 and move horizontally across the page, the random order of single digits would be 3, 2, 9, 4, 2, . . . . If we wish to use two-digit numbers, the random order would be 32, 94, 29, 54, 16, . . . .

Since the digits in the table are random, they may be used vertically in both directions and horizontally in both directions. The direction to be used should be specified before entering the table. To use the table properly, it should be entered randomly. One way would be to make cards with row and column numbers and place the cards in a box, mix them up, and then pick a row number and a column number. The intersection of the row and column would be the location of the first random number. The remaining numbers would be located by moving from the first number in the direction specified prior to entering the table. To illustrate, suppose we wanted to form a random sample of 3 subjects from a population of 10 subjects.* For this example, we have decided to move horizontally to the right in the table. To choose the sample, we would first assign each individual in the population a number from 0 to 9. Next, the table would be entered randomly to locate the first number. Let's assume the entry turns out to be the first number of row 7, p. 550, which is 3. This number designates the first subject in the sample. Thus, the first subject in the sample would be the subject bearing the number 3. We have already decided to move to the right in the table, so the next two numbers are 5 and 6. Thus, the individuals bearing the numbers 5 and 6 would complete the sample.

Next, let's do a problem where there are more individuals in the population. For purposes of illustration, we shall assume that a random sample of 15 subjects is desired from a population of 100. To vary things a bit, we have decided to move vertically down in the table for this problem, rather than horizontally to the right. As before, we need to assign a number to each member of

---

*Of course, in real experiments, the number of elements in the population is much greater than 10. We are using 10 in the first example to help understand how to use the table.

the population. This time, the numbers assigned are from 00 to 99 instead of from 0 to 9. Again the table is entered randomly. This time, let's assume the entry occurs at the intersection of the first two-digit number of column 3 with row 12. The two-digit number located at this intersection is 70. Thus, the first subject in the sample is the individual bearing the number 70. The next subject would be located by moving vertically down from 70. Thus, the second subject in the sample would be the individual bearing the number 33. This process would be continued until 15 subjects have been selected. The complete set of subject numbers would be 70, 33, 82, 22, 96, 35, 14, 12, 13, 59, 97, 37, 54, 42, and 89. In arriving at this set of numbers, the number 82 appeared twice in the table. Since the same individual cannot be in the sample more than once, the repeated number was not included.

## Sampling With or Without Replacement

So far, we have defined a random sample, discussed the importance of random sampling, and presented some techniques for producing random samples. To complete our discussion, we need to distinguish between "sampling with replacement" and "sampling without replacement." To illustrate the difference between these two methods of sampling, let's assume we wish to form a sample of two scores from a population composed of the scores 4, 5, 8, and 10. One way would be to randomly draw one score from the population, record its value, and then place it back in the population before drawing the second score. Thus, the first score would be eligible for selection again on the second draw. This method of sampling is called *sampling with replacement*. A second method would be to randomly draw one score from the population and not replace it before drawing the second one. Thus, the same member of the population could appear in the sample only once. This method of sampling is called *sampling without replacement*.

definitions
- **Sampling with replacement** *is defined as a method of sampling in which each member of the population selected for the sample is returned to the population before the next member is selected.*

- **Sampling without replacement** *is defined as a method of sampling in which the members of the sample are not returned to the population before subsequent members are selected.*

When subjects are being selected to participate in an experiment, sampling without replacement must be used because the same individual can't be in the sample more than once. You will probably recognize this as the method we used in the preceding section. Sampling with replacement forms the mathematical basis for many of the inference tests discussed later in the textbook. Although the two methods do not yield identical results, when sample size is small relative to population size, the differences are negligible and "with-replacement" techniques are much easier to use in providing the mathematical basis for inference. Let's now move on to the topic of probability.

figure 8.1 A pair of dice.

## PROBABILITY

Probability may be approached in two ways: (1) from an *a priori*, or classical, viewpoint and (2) from an *a posteriori*, or empirical, viewpoint. *A priori* means that which can be deduced from reason alone, without experience. From the *a priori*, or classical, viewpoint, probability is defined as

$$p(A) = \frac{\text{Number of events classifiable as } A}{\text{Total number of possible events}} \qquad \textit{a priori probability}$$

The symbol $p(A)$ is read "the probability of occurrence of event $A$." Thus, the equation states that the probability of occurrence of event $A$ is equal to the number of events classifiable as $A$ divided by the number of possible events. To illustrate how this equation is used, let's look at an example involving dice. Figure 8.1 shows a pair of dice. Each die (the singular of dice is die) has six sides with a different number of spots painted on each side. The spots vary from one to six. These innocent-looking cubes are used for gambling in a game called *craps*. They have been the basis of many tears and much happiness depending on the "luck" of the gambler.

Returning to *a priori* probability, suppose we are going to roll a die once. What is the probability it will come to rest with a 2 (the side with two spots on it) facing upward? Since there are six possible numbers that might occur and only one of these is 2, the probability of a 2 in one roll of one die is

$$p(A) = p(2) = \frac{\text{Number of events classifiable as 2}}{\text{Total number of possible events}} = \frac{1}{6} = 0.1667^{*}$$

Let's try one more problem using the *a priori* approach. What is the probability of getting a number greater than 4 in one roll of one die? This time there are two events classifiable as $A$ (rolling 5 or 6). Thus,

$$p(A) = p(5 \text{ or } 6) = \frac{\text{Number of events classifiable as 5 or 6}}{\text{Total number of possible events}} = \frac{2}{6} = 0.3333$$

Note that the previous two problems were solved by reason alone, without recourse to any data collection. This approach is to be contrasted with the *a posteriori*, or empirical, approach to probability. *A posteriori* means "after the fact," and in the context of probability, it means after some data have been collected. From the *a posteriori*, or empirical, viewpoint, probability is defined as

$$p(A) = \frac{\text{Number of times } A \text{ has occurred}}{\text{Total number of occurrences}} \qquad \textit{a posteriori probability}$$

To determine the probability of a 2 in one roll of one die using the empirical approach, we would have to take the actual die, roll it many times, and count

---

*In this and all other problems involving dice, we shall assume that the dice will not come to rest on any of their edges.

the number of times a 2 has occurred. The more times we roll the die, the better. Let's assume for this problem that we roll the die 100,000 times and that a 2 occurs 16,000 times. The probability of a 2 occurring in one roll of the die is found by

$$p(2) = \frac{\text{Number of times 2 has occurred}}{\text{Total number of occurrences}} = \frac{16,000}{100,000} = 0.1600$$

Note that, with this approach, it is necessary to have the actual die and to collect some data before determining the probability. The interesting thing is that if the die is evenly balanced (spoken of as a fair die), when we roll the die many, many times, the *a posteriori* probability approaches the *a priori* probability. If we roll an infinite number of times, the two probabilities will equal each other. Note also that, if the die is loaded (weighted so that one side comes up more often than the others), the *a posteriori* probability will differ from the *a priori* determination. For example, if the die is heavily weighted for a 6 to come up, a 2 might never appear. We can see now that the *a priori* equation assumes that each possible outcome has an equal chance of occurrence. For most of the problems in this chapter and the next, we shall use the *a priori* approach to probability.

## Some Basic Points Concerning Probability Values

Since probability is fundamentally a proportion, it ranges in value from 0.00 to 1.00. If the probability of an event occurring equals 1.00, then the event is certain to occur. If the probability equals 0.00, then the event is certain *not* to occur. For example, an ordinary die does not have a side with 7 dots on it. Therefore, the probability of rolling a 7 with a single die equals 0.00. Rolling a 7 is certain not to occur. On the other hand, the probability that a number from 1 to 6 will occur equals 1.00. It is certain that one of the numbers 1, 2, 3, 4, 5, or 6 will occur.

The probability of occurrence of an event is expressed as a fraction or a decimal number. For example, the probability of randomly picking the ace of spades in one draw from a deck of ordinary playing cards is $\frac{1}{52}$, or 0.0192.[*] The answer may be left as a fraction ($\frac{1}{52}$) but usually is converted to its decimal equivalent (0.0192).

Sometimes probability is expressed as "chances in 100." For example, someone might say the probability that event *A* will occur is 5 chances in 100. What he really means is $p(A) = 0.05$. Occasionally, probability is also expressed as the odds for or against an event occurring. For example, a betting person might say that the odds are 3 to 1 favoring Fred to win the race. In probability terms, $p(\text{Fred's winning}) = \frac{3}{4} = 0.75$. If the odds were 3 to 1 against Fred's winning, $p(\text{Fred's winning}) = \frac{1}{4} = 0.25$.

## Computing Probability

Determining the probability of events can be complex. In fact, whole courses are devoted to this topic, and they are quite difficult. Fortunately, for our purposes, there are only two major probability rules we need to learn: the addition rule and the multiplication rule. These rules provide the foundation necessary for understanding the statistical inference tests that follow in this textbook.

---

[*]For the uninitiated, a deck of ordinary playing cards is composed of 52 cards; 4 suits (spades, hearts, diamonds, and clubs), and 13 cards in each suit (Ace, 2, 3, 4, 5, 6, 7, 8, 9, 10, Jack, Queen, and King).

## The Addition Rule

The addition rule is concerned with determining the probability of occurrence of any one of several possible events. To begin our discussion, let's assume there are only two possible events, *A* and *B*. When there are two events, the addition rule states:

---

**definition** ■ *The* **probability of occurrence of** ***A*** **or** ***B*** *is equal to the probability of occurrence of A plus the probability of occurrence of B minus the probability of occurrence of both A and B.*

---

In equation form, the addition rule states:

$$p(A \text{ or } B) = p(A) + p(B) - p(A \text{ and } B)$$

*addition rule for two events— general equation*

Let's illustrate how this rule is used. Suppose we want to determine the probability of picking an ace or a club in one draw from a deck of ordinary playing cards. The problem has been solved in two ways in Figure 8.2. Refer to the figure as you read this paragraph. The first way is by enumerating all the events classifiable as an ace or a club and using the basic equation for probability. There are 16 ways to get an ace or a club, so the probability of getting an ace or a club $= \frac{16}{52} = 0.3077$. The second method uses the addition rule. The probability of getting an ace $= \frac{4}{52}$, and the probability of getting a club $= \frac{13}{52}$. The probability of getting both ace and a club $= \frac{1}{52}$. By the addition rule, the probability of getting an ace or a club $= \frac{4}{52} + \frac{13}{52} - \frac{1}{52} = \frac{16}{52} = 0.3077$. Why do we need to subtract the probability of getting both an ace and a club? Because we have already counted the ace of clubs twice. Without subtracting it, we would be misled into thinking there are 17 favorable events rather than just 16.

In this course, we shall be using the addition rule almost entirely in situations where the events are *mutually exclusive*.

---

**definition** ■ **Two events are mutually exclusive** *if both cannot occur together.* Another way of saying this is that **two events are mutually exclusive** *if the occurrence of one precludes the occurrence of the other.*

---

The events of rolling a 1 and of rolling a 2 in one roll of a die are mutually exclusive. If the roll ends with a 1, it cannot also be a 2. The events of picking an ace and a king in one draw from a deck of ordinary playing cards are mutually exclusive. If the card is an ace, it precludes the card also being a king. This can be contrasted with the events of picking an ace and a club in one draw from the deck. These events are not mutually exclusive because there is a card that is both an ace and a club (the ace of clubs).

When the events are mutually exclusive, the probability of both events occurring together is zero. Thus, $p(A \text{ and } B) = 0$ when *A* and *B* are mutually exclusive. Under these conditions, the addition rule simplifies to:

$$p(A \text{ or } B) = p(A) + p(B)$$    *addition rule when A and B are mutually exclusive*

Let's practice solving some problems involving situations in which *A* and *B* are mutually exclusive.

**(a) By enumeration using the basic definition of probability**

$$p(A) = \frac{\text{Number of events favorable to } A}{\text{Total number of possible events}}$$

$$= \frac{16}{52} = 0.3077$$

*where*    *A* = drawing an ace or a club

Ace or club

*Events favorable to A*

16

**(b) By the addition rule**

$$p(A \text{ or } B) = p(A) + p(B) - p(A \text{ and } B)$$

$$= \frac{4}{52} + \frac{13}{52} - \frac{1}{52}$$

$$= \frac{16}{52} = 0.3077$$

*where*    *A* = drawing an ace
         *B* = drawing a club

*Events favorable to A*

*Events favorable to B*

*Events favorable to A and B*

**figure 8.2** Determining the probability of randomly picking an ace or a club in one draw from a deck of ordinary playing cards.

## Practice Problem 8.1

What is the probability of randomly picking a 10 or a 4 in one draw from a deck of ordinary playing cards?

**SOLUTION**

The solution is shown in the following figure. Since we want either a 10 *or* a 4 and these two events are mutually exclusive, the addition rule with mutually exclusive events is appropriate. Thus, $p(10 \text{ or } 4) = p(10) + p(4)$. There are four 10s, four 4s, and 52 cards, so $p(10) = \frac{4}{52}$ and $p(4) = \frac{4}{52}$. Thus, $p(10 \text{ or } 4) = \frac{4}{52} + \frac{4}{52} = \frac{8}{52} = 0.1538$.

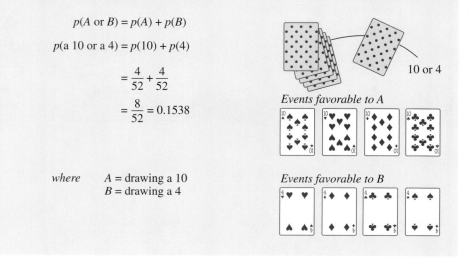

$$p(A \text{ or } B) = p(A) + p(B)$$

$$p(a\ 10 \text{ or a } 4) = p(10) + p(4)$$

$$= \frac{4}{52} + \frac{4}{52}$$

$$= \frac{8}{52} = 0.1538$$

where    $A$ = drawing a 10
         $B$ = drawing a 4

10 or 4

*Events favorable to A*

*Events favorable to B*

## Practice Problem 8.2

In rolling a fair die once, what is the probability of rolling a 1 or an even number?

**SOLUTION**

The solution is shown in the accompanying figure. Since the events are mutually exclusive and the problem asks for either a 1 *or* an even number, the addition rule with mutually exclusive events applies. Thus, $p(1 \text{ or an even number}) = p(1) + p(\text{an even number})$. There is one way to roll a 1, three ways to roll an even number (2, 4, 6), and six possible outcomes. Thus, $p(1) = \frac{1}{6}, p(\text{an even number}) = \frac{3}{6}$, and $p(1 \text{ or an even number}) = \frac{1}{6} + \frac{3}{6} = \frac{4}{6} = 0.6667$

$$p(A \text{ or } B) = p(A) + p(B)$$

$$p(1 \text{ or an even number}) = p(1) + p(\text{an even number})$$

$$= \frac{1}{6} + \frac{3}{6} = \frac{4}{6}$$

$$= 0.6667$$

*where*    $A$ = rolling a 1
            $B$ = rolling an even number

*Events favorable to A*

*Events favorable to B*

## Practice Problem 8.3

Suppose you are going to randomly sample 1 individual from a population of 130 people. In the population, there are 40 children younger than 12, 60 teenagers, and 30 adults. What is the probability the individual you select will be a teenager or an adult?

### SOLUTION

The solution is shown in the accompanying figure. Since the events are mutually exclusive and we want a teenager or an adult, the addition rule with mutually exclusive events is appropriate. Thus, $p(\text{teenager or adult}) = p(\text{teenager}) + p(\text{adult})$. Since there are 60 teenagers, 30 adults, and 130 people in the population, $p(\text{teenager}) = \frac{60}{130}$ and $p(\text{adult}) = \frac{30}{130}$. Thus, $p(\text{teenager or adult}) = \frac{60}{130} + \frac{30}{130} = \frac{90}{130} = 0.6923$.

$$p(A \text{ or } B) = p(A) + p(B)$$

$$p(\text{a teenager or an adult}) = p(\text{a teenager}) + p(\text{an adult})$$

$$= \frac{60}{130} + \frac{30}{130}$$

$$= \frac{90}{130} = 0.6923$$

*where*    $A$ = a teenager
            $B$ = an adult

Teenager or Adult

Population →

40 children younger than 12

60 teenagers

30 adults

The addition rule may also be used when there are more than two events. This is accomplished by a simple extension of the equation used for two events. Thus, when there are more than two events and the events are mutually exclusive, the probability of occurrence of any one of the events is equal to the sum of the probability of each event. In equation form,

$$p(A \text{ or } B \text{ or } C \ldots \text{ or } Z) = p(A) + p(B) + p(C) + \cdots + p(Z)$$

*addition rule with more than two mutually exclusive events*

*where*  $Z$ = the last event

Very often we shall encounter situations in which the events are not only mutually exclusive but also exhaustive. We have already defined mutually exclusive but not *exhaustive*.

**definition**  ■  *A set of events is **exhaustive** if the set includes all of the possible events.*

For example, in rolling a die once, the set of events of getting a 1, 2, 3, 4, 5, or 6 is exhaustive because the set includes all of the possible events. When a set of events is both exhaustive and mutually exclusive, a very useful relationship exists. Under these conditions, the sum of the individual probabilities of each event in the set must equal 1. Thus,

$$p(A) + p(B) + p(C) + \cdots + p(Z) = 1.00$$   *when events are exhaustive and mutually exclusive*

*where*  $A, B, C, \ldots, Z$ = the events

To illustrate this relationship, let's consider the set of events of getting a 1, 2, 3, 4, 5, or 6 in rolling a fair die once. Since the events are exhaustive and mutually exclusive, the sum of their probabilities must equal 1. We can see this is true because $p(1) = \frac{1}{6}$, $p(2) = \frac{1}{6}$, $p(3) = \frac{1}{6}$, $p(4) = \frac{1}{6}$, $p(5) = \frac{1}{6}$, and $p(6) = \frac{1}{6}$. Thus,

$$p(1) + p(2) + p(3) + p(4) + p(5) + p(6) = 1.00$$
$$\tfrac{1}{6} + \tfrac{1}{6} + \tfrac{1}{6} + \tfrac{1}{6} + \tfrac{1}{6} + \tfrac{1}{6} = 1.00$$

When there are only two events and the events are mutually exclusive, it is customary to assign the symbol $P$ to the probability of occurrence of one of the events and $Q$ to the probability of occurrence of the other event. For example, if I were flipping a penny and only allowed it to come up heads or tails, this would be a situation in which there are only two possible events (a head or a tail) with each flip, and the events are mutually exclusive (if it is a head, it can't be a tail and vice versa). It is customary to let $P$ equal the probability of occurrence of one of the events, say, a head, and $Q$ equal the probability of occurrence of the other event, a tail. In this case, if the coin were a fair coin, $P = \frac{1}{2}$ and $Q = \frac{1}{2}$. Since the events are exhaustive and mutually exclusive, their probabilities must equal 1. Thus,

$$P + Q = 1.00$$   *when two events are exhaustive and mutually exclusive*

We shall be using the symbols $P$ and $Q$ extensively in Chapter 9 in conjunction with the binomial distribution.

## The Multiplication Rule

Whereas the addition rule gives the probability of occurrence of any one of several events, the multiplication rule is concerned with the joint or successive occurrence of several events. Note that the multiplication rule often deals with what happens on more than one roll or draw, whereas the addition rule covers just one roll or one draw. If we are interested in the joint or successive occurrence of two events $A$ and $B$, the multiplication rule states the following:

| definition | ■ | *The* **probability of occurrence of both $A$ and $B$** *is equal to the probability of occurrence of A times the probability of occurrence of B given A has occurred.* |

In equation form, the multiplication rule is

$$p(A \text{ and } B) = p(A)p(B|A)$$ *multiplication rule with two events—general equation*

Note that the symbol $p(B|A)$ is read "probability of occurrence of $B$ given $A$ has occurred." It does not mean $B$ divided by $A$. Note also that the multiplication rule is concerned with the occurrence of $A$ *and* $B$, whereas the addition rule applies to the occurrence of $A$ *or* $B$.

In discussing the multiplication rule, it is useful to distinguish among three conditions: when the events are mutually exclusive, when the events are independent, and when the events are dependent.

**Multiplication rule: Mutually exclusive events** We have already discussed the joint occurrence of $A$ and $B$ when $A$ and $B$ are mutually exclusive. You will recall that if $A$ and $B$ are mutually exclusive,

$$p(A \text{ and } B) = 0$$ *multiplication rule with mutually exclusive events*

because when events are mutually exclusive, the occurrence of one precludes the occurrence of the other. The probability of their joint occurrence is zero.

**Multiplication rule: Independent events** To understand how the multiplication rule applies in this situation, we must first define *independent*.

| definition | ■ | **Two events are independent** *if the occurrence of one has no effect on the probability of occurrence of the other.* |

Sampling with replacement illustrates this condition well. For example, suppose we are going to draw two cards, one at a time, with replacement, from a deck of ordinary playing cards. We can let $A$ be the card drawn first and $B$ be the card drawn second. Since *A* is replaced before drawing *B,* the occurrence of *A* on the first draw has no effect on the probability of occurrence of *B*. For instance, if *A* were an ace, because it is replaced in the deck before picking the second card, the occurrence of an ace on the first draw has no effect on the probability of occurrence of the card picked on the second draw. If *A* and *B* are independent, then the probability of *B* occurring is unaffected by *A*. Therefore, $p(B|A) = p(B)$. Under this condition, the multiplication rule becomes

$$p(A \text{ and } B) = p(A)p(B|A) = p(A)p(B)$$   *multiplication rule with independent events*

Let's see how to use this equation. Suppose we are going to randomly draw two cards, one at a time, with replacement, from a deck of ordinary playing cards. What is the probability both cards will be aces?

The solution is shown in Figure 8.3. Since the problem requires an ace on the first draw *and* an ace on the second draw, the multiplication rule is appropriate. We can let *A* be an ace on the first draw and *B* be an ace on the second draw. Since sampling is with replacement, *A* and *B* are independent. Thus, $p$(an ace on first draw and an ace on second draw) = $p$(an ace on first draw)$p$(an ace on second draw). There are four aces possible on the first draw, four aces possible on the second draw (sampling is *with* replacement), and 52 cards in the deck, so $p$(an ace on first draw) = $\frac{4}{52}$ and $p$(an ace on second draw) = $\frac{4}{52}$. Thus, $p$(an ace on first draw and an ace on second draw) = $\frac{4}{52}(\frac{4}{52}) = \frac{16}{2704} = 0.0059$.

Let's do a few more problems for practice.

figure 8.3 Determining the probability of randomly sampling two aces in two draws from a deck of ordinary playing cards. Sampling is one at a time with replacement: multiplication rule with independent events.

## Practice Problem 8.4

Suppose we roll a pair of fair dice once. What is the probability of obtaining a 2 on die 1 and a 4 on die 2?

**SOLUTION**

The solution is shown in the following figure. Since there is independence between the dice and the problem asks for a 2 *and* a 4, the multiplication rule with independent events applies. Thus, $p$(a 2 on die 1 and a 4 on die 2) = $p$(a 2 on die 1)$p$(a 4 on die 2). There is one way to get a 2 on die 1, one way to get a 4 on die 2, and six possible outcomes with each die. Therefore, $p$(2 on die 1) = $\frac{1}{6}$, $p$(4 on die 2) = $\frac{1}{6}$, and $p$(2 on die 1 and 4 on die 2) = $\frac{1}{6}(\frac{1}{6}) = \frac{1}{36} = 0.0278$.

$$p(2 \text{ on die 1 and 4 on die 2}) = p(2 \text{ on die 1})p(4 \text{ on die 2})$$

$$= \left(\frac{1}{6}\right)\left(\frac{1}{6}\right) = \frac{1}{36} = 0.0278$$

*Events favorable to A*
*Die 1*

*Events favorable to B*
*Die 2*

*where*    $A$ = a 2 on die 1
            $B$ = a 4 on die 2

## Practice Problem 8.5

If two pennies are flipped once, what is the probability both pennies will turn up heads? Assume that the pennies are fair coins and that a head or tail is the only possible outcome with each coin.

**SOLUTION**

The solution is shown in the accompanying figure. Since the outcome with the first coin has no effect on the outcome of the second coin, there is independence between events. The problem requires a head with the first coin *and* a head with the second coin, so the multiplication rule with independent events is appropriate. Thus, $p$(a head with the first penny and a

*(continued)*

head with the second penny) = $p$(a head with first penny)$p$(a head with second penny). Since there is only one way to get a head with each coin and two possibilities with each coin (a head or a tail), $p$(a head with first penny) = $\frac{1}{2}$ and $p$(a head with second penny) = $\frac{1}{2}$. Thus, $p$(head with first penny and head with second penny) = $\frac{1}{2}(\frac{1}{2}) = \frac{1}{4} = 0.2500$.

$$p(A \text{ and } B) = p(A)p(B)$$

$$\begin{bmatrix} p\text{(a head with 1st penny and} \\ \text{a head with 2nd penny)} \end{bmatrix} = p\text{(a head with 1st penny)}p\text{(a head with 2nd penny)}$$

$$= \left(\frac{1}{2}\right)\left(\frac{1}{2}\right) = 0.2500$$

*where*  $A$ = a head with 1st penny          *Events favorable to A*
     $B$ = a head with 2nd penny          *First penny*

*Events favorable to B*
*Second penny*

## Practice Problem 8.6

Suppose you are randomly sampling from a bag of fruit. The bag contains four apples, six oranges, and five peaches. If you sample two fruits, one at a time, with replacement, what is the probability you will get an orange and an apple in that order?

### SOLUTION

The solution is shown in the accompanying figure. Since there is independence between draws (sampling is with replacement) and we want an orange *and* an apple, the multiplication rule with independent events applies. Thus, $p$(an orange on first draw and an apple on second draw) = $p$(an orange on first draw)$p$(an apple on second draw). Since there are 6 oranges and 15 pieces of fruit in the bag, $p$(an orange on first draw) = $\frac{6}{15}$. Because the fruit selected on the first draw is replaced before the second draw, it has no effect on the fruit picked on the second draw. There are 4 apples and 15 pieces of fruit, so $p$(an apple on second draw) $= \frac{4}{15}$. Therefore, $p$(an orange on first draw and an apple on second draw) $= \frac{6}{15}(\frac{4}{15}) = 0.1067$.

$$p(A \text{ and } B) = p(A)p(B)$$

$$\begin{bmatrix} p(\text{an orange on 1st draw and} \\ \text{an apple on 2nd draw}) \end{bmatrix} = p(\text{an orange on 1st draw})p(\text{an apple on 2nd draw})$$

$$= \left(\frac{6}{15}\right)\left(\frac{4}{15}\right)$$

$$= \frac{24}{225} = 0.1067$$

*where*    $A$ = an orange on 1st draw
           $B$ = an apple on 2nd draw

*Events favorable to A*
*Oranges*

*Events favorable to B*
*Apples*

## Practice Problem 8.7

Suppose you are randomly sampling 2 individuals from a population of 110 men and women. There are 50 men and 60 women in the population. Sampling is one at a time, with replacement. What is the probability the sample will contain all women?

### SOLUTION

The solution is shown in the accompanying figure. Since the problem requires a woman on the first draw and a woman on the second draw and there is independence between these two events (sampling is with replacement), the multiplication rule with independent events is appropriate.

*(continued)*

Thus, $p$(a woman on first draw and a woman on second draw) $= p$(a woman on first draw)$p$(a woman on second draw). There are 60 women and 110 people in the population, so $p$(a woman on first draw) $= \frac{60}{110}$, and $p$(a woman on second draw) $= \frac{60}{110}$. Therefore, $p$(a woman on first draw and a woman on second draw) $= \frac{60}{110}\left(\frac{60}{110}\right) = \frac{3600}{12,100} = 0.2975$.

$$\begin{bmatrix} p(\text{a woman on 1st draw and} \\ \text{a woman on 2nd draw}) \end{bmatrix} = p(\text{a woman on 1st draw})p(\text{a woman on 2nd draw})$$

$$= \left(\frac{60}{110}\right)\left(\frac{60}{110}\right)$$

$$= \frac{3600}{12,100} = 0.2975$$

*where*  $A$ = a woman on 1st draw
  $B$ = a woman on 2nd draw

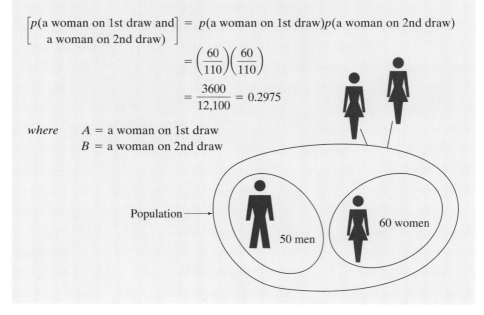

The multiplication rule with independent events also applies to situations in which there are more than two events. In such cases, the probability of the joint occurrence of the events is equal to the product of the individual probabilities of each event. In equation form,

$$p(A \text{ and } B \text{ and } C \text{ and } \ldots \text{ and } Z) = p(A)p(B)p(C) \cdots p(Z)$$

*multiplication rule with more than two independent events*

To illustrate the use of this equation, let's suppose that instead of sampling 2 individuals from the population in Practice Problem 8.7, you are going to sample 4 persons. Otherwise the problem is the same. The population is composed of 50 men and 60 women. As before, sampling is one at a time, with replacement. What is the probability you will pick 3 women and 1 man in that order? The solution is shown in Figure 8.4. Since the problem requires a woman on the first *and* second *and* third draws *and* a man on the fourth draw and sampling is with replacement, the multiplication rule with more than two independent events is appropriate. This rule is just like the multiplication rule with two independent events except there are more terms to multiply. Thus, $p$(a woman on first draw and a woman on second draw and a woman on third draw and a man on fourth draw) $= p$(a woman on first draw)$p$(a woman on second draw)$p$(a woman on third draw)$p$(a man on fourth draw). There are 60 women, 50 men, and 110 people in the population. Since sampling is with replacement, $p$(a woman on first draw) $= \frac{60}{110}$, $p$(a woman on second draw) $= \frac{60}{110}$, $p$(a woman on third draw) $= \frac{60}{110}$, and $p$(a man on fourth draw) $= \frac{50}{110}$. Thus, $p$(a woman on first draw and a woman on second draw

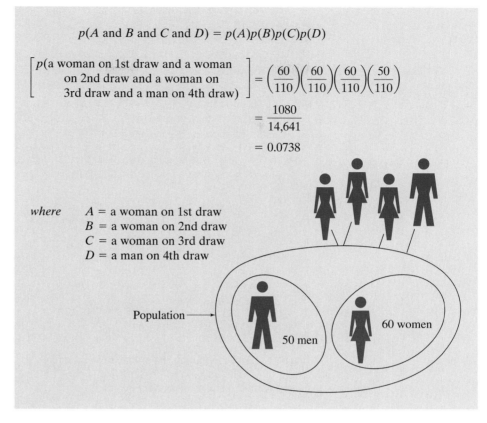

$$p(A \text{ and } B \text{ and } C \text{ and } D) = p(A)p(B)p(C)p(D)$$

$$\begin{bmatrix} p(\text{a woman on 1st draw and a woman} \\ \text{on 2nd draw and a woman on} \\ \text{3rd draw and a man on 4th draw}) \end{bmatrix} = \left(\frac{60}{110}\right)\left(\frac{60}{110}\right)\left(\frac{60}{110}\right)\left(\frac{50}{110}\right)$$

$$= \frac{1080}{14,641}$$

$$= 0.0738$$

*where*  $A$ = a woman on 1st draw
$B$ = a woman on 2nd draw
$C$ = a woman on 3rd draw
$D$ = a man on 4th draw

Population ⟶

50 men

60 women

f i g u r e  8.4  Determining the probability of randomly sampling 3 women and 1 man, in that order, in four draws from a population of 50 men and 60 women. Sampling is one at a time with replacement: multiplication rule with several independent events.

and a woman on third draw and a man on fourth draw) $= \frac{60}{110}\left(\frac{60}{110}\right)\left(\frac{60}{110}\right)\left(\frac{50}{110}\right) = 1080/14,641 = 0.0738$.

**Multiplication rule: Dependent events**  When $A$ and $B$ are dependent, the probability of occurrence of $B$ is affected by the occurrence of $A$. In this case, we cannot simplify the equation for the probability of $A$ and $B$. We must use it in its original form. Thus, if $A$ and $B$ are dependent,

$$p(A \text{ and } B) = p(A)p(B|A) \qquad \textit{multiplication rule with dependent events}$$

Sampling without replacement provides a good illustration for dependent events. Suppose you are going to draw two cards, one at a time, *without* replacement, from a deck of ordinary playing cards. What is the probability both cards will be aces?

The solution is shown in Figure 8.5. We can let $A$ be an ace on the first draw and $B$ be an ace on the second draw. Since sampling is without replacement (whatever card is picked the first time is kept out of the deck), the occurrence of $A$ *does* affect the probability of $B$. $A$ and $B$ are dependent. Since the problem asks for an ace on the first *and* an ace on the second draw, and these events are dependent, the multiplication rule with dependent events is appropriate. Thus, $p(\text{an ace on first draw and an ace on second draw}) = p(\text{an ace on first draw})p(\text{an ace on second draw, given an ace was obtained on first draw})$. For the first draw, there are 4 aces and 52 cards. Therefore, $p(\text{an ace on first draw}) = \frac{4}{52}$.

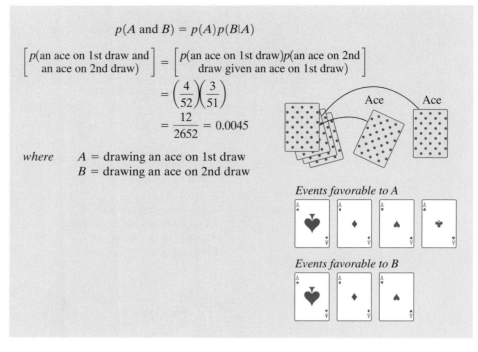

$$p(A \text{ and } B) = p(A)p(B|A)$$

$$\begin{bmatrix} p(\text{an ace on 1st draw and} \\ \text{an ace on 2nd draw}) \end{bmatrix} = \begin{bmatrix} p(\text{an ace on 1st draw})p(\text{an ace on 2nd} \\ \text{draw given an ace on 1st draw}) \end{bmatrix}$$

$$= \left(\frac{4}{52}\right)\left(\frac{3}{51}\right)$$

$$= \frac{12}{2652} = 0.0045$$

*where*    $A$ = drawing an ace on 1st draw
$B$ = drawing an ace on 2nd draw

*Events favorable to A*

*Events favorable to B*

**f i g u r e  8.5**  Determining the probability of randomly picking two aces in two draws from a deck of ordinary playing cards. Sampling is one at a time without replacement: multiplication rule with dependent events.

Since sampling is without replacement, $p$(an ace on second draw given an ace on first draw) = $\frac{3}{51}$. Thus, $p$(an ace on first draw and an ace on second draw) = $\frac{4}{52}\left(\frac{3}{51}\right) = \frac{12}{2652} = 0.0045$.

## Practice Problem 8.8

Suppose you are randomly sampling two fruits, one at a time, from the bag of fruit in Practice Problem 8.6. As before, the bag contains four apples, six oranges, and five peaches. However, this time you are sampling *without* replacement. What is the probability you will get an orange and an apple in that order?

### SOLUTION

The solution is shown in the accompanying figure. Since the problem requires an orange *and* an apple and sampling is without replacement, the multiplication rule with dependent events applies. Thus, $p$(an orange on first draw and an apple on second draw) = $p$(an orange on first draw)$p$(an apple on second draw given an orange was obtained on first draw). On the first draw, there are 6 oranges and 15 fruits. Therefore, $p$(an orange on first draw) $= \frac{6}{15}$. Since sampling is without replacement, $p$(an apple on second draw given an orange on first draw) $= \frac{4}{14}$. Therefore, $p$(an orange on first draw and an apple on second draw) $= \frac{6}{15}\left(\frac{4}{14}\right) = \frac{24}{210} = 0.1143$.

$$p(A \text{ and } B) = p(A)p(B \mid A)$$

$$\begin{bmatrix} p(\text{an orange on 1st draw and} \\ \text{an apple on 2nd draw}) \end{bmatrix} = \begin{bmatrix} p(\text{an orange on 1st draw})p(\text{an apple on} \\ \text{2nd draw given an orange on 1st draw}) \end{bmatrix}$$

$$= \left(\frac{6}{15}\right)\left(\frac{4}{14}\right)$$

$$= \frac{24}{210} = 0.1143$$

*where*   $A =$ an orange on 1st draw
$B =$ an apple on 2nd draw

Orange    Apple

*Events favorable to A*
*Oranges*

*Events favorable to B*
*Apples*

## Practice Problem 8.9

In a particular college class, there are 15 music majors, 24 history majors, and 46 psychology majors. If you randomly sample 2 students from the class, what is the probability they will both be history majors? Sampling is one at a time, without replacement.

### SOLUTION

The solution is shown in the accompanying figure. Since the problem requires a history major on the first draw *and* a history major on the second draw and sampling is without replacement, the multiplication rule with dependent events is appropriate. Thus, $p$(a history major on first draw and a history major on second draw) $= p$(a history major on first draw)$p$(a history major on second draw given a history major was obtained on first draw). On

*(continued)*

the first draw, there were 24 history majors and 85 people in the population. Therefore, $p$(a history major on first draw) $= \frac{24}{85}$. Since sampling is without replacement, $p$(a history major on second draw given a history major on first draw) $= \frac{23}{84}$. Therefore, $p$(a history major on first draw and a history major on second draw) $= \frac{24}{85}(\frac{23}{84}) = \frac{552}{7140} = 0.0773$.

$$p(A \text{ and } B) = p(A)p(B \mid A)$$

$$\begin{bmatrix} p(\text{a history major on 1st draw and} \\ \text{a history major on 2nd draw}) \end{bmatrix} = \begin{bmatrix} p(\text{a history major on 1st draw and})p(\text{a history} \\ \text{major on 2nd draw given a history major} \\ \text{on 1st draw}) \end{bmatrix}$$

$$= \left(\frac{24}{85}\right)\left(\frac{23}{84}\right)$$

$$= \frac{552}{7140} = 0.0773$$

*where*   $A$ = a history major on 1st draw
$B$ = a history major on 2nd draw

Like the multiplication rule with independent events, the multiplication rule with dependent events also applies to situations in which there are more than two events. In such cases, the equation becomes

$$p(A \text{ and } B \text{ and } C \text{ and } \ldots \text{ and } Z) = p(A)p(B|A)p(C|AB) \cdots p(Z|ABC \ldots)$$

*multiplication rule with more than two dependent events*

*where*       $p(A)$ = probability of $A$
$p(B|A)$ = probability of $B$ given $A$ has occurred
$p(C|AB)$ = probability of $C$ given $A$ and $B$ have occurred
$p(Z|ABC \ldots)$ = probability of $Z$ given $A$, $B$, $C$, and all other events have occurred

To illustrate how to use this equation, let's do a problem that involves more than two dependent events. Suppose you are going to sample 4 students from the college class given in Practice Problem 8.9. In that class, there were 15 music majors, 24 history majors, and 46 psychology majors. If sampling is one at a time, without replacement, what is the probability you will obtain 4 history majors?

The solution is shown in Figure 8.6. Since the problem requires a history major on the first *and* second *and* third *and* fourth draws and sampling is without replacement, the multiplication rule with more than two dependent events is

$$p(A \text{ and } B \text{ and } C \text{ and } D) = p(A)p(B|A)p(C|AB)p(D|ABC)$$

$$= \left(\frac{24}{85}\right)\left(\frac{23}{84}\right)\left(\frac{22}{83}\right)\left(\frac{21}{82}\right)$$

$$= \frac{255{,}024}{48{,}594{,}840} = 0.0052$$

*where*   $A$ = a history major on 1st draw
$B$ = a history major on 2nd draw
$C$ = a history major on 3rd draw
$D$ = a history major on 4th draw

History majors

Population

15
music
majors

46
psychology
majors

24
history
majors

**f i g u r e 8.6**   Determining the probability of randomly sampling 4 history majors on four draws from a population of 15 music majors, 24 history majors, and 46 psychology majors. Sampling is one at a time without replacement: multiplication rule with several dependent events.

appropriate. This rule is very much like the multiplication rule with two dependent events, except more multiplying is required. Thus, for this problem, $p$(a history major on first draw and a history major on second draw and a history major on third draw and a history major on fourth draw) = $p$(a history major on first draw)$p$(a history major on second draw given a history major on first draw)$p$(a history major on third draw given a history major on first and second draws)$p$(a history major on fourth draw given a history major on first, second, and third draws). On the first draw, there are 24 history majors and 85 individuals in the population. Thus, $p$(a history major on first draw) = $\frac{24}{85}$. Since sampling is without replacement, $p$(a history major on second draw given a history major on first draw) = $\frac{23}{84}$, $p$(a history major on third draw given a history major on first and second draws) = $\frac{22}{83}$, and $p$(a history major on fourth draw given a history major on first, second, and third draws) = $\frac{21}{82}$. Therefore, $p$(a history major on first draw and a history major on second draw and a history major on third draw and a history major on fourth draw) = $\frac{24}{85}\left(\frac{23}{84}\right)\left(\frac{22}{83}\right)\left(\frac{21}{82}\right)$ = 255,024/48,594,840 = 0.0052.

## Multiplication and Addition Rules

Some situations require that we use both the multiplication and addition rules for their solution. For example, suppose that I am going to roll two fair dice once. What is the probability the sum of the numbers showing on the dice will equal 11? The solution is shown in Figure 8.7. There are two possible outcomes that

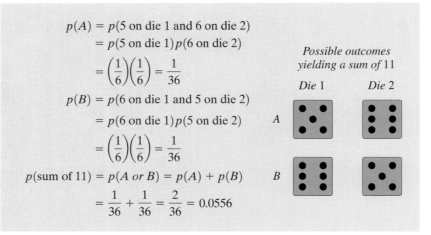

$$p(A) = p(\text{5 on die 1 and 6 on die 2})$$
$$= p(\text{5 on die 1})\,p(\text{6 on die 2})$$
$$= \left(\frac{1}{6}\right)\left(\frac{1}{6}\right) = \frac{1}{36}$$
$$p(B) = p(\text{6 on die 1 and 5 on die 2})$$
$$= p(\text{6 on die 1})\,p(\text{5 on die 2})$$
$$= \left(\frac{1}{6}\right)\left(\frac{1}{6}\right) = \frac{1}{36}$$
$$p(\text{sum of 11}) = p(A \ or \ B) = p(A) + p(B)$$
$$= \frac{1}{36} + \frac{1}{36} = \frac{2}{36} = 0.0556$$

*Possible outcomes yielding a sum of 11*

f i g u r e **8.7** Determining the probability of rolling a sum of 11 in one roll of two fair dice: multiplication and addition rules.

yield a sum of 11 (die 1 = 5 and die 2 = 6, which we shall call outcome *A*; and die 1 = 6 and die 2 = 5, which we shall call outcome *B*). Since the dice are independent, we can use the multiplication rule with independent events to find the probability of each outcome. By using this rule, $p(A) = \frac{1}{6}(\frac{1}{6}) = \frac{1}{36}$, and $p(B) = \frac{1}{6}(\frac{1}{6}) = \frac{1}{36}$. Since either of the outcomes yields a sum of 11, $p(\text{sum of 11})$ $= p(A \ or \ B)$. These outcomes are mutually exclusive, so we can use the addition rule with mutually exclusive events to find $p(A \ or \ B)$. Thus, $p(\text{sum of 11}) = p(A \ or \ B) = p(A) + p(B) = \frac{1}{36} + \frac{1}{36} = \frac{2}{36} = 0.0556$.

Let's try one more problem that involves both the multiplication and addition rules.

## Practice Problem 8.10

Suppose you have arrived in Las Vegas and you are going to try your "luck" on a one-armed bandit (slot machine). In case you are not familiar with slot machines, basically a slot machine has three wheels that rotate independently. Each wheel contains pictures of different objects. Let's assume the one you are playing has seven different fruits on wheel 1: a lemon, a plum, an apple, an orange, a pear, some cherries, and a banana. Wheels 2 and 3 have the same fruits as wheel 1. When the lever is pulled down, the three wheels rotate independently and then come to rest. On the slot machine, there is a window in front of each wheel. The pictures of the fruits pass under the window during rotation. When the wheel stops, one of the fruits from each wheel will be in view. We shall assume that each fruit on a wheel has an equal probability of appearing under the window at the end of rotation. You insert your silver dollar and pull down the lever. What is the probability that two lemons and a pear will appear? Order is not important; all you care about is getting two lemons and a pear, in any order.

**SOLUTION**

The solution is shown in the accompanying figure. There are three possible orders of two lemons and a pear: lemon, lemon, pear; lemon, pear, lemon; and pear, lemon, lemon. Since the wheels rotate independently, we can use the multiplication rule with independent events to determine the probability of each order. Since each fruit is equally likely, $p$(lemon and lemon and pear) $= p$(lemon)$p$(lemon)$p$(pear) $= \frac{1}{7}(\frac{1}{7})(\frac{1}{7}) = \frac{1}{343}$. The same probability also applies to the other two orders. Since the three orders give two lemons and a pear, $p$(two lemons and a pear) $= p$(order 1, 2, or 3). By using the addition rule with independent events, $p$(order 1, 2, or 3) $= \frac{3}{343} = 0.0087$. Thus, the probability of getting two lemons and a pear, without regard to order, equals 0.0087.

$p$(order 1) $= p$(lemon on wheel 1 and lemon on wheel 2 and pear on wheel 3)
           $= p$(lemon on wheel 1)$p$(lemon on wheel 2)$p$(pear on wheel 3)

$$= \left(\frac{1}{7}\right)\left(\frac{1}{7}\right)\left(\frac{1}{7}\right) = \frac{1}{343}$$

$p$(order 2) $= p$(lemon on wheel 1 and pear on wheel 2 and lemon on wheel 3)
           $= p$(lemon on wheel 1)$p$(pear on wheel 2)$p$(lemon on wheel 3)

$$= \left(\frac{1}{7}\right)\left(\frac{1}{7}\right)\left(\frac{1}{7}\right) = \frac{1}{343}$$

$p$(order 3) $= p$(pear on wheel 1 and lemon on wheel 2 and lemon on wheel 3)
           $= p$(pear on wheel 1)$p$(lemon on wheel 2)$p$(lemon on wheel 3)

$$= \left(\frac{1}{7}\right)\left(\frac{1}{7}\right)\left(\frac{1}{7}\right) = \frac{1}{343}$$

(*continued*)

$$\left.\begin{pmatrix} p(2 \text{ lemons} \\ \text{and a pear}) \end{pmatrix}\right) = p(\text{order 1 or 2 or 3}) = p(\text{order 1}) + p(\text{order 2}) + p(\text{order 3})$$

$$= \frac{1}{343} + \frac{1}{343} + \frac{1}{343} = \frac{3}{343} = 0.0087$$

## Probability and Normally Distributed Continuous Variables

So far in our discussion of probability, we have considered variables that have been discrete, such as sampling from a deck of cards or rolling a pair of dice. However, many of the dependent variables that are evaluated in experiments are continuous, not discrete. When a variable is continuous

$$p(A) = \frac{\text{Area under the curve corresponding to } A}{\text{Total area under the curve}} \qquad \textit{probability of A with a} \\ \textit{continuous variable}$$

Often (although not always) these variables are normally distributed, so we shall concentrate our discussion on normally distributed continuous variables.

To illustrate the use of probability with continuous variables that are normally distributed, suppose we have measured the weights of all the sophomore women at your college. Let's assume this is a population set of scores that is normally distributed, with a mean of 120 pounds and a standard deviation of 8 pounds. If we randomly sampled one score from the population, what is the probability it would be equal to or greater than a score of 134?

The population is drawn in Figure 8.8. The mean of 120 and the score of 134 are located on the $X$ axis. The shaded area represents all the scores that are equal to or greater than 134. Since sampling is random, each score has an equal chance of being selected. Thus, the probability of obtaining a score equal to or greater than 134 can be found by determining the proportion of the total scores that are contained in the shaded area. The scores are normally distributed, so we can find

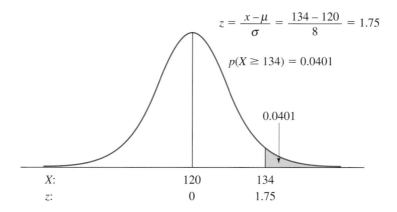

figure 8.8  Probability of obtaining $X \geq 134$ if randomly sampling one score from a normal population, with $\mu = 120$ and $\sigma = 8$.

this proportion by converting the raw score to its $z$-transformed value and then looking up the area in Table A in Appendix D. Thus,

$$z = \frac{X - \mu}{\sigma} = \frac{134 - 120}{8} = \frac{14}{8} = 1.75$$

From Table A, column C,

$$p(X \geq 134) = 0.0401$$

We are sure you will recognize that this type of problem is quite similar to those presented in Chapter 5 when dealing with standard scores. The main difference is that, in this chapter, the problem has been cast in terms of probability rather than asking for the proportion or percentage of scores as was done in Chapter 5. Since you are already familiar with this kind of problem, we don't think it necessary to give a lot of practice problems. However, let's try a couple just to be sure.

## Practice Problem 8.11

Consider the same population of sophomore women just discussed in the text. If one score is randomly sampled from the population, what is the probability it will be equal to or less than 110?

### SOLUTION

The solution is presented in the accompanying figure. The shaded area represents all the scores that are equal to or less than 110. Since sampling is random, each score has an equal chance of being selected. To find $p(X \leq 110)$, first we must transform the raw score of 110 to its $z$ score. Then we can find the proportion of the total scores that are contained in the shaded area by using Table A. Thus,

$$z = \frac{X - \mu}{\sigma} = \frac{110 - 120}{8} = -1.25$$

$$p(X \leq 110) = 0.1056$$

0.1056

| X: | 110 | 120 |
| z: | −1.25 | 0 |

## Practice Problem 8.12

Considering the same population again, what is the probability of randomly sampling a score that is as far or farther from the mean than a score of 138?

### SOLUTION

The solution is shown in the accompanying figure. The score of 138 is 18 units above the mean. Since the problem asks for scores as far or farther from the mean, we must also consider scores that are 18 units or more below the mean. The shaded areas contain all of the scores that are 18 units or more away from the mean. Since sampling is random, each score has an equal chance of being selected. To find $p(X \leq 102 \text{ or } X \geq 138)$, first we must transform the raw scores of 102 and 138 to their z scores. Then we can find the proportion of the total scores that are contained in the shaded areas by using Table A. $p(X \leq 102 \text{ or } X \geq 138)$ equals this proportion. Thus,

$$z = \frac{X - \mu}{\sigma} = \frac{102 - 120}{8} = -\frac{18}{8} \qquad z = \frac{X - \mu}{\sigma} = \frac{138 - 120}{8} = \frac{18}{8}$$

$$= -2.25 \qquad\qquad\qquad = 2.25$$

From Table A, column C,

$$p(X \leq 102 \text{ or } X \geq 138) = 0.0122 + 0.0122 = 0.0244$$

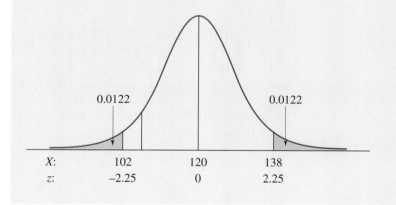

| X: | 102 | 120 | 138 |
| z: | −2.25 | 0 | 2.25 |

# "Not Guilty, I'm a Victim of Coincidence": Gutsy Plea or Truth?

**D**espite a tradition of qualitatively rather than quantitatively based decision making, the legal field is increasingly using statistics as a basis for decisions. The following case from Sweden is an example.

In a Swedish trial, the defendant was contesting a charge of overtime parking. An officer had marked the position of the valves of the front and rear tires of the accused driver's car, according to a clock representation (e.g., front valve to one o'clock and rear valve to six o'clock), in both cases to the nearest hour (see diagram). After the allowed time had elapsed, the car was still there, with the two valves pointing to one and six o'clock as before. The accused was given a parking ticket.

In court, however, he pleaded innocent, claiming that he had left the parking spot in time, but returned to it later, and the valves had just happened to come to rest in the same position as before. The judge, not having taken a basic course in statistics, called in a statistician to evaluate the defendant's claim of coincidence. Is the defendant's claim reasonable? Assume you are the statistician. What would you tell the judge? In formulating your answer, assume independence between the wheels, as did the statistician who advised the judge.

*Answer*    As a statistician, your job is to determine how reasonable the plea of coincidence really is. If we assume the defendant's story is true about leaving and coming back to the parking spot, what is the probability of the two valves returning to their one and six o'clock positions? Since there are 12 possible positions for each valve, assuming independence between the wheels, using the multiplication rule,

$$p(\text{one and six}) = \left(\tfrac{1}{12}\right)\left(\tfrac{1}{12}\right) = \tfrac{1}{144}$$
$$= 0.0069$$

Thus, if coincidence (or chance alone) is at work, the probability of the valves returning to their original positions is about 7 times in 1000. What do you think the judge did when given this information? Believe it or not, the judge acquitted the defendant, saying that if all four wheels had been checked and found to point in the same directions as before ($p = \tfrac{1}{12} \times \tfrac{1}{12} \times \tfrac{1}{12} \times \tfrac{1}{12} = \tfrac{1}{20736} = 0.00005$), then the coincidence claim would have been rejected as too improbable and the defendant convicted. Thus, the judge considered the coincidence explanation as too probable to reject, even though the results would be obtained only 1 out of 144 times if coincidence was at work. Actually, because the wheels do not rotate independently, the formulas used most likely understate somewhat the probability of a chance return to the original position. (How did you do? Can we call on you in the future as a statistical expert to help mete out justice?)

## WHAT IS THE TRUTH?

# Sperm Count Decline—Male or Sampling Inadequacy?

The headline of an article that appeared in 1995 in a leading metropolitan newspaper read, "20-year study shows sperm count decline among fertile men." Excerpts from the article are reproduced here.

*A new study has found a marked decline in sperm counts among fertile men over the past 20 years. . . .*

*The paper, published today in* The New England Journal of Medicine, *was based on data collected over a 20-year period at a* Paris sperm bank. Some experts in the United States took strong exception to the findings. . . .

*The new study, by Dr. Pierre Jouannet of the Center for the Study of the Conservation of Human Eggs and Sperm in Paris, examined semen collected by a sperm bank in Paris beginning in 1973. They report that sperm counts fell by an average of 2.1 percent a year, going from 89 million sperm per milliliter in 1973 to an average of 60 million per milliliter in 1992. At the same time they found the percentages of sperm that moved normally and were properly formed declined by 0.5 to 0.6 of 1 percent a year.*

*The paper is accompanied by an invited editorial by an expert on male infertility, Dr. Richard Sherins, director of the division of andrology at the Genetics and IVF* institute in Fairfax, Va., who said the current studies and several preceding it suffered from methodological flaws that made their data uninterpretable.

Sherins said that the studies did not look at sperm from randomly selected men and that sperm counts and sperm quality vary so much from week to week that it is hazardous to rely on single samples to measure sperm quality, as these studies did.

What do you think? Why might it be important to use samples from randomly selected men rather than from men who deposit their sperm at a sperm bank? Why might large week-to-week variability in sperm counts and sperm quality complicate interpretation of the data?

# WHAT IS THE TRUTH?

## A Sample of a Sample

The following article on polling appeared in a recent issue of *The New York Times* on the Web. I found the article very interesting and hope it is to you as well. The article is presented in its entirety.

### How the 'Typical' Respondent Is Found

**By MICHAEL KAGAY**

*"What kind of people do you call for your polls? You must not be polling anyone around here in Texas."*

*Pollsters receive a lot of calls like this, usually from people who are genuinely puzzled to find that their own views on some controversial issue, or even the views of most people in their particular locality, are not in the majority nationwide—according to the polls.*

*But most pollsters take enormous care to ensure a representative sample of respondents to their polls. Good question writing may still be an art, and skillful interviewing may be a craft, but proper sampling is what puts the science into polling.*

*Random Digit Dialing, or RDD, is the standard sampling procedure in use throughout the polling profession today. The objective is to give every residential telephone*

*number in the United States an equal chance of being called for an interview. Almost every polling organization uses some form of RDD.*

*The New York Times/CBS News Poll, for example, relies on the GENESYS system, developed and maintained by Marketing Systems Group of Philadelphia. That system consists of a database of over 42,000 residential telephone exchanges throughout the United States, updated every few months to include newly created area codes and exchanges.*

*That system also contains computer software to draw a random sample of those exchanges for each new poll, and to randomly make up the last four digits of each individual telephone number to be called.*

*That random choice from the universe of all possible telephone numbers is what guarantees the representativeness of the sample of households called for a poll.*

*In the case of the poll the caller was inquiring about, Texans constitute about seven percent of all Americans, but they formed six percent of the respondents in that particular poll. Pretty close to the mark, but a little bit short.*

#### Pursuing Respondents Vigorously

*Some types of people are harder to reach and to interview than others. How can bias in the results be reduced or avoided?*

*The first remedy is vigorous pursuit of the household and then of the designated individual respondent within the household.*

*Most polls make multiple calls to the household over the course of the poll, which often includes daytime calling, nighttime calling, weekdays and weekends. Interviewers leave messages on answering machines about why they are calling, make appointments when the designated individual is not at home, and offer to call back at a time more convenient to the respondent.*

*For respondents who refuse to be interviewed, many polls also employ a special squad of interviewers who make an additional callback to try to convert the refusal into a completed interview. That task takes special skills—the ability to convince the respondent of the importance of the interview and the right personality—an ability to tolerate possible rejection.*

#### Weighting or Balancing After the Interview

*Still, just about every poll contains a few too many women, retired people, college graduates, and whites— compared to what the Census Bureau calculates the U.S. population contains at any given time.*

*This occurs because people vary in how frequently they are at home, how willing they are to talk to strangers*

*(continued)*

## WHAT IS THE TRUTH?

# A Sample of a Sample *(continued)*

*on the phone, and how confident they feel in sharing their views about political and social issues.*

*Therefore, most polls mildly weight their respondents—slightly upping the proportion of men, younger people, those with less education, and racial minorities—to bring the proportions into proper balance. Some pollsters refer to this procedure as balancing.*

*At the same time the* Times/CBS News Poll *also takes the opportunity to make a slight adjustment for the size of household and the number of telephone lines into the residence. This equalizes the probability of selection for individuals in situations where some households have multiple telephone lines and when some households have more adult residents than others.*

*All these minor adjustments serve to make a good sample even better, and more representative.*

### A Sample That Looks Like America

*So what do the respondents in a typical* New York Times/CBS News Poll *look like? After all the random dialing, the callbacks, the refusal conversion, and the weighting, here is what a typical poll consists of:*

- *In terms of geography, respondents are 22 percent living in the northeast, 33 percent in the south, 24 percent in the mid-west, and 21 percent in the west.*
- *In terms of gender, they are 47 percent men and 53 percent women.*
- *In terms of race, they are 80 percent white, 11 percent black, 1 percent Asian, and 6 percent other.*
- *In education, they are 24 percent college graduates, another 27 percent with some college or trade schooling, 37 percent who did not go beyond high school, and 12 percent who did not graduate from high school.*
- *In politics the mood shifts from time to time, but recently 27 percent consider themselves Republicans, while 36 percent think of themselves as Democrats, and another 30 percent call themselves Independents.*
- *In political philosophy, 20 percent typically call themselves liberals, while 42 percent call themselves moderates, and 32 percent call themselves conservatives.*

*And that's a sample that pretty much reflects America.*

*Or, at least, English-speaking America, for most national polls today are conducted only in English. That is one limitation of polls that must be kept in mind, as the Spanish-speaking population in the U.S. grows. And that may explain why the* Times/CBS News Poll *was a little bit short on Texans in that poll the caller inquired about; Texas is a state with a large Spanish-speaking population.*

*Polls also have other limitations and problems, and future Poll Watch columns will touch on these, too.*

*Source:* Copyright © 1999 by the New York Times Co. Reprinted by permission.

## SUMMARY

In this chapter, we have discussed the topics of random sampling and probability. A random sample is defined as a sample that has been selected from a population by a process that ensures that (1) each possible sample of a given size has an equal chance of being selected and (2) all members of the population have an equal chance of being selected into the sample. After defining and discussing the importance of random sampling, we described various methods for obtaining a random sample. In the last section on random sampling, we discussed sampling with and without replacement.

In presenting probability, we pointed out that probability may be approached from two viewpoints: *a priori* and *a posteriori*. According to the *a priori* view, $p(A)$ is defined as

$$p(A) = \frac{\text{Number of events classifiable as } A}{\text{Total number of possible events}}$$

From an *a posteriori* standpoint, $p(A)$ is defined as

$$p(A) = \frac{\text{Number of times } A \text{ has occurred}}{\text{Total number of occurrences}}$$

Since probability is fundamentally a proportion, it ranges from 0.00 to 1.00. Next, we presented two probability rules necessary for understanding inferential statistics: the addition rule and the multiplication rule. Assuming there are two events ($A$ and $B$), the addition rule gives the probability of $A$ or $B$, whereas the multiplication rule gives the probability of $A$ and $B$. The addition rule states the following:

$$p(A \text{ or } B) = p(A) + p(B) - p(A \text{ and } B)$$

If the events are mutually exclusive,

$$p(A \text{ or } B) = p(A) + p(B)$$

If the events are mutually exclusive and exhaustive,

$$p(A) + p(B) = 1.00$$

The multiplication rule states the following:

$$p(A \text{ and } B) = p(A)p(B \mid A)$$

If the events are mutually exclusive,

$$p(A \text{ and } B) = 0$$

If the events are independent,

$$p(A \text{ and } B) = p(A)p(B)$$

If the events are dependent, we must use the general equation

$$p(A \text{ and } B) = p(A)p(B \mid A)$$

In addition, we discussed (1) the generalization of these equations to situations in which there were more than two events and (2) situations that required both the addition and multiplication rules for their solution. Finally, we discussed the probability of $A$ with continuous variables and described how to find $p(A)$ when the variable was both normally distributed and continuous. The equation for determining the probability of $A$ when the variable is continuous is

$$p(A) = \frac{\text{Area under the curve corresponding to } A}{\text{Total area under the curve}}$$

## IMPORTANT TERMS

Addition rule (p. 170)
*A posteriori* (p. 168)
*A priori* (p. 168)
Exhaustive set of events (p. 174)
Independence of two events
   (p. 175)

Multiplication rule (p. 175)
Mutually exclusive events
   (p. 170)
Probability (p. 168)
Probability of occurrence of $A$ or $B$
   (p. 170)

Probability of occurrence of both $A$
   and $B$ (p. 175)
Random sample (p. 164)
Sampling with replacement (p. 167)
Sampling without replacement
   (p. 167)

## QUESTIONS AND PROBLEMS

1. Define or identify each term in the Important Terms section.
2. What two purposes does random sampling serve?

3. Assume you want to form a random sample of 20 subjects from a population of 400 individuals. Sampling will be without replacement, and you plan to use Table J in Appendix D to accomplish

the randomization. Explain how you would use the table to select the sample.

4. A developmental psychologist is interested in assessing the "emotional intelligence" of college students. The experimental design calls for administering a questionnaire that measures emotional intelligence to a sample of 100 undergraduate student volunteers who are enrolled in an introductory psychology course currently being taught at her university. Assume this is the only sample being used for this study and discuss the adequacy of the sample.

5. What is the difference between *a priori* and *a posteriori* probability?

6. The addition rule gives the probability of occurrence of any one of several events, whereas the multiplication rule gives the probability of the joint or successive occurrence of several events. Is this statement correct? Explain, using examples to illustrate your explanation.

7. When solving problems involving the multiplication rule, is it useful to distinguish among three conditions? What are these conditions? Why is it useful to distinguish among them?

8. What is the definition of probability when the variable is continuous?

9. Which of the following are examples of independent events?
    a. Obtaining a 3 and a 4 in one roll of two fair dice
    b. Obtaining an ace and a king in that order by drawing twice without replacement from a deck of cards
    c. Obtaining an ace and a king in that order by drawing twice with replacement from a deck of cards
    d. A cloudy sky followed by rain
    e. A full moon and eating a hamburger

10. Which of the following are examples of mutually exclusive events?
    a. Obtaining a 4 and a 7 in one draw from a deck of ordinary playing cards
    b. Obtaining a 3 and a 4 in one roll of two fair dice
    c. Being male and becoming pregnant
    d. Obtaining a 1 and an even number in one roll of a fair die
    e. Getting married and remaining a bachelor

11. Which of the following are examples of exhaustive events?
    a. Flipping a coin and obtaining a head or a tail (edge not allowed)
    b. Rolling a die and obtaining a 2

    c. Taking an exam and either passing or failing
    d. Going out on a date and having a good time

12. At the beginning of the baseball season in a particular year, the odds that the New York Yankees will win the American League pennant are 3 to 2.
    a. What are the odds that the Yankees will lose the pennant?
    b. What is the probability that the Yankees will win the pennant? Express your answer as a decimal.
    c. What is the probability that the Yankees will lose the pennant? Express your answer as a decimal. other

13. If you draw a single card once from a deck of ordinary playing cards, what is the probability that it will be
    a. The ace of diamonds?
    b. A 10?
    c. A queen or a heart?
    d. A 3 or a black card? other

14. If you roll two fair dice once, what is the probability that you will obtain
    a. A 2 on die 1 and a 5 on die 2?
    b. A 2 and a 5 without regard to which die has the 2 or 5?
    c. At least one 2 or one 5?
    d. A sum of 7? other

15. If you are randomly sampling one at a time with replacement from a bag that contains eight blue marbles, seven red marbles, and five green marbles, what is the probability of obtaining
    a. A blue marble in one draw from the bag?
    b. Three blue marbles in three draws from the bag?
    c. A red, a green, and a blue marble in that order in three draws from the bag?
    d. At least two red marbles in three draws from the bag? other

16. Answer the same questions as in Problem 15, except sampling is one at a time without replacement. other

17. You are playing the one-armed bandit (slot machine) described in Practice Problem 8.10, p. 186. There are three wheels, and on each wheel there is a picture of a lemon, a plum, an apple, an orange, a pear, cherries, and a banana (seven different pictures). You insert your silver dollar and pull down the lever. What is the probability that
    a. Three oranges will appear?
    b. Two oranges and a banana will appear, without regard to order?
    c. At least two oranges will appear? other

18. You want to call a friend on the telephone. You remember the first three digits of her phone number, but you have forgotten the last four digits. What is the probability that you will get the correct number merely by guessing once? other

19. You are planning to make a "killing" at the race track. In a particular race, there are seven horses entered. If the horses are all equally matched, what is the probability of your correctly picking the winner and runner-up? other

20. A gumball dispenser has 38 orange gumballs, 30 purple ones, and 18 yellow ones. The dispenser operates such that one quarter delivers 1 gumball.
    a. Using three quarters, what is the probability of obtaining 3 gumballs in the order orange, purple, orange?
    b. Using one quarter, what is the probability of obtaining 1 gumball that is either purple or yellow?
    c. Using three quarters, what is the probability that of the 3 gumballs obtained, exactly 1 will be purple and 1 will be yellow? other

21. If two cards are randomly drawn from a deck of ordinary playing cards, one at a time, with replacement, what is the probability of obtaining at least one ace? other

22. A state lottery is paying $1 million to the holder of the ticket with the correct eight-digit number. Tickets cost $1 apiece. If you buy one ticket, what is the probability you will win? Assume there is only one ticket for each possible eight-digit number and the winning number is chosen by a random process. other

23. Given a population comprised of 30 bats, 15 gloves, and 60 balls, if sampling is random and one at a time without replacement,
    a. What is the probability of obtaining a glove if one object is sampled from the population?
    b. What is the probability of obtaining a bat and a ball in that order if two objects are sampled from the population?
    c. What is the probability of obtaining a bat, a glove, and a bat in that order if three objects are sampled from the population? other

24. A distribution of scores is normally distributed with a mean $\mu = 85$ and a standard deviation $\sigma = 4.6$. If one score is randomly sampled from the distribution, what is the probability that it will be
    a. Greater than 96?
    b. Between 90 and 97?
    c. Less than 88? other

25. Assume the IQ scores of the students at your university are normally distributed, with $\mu = 115$ and $\sigma = 8$. If you randomly sample one score from this distribution, what is the probability it will be
    a. Higher than 130?
    b. Between 110 and 125?
    c. Lower than 100? cognitive

26. A standardized test measuring mathematics proficiency in sixth graders is administered nationally. The results show a normal distribution of scores, with $\mu = 50$ and $\sigma = 5.8$. If one score is randomly sampled from this population, what is the probability it will be
    a. Higher than 62?
    b. Between 40 and 65?
    c. Lower than 45? education

27. Assume we are still dealing with the population of Question 24. If, instead of randomly sampling from the population, the single score was sampled, using a nonrandom process, would that affect any of the answers to Problem 24 part **a, b,** or **c**? Explain. other

28. An ethologist is interested in how long it takes a certain species of water shrew to catch its prey. On 20 occasions each day, he lets a dragonfly loose inside the cage of a shrew and times how long it takes until the shrew catches the dragonfly. After months of research, the ethologist concludes that the mean prey-catching time was 30 seconds, the standard deviation was 5.5 seconds, and the scores were normally distributed. Based on the shrew's past record, what is the probability
    a. It will catch a dragonfly in less than 18 seconds?
    b. It will catch a dragonfly in between 22 and 45 seconds?
    c. It will take longer than 40 seconds to catch a dragonfly? biological

29. An instructor at the U.S. Navy's underwater demolition school believes he has developed a new technique for staying under water longer. The school commandant gives him permission to try his technique with a student who has been randomly selected from the current class. As part of their qualifying exam, all students are tested to see how long they can stay under water without an air tank. Past records show that the scores are normally distributed with a mean $\mu = 130$ seconds and a standard deviation $\sigma = 14$ seconds. If the new technique has no additional effect, what

is the probability that the randomly selected student will stay under water for

a. More than 150 seconds?

b. Between 115 and 135 seconds?

c. Less than 90 seconds? education

30. If you are randomly sampling two scores one at a time with replacement from a population comprised of the scores 2, 3, 4, 5, and 6, what is the probability that

a. The mean of the sample ($\overline{X}$) will equal 6.0?

b. $\overline{X} \geq 5.5$?

c. $\overline{X} \leq 2.0$?

*Hint*: All of the possible samples of size 2 are listed on p. XXX. other

## NOTES

8.1 We realize that if the process ensures that each possible sample of a given size has an equal chance of being selected, then it also ensures that all the members of the population have an equal chance of being selected into the sample. We included the latter statement in the definition because we believed it is sufficiently important to deserve this special emphasis.

### BOOK COMPANION WEBSITE

Go to www.thomsonedu.com/psychology/pagano for:

- Flash cards for review of terms
- Chapter quiz
- Statistical workshops
- And more

### WebTUTOR

Available via WebTutor for this chapter:

- Detailed chapter outline
- *Know and Be Able To Do* section
- Drag & Drop game for review of terms
- Flash cards for review of terms
- Audio flash cards for MP3 player
- More practice problems using computational equations
- Chapter quiz

# Binomial Distribution

CHAPTER **9**

## INTRODUCTION

In Chapter 10, we'll discuss the topic of hypothesis testing. This topic is a very important one. It forms the basis for most of the material taken up in the remainder of the textbook. For reasons explained in Chapter 10, we've chosen to introduce the concepts of hypothesis testing by using a simple inference test called the sign test. However, to understand and use the sign test, we must first discuss a probability distribution called the binomial distribution.

## DEFINITION AND ILLUSTRATION OF THE BINOMIAL DISTRIBUTION

The binomial distribution may be defined as follows:

*The **binomial distribution** is a probability distribution that results when the following five conditions are met: (1) There is a series of N trials; (2) on each trial, there are only two possible outcomes; (3) on each trial, the two possible outcomes are mutually exclusive; (4) there is independence between the outcomes of each trial; and (5) the probability of each possible outcome on any trial stays the same from trial to trial. When these requirements are met, the binomial distribution tells us each possible outcome of the N trials and the probability of getting each of these outcomes.*

Let's use coin flipping as an illustration for generating the binomial distribution. Suppose we flip a fair or unbiased penny once. Suppose further that we restrict the possible outcomes at the end of the flip to either a head or a tail. You will recall from Chapter 8 that a fair coin means the probability of a head with the coin equals the probability of a tail. Since there are only two possible outcomes in one flip,

$$p(\text{head}) = p(H) = \frac{\text{Number of outcomes classifiable as heads}}{\text{Total number of outcomes}}$$

$$= \frac{1}{2} = 0.5000$$

$$p(\text{tail}) = p(T) = \frac{\text{Number of outcomes classifiable as tails}}{\text{Total number of outcomes}}$$

$$= \frac{1}{2} = 0.5000$$

Now suppose we flip two pennies that are unbiased. The flip of each penny is considered a trial. Thus, with two pennies, there are two trials ($N = 2$). The possible outcomes of flipping two pennies are given in Table 9.1. There are four possible outcomes: one in which there are 2 heads (row 1), two in which there are 1 head and 1 tail (rows 2 and 3), and one in which there are 2 tails (row 4).

Next, let's determine the probability of getting each of these outcomes due to chance. If chance alone is operating, then each of the outcomes is equally likely. Thus,

$$p(2\,\text{heads}) = p(HH) = \frac{\text{Number of outcomes classifiable as 2 heads}}{\text{Total number of outcomes}}$$

$$= \frac{1}{4} = 0.2500$$

$$p(1\,\text{head}) = p(HT\,\text{or}\,TH) = \frac{\text{Number of outcomes classifiable as 1 head}}{\text{Total number of outcomes}}$$

$$= \frac{2}{4} = 0.5000$$

$$p(0\,\text{head}) = p(TT) = \frac{\text{Number of outcomes classifiable as 0 heads}}{\text{Total number of outcomes}}$$

$$= \frac{1}{4} = 0.2500$$

**t a b l e  9.1**  All possible outcomes of flipping
two coins once

| Row No. | Penny 1 | Penny 2 | No. of Outcomes |
|---------|---------|---------|-----------------|
| 1 | *H* | *H* | 1 |
| 2 | *H* | *T* | 2 |
| 3 | *T* | *H* | |
| 4 | *T* | *T* | 1 |
| | | Total outcomes | 4 |

You should note that we could have also found these probabilities from the multiplication and addition rules. For example, $p(1 \text{ head})$ could have been found from a combination of the addition and multiplication rules as follows:

$$p(1 \text{ head}) = p(HT \text{ or } TH)$$

Using the multiplication rule, we obtain

$$p(HT) = p(\text{head on coin 1 and tail on coin 2})$$
$$= p(\text{head on coin 1})p(\text{tail on coin 2})$$
$$= \tfrac{1}{2}\left(\tfrac{1}{2}\right) = \tfrac{1}{4}$$
$$p(TH) = p(\text{tail on coin 1 and head on coin 2})$$
$$= p(\text{tail on coin 1})p(\text{head on coin 2})$$
$$= \tfrac{1}{2}\left(\tfrac{1}{2}\right) = \tfrac{1}{4}$$

Using the addition rule, we obtain

$$p(1 \text{ head}) = p(HT \text{ or } TH)$$
$$= p(HT) + p(TH)$$
$$= \tfrac{1}{4} + \tfrac{1}{4} = \tfrac{2}{4} = 0.5000$$

Next, suppose we increase $N$ from 2 to 3. The possible outcomes of flipping three unbiased pennies once are shown in Table 9.2. This time there are eight possible outcomes: one way to get 3 heads (row 1), three ways to get 2 heads and 1 tail (rows 2, 3, and 4), three ways to get 1 head and 2 tails (rows 5, 6, and 7), and one way to get 0 heads (row 8). Since each outcome is equally likely,

$$p(3 \text{ heads}) = \tfrac{1}{8} = 0.1250$$
$$p(2 \text{ heads}) = \tfrac{3}{8} = 0.3750$$
$$p(1 \text{ head}) = \tfrac{3}{8} = 0.3750$$
$$p(0 \text{ heads}) = \tfrac{1}{8} = 0.1250$$

The distributions resulting from flipping one, two, or three fair pennies are shown in Table 9.3. These are binomial distributions because they are probability distributions that have been generated by a situation in which there is a series of trials ($N = 1, 2,$ or 3), where on each trial there are only two possible outcomes (head or tail), on each trial the possible outcomes are mutually exclusive (if it's a table 9.2   All possible outcomes of flipping three pennies once

| Row No. | Penny 1 | Penny 2 | Penny 3 | No. of Outcomes |
|---------|---------|---------|---------|-----------------|
| 1 | H | H | H | 1 |
| 2 | H | H | T | |
| 3 | H | T | H | 3 |
| 4 | T | H | H | |
| 5 | T | T | H | |
| 6 | T | H | T | 3 |
| 7 | H | T | T | |
| 8 | T | T | T | 1 |
| | | | Total outcomes | 8 |

table 9.3   Binomial distribution for coin flipping when the number of coins equals 1, 2, or 3

| N | Possible Outcomes | Probability |
|---|-------------------|-------------|
| 1 | 1 H | 0.5000 |
| | 0 H | 0.5000 |
| 2 | 2 H | 0.2500 |
| | 1 H | 0.5000 |
| | 0 H | 0.2500 |
| 3 | 3 H | 0.1250 |
| | 2 H | 0.3750 |
| | 1 H | 0.3750 |
| | 0 H | 0.1250 |

head, it cannot be a tail), there is independence between trials (there is independence between the outcomes of each coin), and the probability of a head or tail on any trial stays the same from trial to trial. Note that each distribution gives two pieces of information: (1) all possible outcomes of the $N$ trials and (2) the probability of getting each of the outcomes.

## GENERATING THE BINOMIAL DISTRIBUTION FROM THE BINOMIAL EXPANSION

We could continue this enumeration process for larger values of $N$, but it becomes too laborious. It would indeed be a dismal prospect if we had to use enumeration for every value of $N$. Think about what happens when $N$ gets to 15. With 15 pennies, there are $(2)^{15} = 32,768$ different ways that the 15 coins could fall. Fortunately, there is a mathematical expression that allows us to generate in a simple way everything we've been considering. The expression is called the *binomial expansion*. The binomial expansion is given by

$$(P + Q)^N \qquad \textit{binomial expansion}$$

*where*    $P$ = probability of one of the two possible outcomes on a trial

$Q$ = probability of the other possible outcome

$N$ = number of trials

To generate the possible outcomes and associated probabilities we arrived at in the previous coin-flipping experiments, all we need to do is expand the expression $(P + Q)^N$ for the number of coins in the experiment and evaluate each term in the expansion. For example, if there are two coins, $N = 2$ and

$$2\,P \; events \qquad 1\,P \; and \; 1\,Q \; event \qquad 2\,Q \; events$$

$$(P + Q)^N = (P + Q)^2 = P^2 + 2P^1Q^1 + Q^2$$

The terms $P^2, 2P^1Q^1$, and $Q^2$ represent all the possible outcomes of flipping two coins once.

*The letters of each term ($P$ or $PQ$ or $Q$) tell us the kinds of events that comprise the outcome, the exponent of each letter tells us how many of that kind of event there are in the outcome, and the coefficient of each term tells us how many ways there are of obtaining the outcome.*

Thus,

1. $P^2$ indicates that one possible outcome is composed of two $P$ events. The $P$ alone tells us this outcome is composed entirely of $P$ events. The exponent 2 indicates there are two of this kind of event. If we associate $P$ with heads, $P^2$ tells us one possible outcome is two heads.
2. $2P^1Q^1$ indicates that another possible outcome is one $P$ and one $Q$ event, or one head and one tail. The coefficient 2 tells us there are two ways to obtain one $P$ and one $Q$ event.
3. $Q^2$ represents an outcome of two $Q$ events, or two tails (zero heads).

The probability of getting each of these possible outcomes is found by evaluating their respective terms using the numerical values of $P$ and $Q$. If the coins are fair, then $P = Q = 0.50$. Thus,

$$p(2 \text{ heads}) = P^2 = (0.50)^2 = 0.2500$$
$$p(1 \text{ head}) = 2P^1Q^1 = 2(0.50)(0.50) = 0.5000$$
$$p(0 \text{ heads}) = Q^2 = (0.50)^2 = 0.2500$$

These results are the same as those obtained by enumeration. Note that in using the binomial expansion to find the probability of each possible outcome, we do not add the terms but use them separately. At this point, it probably seems much easier to use enumeration than the binomial expansion. However, the situation reverses itself quickly as $N$ gets larger.

Let's do one more example, this time with $N = 3$. As before, we need to expand $(P + Q)^N$ and evaluate each term in the expansion using $P = Q = 0.50$.[*] Thus,

$$(P + Q)^N = (P + Q)^3 = P^3 + 3P^2Q + 3PQ^2 + Q^3$$

The terms $P^3, 3P^2Q, 3PQ^2$, and $Q^3$ represent all of the possible outcomes of flipping three pennies once. $P^3$ tells us there are three $P$ events, or 3 heads. The term $3P^2Q$ indicates that this outcome has two $P$ events and one $Q$ event, or 2 heads

---

[*]See Note 9.1 for the general equation to expand $(P + Q)^N$.

and 1 tail. The term $3PQ^2$ represents one $P$ event and two $Q$ events, or 1 head and 2 tails. Finally, the term $Q^3$ designates three $Q$ events and zero $P$ events, or 3 tails and 0 heads. We can find the probability of each of these outcomes by evaluation of their respective terms. Since each coin is a fair coin, $P = Q = 0.50$. Thus,

$$p(3 \text{ heads}) = P^3 = (0.50)^3 = 0.1250$$
$$p(2 \text{ heads}) = 3P^2Q = 3(0.50)^2(0.50) = 0.3750$$
$$p(1 \text{ head}) = 3PQ^2 = 3(0.50)(0.50)^2 = 0.3750$$
$$p(0 \text{ heads}) = Q^3 = (0.50)^3 = 0.1250$$

These are the same results we derived previously by enumeration.

The binomial distribution may be generated for any $N$, $P$, and $Q$ by using the binomial expansion. We have graphed the binomial distributions for $N = 3, 8$, and 15 in Figure 9.1. $P = Q = 0.50$ for each of these distributions.

Note that (1) with $P = 0.50$, the binomial distribution is symmetrical; (2) it has two tails (i.e., it tails off as we go from the center toward either end); (3) it involves a discrete variable (e.g., we can't have $2\frac{1}{2}$ heads); and (4) as $N$ increases, the binomial distribution gets closer to the shape of a normal curve.

## USING THE BINOMIAL TABLE

Although in principle any problem involving binomial data can be answered by directly substituting into the binomial expansion, mathematicians have saved us the work. They have solved the binomial expansion for many values of $N$ and reported the results in tables. One such table is Table B in Appendix D. This table gives the binomial distribution for values of $N$ up to 20. Glancing at Table B (p. 533), you observe that $N$ (the number of trials) is given in the first column and the possible outcomes are given in the second column, which is headed by "No. of $P$ or $Q$ Events." The rest of the columns contain probability entries for various values of $P$ or $Q$. The values of $P$ or $Q$ are given at the top of each column. Thus, the second column contains probability values for $P$ or $Q = 0.10$ and the last column has the values for $P$ or $Q = 0.50$. In practice, any problem involving binomial data can be solved by looking up the appropriate probability in this table. This, of course, applies only for $N \leq 20$ and the $P$ or $Q$ values given in the table.

The reader should note that Table B can be used to solve problems in terms of $P$ or $Q$. Thus, with the exception of the first column, the column headings are given in terms of $P$ or $Q$. To emphasize which we are using ($P$ or $Q$) in a given problem, if we are entering the table under $P$ and the number of $P$ events, we shall refer to the second column as "number of $P$ events" and the remaining column headings as "$P$" probability values. If we are entering Table B under $Q$ and the number of $Q$ events, we shall refer to the second column heading as "number of $Q$ events" and the rest of the column headings as "$Q$" probability values. Let's now see how to use this table to solve problems involving binomial situations.

**example**

If I flip three unbiased coins once, what is the probability of getting 2 heads and 1 tail? Assume each coin can only be a head or tail.

**SOLUTION**

In this problem, $N$ is the number of coins, which equals 3. We can let $P$ equal the probability of a head in one flip of any coin. The coins are unbiased, so $P = 0.50$. Since we want to determine the probability of getting 2 heads, the number of *P* events equals 2. Having determined the foregoing, all we need do is enter Table B under *N* = 3. Next, we locate the 2 in the number of *P* events column. The answer is found where the row containing the 2 intersects the column headed by *P* = 0.50. This is shown in Table 9.4. Thus,

t a b l e  9.4  Table B entry

| *N* | No. of *P* Events | *P* **0.50** |
|---|---|---|
| 3 | 2 | 0.3750 |

$$p(2 \text{ heads and 1 tail}) = 0.3750$$

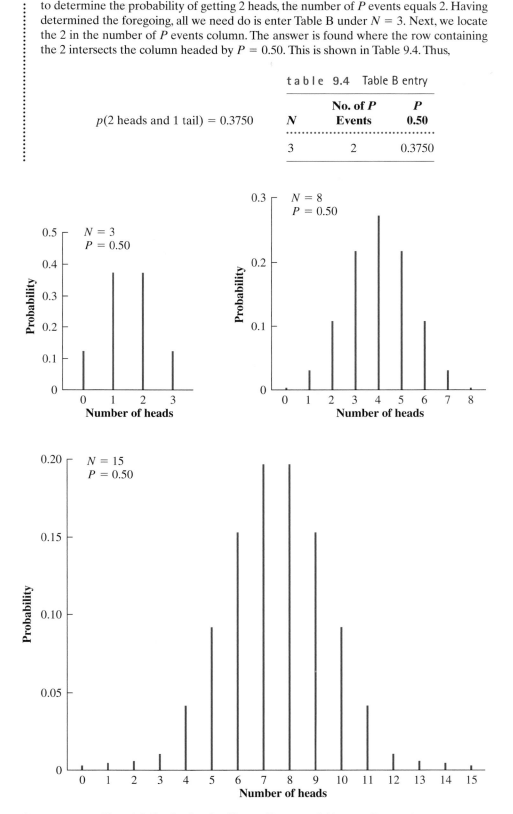

f i g u r e  9.1   Binomial distribution for *N* = 3, *N* = 8, and *N* = 15; *P* = 0.50.

Note that this is the same answer we arrived at before. In fact, if you look at the remaining entries in that column ($P = 0.50$) for $N = 2$ and 3, you will see that they are the same as we arrived at earlier using the binomial expansion—and they ought to be because the table entries are taken from the binomial expansion. Let's try some practice problems using this table.

## Practice Problem 9.1

If six unbiased coins are flipped once, what is the probability of getting
**a.** Exactly 6 heads?
**b.** 4, 5, or 6 heads?

**SOLUTION**

**a.** Given there are six coins, $N = 6$. Again, we can let $P =$ the probability of a head in one flip of any coin. The coins are unbiased, so $P = 0.50$. Since we want to know the probability of getting exactly 6 heads, the number of $P$ events = 6. Entering Table B under $N = 6$, number of $P$ events = 6 and $P = 0.50$, we find

Table B entry

| | $N$ | No. of $P$ Events | $P$ 0.50 |
|---|---|---|---|
| $p$(exactly 6 heads) = 0.0156 | 6 | 6 | 0.0156 |

**b.** Again, $N = 6$ and $P = 0.50$. We can find the probability of 4, 5, and 6 heads by entering Table B under number of $P$ events = 4, 5, and 6, respectively. Thus,

Table B entry

| | $N$ | No. of $P$ Events | $P$ 0.50 |
|---|---|---|---|
| $p$(4 heads) = 0.2344 | 6 | 4 | 0.2344 |
| $p$(5 heads) = 0.0938 | | 5 | 0.0938 |
| $p$(6 heads) = 0.0156 | | 6 | 0.0156 |

From the addition rule with mutually exclusive events,

$$p(4, 5, \text{ or } 6 \text{ heads}) = p(4) + p(5) + p(6)$$
$$= 0.2344 + 0.0938 + 0.0156$$
$$= 0.3438$$

## Practice Problem 9.2

If 10 unbiased coins are flipped once, what is the probability of getting a result as extreme or more extreme than 9 heads?

**SOLUTION**

There are 10 coins, so $N = 10$. As before, we shall let $P =$ the probability of getting a head in one flip of any coin. The coins are unbiased, so $P = Q = 0.50$. The phrase "as extreme or more extreme than" means "as far from the center of the distribution or farther from the center of the distribution than." Thus, "as extreme or more extreme than 9 heads" means results that are as far from the center of the distribution or farther from the center of the distribution than 9 heads. Thus, the number of $P$ events $= 0, 1, 9,$ or $10$. In Table B under $N = 10$, number of $P$ events $= 0, 1, 9,$ or $10$, and $P = 0.50$, we find

Table B entry

| $N$ | No. of $P$ Events | $P$ 0.50 |
|-----|-------------------|----------|
| 10  | 0                 | 0.0010   |
|     | 1                 | 0.0098   |
|     | 9                 | 0.0098   |
|     | 10                | 0.0010   |

$$p\begin{pmatrix} \text{as extreme or} \\ \text{more extreme} \\ \text{than 9 heads} \end{pmatrix} = p(0, 1, 9, \text{or } 10)$$
$$= p(0) + p(1) + p(9) + p(10)$$
$$= 0.0010 + 0.0098 + 0.0098$$
$$\quad + 0.0010$$
$$= 0.0216$$

The binomial expansion is very general. It is not limited to values where $P = 0.50$. Thus, Table B also lists probabilities for values of $P$ other than 0.50. Let's try some problems where $P$ is not equal to 0.50.

## Practice Problem 9.3

Assume you have eight biased coins. Each coin is weighted such that the probability of a head with it is 0.30. If the eight biased coins are flipped once, what is the probability of getting

**a.** 7 heads?
**b.** 7 or 8 heads?
**c.** The probability found in part **a** comes from evaluating which of the term(s) in the following binomial expansion?

$$P^8 + 8P^7Q^1 + 28P^6Q^2 + 56P^5Q^3 + 70P^4Q^4 + 56P^3Q^5 + 28P^2Q^6 + 8P^1Q^7 + Q^8$$

*(continued)*

**d.** With your calculator, evaluate the term(s) selected in part **c** using $P = 0.30$. Compare your answer with the answer in part **a**. Explain.

**SOLUTION**

**a.** Given there are eight coins, $N = 8$. Let $P =$ the probability of getting a head in one flip of any coin. Since the coins are biased such that the probability of a head on any coin is 0.30, $P = 0.30$. Since we want to determine the probability of getting exactly 7 heads, the number of $P$ events $= 7$. In Table B under $N = 8$, number of $P$ events $= 7$, and $P = 0.30$, we find the following:

Table B entry

$p$(exactly 7 heads) = 0.0012

| $N$ | No. of $P$ Events | $P$ 0.30 |
|---|---|---|
| 8 | 7 | 0.0012 |

**b.** Again, $N = 8$ and $P = 0.30$. We can find the probability of 7 and 8 heads in Table B under number of $P$ events $= 7$ and 8, respectively. Thus,

Table B entry

$p$(7 heads) = 0.0012
$p$(8 heads) = 0.0001

| $N$ | No. of $P$ Events | $P$ 0.30 |
|---|---|---|
| 8 | 7 | 0.0012 |
|  | 8 | 0.0001 |

From the addition rule with mutually exclusive events,

$$p(7 \text{ or } 8 \text{ heads}) = p(7) + p(8)$$
$$= 0.0012 + 0.0001$$
$$= 0.0013$$

**c.** $8P^7Q^1$

**d.** $8P^7Q^1 = 8(0.30)^7(0.7) = 0.0012$. As expected, the answers are the same. The table entry was computed using $8P^7Q^1$ with $P = 0.30$ and $Q = 0.70$.

Thus, using Table B when $P$ is less than 0.50 is very similar to using it when $P = 0.50$. We just look in the table under the new $P$ value rather than under $P = 0.50$.

Table B can also be used when $P > 0.50$. To illustrate, consider the following example.

example

## (P > 0.50)

If five biased coins are flipped once, what is the probability of getting (a) 5 heads and (b) 4 or 5 heads? Each coin is weighted such that the probability of a head on any coin is 0.75.

### SOLUTION

a. 5 heads. There are five coins, so $N = 5$. Again, let $P$ = the probability of getting a head in one flip of any coin. Since the bias is such that the probability of a head on any coin is 0.75, $P = 0.75$. Since we want to determine the probability of getting 5 heads, the number of $P$ events equals 5. Following our usual procedure, we would enter Table B under $N = 5$, number of $P$ events = 5, and $P = 0.75$. However, Table B does not have a column headed by 0.75. All of the column headings are equal to or less than 0.50. Nevertheless, we can use Table B to solve this problem.

   When $P > 0.50$, all we need do is solve the problem in terms of $Q$ and the number of $Q$ events, rather than $P$ and the number of $P$ events. Since the probability values given in Table B are for either $P$ or $Q$, once the problem is put in terms of $Q$, we can refer to Table B using $Q$ rather than $P$. Translating the problem into $Q$ terms involves two steps: determining $Q$ and determining the number of $Q$ events. Let's follow these steps using the present example:

1. *Determining Q.*

$$Q = 1 - P = 1 - 0.75 = 0.25$$

2. *Determining the number of Q events.*

$$\textit{Number of Q events} = N - \textit{Number of P events} = 5 - 5 = 0$$

Thus, to solve this example, we refer to Table B under $N = 5$, number of $Q$ events = 0, and $Q = 0.25$. The Table B entry is shown in Table 9.5. Thus,

$p(5 \text{ heads}) = p(0 \text{ tails}) = 0.2373$

table 9.5   Table B entry

| N | No. of Q Events | Q 0.25 |
|---|---|---|
| 5 | 0 | 0.2373 |

b. 4 or 5 heads. Again, $N = 5$ and $Q = 0.25$. This time, the number of $Q$ events = 0 or 1. The Table B entry is shown in Table 9.6. Thus,

$p(4 \text{ or } 5 \text{ heads}) = p(0 \text{ or } 1 \text{ tail})$

$= 0.2373 + 0.3955$

$= 0.6328$

table 9.6   Table B entry

| N | No. of Q Events | Q 0.25 |
|---|---|---|
| 5 | 0 | 0.2373 |
|   | 1 | 0.3955 |

We are now ready to try a practice problem.

## Practice Problem 9.4

If 12 biased coins are flipped once, what is the probability of getting
**a.** Exactly 10 heads?
**b.** 10 or more heads?
The coins are biased such that the probability of a head with any coin equals 0.65.

**SOLUTION**

**a.** Given there are 12 coins, $N = 12$. Let $P =$ the probability of a head in one flip of any coin. Since the probability of a head with any coin equals 0.65, $P = 0.65$. Since $P > 0.50$, we shall enter Table B with $Q$ rather than $P$. If there are 10 $P$ events, there must be 2 $Q$ events ($N = 12$). If $P = 0.65$, then $Q = 0.35$. Using $Q$ in Table B, we obtain

Table B entry

$p(10 \text{ heads}) = 0.1088$

| $N$ | No. of $Q$ Events | $Q$ 0.35 |
|-----|-------------------|----------|
| 12  | 2                 | 0.1088   |

**b.** Again, $N = 12$ and $P = 0.65$. This time, the number of $P$ events equals 10, 11, or 12. Since $P > 0.50$, we must use $Q$ in Table B rather than $P$. With $N = 12$, the number of $Q$ events equals 0, 1, or 2 and $Q = 0.35$. Using $Q$ in Table B, we obtain

Table B entry

$p(10, 11, \text{ or } 12 \text{ heads}) = 0.1088 + 0.0368$
$\qquad\qquad\qquad\qquad + 0.0057$
$\qquad\qquad\qquad = 0.1513$

| $N$ | No. of $Q$ Events | $Q$ 0.35 |
|-----|-------------------|----------|
| 12  | 0                 | 0.0057   |
|     | 1                 | 0.0368   |
|     | 2                 | 0.1088   |

So far, we have dealt exclusively with coin flipping. However, the binomial distribution is not just limited to coin flipping. It applies to all situations involving a series of trials where on each trial there are only two possible outcomes, the possible outcomes on each trial are mutually exclusive, there is independence between the outcomes of each trial, and the probability of each possible outcome on any trial stays the same from trial to trial. There are many situations that fit these requirements. To illustrate, let's do a couple of practice problems.

## Practice Problem 9.5

A student is taking a multiple-choice exam with 15 questions. Each question has five choices. If the student guesses on each question, what is the probability of passing the test? The lowest passing score is 60% of the questions answered correctly. Assume that the choices for each question are equally likely.

**SOLUTION**

This problem fits the binomial requirements. There is a series of trials (questions). On each trial, there are only two possible outcomes. The student is either right or wrong. The possible outcomes are mutually exclusive. If she is right on a question, she can't be wrong. There is independence between the outcomes of each trial. If she is right on question 1, it has no effect on the outcome of question 2. Finally, if we assume the student guesses on each trial, then the probability of being right and the probability of being wrong on any trial stay the same from trial to trial. Thus, the binomial distribution and Table B apply.

We can consider each question a trial (no pun intended). Given there are 15 questions, $N = 15$. We can let $P =$ the probability that she will guess correctly on any question. Since there are five choices that are equally likely on each question, $P = 0.20$. A passing grade equals 60% correct answers or more. Therefore, a student will pass if she gets 9 or more answers correct (60% of 15 is 9). Thus, the number of $P$ events equals 9, 10, 11, 12, 13, 14, and 15. Looking in Table B under $N = 15$, number of $P$ events = 9, 10, 11, 12, 13, 14, and 15, and $P = 0.20$, we obtain

$$p(9, 10, 11, 12, 13, 14,$$
$$\text{or } 15 \text{ correct guesses}) = 0.0007 + 0.0001$$
$$= 0.0008$$

Table B entry

| $N$ | No. of $P$ Events | $P$ 0.20 |
|-----|-------------------|----------|
| 15  | 9                 | 0.0007   |
|     | 10                | 0.0001   |
|     | 11                | 0.0000   |
|     | 12                | 0.0000   |
|     | 13                | 0.0000   |
|     | 14                | 0.0000   |
|     | 15                | 0.0000   |

Your friend claims to be a coffee connoisseur. She always drinks Starbucks and claims no other coffee even comes close to tasting so good. You suspect she is being a little grandiose. In fact, you wonder whether she can even taste the difference between Starbucks and the local roaster's coffee. Your friend agrees to the following experiment. While blindfolded, she is given six opportunities to taste from two cups of coffee and tell you which of the two cups contains Starbucks. The cups are identical and contain the same type of coffee except that one contains coffee made from beans supplied and roasted by Starbucks and the other by the local roaster. After each tasting of the two cups, you remove any telltale signs and randomize which of the two cups she is given first for the next trial. Believe it or not, your friend correctly identifies Starbucks on all six trials! What do you conclude? Can you think of a way to increase your confidence in the conclusion?

### SOLUTION

The logic of our analysis is as follows. We will assume that your friend really can't tell the difference between the two coffees. She must then be guessing on each trial. We will compute the probability of getting six out of six correct, assuming guessing on each trial. If this probability is very low, we will reject guessing as a reasonable explanation and conclude that your friend can really taste the difference.

This experiment fits the requirements for the binomial distribution. Each comparison of the two coffees can be considered a trial (again, no pun intended). On each trial, there are only two possible outcomes. Your friend is either right or wrong. The outcomes are mutually exclusive. There is independence between trials. If your friend is correct on trial 1, it has no effect on the outcome of trial 2. Finally, if we assume your friend guesses on any trial, then the probability of being correct and the probability of being wrong stay the same from trial to trial.

Given each comparison of coffees is a trial, $N = 6$. We can let $P =$ the probability your friend will guess correctly on any trial. There are only two coffees, so $P = 0.50$. Your friend was correct on all six trials. Therefore, the number of $P$ events = 6. Thus,

$p$(6 correct guesses) = 0.0156

Table B entry

| $N$ | No. of $P$ Events | $P$ 0.50 |
|---|---|---|
| 6 | 6 | 0.0156 |

Assuming your friend is guessing, the probability of her getting six out of six correct is 0.0156. Since this is a fairly low value, you would probably reject guessing because it is an unreasonable explanation and conclude that your friend can really taste the difference. To increase your confidence in rejecting guessing, you could include more brands of coffee on each trial, or you could increase the number of trials. For example, even with only two coffees, the probability of guessing correctly on 12 out of 12 trials is 0.0002.

## SUMMARY

In this chapter, we have discussed the binomial distribution. The binomial distribution is a probability distribution that results when the following conditions are met: (1) There is a series of $N$ trials; (2) on each trial, there are only two possible outcomes; (3) the outcomes are mutually exclusive; (4) there is independence between trials; and (5) the probability of each possible outcome on any trial stays the same from trial to trial. When these conditions are met, the binomial distribution tells us each possible outcome of the $N$ trials and the probability of getting each of these outcomes.

We illustrated the binomial distribution through coin-flipping experiments and then showed how the binomial distribution could be generated through the binomial expansion. The binomial expansion is given by $(P + Q)^N$, where $P$ = the probability of occurrence of one of the events and $Q$ = the probability of occurrence of the other event. Finally, we showed how to use the binomial table (Table B in Appendix D) to solve problems involving the binomial distribution. The binomial distribution is appropriate whenever the five conditions listed at the beginning of this summary are met.

## IMPORTANT TERMS

Biased coins (p. 207)
Binomial distribution (p. 199)
Binomial expansion (p. 202)

Binomial table (p. 204)
Fair coins (p. 200)

Number of $P$ events (p. 203)
Number of $Q$ events (p. 203)

## QUESTIONS AND PROBLEMS

1. Briefly define or explain each of the terms in the "Important Terms" section.
2. What are the five conditions necessary for the binomial distribution to be appropriate?
3. In a binomial situation, if $P = 0.10$, $Q = $ _____.
4. Using Table B, if $N = 6$ and $P = 0.40$,
   a. The probability of getting exactly five $P$ events = _____.
   b. This probability comes from evaluating which of the terms in the following equation?

   $$P^6 + 6P^5Q + 15P^4Q^2 + 20P^3Q^3 + 15P^2Q^4 + 6PQ^5 + Q^6$$

   c. Evaluate the term(s) of your answer in part **b** using $P = 0.40$ and compare your answer with part **a.**
5. Using Table B, if $N = 12$ and $P = 0.50$,
   a What is the probability of getting exactly 10 $P$ events?
   b. What is the probability of getting 11 or 12 $P$ events?
   c. What is the probability of getting at least 10 $P$ events?
   d. What is the probability of getting a result as extreme as or more extreme than 10 $P$ events?
6. Using Table B, if $N = 14$ and $P = 0.70$,
   a. What is the probability of getting exactly 13 $P$ events?

   b. What is the probability of getting at least 13 $P$ events?
   c. What is the probability of getting a result as extreme as or more extreme than 13 $P$ events?
7. Using Table B, if $N = 20$ and $P = 0.20$,
   a. What is the probability of getting exactly two $P$ events?
   b. What is the probability of getting two or fewer $P$ events?
   c. What is the probability of getting a result as extreme as or more extreme than two $P$ events?
8. An individual flips nine fair coins. If she allows only a head or a tail with each coin,
   a. What is the probability they all will fall heads?
   b. What is the probability there will be seven or more heads?
   c. What is the probability there will be a result as extreme as or more extreme than seven heads?
9. Someone flips 15 biased coins once. The coins are weighted such that the probability of a head with any coin is 0.85.
   a. What is the probability of getting exactly 14 heads?
   b. What is the probability of getting at least 14 heads?
   c. What is the probability of getting exactly 3 tails?
10. A key shop advertises that the keys made there have a $P = 0.90$ of working effectively. If you

bought 10 keys from the shop, what is the probability that all of the keys would work effectively?

11. A student is taking a true/false exam with 15 questions. If he guesses on each question, what is the probability he will get at least 13 questions correct? education

12. A student is taking a multiple-choice exam with 16 questions. Each question has five alternatives. If the student guesses on 12 of the questions, what is the probability she will guess at least 8 correct? Assume all of the alternatives are equally likely for each question on which the student guesses. education

13. You are interested in determining whether a particular child can discriminate the color green from blue. Therefore, you show the child five wooden blocks. The blocks are identical except that two are green and three are blue. You randomly arrange the blocks in a row and ask him to pick out a green block. After a block is picked, you replace it and randomize the order of the blocks once more. Then you again ask him to pick out a green block. This procedure is repeated until the child has made 14 selections. If he really can't discriminate green from blue, what is the probability he will pick a green block at least 11 times? cognitive

14. Let's assume you are an avid horse race fan. You are at the track and there are eight races. On this day, the horses and their riders are so evenly matched that chance alone determines the finishing order for each race. There are 10 horses in every race. If, on each race, you bet on one horse to show (to finish third, second, or first),
    a. What is the probability that you will win your bet in all eight races?
    b. What is the probability that you will win in at least six of the races? other

15. A manufacturer of valves admits that its quality control has gone radically "downhill" such that currently the probability of producing a defective valve is 0.50. If it manufactures 1 million valves in a month and you randomly sample from these valves 10,000 samples, each composed of 15 valves,
    a. In how many samples would you expect to find exactly 13 good valves?
    b. In how many samples would you expect to find at least 13 good valves? I/O

16. Assume that 15% of the population is left-handed and the remainder is right-handed (there are no ambidextrous individuals). If you stop the next five persons you meet, what is the probability that
    a. All will be left-handed?
    b. All will be right-handed?
    c. Exactly two will be left-handed?
    d. At least one will be left-handed?
    For the purposes of this problem, assume independence in the selection of the five individuals. other

17. In your voting district, 25% of the voters are against a particular bill and the rest favor it. If you randomly poll four voters from your district, what is the probability that
    a. None will favor the bill?
    b. All will favor the bill?
    c. At least one will be against the bill? I/O

18. At your university, 30% of the undergraduates are from out of state. If you randomly select eight of the undergraduates, what is the probability that
    a. All are from within the state?
    b. All are from out of state?
    c. Exactly two are from within the state?
    d. At least five are from within the state? education

19. Twenty students living in a college dormitory participated in a taste contest between the two leading colas.
    a. If there really is no preference, what is the probability that all 20 would prefer Brand X to Brand Y?
    b. If there really is no preference, what is the probability that at least 17 would prefer Brand X to Brand Y?
    c. How many of the 20 students would have to prefer Brand X before you would be willing to conclude that there really is a preference for Brand X? other

20. A large bowl contains 1 million marbles. Half of the marbles have a plus (+) painted on them and the other half has a minus (−).
    a. If you randomly sample 10 marbles, one at a time with replacement from the bowl, what is the probability you will select 9 marbles with pluses and 1 with a minus?
    b. If you take 1000 random samples of 10 marbles, one at a time with replacement, how many of the samples would you expect to be all pluses? other

## NOTES

9.1 The equation for expanding $(P + Q)^N$ is

$$(P + Q)^N = P^N + \frac{N}{1}P^{N-1}Q + \frac{N(N-1)}{1(2)} P^{N-2}Q^2$$

$$+ \frac{N(N-1)(N-2)}{1(2)(3)} P^{N-3}Q^3$$

$$+ \cdots + Q^N$$

### BOOK COMPANION WEBSITE

Go to www.thomsonedu.com/psychology/pagano for:

- Flash cards for review of terms
- Chapter quiz
- Statistical workshops
- And more

### WebTUTOR

Available via WebTutor for this chapter:

- Detailed chapter outline
- *Know and Be Able To Do* section
- Drag & Drop game for review of terms
- Flash cards for review of terms
- Audio flash cards for MP3 player
- More practice problems using computational equations
- Chapter quiz

# Introduction to Hypothesis Testing Using the Sign Test

CHAPTER **10**

## INTRODUCTION

We pointed out previously that inferential statistics has two main purposes:
(1) hypothesis testing and (2) parameter estimation. By far, most of the applications of inferential statistics are in the area of hypothesis testing. As discussed in

Chapter 1, scientific methodology depends on this application of inferential statistics. Without objective verification, science would cease to exist, and objective verification is often impossible without inferential statistics. You will recall that at the heart of scientific methodology is an experiment. Usually, the experiment has been designed to test a hypothesis, and the resulting data must be analyzed. Occasionally, the results are so clear-cut that statistical inference is not necessary. However, such experiments are rare. Because of the variability that is inherent from subject to subject in the variable being measured, it is often difficult to detect the effect of the independent variable without the help of inferential statistics. In this chapter, we shall begin the fascinating journey into how experimental design, in conjunction with mathematical analysis, can be used to verify truth assertions or hypotheses, as we have been calling them. We urge you to apply yourself to this chapter with special rigor. The material it contains applies to all of the inference tests we shall take up (which constitutes most of the remaining text).

## AN EXPERIMENT: MARIJUANA AND THE TREATMENT OF AIDS PATIENTS

Let's assume that you are a social scientist working in a metropolitan hospital that services a very large population of AIDS patients. You are very concerned about the pain and suffering that afflict these patients. In particular, although you are not yet convinced, you think there may be an ethically proper place for using marijuana in the treatment of these patients, particularly in the more advanced stages of the illness. Of course, before seriously considering the other issues involved in advocating the use of marijuana for this purpose, you must be convinced that it does have important positive effects. Thus far, although there have been many anecdotal reports from AIDS patients that using marijuana decreases their nausea, increases their appetite, and increases their desire to socialize, there have not been any scientific experiments to shore up these reports.

As a scientist, you realize that although personal reports are suggestive, they are not conclusive. Experiments must be done before one can properly assess cause and effect—in this case, the effects claimed for marijuana. This is very important to you, so you decide to embark on a research program directed to this end. The first experiment you plan is to investigate the effect of marijuana on appetite in AIDS patients. Of course, if marijuana actually decreases appetite rather than increases it, you want to be able to detect this as well because it has important practical consequences. Therefore, this will be a basic fact-finding experiment in which you attempt to determine whether marijuana has any effect at all, either to increase or to decrease appetite. The first experiment will be a modest one. You plan to randomly sample 10 individuals from the population of AIDS patients who are being treated at your hospital. You realize that the generalization will be limited to this population, but for many reasons, you are willing to accept this limitation for this initial experiment. After getting permission from the appropriate authorities, you conduct the following experiment.

A random sample of 10 AIDS patients who agree to participate in the experiment is selected from a rather large population of AIDS patients being treated on an outpatient basis at your hospital. None of the patients in this population are being treated with marijuana. Each patient is admitted to the hospital for a week to participate in the experiment. The first 2 days are used to allow each patient to get used to the hospital. On the third day, half of the patients receive a pill containing a synthetic form of marijuana's active ingredient, THC, prior to eating each meal, and on the sixth day, they receive a placebo pill before each meal. The other half of the patients are treated the same as in the experimental condition, except that they receive the pills in the reverse order, that is, the placebo pills on the third day and the THC pills on the sixth day. The dependent variable is the amount of food eaten by each patient on day 3 and day 6.

In this experiment, each subject is tested under two conditions: an experimental condition and a control condition. We have labeled the condition in which the subject receives the THC pills as the experimental condition and the condition in which the subject receives the placebo pills as the control condition. Thus, there are two scores for each subject: the amount of food eaten (calories) in the experimental condition and the amount of food eaten in the control condition. If marijuana really does affect appetite, we would expect different scores for the two conditions. For example, if marijuana increases appetite, then more food should be eaten in the experimental condition. If the control score for each subject is subtracted from the experimental score, we would expect a predominance of positive difference scores. The results of the experiment are given in Table 10.1.

These data could be analyzed with several different statistical inference tests such as the sign test, Wilcoxon matched-pairs signed ranks test, and Student's *t* test for correlated groups. The choice of which test to use in an actual experiment is an important one. It depends on the sensitivity of the test and on whether the data of the experiment meet the assumptions of the test. We shall discuss each of these points in subsequent chapters. In this chapter, we shall analyze the data of your experiment with the sign test. We have chosen the sign test because (1) it is easy to understand and (2) all of the major concepts concerning hypothesis testing can be illustrated clearly and simply.

The sign test ignores the magnitude of the difference scores and considers only their direction or sign. This omits a lot of information, which makes the test rather insensitive (but much easier to understand). If we consider only the signs

**t a b l e  10.1**   Results of the marijuana experiment

| Patient No. | Experimental Condition THC Pill Food Eaten (calories) | Control Condition Placebo Pill Food Eaten (calories) | Difference Score (calories) |
|---|---|---|---|
| 1 | 1325 | 1012 | +313 |
| 2 | 1350 | 1275 | + 75 |
| 3 | 1248 | 950 | +298 |
| 4 | 1087 | 840 | +247 |
| 5 | 1047 | 942 | +105 |
| 6 | 943 | 860 | + 83 |
| 7 | 1118 | 1154 | − 36 |
| 8 | 908 | 763 | +145 |
| 9 | 1084 | 920 | +164 |
| 10 | 1088 | 876 | +212 |

of the difference scores, then your experiment produced 9 out of 10 pluses. The amount of food eaten in the experimental condition was greater after taking the THC pill in all but one of the patients. Are we therefore justified in concluding that marijuana produces an increase in appetite? Not necessarily.

Suppose that marijuana has absolutely no effect on appetite. Isn't it still possible to have obtained 9 out of 10 pluses in your experiment? Yes, it is. If marijuana has no effect on appetite, then each subject would have received two conditions that were identical except for chance factors. Perhaps when subject 1 was run in the THC condition, he had slept better the night before and his appetite was higher than when run in the control condition before any pills were taken. If so, we would expect him to eat more food in the THC condition even if THC has no effect on appetite. Perhaps subject 2 had a cold when run in the placebo condition, which blunted her appetite relative to when run in the experimental condition. Again we would expect more food to be eaten in the experimental condition even if THC has no effect.

We could go on giving examples for the other subjects. The point is that these explanations of the greater amount eaten in the THC condition are chance factors. They are different factors, independent of one another, and they could just as easily have occurred on either of the two test days. It seems unlikely to get 9 out of 10 pluses simply as a result of chance factors. The crucial question really is, "How unlikely is it?" Suppose we know that if chance alone is responsible, we shall get 9 out of 10 pluses only 1 time in 1 billion. This is such a rare occurrence, we would no doubt reject chance and, with it, the explanation that marijuana has no effect on appetite. We would then conclude by accepting the hypothesis that marijuana affects appetite because it is the only other possible explanation. Since the sample was a random one, we can assume it was representative of the AIDS patients being treated at your hospital, and we therefore would generalize the results to that population.

Suppose, however, that the probability of getting 9 out of 10 pluses due to chance alone is really 1 in 3, not 1 in 1 billion. Can we reject chance as a cause of the data? The decision is not as clear-cut this time. What we need is a rule for determining when the obtained probability is small enough to reject chance as an underlying cause. We shall see that this involves setting a critical probability level (called the alpha level) against which to compare the results.

Let's formalize some of the concepts we've been presenting.

## Repeated Measures Design

The experimental design that we have been using is called the repeated measures, replicated measures, or correlated groups design. *The essential features are that there are paired scores in the conditions and the differences between the paired scores are analyzed.* In the marijuana experiment, we used the same subjects in each condition. Thus, the subjects served as their own controls. Their scores were paired, and the differences between these pairs were analyzed. Instead of the same subjects, we could have used identical twins or subjects who were matched in some other way. In animal experimentation, littermates have often been used for pairing. The most basic form of this design employs just two conditions: an experimental and a control condition. The two conditions are kept as identical as possible except for values of the independent variable, which, of course, are intentionally made different. In our example, marijuana is the independent variable.

## Alternative Hypothesis ($H_1$)

In any experiment, there are two hypotheses that compete for explaining the results: the *alternative hypothesis* and the *null hypothesis*. The alternative hypothesis is the one that claims the difference in results between conditions is due to the independent variable. In this case, it is the hypothesis that claims "marijuana affects appetite." The alternative hypothesis can be directional or nondirectional. The hypothesis "marijuana affects appetite" is nondirectional because it does not specify the direction of the effect. If the hypothesis specifies the direction of the effect, it is a directional hypothesis. "Marijuana increases appetite" is an example of a directional alternative hypothesis.

## Null Hypothesis ($H_0$)

The null hypothesis is set up to be the logical counterpart of the alternative hypothesis such that if the null hypothesis is false, the alternative hypothesis must be true. Therefore, these two hypotheses must be mutually exclusive and exhaustive. If the alternative hypothesis is nondirectional, it specifies that the independent variable has an effect on the dependent variable. For this nondirectional alternative hypothesis, the null hypothesis asserts that the independent variable has *no* effect on the dependent variable. In the present example, since the alternative hypothesis is nondirectional, the null hypothesis specifies that "marijuana does not affect appetite." We pointed out previously that the alternative hypothesis specifies "marijuana affects appetite." You can see that these two hypotheses are mutually exclusive and exhaustive. If the null hypothesis is false, then the alternative hypothesis must be true. As you will see, we always first evaluate the null hypothesis and try to show that it is false. If we can show it to be false, then the alternative hypothesis must be true.[*]

If the alternative hypothesis is directional, the null hypothesis asserts that the independent variable does not have an effect in the direction specified by the alternative hypothesis.[†] For example, for the alternative hypothesis "marijuana increases appetite," the null hypothesis asserts that "marijuana does not increase appetite." Again, note that the two hypotheses are mutually exclusive and exhaustive. If the null hypothesis is false, the alternative hypothesis must be true.

## Decision Rule ($\alpha$ Level)

We always evaluate the results of an experiment by assessing the null hypothesis. The reason we directly assess the null hypothesis instead of the alternative hypothesis is that we can calculate the probability of chance events, but there is no way to calculate the probability of the alternative hypothesis. We evaluate the null hypothesis by assuming it is true and testing the reasonableness of this assumption by calculating the probability of getting the results *if chance alone is operating*. If the obtained probability turns out to be equal to or less than a critical probability level called the *alpha ($\alpha$) level,* we reject the null hypothesis. Rejecting the null hypothesis allows us, then, to accept indirectly the alternative

---

[*]See Note 10.1.
[†]See Note 10.2.

hypothesis because, if the experiment is done properly, it is the only other possible explanation. When we reject $H_0$, we say the results are *significant* or *reliable*. If the obtained probability is greater than the alpha level, we conclude by failing to reject $H_0$. Since the experiment does not allow rejection of $H_0$, we retain $H_0$ as a reasonable explanation of the data. Throughout the text, we shall use the expressions "failure to reject $H_0$" and "retain $H_0$" interchangeably. When we retain $H_0$, we say the results are not significant or reliable. Of course, when the results are not significant, we cannot accept the alternative hypothesis. Thus, the decision rule states:

> If the obtained probability $\leq \alpha$, reject $H_0$.
> If the obtained probability $> \alpha$, fail to reject $H_0$, retain $H_0$.

The alpha level is set at the beginning of the experiment. Commonly used alpha levels are $\alpha = 0.05$ and $\alpha = 0.01$. Later in this chapter, we shall discuss the rationale underlying the use of these levels.

For now let's assume $\alpha = 0.05$ for the marijuana data. Thus, to evaluate the results of the marijuana experiment, we need to (1) determine the probability of getting 9 out of 10 pluses if chance alone is responsible and (2) compare this probability with alpha.

## Evaluating the Marijuana Experiment Using the Binomial Distribution

The data of this experiment fit the requirements for the binomial distribution. The experiment consists of a series of trials (the exposure of each patient to the experimental and control conditions is a trial). On each trial, there are only two possible outcomes: a plus and a minus. Note that this model does not allow ties. If any ties occur, they must be discarded and the $N$ reduced accordingly. The outcomes are mutually exclusive (a plus and a minus cannot occur simultaneously), there is independence between trials (the score of patient 1 in no way influences the score of patient 2, etc.), and the probability of a plus and the probability of a minus stay the same from trial to trial. Since the binomial distribution is appropriate, we can use Table B in Appendix D (Table 10.2) to determine the probability of getting 9 pluses out of 10 trials when chance alone is responsible. We solve this problem in the same way we did with the coin-flipping problems in Chapter 9.

Given there are 10 patients, $N = 10$. We can let $P =$ the probability of getting a plus with any patient.[*] If chance alone is operating, the probability of a plus is equal to the probability of a minus. There are only two equally likely alternatives, so $P = 0.50$. Since we want to determine the probability of 9 pluses, the number of $P$ events = 9. In Table B under $N = 10$, number of $P$ events = 9, and $P = 0.50$, we obtain

$p(9 \text{ pluses}) = 0.0098$

t a b l e  10.2   Table B entry

| $N$ | No. of $P$ Events | $P$ 0.50 |
|---|---|---|
| 10 | 9 | 0.0098 |

---

[*]Throughout this chapter and the next, whenever using the sign test, we shall always let $P =$ the probability of a *plus* with any subject. This is arbitrary; we could have chosen $Q$. However, using the same letter ($P$ or $Q$) to designate the probability of a plus for all problems does avoid unnecessary confusion.

Alpha has been set at 0.05. The analysis shows that only 98 times in 10,000 would we get 9 pluses if chance alone is the cause. Since 0.0098 is lower than alpha, we reject the null hypothesis.[*] It does not seem to be a reasonable explanation of the data. Therefore, we conclude by accepting the alternative hypothesis that marijuana affects appetite. It appears to increase it. Since the sample was randomly selected, we assume the sample is representative of the population. Therefore, it is legitimate to assume that this conclusion applies to the *population* of AIDS patients being treated at your hospital.

It is worth noting that very often in practice the results of an experiment are generalized to groups that were not part of the population from which the sample was taken. For instance, on the basis of this experiment, we might be tempted to claim that marijuana would increase the appetites of AIDS patients being treated at other hospitals. Strictly speaking, the results of an experiment apply only to the population from which the sample was randomly selected. Therefore, generalization to other groups should be made with caution. This caution is necessary because the other groups may differ from the subjects in the original population in some way that would cause a different result. Of course, as the experiment is replicated in different hospitals with different patients, the legitimate generalization becomes much broader.

## TYPE I AND TYPE II ERRORS

When making decisions regarding the null hypothesis, it is possible to make errors of two kinds. These are called *Type I* and *Type II errors*.

definitions    ■ A **Type I error** *is defined as a decision to reject the null hypothesis when the null hypothesis is true. A* **Type II error** *is defined as a decision to retain the null hypothesis when the null hypothesis is false.*

To illustrate these concepts, let's return to the marijuana example. Recall the logic of the decision process. First, we assume $H_0$ is true and evaluate the probability of getting the obtained score differences between conditions if chance alone is responsible. If the obtained probability $\leq \alpha$, we reject $H_0$. If the obtained probability $> \alpha$, we retain $H_0$. In the marijuana experiment, the obtained probability $[p(9\text{ pluses})] = 0.0098$. Since this was lower than alpha, we rejected $H_0$ and concluded that marijuana was responsible for the results. Can we be certain that we made the correct decision? How do we know that chance wasn't really responsible? Perhaps the null hypothesis is really true. Isn't it possible that this was one of those 98 times in 10,000 we would get 9 pluses and 1 minus if chance alone was operating? *The answer is that we never know for sure that*

---

[*]This is really a simplification made here for clarity. In actual practice, we evaluate the probability of getting the obtained result *or any more extreme*. The point is discussed in detail later in this chapter in the section titled "Evaluating the Tail of the Distribution."

*chance wasn't responsible.* It is possible that the 9 pluses and 1 minus were really due to chance. If so, then we made an error by rejecting $H_0$. This is a Type I error—a rejection of the null hypothesis when it is true.

A Type II error occurs when we retain $H_0$ and it is false. Suppose that in the marijuana experiment $p(9 \text{ pluses}) = 0.2300$ instead of 0.0098. In this case, $0.2300 > \alpha$, so we would retain $H_0$. If $H_0$ is false, we have made a Type II error, that is, retaining $H_0$ when it is false.

To help clarify the relationship between the decision process and possible error, we've summarized the possibilities in Table 10.3. The column heading is "State of Reality." This means the correct state of affairs regarding the null hypothesis. There are only two possibilities. Either $H_0$ is true or it is false. The row heading is the decision made when analyzing the data. Again, there are only two possibilities. Either we reject $H_0$ or we retain $H_0$. If we retain $H_0$ and $H_0$ is true, we've made a correct decision (see the first cell in the table). If we reject $H_0$ and $H_0$ is true, we've made a Type I error. This is shown in cell 3. If we retain $H_0$ and $H_0$ is false, we've made a Type II error (cell 2). Finally, if we reject $H_0$ and $H_0$ is false, we've made a correct decision (cell 4). Note that when we reject $H_0$, the only possible error is a Type I error. If we retain $H_0$, the only error we may make is a Type II error.

t a b l e 10.3    Possible conclusions and the state of reality

| Decision | State of Reality | |
| --- | --- | --- |
| | $H_0$ *is true* | $H_0$ *is false* |
| **Retain $H_0$** | [1]Correct decision | [2]Type II error |
| **Reject $H_0$** | [3]Type I error | [4]Correct decision |

You may wonder why we've gone to the trouble of analyzing all the logical possibilities. We've done so because it is very important to know the possible errors we may be making when we draw conclusions from an experiment. From the preceding analysis, we know there are only two such possibilities, a Type I error or a Type II error. Knowing these are possible, we can design experiments before conducting them to help minimize the probability of making a Type I or a Type II error. By minimizing the probability of making these errors, we maximize the probability of concluding correctly, regardless of whether the null hypothesis is true or false. We shall see in the next section that alpha limits the probability of making a Type I error. Therefore, by controlling the alpha level we can minimize the probability of making a Type I error. Beta (read "bayta") is defined as the probability of making a Type II error. We shall discuss ways to minimize beta in the next chapter.

## ALPHA LEVEL AND THE DECISION PROCESS

It should be clear that whenever we are using sample data to evaluate a hypothesis, we are never certain of our conclusion. When we reject $H_0$, we don't know for sure that it is false. We take the risk that we may be making a Type I error. Of course, the less reasonable it is that chance is the cause of the results, the more confident we are that we haven't made an error by rejecting the null hypothesis. For example, when the probability of getting the results is 1 in 1 million ($p = 0.000001$) under the assumption of chance, we are more confident that the null hypothesis is false than when the probability is 1 in 10 ($p = 0.10$).

definition ■ *The **alpha level** that the scientist sets at the beginning of the experiment is the level to which he or she wishes to limit the probability of making a Type I error.*

Thus, when a scientist sets $\alpha = 0.05$, he is in effect saying that when he collects the data he will reject the null hypothesis if, under the assumption that chance alone is responsible, the obtained probability is equal to or less than 5 times in 100. In so doing, he is saying that he is willing to limit the probability of rejecting the null hypothesis when it is true to 5 times in 100. Thus, he limits the probability of making a Type I error to 0.05.

There is no magical formula that tells us what the alpha level should be to arrive at truth in each experiment. To determine a reasonable alpha level for an experiment, we must consider the consequences of making an error. In science, the effects of rejecting the null hypothesis when it is true (Type I error) are costly. When a scientist publishes an experiment in which he rejects the null hypothesis, other scientists either attempt to replicate the results or accept the conclusion as valid and design experiments based on the scientist having made a correct decision. Since many work-hours and dollars go into these follow-up experiments, scientists would like to minimize the possibility that they are pursuing a false path. Thus, they set rather conservative alpha levels: $\alpha = 0.05$ and $\alpha = 0.01$ are commonly used. You might ask, "Why not set even more stringent criteria, such as $\alpha = 0.001$?" Unfortunately, when alpha is made more stringent, the probability of making a Type II error increases.

We can see this by considering an example. This example is best understood in conjunction with Table 10.4. Suppose we do an experiment and set $\alpha = 0.05$ (top row of Table 10.4). We evaluate chance and get an obtained probability of 0.02. We reject $H_0$. If $H_0$ is true, we have made a Type I error (cell 1). Suppose, however, that alpha had been set at $\alpha = 0.01$ instead of 0.05 (bottom row of Table 10.4). In this case, we would retain $H_0$ and no longer would be making a Type I error (cell 3). Thus, the more stringent the alpha level, the lower the probability of making a Type I error.

On the other hand, what happens if $H_0$ is really false (last column of the table)? With $\alpha = 0.05$ and the obtained probability = 0.02, we would reject $H_0$

**Table 10.4** Effect on beta of making alpha more stringent

| Alpha Level | Obtained Probability | Decision | State of Reality | |
| --- | --- | --- | --- | --- |
| | | | *$H_0$ is true* | *$H_0$ is false* |
| 0.05 | 0.02 | **Reject $H_0$** | [1]Type I error | [2]Correct decision |
| 0.01 | 0.02 | **Retain $H_0$** | [3]Correct decision | [4]Type II error |

and thereby make a correct decision (cell 2). However, if we changed alpha to $\alpha = 0.01$, we would retain $H_0$ and we would make a Type II error (cell 4). Thus, making alpha more stringent decreases the probability of making a Type I error but increases the probability of making a Type II error. Because of this interaction between alpha and beta, the alpha level chosen for an experiment depends on the intended use of the experimental results. As mentioned previously, if the results are to communicate a new fact to the scientific community, the consequences of a Type I error are great, and therefore stringent alpha levels are used (0.05 and 0.01). If, however, the experiment is exploratory in nature and the results are to guide the researcher in deciding whether to do a full-fledged experiment, it would be foolish to use such stringent levels. In such cases, alpha levels as high as 0.10 or 0.20 are often used.

Let's consider one more example. Imagine you are the president of a drug company. One of your leading biochemists rushes into your office and tells you that she has discovered a drug that increases memory. You are of course elated, but you still ask to see the experimental results. Let's assume it will require a $30 million outlay to install the apparatus to manufacture the drug. This is quite an expense, but if the drug really does increase memory, the potential benefits and profits are well worth it. In this case, you would want to be very sure that the results are not due to chance. The consequences of a Type I error are great. You stand to lose $30 million. You will probably want to use an extremely stringent alpha level before deciding to reject $H_0$ and risk the $30 million.

We hasten to reassure you that *truth* is not dependent on the alpha level used in an experiment. Either marijuana affects appetite or it doesn't. Either the drug increases memory or it doesn't. Setting a stringent alpha level merely diminishes the possibility that we shall conclude for the alternative hypothesis when the null hypothesis is really true.

Since we never know for sure what the real truth is as a result of a single experiment, replication is a necessary and essential part of the scientific process. Before an "alleged fact" is accepted into the body of scientific knowledge, it must be demonstrated independently in several laboratories. The probability of making a Type I error decreases greatly with independent replication.

## EVALUATING THE TAIL OF THE DISTRIBUTION

In the previous discussion, the obtained probability was found by using just the specific outcomes of the experiment (i.e., 9 pluses and 1 minus). However, we did that to keep things simple for clarity when presenting the other major concepts. In fact, it is incorrect to use *just the specific outcome* when evaluating the results of an experiment. Instead, we must determine the probability of getting the obtained outcome or *any outcome even more extreme*. It is this probability that we compare with alpha to assess the reasonableness of the null hypothesis. In other words, we evaluate the *tail* of the distribution, beginning with the obtained result, rather than just the obtained result itself. If the alternative hypothesis is nondirectional, we evaluate the obtained result or any even more extreme in both directions (both tails). If the alternative hypothesis is directional, we evaluate only the tail of the distribution that is in the direction specified by $H_1$.

To illustrate, let's again evaluate the data in the present experiment, this time evaluating the tails rather than just the specific outcome. Figure 10.1 shows the binomial distribution for $N = 10$ and $P = 0.50$. The distribution has two tails, one containing few pluses and one containing many pluses. The alternative hypothesis is nondirectional, so to calculate the obtained probability, we must determine the probability of getting the obtained result or a result even more extreme *in both directions*. Since the obtained result was 9 pluses, we must include outcomes as extreme as or more extreme than 9 pluses. From Figure 10.1, we can see that the outcome of 10 pluses is more extreme in one direction and the outcomes of 1 plus and 0 plus are as extreme or more extreme in the other direction. Thus, the obtained probability is as follows:

$$p(0, 1, 9, \text{ or } 10 \text{ pluses}) = p(0) + p(1) + p(9) + p(10)$$
$$= 0.0010 + 0.0098 + 0.0098 + 0.0010$$
$$= 0.0216$$

It is this probability (0.0216, not 0.0098) that we compare with alpha to reject or retain the null hypothesis. This probability is called a *two-tailed probability* value because the outcomes we evaluate occur under both tails of the distribution. Thus, alternative hypotheses that are nondirectional are evaluated with two-tailed probability values. If the alternative hypothesis is nondirectional, the alpha level must also be two-tailed. If $\alpha = 0.05_{2 \text{ tail}}$, this means that the two-tailed obtained probability value must be equal to or less than 0.05 to reject $H_0$. In this example, 0.0216 is less than 0.05, so we reject $H_0$ and conclude as we did before that marijuana affects appetite.

If the alternative hypothesis is directional, we evaluate the tail of the distribution that is in the direction predicted by $H_1$. To illustrate this point, suppose the alternative hypothesis was that "marijuana increases appetite" and the obtained result was 9 pluses and 1 minus. Since $H_1$ specifies that marijuana increases appetite, we evaluate the tail with the higher number of pluses. Remember that a plus means more food eaten in the marijuana condition. Thus, if marijuana increases appetite, we expect mostly pluses. The outcome of

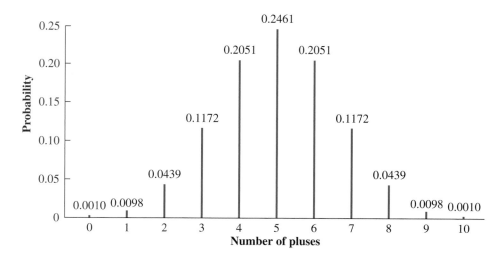

figure 10.1  Binomial distribution for $N = 10$ and $P = 0.50$.

10 pluses is the only possible result in this direction more extreme than 9 pluses. The obtained probability is

$$p(9 \text{ or } 10 \text{ pluses}) = 0.0098 + 0.0010$$
$$= 0.0108$$

This probability is called a *one-tailed probability* because all of the outcomes we are evaluating are under one tail of the distribution. Thus, alternative hypotheses that are directional are evaluated with one-tailed probabilities. If the alternative hypothesis is directional, the alpha level must be one-tailed. Thus, directional alternative hypotheses are evaluated against one-tailed alpha levels. In this example, if $\alpha = 0.05_{1 \text{ tail}}$, we would reject $H_0$ because 0.0108 is less than 0.05.

The reason we evaluate the tail has to do with the alpha level set at the beginning of the experiment. In the example we have been using, suppose the hypothesis is that "marijuana increases appetite." This is a directional hypothesis, so a one-tailed evaluation is appropriate. Assume $N = 10$ and $\alpha = 0.05_{1 \text{ tail}}$. By setting $\alpha = 0.05$ at the beginning of the experiment, the researcher desires to limit the probability of a Type I error to 5 in 100. Suppose the results of the experiment turn out to be 8 pluses and 2 minuses. Is this a result that allows rejection of $H_0$ consistent with the alpha level? Your first impulse is no doubt to answer "yes" because $p(8 \text{ pluses}) = 0.0439$. However, if we reject $H_0$ with 8 pluses, we must also reject it if the results are 9 or 10 pluses. Why? Because these outcomes are even more favorable to $H_1$ than 8 pluses and 2 minuses. Certainly, if marijuana really does increase appetite, obtaining 10 pluses and 0 minuses is better evidence than 8 pluses and 2 minuses, and similarly for 9 pluses and 1 minus. Thus, if we reject with 8 pluses, we must also reject with 9 and 10 pluses. But what is the probability of getting 8, 9, or 10 pluses if chance alone is operating?

$$p(8, 9, \text{ or } 10 \text{ pluses}) = p(8) + p(9) + p(10)$$
$$= 0.0439 + 0.0098 + 0.0010$$
$$= 0.0547$$

The probability is greater than alpha. Therefore, we can't allow 8 pluses to be a result for which we could reject $H_0$; the probability of falsely rejecting $H_0$ would be greater than the alpha level. Note that this is true even though the probability of 8 pluses itself is less than alpha. Therefore, we don't evaluate the exact outcome, but rather we evaluate the tail so as to limit the probability of a Type I error to the alpha level set at the beginning of the experiment. The reason we use a two-tailed evaluation with a nondirectional alternative hypothesis is that results at both ends of the distribution are legitimate candidates for rejecting the null hypothesis.

## ONE– AND TWO–TAILED PROBABILITY EVALUATIONS

When setting the alpha level, we must decide whether the probability evaluation should be one- or two-tailed. When making this decision, use the following rule:

*The evaluation should always be two-tailed unless the experimenter will retain $H_0$ when results are extreme in the direction opposite to the predicted direction.*

In following this rule, there are two situations commonly encountered that warrant directional hypotheses. First, when it makes no practical difference if the results turn out to be in the opposite direction, it is legitimate to use a directional hypothesis and a one-tailed evaluation. For example, if a manufacturer of automobile tires is testing a new type of tire that is supposed to last longer, a one-tailed evaluation is legitimate because it doesn't make any practical difference if the experimental results turn out in the opposite direction. The conclusion will be to retain $H_0$, and the manufacturer will continue to use the old tires. Another situation in which it seems permissible to use a one-tailed evaluation is when there are good theoretical reasons, as well as strong supporting data, to justify the predicted direction. In this case, if the experimental results turn out to be in the opposite direction, the experimenter again will conclude by retaining $H_0$ (at least until the experiment is replicated) because the results fly in the face of previous data and theory.

In situations in which the experimenter will reject $H_0$ if the results of the experiment are extreme in the direction opposite to the prediction direction, a two-tailed evaluation should be used. To understand why, let's assume the researcher goes ahead and uses a directional prediction, setting $\alpha = 0.05_{1\,\text{tail}}$, and the results turn out to be extreme in the opposite direction. If he is unwilling to conclude by retaining $H_0$, what he will probably do is shift, after seeing the data, to using a nondirectional hypothesis employing $\alpha = 0.05_{2\,\text{tail}}$ (0.025 under each tail) to be able to reject $H_0$. In the long run, following this procedure will result in a Type I error probability of 0.075 (0.05 under the tail in the predicted direction and 0.025 under the other tail). Thus, switching alternative hypotheses after seeing the data produces an inflated Type I error probability. It is of course even worse if, after seeing that the data are in the direction opposite to that predicted, the experimenter switches to $\alpha = 0.05_{1\,\text{tail}}$ in the direction of the outcome so as to reject $H_0$. In this case, the probability of a Type I error, in the long run, would be 0.10 (0.05 under each tail). For example, an experimenter following this procedure for 100 experiments, assuming all involved true null hypotheses, would be expected to falsely reject the null hypothesis 10 times. Since each of these rejections would be a Type I error, following this procedure leads to the probability of a Type I error of 0.10 (10/100 = 0.10). Therefore, to maintain the Type I error probability at the desired level, it is important to decide at the beginning of the experiment whether $H_1$ should be directional or nondirectional and to set the alpha level accordingly. If a directional $H_1$ is used, the predicted direction must be adhered to, even if the results of the experiment turn out to be extreme in the opposite direction. Consequently, $H_0$ must be retained in such cases.

For solving the problems and examples contained in this textbook, we shall indicate whether a one- or two-tailed evaluation is appropriate; we would like you to practice both. Be careful when solving these problems. When a scientist conducts an experiment, she is often following a hunch that predicts a directional effect. The problems in this textbook are often stated in terms of the scientist's directional hunch. Nonetheless, *unless the scientist will conclude by retaining $H_0$ if the results turn out to be extreme in the opposite direction,* she should use a nondirectional $H_1$ and a two-tailed evaluation, even though her hunch is directional. Each textbook problem will tell you whether you should use a nondirectional or directional $H_1$ when it asks for the alternative hypothesis. If you are asked for a nondirectional $H_1$, you should assume that the appropriate criterion for a directional alternative hypothesis has not been met, regardless of whether the scientist's hunch in the problem is directional. If you are asked for a directional $H_1$, assume that the appropriate criterion has been met and it is proper to use a directional $H_1$.

We are now ready to do a complete problem in exactly the same way any scientist would if he or she were using the sign test to evaluate the data.

## Practice Problem 10.1

Assume we have conducted an experiment to test the hypothesis that marijuana affects the appetites of AIDS patients. The procedure and population are the same as we described previously, except this time we have sampled 12 AIDS patients. The results are shown here (the scores are in calories):

| Condition | Patient | | | | | | | | | | | |
|---|---|---|---|---|---|---|---|---|---|---|---|---|
| | *1* | *2* | *3* | *4* | *5* | *6* | *7* | *8* | *9* | *10* | *11* | *12* |
| THC | 1051 | 1066 | 963 | 1179 | 1144 | 912 | 1093 | 1113 | 985 | 1271 | 978 | 951 |
| Placebo | 872 | 943 | 912 | 1213 | 1034 | 854 | 1125 | 1042 | 922 | 1136 | 886 | 902 |

**a.** What is the nondirectional alternative hypothesis?
**b.** What is the null hypothesis?
**c.** Using $\alpha = 0.05_{2\,tail}$, what do you conclude?
**d.** What error may you be making by your conclusion in part **c**?
**e.** To what population does your conclusion apply?

The solution follows.

### SOLUTION

**a.** Nondirectional alternative hypothesis:   Marijuana affects appetites of AIDS patients who are being treated at your hospital.
**b.** Null hypothesis:   Marijuana has no effect on appetites of AIDS patients who are being treated at your hospital.
**c.** Conclusion, using $\alpha = 0.05_{2\,tail}$:

STEP 1: **Calculate the number of pluses and minuses.**   The first step is to calculate the number of pluses and minuses in the sample. We have subtracted the "placebo" scores from the corresponding "THC" scores. The reverse could also have been done. There are 10 pluses and 2 minuses.

STEP 2: **Evaluate the number of pluses and minuses.**   Once we have calculated the obtained number of pluses and minuses, we must determine the probability of getting this outcome or any

*(continued)*

even more extreme in both directions because this is a two-tailed evaluation. The binomial distribution is appropriate for this determination. $N$ = the number of difference scores (pluses and minuses) = 12. We can let $P$ = the probability of a plus with any subject. If marijuana has no effect on appetite, chance alone accounts for whether any subject scores a plus or a minus. Therefore, $P = 0.50$. The obtained result was 10 pluses and 2 minuses, so the number of $P$ events = 10. The probability of getting an outcome as extreme as or more extreme than 10 pluses (two-tailed) equals the probability of 0, 1, 2, 10, 11, or 12 pluses. Since the distribution is symmetrical, $p(0, 1, 2, 10, 11,$ or 12 pluses) equals $p(10, 11,$ or 12 pluses) $\times 2$. Thus, from Table B:

| | Table B entry | |
|---|---|---|
| | **No. of $P$** | **$P$** |
| **$N$** | **Events** | **0.50** |
| 12 | 10 | 0.0161 |
| | 11 | 0.0029 |
| | 12 | 0.0002 |

$p(0, 1, 2, 10, 11$ or 12 pluses)

$= p(10, 11,$ or 12 pluses$) \times 2$

$= [p(10) + p(11) + p(12)] \times 2$

$= (0.0161 + 0.0029 + 0.0002) \times 2$

$= 0.0384$

The same value would have been obtained if we had added the six probabilities together rather than finding the one-tailed probability and multiplying by 2. Since $0.0384 < 0.05$, we reject the null hypothesis. It is not a reasonable explanation of the results. Therefore, we conclude that marijuana affects appetite. It appears to increase it.

**d.** Possible error:   By rejecting the null hypothesis, you might be making a Type I error. In reality, the null hypothesis may be true and you have rejected it.

**e.** Population:   These results apply to the population of AIDS patients from which the sample was taken.

## Practice Problem 10.2

You have good reason to believe a particular TV program is causing increased violence in teenagers. To test this hypothesis, you conduct an experiment in which 15 individuals are randomly sampled from the teenagers attending your neighborhood high school. Each subject is run in an experimental and a control condition. In the experimental condition, the teenagers watch the TV program for 3 months, during which you record the number of violent acts committed. The control condition also lasts for

3 months, but the teenagers are not allowed to watch the program during this period. At the end of each 3-month period, you total the number of violent acts committed. The results are given here:

| Condition | Subject | | | | | | | | | | | | | | |
|---|---|---|---|---|---|---|---|---|---|---|---|---|---|---|---|
| | *1* | *2* | *3* | *4* | *5* | *6* | *7* | *8* | *9* | *10* | *11* | *12* | *13* | *14* | *15* |
| Viewing the program | 25 | 35 | 10 | 8 | 24 | 40 | 44 | 18 | 16 | 25 | 32 | 27 | 33 | 28 | 26 |
| Not viewing the program | 18 | 22 | 7 | 11 | 13 | 35 | 28 | 12 | 20 | 18 | 38 | 24 | 27 | 21 | 22 |

**a.** What is the directional alternative hypothesis?
**b.** What is the null hypothesis?
**c.** Using $\alpha = 0.01_{1\,tail}$, what do you conclude?
**d.** What error may you be making by your conclusion in part **c**?
**e.** To what population does your conclusion apply?

The solution follows.

**SOLUTION**

**a.** Directional alternative hypothesis:    Watching the TV program causes increased violence in teenagers.
**b.** Null hypothesis:    Watching the TV program does not cause increased violence in teenagers.
**c.** Conclusion, using $\alpha = 0.01_{1\,tail}$:

STEP 1: **Calculate the number of pluses and minuses.**    The first step is to calculate the number of pluses and minuses in the sample from the data. We have subtracted the scores in the "not viewing" condition from the scores in the "viewing" condition. The obtained result is 12 pluses and 3 minuses.

STEP 2: **Evaluate the number of pluses and minuses.**    Next, we must determine the probability of getting this outcome or any even more extreme in the direction of the alternative hypothesis. This is a one-tailed evaluation because the alternative hypothesis is directional. The binomial distribution is appropriate. $N =$ the number of difference scores $= 15$. Let $P =$ the probability of a plus with any subject. We can evaluate the null hypothesis by assuming chance alone accounts for whether any subject scores a plus or minus. Therefore, $P = 0.50$. The obtained result was 12 pluses and 3 minuses, so the number of $P$ events $= 12$. The probability of 12 pluses or more equals the probability of 12, 13, 14, or 15 pluses. This can be found from Table B. Thus,

*(continued)*

Table B entry

| N | No. of P Events | P 0.50 |
|---|---|---|
| 15 | 12 | 0.0139 |
| | 13 | 0.0032 |
| | 14 | 0.0005 |
| | 15 | 0.0000 |

$p\,(12, 13, 14,$ or 15 pluses)

$$= p\,(12) + p\,(13) + p\,(14) + p\,(15)$$
$$= 0.0139 + 0.0032 + 0.0005 + 0.0000$$
$$= 0.0176$$

Since $0.0176 > 0.01$, we fail to reject the null hypothesis. Therefore, we retain $H_0$ and cannot conclude that the TV program causes increased violence in teenagers.

**d.** Possible error:   By retaining the null hypothesis, you might be making a Type II error. The TV program may actually cause increased violence in teenagers.

**e.** Population:   These results apply to the population of teenagers attending your neighborhood school.

## Practice Problem 10.3

A corporation psychologist believes that exercise affects self-image. To investigate this possibility, 14 employees of the corporation are randomly selected to participate in a jogging program. Before beginning the program, they are given a questionnaire that measures self-image. Then they begin the jogging program. The program consists of jogging at a moderately taxing rate for 20 minutes a day, 4 days a week. Each employee's self-image is measured again after 2 months on the program. The results are shown here (the higher the score, the higher the self-image); a score of 20 is the highest score possible.

| Subject | Before Jogging | After Jogging | Subject | Before Jogging | After Jogging |
|---|---|---|---|---|---|
| 1 | 14 | 20 | 8 | 16 | 13 |
| 2 | 13 | 16 | 9 | 10 | 16 |
| 3 | 8 | 15 | 10 | 14 | 18 |
| 4 | 14 | 12 | 11 | 6 | 14 |
| 5 | 12 | 15 | 12 | 15 | 17 |
| 6 | 7 | 13 | 13 | 12 | 18 |
| 7 | 10 | 12 | 14 | 9 | 15 |

**a.** What is the alternative hypothesis? Use a nondirectional hypothesis.
**b.** What is the null hypothesis?
**c.** Using $\alpha = 0.05_{2\,\text{tail}}$, what do you conclude?
**d.** What error may you be making by your conclusion in part **c**?
**e.** To what population does your conclusion apply?

The solution follows.

**SOLUTION**

**a.** Nondirectional alternative hypothesis:   Jogging affects self-image.
**b.** Null hypothesis:   Jogging has no effect on self-image.
**c.** Conclusion, using $\alpha = 0.05_{2\,\text{tail}}$:

> **STEP 1: Calculate the number of pluses and minuses.**   We have subtracted the "before jogging" from the "after jogging" scores. There are 12 pluses and 2 minuses.
>
> **STEP 2: Evaluate the number of pluses and minuses.**   Because $H_1$ is nondirectional, we must determine the probability of getting a result as extreme as or more extreme than 12 pluses (two-tailed), assuming chance alone accounts for the differences. The binomial distribution is appropriate. $N = 14$, $P = 0.50$, and number of $P$ events = 0, 1, 2, 12, 13, or 14. Thus, from Table B:

$$
\begin{aligned}
p(0, 1, 2, 12, 13, \text{ or } 14 \text{ pluses}) &= p(0) + p(1) + p(2) + p(12) \\
&\quad + p(13) + p(14) \\
&= 0.0001 + 0.0009 + 0.0056 \\
&\quad + 0.0056 + 0.0009 + 0.0001 \\
&= 0.0132
\end{aligned}
$$

Table B entry

| $N$ | No. of $P$ Events | $P$ 0.50 |
|---|---|---|
| 14 | 0 | 0.0001 |
|  | 1 | 0.0009 |
|  | 2 | 0.0056 |
|  | 12 | 0.0056 |
|  | 13 | 0.0009 |
|  | 14 | 0.0001 |

The same value would have been obtained if we had found the one-tailed probability and multiplied by 2. Since $0.0132 < 0.05$, we reject the null hypothesis. It appears that jogging improves self-image.
**d.** Possible error:   By rejecting the null hypothesis, you might be making a Type I error. The null hypothesis may be true, and it was rejected.
**e.** Population:   These results apply to all the employees of the corporation who were employed at the time of the experiment.

## SIZE OF EFFECT: SIGNIFICANT VERSUS IMPORTANT

The procedure we have been following in assessing the results of an experiment is first to evaluate directly the null hypothesis and then to conclude indirectly with regard to the alternative hypothesis. If we are able to reject the null hypothesis, we say the results *significant*. What we really mean by "significant" is "statistically significant." That is, the results are probably not due to chance, the independent variable has had a real effect, and if we repeat the experiment, we would again get results that would allow us to reject the null hypothesis. It might have been better to use the term *reliable* to convey this meaning rather than significant. However, the usage of *significant* is well established, so we will have to live with it. The point is that we must not confuse statistically significant with practically or theoretically "important." A statistically significant effect says little about whether the effect is an important one. For example, suppose the real effect of marijuana is to increase appetite by only 10 calories. Using careful experimental design and a large enough sample, it is possible that we would be able to detect even this small an effect. If so, we would conclude that the result is significant (reliable), but then we still need to ask, "How important is this real effect?" For most purposes, except possibly theoretical ones, the importance of an effect increases directly with the size of the effect. For further discussion of this point, see "What Is the Truth? Much Ado About Almost Nothing," in Chapter 15.

## WHAT IS THE TRUTH?

# Chance or Real Effect?—1

An article appeared in *Time* magazine concerning the "Pepsi Challenge Taste Test." A Pepsi ad, shown on the facing page, appeared in the article. Taste Test participants were Coke drinkers from Michigan who were asked to drink from a glass of Pepsi and another glass of Coke and say which they preferred. To avoid obvious bias, the glasses were not labeled "Coke" or "Pepsi." Instead, to facilitate a "blind" administration of the drinks, the Coke glass was marked with a "Q" and the Pepsi glass with an "M." The results as stated in the ad are, "More than half the Coca-Cola drinkers tested in Michigan preferred Pepsi." Aside from a possible real preference for Pepsi in the population of Michigan Coke drinkers, can you think of any other possible explanation of these sample results?

# WHAT IS THE TRUTH?

## Chance or Real Effect?—1 (*continued*)

***Answer***  The most obvious alternative explanation of these results is that they are due to chance alone; that in the population, the preference for Pepsi and Coke is equal ($P = 0.50$). You, of course, recognize this as the null hypothesis explanation. This explanation could and, in our opinion, should have been ruled out (within the limits of Type I error) by analyzing the sample data with the appropriate inference test. If the results really are significant, it doesn't take much space in an ad to say so. This ad is like many that state sample results favoring their product without evaluating chance as a reasonable explanation.

As an aside, Coke did not cry "chance alone," but instead claimed the study was invalid because people like the letter "M" better than "Q." Coke conducted a study to test its contention by putting Coke in both the "M" and "Q" glasses. Sure enough, more people preferred the drink in the "M" glass, even though it was Coke in both glasses. Pepsi responded by doing another Pepsi Challenge round, only this time revising the letters to "S" and "L," with Pepsi always in the "L" glass. The sample results again favored Pepsi. Predictably, Coke executives again cried foul,

claiming an "L" preference. A noted motivational authority was then consulted and he reported that he knew of no studies showing a bias in favor of the letter "L." As a budding statistician, how might you

design an experiment to determine whether there is a preference for Pepsi or Coke in the population and at the same time eliminate glass-preference as a possible explanation?

© PepsiCo, Inc. 1976. Reproduced with permission.

## WHAT IS THE TRUTH?

# Chance or Real Effect?—2

The research reported in the previous "What Is the Truth?" section did not report any significance levels. Sometimes experiments are reported that do contain significance levels but that nonetheless raise suspicions of Type I error. Consider the following newspaper article on research done at a leading U.S. university.

### Study: Mildly Depressed Women Live Longer

*If you want to live a long, happy life, think again.*

*Researchers at Duke University followed more than 4,000 older people for a decade and found that women who lived longest were mildly depressed. The study is in the May-June issue of* American Journal of Geriatric Psychiatry.

*"We don't quite understand the finding," said Dr. Dan Blazer, a professor of psychiatry and behavioral science at Duke and co-author of the study. This jump in longevity was seen only in women. Women with mild depression, determined by a diagnostic questionnaire, were 40 percent less* likely to die during the study period compared with women with no depression or those with more serious forms of depression. For men, mild depression was found to have no effect on mortality.

*Blazer suspects mild forms of depression could protect against death by slowing people down, giving them more time to pay attention to their minds and bodies.*

Author Unknown. Article from *The Coloradoan*, May 4, 2002, p. A3.

Although the newspaper article didn't state any significance levels, let's assume that in the *American Journal of Geriatric Psychiatry* article, it was stated that using $\alpha = 0.05$, the women with mild depression were *significantly* more likely to die during the study period compared with women with no depression or those with more serious forms of depression. Yes, this result reached significance at the 0.05 level, but it still seems questionable. First, this seems like a surprising, unplanned result that the authors admit they don't understand. Second, neither women with no depression nor women with more serious depression showed it. Finally, mildly depressed men didn't show the result either. What do you think, chance or real effect? The point being made is that just because a result is statistically significant, it does not automatically mean that the result is a real effect. Of course, replication would help resolve the issue.

# WHAT IS THE TRUTH?

## "No Product Is Better Than Our Product"

**O**ften we see advertisements that present no data and make the assertion, "No product is better in doing X than our product." An ad regarding Excedrin, which was published in a national magazine, is an example of this kind of advertisement. The ad showed a large picture of a bottle of Excedrin tablets along with the statements,

"Nothing you can buy is stronger."
"Nothing you can buy works harder."
"Nothing gives you bigger relief."

The question is, "How do we interpret these claims?" Do we rush out and buy Excedrin because it is stronger, works harder, and gives bigger relief than any other headache remedy available? If there are experimental data that form the basis of this ad's claims, we wonder what the results really are. What is your guess?

*Answer*   Of course, we really don't know in every case, and therefore we don't intend our remarks to be directed at any specific ad. We have just chosen the Excedrin ad as an illustration of many such ads. However, we can't help but be suspicious that in most, if not all, cases where sample

data exist, the actual data show that there is no significant difference in doing X between the advertiser's product and the other products tested.

For the sake of discussion, let's call the advertiser's product "A." If the data had shown that "A" was better than the competing products, it seems reasonable that the advertiser would directly claim superiority for its product, rather than implying this indirectly through the weaker statement that no other product is better than theirs.

Why, then, would the advertiser make this weaker statement? Probably because the actual data do not show product "A" to be superior at all. Most likely, the sample data show product "A" to be either equal to or inferior to the others, and the inference test shows no significant difference between the products. Given such

data, rather than saying that the research shows our product to be inferior or, at best, equal to the other products at doing X (which clearly would not sell a whole bunch of product "A"), the results are stated in this more positive, albeit, in our opinion, misleading way. Saying "No other product is better than ours in doing X" will obviously sell more products than "All products tested were equal in doing X." And after all, if you read the weaker statement closely, it does not really say that product "A" is superior to the others.

Thus, in the absence of reported data to the contrary, we believe the most accurate interpretation of the claim "No other competitor's product is superior to ours at doing X" is that *the products are equal at doing X.*

## WHAT IS THE TRUTH?

# Anecdotal Reports Versus Systematic Research

The following article appeared in an issue of *The New York Times* on the Web. It is representative of a fairly common occurrence: individual testimony about a phenomenon conflicts with systematic research concerning the phenomenon. In this case, we are looking at the effects of the hormone secretin on autism. After reading the article, if you were asked if secretin has a beneficial effect on autism, how would you answer? Would you be satisfied with anecdotal reports? Would negative results from systematic research satisfy you? How could the issue be resolved?

### *A Drug Used for Autism Is Under Fire in New Study*

**By SANDRA BLAKESLEE**

*A hormone trumpeted in the news media and on the Internet as a potential cure for autism worked no better than saltwater in its first controlled clinical trial, scientists are reporting.*

*The study, described in the issue of* The New England Journal of

Medicine *that is being published on Thursday, is one of a dozen efforts sponsored by the National Institutes of Health to test the hormone, secretin, which gained wide attention after a 3-year-old New Hampshire boy showed rapid improvement after taking the drug in 1996.*

*"Secretin is in widespread use across the country," said Dr. Marie Bristol-Power, special assistant for autism programs at the Institute of Child Health and Human Development at the N.I.H. "Parents need to know if it is promising and should be pursued or if they are being taken advantage of."*

*The study was not definitive, Dr. Bristol-Power said, and researchers*

*will know more by the middle of next year, when other studies are completed.*

*Defenders of secretin were quick to denounce the new study, saying it did not give the drug a fair test.*

*"No one has ever claimed that secretin is a miracle cure for autism," said Victoria Beck, the mother of the boy who improved after taking it.*

*Ms. Beck, who has written a book on secretin, called the hormone "a clue that deserves careful investigation and not dismissal from autism gurus, who have a vested interest in the way things have been done in the past."*

*Autism is a serious brain disorder that begins in infancy and*

## WHAT IS THE TRUTH?

# Anecdotal Reports Versus Systematic Research (*continued*)

prevents children from developing normally. Symptoms, which can be mild to severe, include an inability to communicate, a refusal to make eye contact, repetitive behavior like head banging or hand flapping, and a preoccupation with unusual activities or interests.

Half a million Americans have the disorder, which is typically treated with educational and behavioral therapy; while intensive therapy has proved effective in some patients, two-thirds of adults with autism cannot live independently.

Secretin is a hormone made in the intestine that stimulates the release of digestive fluids. Ms. Beck's son, Parker, was given an injection to explore the cause of his chronic diarrhea. Soon afterward, his behavior improved; he could hold still and interact better with adults.

When his story was reported on television, in newspapers and on the Internet last year, parents began clamoring to get the drug.

Dr. Bristol-Power said that the supply of secretin was soon

exhausted and that a black market developed involving sham secretin, price gouging and other forms of profiteering; Ms. Beck said that these stories were exaggerated and that no one today had any problem obtaining secretin at a fair price, which is about $200 an injection.

Anecdotes about secretin are thriving on the Internet. Some parents report dramatic effects, others see no effect and some report that their child's symptoms have worsened. Both sides in the secretin controversy estimate that 2,000 to 3,000 children have taken or are taking the drug.

The controlled study of secretin was led by Dr. James Bodfish of the Western Carolina Center and the University of North Carolina, and by Dr. Adrian Sandler of the Center for Child Development at Thoms Rehabilitation Hospital in Asheville, N.C.

In all, 56 autistic children 3 to 14 years of age took part in the study. Half received a single injection of synthetic human secretin, and the rest were injected with saltwater. Researchers administered a battery of behavioral tests at intervals of one day, one week and four weeks after the treatment. Statistically, the two groups showed no differences, Dr. Sandler said.

A third of the children in both the placebo and treatment groups improved on some of the same measures. The only explanation, Dr. Sandler said, is a "significant placebo effect."

"Parents are extremely invested in the possibility of new treatments and have high expectancies," he said. "They are looking for subtle improvements.

Kids with autism show variability in their day-to-day behavior and it would be easy to attribute normal variations to the secretin."

Ms. Beck disputes this interpretation, contending that by concentrating on standard behavioral tests the researchers have failed to look [at] a wide range of physiological responses seen in children given secretin, and that those should be studied.

"It really bothers me that parents are portrayed as this desperate group of people with vacant minds," she said. "They claim we can't tell the difference between an improvement and a mirage. But when a child stops vomiting, sleeps through the night and makes eye contact, we know something is happening."

## SUMMARY

In this chapter, we have discussed the topic of hypothesis testing, using the sign test as our vehicle. The sign test is used in conjunction with the repeated measures design. The essential features of the repeated measures design are that there are paired scores between conditions and difference scores are analyzed.

In any hypothesis-testing experiment, there are always two hypotheses that compete to explain the results: the alternative hypothesis and the null hypothesis. The alternative hypothesis specifies that the independent variable is responsible for the differences in score values between the conditions. The alternative hypothesis may be directional or nondirectional. It is legitimate to use a directional hypothesis when there is a good theoretical basis and good supporting evidence in the literature. If the experiment is a basic fact-finding experiment, ordinarily a nondirectional hypothesis should be used. A directional alternative hypothesis is evaluated with a one-tailed probability value and a nondirectional hypothesis with a two-tailed probability value.

The null hypothesis is the logical counterpart to the alternative hypothesis such that if the null hypothesis is false, the alternative hypothesis must be true. If the alternative hypothesis is nondirectional, the null hypothesis specifies that the independent variable has no effect on the dependent variable. If the alternative hypothesis is directional, the null hypothesis states that the independent variable has no effect in the direction specified.

In evaluating the data from an experiment, we never directly evaluate the alternative hypothesis. We always first evaluate the null hypothesis. The null hypothesis is evaluated by assuming chance alone is responsible for the differences in scores between conditions. In doing this evaluation, we calculate the probability of getting the obtained result or a result even more extreme if chance alone is responsible. If this obtained probability is equal to or lower than the alpha level, we consider the null hypothesis explanation unreasonable and reject the null hypothesis. We

conclude by accepting the alternative hypothesis because it is the only other explanation. If the obtained probability is greater than the alpha level, we retain the null hypothesis. It is still considered a reasonable explanation of the data. Of course, if the null hypothesis is not rejected, the alternative hypothesis cannot be accepted. The conclusion applies legitimately only to the population from which the sample was randomly drawn. We must be careful to distinguish "statistically significant" from practically or theoretically "important."

The alpha level is usually set at 0.05 or 0.01 to minimize the probability of making a Type I error. A Type I error occurs when the null hypothesis is rejected and it is actually true. The alpha level limits the probability of making a Type I error. It is also possible to make a Type II error. This occurs when we retain the null hypothesis and it is false. Beta is defined as the probability of making a Type II error. When alpha is made more stringent, beta increases. By minimizing alpha and beta, it is possible to have a high probability of correctly concluding from an experiment regardless of whether $H_0$ or $H_1$ is true. A significant result really says that it is a reliable result but gives little information about the size of the effect. The larger the effect, the more likely it is to be an important effect.

In analyzing the data of an experiment with the sign test, we ignore the magnitude of difference scores and just consider their direction. There are only two possible scores for each subject: a plus or a minus. We sum the pluses and minuses for all subjects, and the obtained result is the total number of pluses and minuses. To test the null hypothesis, we calculate the probability of getting the total number of pluses or a number of pluses even more extreme if chance alone is responsible. The binomial distribution with $P$(the probability of a plus) $= 0.50$ and $N =$ the number of difference scores is appropriate for making this determination. An illustrative problem and several practice problems were given to show how to evaluate the null hypothesis using the binomial distribution.

## IMPORTANT TERMS

Alpha ($\alpha$) level (p. 220, 224)
Alternative hypothesis ($H_1$) (p. 220)
Beta ($\beta$) (p. 223)
Binomial distribution (p. 221)
Correct decision (p. 224)
Correlated groups design (p. 219)
Directional hypothesis (p. 220)
Fail to reject null hypothesis (p. 221)

Important size of effect (p. 234)
Nondirectional hypothesis (p. 220)
Null hypothesis ($H_0$) (p. 220)
One-tailed probability (p. 227)
Reject null hypothesis (p. 222)
Repeated measures design (p. 219)
Replicated measures design (p. 219)
Retain null hypothesis (p. 221)

Sign test (p. 216)
Significant (p. 221)
Size of effect (p. 234)
State of reality (p. 223)
Two-tailed probability (p. 226)
Type I error (p. 222)
Type II error (p. 222)

## QUESTIONS AND PROBLEMS

1. Briefly define or explain each of the terms in the Important Terms section.
2. Briefly describe the process involved in hypothesis testing. Be sure to include the alternative hypothesis, the null hypothesis, the decision rule, the possible type of error, and the population to which the results can be generalized.
3. Explain in your own words why it is important to know the possible errors we might make when rejecting or failing to reject the null hypothesis.
4. Does the null hypothesis for a nondirectional $H_1$ differ from the null hypothesis for a directional $H_1$? Explain.
5. Under what conditions is it legitimate to use a directional $H_1$? Why is it not legitimate to use a directional $H_1$ just because the experimenter has a "hunch" about the direction?
6. If the obtained probability in an experiment equals 0.0200, does this mean that the probability that $H_0$ is true equals 0.0200? Explain.
7. Discuss the difference between "significant" and "important." Include "effect size" in your discussion.
8. What considerations go into determining the best alpha level to use? Discuss.
9. A primatologist believes that rhesus monkeys possess curiosity. She reasons that, if this is true, then they should prefer novel stimulation to repetitive stimulation. An experiment is conducted in which 12 rhesus monkeys are randomly

selected from the university colony and taught to press two bars. Pressing bar 1 always produces the same sound, whereas bar 2 produces a novel sound each time it is pressed. After learning to press the bars, the monkeys are tested for 15 minutes, during which they have free access to both bars. The number of presses on each bar during the 15 minutes is recorded. The resulting data are as follows:

| Subject | Bar 1 | Bar 2 |
|---------|-------|-------|
| 1 | 20 | 40 |
| 2 | 18 | 25 |
| 3 | 24 | 38 |
| 4 | 14 | 27 |
| 5 | 5 | 31 |
| 6 | 26 | 21 |
| 7 | 15 | 32 |
| 8 | 29 | 38 |
| 9 | 15 | 25 |
| 10 | 9 | 18 |
| 11 | 25 | 32 |
| 12 | 31 | 28 |

a. What is the alternative hypothesis? In this case, assume a nondirectional hypothesis is appropriate because there is insufficient empirical basis to warrant a directional hypothesis.

b. What is the null hypothesis?

c. Using $\alpha = 0.05_{2\ tail}$, what is your conclusion?

d. What error may you be making by your conclusion in part **c**?

e. To what population does your conclusion apply? cognitive, biological

10. A school principal is interested in a new method for teaching eighth-grade social studies, which he believes will increase the amount of material learned. To test this method, the principal conducts the following experiment. The eighth-grade students in the school district are grouped into pairs based on matching their IQs and past grades. Twenty matched pairs are randomly selected for the experiment. One member of each pair is randomly assigned to a group that receives the new method, and the other member of each pair to a group that receives the standard instruction. At the end of the course, all students take a common final exam. The following are the results:

| Pair No. | New Method | Standard Instruction |
|---|---|---|
| 1 | 95 | 83 |
| 2 | 75 | 68 |
| 3 | 73 | 80 |
| 4 | 85 | 82 |
| 5 | 78 | 84 |
| 6 | 86 | 78 |
| 7 | 93 | 85 |
| 8 | 88 | 82 |
| 9 | 75 | 84 |
| 10 | 84 | 68 |
| 11 | 72 | 81 |
| 12 | 84 | 91 |
| 13 | 75 | 72 |
| 14 | 87 | 81 |
| 15 | 94 | 83 |
| 16 | 82 | 87 |
| 17 | 70 | 65 |
| 18 | 84 | 76 |
| 19 | 72 | 63 |
| 20 | 83 | 80 |

a. What is the alternative hypothesis? Use a directional hypothesis.

b. What is the null hypothesis?

c. Using $\alpha = 0.05_{1\ tail}$, what is your conclusion?

d. What error may you be making by your conclusion in part **c**?

e. To what population does your conclusion apply? education

11. A physiologist believes that the hormone angiotensin II is important in regulating thirst. To investigate this belief, she randomly samples 16 rats from the vivarium of the drug company where she works and places them in individual cages with free access to food and water. After they have grown acclimated to their new "homes," the experimenter measures the amount of water each rat drinks in a 20-minute period. Then she injects each animal intravenously with a known concentration (100 micrograms per kilogram) of angiotensin II. The rats are then put back into their home cages, and the amount each drinks for another 20-minute period is measured. The results are shown in the following table. Scores are in milliliters drunk per 20 minutes.

| Subject | Before Injection | After Injection |
|---|---|---|
| 1 | 1.2 | 11.3 |
| 2 | 0.8 | 10.7 |
| 3 | 0.5 | 10.3 |
| 4 | 1.3 | 11.5 |
| 5 | 0.6 | 9.6 |
| 6 | 3.5 | 3.3 |
| 7 | 0.7 | 10.5 |
| 8 | 0.4 | 11.4 |
| 9 | 1.1 | 12.0 |
| 10 | 0.3 | 12.8 |
| 11 | 0.6 | 11.4 |
| 12 | 0.3 | 9.8 |
| 13 | 0.5 | 10.6 |
| 14 | 4.1 | 3.2 |
| 15 | 0.4 | 12.1 |
| 16 | 1.0 | 11.2 |

a. What is the nondirectional alternative hypothesis?

b. What is the null hypothesis?

c. Using $\alpha = 0.05_{2\ \text{tail}}$, what is your conclusion? Assume the injection itself had no effect on drinking behavior.

d. What error may you be making by your conclusion in part **c**?

e. To what population does your conclusion apply? biological

12. A leading toothpaste manufacturer advertises that, in a recent medical study, 70% of the people tested had brighter teeth after using its toothpaste (called Very Bright) as compared to using the leading competitor's brand (called Brand X). The advertisement continues, "Therefore, use Very Bright and get brighter teeth." In point of fact, the data upon which these statements were based were collected from a random sample of 10 employees from the manufacturer's Pasadena plant. In the experiment, each employee used both toothpastes. Half of the employees used Brand X for 3 weeks, followed by Very Bright for the same time period. The other half used Very Bright first, followed by Brand X. A brightness test was given at the end of each 3-week period. Thus, there were two scores for each employee, one from the brightness test following the use of Brand X and one following the use of Very Bright. The following table shows the scores (the higher, the brighter):

| Subject | Very Bright | Brand X |
|---------|-------------|---------|
| 1 | 5 | 4 |
| 2 | 4 | 3 |
| 3 | 4 | 2 |
| 4 | 2 | 3 |
| 5 | 3 | 1 |
| 6 | 4 | 1 |
| 7 | 1 | 3 |
| 8 | 3 | 4 |
| 9 | 6 | 5 |
| 10 | 6 | 4 |

a. What is the alternative hypothesis? Use a directional hypothesis.

b. What is the null hypothesis?

c. Using $\alpha = 0.05_{1\ \text{tail}}$, what do you conclude?

d. What error may you be making by your conclusion in part **c**?

e. To what population does your conclusion apply?

f. Does the advertising seem misleading? I/O

13. A researcher is interested in determining whether acupuncture affects pain tolerance. An experiment is performed in which 15 students are randomly chosen from a large pool of university undergraduate volunteers. Each subject serves in two conditions. In both conditions, each subject receives a short-duration electric shock to the pulp of a tooth. The shock intensity is set to produce a moderate level of pain to the unanesthetized subject. After the shock is terminated, each subject rates the perceived level of pain on a scale of 0–10, with 10 being the highest level. In the experimental condition, each subject receives the appropriate acupuncture treatment prior to receiving the shock. The control condition is made as similar to the experimental condition as possible, except a placebo treatment is given instead of acupuncture. The two conditions are run on separate days at the same time of day. The pain ratings in the accompanying table are obtained.

a. What is the alternative hypothesis? Assume a nondirectional hypothesis is appropriate.

b. What is the null hypothesis?

c. Using $\alpha = 0.05_{2\ \text{tail}}$, what is your conclusion?

d. What error may you be making by your conclusion in part **c**?

e. To what population does your conclusion apply?

| Subject | Acupuncture | Placebo |
|---------|-------------|---------|
| 1 | 4 | 6 |
| 2 | 2 | 5 |
| 3 | 1 | 5 |
| 4 | 5 | 3 |
| 5 | 3 | 6 |
| 6 | 2 | 4 |
| 7 | 3 | 7 |
| 8 | 2 | 6 |
| 9 | 1 | 8 |
| 10 | 4 | 3 |
| 11 | 3 | 7 |
| 12 | 4 | 8 |
| 13 | 5 | 3 |
| 14 | 2 | 5 |
| 15 | 1 | 4 |

cognitive, health

## NOTES

10.1 If the null hypothesis is false, then chance does not account for the results. Strictly speaking, this means that something systematic differs between the two groups. Ideally, the only systematic difference is due to the independent variable. Thus, we say that if the null hypothesis is false, the alternative hypothesis must be true. Practically speaking, however, the reader should be aware that it is hard to do the perfect experiment. Consequently, in addition to the alternative hypothesis, there are often additional possible explanations of the systematic difference. Therefore, when we say "we accept $H_1$," you should be aware that there may be additional explanations of the systematic difference.

10.2 If the alternative hypothesis is directional, the null hypothesis asserts that the independent variable does not have an effect in the direction specified by the alternative hypothesis. This is true in the overwhelming number of experiments conducted. Occasionally, an experiment is conducted where the alternative hypothesis specifies not only the direction but also the magnitude of the effect. For example, in connection with the marijuana experiment, an alternative hypothesis of this type might be "Marijuana increases appetite so as to increase average daily eating by more than 200 calories." The null hypothesis for this alternative hypothesis is "Marijuana increases appetite so as to increase daily eating by 200 or less calories."

## BOOK COMPANION WEBSITE

Go to www.thomsonedu.com/psychology/pagano for:

- Flash cards for review of terms
- Chapter quiz
- Statistical workshops
- And more

## WebTUTOR

Available via WebTutor for this chapter:

- Detailed chapter outline
- *Know and Be Able To Do* section
- Drag & Drop game for review of terms
- Flash cards for review of terms
- Audio flash cards for MP3 player
- More practice problems using computational equations
- Chapter quiz

# Power

## INTRODUCTION

We have seen in Chapter 10 that there are two errors we might make when testing hypotheses. We have called them Type I and Type II errors. We have further pointed out that the alpha level limits the probability of making a Type I error. By setting alpha to 0.05 or 0.01, experimenters can limit the probability that they will falsely reject the null hypothesis to these low levels. But what about Type II errors? We defined beta ($\beta$) as the probability of making a Type II error. We shall see later in this chapter that $\beta = 1 -$ power. By maximizing power, we minimize beta, which means we minimize the probability of making a Type II error. Thus, power is a very important topic.

## WHAT IS POWER?

Conceptually, the power of an experiment is a measure of the sensitivity of the experiment to detect a *real effect* of the independent variable. *By "a real effect of the independent variable," we mean an effect that produces a change in the dependent variable.* If the independent variable does not produce a change in the dependent variable, it has no effect and we say that the independent variable does not have a real effect.

In analyzing the data from an experiment, we "detect" a real effect of the independent variable by rejecting the null hypothesis. Thus, power is defined in terms of rejecting $H_0$.

definition    ■   *Mathematically,* **the power of an experiment** *is defined as the probability that the results of an experiment will allow rejection of the null hypothesis if the independent variable has a real effect.*

Another way of stating the definition is that the power of an experiment is the probability that the results of an experiment will allow rejection of the null hypothesis if the null hypothesis is false.

Since power is a probability, its value can vary from 0.00 to 1.00. The higher the power, the more sensitive the experiment to detect a real effect of the independent variable. Experiments with power as high as 0.80 or higher are very desirable but rarely seen in the behavioral sciences. Values of 0.40 to 0.60 are much more common. It is especially useful to determine the power of an experiment when (1) initially designing the experiment and (2) interpreting the results of experiments that fail to detect any real effects of the independent variable (i.e., experiments that retain $H_0$).

## $P_{\text{null}}$ AND $P_{\text{real}}$

When computing the power of an experiment using the sign test, it is useful to distinguish between $P_{\text{null}}$ and $P_{\text{real}}$.

definitions    ■   $P_{\text{null}}$ *is the probability of getting a plus with any subject in the sample of the experiment when the independent variable has no effect.*

■   $P_{\text{real}}$ *is the probability of getting a plus with any subject in the sample of the experiment when the independent variable has a real effect.*

$P_{null}$ always equals 0.50. For experiments where $H_1$ is nondirectional, $P_{real}$ equals any one of the other possible values of $P$ (i.e., any value of $P$ that does not equal 0.50).

### $P_{real}$: A Measure of the Size and Direction of the Real Effect

The actual value of $P_{real}$ will depend on the size and direction of the real effect. To illustrate, let's use the marijuana experiment of Chapter 10. (Refer to Figure 11.1 for the rest of this discussion.) Let us for the moment assume that the marijuana experiment was conducted on the entire population of 10,000 AIDS patients being treated at your hospital, not just on the sample of 10. If the effect of marijuana is to increase appetite and the size of the real effect is large enough to overcome all the variables that might be acting to decrease appetite, we would get pluses from all 10,000 patients. Accordingly, there would be 10,000 pluses and 0 minuses in the population. Thus, for this size and direction of marijuana effect, $P_{real} = 1.00$. This is because there are all pluses in the population and the scores of the 10 subjects in the actual experiment would have to be a random sample from this population of scores. We can now elaborate further on the definition of $P_{real}$.

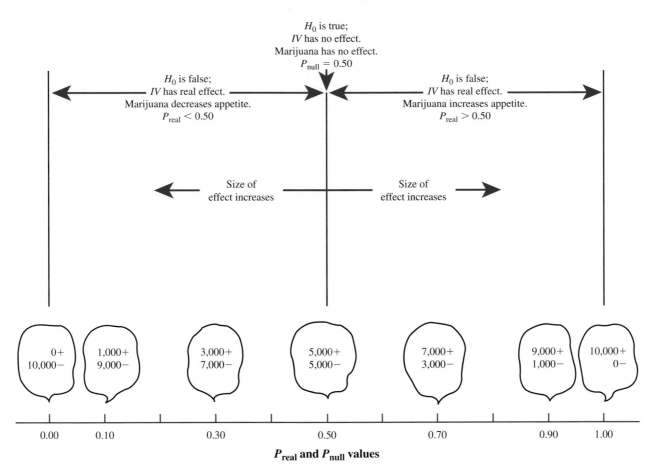

**figure 11.1**   Relationship among null hypothesis, size of marijuana effect, and $P$ values for a nondirectional $H_1$.

definition   ■   *As we defined it earlier, $P_{real}$ is the probability of a plus with any subject in the sample of the experiment if the independent variable has a real effect. However, it is also the proportion of pluses in the population if the experiment were done on the entire population and the independent variable has a real effect.*

Of course, the value $P_{real}$ is the same whether defined in terms of the population proportion of pluses or the probability of a plus with any subject in the sample. Let us return now to our discussion of $P_{real}$ and the magnitude of the effect of the independent variable.

If marijuana increases appetite less strongly than to produce all pluses—say, to produce 9 pluses for every 1 minus—in the population, there would be 9000 pluses and 1000 minuses and $P_{real} = 0.90$.[*] If the increasing effect of marijuana were of even smaller size—say, 7 pluses for every 3 minuses—the population would have 7000 pluses and 3000 minuses. In this case, $P_{real} = 0.70$. Finally, if marijuana had no effect on appetite, then there would be 5000 pluses and 5000 minuses, and $P_{null} = 0.50$. Of course, this is the chance alone prediction.

On the other hand, if marijuana decreases appetite, we would expect fewer pluses than minuses. Here, $P_{real} < 0.50$. To illustrate, if the decreasing effect on appetite is large enough, there would be all minuses (10,000 minuses and 0 pluses) in the population and $P_{real} = 0.00$. A decreasing effect of smaller size, such that there were 1000 pluses and 9000 minuses, would yield $P_{real} = 0.10$. A still weaker decreasing effect on appetite—say, 3 pluses for every 7 minuses—would yield $P_{real} = 0.30$. As the decreasing effect on appetite weakens still further, we finally return to the null hypothesis specification of $P_{null} = 0.50$ (marijuana has no effect).

From the previous discussion, we can see that $P_{real}$ is a measure of the size and direction of the independent variable's real effect. The further $P_{real}$ is from 0.50, the greater is the size of the real effect. It turns out that the power of the experiment varies with the size of the real effect. Thus, when doing a power analysis with the sign test, we must consider all $P_{real}$ values of possible interest.

## POWER ANALYSIS OF THE AIDS EXPERIMENT

Suppose you are planning an experiment to test the hypothesis that "marijuana affects appetite in AIDS patients." You plan to randomly select five AIDS patients from your hospital AIDS population and conduct the experiment as previously described. Since you want to limit the probability of falsely rejecting the null hypothesis to a low level, you set $\alpha = 0.05_{2tail}$. Given this stringent alpha level, if you reject $H_0$, you can be reasonably confident your results are due to marijuana and not to chance. But what is the probability that you will reject the

---

[*]The reader should note that, even though there are minuses in the population, we assume that the effect of marijuana is the same on all subjects (namely, it increases appetite in all subjects). The minuses are assumed to have occurred due to randomly occurring variables that decrease appetite.

null hypothesis as a result of doing this experiment? To answer this question, we must first determine what sample results, if any, will allow $H_0$ to be rejected. The results most favorable for rejecting the null hypothesis are all pluses or all minuses. Suppose you got the strongest possible result—all pluses in the sample. Could you reject $H_0$? Since $H_1$ is nondirectional, a two-tailed evaluation is appropriate. With $N = 5$ and $P_{null} = 0.50$, from Table B in Appendix D,

$p(5$ pluses or 5 minuses$) = p(5$ pluses or 0 pluses$)$

$= 0.0312 + 0.0312$

$= 0.0624$

Table B entry

| $N$ | No. of $P$ Events | $P$ 0.50 |
|---|---|---|
| 5 | 0 | 0.0312 |
|   | 5 | 0.0312 |

Since 0.0624 is greater than alpha, if we obtained these results in the experiment, we must conclude by retaining $H_0$. Thus, even if the results were the *most favorable possible for rejecting $H_0$*, we still can't reject it!

Let's look at the situation a little more closely. Suppose, in fact, that marijuana has a very strong effect on appetite and that it increases appetite so much that, if the experiment were conducted on the entire population, there would be all pluses. For example, if the population were 10,000 patients, there would be 10,000 pluses. The five scores in the sample would be a random sample from this population of scores, and the sample would have all pluses. But we've just determined that, even with five pluses in the sample, we would be unable to reject the null hypothesis. Thus, no matter how large the marijuana effect really is, we would not be able to reject $H_0$. With $N = 5$ and $\alpha = 0.05_{2\,tail}$, there is no sample result that would allow $H_0$ to be rejected. This is the most insensitive experiment possible. Power has been defined as the probability of rejecting the null hypothesis if the independent variable has a real effect. In this experiment, the probability of rejecting the null hypothesis is zero, no matter how large the independent variable effect really is. *Thus, the power of this experiment is zero for all $P_{real}$ values.* We can place very little value on results from such an insensitive experiment.

## Effect of $N$ and Size of Real Effect

Next, suppose $N$ is increased to 10. Are there now any sample results that will allow us to reject the null hypothesis? The solution is shown in Table 11.1. If the sample outcome is 0 pluses, from Table B, with $N = 10$ and using $P_{null} = 0.50$, $p(0$ or 10 pluses$) = 0.0020$. Note we included 10 pluses because the alternative hypothesis is nondirectional, requiring a two-tailed evaluation. Since 0.0020 is less than alpha, we would reject $H_0$ if we got this sample outcome. Since the two-tailed probability for 10 pluses is also 0.0020, we would also reject $H_0$ with this outcome. From Table B, we can see that, if the sample outcome were 1 plus or 9 pluses, we would also reject $H_0$ ($p = 0.0216$). However, if the sample outcome were 2 pluses or 8 pluses, the two-tailed probability t a b l e 11.1   Determining the sample outcomes that will allow rejection of the null hypothesis with $N = 10$, $P_{null} = 0.50$, and $\alpha = 0.05_{2\ tail}$

| Sample Outcome | Probability | Decision |
|---|---|---|
| 0 pluses | $p(0 \text{ or } 10 \text{ pluses}) = 2(0.0010)$ <br> $= 0.0020$ | Reject $H_0$ |
| 10 pluses | $p(0 \text{ or } 10 \text{ pluses}) = 2(0.0010)$ <br> $= 0.0020$ | Reject $H_0$ |
| 1 plus | $p(0, 1, 9, \text{ or } 10 \text{ pluses}) = 2(0.0010 + 0.0098)$ <br> $= 0.0216$ | Reject $H_0$ |
| 9 pluses | $p(0, 1, 9, \text{ or } 10 \text{ pluses}) = 2(0.0010 + 0.0098)$ <br> $= 0.0216$ | Reject $H_0$ |
| 2 pluses | $p(0, 1, 2, 8, 9, \text{ or } 10 \text{ pluses}) = 2(0.0010 + 0.0098 + 0.0439)$ <br> $= 0.1094$ | Retain $H_0$ |
| 8 pluses | $p(0, 1, 2, 8, 9, \text{ or } 10 \text{ pluses}) = 2(0.0010 + 0.0098 + 0.0439)$ <br> $= 0.1094$ | Retain $H_0$ |

value (0.1094) would be greater than alpha. Hence, we would retain $H_0$ with 2 or 8 pluses. If we can't reject $H_0$ with 2 or 8 pluses, we certainly can't reject $H_0$ if we get an outcome less extreme, such as 3, 4, 5, 6, or 7 pluses. Thus, the only outcomes that will allow us to reject $H_0$ are 0, 1, 9, or 10 pluses. Note that, in making this determination, since we were evaluating the null hypothesis, we used $P_{null} = 0.50$ (which assumes no effect) and began at the extremes, working in toward the center of the distribution until we reached the first outcome for which the two-tailed probability exceeded alpha. The outcomes allowing rejection of $H_0$ are the ones more extreme than this first outcome for which we retain $H_0$.

How can we use these outcomes to determine power? Power equals the probability of rejecting $H_0$ if the independent variable has a real effect. We've just determined that the only way we shall reject $H_0$ is if we obtain a sample outcome of 0, 1, 9, or 10 pluses. Therefore, power equals the probability of getting 0, 1, 9, or 10 pluses in our sample if the independent variable has a real effect. Thus,

Power = probability of rejecting $H_0$ if the independent variable (*IV*) has a real effect

= $p(0, 1, 9, \text{ or } 10 \text{ pluses})$ if *IV* has a real effect

But the probability of getting 0, 1, 9, or 10 pluses depends on the size of marijuana's real effect on appetite. Therefore, power will differ for different sizes of effect. To illustrate this point, we shall calculate power for several possible sizes of real effect. Using $P_{real}$ as our measure of the magnitude and direction of the marijuana effect, we will calculate power for $P_{real} = 1.00, 0.90, 0.70, 0.30, 0.10$, and 0.00. These values have been chosen to span the full range of possible real effects.

First, let's assume marijuana has such a strong increasing effect on appetite that, if it were given to the entire population, it would produce all pluses. In this case, $P_{real} = 1.00$. Determining power for $P_{real} = 1.00$ is as follows:

Power = probability of rejecting $H_0$ if *IV* has a real effect

$\quad = p(0, 1, 9, \text{or } 10 \text{ pluses})$ as the sample outcome if $P_{real} = 1.00$

$\quad = p(0) + p(1) + p(9) + p(10) \quad$ if $P_{real} = 1.00$

$\quad = 0.0000 + 0.0000 + 0.0000 + 1.0000$

$\quad = 1.0000$

If $P_{real} = 1.00$, the only possible scores are pluses. Therefore, the sample of 10 scores must be all pluses. Thus, $p(0 \text{ pluses}) = p(1 \text{ plus}) = p(9 \text{ pluses}) = 0.0000$, and $p(10 \text{ pluses}) = 1.0000$. Thus, by the addition rule, power = 1.0000. The probability of rejecting the null hypothesis when it is false such that $P_{real} = 1.00$ is equal to 1.0000. It is certain that if the effect of marijuana is as large as described, the experiment with 10 subjects will detect its effect. $H_0$ will be rejected with certainty.

Suppose, however, that the effect of marijuana on appetite is not quite as large as has been described—that is, if it were given to the population, there would still be many more pluses than minuses, but this time there would be 9 pluses on the average for every 1 minus. In this case, $P_{real} = 0.90$. The power for this somewhat lower magnitude of real effect is found from Table B, using $P = 0.90$ ($Q = 0.10$). Thus,

Power = probability of rejecting $H_0$ if *IV* has a real effect

$\quad = p(0, 1, 9, \text{or } 10 \text{ pluses})$ as the sample outcome if $P_{real} = 0.90$

$\quad = p(0) + p(1) + p(9) + p(10) \quad$ if $P_{real} = 0.90$

$\quad = 0.0000 + 0.0000 + 0.3874 + 0.3487$

$\quad = 0.7361$

Table B entry

| N | No. of Q Events | Q 0.10 |
|---|---|---|
| 10 | 0 | 0.3487 |
| | 1 | 0.3874 |
| | 9 | 0.0000 |
| | 10 | 0.0000 |

The power of this experiment to detect an effect represented by $P_{real} = 0.90$ is 0.7361. Thus, the power of the experiment has decreased. Note that in determining the power for $P_{real} = 0.90$, the sample outcomes for rejecting $H_0$ haven't changed. As before, they are 0, 1, 9, or 10 pluses. Since these are the outcomes that will allow rejection of $H_0$, they are dependent on only $N$ and $\alpha$. Remember that we find these outcomes for the given $N$ and $\alpha$ level by assuming chance alone is at work ($P_{null} = 0.50$) and determining the sample outcomes for which the obtained probability is equal to or less than $\alpha$ using $P_{null}$.

What happens to the power of the experiment if the marijuana has only a moderate effect such that $P_{real} = 0.70$?

Power = probability of rejecting $H_0$ if *IV* has a real effect

= $p(0, 1, 9,$ or $10$ pluses$)$ as the sample outcome if $P_{real} = 0.70$

= $p(0) + p(1) + p(9) + p(10)$      if $P_{real} = 0.70$

= $0.0000 + 0.0001 + 0.1211 + 0.0282$

= $0.1494$

Table B entry

| $N$ | No. of $Q$ Events | $Q$ 0.30 |
|---|---|---|
| 10 | 0 | 0.0282 |
|  | 1 | 0.1211 |
|  | 9 | 0.0001 |
|  | 10 | 0.0000 |

Power has decreased to 0.1494. Power calculations have also been made for effect sizes represented by $P_{real} = 0.30$, $P_{real} = 0.10$, and $P_{real} = 0.00$. The results are summarized in Table 11.2.

t a b l e 11.2   Calculation of power and beta

| $N$ | $H_0$ | $\alpha$ | Sample Outcomes[*] | Size of Marijuana Effect | Power | $\beta$ |
|---|---|---|---|---|---|---|
| 5 | $P_{null} = 0.50$ | $0.05_{2\,tail}$ | None | For all $P_{real}$ values | 0 | 1.0000 |
| 10 | $P_{null} = 0.50$ | $0.05_{2\,tail}$ | 0, 1, 9, or 10 pluses | $P_{real} = 1.00$ | 1.0000 | 0.0000 |
|  |  |  |  | $P_{real} = 0.90$ | 0.7361 | 0.2639 |
|  |  |  |  | $P_{real} = 0.70$ | 0.1494 | 0.8506 |
|  |  |  |  | $P_{null} = 0.50$ | [†] |  |
|  |  |  |  | $P_{real} = 0.30$ | 0.1494 | 0.8506 |
|  |  |  |  | $P_{real} = 0.10$ | 0.7361 | 0.2639 |
|  |  |  |  | $P_{real} = 0.00$ | 1.0000 | 0.0000 |
| 20 | $P_{null} = 0.50$ | $0.05_{2\,tail}$ | 0–5 or 15–20 pluses | $P_{real} = 0.30$ | 0.4163 | 0.5837 |
| 20 | $P_{null} = 0.50$ | $0.01_{2\,tail}$ | 0–3 or 17–20 pluses | $P_{real} = 0.30$ | 0.1070 | 0.8930 |

[*]Sample outcomes that would result in rejecting $H_0$.
[†]See Note 11.1.

At this point, several generalizations are possible. First, as $N$ increases, power goes up. Second, for a particular $N$, say $N = 10$, power varies directly with the magnitude of the real effect. As the magnitude decreases, the power of the experiment decreases. When the magnitude of the effect approaches that predicted by the null hypothesis, power gets very low. This relationship is shown in Figure 11.2.

## Power and Beta ($\beta$)

As the power of an experiment increases, the probability of making a Type II error decreases. This can be shown as follows.

When we conclude from an experiment, there are only two possibilities: We either reject $H_0$ or retain $H_0$. These possibilities are also mutually exclusive. Therefore, the sum of their probabilities must equal 1. Assuming $H_0$ is false,

$$p(\text{rejecting } H_0 \text{ if it is false}) + p(\text{retaining } H_0 \text{ if it is false}) = 1$$

but

$$\text{Power} = p(\text{rejecting } H_0 \text{ if it is false})$$
$$\text{Beta} = p(\text{retaining } H_0 \text{ if it is false})$$

Thus,

$$\text{Power} + \text{Beta} = 1$$

or

$$\text{Beta} = 1 - \text{Power}$$

Thus, as power increases, beta decreases. The appropriate beta values are shown in the last column of Table 11.2.

You will note that Table 11.2 has some additional entries. When $N = 20$, the power for this experiment to detect an effect of $P_{\text{real}} = 0.30$ is equal to 0.4163.

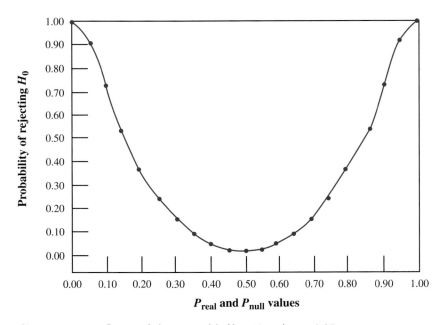

figure   11.2   Power of sign test with $N = 10$ and $\alpha = 0.05_{2 \text{ tail}}$.

When $N = 10$, the power is only 0.1494. This is another demonstration that as $N$ increases, power increases.

## Power and Alpha ($\alpha$)

The last row of Table 11.2 demonstrates the fact that, by making alpha more stringent, power goes down and beta is increased. With $N = 20$, $P_{real} = 0.30$, and $\alpha = 0.01_{2\,tail}$:

Power = $p$(0–3 or 17–20 pluses)

= 0.1070

$\beta = 1 - $ Power

= $1 - 0.1070$

= 0.8930

Table B entry

| $N$ | No. of $P$ Events | $P$ 0.30 |
|---|---|---|
| 20 | 0 | 0.0008 |
| | 1 | 0.0068 |
| | 2 | 0.0278 |
| | 3 | 0.0716 |
| | 17 | 0.0000 |
| | 18 | 0.0000 |
| | 19 | 0.0000 |
| | 20 | 0.0000 |

By making alpha more stringent, the possible sample outcomes for rejecting $H_0$ are decreased. Thus, for $\alpha = 0.01_{2\,tail}$, only 0–3 or 17–20 pluses will allow rejection of $H_0$, whereas for $\alpha = 0.05_{2\,tail}$, 0–5 or 15–20 pluses will result in rejection of $H_0$. This naturally reduces the probability of rejecting the null hypothesis. The decrease in power results in an increase in beta.

Let's summarize a little.

1. The power of an experiment is the probability that the experiment will result in rejecting the null hypothesis if the independent variable has a real effect.
2. Power = 1 – Beta. Therefore, the higher the power is, the lower is beta.
3. Power varies directly with $N$. Increasing $N$ increases power.
4. Power varies directly with the size of the real effect of the independent variable.
5. Power varies directly with alpha level. Power decreases with more stringent alpha levels.

The reader should be aware that the experimenter never knows how strong the effect of the independent variable actually is before doing the experiment. Otherwise, why do the experiment? In practice, we estimate its strength from pilot work or other research and then design an experiment that has high power to detect that strength. For example, if a moderate effect ($P_{real} = 0.70$) is expected, by selecting the appropriate $N$ we can arrive at a decent sensitivity (e.g., power = 0.8000 or higher). How high should power be? What strength of effect should be expected? These are questions that must be answered by the researcher based on experience and available resources. It should be pointed out that by designing the experiment to have a power = 0.8000 for $P_{real} = 0.70$, the power of the experiment will be even higher if the effect of the independent variable is stronger than expected. *Thus, the strategy is to design the experiment for the maximum power that resources will allow for the minimum size of real effect expected.*

## ALPHA–BETA AND REALITY

When one does an experiment, there are only two possibilities: Either $H_0$ is really true or it is false. By minimizing alpha and beta, we maximize the likelihood that our conclusions will be correct. For example, if $H_0$ is really true, the probability of correctly concluding from the experiment is

$$p(\text{correctly concluding}) = p(\text{retaining } H_0) = 1 - \alpha$$

If alpha is at a stringent level (say, 0.05), then $p(\text{correctly concluding})$ is

$$p(\text{correctly concluding}) = 1 - \alpha = 1 - 0.05 = 0.95$$

On the other hand, if $H_0$ is really false, the probability of correctly concluding is

$$p(\text{correctly concluding}) = p(\text{rejecting } H_0) = \text{power} = 1 - \beta$$

If beta is low (say, equal to 0.10 for the minimum real effect of interest), then

$$p(\text{correctly concluding}) = 1 - \beta = 1 - 0.10 = 0.90$$

Thus, whichever is the true state of affairs ($H_0$ is true or $H_0$ is false), there is a high probability of correctly concluding when $\alpha$ is set at a stringent level and $\beta$ is low. One way of achieving a low beta level when $\alpha$ is set at a stringent level is to have a large $N$. Another way is to use the statistical inference test that is the most powerful for the data. A third way is to control the external conditions of the experiment such that the variability of the data is reduced. We shall discuss the latter two methods when we cover Student's $t$ test in Chapters 13 and 14.

## INTERPRETING NONSIGNIFICANT RESULTS

Although power aids in designing an experiment, it is much more often used when interpreting the results of an experiment that has already been conducted and that has yielded nonsignificant results. Failure to reject $H_0$ may occur because (1) $H_0$ is in fact true or (2) $H_0$ is false, but the experiment was of low power. It is due to the second possible reason that we can *never accept $H_0$* as being correct when an experiment fails to yield significance. Instead, we say the experiment has failed to allow the null hypothesis to be rejected. It is possible that $H_0$ is indeed false, but the experiment was insensitive; that is, it didn't give $H_0$ much of a chance to be rejected. A case in point is the example we presented before with $N = 5$. In that experiment, whatever results we obtained, they would not reach significance. We could not reject $H_0$ no matter how strong the real effect actually was. It would be a gross error to accept $H_0$ as a result of doing that experiment. The experiment did not give $H_0$ any chance of being rejected. *From this viewpoint, we can see that every experiment exists to give $H_0$ a chance to be rejected. The higher the power, the more the experiment allows $H_0$ to be rejected if it is false.*

Perhaps an analogy will help in understanding this point. We can liken the power of an experiment to the use of a microscope. Physiological psychologists have long been interested in what happens in the brain to allow the memory of an event to be recorded. One hypothesis states that a group of neurons fires together as a result of the stimulus presentation. With repeated firings (trials), there is growth across the synapses of the cells, so after a while, they become activated together whenever the stimulus is presented. This "cell assembly" then becomes the physiological engram of the stimuli (i.e., it is the memory trace).

To test this hypothesis, an experiment is done involving visual recognition. After some animals have practiced a task, the appropriate brain cells from each are prepared on slides so as to look for growth across the synapses. $H_0$ predicts no growth; $H_1$ predicts growth. First, the slides are examined with the naked eye; no growth is seen. Can we therefore accept $H_0$? No, because the eye is not powerful enough to see growth even if it were there. The same holds true for a low-power experiment. If the results are not significant, we cannot conclude by accepting $H_0$ because even if $H_0$ is false, the low power makes it unlikely that we would reject the null hypothesis. So next, a light microscope is used, and still there is no growth seen between synapses. Even though this is a more powerful experiment, can we conclude that $H_0$ is true? No, because a light microscope doesn't have enough power to see the synapses clearly. So finally, an electron microscope is used, producing a very powerful experiment in which all but the most minute structures at the synapse can be seen clearly. If $H_0$ is false (that is, if there is growth across the synapse), this powerful experiment has a higher probability of detecting it. Thus, the higher the power of an experiment is, the more the experiment allows $H_0$ to be rejected if it is false.

In light of the foregoing discussion, whenever an experiment fails to yield significant results, we must be careful in our interpretation. Certainly, we can't assert that the null hypothesis is correct. However, if the power of the experiment is high, we can say a little more than just that the experiment has failed to allow rejection of $H_0$. For example, if power is 1.0000 for an effect represented by $P_{real} = 1.00$ and we fail to reject $H_0$, we can at least conclude that the independent variable is not that strong. If the power is, say, 0.8000 for a moderate effect ($P_{real} = 0.70$), we can be reasonably confident the independent variable is not that effective. On the other hand, if power is low, nonsignificant results tell us little about the true state of reality. Thus, a power analysis tells us how much confidence to place in experiments that fail to reject the null hypothesis. When we fail to reject the null hypothesis, the higher the power to detect a given real effect, the more confident we are that the independent variable is not that strong. However, note that as the real effect of the independent variable gets very weak, the power of the experiment to detect it also gets very low (see Figure 11.2). *Thus, it is impossible to ever prove that the null hypothesis is true because the power to detect very weak but real effects of the independent variable is always low.*

## CALCULATION OF POWER

Calculation of power involves a two-step process for each level of $P_{real}$:

**STEP 1:** Assume the null hypothesis is true. Using $P_{null} = 0.50$, determine the possible sample outcomes in the experiment that allow $H_0$ to be rejected.

**STEP 2:** For the level of $P_{real}$ under consideration (e.g., $P_{real} = 0.30$), determine the probability of getting any of the above sample outcomes. This probability is the power of the experiment to detect this level of real effect.

## Practice Problem 11.1

You are interested in determining whether word recall is better when (1) the words are just directly memorized or (2) a story that includes all the words is made up by the subjects. In the second method, the story, from which the words could be recaptured, would be recalled. You plan to run 14 subjects in a repeated measures experiment and analyze the data with the sign test. Each subject will use both methods with equivalent sets of words. The number of words remembered in each condition will be the dependent variable; $\alpha = 0.05_{2\,\text{tail}}$.

**a.** What is the power of the experiment to detect a moderate[*] effect ($P_{\text{real}} = 0.80$ or $0.20$)?

**b.** What is the probability of a Type II error?

The solution follows. From the solution, we see that the power to detect a moderate difference in the effect on word recall between memorizing the words and making up a story including the words is 0.4480. This means that we have about a 45% chance of rejecting $H_0$ if the effect is moderate ($P_{\text{real}} = 0.80$ or $0.20$) and a 55% chance of making a Type II error. If the effect is weaker than moderate, then the probability of making a Type II error is even higher. Of course, increasing $N$ in the experiment will increase the probability of rejecting $H_0$ and decrease the probability of making a Type II error.

### SOLUTION

**a.** Calculation of power:    Calculation of power involves a two-step process:

**STEP 1: Assume the null hypothesis is true ($P_{\text{null}} = 0.50$) and determine the possible sample outcomes in the experiment that will allow $H_0$ to be rejected.** $\alpha = 0.05_{2\,\text{tail}}$. With $N = 14$ and $P = 0.50$, from Table B,

| | | | | |
|---|---|---|---|---|
| $p(0\ \text{pluses})$ | $= 0.0001$ | | $p(0\ \text{pluses})$ | $= 0.0001$ |
| $p(1\ \text{plus})$ | $= 0.0009$ | | $p(1\ \text{plus})$ | $= 0.0009$ |
| $p(2\ \text{pluses})$ | $= 0.0056$ | | $p(2\ \text{pluses})$ | $= 0.0056$ |
| $p(12\ \text{pluses})$ | $= 0.0056$ | | $p(3\ \text{pluses})$ | $= 0.0222$ |
| $p(13\ \text{pluses})$ | $= 0.0009$ | | $p(11\ \text{pluses})$ | $= 0.0222$ |
| $p(14\ \text{pluses})$ | $= 0.0001$ | | $p(12\ \text{pluses})$ | $= 0.0056$ |
| $p(0, 1, 2, 12, 13,\ \text{or}\ 14) = 0.0132$ | | | $p(13\ \text{pluses})$ | $= 0.0009$ |
| | | | $p(14\ \text{pluses})$ | $= 0.0001$ |
| | | | $p(0, 1, 2, 3, 11, 12, 13,\ \text{or}\ 14)$ | $= 0.0576$ |

---

[*]We have divided the magnitude range into the following three intervals: a strong effect such that $P_{\text{real}} = 0.00\text{--}0.15$ or $0.85\text{--}1.00$, a moderate effect such that $P_{\text{real}} = 0.15\text{--}0.35$ or $0.65\text{--}0.85$, and a weak effect such that $P_{\text{real}} = 0.35\text{--}0.49$ or $0.51\text{--}0.65$.          (*continued*)

Beginning at the extremes and moving toward the middle of the distribution, we find that we can reject $H_0$ if we obtain 2 or 12 pluses ($p = 0.0132$), but we fail to reject $H_0$ if we obtain 3 or 11 pluses ($p = 0.0576$) in the sample. Therefore, the outcomes that will allow rejection of $H_0$ are 0, 1, 2, 12, 13, or 14 pluses.

STEP 2: **For $P_{real} = 0.20$, determine the probability of getting any of the aforementioned sample outcomes.** This probability is the power of the experiment to detect this hypothesized real effect. With $N = 14$ and $P_{real} = 0.20$, from Table B,

Power = probability of rejecting $H_0$ if $IV$ has a real effect

= $p(0, 1, 2, 12, 13,$ or $14$ pluses) as sample outcomes if $P_{real} = 0.20$

= $0.0440 + 0.1539 + 0.2501 + 0.0000 + 0.0000 + 0.0000$

= $0.4480$

Table B entry

| $N$ | No. of $P$ Events | $P$ 0.20 |
|---|---|---|
| 14 | 0 | 0.0440 |
| | 1 | 0.1539 |
| | 2 | 0.2501 |
| | 12 | 0.0000 |
| | 13 | 0.0000 |
| | 14 | 0.0000 |

Note that the same answer would result for $P_{real} = 0.80$.

**b.** Calculation of beta:

$$\beta = 1 - \text{Power}$$
$$= 1 - 0.4480$$
$$= 0.5520$$

## Practice Problem 11.2

Assume you are planning an experiment to evaluate a drug. The alternative hypothesis is directional, in the direction to produce mostly pluses. You will use the sign test to analyze the data; $\alpha = 0.05_{1\,tail}$. You want to be able to detect a weak effect (say, $P_{real} = 0.60$) in the same direction as the alternative hypothesis. There will be 16 subjects in the experiment.

**a.** What is power of the experiment to detect this weak effect?
**b.** What is the probability of making a Type II error?

**SOLUTION**

**a.** Calculation of power:    There are two steps involved in calculating power:

**STEP 1:** **Assume the null hypothesis is true ($P_{null} = 0.50$) and determine the possible sample outcomes in the experiment that will allow $H_0$ to be rejected.** $\alpha = 0.05_{1\,tail}$. With $N = 16$ and $P = 0.50$, from Table B,

| | | | |
|---|---|---|---|
| $p$(12 pluses) | $= 0.0278$ | $p$(11 pluses) | $= 0.0667$ |
| $p$(13 pluses) | $= 0.0085$ | $p$(12 pluses) | $= 0.0278$ |
| $p$(14 pluses) | $= 0.0018$ | $p$(13 pluses) | $= 0.0085$ |
| $p$(15 pluses) | $= 0.0002$ | $p$(14 pluses) | $= 0.0018$ |
| $p$(16 pluses) | $= 0.0000$ | $p$(15 pluses) | $= 0.0002$ |
| $p$(12, 13, 14, 15, or 16) | $= 0.0383$ | $p$(16 pluses) | $= 0.0000$ |
| | | $p$(11, 12, 13, 14, 15, or 16) | $= 0.1050$ |

Since the alternative hypothesis is in the direction of mostly pluses, outcomes for rejecting $H_0$ are found under the tail with the higher numbers of pluses. Beginning with 16 pluses and moving toward the middle of the distribution, we find that we shall reject $H_0$ if we obtain 12 pluses ($p = 0.0383$), but we shall fail to reject $H_0$ if we obtain 11 pluses ($p = 0.1050$) in the sample. Therefore, the outcomes that will allow rejection of $H_0$ are 12, 13, 14, 15, or 16 pluses.

**STEP 2:** **For $P_{real} = 0.60$, determine the probability of getting any of the aforementioned sample outcomes.**    This probability is the power of the experiment to detect this hypothesized real effect. With $N = 16$ and $P_{real} = 0.60$ ($Q = 0.40$), from Table B,

Power $=$ probability of rejecting $H_0$ if *IV* has a real effect

$= p$(12, 13, 14, 15, or 16 pluses) as sample outcomes if $P_{real} = 0.60$

$= 0.1014 + 0.0468 + 0.0150 + 0.0030 + 0.0003$

$= 0.1665$

Table B entry

| $N$ | No. of $Q$ Events | $Q$ 0.40 |
|---|---|---|
| 16 | 0 | 0.0003 |
| | 1 | 0.0030 |
| | 2 | 0.0150 |
| | 3 | 0.0468 |
| | 4 | 0.1014 |

**b.** Calculation of beta:

$\beta = 1 - \text{Power}$

$= 1 - 0.1665$

$= 0.8335$

*(continued)*

This experiment is very insensitive to a weak drug effect. The probability of a Type II error is too high. The $N$ should be made larger to increase the power of the experiment to detect the weak drug effect.

## Practice Problem 11.3

In Practice Problem 10.2 (p. 230), you conducted an experiment testing the directional alternative hypothesis that watching a particular TV program caused increased violence in teenagers. The experiment included 15 subjects, and $\alpha = 0.01_{1\text{tail}}$. The data were analyzed with the sign test, and we retained $H_0$.

**a.** In that experiment, what was the power to detect a moderate effect of $P_{\text{real}} = 0.70$ in the direction of the alternative hypothesis?

**b.** What was the probability of a Type II error?

### SOLUTION

**a.** Calculation of power:  There are two steps involved in calculating power:

**STEP 1:  Assume the null hypothesis is true ($P_{\text{null}} = 0.50$) and determine the possible sample outcomes in the experiment that will allow $H_0$ to be rejected.** $\alpha = 0.01_{1\text{tail}}$. With $N = 15$ and $P = 0.50$, from Table B,

| | | | |
|---|---|---|---|
| $p(13$ pluses$)$ | $= 0.0032$ | $p(12$ pluses$)$ | $= 0.0139$ |
| $p(14$ pluses$)$ | $= 0.0005$ | $p(13$ pluses$)$ | $= 0.0032$ |
| $p(15$ pluses$)$ | $= 0.0000$ | $p(14$ pluses$)$ | $= 0.0005$ |
| $p(13, 14,$ or $15) = 0.0037$ | | $p(15$ pluses$)$ | $= 0.0000$ |
| | | $p(12, 13, 14,$ or $15) = 0.0176$ | |

Since the alternative hypothesis is in the direction of mostly pluses, outcomes for rejecting $H_0$ are found under the tail with the higher numbers of pluses. Beginning with 15 pluses and moving toward the middle of the distribution, we find that we shall reject $H_0$ if we obtain 13 pluses ($p = 0.0037$), but we shall retain $H_0$ if we obtain 12 pluses ($p = 0.0176$) in the sample. Therefore, the outcomes that will allow rejection of $H_0$ are 13, 14, or 15 pluses.

STEP 2: **For $P_{real} = 0.70$, determine the probability of getting any of the aforementioned sample outcomes.** This probability is the power of the experiment to detect this hypothesized real effect. With $N = 15$ and $P_{real} = 0.70$, from Table B,

Power = probability of rejecting $H_0$ if $IV$ has a real effect

= $p(13, 14,$ or $15$ pluses) as sample outcomes if $P_{real} = 0.70$

= $0.0916 + 0.0305 + 0.0047$

= $0.1268$

Table B entry

| $N$ | No of $Q$ Events | $Q$ 0.30 |
|-----|-----------------|----------|
| 15  | 0               | 0.0047   |
|     | 1               | 0.0305   |
|     | 2               | 0.0916   |

**b.** Calculation of beta:

$\beta = 1 -$ Power

$= 1 - 0.1268$

$= 0.8732$

Note that since the power to detect a moderate effect is very low, even though we retained $H_0$ in the experiment, we can't conclude that the program does not affect violence. The experiment should be redone with increased power to allow a better evaluation of the program's effect on violence.

# WHAT IS THE TRUTH?

## Astrology and Science

A newspaper article appeared in a recent issue of the Pittsburgh *Post-Gazette* with the headline, "When Clinical Studies Mislead." Excerpts from the article are reproduced here:

*Shock waves rolled through the medical community two weeks ago when researchers announced that a frequently prescribed triad of drugs previously shown to be helpful after a heart attack had proved useless in new studies. . . .*

*"People are constantly dazzled by numbers, but they don't know what lies behind the numbers," said Alvan R. Feinstein, a professor of medicine and epidemiology at the Yale University School of Medicine. "Even scientists and physicians have been brainwashed into thinking that the magic phrase 'statistical significance' is the answer to everything."*

*The recent heart-drug studies belie that myth. Clinical trials involving thousands of patients over a period of several years had shown previously that nitrate-containing drugs such as nitroglycerine, the enzyme inhibitor captopril and magnesium all helped save lives when administered after a heart attack.*

*Comparing the life spans of those who took the medicines with those who didn't, researchers found the difference to be statistically significant, and the drugs became part of the standard medical practice. In the United States, more than 80 percent of heart attack patients are given nitrate drugs.*

*But in a new study involving more than 50,000 patients, researchers found no benefit from nitrates or magnesium and*

*captopril's usefulness was marginal. Oxford epidemiologist Richard Peto, who oversaw the latest study, said the positive results from the previous trial must have been due to "the play of chance." . . . Faulty number crunching, Peto said, can be a matter of life and death.*

*He and his colleagues drove that point home in 1988 when they submitted a paper to the British medical journal* The Lancet. *Their landmark report showed that heart*

PRESCRIPTIONS
AND
ASTROLOGICAL ASPIRIN
FORECASTS
———————————
SAGITTARIUS-NO   ARIES-NO
CANCER-MAYBE    TAURUS-NO
LEO-SURE        GEMINI-N
VIRGO-YES       LI
CAPICORN-NOPE
RIUS-YES
SCES-NOT YET
CORPIO-LATER

## WHAT IS THE TRUTH?

attack victims had a better chance of surviving if they were given aspirin within a few hours after their attacks. As Peto tells the story, the journal's editors wanted the researchers to break down the data into various subsets, to see whether certain kinds of patients who differed from each other by age or other characteristics were more or less likely to benefit from aspirin.

Peto objected, arguing that a study's validity could be compromised by breaking it into too many pieces. If you compare enough subgroups, he said, you're bound to get some kind of correlation by chance alone. When the editors insisted, Peto capitulated, but among other things he divided his patients by zodiac birth signs and demanded that his findings be included in the published paper. Today, like a

warning sign to the statistically uninitiated, the wacky numbers are there for all to see: Aspirin is useless for Gemini and Libra heart attack victims but is a lifesaver for people born under any other sign. . . .

Studies like these exemplify two of the more common statistical offenses committed by scientists—making too many comparisons and paying too little attention to whether something makes sense—said James L. Mills, chief of the pediatric epidemiology section of the National Institute of Child Health and Human Development.

"People search through their results for the most exciting and positive things," he said. "But you also have to look at the biological plausibility. A lot of findings that don't withstand the test of time didn't really make any sense in the first place. . . ."

In the past few years, many scientists have embraced larger and larger clinical trials to minimize the chances of being deceived by a fluke.

What do you think? If you were a physician, would you continue to prescribe nitrates to heart attack patients? Is it really true that the early clinical trials are an example of Type I error, as suggested by Dr. Peto? Will larger and larger clinical trials minimize the chances of being deceived by a fluke? Finally, is aspirin really useless for Gemini and Libra heart attack victims but a lifesaver for people born under any other sign?

## SUMMARY

In this chapter, we have discussed the topic of power. Power is defined as the probability of rejecting the null hypothesis when the independent variable has a real effect. Since power varies with the size of the real effect, it should be calculated for the smallest real effect of interest. The power will be even higher for larger effects. Calculation of power involves two steps. In the first step, the null hypothesis is assumed true ($P_{null} = 0.50$), and all the possible sample outcomes in the experiment that would allow the null hypothesis to be rejected are determined. Next, for the real effect under consideration (e.g., the effect represented by $P_{real} = 0.30$), the probability of getting any of these sample outcomes is calculated. This probability is the power of the experiment to detect this effect ($P_{real} = 0.30$).

Other factors held constant, power increases with increases in $N$ and with increases in the size of the real effect of the independent variable. Power decreases as the alpha level is made more stringent. Power equals $1 - $ beta, so maximizing power mini-mizes the probability of a Type II error. Thus, by minimizing alpha and beta, we maximize the probability of correctly determining the true effect of the independent variable, no matter what the state of reality.

A power analysis is useful when (1) initially designing an experiment and (2) interpreting the results of experiments that retain the null hypothesis. When an experiment is conducted and the results are not significant, it may be because the null hypothesis is true or because the experiment has low power. It is for this reason that, when the results are not significant, we do not conclude by *accepting* the null hypothesis but rather by *failing to reject* it. The null hypothesis actually may be false, but the experiment did not have high enough power to detect it. Every experiment exists to give the null hypothesis a chance to be rejected. The more powerful the experiment, the higher the probability the null hypothesis will be rejected if it is false. Since power gets low as the real effect of the independent variable decreases, it is impossible to prove that $H_0$ is true.

## IMPORTANT TERMS

Alpha  (p. 255)
Beta  (p. 246)
Correct decision  (p. 255)
Nonsignificant  (p. 255)
Null hypothesis  (p. 255)

$P_{null}$  (p. 246)
$P_{real}$  (p. 246)
Power  (p. 246)
Real effect  (p. 246)
Significant results  (p. 256)

State of reality  (p. 255)
Type I error  (p. 245)
Type II error  (p. 245)

## QUESTIONS AND PROBLEMS

1. What is power? How is it defined?
2. In what two situations is a power analysis especially useful? Explain.
3. In hypothesis testing experiments, why is the conclusion "We retain $H_0$" preferable to "We accept $H_0$ as true"?
4. In hypothesis testing experiments, is it ever correct to conclude that the independent variable has had *no* effect? Explain.
5. In computing power, why do we always compute the sample outcomes that will allow rejection of $H_0$?
6. Using $\alpha$ and $\beta$, explain how we can maximize the probability of correctly concluding from an experiment, regardless of whether $H_0$ is true or false. As part of your explanation, choose values for $\alpha$ and $\beta$ and determine the probability of correctly concluding when $H_0$ is true and when $H_0$ is false.

7. You are considering testing a new drug that is supposed to facilitate learning in mentally retarded children. Because there is relatively little known about the drug, you plan to use a nondirectional alternative hypothesis. Your resources are limited, so you can test only 15 subjects. The subjects will be run in a repeated measures design and the data analyzed with the sign test using $\alpha = 0.05_{2\,tail}$. If the drug has a moderate effect on learning such that $P_{real} = 0.70$, what is the probability you will detect it when doing your experiment? What is the probability of a Type II error? cognitive
8. In Chapter 10, Problem 10 (p. 242), a new teaching method was evaluated. Twenty pairs of subjects were run in a repeated measures design. The results were in favor of the new method but did not reach significance ($H_0$ was not rejected) using the sign test with $\alpha = 0.05_{1\,tail}$. In trying to interpret

why the results were not significant, you reason that there are two possibilities: either (1) the two teaching methods are really equal in effectiveness ($H_0$ is true) or (2) the new method is better, but the experiment was insensitive. To evaluate the latter possibility, you conduct an analysis to determine the power of the experiment to detect a moderate difference favoring the new method such that $P_{real} = 0.80$. What is the power of the experiment to detect this effect? What is beta? education

9. A researcher is going to conduct an experiment to determine whether one night's sleep loss affects performance. Assume the requirements are met for a directional alternative hypothesis. Fourteen subjects will be run in a repeated measures design. The data will be analyzed with the sign test, using $\alpha = 0.05_{1\,tail}$. Each subject will receive two conditions: condition 1, where the performance of the subject is measured after a good night's sleep, and condition 2, where performance is measured after one night's sleep deprivation. The better the performance, the higher the score. When the data are analyzed, the scores of condition 2 will be subtracted from those of condition 1. If one night's loss of sleep has a strong detrimental effect on performance such that $P_{real} = 0.90$, what is the power of the experiment to detect this effect? What is the probability of a Type II error? cognitive

10. In Chapter 10, Problem 12 (p. 243), what is the power of the experiment to detect a moderate effect such that $P_{real} = 0.70$? education

11. A psychiatrist is planning an experiment to determine whether stimulus isolation affects depression. Eighteen subjects will be run in a repeated measures design. The data will be analyzed with the sign test, using $\alpha = 0.05_{2\,tail}$. Each subject will receive two conditions: condition 1, one week of living in an environment with a normal amount of external stimulation, and condition 2, one week in an environment where external stimulation has been radically curtailed. A questionnaire measuring depression will be administered after each condition. The higher the score on the questionnaire, the greater the subject's depression. In analyzing the data, the scores of condition 1 will be subtracted from the scores of condition 2. If one week of stimulus isolation has an effect on depression such that $P_{real} = 0.60$, what is the power of the experiment to detect this weak effect? What is beta? If the results of the experiment are not significant, is it legitimate for the psychiatrist to conclude that stimulus isolation has no effect on depression? Why? cognitive, clinical, health

12. In Chapter 10, Practice Problem 10.2, an experiment was conducted to determine whether watching a particular TV program resulted in increased violence in teenagers. In that experiment, 15 subjects were run with each subject serving in an experimental and control condition. The sign test was used to analyze the data, with $\alpha = 0.01_{1\,tail}$. Suppose the TV program does increase violence moderately ($P_{real} = 0.70$). Before running the experiment, what is the probability that the experiment will detect at least this level of real effect? What is the probability of a Type II error? The data collected in this experiment failed to allow rejection of $H_0$. Are we therefore justified in concluding that the TV program has no effect on violence in teenagers? Explain. social

## NOTES

11.1 This probability is not equal to power because when $P = 0.50$, $H_0$ is true. Power is calculated when $H_0$ is false. The probability of rejecting $H_0$ when $H_0$ is true is defined as the probability of making a Type I error. For this example:

$$p(\text{reject } H_0 \text{ when } P = 0.50) = p(\text{Type I error})$$
$$= p(0) + p(1) + p(9) + p(10)$$
$$= 0.0010 + 0.0098 + 0.0098 + 0.0010$$
$$= 0.0216$$

Note that the probability of making a Type I error (0.0216) is not equal to the $\alpha$ level (0.05) because the number of pluses is a discrete variable rather than a continuous variable. To have $p(\text{Type I error})$ equal alpha, we would need an outcome between 8 and 9 pluses. Of course, this is impossible because the number of pluses can only be 8 or 9 (discrete values). The probability of making a Type I error is equal to alpha when the variable is continuous.

**BOOK COMPANION WEBSITE**

Go to www.thomsonedu.com/psychology/pagano for:

• Flash cards for review of terms
• Chapter quiz
• Statistical workshops
• And more

**WebTUTOR**

Available via WebTutor for this chapter:

• Detailed chapter outline
• *Know and Be Able To Do* section
• Drag & Drop game for review of equations, concepts, and other material
• Flash cards for review of terms
• Audio flash cards for MP3 player
• More practice problems using computational equations
• Chapter quiz

# Sampling Distributions, Sampling Distribution of the Mean, the Normal Deviate ($z$) Test

**CHAPTER 12**

## INTRODUCTION

In Chapters 10 and 11, we have seen how to use the scientific method to investigate hypotheses. We have introduced the replicated measures and the independent groups designs and discussed how to analyze the resulting data. At the heart of the analysis is the ability to answer the question, *What is the probability of getting the obtained result or results even more extreme if chance alone is responsible for the differences between the experimental and control scores?*

Although it hasn't been emphasized, the answer to this question involves two steps: (1) calculating the appropriate statistic and (2) evaluating the statistic based on its sampling distribution. In this chapter, we shall more formally discuss the topic of a statistic and its sampling distribution. Then we shall begin our analysis of single sample experiments, using the mean of the sample as a statistic. This involves the sampling distribution of the mean and the normal deviate (*z*) test.

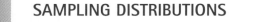

## SAMPLING DISTRIBUTIONS

What is a sampling distribution?

definition ■ *The* **sampling distribution of a statistic** *gives* (1) *all the values that the statistic can take and* (2) *the probability of getting each value under the assumption that it resulted from chance alone.*

In the replicated measures design, we used the sign test to analyze the data. The statistic calculated was the *number of pluses* in the sample of *N* difference scores. In one version of the "marijuana and appetite" experiment, we obtained nine pluses and one minus. This result was evaluated by using the binomial distribution. The binomial distribution with $P = 0.50$ lists all the possible values of the statistic, the number of pluses, along with the probability of getting each value under the assumption that chance alone produced it. *The binomial distribution with $P = 0.50$ is the sampling distribution of the statistic used in the sign test.* Note that there is a different sampling distribution for each sample size (*N*).

Generalizing from this example, it can be seen that data analysis basically involves two steps:

1. Calculating the appropriate statistic—for example, number of pluses and minuses for the sign test
2. Evaluating the statistic based on its sampling distribution

If the probability of getting the obtained value of the statistic or any value more extreme is equal to or less than the alpha level, we reject $H_0$ and accept $H_1$. If not, we retain $H_0$. If we reject $H_0$ and it is true, we've made a Type I error. If we retain $H_0$ and it's false, we've made a Type II error. This process applies to all experiments involving hypothesis testing. *What changes from experiment to experiment is the statistic used and its accompanying sampling distribution.* Once you understand this concept, you can appreciate that a large part of teaching inferential statistics is devoted to presenting the most often used statistics, their sampling distributions, and the conditions under which each statistic is appropriately used.

### Generating Sampling Distributions

We have defined a sampling distribution as a probability distribution of all the possible values of a statistic under the assumption that chance alone is operating. One way of deriving sampling distributions is from basic probability considerations. We used this approach in generating the binomial distribution. Sampling distributions can also be derived from an empirical sampling approach. In this approach, we have an actual or theoretical set of population scores that exists if the independent variable has no effect. We derive the sampling distribution of the statistic by

1. Determining all the possible different samples of size $N$ that can be formed from the population of scores
2. Calculating the statistic for each of the samples
3. Calculating the probability of getting each value of the statistic if chance alone is operating

To illustrate the sampling approach, let's suppose we are conducting an experiment with a sample size $N = 2$, using the sign test for analysis. We can imagine a theoretical set of scores that would result if the experiment were done on the entire population and the independent variable had no effect. This population set of scores is called the *null-hypothesis population*.

definition ■ *The* **null-hypothesis population** *is an actual or theoretical set of population scores that would result if the experiment were done on the entire population and the independent variable had no effect. It is called the null-hypothesis population because it is used to test the validity of the null hypothesis.*

In the case of the sign test, if the independent variable had no effect, the null-hypothesis population would have an equal number of pluses and minuses ($P = Q = 0.50$).

For computational ease in generating the sampling distribution, let's assume there are only six scores in the population: three pluses and three minuses. To derive the sampling distribution of "the number of pluses" with $N = 2$, we must first determine all the different samples of size $N$ that can be formed from the population. Sampling is one at a time, with replacement. Figure 12.1 shows the population and, schematically, the different samples of size 2 that can be drawn from it. It turns out that there are 36 different samples of size 2 possible. These are listed in the table of Figure 12.1, column 2. Next, we must calculate the value of the statistic for each sample. This information is presented in the table of Figure 12.1, columns 3 and 4. Note that of the 36 different samples possible, 9 have two pluses, 18 have one plus, and 9 have no pluses. The last step is to calculate the probability of getting each value of the statistic. If chance alone is operating, each sample is equally likely. Thus,

$$p(2 \text{ pluses}) = \tfrac{9}{36} = 0.2500$$

$$p(1 \text{ plus}) = \tfrac{18}{36} = 0.5000$$

$$p(0 \text{ pluses}) = \tfrac{9}{36} = 0.2500$$

We have now derived the sampling distribution for $N = 2$ of the statistic "number of pluses." The distribution is plotted in Figure 12.2. In this example, we used a population in which there were only six scores. The identical sampling

| Sample Composition | | | | Sample Composition | | | |
|---|---|---|---|---|---|---|---|
| Sample number (1) | Element numbers (2) | Actual scores (3) | Statistic, no. of pluses (4) | Sample number (1) | Element numbers (2) | Actual scores (3) | Statistic, no. of pluses (4) |
| 1 | 1, 1 | + + | 2+ | 19 | 4, 1 | − + | 1+ |
| 2 | 1, 2 | + + | 2+ | 20 | 4, 2 | − + | 1+ |
| 3 | 1, 3 | + + | 2+ | 21 | 4, 3 | − + | 1+ |
| 4 | 1, 4 | + − | 1+ | 22 | 4, 4 | − − | 0+ |
| 5 | 1, 5 | + − | 1+ | 23 | 4, 5 | − − | 0+ |
| 6 | 1, 6 | + − | 1+ | 24 | 4, 6 | − − | 0+ |
| 7 | 2, 1 | + + | 2+ | 25 | 5, 1 | − + | 1+ |
| 8 | 2, 2 | + + | 2+ | 26 | 5, 2 | − + | 1+ |
| 9 | 2, 3 | + + | 2+ | 27 | 5, 3 | − + | 1+ |
| 10 | 2, 4 | + − | 1+ | 28 | 5, 4 | − − | 0+ |
| 11 | 2, 5 | + − | 1+ | 29 | 5, 5 | − − | 0+ |
| 12 | 2, 6 | + − | 1+ | 30 | 5, 6 | − − | 0+ |
| 13 | 3, 1 | + + | 2+ | 31 | 6, 1 | − + | 1+ |
| 14 | 3, 2 | + + | 2+ | 32 | 6, 2 | − + | 1+ |
| 15 | 3, 3 | + + | 2+ | 33 | 6, 3 | − + | 1+ |
| 16 | 3, 4 | + − | 1+ | 34 | 6, 4 | − − | 0+ |
| 17 | 3, 5 | + − | 1+ | 35 | 6, 5 | − − | 0+ |
| 18 | 3, 6 | + − | 1+ | 36 | 6, 6 | − − | 0+ |

**f i g u r e  12.1**  All of the possible samples of size 2 that can be drawn from a population of three pluses and three minuses. Sampling is one at a time, with replacement.

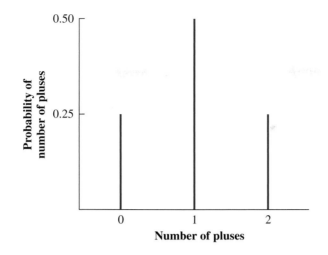

**figure 12.2**   Sampling distribution of "number of pluses" with $N = 2$ and $P = 0.50$.

distribution would have resulted (even though there would be many more "different" samples) had we used a larger population as long as the number of pluses equaled the number of minuses and the sample size equaled 2. Note that this is the same sampling distribution we arrived at through basic probability considerations when we were discussing the binomial distribution with $N = 2$ (see Figure 12.3 for a comparison). This time, however, we generated it by sampling from the null-hypothesis population. The sampling distribution of a statistic is often defined in terms of this process. Viewed in this manner, we obtain the following definition.

| **Empirical Sampling Approach** | | | **A Priori Approach** | | |
|---|---|---|---|---|---|
| *Draw 1* | *Draw 2* | *Number of ways* | *Coin 1* | *Coin 2* | *Number of ways* |
| + | + | 9 | H | H | 1 |
| + / − | − / + | 18 | H / T | T / H | 2 |
| − | − | 9 | T | T | 1 |
| | | 36 | | | 4 |

$$p(2\,+\,) = \frac{9}{36} = 0.2500 \qquad p(2\text{H}) = \frac{1}{4} = 0.2500$$

$$p(1\,+\,) = \frac{18}{36} = 0.5000 \qquad p(1\text{H}) = \frac{2}{4} = 0.5000$$

$$p(0\,+\,) = \frac{9}{36} = 0.2500 \qquad p(0\text{H}) = \frac{1}{4} = 0.2500$$

**figure 12.3**   Comparison of empirical sampling approach and *a priori* approach for generating sampling distributions.

definition ■ *A **sampling distribution** gives all the values a statistic can take, along with the probability of getting each value if sampling is random from the null-hypothesis population.*

## THE NORMAL DEVIATE ($z$) TEST

Although much of the foregoing has been abstract and seemingly impractical, it is necessary to understand the sampling distributions underlying many of the statistical tests that follow. One such test, the normal deviate ($z$) test, is a test that is used when we know the parameters of the null-hypothesis population. The $z$ test uses the mean of the sample as a basic statistic. Let's consider an experiment where the $z$ test is appropriate.

an experiment

### Evaluating the Reading Program at the Local Public Schools

Assume you are superintendent of public schools for the city in which you live. Recently, local citizens have been concerned that the reading program in the public schools may be an inferior one. Since this is a serious issue, you decide to conduct an experiment to investigate the matter. You set $\alpha = 0.05_{1\,\text{tail}}$ for making your decision. You begin by comparing the reading level of current high school seniors with established norms. The norms are based on scores from a reading proficiency test administered nationally to a large number of high school seniors. The scores of this population are normally distributed with $\mu = 75$ and $\sigma = 16$. For your experiment, you administer the reading test to 100 randomly selected high school seniors in your city. The obtained mean of the sample ($\overline{X}_{\text{obt}}$) = 72. What is your conclusion?

There is no doubt that the sample mean of 72 is lower than the national population mean of 75. Is it significantly lower, however? If chance alone is at work, then we can consider the 100 sample scores to be a random sample from a population with $\mu = 75$. The null hypothesis for this experiment asserts that such is the case. What is the probability of getting a mean score as low as or even lower than 72 if the 100 scores are a random sample from a normally distributed population having a mean of 75 and standard deviation of 16? If the probability is equal to or lower than alpha, we reject $H_0$ and accept $H_1$. If not, we retain $H_0$. It is clear that the statistic we are using is the *mean* of the sample. To determine the appropriate probability, we must know the *sampling distribution of the mean.*

In the following section, we shall discuss the sampling distribution of the mean. For the time being, set aside the "Super" and his problem. We shall return to him soon enough. For now, it is sufficient to realize that we are going to use the mean of a sample to evaluate $H_0$, and to do that, we must know the sampling distribution of the mean.

## Sampling Distribution of the Mean

Applying the definition of the sampling distribution of a statistic to the mean, we obtain the following:

definition ■ *The* **sampling distribution of the mean** *gives all the values the mean can take, along with the probability of getting each value if sampling is random from the null-hypothesis population.*

The sampling distribution of the mean can be determined empirically and theoretically, the latter through use of the Central Limit Theorem. The theoretical derivation is complex and beyond the level of this textbook. Therefore, for pedagogical reasons, we prefer to present the empirical approach. When we follow this approach, we can determine the sampling distribution of the mean by actually taking a specific population of raw scores having a mean $\mu$ and standard deviation $\sigma$ and (1) drawing all possible different samples of a fixed size $N$, (2) calculating the mean of each sample, and (3) calculating the probability of getting each mean value if chance alone were operating. This process is shown in Figure 12.4. After performing these three steps, we would have derived the sampling distrib-

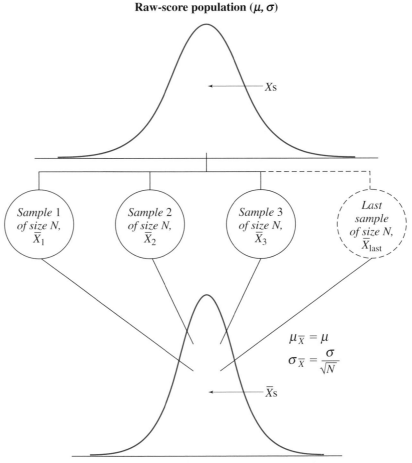

**figure 12.4**   Generating the sampling distribution of the mean for samples of size $N$ taken from a population of raw scores.

ution of the mean for samples of size $N$ taken from a specific population with mean $\mu$ and standard deviation $\sigma$. This sampling distribution of the mean would give all the values that the mean could take for samples of size $N$, along with the probability of getting each value if sampling is random from the specified population. By repeating the three-step process for populations of different score values and by systematically varying $N$, we can determine that the sampling distribution of the mean has the following general characteristics. For samples of any size $N$, the sampling distribution of the mean

1. Is a distribution of scores, each score of which is a sample mean of $N$ scores. This distribution has a mean and a standard deviation. The distribution is shown in the bottom part of Figure 12.4. You should note that this is a *population* set of scores even though the scores are based on samples, because the distribution contains the *complete* set of sample means. We shall symbolize the mean of the distribution as $\mu_{\bar{X}}$ and the standard deviation as $\sigma_{\bar{X}}$. Thus,

   $\mu_{\bar{X}}$ = mean of the sampling distribution of the mean

   $\sigma_{\bar{X}}$ = standard deviation of the sampling distribution of the mean

   $\sigma_{\bar{X}}$ is also called the *standard error of the mean* because each sample mean can be considered an estimate of the mean of the raw-score population. Variability between sample means then occurs due to errors in estimation— hence the phrase standard *error* of the mean for $\sigma_{\bar{X}}$.

2. Has a mean equal to the mean of the raw-score population. In equation form,

   $$\mu_{\bar{X}} = \mu$$

3. Has a standard deviation equal to the standard deviation of the raw-score population divided by $\sqrt{N}$. In equation form,

   $$\sigma_{\bar{X}} = \frac{\sigma}{\sqrt{N}}$$

4. Is normally shaped, depending on the shape of the raw-score population and on sample size.

The first characteristic is rather obvious. It merely states that the sampling distribution of the mean is made up of sample mean scores. As such, it, too, must have a mean and a standard deviation. The second characteristic says that the mean of the sampling distribution of the mean is equal to the mean of the raw scores ($\mu_{\bar{X}} = \mu$). We can gain some insight into this relationship by recognizing that each sample mean is an estimate of the mean of the raw-score population. Each will differ from the mean of the raw-score population due to chance. Sometimes the sample mean will be greater than the population mean, and sometimes it will be smaller because of chance factors. As we take more sample means, the average of these sample means will get closer to the mean of the raw-score population because the chance factors will cancel. Finally, when we have all of the possible different sample means, their average will equal the mean of the raw-score population ($\mu_{\bar{X}} = \mu$).

The third characteristic says that the standard deviation of the sampling distribution of the mean is equal to the standard deviation of the raw-score population divided by $\sqrt{N}$ ($\sigma_{\bar{X}} = \sigma/\sqrt{N}$). This says that the standard deviation of the sampling distribution of the mean varies directly with the standard deviation of the raw-score population and inversely with $\sqrt{N}$. It is fairly obvious why $\sigma_{\bar{X}}$ should vary directly with $\sigma$. If the scores in the population are more variable, $\sigma$ goes up and so does the variability between the means based on these scores. Understanding why $\sigma_{\bar{X}}$ varies inversely with $\sqrt{N}$ is a little more difficult. Recognizing that each sample mean is an estimate of the mean of the raw-score population is the key. As $N$ (the number of scores in each sample) goes up, each sample mean becomes a more accurate estimate of $\mu$. Since the sample means are more accurate, they will vary less from sample to sample, causing the variance $(\sigma_{\bar{X}}^2)$ of the sample means to decrease. Thus, $\sigma_{\bar{X}}^2$ varies inversely with $N$. Since $\sigma_{\bar{X}} = \sqrt{\sigma_{\bar{X}}^2}$, then $\sigma_{\bar{X}}$ varies inversely with $\sqrt{N}$. We would like to further point out that, since the standard deviation of the sampling distribution of the mean $(\sigma_{\bar{X}})$ changes with sample size, there is a different sampling distribution of the mean for each different sample size. This seems reasonable, because if the sample size changes, then the scores in each sample change and, consequently, so do the sample means. Thus, the sampling distribution of the mean for samples of size 10 should be different from the sampling distribution of the mean for samples of size 20 and so forth.

Regarding the fourth point, there are two factors that determine the shape of the sampling distribution of the mean: (1) the shape of the population raw scores and (2) the sample size ($N$). Concerning the first factor, if the population of raw scores is normally distributed, the sampling distribution of the mean will also be normally distributed, regardless of sample size. However, if the population of raw scores is not normally distributed, the shape of the sampling distribution depends on the sample size. *The Central Limit Theorem tells us that, regardless of the shape of the population of raw scores, the sampling distribution of the mean approaches a normal distribution as sample size N increases.* If $N$ is sufficiently large, the sampling distribution of the mean is approximately normal. How large must $N$ be for the sampling distribution of the mean to be considered normal? This depends on the shape of the raw-score population. The further the raw scores deviate from normality, the larger the sample size must be for the sampling distribution of the mean to be normally shaped. If $N \geq 300$, the shape of the population of raw scores is no longer important. With this size $N$, regardless of the shape of the raw-score population, the sampling distribution of the mean will deviate so little from normality that, for statistical calculations, we can consider it normally distributed. Since most populations encountered in the behavioral sciences do not differ greatly from normality, if $N \geq 30$, it is usually assumed that the sampling distribution of the mean will be normally shaped.[*]

Although it is beyond the scope of this text to prove these characteristics, we can demonstrate them, as well as gain more understanding about the sampling distribution of the mean, by considering a population and deriving the sampling distribution of the mean for samples taken from it. To simplify computation, let's use a population with a small number of scores. For the purposes of this illustration, assume the population raw scores are 2, 3, 4, 5, and 6. The mean of the population ($\mu$) equals 4.00, and the standard deviation ($\sigma$) equals 1.41. We want to derive the sampling distribution of the mean for samples of size 2 taken from this population. Again, assume sampling is one score at a time, with replacement. The first step is to draw all possible different samples of size 2 from the population.

---

[*]There are some notable exceptions to this rule, such as reaction-time scores.

| Sample Number (1) | Sample Scores (2) | $\overline{X}$ (3) | Sample Number (1) | Sample Scores (2) | $\overline{X}$ (3) |
|---|---|---|---|---|---|
| 1 | 2, 2 | 2.0 | 14 | 4, 5 | 4.5 |
| 2 | 2, 3 | 2.5 | 15 | 4, 6 | 5.0 |
| 3 | 2, 4 | 3.0 | 16 | 5, 2 | 3.5 |
| 4 | 2, 5 | 3.5 | 17 | 5, 3 | 4.0 |
| 5 | 2, 6 | 4.0 | 18 | 5, 4 | 4.5 |
| 6 | 3, 2 | 2.5 | 19 | 5, 5 | 5.0 |
| 7 | 3, 3 | 3.0 | 20 | 5, 6 | 5.5 |
| 8 | 3, 4 | 3.5 | 21 | 6, 2 | 4.0 |
| 9 | 3, 5 | 4.0 | 22 | 6, 3 | 4.5 |
| 10 | 3, 6 | 4.5 | 23 | 6, 4 | 5.0 |
| 11 | 4, 2 | 3.0 | 24 | 6, 5 | 5.5 |
| 12 | 4, 3 | 3.5 | 25 | 6, 6 | 6.0 |
| 13 | 4, 4 | 4.0 | | | |

**f i g u r e 12.5** All of the possible samples of size 2 that can be drawn from a population comprising the raw scores 2, 3, 4, 5, and 6. Sampling is one at a time, with replacement.

Figure 12.5 shows the population raw scores and, schematically, the different samples of size 2 that can be drawn from it. There are 25 different samples of size 2 possible. These are listed in the table of Figure 12.5, column 2. Next, we must calculate the mean of each sample. The results are shown in column 3 of this table. It is now a simple matter to calculate the probability of getting each mean value. Thus,

$$p(\overline{X} = 2.0) = \frac{\text{Number of possible } \overline{X}\text{s of 2.0}}{\text{Total number of } \overline{X}\text{s}} = \frac{1}{25} = 0.04$$

$$p(\overline{X} = 2.5) = \tfrac{2}{25} = 0.08$$

$$p(\overline{X} = 3.0) = \tfrac{3}{25} = 0.12$$

$$p(\overline{X} = 3.5) = \tfrac{4}{25} = 0.16$$

$$p(\overline{X} = 4.0) = \tfrac{5}{25} = 0.20$$

$$p(\overline{X} = 4.5) = \tfrac{4}{25} = 0.16$$

$$p(\overline{X} = 5.0) = \tfrac{3}{25} = 0.12$$

$$p(\overline{X} = 5.5) = \tfrac{2}{25} = 0.08$$

$$p(\overline{X} = 6.0) = \tfrac{1}{25} = 0.04$$

We have now derived the sampling distribution of the mean for samples of $N = 2$ taken from a population comprising the raw scores 2, 3, 4, 5, and 6. We have determined all the mean values possible from sampling two scores from the given population, along with the probability of obtaining each mean value if sampling is random from the population. The complete sampling distribution is shown in Table 12.1.

Suppose, for some reason, we wanted to know the probability of obtaining an $\overline{X} \geq 5.5$ due to randomly sampling two scores, one at a time, with replacement, from the raw-score population. We can determine the answer by consulting the sampling distribution of the mean for $N = 2$. Why? Because this distribution contains all of the possible sample mean values and their probability under the assumption of random sampling. Thus,

$$p(\overline{X} \geq 5.5) = 0.08 + 0.04 = 0.12$$

Now, let's consider the characteristics of this distribution: first, its shape. The original population of raw scores and the sampling distribution have been plotted in Figure 12.6(a) and (b). In part (c), we have plotted the sampling distribution of the mean with $N = 3$. Note that the shape of the two sampling distributions differs greatly from the population of raw scores. *Even with an N as small as 3 and a very nonnormal population of raw scores, the sampling distribution of the mean has a shape that approaches normality.* This is an illustration of what the Central Limit Theorem is telling us—namely, that as $N$ increases, the shape of the sampling distribution of the mean approaches that of a normal distribution. Of course, if the shape of the raw-score population were normal, the shape of the sampling distribution of the mean would be too.

Next, let's demonstrate that $\mu_{\overline{X}} = \mu$:

**table 12.1** Sampling distribution of the mean with $N = 2$ and population scores of 2, 3, 4, 5, and 6

| $\overline{X}$ | $p(\overline{X})$ |
| --- | --- |
| 2.0 | 0.04 |
| 2.5 | 0.08 |
| 3.0 | 0.12 |
| 3.5 | 0.16 |
| 4.0 | 0.20 |
| 4.5 | 0.16 |
| 5.0 | 0.12 |
| 5.5 | 0.08 |
| 6.0 | 0.04 |

$$\mu = \frac{\Sigma X}{\text{Number of raw scores}} \qquad \mu_{\overline{X}} = \frac{\Sigma \overline{X}}{\text{Number of mean scores}}$$

$$= \tfrac{20}{5} = 4.00 \qquad\qquad = \tfrac{100}{25} = 4.00$$

Thus,

$$\mu_{\overline{X}} = \mu$$

The mean of the raw scores is found by dividing the sum of the raw scores by the number of raw scores: $\mu = 4.00$. The mean of the sampling distribution of the

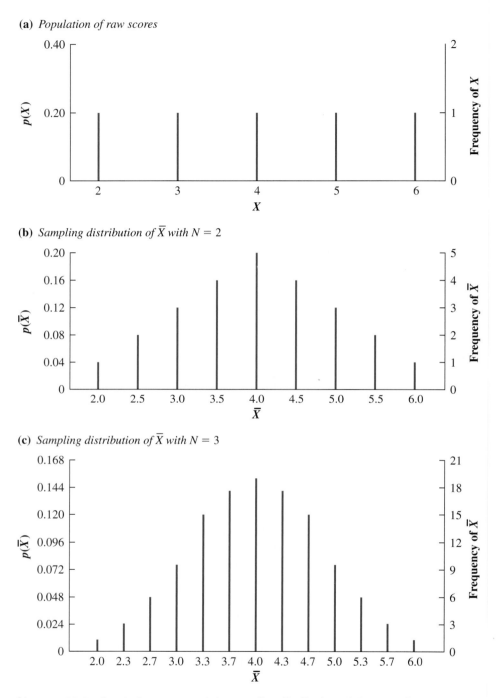

**(a)** *Population of raw scores*

**(b)** *Sampling distribution of $\overline{X}$ with N = 2*

**(c)** *Sampling distribution of $\overline{X}$ with N = 3*

f i g u r e  **12.6**   Population scores and the sampling distribution of the mean for samples of size *N* = 2 and *N* = 3.

mean is found by dividing the sum of the sample mean scores by the number of mean scores: $\mu_{\overline{X}} = 4.00$. Thus, $\mu_{\overline{X}} = \mu$.

Finally, we need to show that $\sigma_{\overline{X}} = \sigma/\sqrt{N}$. $\sigma_{\overline{X}}$ can be calculated in two ways: (1) from the equation $\sigma_{\overline{X}} = \sigma/\sqrt{N}$ and (2) directly from the sample mean scores themselves. Our demonstration will involve calculating $\sigma_{\overline{X}}$ in both ways, showing that they lead to the same value. The calculations are shown in Table 12.2. Since both methods yield the same value ($\sigma_{\overline{X}} = 1.00$), we have demonstrated that

$$\sigma_{\overline{X}} = \frac{\sigma}{\sqrt{N}}$$

Note that $N$ in the previous equation is the number of scores in each sample. Thus, we have demonstrated that

1. $\mu_{\overline{X}} = \mu$
2. $\sigma_{\overline{X}} = \sigma/\sqrt{N}$
3. The sampling distribution of the mean takes on a shape similar to normal even if the raw scores are nonnormal.

## The Reading Proficiency Experiment Revisited

We are now in a position to return to the "Super" and evaluate the data from the experiment evaluating reading proficiency. Let's restate the experiment.

> You are superintendent of public schools and have conducted an experiment to investigate whether the reading proficiency of high school seniors living in your city is deficient. A random sample of 100 high school seniors from this population had a mean reading score of 72 ($\overline{X}_{\text{obt}} = 72$). National norms of reading proficiency for high school seniors show a normal distribution of scores with a mean of 75 ($\mu = 75$) and a standard deviation of 16 ($\sigma = 16$). Is it reasonable to consider the 100 scores a random sample from a normally distributed population of reading scores where $\mu = 75$ and $\sigma = 16$? Use $\alpha = 0.05_{1 \text{ tail}}$.

If we take all possible samples of size 100 from the population of normally distributed reading scores, we can determine the sampling distribution of the mean samples with $N = 100$. From what has been said before, this distribution (1) is normally shaped, (2) has a mean $\mu_{\overline{X}} = \mu = 75$, and (3) has a standard deviation $\sigma_{\overline{X}} = \sigma/\sqrt{N} = 16/\sqrt{100} = 1.6$. The two distributions are shown in Figure 12.7. Note that the sampling distribution of the mean contains all the possible mean scores from samples of size 100 drawn from the null-hypothesis population ($\mu = 75, \sigma = 16$). For the sake of clarity in the following exposition, we have redrawn the sampling distribution of the mean alone in Figure 12.8.

The shaded area of Figure 12.8 contains all the mean values of samples of $N = 100$ that are as low as or lower than $\overline{X}_{\text{obt}} = 72$. The proportion of shaded area to total area will tell us the probability of obtaining a sample mean equal to

**t a b l e 12.2**  Demonstration that $\sigma_{\overline{X}} = \dfrac{\sigma}{\sqrt{N}}$

| **Using $\sigma_{\overline{X}} = \sigma/\sqrt{N}$** | **Using the Sample Mean Scores** |
|---|---|
| $\sigma_{\overline{X}} = \dfrac{\sigma}{\sqrt{N}}$ | $\sigma_{\overline{X}} = \sqrt{\dfrac{\Sigma(\overline{X} - \mu_{\overline{X}})^2}{\text{Number of mean scores}}}$ |
| $= \dfrac{1.41}{\sqrt{2}}$ | $= \sqrt{\dfrac{(2.0 - 4.0)^2 + (2.5 - 4.0)^2 + \cdots + (6.0 - 4.0)^2}{25}}$ |
| $= 1.00$ | $= \sqrt{\dfrac{25}{25}} = 1.00$ |

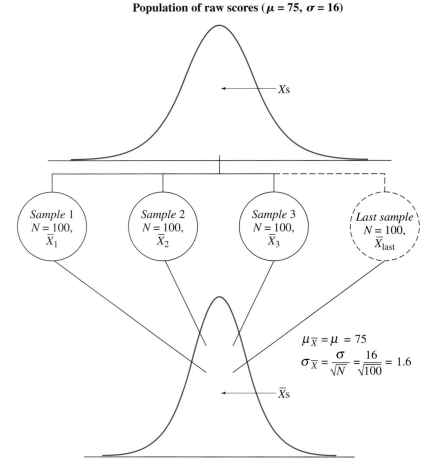

**Population of raw scores ($\mu = 75$, $\sigma = 16$)**

$X$s

*Sample 1*
$N = 100,$
$\overline{X}_1$

*Sample 2*
$N = 100,$
$\overline{X}_2$

*Sample 3*
$N = 100,$
$\overline{X}_3$

*Last sample*
$N = 100,$
$\overline{X}_{last}$

$\mu_{\overline{X}} = \mu = 75$

$\sigma_{\overline{X}} = \dfrac{\sigma}{\sqrt{N}} = \dfrac{16}{\sqrt{100}} = 1.6$

$\overline{X}$s

**Sampling distribution of the mean for samples with $N = 100$**

f i g u r e  **12.7**  Sampling distribution of the mean for samples of size $N = 100$ drawn from a population of raw scores with $\mu = 75$ and $\sigma = 16$.

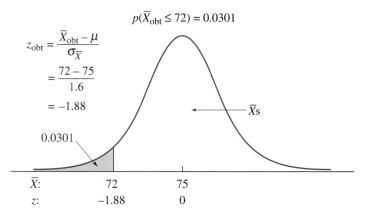

$p(\overline{X}_{obt} \leq 72) = 0.0301$

$z_{obt} = \dfrac{\overline{X}_{obt} - \mu}{\sigma_{\overline{X}}}$

$= \dfrac{72 - 75}{1.6}$

$= -1.88$

0.0301

$\overline{X}$s

| $\overline{X}$: | 72 | 75 |
|---|---|---|
| $z$: | $-1.88$ | 0 |

f i g u r e  **12.8**  Evaluation of reading proficiency data comparing the obtained probability with the alpha level.

or less than 72 if chance alone is at work (another way of saying this is, "if the sample is a random sample from the null-hypothesis population"). Since the sampling distribution of the mean is normally shaped, we can find the proportion of the shaded area by (1) calculating the $z$ transform ($z_{obt}$) for $\overline{X}_{obt} = 72$ and (2) determining the appropriate area from Table A, Appendix D, using $z_{obt}$.

The equation for $z_{obt}$ is very similar to the $z$ equation in Chapter 5, but instead of dealing with raw scores, we are dealing with mean values. The two equations are shown in Table 12.3.

table 12.3    *z* equations

| **Raw Scores** | **Mean Scores** |
| --- | --- |
| $z = \dfrac{X - \mu}{\sigma}$ | $z_{obt} = \dfrac{\overline{X}_{obt} - \mu_{\overline{X}}}{\sigma_{\overline{X}}}$ |

Since $\mu_{\overline{X}} = \mu$, the $z_{obt}$ equation for sample means simplifies to

$$z_{obt} = \frac{\overline{X}_{obt} - \mu}{\sigma_{\overline{X}}} \qquad z \ transformation \ for \ \overline{X}_{obt}$$

Calculating $z_{obt}$ for the present experiment, we obtain

$$z_{obt} = \frac{\overline{X}_{obt} - \mu}{\sigma_{\overline{X}}}$$
$$= \frac{72 - 75}{1.6}$$
$$= -1.88 \qquad for \ \overline{X}_{obt} = 72$$

From Table A, column C, in Appendix D,

$$p(\overline{X}_{obt} \leq 72) = 0.0301$$

Since $0.0301 < 0.05$, we reject $H_0$ and conclude that it is unreasonable to assume that the 100 scores are a random sample from a population where $\mu = 75$. The reading proficiency of high school seniors in your city appears deficient.

## Alternative Solution Using $z_{obt}$ and the Critical Region for Rejection of $H_0$

The results of this experiment can be analyzed in another way. This method is actually the preferred method because it is simpler and it sets the pattern for the inference tests to follow. However, it builds upon the previous method and therefore couldn't be presented until now. To use this method, we must first define some terms.

definitions  ■  *The **critical region for rejection of the null hypothesis** is the area under the curve that contains all the values of the statistic that allow rejection of the null hypothesis.*

■  *The **critical value of a statistic** is the value of the statistic that bounds the critical region.*

To analyze the data using the alternative method, all we need do is calculate $z_{obt}$, determine the critical value of $z$ ($z_{crit}$), and assess whether $z_{obt}$ falls within the critical region for rejection of $H_0$. We already know how to calculate $z_{obt}$.

The critical region for rejection of $H_0$ is determined by the alpha level. For example, if $\alpha = 0.05_{1\,tail}$ in the direction predicting a negative $z_{obt}$ value, as in the previous example, then the critical region for rejection of $H_0$ is the area under the left tail of the curve that equals 0.0500. We find $z_{crit}$ for this area by using Table A in a reverse manner. Referring to Table A and skimming column C until we locate 0.0500, we can determine the $z$ value that corresponds to 0.0500. It turns out that 0.0500 falls midway between the $z$ scores of 1.64 and 1.65. Therefore, the $z$ value corresponding to 0.0500 is 1.645. Since we are dealing with the left tail of the distribution,

$$z_{crit} = -1.645$$

This score defines the critical region for rejection of $H_0$ and, hence, is called $z_{crit}$. If $z_{obt}$ falls in the critical region for rejection, we will reject $H_0$. These relationships are shown in Figure 12.9(a). If $\alpha = 0.05_{1\,tail}$ in the direction predicting a positive $z_{obt}$ value, then

$$z_{crit} = 1.645$$

This is shown in Figure 12.9(b). If $\alpha = 0.05_{2\,tail}$, then the combined area under the two tails of the curve must equal 0.0500. Thus, the area under each tail must equal 0.0250, as in Figure 12.9(c). For this area,

$$z_{crit} = \pm 1.96$$

To reject $H_0$, the obtained sample mean ($\overline{X}_{obt}$) must have a $z$-transformed value ($z_{obt}$) that falls within the critical region for rejection.

Let's now use these concepts to analyze the reading data. First, we calculate $z_{obt}$:

$$z_{obt} = \frac{\overline{X}_{obt} - \mu}{\sigma_{\overline{X}}}$$

$$= \frac{72 - 75}{1.6} = \frac{-3}{1.6}$$

$$= -1.88$$

The next step is to determine $z_{crit}$. Since $\alpha = 0.05_{1\,tail}$, the area under the left tail equals 0.0500. For this area, from Table A we obtain

$$z_{crit} = -1.645$$

Finally, we must determine whether $z_{obt}$ falls within the critical region. If it does, we reject the null hypothesis. If it doesn't, we retain the null hypothesis. The decision rule states the following:

*If $|z_{obt}| \geq |z_{crit}|$, reject the null hypothesis. If not, retain the null hypothesis.*

Note that this equation is just a shorthand way of specifying that, if $z_{obt}$ is positive, it must be equal to or greater than $+z_{crit}$ to fall within the critical region. If $z_{obt}$ is negative, it must be equal to or less than $-z_{crit}$ to fall within the critical region.

In the present example, since $|z_{obt}| > 1.645$, we reject the null hypothesis. The complete solution using this method is shown in Figure 12.10. We would like to point out that, in using this method, we are following the two-step procedure out-

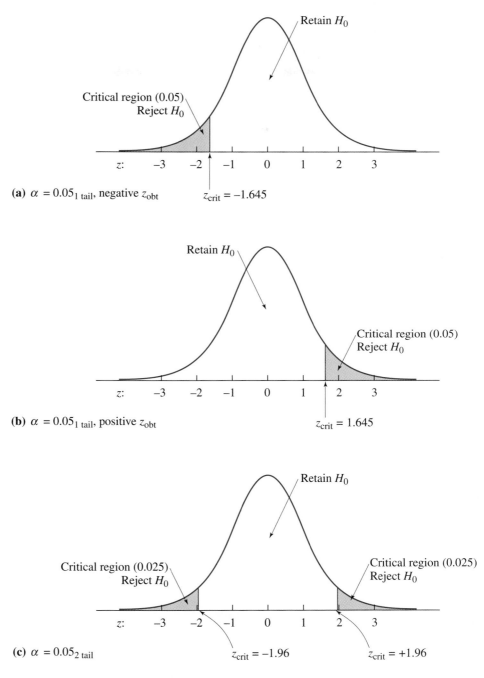

(a) $\alpha = 0.05_{1\,\text{tail}}$, negative $z_{\text{obt}}$

(b) $\alpha = 0.05_{1\,\text{tail}}$, positive $z_{\text{obt}}$

(c) $\alpha = 0.05_{2\,\text{tail}}$

Adapted from *Fundamental Statistics for Behavioral Sciences* by Robert B. McCall, © 1998 by Brooks/Cole.

f i g u r e 12.9 Critical region of rejection for $H_0$ for (a) $\alpha = 0.05_{1\,\text{tail}}$, $z_{\text{obt}}$ negative; (b) $\alpha = 0.05_{1\,\text{tail}}$, $z_{\text{obt}}$ positive; and (c) $\alpha = 0.05_{2\,\text{tail}}$.

lined previously in this chapter for analyzing data: (1) calculating the appropriate statistic and (2) evaluating the statistic based on its sampling distribution. Actually, the experimenter calculates two statistics: $\overline{X}_{\text{obt}}$ and $z_{\text{obt}}$. The final one evaluated is $z_{\text{obt}}$. If the sampling distribution of $\overline{X}$ is normally shaped, then the $z$ distribution will also be normal and the appropriate probabilities given by Table A.

**STEP 1:** Calculate the appropriate statistic:

$$z_{obt} = \frac{\overline{X}_{obt} - \mu}{\sigma_{\overline{X}}} = \frac{72 - 75}{1.6} = -1.88$$

**STEP 2:** Evaluate the statistic based on its sampling distribution. The decision rule is as follows: If $|z_{obt}| \geq |z_{crit}|$, reject $H_0$. Since $\alpha = 0.05_{1\,tail}$, from Table A,

$$z_{crit} = -1.645$$

Since $|z_{obt}| > 1.645$, it falls within the critical region for rejection of $H_0$. Therefore, we reject $H_0$.

$\mu_{\overline{X}} = \mu = 75$

$\sigma_{\overline{X}} = \dfrac{\sigma}{\sqrt{N}} = \dfrac{16}{\sqrt{100}} = 1.6$

$z_{crit}$

| $z$: | $-1.88$ | $-1.645$ | 0 |
| $\overline{X}$: | 72 | | 75 |

$z_{obt}$ *or* $\overline{X}_{obt}$

**figure 12.10** Solution to reading proficiency experiment using $z_{obt}$ and the critical region.

Of course, the $z$ distribution has a mean of 0 and a standard deviation of 1, as discussed in Chapter 5.

Let's try another problem using this approach.

## Practice Problem 12.1

A university president believes that, over the past few years, the average age of students attending his university has changed. To test this hypothesis, an experiment is conducted in which the age of 150 students who have been randomly sampled from the student body is measured. The mean age is 23.5 years. A complete census taken at the university a few years before the experiment showed a mean age of 22.4 years, with a standard deviation of 7.6.

**a.** What is the nondirectional alternative hypothesis?
**b.** What is the null hypothesis?
**c.** Using $\alpha = 0.05_{2\,tail}$, what is the conclusion?

**SOLUTION**

a. Nondirectional alternative hypothesis:　Over the past few years, the average age of students at the university has changed. Therefore, the sample with $\overline{X}_{obt} = 23.5$ is a random sample from a population where $\mu \neq 22.4$.

b. Null hypothesis:　The null hypothesis asserts that it is reasonable to consider the sample with $\overline{X}_{obt} = 23.5$ a random sample from a population with $\mu = 22.4$.

c. Conclusion, using $\alpha = 0.05_{2\,tail}$:

> **STEP 1: Calculate the appropriate statistic.**　The data are given in the problem.

$$z_{obt} = \frac{\overline{X}_{obt} - \mu}{\sigma_{\overline{X}}}$$

$$= \frac{\overline{X}_{obt} - \mu}{\sigma/\sqrt{N}} = \frac{23.5 - 22.4}{7.6/\sqrt{150}}$$

$$= \frac{1.1}{0.6205} = 1.77$$

> **STEP 2: Evaluate the statistic based on its sampling distribution.**　The decision rule is as follows: If $|z_{obt}| \geq |z_{crit}|$, reject $H_0$. If not, retain $H_0$. Since $\alpha = 0.05_{2\,tail,}$ from Table A,

$$z_{crit} = \pm 1.96$$

Since $|z_{obt}| < 1.96$, it does not fall within the critical region for rejection of $H_0$. Therefore, we retain $H_0$. We cannot conclude that the average age of students attending the university has changed.

## Practice Problem 12.2

A gasoline manufacturer believes a new additive will result in more miles per gallon. A large number of mileage measurements on the gasoline without the additive have been made by the company under rigorously controlled conditions. The results show a mean of 24.7 miles per gallon and a standard deviation of 4.8. Tests are conducted on a sample of 75 cars using the gasoline plus the additive. The sample mean equals 26.5 miles per gallon.

a. Let's assume there is adequate basis for a one-tailed test. What is the directional alternative hypothesis?

b. What is the null hypothesis?

c. What is the conclusion? Use $\alpha = 0.05_{1\,tail}$.

*(continued)*

**SOLUTION**

**a.** Directional alternative hypothesis:  The new additive increases the number of miles per gallon. Therefore, the sample with $\overline{X}_{obt} = 26.5$ is a random sample from a population where $\mu > 24.7$.

**b.** Null hypothesis: $H_0$:  The sample with $\overline{X}_{obt} = 26.5$ is a random sample from a population with $\mu \leq 24.7$.

**c.** Conclusion, using $\alpha = 0.05_{1\,tail}$:

> **STEP 1: Calculate the appropriate statistic.** The data are given in the problem.
>
> $$z_{obt} = \frac{\overline{X}_{obt} - \mu}{\sigma/\sqrt{N}}$$
>
> $$= \frac{26.5 - 24.7}{4.8/\sqrt{75}} = \frac{1.8}{0.5543}$$
>
> $$= 3.25$$

> **STEP 2: Evaluate the statistic based on its sampling distribution.** The decision rule states that if $|z_{obt}| \geq |z_{crit}|$, reject $H_0$. If not, retain $H_0$. Given $\alpha = 0.05_{1\,tail}$, from Table A,
>
> $$z_{crit} = 1.645$$

Since $|z_{obt}| > 1.645$, it falls within the critical region for rejection of $H_0$. Therefore, we reject the null hypothesis and conclude that the gasoline additive does increase miles per gallon.

## Conditions Under Which the *z* Test Is Appropriate

The *z* test is appropriate when the experiment involves a single sample mean ($\overline{X}_{obt}$) and the parameters of the null-hypothesis population are known (i.e., when $\mu$ and $\sigma$ are known). In addition, to use this test, the sampling distribution of the mean should be normally distributed. This, of course, requires that $N \geq 30$ or that the null-hypothesis population itself be normally distributed.[*] This normality requirement is spoken of as "the mathematical assumption underlying the *z* test."

## Power and the *z* Test

In Chapter 11, we discussed power in conjunction with the sign test. Let's review some of the main points made in that chapter.

1. Conceptually, power is the sensitivity of the experiment to detect a real effect of the independent variable, if there is one.

---

[*]Many authors would limit the use of the *z* test to data that are of interval or ratio scaling. Please see the footnote in Chapter 2, p. 31, for references discussing this point.

2. Power is defined mathematically as the probability that the experiment will result in rejecting the null hypothesis if the independent variable has a real effect.
3. Power + Beta = 1. Thus, power varies inversely with beta.
4. Power varies directly with $N$. Increasing $N$ increases power.
5. Power varies directly with the size of the real effect of the independent variable. The power of an experiment is greater for large effects than for small effects.
6. Power varies directly with alpha level. If alpha is made more stringent, power decreases.

These points about power are true regardless of the inference test. In this section, we will again illustrate these conclusions, only this time in conjunction with the normal deviate test. We will begin with a discussion of power and a sample size.

example

## Power and Sample Size ($N$)

Let's return to the illustrative experiment at the beginning of this chapter. We'll assume you are again wearing the hat of superintendent of public schools. This time, however, you are just designing the experiment. It has not yet been conducted. You want to determine whether the reading program for high school seniors in your city is deficient. As described previously, the national norms of reading proficiency of high school seniors is a normal distribution of population scores with $\mu = 75$ and $\sigma = 16$. You plan to test a random sample of high school seniors from your city, and you are trying to determine how large the sample size should be. You will use $\alpha = 0.05_{1\ tail}$ in evaluating the data when collected. You want to be able to detect proficiency deficiencies in your program of 3 or more mean points from the national norms. That is, if the mean reading proficiency of the population of high school seniors in your city is lower than the national norms by 3 or more points, you want your experiment to have a high probability to detect it.

a. If you decide to use a sample size of 25 ($N = 25$), what is the power of your experiment to detect a population deficiency in reading proficiency of 3 mean points from the national norms?
b. If you increase the sample size to $N = 100$, what is the power now to detect a population deficiency in reading proficiency of 3 mean points?
c. What size $N$ should you use for the power to be approximately 0.9000 to detect a population deficiency in reading proficiency of 3 mean points?

### SOLUTION

a. Power with $N = 25$.

As discussed in Chapter 11, power is the probability of rejecting $H_0$ if the independent variable has a real effect. In computing the power to detect a hypothesized real effect, we must first determine the sample outcomes that will allow rejection of $H_0$. Then, we must determine the probability of getting any of these sample outcomes if the independent variable has the hypothesized real effect. The resulting probability is the power to detect the hypothesized real effect. Thus, there are two steps in computing power:

**STEP 1:** Determine the possible sample mean outcomes in the experiment that would allow $H_0$ to be rejected. With the $z$ test, this means determining the critical region for rejection of $H_0$, using $\overline{X}$ as the statistic.

**STEP 2:** Assuming the hypothesized real effect of the independent variable is the true state of affairs, determine the probability of getting a sample mean in the critical region for rejection of $H_0$.

Let's now compute the power to detect a population deficiency in reading proficiency of 3 mean points from the national norms, using $N = 25$.

**STEP 1:** Determine the possible sample mean outcomes in the experiment that would allow $H_0$ to be rejected. With the *z* test, this means determining the critical region for rejection of $H_0$, using $\overline{X}$ as the statistic.

When evaluating $H_0$ with the *z* test, we assume the sample is a random sample from the null-hypothesis population. We will symbolize the mean of the null-hypothesis population as $\mu_{\text{null}}$. In the present example, the null-hypothesis population is the set of scores established by national testing, that is, a normal population of scores with $\mu_{\text{null}} = 75$. With $\alpha = 0.05_{1\text{ tail}}$, $z_{\text{crit}} = -1.645$. To determine the critical value of $\overline{X}$, we can use the *z* equation solved for $\overline{X}_{\text{crit}}$:

$$z_{\text{crit}} = \frac{\overline{X}_{\text{crit}} - \mu_{\text{null}}}{\sigma_{\overline{X}}}$$

$$\overline{X}_{\text{crit}} = \mu_{\text{null}} + \sigma_{\overline{X}}(z_{\text{crit}})$$

Substituting the data with $N = 25$,

$$\overline{X}_{\text{crit}} = 75 + 3.2(-1.645) \qquad \sigma_{\overline{X}} = \frac{\sigma}{\sqrt{N}} = \frac{16}{\sqrt{25}} = 3.2$$

$$= 75 - 5.264$$

$$= 69.74$$

Thus, with $N = 25$, we will reject $H_0$ if, when we conduct the experiment, the mean of the sample $(\overline{X}_{\text{obt}}) \leq 69.74$. See Figure 12.11 for a pictorial representation of these relationships.

**STEP 2:** Assuming the hypothesized real effect of the independent variable is the true state of affairs, determine the probability of getting a sample mean in the critical region for rejection of $H_0$.

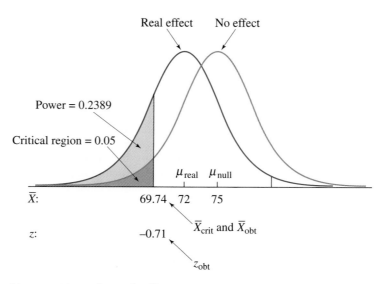

f i g u r e 12.11   Power for $N = 25$.

If the independent variable has the hypothesized real effect, then the sample scores in your experiment are not a random sample from the null-hypothesis population. Instead, they are a random sample from a population having a mean as specified by the hypothesized real effect. We shall symbolize this mean as $\mu_{real}$. Thus, if the reading proficiency of the population of seniors in your city is 3 mean points lower than the national norms, then the sample in your experiment is a random sample from a population where $\mu_{real} = 72$. The probability of your sample mean falling in the critical region if the sample is actually a random sample from a population where $\mu_{real} = 72$ is found by obtaining the $z$ transform for $\overline{X}_{obt} = 69.74$ and looking up its corresponding area in Table A. Thus,

$$z_{obt} = \frac{\overline{X}_{obt} - \mu_{real}}{\sigma_{\overline{X}}} \qquad \sigma_{\overline{X}} = \frac{\sigma}{\sqrt{N}} = \frac{16}{\sqrt{25}} = 3.2$$

$$= \frac{69.74 - 72}{3.2}$$

$$= -0.71$$

From Table A,

$$p(\overline{X}_{obt} \leq 69.74) = p(z_{obt} \leq -0.71) = 0.2389$$

Thus,

$$\text{Power} = 0.2389$$

$$\text{Beta} = 1 - \text{Power} = 1 - 0.2389 = 0.7611$$

Thus, the power to detect a deficiency of 3 mean points with $N = 25$ is 0.2389 and beta = 0.7611.

Since the probability of a Type II error is too high, you decide not to go ahead and run the experiment with $N = 25$. Let's now see what happens to power and beta if $N$ is increased to 100.

b. If $N = 100$, what is the power to detect a population difference in reading proficiency of 3 mean points?

**STEP 1:** Determine the possible sample mean outcomes in the experiment that would allow $H_0$ to be rejected. With the $z$ test, this means determining the critical region for rejection of $H_0$, using $\overline{X}$ as the statistic:

$$\overline{X}_{crit} = \mu_{null} + \sigma_{\overline{X}}(z_{crit}) \qquad \sigma_{\overline{X}} = \frac{\sigma}{\sqrt{N}} = \frac{16}{\sqrt{100}} = 1.6$$

$$= 75 + 1.6(-1.645)$$

$$= 75 - 2.632$$

$$= 72.37$$

**STEP 2:** Assuming the hypothesized real effect of the independent variable is the true state of affairs, determine the probability of getting a sample mean in the critical region for rejection of $H_0$.

$$z_{obt} = \frac{\overline{X}_{obt} - \mu_{real}}{\sigma_{\overline{X}}} \qquad \sigma_{\overline{X}} = \frac{\sigma}{\sqrt{N}} = \frac{16}{\sqrt{100}} = 1.6$$

$$= \frac{72.37 - 72}{1.6}$$

$$= 0.23$$

From Table A,

$$p(\overline{X}_{obt} \leq 72.37) = 0.5000 + 0.0910 = 0.5910$$

Thus,

$$\text{Power} = 0.5910$$

$$\text{Beta} = 1 - \text{Power} = 1 - 0.5910 = 0.4090$$

Thus, by increasing $N$ from 25 to 100, the power to detect a deficiency of 3 mean points has increased from 0.2389 to 0.5910. Beta has decreased from 0.7611 to 0.4090. This is a demonstration that power varies directly with $N$ and beta varies inversely with $N$. Thus, increasing $N$ causes an increase in power and a decrease in beta. Figure 12.12 summarizes the relationships for this problem.

c. What size $N$ should you use for the power to be approximately 0.9000?

For the power to be 0.9000 to detect a population deficiency of 3 mean points, the probability that $\overline{X}_{obt}$ will fall in the critical region must be equal to 0.9000. As shown in Figure 12.13, this dictates that the area between $z_{obt}$ and $\mu_{real} = 0.4000$. From Table A, $z_{obt} = 1.28$. (Note that we have taken the closest table reading rather than interpolating. This will result in a power close to 0.9000, but not exactly equal to 0.9000.) By solving the $z_{obt}$ equation for $\overline{X}_{obt}$ and setting $\overline{X}_{obt}$ equal to $\overline{X}_{crit}$, we can determine $N$. Thus,

$$\overline{X}_{obt} = \mu_{real} + \sigma_{\overline{X}}(z_{obt})$$

$$\overline{X}_{crit} = \mu_{null} + \sigma_{\overline{X}}(z_{crit})$$

Setting $\overline{X}_{obt} = \overline{X}_{crit}$, we have,

$$\mu_{real} + \sigma_{\overline{X}}(z_{obt}) = \mu_{null} + \sigma_{\overline{X}}(z_{crit})$$

Solving for $N$,

$$\mu_{real} - \mu_{null} = \sigma_{\overline{X}}(z_{crit}) - \sigma_{\overline{X}}(z_{obt})$$

$$\mu_{real} - \mu_{null} = \sigma_{\overline{X}}(z_{crit} - z_{obt})$$

$$\mu_{real} - \mu_{null} = \frac{\sigma}{\sqrt{N}}(z_{crit} - z_{obt})$$

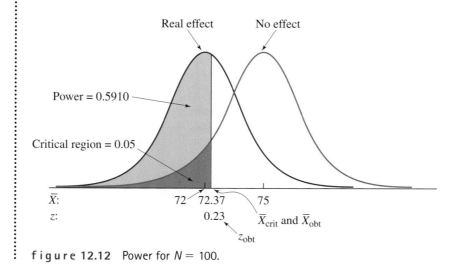

**figure 12.12** Power for $N = 100$.

**figure 12.13**   Determining $N$ for power $= 0.9000$.

$$\sqrt{N}(\mu_{\text{real}} - \mu_{\text{null}}) = \sigma(z_{\text{crit}} - z_{\text{obt}})$$

$$N = \left[ \frac{\sigma(z_{\text{crit}} - z_{\text{obt}})}{\mu_{\text{real}} - \mu_{\text{null}}} \right]^2$$

Thus, to determine $N$, the equation we use is

$$N = \left[ \frac{\sigma(z_{\text{crit}} - z_{\text{obt}})}{\mu_{\text{real}} - \mu_{\text{null}}} \right]^2 \qquad \textit{equation for determining N}$$

Applying this equation to the problem we have been considering, we get

$$N = \left[ \frac{\sigma(z_{\text{crit}} - z_{\text{obt}})}{\mu_{\text{real}} - \mu_{\text{null}}} \right]^2$$

$$= \left[ \frac{16(-1.645 - 1.28)}{72 - 75} \right]^2$$

$$= 243$$

Thus, if you increase $N$ to 243 subjects, the power will be approximately 0.9000 (power $= 0.8997$) to detect a population deficiency in reading proficiency of 3 mean points. I suggest you confirm this power calculation yourself using $N = 243$ as a practice exercise.

**Power and alpha level**   Next, let's take a look at the relationship between power and alpha. Suppose you had set $\alpha = 0.01_{1\,\text{tail}}$ instead of $0.05_{1\,\text{tail}}$. What happens to the resulting power? (We'll assume $N = 100$ in this question.)

**SOLUTION**

**STEP 1:**   Determine the possible sample mean outcomes in the experiment that would allow $H_0$ to be rejected. With the $z$ test, this means determining the critical region for rejection of $H_0$, using $\overline{X}$ as the statistic:

$$\overline{X}_{\text{crit}} = \mu_{\text{null}} + \sigma_{\overline{X}}(z_{\text{crit}}) \qquad \sigma_{\overline{X}} = \frac{\sigma}{\sqrt{N}} = \frac{16}{100} = 1.6$$

$$= 75 + 1.6(-2.33) \qquad z_{\text{crit}} = -2.33$$

$$= 71.27$$

**STEP 2:** Assuming the hypothesized real effect of the independent variable is the true state of affairs, determine the probability of getting a sample mean in the critical region for rejection of $H_0$.

$$z_{\text{obt}} = \frac{\overline{X}_{\text{obt}} - \mu_{\text{real}}}{\sigma_{\overline{X}}} \qquad \sigma_{\overline{X}} = \frac{\sigma}{\sqrt{N}} = \frac{16}{100} = 1.6$$

$$= \frac{71.27 - 72}{1.6}$$

$$= -0.46$$

From Table A,

$$p(\overline{X}_{\text{obt}} \leq 71.27) = 0.3228$$

Thus,

$$\text{Power} = 0.3228$$

$$\text{Beta} = 1 - \text{Power} = 0.6772$$

Thus, by making alpha more stringent (changing it from $0.05_{1\,\text{tail}}$ to $0.01_{1\,\text{tail}}$), power has decreased from 0.5910 to 0.3228. Beta has increased from 0.4090 to 0.6772. This demonstrates that there is a direct relationship between alpha and power and an inverse relationship between alpha and beta. Figure 12.14 shows the relationships for this problem.

**Relationship between size of real effect and power**   Next, let's investigate the relationship between the size of the real effect and power. To do this, let's calculate the power to detect a population deficiency in reading proficiency of 5 mean points from the national norms. We'll assume $N = 100$ and $\alpha = 0.05_{1\,\text{tail}}$. Figure 12.15 shows the relationships for this problem.

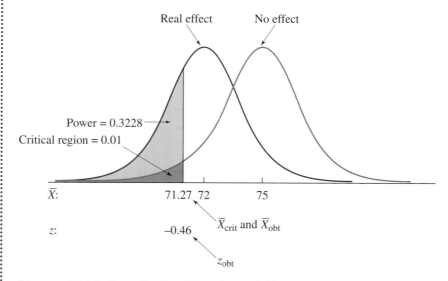

**figure 12.14**  Power for $N = 100$ and $\alpha = 0.01_{1\,\text{tail}}$.

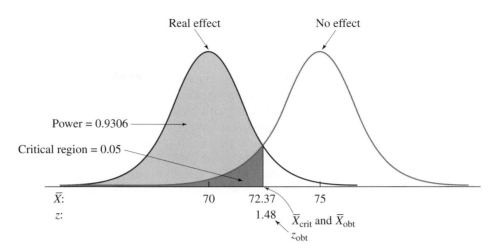

**figure 12.15** Power for $N = 100$ and $\mu_{real} = 70$.

**SOLUTION**

**STEP 1:** Determine the possible sample mean outcomes in the experiment that would allow $H_0$ to be rejected. With the z test, this means determining the critical region for rejection of $H_0$, using $\overline{X}$ as the statistic:

$$\overline{X}_{crit} = \mu_{null} + \sigma_{\overline{X}}(z_{crit}) \qquad \sigma_{\overline{X}} = \frac{\sigma}{\sqrt{N}} = \frac{16}{100} = 1.6$$

$$= 75 + 1.6(-1.645)$$

$$= 72.37$$

**STEP 2:** Assuming the hypothesized real effect of the independent variable is the true state of affairs, determine the probability of getting a sample mean in the critical region for rejection of $H_0$:

$$z_{obt} = \frac{\overline{X}_{obt} - \mu_{real}}{\sigma_{\overline{X}}} \qquad \sigma_{\overline{X}} = \frac{\sigma}{\sqrt{N}} = \frac{16}{100} = 1.6$$

$$= \frac{72.37 - 70}{1.6}$$

$$= 1.48$$

From Table A,

$$p(\overline{X}_{obt} \leq 72.37) = 0.5000 + 0.4306 = 0.9306$$

Thus,

$$\text{Power} = 0.9306$$

$$\text{Beta} = 1 - \text{Power} = 1 - 0.9306 = 0.0694$$

Thus, by increasing the size of the real effect from 3 to 5 mean points, power has increased from 0.5910 to 0.9306. Beta has decreased from 0.4090 to 0.0694. This demonstrates that there is a direct relationship between the size of the real effect and the power to detect it.

## SUMMARY

In this chapter, we have discussed the topics of the sampling distribution of a statistic, how to generate sampling distributions from an empirical sampling approach, the sampling distribution of the mean, and how to analyze single sample experiments with the z test. We pointed out that the procedure for analyzing data in most hypothesis-testing experiments is to calculate the appropriate statistic and then evaluate the statistic based on its sampling distribution. The sampling distribution of a statistic gives all the values that the statistic can take, along with the probability of getting each value if sampling is random from the null-hypothesis population. The sampling distribution can be generated theoretically with the Central Limit Theorem or empirically by (1) determining all the possible different samples of size N that can be formed from the raw-score population, (2) calculating the statistic for each of the samples, and (3) calculating the probability of getting each value of the statistic if sampling is random from the null-hypothesis population.

The sampling distribution of the mean is a distribution of sample mean values having a mean $(\mu_{\bar{X}})$ equal to $\mu$ and a standard deviation $(\sigma_{\bar{X}})$ equal to $\sigma/\sqrt{N}$. It is normally distributed if the raw-score population is normally distributed or if $N \geq 30$, assuming the raw-score population is not radically different from normality. The z test is appropriate for analyzing single sample experiments, where $\mu$ and $\sigma$ are known and the sample mean is used as the basic statistic. When this test is used, $z_{\mathrm{obt}}$ is calculated and then evaluated to determine whether it falls in the critical region for rejecting the null hypothesis. To use the z test, the sampling distribution of the mean must be normally distributed. This in turn requires that the null-hypothesis population be normally distributed or that $N \geq 30$.

Finally, we discussed power in conjunction with the z test. Power is the probability of rejecting $H_0$ if the independent variable has a real effect. To calculate power, we followed a two-step procedure: determining the possible sample means that allowed rejection of $H_0$ and finding the probability of getting any of these sample means, assuming the hypothesized real effect of the independent variable is true. Power varies directly with N, alpha, and the size of the real effect of the independent variable. Power varies inversely with beta.

## IMPORTANT TERMS

Critical region  (p. 281)
Critical value(s) of a statistic
    (p. 281)
Critical value(s) of $\bar{X}$  (p. 288)
Critical value(s) of z  (p. 282)

Mean of the sampling distribution
    of the mean  (p. 274)
Null-hypothesis population  (p. 269)
Power  (p. 286)
Sampling distribution of a statistic
    (p. 268)

Sampling distribution of the mean
    (p. 272)
Standard error of the mean  (p. 274)
$\mu_{\mathrm{null}}$  (p. 288)
$\mu_{\mathrm{real}}$  (p. 289)

## QUESTIONS AND PROBLEMS

1. Define each of the terms in the Important Terms section.
2. Why is the sampling distribution of a statistic important to be able to use the statistic in hypothesis testing? Explain in a short paragraph.
3. How are sampling distributions generated using the empirical sampling approach?
4. What are the two basic steps used when analyzing data?
5. What are the assumptions underlying the use of the z test?
6. What are the characteristics of the sampling distribution of the mean?

7. Explain why the standard deviation of the sampling distribution of the mean is sometimes referred to as the "standard error of the mean."
8. How do each of the following differ?
    a. $s$ and $s_{\bar{X}}$      b. $s^2$ and $\sigma^2$
    c. $\mu$ and $\mu_{\bar{X}}$      d. $\sigma$ and $\sigma_{\bar{X}}$
9. Explain why $\sigma_{\bar{X}}$ should vary directly with $\sigma$ and inversely with $N$.
10. Why should $\mu_{\bar{X}} = \mu$?
11. Is the shape of the sampling distribution of the mean always the same as the shape of the null-hypothesis population? Explain.

12. When using the $z$ test, why is it important that the sampling distribution of the mean be normally distributed?

13. If the assumptions underlying the $z$ test are met, what are the characteristics of the sampling distribution of $z$?

14. Define power, both conceptually and mathematically.

15. Explain what happens to the power of the $z$ test when each of the following variables increases.
    a. $N$
    b. Alpha level
    c. Size of real effect of the independent variable
    d. $\sigma$

16. How does increasing the $N$ of an experiment affect the following?
    a. Power
    b. Beta
    c. Alpha
    d. Size of real effect

17. Given the population set of scores 3, 4, 5, 6, 7,
    a. Determine the sampling distribution of the mean for sample sizes of 2. Assume sampling is one at a time, with replacement.
    b. Demonstrate that $\mu_{\bar{X}} = \mu$.
    c. Demonstrate that $\sigma_{\bar{X}} = \sigma/\sqrt{N}$.

18. If a population of raw scores is normally distributed and has a mean $\mu = 80$ and a standard deviation $\sigma = 8$, determine the parameters ($\mu_{\bar{X}}$ and $\sigma_{\bar{X}}$) of the sampling distribution of the mean for the following sample sizes.
    a. $N = 16$
    b. $N = 35$
    c. $N = 50$
    d. Explain what happens as $N$ gets larger. other

19. Is it reasonable to consider a sample of 40 scores with $\bar{X}_{obt} = 65$ to be a random sample from a population of scores that is normally distributed, with $\mu = 60$ and $\sigma = 10$? Use $\alpha = 0.05_{2\ tail}$ in making your decision. other

20. A set of sample scores from an experiment has an $N = 30$ and an $\bar{X}_{obt} = 19$.
    a. Can we reject the null hypothesis that the sample is a random sample from a normal population with $\mu = 22$ and $\sigma = 8$? Use $\alpha = 0.01_{1\ tail}$. Assume the sample mean is in the correct direction.
    b. What is the power of the experiment to detect a real effect such that $\mu_{real} = 20$?
    c. What is the power to detect a $\mu_{real} = 20$ if $N$ is increased to 100?

d. What value does $N$ have to equal to achieve a power of 0.8000 to detect a $\mu_{real} = 20$? Use the nearest table value for $z_{obt}$. other

21. On the basis of her newly developed technique, a student believes she can reduce the amount of time schizophrenics spend in an institution. As director of training at a nearby institution, you agree to let her try her method on 20 schizophrenics, randomly sampled from your institution. The mean duration that schizophrenics stay at your institution is 85 weeks, with a standard deviation of 15 weeks. The scores are normally distributed. The results of the experiment show that the patients treated by the student stay a mean duration of 78 weeks, with a standard deviation of 20 weeks.
    a. What is the alternative hypothesis? In this case, assume a nondirectional hypothesis is appropriate because there are insufficient theoretical and empirical bases to warrant a directional hypothesis.
    b. What is the null hypothesis?
    c. What do you conclude about the student's technique? Use $\alpha = 0.05_{2\ tail}$. clinical, health

22. A professor has been teaching statistics for many years. His records show that the overall mean for final exam scores is 82, with a standard deviation of 10. The professor believes that this year's class is superior to his previous ones. The mean for final exam scores for this year's class of 65 students is 87. What do you conclude? Use $\alpha = 0.05_{1\ tail}$. education

23. An automotive engineer believes that her newly designed engine will be a great gas saver. A large number of tests on engines of the old design yielded a mean gasoline consumption of 27.5 miles per gallon, with a standard deviation of 5.2. Fifteen new engines are tested. The mean gasoline consumption is 29.6 miles per gallon. What is your conclusion? Use $\alpha = 0.05_{1\ tail}$. other

24. In Problem 12.2, we presented data testing a new gasoline additive. A large number of mileage measurements on the gasoline without the additive showed a mean of 24.7 miles per gallon and a standard deviation of 4.8. An experiment was performed in which 75 cars were tested using the gasoline plus the additive. The results showed a sample mean of 26.5 miles per gallon. To evaluate these data, a directional test with $\alpha = 0.05_{1\ tail}$ was used. Suppose that before doing the experiment, the manufacturer wants

to determine the probability that he will be able to detect a real mean increase of 2.0 miles per gallon with the additive if the additive is at least that effective.

a. If he tests 20 cars, what is the power to detect a mean increase of 2.0 miles per gallon?

b. If he increases the *N* to 75 cars, what is the power to detect a mean increase of 2.0 miles per gallon?

c. How many cars should he use if he wants to have a 99% chance of detecting a mean increase of 2.0 miles per gallon? I/O

25. A physical education professor believes that exercise can slow the aging process. For the past 10 years, he has been conducting an exercise class for 14 individuals who are currently 50 years old. Normally, as one ages, maximum oxygen consumption decreases. The national norm for maximum oxygen consumption in 50-year-old individuals is 30 milliliters per kilogram per minute, with a standard deviation of 8.6. The mean of the 14 individuals is 40 milliliters per kilogram per minute. What do you conclude? Use $\alpha = 0.05_{1\,tail}$. biological, health

# Student's *t* Test for Single Samples

## INTRODUCTION

In Chapter 12, we discussed the *z* test and determined that it was appropriate in situations in which both the mean and the standard deviation of the null-hypothesis population were known. However, these situations are relatively rare. It is more common to encounter situations in which the mean of the null-hypothesis population can be specified and the standard deviation is *unknown*. In these

**table 13.1** Comparison of equations for the *z* and *t* tests

| *z* Test | *t* Test |
|---|---|
| $z_{obt} = \dfrac{\overline{X}_{obt} - \mu}{\sigma/\sqrt{N}}.$ | $t_{obt} = \dfrac{\overline{X}_{obt} - \mu}{s/\sqrt{N}}.$ |
| $= \dfrac{\overline{X}_{obt} - \mu}{\sigma_{\overline{X}}}$ | $= \dfrac{\overline{X}_{obt} - \mu}{s_{\overline{X}}}$ |

*where* $s$ = estimate of $\sigma$

$s_{\overline{X}}$ = estimate of $\sigma_{\overline{X}}$

cases, the *z* test cannot be used. Instead, another test, called *Student's t test,* is employed. The *t* test is very similar to the *z* test. It was developed by W. S. Gosset, writing under the pen name of "Student." Student's *t* test is a practical, quite powerful test widely used in the behavioral sciences. In this chapter, we shall discuss the *t* test in conjunction with experiments involving a single sample. In Chapter 14, we shall discuss the *t* test as it applies to experiments using two samples or conditions.

## COMPARISON OF THE *z* AND *t* TESTS

The *z* and *t* tests for single sample experiments are quite alike. The equations for each are shown in Table 13.1.

In comparing these equations, we can see that the only difference is that the *z* test uses the standard deviation of the null-hypothesis population ($\sigma$), whereas the *t* test uses the standard deviation of the sample (*s*). When $\sigma$ is unknown, we estimate it using the estimate given by *s,* and the resulting statistic is called *t.* Thus, the denominator of the *t* test is $s/\sqrt{N}$ rather than $\sigma/\sqrt{N}$. The symbol $s_{\overline{X}}$ replaces $\sigma_{\overline{X}}$ where

$$s_{\overline{X}} = \frac{s}{\sqrt{N}} \qquad \textit{estimated standard error of the mean}$$

We are ready now to consider an experiment using the *t* test to analyze the data.

an experiment

### Technique for Increasing Early Speaking in Children

Suppose you have a technique that you believe will affect the age at which children begin speaking. In your locale, the average age of first word utterances is 13.0 months. The standard deviation is unknown. You apply your technique to a random sample of 15 children. The results show that the sample mean age of first word utterances is 11.0 months, with a standard deviation of 3.34.

1. What is the nondirectional alternative hypothesis?
2. What is the null hypothesis?
3. Did the technique work? Use $\alpha = 0.05_{2\ tail}$.

**SOLUTION**

1. Alternative hypothesis: The technique affects the age at which children begin speaking. Therefore, the sample with $\overline{X}_{\text{obt}} = 11.0$ is a random sample from a population where $\mu \neq 13.0$.

2. Null hypothesis: $H_0$: The sample with $\overline{X}_{\text{obt}} = 11.0$ is a random sample from a population with $\mu = 13.0$.

3. Conclusion using $\alpha = 0.05_{2\text{ tail}}$:

**STEP 1: Calculate the appropriate statistic.**   Since $\sigma$ is unknown, it is impossible to determine $z_{\text{obt}}$. However, $s$ is known, so we can calculate $t_{\text{obt}}$. Thus,

$$t_{\text{obt}} = \frac{\overline{X}_{\text{obt}} - \mu}{s/\sqrt{N}}$$

$$= \frac{11.0 - 13.0}{3.34/\sqrt{15}}$$

$$= \frac{-2}{0.862}$$

$$= -2.32$$

The next step ordinarily would be to evaluate $t_{\text{obt}}$ using the sampling distribution of *t*. However, because this distribution is not yet familiar, we need to discuss it before we can proceed with the evaluation.

# THE SAMPLING DISTRIBUTION OF *t*

Using the definition of sampling distribution developed in Chapter 12, we note the following.

**definition**  ■  *The **sampling distribution of t** is a probability distribution of the t values that would occur if all possible different samples of a fixed size N were drawn from the null-hypothesis population. It gives (1) all the possible different t values for samples of size N and (2) the probability of getting each value if sampling is random from the null-hypothesis population.*

As with the sampling distribution of the mean, the sampling distribution of *t* can be determined theoretically or empirically. Again, for pedagogical reasons, we prefer the empirical approach. The sampling distribution of *t* can be derived empirically by taking a specific population of raw scores, drawing all possible different samples of a fixed size *N*, and then calculating the *t* value for each sample. Once all the possible *t* values are obtained, it is a simple matter to calculate the probability of getting each different *t* value under the assumption of random sampling from the population. By varying *N* and the population scores, one can derive sampling distributions for various populations and sample sizes. Empirically or theoretically, it turns out that, if the null-hypothesis population is normally shaped, or if $N \geq 30$, the *t* distribution looks very much like the *z* distribution except that there is a *family* of *t* curves that vary with sample size. You will recall that the *z* distribution has only one curve for all sample sizes (the values represented in Table A in Appendix D). On the other hand, the *t* distribution, like the sampling distribution of the mean, has many curves depending on sample size. Since we are estimating σ by using *s* in the *t* equation and the size of the sample influences the accuracy of the estimate, it makes sense that there should be a different sampling distribution of *t* for different sample sizes.

## Degrees of Freedom

Although the *t* distribution varies with sample size, Gosset found that it varies *uniquely* with the *degrees of freedom* associated with *t,* rather than simply with sample size. Why this is so will not be apparent until Chapter 14. For now, let's just pursue the concept of degrees of freedom.

definition ■ *The* **degrees of freedom (df)** *for any statistic is the number of scores that are free to vary in calculating that statistic.*

For example, there are *N* degrees of freedom associated with the mean. How do we know this? For any set of scores, *N* is given. If there are three scores and we know the first two scores, the last score can take on any value. It has no restrictions. There is no way to tell what it must be by knowing the other two scores. The same is true for the first two scores. Thus, all three scores are free to vary when calculating the mean. Thus, there are *N* degrees of freedom.

Contrast this with calculating the standard deviation:

$$s = \sqrt{\frac{\Sigma (X - \overline{X})^2}{N - 1}}$$

Since the sum of deviations about the mean must equal zero, only $N - 1$ of the deviation scores are free to take on any value. Thus, there are $N - 1$ degrees of freedom associated with *s*. Why is this so? Consider the raw scores 4, 8, and 12. The mean is 8. Table 13.2 shows what happens when calculating *s*.

Since the mean is 8, the deviation score for the raw score of 4 is −4 and for the raw score of 8 is 0. Since $\Sigma (X - \overline{X}) = 0$, the last deviation is fixed by the other deviations. It must be +4 (see the "?" in Table 13.2). It cannot take on any value; instead it is fixed at +4 by the other two deviation scores. Therefore, only two of the three deviation scores are free to vary. Whatever value these take, the third is fixed. In calculating *s,* only $N - 1$ deviation scores are free to vary. Thus, there are $N - 1$ degrees of freedom associated with the standard deviation.

table 13.2 Number of deviation scores free to vary

| *X* | $\overline{X}$ | $X - \overline{X}$ |
| --- | --- | --- |
| 4 | 8 | −4 |
| 8 | 8 | 0 |
| 12 | 8 | ? |

In calculating *t* for single samples, we must first calculate *s*. We lose 1 degree of freedom in calculating *s,* so there are $N - 1$ degrees of freedom associated with *t*. Thus, for the *t* test,

$$df = N - 1 \qquad \textit{degrees of freedom for t test (single sample)}$$

## *t* AND *z* DISTRIBUTIONS COMPARED

Figure 13.1 shows the *t* distribution for various degrees of freedom. The *t* distribution is symmetrical about zero and becomes closer to the normally distributed *z* distribution with increasing df. Notice how quickly it approaches the normal curve. Even with df as small as 20, the *t* distribution rather closely approximates the normal curve. Theoretically, when df = ∞,[*] the *t* distribution is identical to the *z* distribution. This makes sense because as the df increases, sample size increases and the estimate *s* gets closer to σ. At any df other than ∞, the *t* distribution has more extreme *t* values than the *z* distribution, since there is more variability in *t* because we used *s* to estimate σ. Another way of saying this is that the tails of the *t* distribution are elevated relative to the *z* distribution. Thus, for a given alpha level, the critical value of *t* is higher than for *z,* making the *t* test less

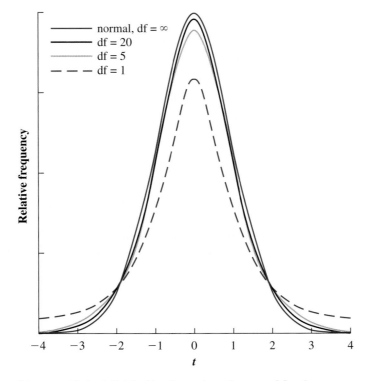

f i g u r e **13.1**  *t* distribution for various degrees of freedom.

---

[*]As df approaches infinity, the *t* distribution approaches the normal curve.

**t a b l e  13.3**  Critical values of *z* and *t* at the 0.05 and 0.01 alpha levels, one-tailed

| *df* | $z_{0.05}$ | $t_{0.05}$ | $z_{0.01}$ | $t_{0.01}$ |
|------|------------|------------|------------|------------|
| 5    | 1.645      | 2.015      | 2.326      | 3.365      |
| 30   | 1.645      | 1.697      | 2.326      | 2.457      |
| 60   | 1.645      | 1.671      | 2.326      | 2.390      |
| ∞    | 1.645      | 1.645      | 2.326      | 2.326      |

sensitive than the *z* test. That is, for any alpha level, $t_{obt}$ must be higher than $z_{obt}$ to reject the null hypothesis. Table 13.3 shows the critical values of *z* and *t* at the 0.05 and 0.01 alpha levels. As the df increases, the critical value of *t* approaches that of *z*. The critical *z* value, of course, doesn't change with sample size. Critical values of *t* for various alpha levels and df are contained in Table D of Appendix D. These values have been obtained from the sampling distribution of *t* for each df. The table may be used for evaluating $t_{obt}$ for any experiment. We are now ready to return to the illustrative example.

## FIRST WORD UTTERANCES EXPERIMENT REVISITED

You are investigating a technique purported to affect the age at which children begin speaking: $\mu = 13.0$ months; $\sigma$ is unknown; the sample of 15 children using your technique has a mean for first word utterances of 11.0 months and a standard deviation of 3.34.

1. What is the nondirectional alternative hypothesis?
2. What is the null hypothesis?
3. Did the technique work? Use $\alpha = 0.05_{2\,tail}$.

**SOLUTION**

1. Alternative hypothesis: The technique affects the age at which children begin speaking. Therefore, the sample with $\overline{X}_{obt} = 11.0$ is a random sample from a population where $\mu \neq 13.0$.
2. Null hypothesis: $H_0$: The sample with $\overline{X}_{obt} = 11.0$ is a random sample from a population with $\mu = 13.0$.
3. Conclusion using $\alpha = 0.05_{2\,tail}$:

   **STEP 1: Calculate the appropriate statistic.**  Since this is a single sample experiment with unknown $\sigma$, $t_{obt}$ is appropriate:

$$t_{obt} = \frac{\overline{X}_{obt} - \mu}{s/\sqrt{N}}$$

$$= \frac{11.0 - 13.0}{3.34/\sqrt{15}}$$

$$= -2.32$$

**STEP 1: Calculate the appropriate statistic.** Since $\sigma$ is unknown, $t_{obt}$ is appropriate.

$$t_{obt} = \frac{\overline{X}_{obt} - \mu}{s/\sqrt{N}} = \frac{11.0 - 13.00}{3.34/\sqrt{15}} = -2.32$$

**STEP 2: Evaluate the statistic.** If $|t_{obt}| \geq |t_{crit}|$, reject $H_0$. Since $\alpha = 0.05_{2\ tail}$ and df $= N - 1 = 15 - 1 = 14$, from Table D,

$$t_{crit} = \pm 2.145$$

Since $|t_{obt}| > 2.145$, it falls within the critical region. Therefore, we reject $H_0$.

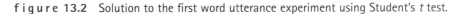

f i g u r e **13.2** Solution to the first word utterance experiment using Student's $t$ test.

**STEP 2: Evaluate the statistic based on its sampling distribution.** Just as with the $z$ test, if

$$|t_{obt}| \geq |t_{crit}|$$

then it falls within the critical region for rejection of the null hypothesis. $t_{crit}$ is found in Table D under the appropriate alpha level and df. For this example, with $\alpha = 0.05_{2\ tail}$ and df $= N - 1 = 15 - 1 = 14$, from Table D,

$$t_{crit} = \pm 2.145$$

Since $|t_{obt}| > 2.145$, we reject $H_0$ and conclude that the technique does affect the age at which children in your locale first begin speaking. The solution is shown in Figure 13.2.

## CALCULATING $t_{obt}$ FROM ORIGINAL SCORES

If in a given situation the original scores are available, $t$ can be calculated directly without first having to calculate $s$. The appropriate equation is given here:[*]

---

[*]The derivation is presented in Note 13.1.

$$t_{obt} = \frac{\overline{X}_{obt} - \mu}{\sqrt{\dfrac{SS}{N(N-1)}}} \qquad \textit{equation for computing } t_{obt} \textit{ from raw scores}$$

$$\textit{where} \qquad SS = \Sigma(X - \overline{X})^2 = \Sigma X^2 - \frac{(\Sigma X)^2}{N}$$

**example**

Suppose the original data in the previous problem were as shown in Table 13.4. Let's calculate $t_{obt}$ directly from these raw scores.

**SOLUTION**

$$t_{obt} = \frac{\overline{X}_{obt} - \mu}{\sqrt{\dfrac{SS}{N(N-1)}}} \qquad SS = \Sigma X^2 - \frac{(\Sigma X)^2}{N}$$

$$= \frac{11.0 - 13.0}{\sqrt{\dfrac{156}{15(14)}}} \qquad = 1971 - \frac{(165)^2}{15}$$

$$= \frac{-2}{0.862} = -2.32 \qquad = 156$$

**table 13.4**  Raw scores for first word utterances example

| Age (months) X | Computation of $X^2$ |
|:---:|:---:|
| 8 | 64 |
| 9 | 81 |
| 10 | 100 |
| 15 | 225 |
| 18 | 324 |
| 17 | 289 |
| 12 | 144 |
| 11 | 121 |
| 7 | 49 |
| 8 | 64 |
| 10 | 100 |
| 11 | 121 |
| 8 | 64 |
| 9 | 81 |
| 12 | 144 |
| 165 | 1971 |
| $N = 15$ | $\overline{X}_{obt} = \frac{165}{15} = 11.0$ |

This is the same value arrived at previously. Note that it is all right to first calculate $s$ and then use the original $t_{obt}$ equation. However, the answer is more subject to rounding error.

Let's try another problem.

## Practice Problem 13.1

A researcher believes that in recent years women have been getting taller. She knows that 10 years ago the average height of young adult women living in her city was 63 inches. The standard deviation is unknown. She randomly samples eight young adult women currently residing in her city and measures their heights. The following data are obtained:

| Height (in.) $X$ | Calculation of $X^2$ |
|---|---|
| 64 | 4,096 |
| 66 | 4,356 |
| 68 | 4,624 |
| 60 | 3,600 |
| 62 | 3,844 |
| 65 | 4,225 |
| 66 | 4,356 |
| 63 | 3,969 |
| 514 | 33,070 |
| $N = 8$ | $\overline{X}_{obt} = \frac{514}{8} = 64.25$ |

a. What is the alternative hypothesis? In evaluating this experiment, assume a nondirectional hypothesis is appropriate because there are insufficient theoretical and empirical bases to warrant a directional hypothesis.
b. What is the null hypothesis?
c. What is your conclusion? Use $\alpha = 0.01_{2\,tail}$.

**SOLUTION**

a. Nondirectional alternative hypothesis: In recent years, the height of women has been changing. Therefore, the sample with $\overline{X}_{obt} = 64.25$ is a random sample from a population where $\mu \neq 63$.
b. Null hypothesis: The null hypothesis asserts that it is reasonable to consider the sample with $\overline{X}_{obt} = 64.25$ a random sample from a population with $\mu = 63$.
c. Conclusion, using $\alpha = 0.01_{2\,tail}$:

*(continued)*

**STEP 1: Calculate the appropriate statistic.**   The data were given previously. Since $\sigma$ is unknown, $t_{obt}$ is appropriate. There are two ways to find $t_{obt}$: (1) by calculating $s$ first and then $t_{obt}$ and (2) by calculating $t_{obt}$ directly from the raw scores. Both methods are shown here:

*s first and then $t_{obt}$:*

$$s = \sqrt{\frac{SS}{N-1}} = \sqrt{\frac{45.5}{7}} \qquad SS = \Sigma X^2 - \frac{(\Sigma X)^2}{N} = 33{,}070 - \frac{(514)^2}{8}$$

$$= \sqrt{6.5} = 2.550 \qquad\qquad = 33{,}070 - 33{,}024.5 = 45.5$$

$$t_{obt} = \frac{\overline{X}_{obt} - \mu}{s/\sqrt{N}} = \frac{64.25 - 63}{2.550/\sqrt{8}}$$

$$= \frac{1.25}{0.902} = 1.39$$

*directly from the raw scores:*

$$t_{obt} = \frac{\overline{X}_{obt} - \mu}{\sqrt{\dfrac{SS}{N(N-1)}}} = \frac{64.25 - 63}{\sqrt{\dfrac{45.5}{8(7)}}} \qquad SS = \Sigma X^2 - \frac{(\Sigma X)^2}{N}$$

$$= \frac{1.25}{\sqrt{0.812}} = 1.39 \qquad\qquad = 33{,}070 - \frac{(514)^2}{8}$$

$$= 33{,}070 - 33{,}024.5 = 45.5$$

**STEP 2: Evaluate the statistic.**   If $|t_{obt}| \geq |t_{crit}|$, reject $H_0$. If not, retain $H_0$. With $\alpha = 0.01_{2\,tail}$ and df $= N - 1 = 8 - 1 = 7$, from Table D,

$$t_{crit} = \pm 3.499$$

Since $|t_{obt}| < 3.499$, it doesn't fall in the critical region. Therefore, we retain $H_0$. We cannot conclude that young adult women in the researcher's city have been changing in height in recent years.

## Practice Problem 13.2

A friend of yours has been "playing" the stock market. He claims he has spent years doing research in this area and has devised an empirically successful method for investing. Since you are not averse to becoming a little richer, you are considering giving him some money to invest for you. However, before you do, you decide to evaluate his method. He agrees to a "dry run" during which he will use his method, but instead of actually buying and selling, you will just monitor the stocks he recommends to see whether his method really works. During the trial time period, the recommended stocks showed the following price changes (a plus score means an increase in price, and a minus indicates a decrease):

| Stock | Price Change ($) X | Calculation of $X^2$ |
|-------|--------------------|----------------------|
| A | +4.52 | 20.430 |
| B | +5.15 | 26.522 |
| C | +3.28 | 10.758 |
| D | +4.75 | 22.562 |
| E | +6.03 | 36.361 |
| F | +4.09 | 16.728 |
| G | +3.82 | 14.592 |
|   | 31.64 | 147.953 |

$$N = 7 \qquad \overline{X}_{obt} = 4.52$$

During the same time period, the average price change of the stock market as a whole was +$3.25. Since you want to know whether the method does better or worse than chance, you decide to use a two-tailed evaluation.

**a.** What is the nondirectional alternative hypothesis?
**b.** What is the null hypothesis?
**c.** What is your conclusion? Use $\alpha = 0.05_{2\,tail}$.

**SOLUTION**

**a.** Nondirectional alternative hypothesis: Your friend's method results in a choice of stocks whose change in price differs from that expected due to random sampling from the stock market in general. Thus, the sample with $\overline{X}_{obt} = \$4.52$ cannot be considered a random sample from a population where $\mu = \$3.25$.

**b.** Null hypothesis: Your friend's method results in a choice of stocks whose change in price doesn't differ from that expected due to random sampling from the stock market in general. Therefore, the sample with $\overline{X}_{obt} = \$4.52$ can be considered a random sample from a population where $\mu = \$3.25$.

**c.** Conclusion, using $\alpha = 0.05_{2\,tail}$:

**STEP 1: Calculate the appropriate statistic.** The data are given in the previous table. Since $\sigma$ is unknown, $t_{obt}$ is appropriate.

$$t_{obt} = \frac{\overline{X}_{obt} - \mu}{\sqrt{\dfrac{SS}{N(N-1)}}} \qquad SS = \Sigma X^2 - \frac{(\Sigma X)^2}{N}$$

$$= \frac{4.52 - 3.25}{\sqrt{\dfrac{4.940}{7(6)}}} \qquad = 147.953 - \frac{(31.64)^2}{7}$$

$$= \frac{1.27}{0.343} = 3.70 \qquad = 4.940$$

*(continued)*

> **STEP 2: Evaluate the statistic.** With $\alpha = 0.05_{2\,\text{tail}}$ and df $= N - 1 = 7 - 1 = 6$, from Table D,
>
> $$t_{\text{crit}} = \pm 2.447$$
>
> Since $|t_{\text{obt}}| > 2.447$, we reject $H_0$. Your friend appears to be a winner. His method does seem to work! However, before investing heavily, we suggest you run the experiment at least one more time to guard against Type I error. Remember that replication is essential before accepting a result as factual. Better to be safe than poor.

## CONDITIONS UNDER WHICH THE *t* TEST IS APPROPRIATE

The *t* test (single sample) is appropriate when the experiment has only one sample, $\mu$ is specified, $\sigma$ is unknown, and the mean of the sample is used as the basic statistic. Like the *z* test, the *t* test requires that the sampling distribution of $\overline{X}$ be normal. For the sampling distribution of $\overline{X}$ to be normal, *N* must be $\geq 30$ or the population of raw scores must be normal.*

## *t* DISTRIBUTION: CONFIDENCE INTERVALS FOR THE POPULATION MEAN

Sometimes it is desirable to know the value of a population mean. Since it is very uneconomical to measure everyone in the population, a random sample is taken and the sample mean is used as an estimate of the population mean. To illustrate, suppose a university administrator is interested in the average IQ of professors at her university. A random sample is taken, and $\overline{X} = 135$. The estimate, then, would be 135. The value 135 is called a *point estimate* because it uses only one value for the estimate. However, if we asked the administrator whether she thought the population mean was exactly 135, her answer would almost certainly be "no." Well, then, how close is 135 to the population mean?

The usual way to answer this question is to give a range of values for which one is reasonably confident that the range includes the population mean. This is called *interval* estimation. For example, the administrator might have some confidence that the population mean lies within the range 130–140. Certainly, she would have more confidence in the range of 130–140 than in the single value of 135. How about the range 110–160? Clearly, there would be more confidence in this range than in the range 130–140. Thus, the wider the range, the greater the confidence that it contains the population mean.

---

*Many authors would limit the use of the *t* test to data that are of interval or ratio scaling. Please see the footnote in Chapter 2, p. 31, for references discussing this point.

definitions

■ *A **confidence interval** is a range of values that probably contains the population value.*

■ ***Confidence limits** are the values that bound the confidence interval.*

It is possible to be more quantitative about the degree of confidence we have that the interval contains the population mean. In fact, we can construct confidence intervals about which there are specified degrees of confidence. For example, we could construct the 95% confidence interval:

*The 95% confidence interval is an interval such that the probability is 0.95 that the interval contains the population value.*

Although there are many different intervals we could construct, in practice the 95% and 99% confidence intervals are most often used. Let's consider how to construct these intervals.

## Construction of the 95% Confidence Interval

Suppose we have randomly sampled a set of $N$ scores from a population of raw scores having a mean $= \mu$ and have calculated $t_{obt}$. Assuming the assumptions of $t$ are met, we see that the probability is 0.95 that the following inequality is true:

$$-t_{0.025} \leq t_{obt} \leq +t_{0.025}$$

$t_{0.025}$ is the critical value of $t$ for $\alpha = 0.025_{1\ tail}$ and df $= N - 1$. All this inequality says is that if we randomly sample $N$ scores from a population of raw scores having a mean of $\mu$ and calculate $t_{obt}$, the probability is 0.95 that $t_{obt}$ will lie between $-t_{0.025}$ and $+t_{0.025}$. The truth of this statement can be understood best by referring to Figure 13.3. This figure shows the $t$ distribution for $N - 1$ degrees of freedom. We've located $+t_{0.025}$ and $-t_{0.025}$ on the distribution. Remember that these values are the critical values of $t$ for $\alpha = 0.025_{1\ tail}$. By definition, 2.5% of the $t$ values must lie under each tail, and 95% of the values must lie between $-t_{0.025}$ and $+t_{0.025}$. It follows, then, that the probability is 0.95 that $t_{obt}$ will lie between $-t_{0.025}$ and $+t_{0.025}$.

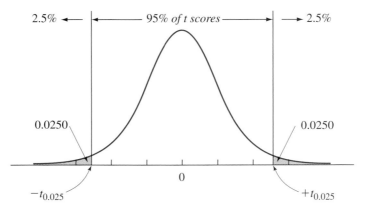

**figure 13.3**   Percentage of $t$ scores between $\pm t_{crit}$ for $\alpha = 0.05_{2\ tail}$ and df $= N - 1$.

We can use the previously given inequality to derive an equation for estimating the value of an unknown $\mu$. Thus,

$$-t_{0.025} \leq t_{\text{obt}} \leq t_{0.025}$$

but

$$t_{\text{obt}} = \frac{\overline{X}_{\text{obt}} - \mu}{s_{\overline{X}}}$$

Therefore,

$$-t_{0.025} \leq \frac{\overline{X}_{\text{obt}} - \mu}{s_{\overline{X}}} \leq t_{0.025}$$

Solving this inequality for $\mu$, we obtain[*]

$$\overline{X}_{\text{obt}} - s_{\overline{X}} t_{0.025} \leq \mu \leq \overline{X}_{\text{obt}} + s_{\overline{X}} t_{0.025}$$

This states that the chances are 95 in 100 that the interval $\overline{X}_{\text{obt}} \pm s_{\overline{X}} t_{0.025}$ contains the population mean. Thus, the interval $\overline{X}_{\text{obt}} \pm s_{\overline{X}} t_{0.025}$ is the 95% confidence interval. The lower and upper confidence limits are given by

$$\mu_{\text{lower}} = \overline{X}_{\text{obt}} - s_{\overline{X}} t_{0.025} \qquad \textit{lower limit for 95\% confidence interval}$$

$$\mu_{\text{upper}} = \overline{X}_{\text{obt}} + s_{\overline{X}} t_{0.025} \qquad \textit{upper limit for 95\% confidence interval}$$

We are now ready to do an example. Let's return to the university administrator.

example

## Estimating the Mean IQ of Professors at a University

Suppose a university administrator is interested in determining the average IQ of professors at her university. It is too costly to test all of the professors, so a random sample of 20 is drawn from the population. Each professor is given an IQ test, and the results show a sample mean of 135 and a sample standard deviation of 8. Construct the 95% confidence interval for the population mean.

### SOLUTION

The 95% confidence interval for the population mean can be found by solving the equations for the upper and lower confidence limits. Thus,

$$\mu_{\text{lower}} = \overline{X}_{\text{obt}} - s_{\overline{X}} t_{0.025} \quad \text{and} \quad \mu_{\text{upper}} = \overline{X}_{\text{obt}} + s_{\overline{X}} t_{0.025}$$

Solving for $s_{\overline{X}}$,

$$s_{\overline{X}} = \frac{s}{\sqrt{N}} = \frac{8}{\sqrt{20}} = 1.789$$

From Table D, with $\alpha = 0.025_{1\,\text{tail}}$ and df $= N - 1 = 20 - 1 = 19$,

$$t_{0.025} = 2.093$$

---

[*]See Note 13.2 for the intermediate steps in this derivation.

Substituting the values for $s_{\overline{X}}$ and $t_{0.025}$ in the confidence limit equations, we obtain

$$\mu_{\text{lower}} = \overline{X}_{\text{obt}} - s_{\overline{X}}\, t_{0.025} \qquad \text{and} \qquad \mu_{\text{upper}} = \overline{X}_{\text{obt}} + s_{\overline{X}}\, t_{0.025}$$

$$= 135 - 1.789(2.093) \qquad\qquad\qquad = 135 + 1.789(2.093)$$

$$= 135 - 3.744 \qquad\qquad\qquad\qquad = 135 + 3.744$$

$$= 131.26 \quad \textit{lower limit} \qquad\qquad = 138.74 \quad \textit{upper limit}$$

Thus, the 95% confidence interval = 131.26–138.74.

What precisely does it mean to say that the 95% confidence interval equals a certain range? In the case of the previous sample, the range is 131.26–138.74. A second sample would yield a different $\overline{X}_{\text{obt}}$ and a different range, perhaps $\overline{X}_{\text{obt}} = 138$ and a range of 133.80–142.20. If we took all of the different possible samples of $N = 20$ from the population, we would have derived the sampling distribution of the 95% confidence interval for samples of size 20. *The important point here is that 95% of these intervals will contain the population mean; 5% of the intervals will not.* Thus, when we say "the 95% confidence interval is 131.26–138.74," we mean the probability is 0.95 that the interval contains the population mean. Note that the probability value applies to the interval and not to the population mean. The population mean is constant. What varies from sample to sample is the interval. Thus, it is not technically proper to state "the probability is 0.95 that the population mean lies within the interval." Rather, the proper statement is "the probability is 0.95 that the interval contains the population mean."

## General Equations for Any Confidence Interval

The equations we have presented thus far deal only with the 95% confidence interval. However, they are easily extended to form general equations for any confidence interval. Thus,

$$\mu_{\text{lower}} = \overline{X}_{\text{obt}} - s_{\overline{X}}\, t_{\text{crit}} \qquad \textit{general equation for lower confidence limit}$$

$$\mu_{\text{upper}} = \overline{X}_{\text{obt}} + s_{\overline{X}}\, t_{\text{crit}} \qquad \textit{general equation for upper confidence limit}$$

where $t_{\text{crit}} =$ the critical one-tailed value of $t$ corresponding to the desired confidence interval.

Thus, if we were interested in the 99% confidence interval, $t_{\text{crit}} = t_{0.005} =$ the critical value of $t$ for $\alpha = 0.005_{1\,\text{tail}}$. To illustrate, let's solve the previous problem for the 99% confidence interval.

### SOLUTION

From Table D, with df $= 19$ and $\alpha = 0.005_{1\,\text{tail}}$,

$$t_{0.005} = 2.861$$

From the previous solution, $s_{\overline{X}} = 1.789$. Substituting these values into the equations for confidence limits, we have

$$\mu_{\text{lower}} = \overline{X}_{\text{obt}} - s_{\overline{X}}\, t_{\text{crit}} \qquad \text{and} \qquad \mu_{\text{upper}} = \overline{X}_{\text{obt}} + s_{\overline{X}}\, t_{\text{crit}}$$

$$= \overline{X}_{\text{obt}} - s_{\overline{X}}\, t_{0.005} \qquad\qquad\qquad = \overline{X}_{\text{obt}} + s_{\overline{X}}\, t_{0.005}$$

$$= 135 - 1.789(2.861) \qquad = 135 + 1.789(2.861)$$
$$= 135 - 5.118 \qquad\qquad = 135 + 5.118$$
$$= 129.88 \quad \textit{lower limit} \qquad = 140.12 \quad \textit{upper limit}$$

Thus, the 99% confidence interval = 129.88–140.12.

Note that this interval is larger than the 95% confidence interval (131.26–138.74). As discussed previously, the larger the interval, the more confidence we have that it contains the population mean.

Let's try a practice problem.

## Practice Problem 13.3

An ethologist is interested in determining the average weight of adult Olympic marmots (found only on the Olympic Peninsula in Washington). It would be expensive and impractical to trap and measure the whole population, so a random sample of 15 adults is trapped and weighed. The sample has a mean of 7.2 kilograms and a standard deviation of 0.48. Construct the 95% confidence interval for the population mean.

### SOLUTION

The data are given in the problem. The 95% confidence interval for the population mean is found by determining the upper and lower confidence limits. Thus,

$$\mu_{\text{lower}} = \overline{X}_{\text{obt}} - s_{\overline{X}} t_{0.025} \quad \text{and} \quad \mu_{\text{upper}} = \overline{X}_{\text{obt}} + s_{\overline{X}} t_{0.025}$$

Solving for $s_{\overline{X}}$,

$$s_{\overline{X}} = \frac{s}{\sqrt{N}} = \frac{0.48}{\sqrt{15}} = 0.124$$

From Table D, with $\alpha = 0.025_{1\,\text{tail}}$ and df $= N - 1 = 15 - 1 = 14$,

$$t_{0.025} = 2.145$$

Substituting the values for $s_{\overline{X}}$ and $t_{0.025}$ in the confidence limit equations, we obtain

$$\mu_{\text{lower}} = \overline{X}_{\text{obt}} - s_{\overline{X}} t_{0.025} \qquad \text{and} \qquad \mu_{\text{upper}} = \overline{X}_{\text{obt}} + s_{\overline{X}} t_{0.025}$$
$$= 7.2 - 0.124(2.145) \qquad\qquad = 7.2 + 0.124(2.145)$$
$$= 7.2 - 0.266 \qquad\qquad\qquad = 7.2 + 0.266$$
$$= 6.93 \quad \textit{lower limit} \qquad\quad = 7.47 \quad \textit{upper limit}$$

Thus, the 95% confidence interval = 6.93–7.47 kilograms.

## Practice Problem 13.4

To estimate the average life of their 100-watt light bulbs, the manufacturer randomly samples 200 light bulbs and keeps them lit until they burn out. The sample has a mean life of 215 hours and a standard deviation of 8 hours. Construct the 99% confidence limits for the population mean. In solving this problem, use the closest table value for degrees of freedom.

### SOLUTION

The data are given in the problem.

$$\mu_{\text{lower}} = \overline{X}_{\text{obt}} - s_{\overline{X}} t_{0.005} \quad \text{and} \quad \mu_{\text{upper}} = \overline{X}_{\text{obt}} + s_{\overline{X}} t_{0.005}$$

$$s_{\overline{X}} = \frac{s}{\sqrt{N}} = \frac{8}{\sqrt{200}} = 0.567$$

From Table D, with $\alpha = 0.005_{1\,\text{tail}}$ and df $= N - 1 = 200 - 1 = 199$,

$$t_{0.005} = 2.617$$

Note that this is the closest table value available from Table D. Substituting the values for $s_{\overline{X}}$ and $t_{0.005}$ in the confidence limit equations, we obtain

$$\mu_{\text{lower}} = \overline{X}_{\text{obt}} - s_{\overline{X}} t_{0.005} \quad \text{and} \quad \mu_{\text{upper}} = \overline{X}_{\text{obt}} + s_{\overline{X}} t_{0.005}$$

$$= 215 - 0.567(2.617) \qquad\qquad = 215 + 0.567(2.617)$$

$$= 213.52 \quad \textit{lower limit} \qquad\qquad = 216.48 \quad \textit{upper limit}$$

Thus, the 99% confidence interval = 213.52–216.48 hours.

## TESTING THE SIGNIFICANCE OF PEARSON *r*

When a correlational study is conducted, it is rare for the whole population to be involved. Rather, the usual procedure is to randomly sample from the population and calculate the correlation coefficient on the sample data. To determine whether a correlation exists in the population, we must test the significance of the obtained $r$ ($r_{\text{obt}}$). Of course, this is the same procedure we have used all along for testing hypotheses. The population correlation coefficient is symbolized by the Greek letter $\rho$ (rho). A nondirectional alternative hypothesis asserts that $\rho \neq 0$. A directional alternative hypothesis asserts that $\rho$ is positive or negative depending on the predicted direction of the relationship. The null hypothesis is tested by assuming that the sample set of $X$ and $Y$ scores having a correlation equal to $r_{\text{obt}}$ is a random sample from a population where $\rho = 0$. The sampling distribution of $r$ can be generated empirically by taking all samples of size $N$ from a population in which $\rho = 0$ and calculating $r$ for each sample. By systematically varying the population scores and $N$, the sampling distribution of $r$ is generated.

The significance of *r* can be evaluated using the *t* test. Thus,

$$t_{obt} = \frac{r_{obt} - \rho}{s_r} \qquad \textit{t test for testing the significance of r}$$

*where* $r_{obt}$ = correlation obtained on a sample of *N* subjects
$\rho$ = population correlation coefficient
$s_r$ = estimate of the standard deviation of the sampling distribution of *r*

Note that this is very similar to the *t* equation used when dealing with the mean of a single sample. The only difference is that the statistic we are dealing with is *r* rather than $\overline{X}$.

$$t_{obt} = \frac{r_{obt} - \rho}{s_r} = \frac{r_{obt}}{\sqrt{\dfrac{1 - r_{obt}^2}{N - 2}}}$$

*where* $\rho = 0$
$s_r = \sqrt{(1 - r_{obt}^2)/(N - 2)}$
df = $N - 2$

Let's use this equation to test the significance of the correlation obtained in the "IQ and grade point average" problem presented in Chapter 6, p. 116. Assume that the 12 students were a random sample from a population of university undergraduates and that we want to determine whether there is a correlation in the population. We'll use $\alpha = 0.05_{2\,tail}$ in making our decision.

Ordinarily, the first step in a problem of this sort is to calculate $r_{obt}$. However, we have already done this and found that $r_{obt} = 0.856$. Substituting this value into the *t* equation, we obtain

$$t_{obt} = \frac{r_{obt}}{\sqrt{\dfrac{1 - r_{obt}^2}{N - 2}}} = \frac{0.856}{\sqrt{\dfrac{1 - (0.856)^2}{10}}} = \frac{0.856}{0.163} = 5.252 = 5.25$$

From Table D, with df = $N - 2 = 10$ and $\alpha = 0.05_{2\,tail}$,

$$t_{crit} = \pm 2.228$$

Since $|t_{obt}| > 2.228$, we reject $H_0$ and conclude that there is a significant positive correlation in the population.

Although the foregoing method works, there is an even easier way to solve this problem. By substituting $t_{crit}$ into the *t* equation, $r_{crit}$ can be determined for any df and any $\alpha$ level. Once $r_{crit}$ is known, all we need do is compare $r_{obt}$ with $r_{crit}$. The decision rule is

If $|r_{obt}| \geq |r_{crit}|$, reject $H_0$.

Statisticians have already calculated $r_{crit}$ for various df and $\alpha$ levels. These are shown in Table E in Appendix D. This table is used in the same way as the *t* table (Table D) except the entries list $r_{crit}$ rather than $t_{crit}$.

Applying the $r_{crit}$ method to the present problem, we would first calculate $r_{obt}$ and then determine $r_{crit}$ from Table E. Finally, we would compare $r_{obt}$ with $r_{crit}$ using the decision rule. In the present example, we have already determined that $r_{obt} = 0.856$. From Table E, with df = 10 and $\alpha = 0.05_{2\,tail}$,

$$r_{crit} = \pm 0.5760$$

Since $|r_{obt}| > 0.5760$, we reject $H_0$, as before. This solution is preferred because it is shorter and easier than the solution that involves comparing $t_{obt}$ with $t_{crit}$.

Let's try some problems for practice.

## Practice Problem 13.5

Folklore has it that there is an inverse correlation between mathematical and artistic ability. A psychologist decides to determine whether there is anything to this notion. She randomly samples 15 undergraduates and gives them tests measuring these two abilities. The resulting data are shown here. Is there a correlation in the population between mathematical ability and artistic ability? Use $\alpha = 0.01_{2\,tail}$.

| Subject No. | Math Ability, X | Artistic Ability, Y | $X^2$ | $Y^2$ | XY |
|---|---|---|---|---|---|
| 1 | 15 | 19 | 225 | 361 | 285 |
| 2 | 30 | 22 | 900 | 484 | 660 |
| 3 | 35 | 17 | 1,225 | 289 | 595 |
| 4 | 10 | 25 | 100 | 625 | 250 |
| 5 | 28 | 23 | 784 | 529 | 644 |
| 6 | 40 | 21 | 1,600 | 441 | 840 |
| 7 | 45 | 14 | 2,025 | 196 | 630 |
| 8 | 24 | 10 | 576 | 100 | 240 |
| 9 | 21 | 18 | 441 | 324 | 378 |
| 10 | 25 | 19 | 625 | 361 | 475 |
| 11 | 18 | 30 | 324 | 900 | 540 |
| 12 | 13 | 32 | 169 | 1,024 | 416 |
| 13 | 9 | 16 | 81 | 256 | 144 |
| 14 | 30 | 28 | 900 | 784 | 840 |
| 15 | 23 | 24 | 529 | 576 | 552 |
| Total | 366 | 318 | 10,504 | 7,250 | 7,489 |

### SOLUTION

**STEP 1: Calculate the appropriate statistic:**

$$r_{obt} = \frac{\sum XY - \dfrac{(\sum X)(\sum Y)}{N}}{\sqrt{\left[\sum X^2 - \dfrac{(\sum X)^2}{N}\right]\left[\sum Y^2 - \dfrac{(\sum Y)^2}{N}\right]}}$$

*(continued)*

$$= \frac{7489 - \dfrac{366(318)}{15}}{\sqrt{\left[10{,}504 - \dfrac{(366)^2}{15}\right]\left[7{,}250 - \dfrac{(318)^2}{15}\right]}}$$

$$= \frac{-270.2}{894.437}$$

$$= -0.302$$

$$= -0.30$$

**STEP 2: Evaluate the statistic.** From Table E, with df $= N - 2 = 15 - 2 = 13$ and $\alpha = 0.01_{2\,\text{tail}}$,

$$r_{\text{crit}} = \pm 0.6411$$

Since $|r_{\text{obt}}| < 0.6411$, we conclude by retaining $H_0$.

## Practice Problem 13.6

In Chapter 6, Practice Problem 6.2, we calculated the Pearson *r* for the relationship between similarity of attitudes and attraction in a sample of 15 college students. In that example, $r_{\text{obt}} = 0.94$. Using $\alpha = 0.05_{2\,\text{tail}}$, let's now determine whether this is a significant value for $r_{\text{obt}}$.

### SOLUTION

From Table E, with df $= N - 2 = 13$ and $\alpha = 0.05_{2\,\text{tail}}$,

$$r_{\text{crit}} = \pm 0.5139$$

Since $|r_{\text{obt}}| > 0.5139$, we reject $H_0$ and conclude there is a significant correlation in the population.

## SUMMARY

In this chapter, we have discussed the use of Student's *t* test for (1) testing hypotheses involving single sample experiments, (2) estimating the population mean by constructing confidence intervals, and (3) testing the significance of Pearson *r*.

In testing hypotheses involving single sample experiments, the *t* test is appropriate when the mean of the null-hypothesis population is known and the standard deviation is unknown. In this situation, we estimate $\sigma$ by using the sample standard deviation. The equation for calculating $t_{\text{obt}}$ is very similar to $z_{\text{obt}}$, but we use *s* instead of $\sigma$. The sampling distribution of *t* is a family of curves that varies with the degrees of freedom associated with calculating *t*. There are $N - 1$ degrees of freedom associated with the *t* test for single samples. The sampling distribution curves are symmetrical, bell-shaped curves having a mean equal to 0. However, these are elevated at the tails relative to the normal distribution. In using the *t* test, $t_{obt}$ is computed and then evaluated to determine whether it falls within the critical region. The *t* test is appropriate when the sampling distribution of $\overline{X}$ is normal. For the sampling distribution of $\overline{X}$ to be normal, the population of raw scores should be normally distributed, or $N \geq 30$.

Next we discussed constructing confidence intervals for the population mean. A confidence interval was defined as a range of values that probably contains the population value. Confidence limits are the values that bound the confidence interval. In discussing this topic, we showed how to construct confidence intervals about which we have a specified degree of confidence that the interval contains the population mean. Illustrative and practice problems were given for constructing the 95% and 99% confidence intervals.

The last topic involved testing the significance of Pearson *r*. We pointed out that, because most correlative data are collected on samples, we must evaluate the sample *r* value ($r_{obt}$) to see whether there is a correlation in the population. The evaluation involves the *t* test. However, by substituting $t_{crit}$ into the *t* equation, we can determine $r_{crit}$ for any df and any alpha level. The value of $r_{obt}$ is evaluated by comparing it with $r_{crit}$ for the given df and alpha level. Several problems were given for practice in evaluating $r_{obt}$.

## IMPORTANT TERMS

Confidence interval (p. 309)
Confidence limits (p. 309)
Critical value(s) of *r* (p. 314)

Critical value(s) of *t* (p. 302)
Degrees of freedom (p. 300)

Sampling distribution of *t* (p. 299)

## QUESTIONS AND PROBLEMS

1. Define each of the terms in the Important Terms section.
2. Assuming the assumptions underlying the *t* test are met, what are the characteristics of the sampling distribution of *t*?
3. Elaborate on what is meant by *degrees of freedom*. Use an example.
4. What are the assumptions underlying the proper use of the *t* test?
5. Discuss the similarities and differences between the *z* and *t* tests.
6. Explain in a short paragraph why the *z* test is more powerful than the *t* test.
7. Which of the following two statements is technically more correct? (1) We are 95% confident that the population mean lies in the interval 80–90, or (2) We are 95% confident that the interval 80–90 contains the population mean. Explain.
8. Explain why df = $N - 1$ when the *t* test is used with single samples.
9. If the sample correlation coefficient has a value different from zero (e.g., $r = 0.45$), this automatically means that the correlation in the population is also different from zero. Is this statement correct? Explain.
10. For the same set of sample scores, is the 99% confidence interval for the population mean

greater or smaller than the 95% confidence interval? Does this make sense? Explain.
11. A sample set of 30 scores has a mean equal to 82 and a standard deviation of 12. Can we reject the hypothesis that this sample is a random sample from a normal population with $\mu = 85$? Use $\alpha = 0.01_{2\,tail}$ in making your decision. other
12. A sample set of 29 scores has a mean of 76 and a standard deviation of 7. Can we accept the hypothesis that the sample is a random sample from a population with a mean greater than 72? Use $\alpha = 0.01_{1\,tail}$ in making your decision. other
13. Is it reasonable to consider a sample with $N = 22$, $\overline{X}_{obt} = 42$, and $s = 9$ to be a random sample from a normal population with $\mu = 38$? Use $\alpha = 0.05_{1\,tail}$ in making your decision. Assume $\overline{X}_{obt}$ is in the right direction. other
14. Using each of the following random samples, determine the 95% and 99% confidence intervals for the population mean:
    a. $\overline{X}_{obt} = 25$, $s = 6$, $N = 15$
    b. $\overline{X}_{obt} = 120$, $s = 8$, $N = 30$
    c. $\overline{X}_{obt} = 30.6$, $s = 5.5$, $N = 24$
    d. Redo part **a** with $N = 30$. What happens to the confidence interval as $N$ increases? other
15. In Problem 21 of Chapter 12, a student conducted an experiment on 25 schizophrenic pa-

tients to test the effect of a new technique on the amount of time schizophrenics need to stay institutionalized. The results showed that under the new treatment, the 25 schizophrenic patients stayed a mean duration of 78 weeks, with a standard deviation of 20 weeks. Previously collected data on a large number of schizophrenic patients showed a normal distribution of scores, with a mean of 85 weeks and a standard deviation of 15 weeks. These data were evaluated using $\alpha = 0.05_{2\ tail}$. The results showed a significant effect. For the present problem, assume that the standard deviation of the population is unknown. Again, using $\alpha = 0.05_{2\ tail}$, what do you conclude about the new technique? Explain the difference in conclusion between Problem 21 and this one. clinical, health

16. As the principal of a private high school, you are interested in finding out how the training in mathematics at your school compares with that of the public schools in your area. For the last 5 years, the public schools have given all graduating seniors a mathematics proficiency test. The distribution has a mean of 78. You give all the graduating seniors in your school the same mathematics proficiency test. The results show a distribution of 41 scores, with a mean of 83 and a standard deviation of 12.2.
    a. What is the alternative hypothesis? Use a non-directional hypothesis.
    b. What is the null hypothesis?
    c. Using $\alpha = 0.05_{2\ tail}$, what do you conclude? education

17. A college counselor wants to determine the average amount of time first-year students spend studying. He randomly samples 61 students from the freshman class and asks them how many hours a week they study. The mean of the resulting scores is 20 hours, and the standard deviation is 6.5 hours.
    a. Construct the 95% confidence interval for the population mean.
    b. Construct the 99% confidence interval for the population mean. education

18. A professor in the women's studies program believes that the amount of smoking by women has increased in recent years. A complete census taken 2 years ago of women living in a neighboring city showed that the mean number of cigarettes smoked daily by the women was 5.4 with a standard deviation of 2.5. To assess her belief, the professor determined the daily smoking rate of a random sample of 200 women currently living in that city. The data show that the number of cigarettes smoked daily by the 200 women has a mean of 6.1 and a standard deviation of 2.7.
    a. Is the professor's belief correct? Assume a directional $H_1$ is appropriate and use $\alpha = 0.05_{1\ tail}$ in making your decision. Be sure that the most sensitive test is used to analyze the data.
    b. Assume the population mean is unknown and reanalyze the data using the same alpha level. What is your conclusion this time? Explain any differences between part **a** and part **b**. social

19. A cognitive psychologist believes that a particular drug improves short-term memory. The drug is safe, with no side effects. An experiment is conducted in which 8 randomly selected subjects are given the drug and then given a short time to memorize a list of 10 words. The subjects are then tested for retention 15 minutes after the memorization period. The number of words correctly recalled by each subject is as follows: 8, 9, 10, 6, 8, 7, 9, 7. Over the past few years, the psychologist has collected a lot of data using this task with similar subjects. Although he has lost the original data, he remembers that the mean was 6 words correctly recalled and that the data were normally distributed. On the basis of these data, what can we conclude about the effect of the drug on short-term memory? Use $\alpha = 0.05_{2\ tail}$ in making your decision. cognitive

20. A physician employed by a large corporation believes that due to an increase in sedentary life in the past decade, middle-age men have become fatter. In 1995, the corporation measured the percentage of fat in their employees. For the middle-age men, the scores were normally distributed, with a mean of 22%. To test her hypothesis, the physician measures the fat percentage in a random sample of 12 middle-age men currently employed by the corporation. The fat percentages found were as follows: 24, 40, 29, 32, 33, 25, 15, 22, 18, 25, 16, 27. On the basis of these data, can we conclude that middle-age men employed by the corporation have become fatter? Assume a directional $H_1$ is legitimate and use $\alpha = 0.05_{1\ tail}$ in making your decision. health

21. A local business school claims that their graduating seniors get higher-paying jobs than the national average for business school graduates. Last year's figures for salaries paid to all business

school graduates on their first job showed a mean of $10.20 per hour. A random sample of 10 graduates from last year's class of the local business school showed the following hourly salaries for their first job: $9.40, $10.30, $11.20, $10.80, $10.40, $9.70, $9.80, $10.60, $10.70, $10.90. You are skeptical of the business school claim and decide to evaluate the salary of the business school graduates using $\alpha = 0.05_{2 \text{ tail}}$. education

22. You wanted to estimate the mean number of vehicles crossing a busy bridge in your neighborhood each morning during rush hour for the past year. To accomplish this, you stationed yourself and a few assistants at one end of the bridge on 18 randomly selected mornings during the year and counted the number of vehicles crossing the bridge in a 10-minute period during rush hour. You found the mean to be 125 vehicles per minute, with a standard deviation of 32.

   a. Construct the 95% confidence limits for the population mean (vehicles per minute).
   b. Construct the 99% confidence limits for the population mean (vehicles per minute). other

23. In Chapter 6, Problem 17, data were presented from a study conducted to investigate the relationship between cigarette smoking and illness. The number of cigarettes smoked daily and the number of days absent from work in the last year due to illness were determined for 12 individuals employed at the company where the researcher worked. The data are shown again here.

| Subject | Cigarettes Smoked | Days Absent |
|---------|-------------------|-------------|
| 1 | 0 | 1 |
| 2 | 0 | 3 |
| 3 | 0 | 8 |
| 4 | 10 | 10 |
| 5 | 13 | 4 |
| 6 | 20 | 14 |
| 7 | 27 | 5 |
| 8 | 35 | 6 |
| 9 | 35 | 12 |
| 10 | 44 | 16 |
| 11 | 53 | 10 |
| 12 | 60 | 16 |

a. Construct a scatter plot for these data.
b. Calculate the value of Pearson $r$.
c. Is the correlation between cigarettes smoked and days absent significant? Use $\alpha = 0.05_{2 \text{ tail}}$. health

24. In Chapter 6, Problem 18, an educator evaluated the reliability of a test for mechanical aptitude that she had constructed. Two administrations of the test, spaced 1 month apart, were given to 10 students. The data are again shown here.

| Student | Administration 1 | Administration 2 |
|---------|------------------|------------------|
| 1 | 10 | 10 |
| 2 | 12 | 15 |
| 3 | 20 | 17 |
| 4 | 25 | 25 |
| 5 | 27 | 32 |
| 6 | 35 | 37 |
| 7 | 43 | 40 |
| 8 | 40 | 38 |
| 9 | 32 | 30 |
| 10 | 47 | 49 |

a. Calculate the value of Pearson $r$ for the two administrations of the mechanical aptitude test.
b. Is the correlation significant? Use $\alpha = 0.05_{2 \text{ tail}}$. I/O

25. In Chapter 6, Problem 15, a sociology professor gave two exams to 8 students. The results are again shown here.

| Student | Exam 1 | Exam 2 |
|---------|--------|--------|
| 1 | 60 | 60 |
| 2 | 75 | 100 |
| 3 | 70 | 80 |
| 4 | 72 | 68 |
| 5 | 54 | 73 |
| 6 | 83 | 97 |
| 7 | 80 | 85 |
| 8 | 65 | 90 |

a. Calculate the value of Pearson $r$ for the two exams.
b. Using $\alpha = 0.05_{2 \text{ tail}}$, determine whether the correlation is significant. If not, does this mean that $\rho = 0$? Explain.

c. Assume you increased the number of students to 20, and now $r = 0.653$. Using the same alpha level as in part **b**, what do you conclude this time? Explain.  education

26. A developmental psychologist is interested in whether tense parents tend to have tense children. A study is done involving one parent for each of 15 families and the oldest child in each family, measuring tension in each pair. Pearson $r = 0.582$. Using $\alpha = 0.05_{2\,\text{tail}}$, is the relationship significant?  developmental, clinical

## NOTES

13.1

$$t_{\text{obt}} = \frac{\overline{X}_{\text{obt}} - \mu}{s/\sqrt{N}}.$$

*Given*

$$= \frac{\overline{X}_{\text{obt}} - \mu}{\sqrt{\dfrac{SS}{N-1}} \bigg/ \sqrt{N}}.$$

*Substituting* $\sqrt{\dfrac{SS}{N-1}}$ *for s*

$$(t_{\text{obt}})^2 = \frac{(\overline{X}_{\text{obt}} - \mu)^2}{\left(\dfrac{SS}{N-1}\right)\left(\dfrac{1}{N}\right)} = \frac{(\overline{X}_{\text{obt}} - \mu)^2}{\dfrac{SS}{N(N-1)}}$$

*Squaring both sides of the equation and rearranging terms*

$$t_{\text{obt}} = \frac{\overline{X}_{\text{obt}} - \mu}{\sqrt{\dfrac{SS}{N(N-1)}}}$$

*Taking the square root of both sides of the equation*

13.2

$$-t_{0.025} \leq \frac{\overline{X}_{\text{obt}} - \mu}{s_{\overline{X}}} \leq t_{0.025}$$

*Given*

$$-s_{\overline{X}}t_{0.025} \leq \overline{X}_{\text{obt}} - \mu \leq s_{\overline{X}}t_{0.025}$$

*Multiplying by* $s_{\overline{X}}$

$$-\overline{X}_{\text{obt}} - s_{\overline{X}}t_{0.025} \leq -\mu \leq -\overline{X}_{\text{obt}} + s_{\overline{X}}t_{0.025}$$

*Subtracting* $\overline{X}_{\text{obt}}$

$$\overline{X}_{\text{obt}} + s_{\overline{X}}t_{0.025} \geq \mu \geq \overline{X}_{\text{obt}} - s_{\overline{X}}t_{0.025}$$

*Multiplying by* $-1$

$$\overline{X}_{\text{obt}} - s_{\overline{X}}t_{0.025} \leq \mu \leq \overline{X}_{\text{obt}} + s_{\overline{X}}t_{0.025}$$

*Rearranging terms*

## BOOK COMPANION WEBSITE

Go to www.thomsonedu.com/psychology/pagano for:

- SPSS problems and solutions
- Flash cards for review of terms
- Chapter quiz
- Statistical workshops
- And more

## WebTUTOR™

Available via WebTutor for this chapter:

- Detailed chapter outline
- *Know and Be Able To Do* section
- Drag & Drop game for review of equations, concepts, and other material
- Flash cards for review of terms
- Audio flash cards for MP3 player
- Solving problems using Excel
- Solving problems using SPSS
- More practice problems using computational equations
- Chapter quiz

# Student's *t* Test for Correlated and Independent Groups

## INTRODUCTION

In Chapters 12 and 13, we have seen that hypothesis testing basically involves two steps: (1) calculating the appropriate statistic and (2) evaluating the statistic using its sampling distribution. We further discussed how to use the *z* and *t* tests to evaluate hypotheses that have been investigated with single sample experiments. In this chapter, we shall present the *t* test in conjunction with experiments involving two conditions or two samples.

We have already encountered the two-condition experiment when using the sign test. The two-condition experiment, whether of the correlated groups or independent groups design, has great advantages over the single sample experiment previously discussed. A major limitation of the single sample experiment is the requirement that at least one population parameter $(\mu)$ must be specified. In the great majority of cases, this information is not available. As will be shown later in this chapter, the two-treatment experiment completely eliminates the need to measure population parameters when testing hypotheses. This has obvious widespread practical utility.

A second major advantage of the two-condition experiment has to do with interpreting the results of the study. Correct scientific methodology does not often allow an investigator to use previously acquired population data when conducting an experiment. For example, in the illustrative problem involving first word utterances (p. 302), we used a population mean value of 13.0 months. How do we really know the mean is 13.0 months? Suppose the figures were collected 3 to 5 years before performing the experiment. How do we know that infants haven't changed over those years? And what about the conditions under which the population data were collected? Were they the same as in the experiment? Isn't it possible that the people collecting the population data were not as motivated as the experimenter and, hence, were not as careful in collecting the data? Just how were the data collected? By being on hand at the moment that the child spoke the first word? Quite unlikely. The data probably were collected by asking parents when their children first spoke. How accurate, then, is the population mean?

Even if the foregoing problems didn't exist, there are others having to do with the experimental method itself. For example, assuming 13.0 months is accurate and applies properly to the sample of 15 infants, how can we be sure it was the experimenter's technique that produced the early utterances? Couldn't they have been due to the extra attention or handling or stimulation given the children in conjunction with the method rather than the method itself?

Many of these problems can be overcome by the use of the two-condition experiment. By using two groups of infants (arrived at by matched pairs [correlated groups design] or random assignment [independent groups design]), giving each group the same treatment except for the experimenter's particular technique (same in attention, handling, etc.), running both groups concurrently, using the same people to collect the data from both groups, and so forth, most alternative explanations of results can be ruled out. In the discussion that follows, we shall first consider the *t* test for the correlated groups design and then for the independent groups design.

# STUDENT'S *t* TEST FOR CORRELATED GROUPS[*]

You will recall that, in the repeated measures or correlated groups design, each subject gets two or more treatments: A difference score is calculated for each subject, and the resulting difference scores are analyzed. The simplest experiment of this type uses two conditions, often called *control* and *experimental,* or *before* and *after.* In a variant of this design, instead of the same subject being used in both conditions, pairs of subjects that are matched on one or more characteristics serve in the two conditions. Thus, pairs might be matched on IQ, age, gender, and so forth. The difference scores between the matched pairs are then analyzed in the same manner as when the same subject serves in both conditions. This design is also referred to as a *correlated groups design* because the subjects in the groups are not independently assigned; that is, the pairs share specifically matched common characteristics. In the independent groups design, which is discussed later in this chapter, there is no pairing.

We first encountered the correlated groups design when using the sign test. However, the sign test had low power because it ignored the magnitude of the difference scores. We used the sign test because of its simplicity. In the analysis of actual experiments, another test, such as the *t* test, would probably be used. The *t* test for correlated groups allows utilization of *both* the magnitude and direction of the difference scores. Essentially, it treats the difference scores as though they were raw scores and tests the assumption that the difference scores are a random sample from a population of difference scores having a mean of zero. This can best be seen through an example.

**an experiment**

## Brain Stimulation and Eating

To illustrate, suppose a physiological psychologist believes that a brain region called the lateral hypothalamus is involved in eating behavior. One way to test this belief is to use a group of animals (e.g., rats) and electrically stimulate the lateral hypothalamus through a chronically indwelling electrode. If the lateral hypothalamus is involved in eating behavior, electrical stimulation of the lateral hypothalamus might alter the amount of food eaten. To control for the effect of brain stimulation per se, another electrode would be implanted in each animal in a neutral brain area. Each area would be stimulated for a fixed period of time, and the amount of food eaten would be recorded. A difference score for each animal would then be calculated.

Let's assume there is insufficient supporting evidence to warrant a directional alternative hypothesis. Therefore, a two-tailed evaluation is planned. The alternative hypothesis states that electrical stimulation of the lateral hypothalamus affects the amount of food eaten. The null hypothesis specifies that electrical stimulation of the lateral hypothalamus does not affect the amount of food eaten. If $H_0$ is true, the difference score for each rat would be due to chance factors. Sometimes it would be positive, and other times it would be negative; sometimes it would be large in magnitude and other times small. If the experiment were done on a large number of rats, say, the entire population, the mean of the difference scores would equal zero.[†] Figure 14.1 shows such a distribution. Note,

---

*See Note 14.1.
†See Note 14.2.

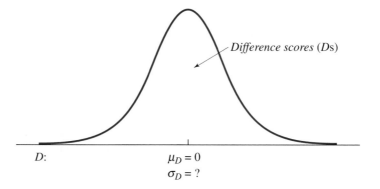

$D$:
$$\mu_D = 0$$
$$\sigma_D = ?$$

**figure 14.1**  Null-hypothesis population of difference scores.

carefully, that the mean of this population is known $(\mu_D = 0)$ and that the standard deviation is unknown $(\sigma_D = ?)$. The chance explanation assumes that the difference scores of the sample in the experiment are a random sample from this population of difference scores. Thus, we have a situation in which there is one set of scores (e.g., the sample difference scores), and we are interested in determining whether it is reasonable to consider these scores a random sample from a population of difference scores having a known mean $(\mu_D = 0)$ and unknown standard deviation.

## Comparison Between the *t* Test for Correlated Groups and the *t* Test for Single Samples

The situation just described is almost identical to those we have previously considered regarding the *t* test with single samples. The only change is that in the correlated groups experiment we are analyzing *difference* scores rather than *raw* scores. It follows, then, that the equations for each should be quite similar. These equations are presented in Table 14.1.

**table 14.1**  *t* Test for single samples and correlated groups

| *t* Test for Single Samples | *t* Test for Correlated Groups |
|---|---|
| $t_{obt} = \dfrac{\overline{X}_{obt} - \mu}{s/\sqrt{N}}$ | $t_{obt} = \dfrac{\overline{D}_{obt} - \mu_D}{s_D/\sqrt{N}}$ |
| $t_{obt} = \dfrac{\overline{X}_{obt} - \mu}{\sqrt{\dfrac{SS}{N(N-1)}}}$ | $t_{obt} = \dfrac{\overline{D}_{obt} - \mu_D}{\sqrt{\dfrac{SS_D}{N(N-1)}}}$ |
| $SS = \Sigma X^2 - \dfrac{(\Sigma X)^2}{N}$ | $SS_D = \Sigma D^2 - \dfrac{(\Sigma D)^2}{N}$ |

*where*

$$D = \text{difference score}$$
$$\overline{D}_{obt} = \text{mean of the sample difference scores}$$
$$\mu_D = \text{mean of the population of difference scores}$$
$$s_D = \text{standard deviation of the sample difference scores}$$
$$N = \text{number of difference scores}$$
$$SS_D = \Sigma(D - \overline{D})^2 = \text{sum of squares of sample difference scores}$$

It is obvious that the two sets of equations are identical except that, in the single sample case, we are dealing with raw scores, whereas in the correlated groups experiment, we are analyzing difference scores. Let's now add some numbers to the brain stimulation experiment and see how to use the *t* test for correlated groups.

## Brain Stimulation Experiment Revisited and Analyzed

A psychologist believes that the lateral hypothalamus is involved in eating behavior. If so, then electrical stimulation of that area might affect the amount eaten. To test this possibility, chronic indwelling electrodes are implanted in 10 rats. Each rat has two electrodes: one implanted in the lateral hypothalamus and the other in an area where electrical stimulation is known to have no effect. After the animals have recovered from surgery, they each receive 30 minutes of electrical stimulation to each brain area, and the amount of food eaten during the stimulation is measured. The amount of food in grams that was eaten during stimulation is shown in Table 14.2.

1. What is the alternative hypothesis? Assume a nondirectional hypothesis is appropriate.
2. What is the null hypothesis?
3. What is the conclusion? Use $\alpha = 0.05_{2\,\text{tail}}$.

**SOLUTION**

1. Alternative hypothesis: The alternative hypothesis specifies that electrical stimulation of the lateral hypothalamus affects the amount of food eaten.

**t a b l e 14.2**   Data from brain stimulation experiment

| | **Food Eaten** | | **Difference** | |
| | *Lateral hypothalamus* (*g*) | *Neutral area* (*g*) | | |
| **Subject** | | | *D* | *D²* |
|---|---|---|---|---|
| 1 | 10 | 6 | 4 | 16 |
| 2 | 18 | 8 | 10 | 100 |
| 3 | 16 | 11 | 5 | 25 |
| 4 | 22 | 14 | 8 | 64 |
| 5 | 14 | 10 | 4 | 16 |
| 6 | 25 | 20 | 5 | 25 |
| 7 | 17 | 10 | 7 | 49 |
| 8 | 22 | 18 | 4 | 16 |
| 9 | 12 | 14 | −2 | 4 |
| 10 | 21 | 13 | 8 | 64 |
| | | | 53 | 379 |

$$N = 10 \qquad \overline{D}_{\text{obt}} = \frac{\Sigma D}{N} = \frac{53}{10} = 5.3$$

The sample difference scores having a mean $\overline{D}_{\text{obt}} = 5.3$ are a random sample from a population of difference scores having a mean $\mu_D \neq 0$.

2. Null hypothesis: The null hypothesis states that electrical stimulation of the lateral hypothalamus has no effect on the amount of food eaten. The sample difference scores having a mean $\overline{D}_{\text{obt}} = 5.3$ are a random sample from a population of difference scores having a mean $\mu_D = 0$.

3. Conclusion, using $\alpha = 0.05_{2\,\text{tail}}$:

STEP 1: **Calculate the appropriate statistic.** Since this is a correlated groups design, we are interested in the difference between the paired scores rather than the scores in each condition per se. The difference scores are shown in Table 14.2. Of the tests covered so far, both the sign test and the *t* test are possible choices. We want to use the test that is most sensitive, so the *t* test has been chosen. From the data table, $N = 10$ and $\overline{D}_{\text{obt}} = 5.3$. The calculation of $t_{\text{obt}}$ is as follows:

$$t_{\text{obt}} = \frac{\overline{D}_{\text{obt}} - \mu_D}{\sqrt{\dfrac{SS_D}{N(N-1)}}} \qquad SS_D = \sum D^2 - \frac{(\sum D)^2}{N}$$

$$= \frac{5.3 - 0}{\sqrt{\dfrac{98.1}{10(9)}}} \qquad\qquad = 379 - \frac{(53)^2}{10}$$

$$= \frac{5.3}{\sqrt{1.09}} \qquad\qquad\quad = 98.1$$

$$= 5.08$$

STEP 2: **Evaluate the statistic.** As with the *t* test for single samples, if $t_{\text{obt}}$ falls within the critical region for rejection of $H_0$, the conclusion is to reject $H_0$. Thus, the same decision rule applies, namely,

$$\text{If } |t_{\text{obt}}| \geq |t_{\text{crit}}|, \text{ reject } H_0.$$

The degrees of freedom are equal to the number of difference scores minus 1. Thus, $\text{df} = N - 1 = 10 - 1 = 9$. From Table D in Appendix D, with $\alpha = 0.05_{2\,\text{tail}}$ and $\text{df} = 9$,

$$t_{\text{crit}} = \pm 2.262$$

Since $|t_{\text{obt}}| > 2.262$, we reject $H_0$ and conclude that electrical stimulation of the lateral hypothalamus affects eating behavior. It appears to increase the amount eaten.

## Practice Problem 14.1

To motivate citizens to conserve gasoline, the government is considering mounting a nationwide conservation campaign. However, before doing so on a national level, it decides to conduct an experiment to evaluate the effectiveness of the campaign. For the experiment, the conservation campaign is conducted in a small but representative geographical area. Twelve families are randomly selected from the area, and the amount of gasoline they use is monitored for 1 month before the advertising campaign and for 1 month after the campaign. The following data are collected:

| Family | Before the Campaign (gal/mo.) | After the Campaign (gal/mo.) | Difference | |
|--------|-------------------------------|------------------------------|:--:|:--:|
| | | | $D$ | $D^2$ |
| A | 55 | 48 | 7 | 49 |
| B | 43 | 38 | 5 | 25 |
| C | 51 | 53 | −2 | 4 |
| D | 62 | 58 | 4 | 16 |
| E | 35 | 36 | −1 | 1 |
| F | 48 | 42 | 6 | 36 |
| G | 58 | 55 | 3 | 9 |
| H | 45 | 40 | 5 | 25 |
| I | 48 | 49 | −1 | 1 |
| J | 54 | 50 | 4 | 16 |
| K | 56 | 58 | −2 | 4 |
| L | 32 | 25 | 7 | 49 |
| | | | 35 | 235 |

$$N = 12 \qquad \overline{D}_{obt} = \frac{\Sigma D}{N} = \frac{35}{12} = 2.917$$

**a.** What is the alternative hypothesis? Use a nondirectional hypothesis.
**b.** What is the null hypothesis?
**c.** What is the conclusion? Use $\alpha = 0.05_{2\,tail}$.

**SOLUTION**

**a.** Alternative hypothesis: The conservation campaign affects the amount of gasoline used. The sample with $\overline{D}_{obt} = 2.917$ is a random sample from a population of difference scores where $\mu_D \neq 0$.
**b.** Null hypothesis: The conservation campaign has no effect on the amount of gasoline used. The sample with $\overline{D}_{obt} = 2.917$ is a random sample from a population of difference scores where $\mu_D = 0$.
**c.** Conclusion, using $\alpha = 0.05_{2\,tail}$:

**STEP 1: Calculate the appropriate statistic.** The difference scores are included in the previous table. We have subtracted the "after" scores from the "before" scores. Assuming the assumptions of $t$ are met, the appropriate statistic is $t_{obt}$. From the data table, $N = 12$ and $\overline{D}_{obt} = 2.917$.

*(continued)*

$$t_{obt} = \frac{\overline{D}_{obt} - \mu_D}{\sqrt{\dfrac{SS_D}{N(N-1)}}} \qquad SS_D = \Sigma D^2 - \frac{(\Sigma D)^2}{N}$$

$$= \frac{2.917 - 0}{\sqrt{\dfrac{132.917}{12(11)}}} \qquad = 235 - \frac{(35)^2}{12}$$

$$= 132.917$$

$$= 2.91$$

**STEP 2: Evaluate the statistic.** Degrees of freedom $= N - 1 = 12 - 1 = 11$. From Table D, with $\alpha = 0.05_{2\,tail}$ and 11 df,

$$t_{crit} = \pm 2.201$$

Since $|t_{obt}| > 2.201$, we reject $H_0$. The conservation campaign affects the amount of gasoline used. It appears to decrease gasoline consumption.

## *t* Test for Correlated Groups and Sign Test Compared

It would have been possible to solve either of the previous two problems using the sign test. We chose the *t* test because it is more sensitive. To illustrate this point, let's use the sign test to solve the problem dealing with gasoline conservation.

**SOLUTION**

**STEP 1: Calculate the statistic.** There are 8 pluses in the sample.

**STEP 2: Evalute the statistic.** With $N = 12$, $P = 0.50$, and $\alpha = 0.05_{2\,tail}$,

$$p(8 \text{ or more pluses}) = p(8) + p(9) + p(10) + p(11) + p(12)$$

From Table B in Appendix D,

$$p(8 \text{ or more pluses}) = 0.1208 + 0.0537 + 0.0161 + 0.0029 + 0.0002$$
$$= 0.1937$$

Since the alpha level is two-tailed,

$$p(\text{outcome as extreme as 8 pluses}) = 2[p(8 \text{ or more pluses})]$$
$$= 2(0.1937)$$
$$= 0.3874$$

Since $0.3874 > 0.05$, we conclude by retaining $H_0$.

We are unable to reject $H_0$ with the sign test, but we were able to reject $H_0$ with the *t* test. Does this mean the campaign is effective if we analyze the data with the *t* test and ineffective if we use the sign test? Obviously not. With the low power of the sign test, there is a high chance of making a Type II error (i.e., retaining $H_0$ when it is false). The *t* test is usually more powerful than the sign test. The additional power gives $H_0$ a better chance to be rejected if it is false. In this case, the additional power resulted in rejection of $H_0$. When several tests are appropriate for analyzing the data, *it is a general rule of statistical analysis to use the most powerful one,* because this gives the highest probability of rejecting $H_0$ when it is false.

## Assumptions Underlying the *t* Test for Correlated Groups

The assumptions are very similar to those underlying the *t* test for single samples. The *t* test for correlated groups requires that the sampling distribution of $\overline{D}$ be normally distributed. This means that N should be $\geq 30$, assuming the population shape doesn't differ greatly from normality, or the population scores themselves should be normally distributed.*

# *z* AND *t* TESTS FOR INDEPENDENT GROUPS

## Independent Groups Design

Two basic experimental designs are used most frequently in studying behavior. The first was introduced when discussing the sign test and the *t* test for correlated groups. This design is called the repeated or replicated measures design. The simplest form of the design uses two conditions: an experimental and a control condition. The essential feature of the design is that there are paired scores between conditions, and *difference* scores from each score pair are analyzed to determine whether chance alone can reasonably explain them.

The other type of design is called the *independent groups design.* Like the correlated groups design, the independent groups design involves experiments using two or more conditions. Each condition uses a different level of the independent variable. The most basic experiment has only two conditions: an experimental and a control condition. In this chapter, we shall consider this basic experiment involving only two conditions. More complicated experiments will be considered in Chapter 15.

In the independent groups design, subjects are randomly selected from the subject population and then randomly assigned to either the experimental or the control condition. There is no basis for pairing of subjects, and each subject is tested only once. All of the subjects in the experimental condition receive the level of the independent variable appropriate for the experimental condition, and the subjects themselves are referred to as the "experimental group." All of the subjects in the control condition receive the level of the independent variable appropriate for the control condition and are referred to as the "control group."

When analyzing the data, since subjects are randomly assigned to conditions, there is no basis for pairing scores between the conditions. Rather, a statistic is computed for each group *separately,* and the two group statistics are compared to determine whether chance alone is a reasonable explanation of the differences between the group statistics. The statistic that is computed on each sample depends on the inference test being used. The *t* test for independent groups computes the mean of each sample and then analyzes the difference between these two sample means to determine whether chance alone is a reasonable explanation of the difference between the two means.

---

*Many authors limit the use of the *t* test to data that are of interval or ratio scaling. Please see the footnote in Chapter 2, p. 31, for references discussing this point.

**$H_1$ and $H_0$**   The sample scores in one of the conditions (say, condition 1) can be considered a random sample from a normally distributed population of scores that would result if all the individuals in the population received that condition (condition 1). Let's call the mean of this hypothetical population $\mu_1$ and the standard deviation $\sigma_1$. Similarly, the sample scores in condition 2 can be considered a random sample from a normally distributed population of scores that would result if all the individuals in the population were given condition 2. We can call the mean of this second population $\mu_2$ and the standard deviation $\sigma_2$. Thus,

$\mu_1$ = mean of the population that receives condition 1

$\sigma_1$ = standard deviation of the population that receives condition 1

$\mu_2$ = mean of the population that receives condition 2

$\sigma_2$ = standard deviation of the population that receives condition 2

Changing the level of the independent variable is assumed to affect the mean of the distribution ($\mu_2$), but not the standard deviation ($\sigma_2$) or variance ($\sigma_2^2$). Thus, under this assumption, if the independent variable has a real effect, the means of the populations will differ but their variances will stay the same. Hence, $\sigma_1^2$ is assumed equal to $\sigma_2^2$. One way in which this assumption would be met is if the independent variable has an equal effect on each individual. A directional alternative hypothesis would predict that the samples are random samples from populations where $\mu_1 > \mu_2$ or $\mu_1 < \mu_2$, depending on the direction of the effect. A nondirectional alternative hypothesis would predict $\mu_1 \neq \mu_2$. If the independent variable has no effect, the samples would be random samples from populations where $\mu_1 = \mu_2$* and chance alone would account for the differences between the sample means.

## *z* TEST FOR INDEPENDENT GROUPS

Before discussing the *t* test for independent groups, we shall present the *z* test. In the two-group situation, the *z* test is almost never used because it requires that $\sigma_1^2$ or $\sigma_2^2$ be known. However, it provides an important conceptual foundation for understanding the *t* test. After presenting the *z* test, we shall move to the *t* test.

Let's begin with an experiment.

an experiment

## **Hormone X and Sexual Behavior**

A physiologist has the hypothesis that hormone X is important in producing sexual behavior. To investigate this hypothesis, 20 male rats were randomly sampled and then randomly assigned to two groups. The animals in group 1 were injected with hormone X and then were placed in individual housing with a sexually receptive female. The

---

*In this case, there would be two null-hypothesis populations: one with a mean $\mu_1$ and a standard deviation of $\sigma_1$ and the other with a mean $\mu_2$ and a standard deviation $\sigma_2$. However, since $\mu_1 = \mu_2$ and $\sigma_1 = \sigma_2$, the populations would be identical.

**t a b l e 14.3** Data from hormone X and sexual behavior experiment

| Hormone X, Group 1 | Placebo, Group 2 |
|:---:|:---:|
| 8 | 5 |
| 10 | 6 |
| 12 | 3 |
| 6 | 4 |
| 6 | 7 |
| 7 | 8 |
| 9 | 6 |
| 8 | 5 |
| 7 | 4 |
| 11 | 8 |
| 84 | 56 |

$n_1 = 10$     $n_2 = 10$
$\overline{X}_1 = 8.4$     $\overline{X}_2 = 5.6$
$\overline{X}_1 - \overline{X}_2 = 2.8$

animals in group 2 were given similar treatment except they were injected with a placebo solution. The number of matings were counted over a 20-minute period. The results are shown in Table 14.3.

As shown in Table 14.3, the mean of group 1 is higher than the mean of group 2. The difference between the means of the two samples is 2.8 and is in the direction that indicates a positive effect. Is it legitimate to conclude that hormone X was responsible for the difference in means? The answer, of course, is no. Before drawing this conclusion, we must evaluate the null-hypothesis explanation. The statistic we are using for this evaluation is the difference between the means of the two samples. As with all other statistics, we must know its sampling distribution before we can evaluate the null hypothesis.

## The Sampling Distribution of the Difference Between Sample Means ($\overline{X}_1 - \overline{X}_2$)

Like the sampling distribution of the mean, this sampling distribution can be determined theoretically or empirically. Again, for pedagogical purposes, we prefer the empirical approach. To empirically derive the sampling distribution of $\overline{X}_1 - \overline{X}_2$, all possible different samples of size $n_1$ would be drawn from a population with a mean of $\mu_1$ and variance of $\sigma_1{}^2$. Likewise, all possible samples of size $n_2$ would be drawn from another population with a mean $\mu_2$ and variance $\sigma_2{}^2$. The values of $\overline{X}_1$ and $\overline{X}_2$ would then be calculated for each sample. Next, $\overline{X}_1 - \overline{X}_2$ would be calculated for all possible pairings of samples of size $n_1$ and $n_2$. The resulting distribution would contain all the possible different $\overline{X}_1 - \overline{X}_2$ scores that could be obtained from the populations when sample sizes are $n_1$ and $n_2$. Once this distribution has been obtained, it is a simple matter to calculate the probability of obtaining each mean difference score ($\overline{X}_1 - \overline{X}_2$), assuming sampling is random of $n_1$ and $n_2$ scores from their respective populations. This then would be the sampling distribution of the difference between sample means for samples of $n_1$ and $n_2$ taken from the specified populations. This process would be repeated for different sample sizes and population scores. Whether determined theoretically or empirically, the sampling distribution of the difference between sample means has the following characteristics:

1. If the populations from which the samples are taken are normal, then the distribution of the difference between sample means is also normal.

2. $\mu_{\overline{X}_1 - \overline{X}_2} = \mu_1 - \mu_2$

   *where*     $\mu_{\overline{X}_1 - \overline{X}_2} =$ the mean of the distribution of the difference between sample means

3. $\sigma_{\overline{X}_1 - \overline{X}_2} = \sqrt{\sigma_{\overline{X}_1}^2 + \sigma_{\overline{X}_2}^2}$

   *where*     $\sigma_{\overline{X}_1 - \overline{X}_2} =$ standard deviation of the sampling distribution of the difference between sample means; alternatively, standard error of the difference between sample means

   $\sigma_{\overline{X}_1}^2 =$ variance of the sampling distribution of the mean for samples of size $n_1$ taken from the first population

   $\sigma_{\overline{X}_2}^2 =$ variance of the sampling distribution of the mean for samples of $n_2$ taken from the second population

If, as mentioned previously, we assume that the variances of the two populations are equal ($\sigma_1^2 = \sigma_2^2$), then the equation for $\sigma_{\bar{X}_1 - \bar{X}_2}$ can be simplified as follows:

$$\sigma_{\bar{X}_1 - \bar{X}_2} = \sqrt{\sigma_{\bar{X}_1}^2 + \sigma_{\bar{X}_2}^2}$$

$$= \sqrt{\frac{\sigma_1^2}{n_1} + \frac{\sigma_2^2}{n_2}}$$

$$= \sqrt{\sigma^2\left(\frac{1}{n_1} + \frac{1}{n_2}\right)}$$

*where*    $\sigma^2 = \sigma_1^2 = \sigma_2^2$ = the variance of each population

The distribution is shown in Figure 14.2. Now let's return to the illustrative example.

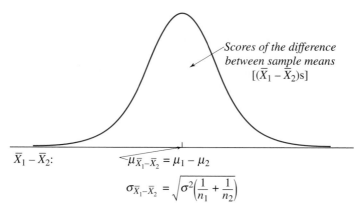

$$\bar{X}_1 - \bar{X}_2:$$

*Scores of the difference between sample means* $[(\bar{X}_1 - \bar{X}_2)s]$

$$\mu_{\bar{X}_1 - \bar{X}_2} = \mu_1 - \mu_2$$

$$\sigma_{\bar{X}_1 - \bar{X}_2} = \sqrt{\sigma^2\left(\frac{1}{n_1} + \frac{1}{n_2}\right)}$$

**figure 14.2**   Sampling distribution of the difference between sample mean scores.

**an experiment**

## Hormone X Experiment Revisited

The results of the experiment showed that 10 rats injected with hormone X had a mean of 8.4 matings, whereas the mean of the 10 rats injected with a placebo was 5.6. Is the mean difference ($\bar{X}_1 - \bar{X}_2 = 2.8$) significant? Use $\alpha = 0.05_{2\,tail}$.

### SOLUTION

The sampling distribution of $\bar{X}_1 - \bar{X}_2$ is shown in Figure 14.3. The shaded area contains all the mean difference scores of +2.8 or more. Assuming the sampling distribution of $\bar{X}_1 - \bar{X}_2$ is normal, if the sample mean difference (2.8) can be converted to its *z* value, we can use the *z* test to solve the problem. The equation for $z_{obt}$ is similar to the other *z* equations we have already considered. However, here the value we are converting is $\bar{X}_1 - \bar{X}_2$. Thus,

$$z_{obt} = \frac{(\bar{X}_1 - \bar{X}_2) - \mu_{\bar{X}_1 - \bar{X}_2}}{\sigma_{\bar{X}_1 - \bar{X}_2}} \qquad equation\ for\ z_{obt},\ independent\ groups\ design$$

If hormone X had no effect on mating behavior, then both samples are random samples from populations where $\mu_1 = \mu_2$ and $\mu_{\bar{X}_1 - \bar{X}_2} = \mu_1 - \mu_2 = 0$. Thus,

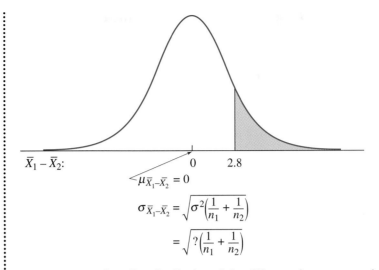

$\overline{X}_1 - \overline{X}_2:$

$\mu_{\overline{X}_1 - \overline{X}_2} = 0$

$$\sigma_{\overline{X}_1 - \overline{X}_2} = \sqrt{\sigma^2\left(\frac{1}{n_1} + \frac{1}{n_2}\right)}$$

$$= \sqrt{?\left(\frac{1}{n_1} + \frac{1}{n_2}\right)}$$

**figure 14.3** Sampling distribution of the difference between sample mean scores for the hormone problem.

$$z_{\text{obt}} = \frac{(\overline{X}_1 - \overline{X}_2) - 0}{\sqrt{\sigma^2\left(\frac{1}{n_1} + \frac{1}{n_2}\right)}} = \frac{2.8}{\sqrt{\sigma^2\left(\frac{1}{10} + \frac{1}{10}\right)}}$$

Note that the variance of the populations ($\sigma^2$) must be known before $z_{\text{obt}}$ can be calculated. Since $\sigma^2$ is almost never known, this limitation severely restricts the practical use of the *z* test in this design. However, as you might guess, $\sigma^2$ can be estimated from the sample data. When this is done, we have the *t* test for independent groups.

# STUDENT'S *t* TEST FOR INDEPENDENT GROUPS

## Comparing the Equations for $z_{\text{obt}}$ and $t_{\text{obt}}$

The equations for the *z* and *t* test are shown in Table 14.4. The *z* and *t* equations are identical except that the *t* equation uses $s_W^2$ to estimate the popula-

**table 14.4**    *z* and *t* equations compared

| *z* Test | *t* Test |
|---|---|
| $z_{\text{obt}} = \dfrac{(\overline{X}_1 - \overline{X}_2) - \mu_{\overline{X}_1 - \overline{X}_2}}{\sigma_{\overline{X}_1 - \overline{X}_2}}$ | $t_{\text{obt}} = \dfrac{(\overline{X}_1 - \overline{X}_2) - \mu_{\overline{X}_1 - \overline{X}_2}}{s_{\overline{X}_1 - \overline{X}_2}}$ |
| $= \dfrac{(\overline{X}_1 - \overline{X}_2) - \mu_{\overline{X}_1 - \overline{X}_2}}{\sqrt{\sigma^2\left(\frac{1}{n_1} + \frac{1}{n_2}\right)}}$ | $= \dfrac{(\overline{X}_1 - \overline{X}_2) - \mu_{\overline{X}_1 - \overline{X}_2}}{\sqrt{s_W^2\left(\frac{1}{n_1} + \frac{1}{n_2}\right)}}$ |

*where*     $s_W^2$ = weighted estimate of $\sigma^2$

$s_{\overline{X}_1 - \overline{X}_2}$ = estimate of $\sigma_{\overline{X}_1 - \overline{X}_2}$ = estimated standard error of the difference between sample means tion variance ($\sigma^2$). This situation is analogous to the *t* test for single samples. You will recall in that situation we used the sample standard deviation(s) to estimate $\sigma$. However, in the *t* test for independent groups, there are two samples, and we wish to estimate $\sigma^2$. Since $s$ is an accurate estimate of $\sigma$, $s^2$ is an accurate estimate of $\sigma^2$. There are two samples, and either could be used to estimate $\sigma^2$, but we can get a more precise estimate by using both. It turns out the most precise estimate of $\sigma^2$ is obtained by using a weighted average of the sample variances $s_1^2$ and $s_2^2$. Weighting is done using degrees of freedom as the weights. Thus,

$$s_W^2 = \frac{\mathrm{df}_1 s_1^2 + \mathrm{df}_2 s_2^2}{\mathrm{df}_1 + \mathrm{df}_2} = \frac{(n_1 - 1)\left(\dfrac{SS_1}{n_1 - 1}\right) + (n_2 - 1)\left(\dfrac{SS_2}{n_2 - 1}\right)}{(n_1 - 1) + (n_2 - 1)} = \frac{SS_1 + SS_2}{n_1 + n_2 - 2}$$

*where*   $s_W^2$ = weighted estimate of $\sigma^2$
$s_1^2$ = variance of the first sample
$s_2^2$ = variance of the second sample
$SS_1$ = sum of squares of the first sample
$SS_2$ = sum of squares of the second sample

Substituting for $s_W^2$ in the *t* equation, we arrive at the computational equation for $t_{\mathrm{obt}}$. Thus,

$$t_{\mathrm{obt}} = \frac{(\overline{X}_1 - \overline{X}_2) - \mu_{\overline{X}_1 - \overline{X}_2}}{\sqrt{s_W^2\left(\dfrac{1}{n_1} + \dfrac{1}{n_2}\right)}} = \frac{(\overline{X}_1 - \overline{X}_2) - \mu_{\overline{X}_1 - \overline{X}_2}}{\sqrt{\left(\dfrac{SS_1 + SS_2}{n_1 + n_2 - 2}\right)\left(\dfrac{1}{n_1} + \dfrac{1}{n_2}\right)}}$$

*computational equation for $t_{\mathrm{obt}}$,*
*independent groups design*

To evaluate the null hypothesis, we assume both samples are random samples from populations having the same mean value ($\mu_1 = \mu_2$). Therefore, $\mu_{\overline{X}_1 - \overline{X}_2} = 0$.[*] The previous equation reduces to

$$t_{\mathrm{obt}} = \frac{\overline{X}_1 - \overline{X}_2}{\sqrt{\left(\dfrac{SS_1 + SS_2}{n_1 + n_2 - 2}\right)\left(\dfrac{1}{n_1} + \dfrac{1}{n_2}\right)}}$$

*computational equation for $t_{\mathrm{obt}}$,*
*assuming $\mu_{\overline{X}_1 - \overline{X}_2} = 0$*

We could go ahead and calculate $t_{\mathrm{obt}}$ for the hormone X example, but to evaluate $t_{\mathrm{obt}}$, we must know the sampling distribution of *t*. It turns out that, when one derives the sampling distribution of *t* for independent groups, the same family of curves is obtained as with the sampling distribution of *t* for single samples, except that there is a different number of degrees of freedom. You will recall that 1 degree of freedom is lost each time a standard deviation is calculated. Since we calculate $s_1^2$ and $s_2^2$ for the two-sample case, we lose 2 degrees of freedom, one from each sample. Thus,

$$\mathrm{df} = (n_1 - 1) + (n_2 - 1) = n_1 + n_2 - 2 = N - 2$$

*where*   $N = n_1 + n_2$

Table D, then, can be used in the same manner as with the *t* test for single samples, except in the two-sample case, we enter the table with $N - 2$ df. Thus,

---

[*]See Note 14.3.

the $t$ distribution varies both with $N$ and degrees of freedom, but it varies uniquely only with degrees of freedom. That is, the $t$ distribution corresponding to 13 df is the same whether it is derived from the single sample situation with $N = 14$ or the two-sample situation with $N = 15$.

## Analyzing the Hormone X Experiment with the $t$ Test for Independent Groups

At long last, we are ready to evaluate the hormone data. The problem and data are restated for convenience.

A physiologist has conducted an experiment to evaluate the effect of hormone X on sexual behavior. Ten rats were injected with hormone X, and 10 other rats received a placebo injection. The number of matings were counted over a 20-minute period.

The results are shown in Table 14.5.

1. What is the alternative hypothesis? Use a nondirectional hypothesis.
2. What is the null hypothesis?
3. What do you conclude? Use $\alpha = 0.05_{2\,tail}$.

t a b l e 14.5  Data from hormone X experiment

| Group 1 Hormone X | | Group 2 Placebo | |
|---|---|---|---|
| $X_1$ | $X_1^2$ | $X_2$ | $X_2^2$ |
| 8 | 64 | 5 | 25 |
| 10 | 100 | 6 | 36 |
| 12 | 144 | 3 | 9 |
| 6 | 36 | 4 | 16 |
| 6 | 36 | 7 | 49 |
| 7 | 49 | 8 | 64 |
| 9 | 81 | 6 | 36 |
| 8 | 64 | 5 | 25 |
| 7 | 49 | 4 | 16 |
| 11 | 121 | 8 | 64 |
| 84 | 744 | 56 | 340 |

$$n_1 = 10 \qquad n_2 = 10$$
$$\overline{X}_1 = 8.4 \qquad \overline{X}_2 = 5.6$$
$$\overline{X}_1 - \overline{X}_2 = 2.8$$

**SOLUTION**

1. Alternative hypothesis: The alternative hypothesis specifies that hormone X affects sexual behavior. The sample mean difference of 2.8 is due to random sampling from populations where $\mu_1 \neq \mu_2$.
2. Null hypothesis: The null hypothesis states that hormone X is not related to sexual behavior. The sample mean difference of 2.8 is due to random sampling from populations where $\mu_1 = \mu_2$.
3. Conclusion, using $\alpha = 0.05_{2\,tail}$:

**STEP 1: Calculate the appropriate statistic.** For now, assume *t* is appropriate. We shall discuss the assumptions of *t* in a later section. From Table 14.5, $n_1 = 10$, $n_2 = 10$, $\overline{X}_1 = 8.4$, and $\overline{X}_2 = 5.6$. Solving for $SS_1$ and $SS_2$,

$$SS_1 = \Sigma X_1^2 - \frac{(\Sigma X_1)^2}{n_1} \qquad SS_2 = \Sigma X_2^2 - \frac{(\Sigma X_2)^2}{n_2}$$

$$= 744 - \frac{(84)^2}{10} \qquad\qquad = 340 - \frac{(56)^2}{10}$$

$$= 38.4 \qquad\qquad\qquad = 26.4$$

Substituting these values in the equation for $t_{obt}$, we have

$$t_{obt} = \frac{\overline{X}_1 - \overline{X}_2}{\sqrt{\left(\dfrac{SS_1 + SS_2}{n_1 + n_2 - 2}\right)\left(\dfrac{1}{n_1} + \dfrac{1}{n_2}\right)}} = \frac{8.4 - 5.6}{\sqrt{\left(\dfrac{38.4 + 26.4}{10 + 10 - 2}\right)\left(\dfrac{1}{10} + \dfrac{1}{10}\right)}} = 3.30$$

**STEP 2: Evaluate the statistic.** As with the previous *t* tests, if $t_{obt}$ falls in the critical region for rejection of $H_0$, we reject $H_0$. Thus,

$$\text{If } |t_{obt}| \geq |t_{crit}|, \text{ reject } H_0.$$

$$\text{If not, retain } H_0.$$

The number of degrees of freedom is df $= N - 2 = 20 - 2 = 18$. From Table D, with $\alpha = 0.05_{2\,\text{tail}}$ and df $= 18$,

$$t_{crit} = \pm 2.101$$

Since $|t_{obt}| > 2.101$, we conclude by rejecting $H_0$.

## Calculating $t_{obt}$ When $n_1 = n_2$

When the sample sizes are equal, the equation for $t_{obt}$ can be simplified. Thus,

$$t_{obt} = \frac{\overline{X}_1 - \overline{X}_2}{\sqrt{\left(\dfrac{SS_1 + SS_2}{n_1 + n_2 - 2}\right)\left(\dfrac{1}{n_1} + \dfrac{1}{n_2}\right)}}$$

but $n_1 = n_2 = n$. Substituting $n$ for $n_1$ and $n_2$ in the equation for $t_{obt}$,

$$t_{obt} = \frac{\overline{X}_1 - \overline{X}_2}{\sqrt{\left(\dfrac{SS_1 + SS_2}{n + n - 2}\right)\left(\dfrac{1}{n} + \dfrac{1}{n}\right)}} = \frac{\overline{X}_1 - \overline{X}_2}{\sqrt{\left(\dfrac{SS_1 + SS_2}{2(n - 1)}\right)\left(\dfrac{2}{n}\right)}} = \frac{\overline{X}_1 - \overline{X}_2}{\sqrt{\dfrac{SS_1 + SS_2}{n(n - 1)}}}$$

Thus,

$$t_{obt} = \frac{\overline{X}_1 - \overline{X}_2}{\sqrt{\dfrac{SS_1 + SS_2}{n(n - 1)}}} \qquad \textit{equation for calculating } t_{obt} \textit{ when } n_1 = n_2$$

Since $n_1 = n_2$ in the previous problem, we can use the simplified equation to calculate $t_{obt}$. Thus,

$$t_{obt} = \frac{\overline{X}_1 - \overline{X}_2}{\sqrt{\dfrac{SS_1 + SS_2}{n(n - 1)}}} = \frac{8.4 - 5.6}{\sqrt{\dfrac{38.4 + 26.4}{10(9)}}} = 3.30$$

This is the same value for $t_{obt}$ that we obtained when using the more complicated equation. Whenever $n_1 = n_2$, it's easier to use the simplified equation. When $n_1 \neq n_2$, the more complicated equation *must* be used.

Let's do one more problem for practice.

## Practice Problem 14.2

A neurosurgeon believes that lesions in a particular area of the brain, called the thalamus, will decrease pain perception. If so, this could be important in the treatment of terminal illness that is accompanied by intense pain. As a first attempt to test this hypothesis, he conducts an experiment in which 16 rats are randomly divided into two groups of eight each. Animals in the experimental group receive a small lesion in the part of the thalamus thought to be involved with pain perception. Animals in the control group receive a comparable lesion in a brain area believed to be unrelated to pain. Two weeks after surgery, each animal is given a brief electrical shock to the paws. The shock is administered in an ascending series, beginning with a very low intensity level and increasing until the animal first flinches. In this manner, the pain threshold to electric shock is determined for each rat. The following data are obtained. Each score represents the current level (milli-amperes) at which flinching is first observed. The higher the current level is, the higher is the pain threshold. Note that one animal died during surgery and was not replaced.

| Neutral Area Lesions Control Group Group 1 | | Thalamic Lesions Experimental Group Group 2 | |
|---|---|---|---|
| $X_1$ | $X_1{}^2$ | $X_2$ | $X_2{}^2$ |
| 0.8 | 0.64 | 1.9 | 3.61 |
| 0.7 | 0.49 | 1.8 | 3.24 |
| 1.2 | 1.44 | 1.6 | 2.56 |
| 0.5 | 0.25 | 1.2 | 1.44 |
| 0.4 | 0.16 | 1.0 | 1.00 |
| 0.9 | 0.81 | 0.9 | 0.81 |
| 1.4 | 1.96 | 1.7 | 2.89 |
| 1.1 | 1.21 | 10.1 | 15.55 |
| 7.0 | 6.96 | | |

$$n_1 = 8 \qquad n_2 = 7$$
$$\overline{X}_1 = 0.875 \qquad \overline{X}_2 = 1.443$$
$$\overline{X}_1 - \overline{X}_2 = -0.568$$

**a.** What is the alternative hypothesis? In this problem, assume there is sufficient theoretical and experimental basis to use a directional hypothesis.
**b.** What is the null hypothesis?
**c.** What do you conclude? Use $\alpha = 0.05_{1\,tail}$.

*(continued)*

**SOLUTION**

a. Alternative hypothesis: The alternative hypothesis states that lesions of the thalamus decrease pain perception. The difference between sample means of $-0.568$ is due to random sampling from populations where $\mu_1 < \mu_2$.

b. Null hypothesis: The null hypothesis states that lesions of the thalamus either have no effect or they increase pain perception. The difference between sample means of $-0.568$ is due to random sampling from populations where $\mu_1 \geq \mu_2$.

c. Conclusion, using $\alpha = 0.05_{1\text{ tail}}$:

STEP 1: **Calculate the appropriate statistic.** Assuming the assumptions of *t* are met, $t_{\text{obt}}$ is the appropriate statistic. From the data table, $n_1 = 8$, $n_2 = 7$, $\overline{X}_1 = 0.875$, and $\overline{X}_2 = 1.443$. Solving for $SS_1$ and $SS_2$, we obtain

$$SS_1 = \Sigma X_1^2 - \frac{(\Sigma X_1)^2}{n_1} \qquad SS_2 = \Sigma X_2^2 - \frac{(\Sigma X_2)^2}{n_2}$$

$$= 6.960 - \frac{(7)^2}{8} \qquad\qquad = 15.550 - \frac{(10.1)^2}{7}$$

$$= 0.835 \qquad\qquad\qquad = 0.977$$

Substituting these values into the general equation for $t_{\text{obt}}$, we have

$$t_{\text{obt}} = \frac{\overline{X}_1 - \overline{X}_2}{\sqrt{\left(\dfrac{SS_1 + SS_2}{n_1 + n_2 - 2}\right)\left(\dfrac{1}{n_1} + \dfrac{1}{n_2}\right)}}$$

$$= \frac{0.875 - 1.443}{\sqrt{\left(\dfrac{0.835 + 0.977}{8 + 7 - 2}\right)\left(\dfrac{1}{8} + \dfrac{1}{7}\right)}} = -2.94$$

STEP 2: **Evaluate the statistic.** Degrees of freedom $= N - 2 = 15 - 2 = 13$. From Table D, with $\alpha = 0.05_{1\text{ tail}}$ and df $= 13$,

$$t_{\text{crit}} = -1.771$$

Since $|t_{\text{obt}}| > 1.771$, we reject $H_0$ and conclude that lesions of the thalamus decrease pain perception.

## Assumptions Underlying the *t* Test for Independent Groups

The assumptions underlying the *t* test for independent groups are as follows:

1. The sampling distribution of $\overline{X}_1 - \overline{X}_2$ is normally distributed. This means the populations from which the samples were taken should be normally distributed.

2. There is *homogeneity of variance*. You will recall that, at the beginning of our discussion concerning the *t* test for independent groups, we pointed

out that the *t* test assumes that the independent variable affects the means of the populations but not their standard deviations ($\sigma_1 = \sigma_2$). Since the variance is just the square of the standard deviation, the *t* test for independent groups also assumes that the variances of the two populations are equal; that is, $\sigma_1^2 = \sigma_2^2$. This is spoken of as the *homogeneity of variance assumption.* If the variances of the samples in the experiment ($s_1^2$ and $s_2^2$) are very different (e.g., if one variance is more than 4 times larger than the other), the two samples probably are not random samples from populations where $\sigma_1^2 = \sigma_2^2$. If this is true, the homogeneity of variance assumption is violated ($\sigma_1^2 \neq \sigma_2^2$).[*]

## Violation of the Assumptions of the t Test for Independent Groups

Experiments have been conducted to determine the effect on the *t* test for independent groups of violating the assumptions of normality of the raw-score populations and homogeneity of variance. Fortunately, it turns out that the *t* test is a *robust* test. *A test is said to be robust if it is relatively insensitive to violations of its underlying mathematical assumptions.* The *t* test is relatively insensitive to violations of normality and homogeneity of variance, depending on sample size and the type and magnitude of the violation.[†] If $n_1 = n_2$ and the size of each sample is equal to or greater than 30, the *t* test for independent groups may be used without appreciable error despite moderate violation of the normality and/or the homogeneity of variance assumptions. If there are extreme violations of these assumptions, then an alternative test such as the Mann–Whitney *U* test should be used. This test is discussed in Chapter 17.

Before leaving this topic, it is worth noting that, when the two samples show large differences in their variances, it may indicate that the independent variable is not having an equal effect on all the subjects within a condition. This can be an important finding in its own right, leading to further experimentation into how the independent variable varies in its effects on different types of subjects.

## Size of Effect

Thus far, we have discussed the *t* test for independent groups and shown how to use it to determine whether the independent variable of interest in a basic independent groups experiment has a real effect on the dependent variable being measured. To determine whether the data show a real effect, we calculate $t_{obt}$; if $t_{obt}$ is significant, we conclude that the independent variable has a real effect. Of course, this gives us very important information. It allows us to support and further delineate theories involving the two variables as well as provide information that may have important practical consequences.

---

[*]There are many inference tests to determine whether the data meet homogeneity of variance assumptions. However, this topic is beyond the scope of this textbook. See R. E. Kirk, *Experimental Design,* 3rd ed., Brooks/Cole, Pacific Grove, CA, 1995, pp. 100–103.

Some statisticians also require that the data be of interval or ratio scaling to use the *z* test, Student's *t* test, and the analysis of variance (covered in Chapter 15). For a discussion of this point, see the references contained in the Chapter 2 footnote on p. 31.

[†]For a review of this topic, see C. A. Boneau, "The Effects of Violations of Assumptions Underlying the *t* Test," *Psychological Bulletin, 57* (1960), 49–64.

In addition to determining whether there is a real effect, it is often desirable to determine the size of the effect. For example, in the experiment investigating the role of the thalamus in pain perception (p. 339), $t_{obt}$ was significant and we were able to conclude that lesions of the thalamus decrease pain perception. Thus, within the limits of Type I error, as a result of conducting this experiment, we can conclude that the thalamus plays a role in pain perception. But surely, it would also be desirable to know how large a role the thalamus plays. Does the thalamus totally control pain perception such that if the relevant thalamic nuclei were completely destroyed, the subject would no longer feel pain? On the other hand, is the effect so small that for any practical purposes, it can be ignored? After all, even small effects are likely to be significant if $N$ is large enough. Determining the size of the thalamic effect would be particularly important for the neurosurgeon doing this research in the hope of developing a treatment for reducing the intense pain felt by some terminal patients.

We have already discussed the size of the effect of the $X$ variable on the $Y$ variable in conjunction with correlational research when we discussed the coefficient of determination ($r^2$) in Chapter 6, p. 120. You will recall that if the $X$ variable is causal with regard to the $Y$ variable, the coefficient of determination is a measure of the size of the effect of $X$ on $Y$. This understanding came about because we showed that $r^2$ is a measure of the variability of $Y$ accounted for by $X$.

The situation is very similar when we are dealing with the independent groups experiment. In the independent groups experiment, the independent variable is the $X$ variable and the dependent variable is the $Y$ variable. Figure 14.4 displays the two situations. In Figure 14.4(a), we have shown the scatter plot that was used to develop an understanding of $r^2$ in Chapter 6. Note that the $X$ variable, "spelling competence," is spread out over many $X$ values. Figure 14.4(b), presents a plot of the data from the thalamus and pain perception experiment. Here, the $X$ variable, "lesions," only has two values: "Lesions of a neutral area—Group 1" and "Lesions of the thalamus—Group 2." Hence, all the data in the basic independent groups design are clustered into two groups.

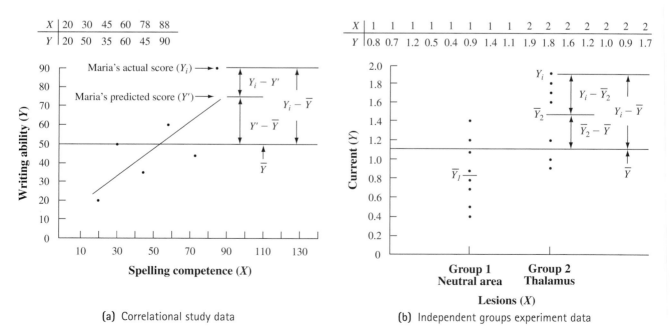

(a) Correlational study data

(b) Independent groups experiment data

**figure 14.4**  *XY* plots of data from a correlational study and an independent groups experiment.

In the correlational study data shown in Figure 14.4(a), the total variability of $Y$ is represented by $Y_i - \overline{Y}$, the variability of $Y$ accounted for by $X$ is represented by $Y' - \overline{Y}$, and the error of prediction is represented by $Y_i - Y'$. $\overline{Y}$ is the average of the $Y$ values of all the scores, and $Y'$ (the predicted value of $Y$) is determined by the regression line relating $X$ and $Y$. The situation is essentially the same with the independent groups data shown in Figure 14.4(b), except that the regression line is replaced by the mean of each group. This is because without knowing group membership, we would predict $\overline{Y}$ for each point, where $\overline{Y}$ is the average of the $Y$ values of all the points in both groups. However, if we knew the group membership of a point (its $X$ value), we would predict the mean of its group $(\overline{Y}_1$ or $\overline{Y}_2)$ for the $Y$ value of the point. Thus, the total variability of $Y$ is represented by $Y_i - \overline{Y}$, the variability of $Y$ accounted for by group membership (i.e., by the independent variable) is represented by $\overline{Y}_2 - \overline{Y}$, and the variability of $Y$ still unaccounted for after knowing group membership is represented by $Y_i - \overline{Y}_2$.

In both situations, the proportion of the total variance of $Y$ that is accounted for by $X$ is a measure of the size of the effect of $X$ on $Y$. Remember that in the independent groups experiment, the $X$ variable is the independent variable. For independent groups designs, omega squared $(\hat{\omega}^2)$ is a statistic that gives a relatively unbiased estimate of the proportion of the total variability of $Y$ in the population that is accounted for by $X$, the independent variable. Hence, we can use $\hat{\omega}^2$ as a measure of the size of effect in experiments using the independent groups design. Omega squared can be computed by using the following equation:

$$\hat{\omega}^2 = \frac{t_{obt}^2 - 1}{t_{obt}^2 + N - 1} \qquad \textit{computational equation for computing omega squared}$$

*where*    $\hat{\omega}^2$ = omega squared
$t_{obt}$ = obtained $t$ value for the data in the independent groups experiment
$N$ = the total number of subjects in both groups = $n_1 + n_2$

For the data of the thalamus and pain perception experiment, $t_{obt} = -2.94$, $n_1 = 8, n_2 = 7$. Therefore,

$$\hat{\omega}^2 = \frac{(-2.94)^2 - 1}{(-2.94)^2 + 15 - 1} = 0.338$$

Thus, the thalamic lesions accounted for about 33.8% of the variability in pain threshold to electric shock. Cohen (1988)* suggests the following scale for interpreting $\hat{\omega}^2$: For a small effect, $\hat{\omega}^2 = 0.01$; for a medium effect, $\hat{\omega}^2 = 0.06$; and for a large effect, $\hat{\omega}^2 = 0.14$. Using this scale, the thalamic lesions had quite a large effect.

## POWER OF THE *t* TEST

The three equations for $t_{obt}$ are as follows:

| Single sample | Correlated groups | Independent groups |
|---|---|---|
| $t_{obt} = \dfrac{\overline{X}_{obt} - \mu}{\sqrt{\dfrac{SS}{N(N-1)}}}$ | $t_{obt} = \dfrac{\overline{D}_{obt} - 0}{\sqrt{\dfrac{SS_D}{N(N-1)}}}$ | $t_{obt} = \dfrac{(\overline{X}_1 - \overline{X}_2) - 0}{\sqrt{\dfrac{SS_1 + SS_2}{n(n-1)}}}$ |

---

*J. Cohen, *Statistical Power Analysis for the Behavioral Sciences,* 2nd ed., Lawrence Erlbaum Associates, Hillsdale, NJ, 1988, pp. 25–26.

It seems fairly obvious that the larger $t_{obt}$ is, the more likely $H_0$ will be rejected. Hence, anything that increases the likelihood of obtaining high values of $t_{obt}$ will result in a more powerful *t* test. This can occur in several ways. First, the larger the real effect of the independent variable is, the more likely $\overline{X}_{obt} - \mu$, $\overline{D}_{obt} - 0$, or $(\overline{X}_1 - \overline{X}_2) - 0$ will be large. Since these difference scores are in the numerator of the *t* equation, it follows that *the greater the effect of the independent variable, the higher the power of the t test* (other factors held constant). Of course, we don't know before doing the experiment what the actual effect of the independent variable is. If we did, then why do the experiment? Nevertheless, this analysis is useful because it suggests that, when designing an experiment, it is desirable to use the level of independent variable that the experimenter believes is the most effective to maximize the chances of detecting its effect. This analysis further suggests that, given meager resources for conducting an experiment, the experiment may still be powerful enough to detect the effect if the independent variable has a large effect.

The denominator of the *t* equation varies as a function of sample size and sample variability. As sample size increases, the denominator decreases. Therefore,

$$\sqrt{\frac{SS}{N(N-1)}}, \quad \sqrt{\frac{SS_D}{N(N-1)}}, \quad \text{and} \quad \sqrt{\frac{SS_1 + SS_2}{n(n-1)}}$$

decrease, causing $t_{obt}$ to increase. *Thus, increasing sample size increases the power of the t test.*

The denominator also varies as a function of sample variability. In the single sample case, $SS$ is the measure of variability. $SS_D$ in the correlated groups experiments and $SS_1 + SS_2$ in the independent groups experiments reflect the variability. As the variability increases, the denominator in each case also increases, causing $t_{obt}$ to decrease. *Thus, high sample variability decreases power.* Therefore, it is desirable to *decrease* variability as much as possible. One way to decrease variability is to carefully control the experimental conditions. For example, in a reaction-time experiment, the experimenter might use a warning signal that directly precedes the stimulus to which the subject must respond. In this way, variability due to attention lapses could be eliminated. Another way is to use the appropriate experimental design. For example, in certain situations, using a correlated groups design rather than an independent groups design will decrease variability.

## CORRELATED GROUPS AND INDEPENDENT GROUPS DESIGNS COMPARED

You are probably aware that many of the hypotheses presented in illustrative examples could have been investigated with either the correlated groups or the independent groups design. For instance, in Practice Problem 14.1, we presented an experiment that was conducted to evaluate the effect of a conservation campaign on gasoline consumption. The experiment used a correlated groups design, and the data were analyzed with the *t* test for correlated groups. For convenience, the data and analysis are provided again in Table 14.6.

t a b l e 14.6   Data and analysis from conservation campaign experiment

| Family | Before the Campaign (gal) (1) | After the Campaign (gal) (2) | Difference $D$ | $D^2$ |
|---|---|---|---|---|
| A | 55 | 48 | 7 | 49 |
| B | 43 | 38 | 5 | 25 |
| C | 51 | 53 | −2 | 4 |
| D | 62 | 58 | 4 | 16 |
| E | 35 | 36 | −1 | 1 |
| F | 48 | 42 | 6 | 36 |
| G | 58 | 55 | 3 | 9 |
| H | 45 | 40 | 5 | 25 |
| I | 48 | 49 | −1 | 1 |
| J | 54 | 50 | 4 | 16 |
| K | 56 | 58 | −2 | 4 |
| L | 32 | 25 | 7 | 49 |
| | | | 35 | 235 |

$$N = 12 \qquad \overline{D}_{\text{obt}} = \frac{\Sigma D}{N} = \frac{35}{12} = 2.917$$

$$t_{\text{obt}} = \frac{\overline{D}_{\text{obt}} - \mu_D}{\sqrt{\dfrac{SS_D}{N(N-1)}}} \qquad SS_D = \Sigma D^2 - \frac{(\Sigma D)^2}{N}$$

$$= \frac{2.917 - 0}{\sqrt{\dfrac{132.917}{12(11)}}} \qquad\qquad = 235 - \frac{(35)^2}{12}$$

$$= 2.907 \qquad\qquad\qquad = 132.917$$

$$= 2.91$$

From Table D, with df = 11 and $\alpha = 0.05_{2\text{ tail}}$,

$$t_{\text{crit}} = \pm 2.201$$

Since $|t_{\text{obt}}| > 2.201$, we rejected $H_0$ and concluded that the conservation campaign does indeed affect gasoline consumption. It significantly lowered the amount of gasoline used.

The conservation campaign could also have been evaluated using the independent groups design. Instead of using the same subjects in each condition, there would be two groups of subjects. One group would be monitored before the campaign and the other group monitored after the campaign. To evaluate the null hypothesis, each sample would be treated as an independent sample randomly selected from populations where $\mu_1 = \mu_2$. The basic statistic calculated would be $\overline{X}_1 - \overline{X}_2$. For the sake of comparison, let's analyze the conservation campaign data as though they were collected by using an independent groups design.

344 CHAPTER 14 Student's *t* Test for Correlated and Independent Groups

Assume there are two different groups. The families in group 1 (before) are monitored for 1 month with respect to the amount of gasoline used before the conservation campaign is conducted, whereas the families in group 2 are monitored for 1 month after the campaign has been conducted.

Since $n_1 = n_2$, we can use the $t_{obt}$ equation for equal $n$. In this experiment, $n_1 = n_2 = 12$. Solving for $\overline{X}_1$, $\overline{X}_2$, $SS_1$, and $SS_2$, we obtain

$$\overline{X}_1 = \frac{\Sigma X_1}{n_1} = \frac{587}{12} = 48.917 \qquad \overline{X}_2 = \frac{\Sigma X_2}{n_2} = \frac{552}{12} = 46.000$$

$$SS_1 = \Sigma X_1^2 - \frac{(\Sigma X_1)^2}{n_1} \qquad\qquad SS_2 = \Sigma X_2^2 - \frac{(\Sigma X_2)^2}{n_2}$$

$$= 29{,}617 - \frac{(587)^2}{12} \qquad\qquad = 26{,}496 - \frac{(552)^2}{12}$$

$$= 902.917 \qquad\qquad\qquad\qquad = 1104$$

Substituting these values into the equation for $t_{obt}$ with equal $n$, we obtain

$$t_{obt} = \frac{\overline{X}_1 - \overline{X}_2}{\sqrt{\dfrac{SS_1 + SS_2}{n(n-1)}}} = \frac{48.917 - 46.000}{\sqrt{\dfrac{902.917 + 1104}{12(11)}}} = 0.748 = 0.75$$

From Table D, with df $= N - 2 = 24 - 2 = 22$ and $\alpha = 0.05_{2\,tail}$,

$$t_{crit} = \pm 2.074$$

Since $|t_{obt}| < 2.074$, we retain $H_0$.

Something seems strange here. When the data were collected with a correlated groups design, we were able to reject $H_0$. However, with an independent groups design, we were unable to reject $H_0$, even though the data were identical. Why? The correlated groups design allows us to use the subjects as their own control. This maximizes the possibility that there will be a high correlation between the scores in the two conditions. In the present illustration, Pearson $r$ for the correlation between the paired before and after scores equals 0.938. When the correlation is high,* the difference scores will be much less variable than the original scores. For example, consider the scores of families A and L. Family A uses quite a lot of gasoline (55 gallons), whereas family L uses much less (32 gallons). As a result of the conservation campaign, the scores of both families decrease by 7 gallons. Their difference scores are identical (7). There is no variability between the difference scores for these families, whereas there is great variability between their raw scores. It is the potential for a high correlation and, hence, decreased variability that causes the correlated groups design to be potentially more powerful than the independent groups design. The decreased variability in the present illustration can be seen most clearly by viewing the two solutions side by side. This is shown in Table 14.7.

The two equations yield the same values except for $SS_D$ in the correlated groups design and $SS_1 + SS_2$ in the independent groups design. $SS_D$ is a measure of the variability of the difference scores. $SS_1 + SS_2$ are measures of the variability of the raw scores. $SS_D = 132.917$, whereas $SS_1 + SS_2 = 2006.917$; $SS_D$ is

---

*See Note 14.4 for a direct comparison between the two *t* equations that involve Pearson *r*.

t a b l e 14.7   Solutions for correlated and independent groups designs

| Correlated Groups | Independent Groups |
|---|---|
| $t_{obt} = \dfrac{\overline{D}}{\sqrt{\dfrac{SS_D}{N(N-1)}}}$ | $t_{obt} = \dfrac{\overline{X}_1 - \overline{X}_2}{\sqrt{\dfrac{SS_1 + SS_2}{n(n-1)}}}$ |
| $= \dfrac{2.917}{\sqrt{\dfrac{132.917}{12(11)}}}$ | $= \dfrac{2.917}{\sqrt{\dfrac{902.917 + 1104}{12(11)}}}$ |
| $= 2.91$ | $= 0.75$ |

much smaller than $SS_1 + SS_2$. It is this decreased variability that causes $t_{obt}$ to be greater in the correlated groups analysis.

If the correlated groups design is potentially more powerful, why not always use this design? First, the independent groups design is much more efficient from a df per measurement analysis. The degrees of freedom are important because the higher the df, the lower $t_{crit}$. In the present illustration, for the correlated groups design, there were 24 measurements taken, but only 11 df resulted. For the independent groups design, there were 24 measurements and 22 df. Thus, the independent groups design results in twice the df for the same number of measurements.

Second, many experiments preclude using the same subject in both conditions. For example, suppose we are interested in investigating whether men and women differ in aggressiveness. Obviously, the same subject could not be used in both conditions. Sometimes the effect of the first condition persists too long over time. If the experiment calls for the two conditions to be administered closely in time, it may not be possible to run the same subject in both conditions without the first condition affecting performance in the second condition. Often, when the subject is run in the first condition, he or she is "used up" or can't be run in the second condition. This is particularly true in learning experiments. For example, if we are interested in the effects of exercise on learning how to ski, we know that once the subjects have learned to ski, they can't be used in the second condition because they already know how to ski. When the same subject can't be used in the two conditions, then it is still possible to match subjects. However, matching is time-consuming and costly. Furthermore, it is often true that the experimenter doesn't know which are the important variables for matching so as to produce a higher correlation. For all these reasons, the independent groups design is used more often than the correlated groups design.

# EVALUATING THE EFFECT OF THE INDEPENDENT VARIABLE USING CONFIDENCE INTERVALS—INDEPENDENT GROUPS DESIGN

Thus far in the inferential statistics part of the textbook, we have been evaluating the effect of the independent variable by determining if it is reasonable to reject the null hypothesis, given the data of the experiment. If it is reasonable to reject $H_0$, then we can conclude by affirming that the independent variable has a real effect. We will call this the null-hypothesis approach. A limitation of the null-hypothesis approach is that by itself it does not tell us anything about the size or the effect.

An alternative approach also allows us to determine if it is reasonable to affirm that the independent variable has a real effect and at the same time gives us an estimate of the size of the real effect. This method uses confidence intervals. Not surprisingly, we will call this method the confidence-interval approach. We will illustrate this confidence-interval approach using the two-group, independent groups design.

You will recall that in Chapter 13, when we were discussing the t test for single samples, we showed how to construct confidence intervals for the population mean $\mu$. Typically, we constructed the 95% or the 99% confidence interval for $\mu$. Of course in that chapter, we were discussing single sample experiments. In the two-group, independent groups design, we have not one but two samples, and each sample is considered to be a random sample from its own population. We have designated the population mean of sample 1 as $\mu_1$ and the population mean of sample 2 as $\mu_2$. The difference $\mu_1 - \mu_2$ is a measure of the real effect of the independent variable. If there is no real effect, then $\mu_1 = \mu_2$ and $\mu_1 - \mu_2 = 0$. By constructing the 95% or 99% confidence interval for the difference $\mu_1 - \mu_2$, we can determine if it is reasonable to affirm that there is a real effect, and if so, we can estimate its size.

## Constructing the 95% Confidence Interval for $\mu_1 - \mu_2$

Constructing the 95% or 99% confidence interval for $\mu_1 - \mu_2$ is very much like constructing these intervals for $\mu$. We will illustrate by comparing the equations for both used to construct the 95% confidence interval. These equations are shown in Table 14.8.

**t a b l e   1 4 . 8** Comparison of equations for constructing the 95% confidence interval for $\mu$ and $\mu_1 - \mu_2$

| **Single Sample Experiment** | **Two Sample Experiment** |
|---|---|
| **95% Confidence Interval for $\mu$** | **95% Confidence Interval for $\mu_1 - \mu_2$** |
| $\mu_{lower} = \overline{X}_{obt} - s_{\overline{X}}t_{0.025}$ | $\mu_{lower} = (\overline{X}_1 - \overline{X}_2) - s_{\overline{X}_1 - \overline{x}_2}t_{0.025}$ |
| $\mu_{upper} = \overline{X}_{obt} + s_{\overline{X}}t_{0.025}$ | $\mu_{upper} = (\overline{X}_1 - \overline{X}_2) + s_{\overline{X}_1 - \overline{x}_2}t_{0.025}$ |
| where $s_{\overline{X}} = \dfrac{s}{\sqrt{n}}$ | where $s_{\overline{X}_1 - \overline{x}_2} = \sqrt{\left(\dfrac{SS_1 + SS_2}{n_1 + n_2 - 2}\right)\left(\dfrac{1}{n_1} + \dfrac{1}{n_2}\right)}$ |

As you can see from the table, the equations for constructing the 95% confidence interval for $\mu$ and for $\mu_1 - \mu_2$ are identical, except that in the two-sample experiment, $(\overline{X}_1 - \overline{X}_2)$ is used instead of $\overline{X}_{obt}$ and $s_{\overline{X}_1} - s_{\overline{X}_2}$ is used instead of $s_{\overline{X}}$.

So far, we have been rather theoretical. Let's now try an example. Let's assume we are interested in analyzing the data from hormone X experiment using the confidence-interval approach. For your convenience, we have repeated the experiment below.

A physiologist has conducted an experiment to evaluate the effect of hormone X on sexual behavior. Ten male rats were injected with hormone X, and 10 other male rats received a placebo injection. The animals were then placed in individual housing with a sexually receptive female. The number of matings were counted over a 20-minute period.

The results are shown in Table 14.9

**t a b l e 14.9**  Results from hormone X experiment

| Group 1, Hormone X | Group 2, Placebo |
|:---:|:---:|
| $X_1$ | $X_2$ |
| 8 | 5 |
| 10 | 6 |
| 12 | 3 |
| 6 | 4 |
| 6 | 7 |
| 7 | 8 |
| 9 | 6 |
| 8 | 5 |
| 7 | 4 |
| 11 | 8 |
| 84 | 744 |
| $n_1 = 10$ | $n_2 = 10$ |
| $\Sigma X_1 = 84$ | $\Sigma X_2 = 56$ |
| $\overline{X}_1 = 84$ | $\overline{X}_2 = 84$ |
| $\Sigma X_1^2 = 744$ | $\Sigma X_2^2 = 340$ |

Evaluate the data of this experiment by constructing the 95% confidence interval for $\mu_1 - \mu_2$. What is your conclusion?

The equations used to construct the 95% confidence interval are

$$\mu_{\text{lower}} = (\overline{X}_1 - \overline{X}_2) - s_{\overline{X}_1 - \overline{X}_2} t_{0.025} \text{ and } \mu_{\text{upper}} = (\overline{X}_1 - \overline{X}_2) + s_{\overline{X}_1 - \overline{X}_2} t_{0.025}$$

Solving first for $SS_1$ and $SS_2$,

$$SS_1 = \Sigma X_1^2 - \frac{(\Sigma X_1)^2}{n_1} \qquad SS_2 = \Sigma X_2^2 + \frac{(\Sigma X_2)^2}{n_2}$$

$$= 744 - \frac{(84)^2}{10} \qquad = 340 + \frac{(56)^2}{10}$$

$$= 38.4 \qquad = 26.4$$

Solving next for $s_{\overline{X}_1 - s_{\overline{X}_2}}$,

$$s_{\overline{X}_1 - \overline{X}_2} = \sqrt{\left(\frac{SS_1 + SS_2}{n_1 + n_2 - 2}\right)\left(\frac{1}{n_1} + \frac{1}{n_2}\right)}$$

$$= \sqrt{\left(\frac{38.4 + 26.4}{10 + 10 - 2}\right)\left(\frac{1}{10} + \frac{1}{10}\right)} = 0.849$$

The last value we need in order to compute $\mu_{\text{lower}}$ and $\mu_{\text{upper}}$ is the value of $t_{0.025}$. From Table D, with $\alpha = 0.025_{1\text{ tail}}$ and df $= N - 2 = 20 - 2 = 18$,

$$t_{0.025} = 2.101$$

We now have all the values we need to compute $\mu_{\text{lower}}$ and $\mu_{\text{upper}}$. For convenience, we've listed them again here. $\overline{X}_1 = 8.4$, $\overline{X}_2 = 5.6$, $s_{\overline{X}_1 - \overline{X}_2} = 0.849$, and $t_{0.025} = 2.101$.

Substituting these values in the equations for $\mu_{\text{lower}}$ and $\mu_{\text{upper}}$, we obtain

$$\mu_{\text{lower}} = (\overline{X}_1 - \overline{X}_2) - s_{\overline{X}_1 - \overline{X}_2} t_{0.025} \qquad \mu_{\text{upper}} = (\overline{X}_1 - \overline{X}_2) + s_{\overline{X}_1 - \overline{X}_2} t_{0.025}$$
$$= (8.4 - 5.6) - 0.849(2.101) \qquad = (8.4 - 5.6) + 0.849(2.101)$$
$$= 1.02 \qquad\qquad\qquad = 4.58$$

Thus, the 95% confidence interval for $\mu_1 - \mu_2 = 1.02 - 4.58$.

## Conclusion Based on the Obtained Confidence Interval

Having computed the 95% confidence interval for $\mu_1 - \mu_2$, we can both come to a conclusion with regard to the null hypothesis and also give an estimate of the size of the real effect of hormone X. The 95% confidence interval corresponds to $\alpha = 0.05_{2\text{ tail}}$ (0.025 under each tail; see Figure 13.3, p. 309). The nondirectional null hypothesis predicts that $\mu_1 - \mu_2 = 0$. Since the obtained 95% confidence interval does not include a value of 0, we can reject the null hypothesis and affirm that hormone X appears to have a real effect. This is the conclusion we reached when we analyzed the data using the null-hypothesis approach with $\alpha = 0.05_{2\text{ tail}}$.

In addition, we have an estimate of the size of the real effect. We are 95% confident that the range of 1.02–4.58 contains the real effect of hormone X. If so, then the real effect of hormone X is to cause 1.0–4.58 more matings than the placebo. Note that if the interval contained the value 0, we would not be able to reject $H_0$, in which case we couldn't affirm that hormone X has a real effect.

## Constructing the 99% Confidence Interval for $\mu_1 - \mu_2$

Constructing the 99% confidence interval for $\mu_1 - \mu_2$ is very much like constructing the 95% confidence interval. The one difference is that for the 99% confidence interval we use $t_{0.005}$ in the equations for the $\mu_{\text{lower}}$ and $\mu_{\text{upper}}$ instead of $t_{0.025}$. This corresponds to $\alpha = 0.01_{2\text{ tail}}$. The equations used to compute the 99% confidence interval are shown here.

$$\mu_{\text{lower}} = (\overline{X}_1 - \overline{X}_2) - s_{\overline{X}_1 - \overline{X}_2} t_{0.005} \text{ and } \mu_{\text{upper}} = (\overline{X}_1 - \overline{X}_2) + s_{\overline{X}_1 - \overline{X}_2} t_{0.005}$$

For the hormone X experiment, $\overline{X}_1 = 8.4$, $\overline{X}_2 = 5.6$, and $s_{\overline{X}_1 - \overline{X}_2} = 0.849$. From Table D, with $\alpha = 0.005_{1\text{ tail}}$ and df $= N - 2 = 20 - 2 = 18$,

$$t_{0.005} = 2.878$$

Using these equations with the data of the hormone X experiment, we obtain

$$\mu_{\text{lower}} = (\overline{X}_1 - \overline{X}_2) - s_{\overline{X}_1 - \overline{X}_2} t_{0.005} \qquad \mu_{\text{upper}} = (\overline{X}_1 - \overline{X}_2) + s_{\overline{X}_1 - \overline{X}_2} t_{0.005}$$
$$= (8.4 - 5.6) - 0.849(2.878) \qquad = (8.4 - 5.6) + 0.849(2.878)$$
$$= 0.36 \qquad\qquad\qquad = 5.24$$

Thus, the 99% confidence interval for the data of the hormone X experiment is 0.36–5.24. Since the obtained 99% confidence interval does not contain the value 0, we can reject $H_0$ at $\alpha = 0.01_{2\text{ tail}}$. In addition, we are 99% confident that the size of the real effect of hormone X falls in the interval of 0.36–5.24. If this interval does contain the real effect, then the real effect is somewhere between 0.36 and 5.24 more matings than the placebo. As was true for the 95% confidence interval, if the 99% confidence interval did contain the value 0, we would not be able to reject $H_0$, and therefore we couldn't affirm $H_1$. Notice also that the 99% confidence interval (0.36–5.24) is larger than the 95% confidence interval (1.02–4.58). This is what we would expect from our discussion in Chapter 13, because the larger the interval, the more confidence we have that it contains the population value being estimated.

# SUMMARY

In this chapter, we have discussed the $t$ test for correlated and independent groups. We pointed out that the $t$ test for correlated groups was really just a special case of the $t$ test for single samples. In the correlated groups design, the differences between paired scores are analyzed. If the independent variable has no effect and chance alone is responsible for the difference scores, then they can be considered a random sample from a population of difference scores where $\mu_D = 0$ and $\sigma_D$ is unknown. But these are the exact conditions in which the $t$ test for single samples applies. The only change is that, in the correlated groups design, we analyze difference scores, whereas in the single sample design, we analyze raw scores. After presenting some illustrative and practice problems, we concluded our discussion of the $t$ test for correlated groups by comparing it with the sign test. We showed that although both are appropriate for the correlated groups design, as long as its assumptions are met, the $t$ test should be used because it is more sensitive.

The $t$ test for independent groups is used when there are two independent groups in the experiment. The statistic that is analyzed is the difference between the means of the two samples ($\overline{X}_1 - \overline{X}_2$). The scores of sample 1 can be considered a random sample from a population having a mean $\mu_1$ and a standard deviation $\sigma_1$. The scores of sample 2 are a random sample from a population having a mean $\mu_2$ and a standard deviation $\sigma_2$.

If the independent variable has a real effect, then the difference between sample means is due to random sampling from populations where $\mu_1 \neq \mu_2$. Changing the level of the independent variable is assumed to affect the means of the populations but not their standard deviations or variances. If the independent variable has no effect and chance alone is responsible for the differences between the two samples, then the difference between sample means is due to random sampling from populations where $\mu_1 = \mu_2$. Under these conditions, the sampling distribution of $\overline{X}_1 - \overline{X}_2$ has a mean of zero and a standard deviation whose value depends on knowing the variance of the populations from which the samples were taken. Since this value is never known, the $z$ test cannot be used. However, we can estimate the variance using a weighted estimate taken from both samples. When this is done, the resulting statistic is $t_{obt}$.

The $t$ statistic, then, is also used for analyzing the data from the two-sample, independent groups experiment. The sampling distribution of $t$ for this design is the same as for the single sample design, except the degrees of freedom are different. In the independent groups design, df $= N - 2$. After presenting some illustrative and practice problems, we discussed the assumptions underlying the $t$ test for independent groups. We pointed out that this test requires that (1) the raw-score populations be normally distributed and (2) there be homogeneity of variance. We also pointed out that the $t$ test is robust with regard to violations of the population normality and homogeneity of variance assumptions. In addition to determining whether there is a significant effect, it is also important to determine the size of the effect. In an independent groups experiment, the size of effect of the independent variable may be estimated by computing $\hat{\omega}^2$.

Next, we discussed the power of the $t$ test. We showed that its power varies directly with the size of the real effect of the independent variable and the $N$ of the experiment but varies inversely with the variability of the sample scores.

Then, we compared the correlated groups and independent groups designs. When the correlation between paired scores is high, the correlated groups design is more sensitive than the independent groups design. However, it is easier and more efficient regarding degrees of freedom to conduct an independent groups experiment. In addition, there are many situations in which the correlated groups design is inappropriate.

Finally, we showed how to evaluate the effect of the independent variable using a confidence-interval approach in experiments employing the two-group, independent groups design. This approach is more complicated than the basic hypothesis testing approach used throughout the inference part this textbook but has the advantage that it allows both the evaluation of $H_0$ and an estimation of the size of effect of the independent variable.

## IMPORTANT TERMS

Confidence-interval approach
(p. 346)
Correlated groups design (p. 323)
Degrees of freedom (p. 334)
Difference between sample means
   (p. 333)
Difference scores (p. 324)

Homogeneity of variance (p. 338)
Independent groups design (p. 329)
Mean of the difference scores (p. 324)
Null-hypothesis approach (p. 346)
Sampling distribution of the
   difference between sample means
   (p. 331)

Size of effect (p. 339)
*t* test for correlated groups (p. 323)
*t* test for independent groups (p. 330)
Variability (p. 342)

## QUESTIONS AND PROBLEMS

1. Identify or define the terms in the Important Terms section.
2. Discuss the advantages of the two-condition experiment compared with the advantages of the single sample experiment.
3. The *t* test for correlated groups can be thought of as a special case of the *t* test for single samples, discussed in the previous chapter. Explain.
4. What is the main advantage of using the *t* test for correlated groups over using the sign test to analyze data from a correlated groups experiment?
5. What are the characteristics of the sampling distribution of the difference between sample means?
6. Why is the *z* test for independent groups never used?
7. What is estimated in the *t* test for independent groups? How is the estimate obtained?
8. It is said that the variance of the sample data has an important bearing on the power of the *t* test. Is this statement true? Explain.
9. What are the advantages and disadvantages of using a correlated groups design as compared with using an independent groups design?
10. What are the assumptions underlying the *t* test for independent groups?
11. Having just made what you believe to be a Type II error, using an independent groups design and a *t* test analysis, name all the things you might do in the next experiment to reduce the probability of a Type II error.
12. Is the size of effect of the independent variable important? Explain.
13. If the effect of the independent variable is significant, does that necessarily mean the effect is a large one? Explain.

*For each of the following problems, unless otherwise told, assume normality in the population.*

14. You are interested in determining whether an experimental birth control pill has the side effect of changing blood pressure. You randomly sample ten women from the city in which you live. You give five of them a placebo for a month and then measure their diastolic blood pressure. Then you switch them to the birth control pill for a month and again measure their blood pressure. The other five women receive the same treatment except they are given the birth control pill first for a month, followed by the placebo for a month. The blood pressure readings are shown here. Note that to safeguard the women from unwanted pregnancy, another means of birth control that does not interact with the pill was used for the duration of the experiment.

| | **Diastolic Blood Pressure** | |
| --- | --- | --- |
| **Subject No.** | **Birth control pill** | **Placebo** |
| 1 | 108 | 102 |
| 2 | 76 | 68 |
| 3 | 69 | 66 |
| 4 | 78 | 71 |
| 5 | 74 | 76 |
| 6 | 85 | 80 |
| 7 | 79 | 82 |
| 8 | 78 | 79 |
| 9 | 80 | 78 |
| 10 | 81 | 85 |

a. What is the alternative hypothesis? Assume a nondirectional hypothesis is appropriate.
b. What is the null hypothesis?
c. What do you conclude? Use $\alpha = 0.01_{2\ tail}$.
social, biological, health

15. Based on previous research and sound theoretical considerations, a cognitive psychologist believes that memory for pictures is superior to memory for words. To test this hypothesis, the psychologist performs an experiment in which students from an introductory psychology class are used as subjects. Eight randomly selected students view 30 slides with nouns printed on them, and another group of eight randomly selected students views 30 slides with pictures of the same nouns. Each slide contains either one noun or one picture and is viewed for 4 seconds. After viewing the slides, subjects are given a recall test, and the number of correctly remembered items is measured. The data follow:

| No. of Pictures Recalled | No. of Nouns Recalled |
|---|---|
| 18 | 12 |
| 21 | 9 |
| 14 | 21 |
| 25 | 17 |
| 23 | 16 |
| 19 | 10 |
| 26 | 19 |
| 15 | 22 |

a. What is the alternative hypothesis? Assume that a directional hypothesis is warranted.
b. What is the null hypothesis?
c. Using $\alpha = 0.05_{1\ tail}$, what is your conclusion?
d. Estimate the size of the real effect. Using Cohen's criterion, is the effect a large one?
cognitive

16. A nurse was hired by a governmental ecology agency to investigate the impact of a lead smelter on the level of lead in the blood of children living near the smelter. Ten children were chosen at random from those living near the smelter. A comparison group of seven children was randomly selected from those living in an area relatively free from possible lead pollution. Blood samples were taken from the children and lead levels determined. The following are the results (scores are in micrograms of lead per 100 milliliters of blood):

| Lead Levels | |
|---|---|
| *Children living near smelter* | *Children living in unpolluted area* |
| 18 | 9 |
| 16 | 13 |
| 21 | 8 |
| 14 | 15 |
| 17 | 17 |
| 19 | 12 |
| 22 | 11 |
| 24 | |
| 15 | |
| 18 | |

a. Using $\alpha = 0.01_{1\ tail}$, what do you conclude?
b. Estimate the size of the real effect. Using Cohen's criterion, is the effect a small one?
health

17. The manager of the cosmetics section of a large department store wants to determine whether newspaper advertising really does affect sales. For her experiment, she randomly selects 15 items currently in stock and proceeds to establish a baseline. The 15 items are priced at their usual competitive values, and the quantity of each item sold for a 1-week period is recorded.

Then, without changing their price, she places a large ad in the newspaper, advertising the 15 items. Again, she records the quantity sold for a 1-week period. The results follow.

| Item | No. Sold Before Ad | No. Sold After Ad |
|------|------|------|
| 1 | 25 | 32 |
| 2 | 18 | 24 |
| 3 | 3 | 7 |
| 4 | 42 | 40 |
| 5 | 16 | 19 |
| 6 | 20 | 25 |
| 7 | 23 | 23 |
| 8 | 32 | 35 |
| 9 | 60 | 65 |
| 10 | 40 | 43 |
| 11 | 27 | 28 |
| 12 | 7 | 11 |
| 13 | 13 | 12 |
| 14 | 23 | 32 |
| 15 | 16 | 28 |

Using $\alpha = 0.05_{2\,tail}$, what do you conclude? I/O

18. Since muscle tension in the head region has been associated with tension headaches, you reason that if the muscle tension could be reduced, perhaps the headaches would decrease or go away altogether. You design an experiment in which nine subjects with tension headaches participate. The subjects keep daily logs of the number of headaches they experience during a 2-week base-line period. Then you train them to lower their muscle tension in the head region, using a biofeedback device. For this experiment, the biofeedback device is connected to the frontalis muscle, a muscle in the forehead region. The device tells the subject the amount of tension in the muscle to which it is attached (in this case, frontalis) and helps them achieve low tension levels. After 6 weeks of training, during which the subjects have become successful at maintaining low frontalis muscle tension, they again keep a 2-week log of the number of headaches experienced. The following are the number of headaches recorded during each 2-week period.

| Subject No. | No. of Headaches Baseline | After training |
|------|------|------|
| 1 | 17 | 3 |
| 2 | 13 | 7 |
| 3 | 6 | 2 |
| 4 | 5 | 3 |
| 5 | 5 | 6 |
| 6 | 10 | 2 |
| 7 | 8 | 1 |
| 8 | 6 | 0 |
| 9 | 7 | 2 |

a. Using $\alpha = 0.05_{2\,tail}$, what do you conclude? Assume the sampling distribution of the mean of the difference scores $(\overline{D})$ is normally distributed. Assume a nondirectional hypothesis is appropriate because there is insufficient empirical basis to warrant a directional hypothesis.

b. If the sampling distribution of $\overline{D}$ is not normally distributed, what other test could you use to analyze the data? What would your conclusion be? clinical, health

19. There is an interpretation difficulty with Problem 18. It is clear that the headaches decreased significantly. However, it is possible that the decrease was not due to the biofeedback training but rather to some other aspect of the situation, such as the attention shown to the subjects. What is really needed is a group to control for this possibility. Assume another group of nine headache patients was run at the same time as the group in Problem 18. This group was treated in the same way except the subjects did not receive any training involving biofeedback. They just talked with you about their headaches each week for 6 weeks, and you showed them lots of warmth, loving care, and attention. The number of headaches for the baseline and 2-week follow-up period for the control group were as follows:

| Subject No. | No. of Headaches | |
| --- | --- | --- |
| | *Baseline* | *Follow-up* |
| 1 | 5 | 4 |
| 2 | 8 | 9 |
| 3 | 14 | 12 |
| 4 | 16 | 15 |
| 5 | 6 | 4 |
| 6 | 5 | 3 |
| 7 | 8 | 7 |
| 8 | 10 | 6 |
| 9 | 9 | 7 |

Evaluate the effect of these other factors, such as attention, on the incidence of headaches. Use $\alpha = 0.05_{2\ tail}$. clinical, health

20. Since the control group in Problem 19 also showed significant reductions in headaches, the interpretation of the results in Problem 18 is in doubt. Did relaxation training contribute to the headache decrease, or was the decrease due solely to other factors, such as attention? To answer this question, we can compare the change scores between the two groups. These scores are shown here:

| Headache Change Scores | |
| --- | --- |
| *Relaxation training group* | *Control group* |
| 14 | 1 |
| 6 | −1 |
| 4 | 2 |
| 2 | 1 |
| −1 | 2 |
| 8 | 2 |
| 7 | 1 |
| 6 | 4 |
| 5 | 2 |

What is your conclusion? Use $\alpha = 0.05_{2\ tail}$. clinical, health

21. The director of human resources at a large company is considering hiring part-time employees to fill jobs previously staffed with full-time workers. However, he wonders if doing so will affect productivity. Therefore, he conducts an experiment to evaluate the idea before implementing it factory-wide. Six full-time job openings, from the parts manufacturing division of the company, are each filled with two employees hired to work half-time. The output of these six half-time pairs is compared with the output of a randomly selected sample of six full-time employees from the same division. Note that all employees in the experiment are engaged in manufacturing the same parts. The average number of parts produced per day by the half-time pairs and full-time workers is shown here:

| Parts Produced per Day | |
| --- | --- |
| *Half-time pairs* | *Full-time workers* |
| 24 | 20 |
| 26 | 28 |
| 46 | 40 |
| 32 | 36 |
| 30 | 24 |
| 36 | 30 |

Does the hiring of part-time workers affect productivity? Use $\alpha = 0.05_{2\ tail}$ in making your decision. I/O

22. On the basis of her experience with clients, a clinical psychologist thinks that depression may affect sleep. She decides to test this idea. The sleep of nine depressed patients and eight normal controls is monitored for three successive nights. The average number of hours slept by each subject during the last two nights is shown in the following table:

| Hours of Sleep | |
|---|---|
| *Depressed patients* | *Normal controls* |
| 7.1 | 8.2 |
| 6.8 | 7.5 |
| 6.7 | 7.7 |
| 7.3 | 7.8 |
| 7.5 | 8.0 |
| 6.2 | 7.4 |
| 6.9 | 7.3 |
| 6.5 | 6.5 |
| 7.2 | |

a. Is the clinician correct? Use $\alpha = 0.05_{2\,tail}$ in making your decision.
b. If the effect is significant, estimate the size of the effect. Using Cohen's criterion, is the effect a large one? clinical, health

23. An educator wants to determine whether early exposure to school will affect IQ. He enlists the aid of the parents of 12 pairs of preschool-age identical twins who agree to let their twins participate in this experiment. One member of each twin pair is enrolled in preschool for 2 years while the other member of each pair remains at home. At the end of the 2 years, the IQs of all the children are measured. The results follow.

| | IQ | |
|---|---|---|
| **Pair** | *Twins at preschool* | *Twins at home* |
| 1 | 110 | 114 |
| 2 | 121 | 118 |
| 3 | 107 | 103 |
| 4 | 117 | 112 |
| 5 | 115 | 117 |
| 6 | 112 | 106 |
| 7 | 130 | 125 |
| 8 | 116 | 113 |
| 9 | 111 | 109 |
| 10 | 120 | 122 |
| 11 | 117 | 116 |
| 12 | 106 | 104 |

Does early exposure to school affect IQ? Use $\alpha = 0.05_{2\,tail}$. cognitive, developmental, education

24. Researchers at a leading university were interested in the effect of sleep on memory consolidation. Twenty-four student volunteers from an introductory psychology course were randomly assigned to either a "Sleep" or "No-Sleep" group, such that there were 12 students in each group. On the first day, all students were flashed pictures of 15 different objects, for 200 milliseconds each, on a computer screen and asked to remember as many of the objects as possible. That night, the "Sleep" group got an ordinary night's sleep. The "No-Sleep" group was kept awake until the second night. All subjects got an ordinary night's sleep on the second and third nights. On the fourth day, all subjects were tested to see how many of the original 15 objects they remembered. The following are the number of objects remembered by each subject on the test:

| Sleep Group | No-Sleep Group |
|---|---|
| 14 | 8 |
| 13 | 9 |
| 8 | 6 |
| 9 | 13 |
| 11 | 7 |
| 10 | 9 |
| 9 | 10 |
| 13 | 12 |
| 12 | 8 |
| 11 | 11 |
| 14 | 9 |
| 13 | 12 |

a. Using $\alpha = 0.05_{2\,tail}$, what do you conclude?
b. Using the confidence-interval approach, construct the 95% confidence interval for $\mu_1 - \mu_2$. What do you conclude regarding $H_0$? What is your estimate of the size of the effect?
c. Using the confidence-interval approach, construct the 99% confidence interval for $\mu_1 - \mu_2$. What do you conclude regarding $H_0$? What is your estimate of the size of the effect? cognitive

25. Developmental psychologists at a prominent California university conducted a longitudinal study investigating the effect of high levels of curiosity in early childhood on intelligence. The local population of 3-year-olds was screened via a test battery assessing curiosity. Twelve of the 3-year-olds scoring in the upper 90% of this variable were given an IQ test at age 3 and again at age 11. The following IQ scores were obtained.

| Subject Number | IQ (Age 3) | IQ (Age 11) |
|---|---|---|
| 1 | 100 | 114 |
| 2 | 105 | 116 |
| 3 | 125 | 139 |
| 4 | 140 | 151 |
| 5 | 108 | 106 |
| 6 | 122 | 119 |
| 7 | 117 | 131 |
| 8 | 112 | 136 |
| 9 | 135 | 148 |
| 10 | 128 | 139 |
| 11 | 104 | 122 |
| 12 | 98 | 113 |

Using $\alpha = 0.01_{2\,tail}$, what do you conclude? In drawing your conclusion, assume that it is well established that IQ stays relatively constant over these years for individuals with average or below-average levels of curiosity. cognitive, developmental

26. Noting that women seem more interested in emotions than men, a researcher in the field of women's studies wondered if women recall emotional events better than men. She decides to gather some data on the matter. An experiment is conducted in which eight randomly selected men and women are shown 20 highly emotional photographs and then asked to recall them 1 week after the showing. The following recall data are obtained. Scores are percent correct; one man failed to show up for the recall test.

| Men | Women |
|---|---|
| 75 | 85 |
| 85 | 92 |
| 67 | 78 |
| 77 | 80 |
| 83 | 88 |
| 88 | 94 |
| 86 | 90 |
| | 89 |

Using $\alpha = 0.05_{2\,tail}$, what do you conclude? cognitive, social

27. Since the results of the experiment in Problem 26 were very close to being significant, the researcher decides to replicate that experiment, only this time increasing the power by increasing $N$. This study included 10 men and 10 women. The following results are obtained.

| Men | Women |
|---|---|
| 74 | 87 |
| 87 | 90 |
| 64 | 80 |
| 76 | 77 |
| 85 | 91 |
| 86 | 95 |
| 84 | 89 |
| 78 | 92 |
| 77 | 90 |
| 80 | 94 |

Using $\alpha = 0.05_{2\,tail}$, what do you conclude this time? cognitive, social

28. A physics instructor believes that natural lighting in classrooms improves student learning. He conducts an experiment in which he teaches the same physics unit to two groups of seven randomly assigned students in each group. Everything is similar for the groups, except that one of the groups receives the instruction in a classroom that admits a lot of natural light in addition to the incandescent lighting while the other uses a classroom with only incandescent lighting. At the end of the unit, both groups are given the same end-of-unit exam. There are 20 possible points

on the exam; the higher the score, the better the performance. The following scores are obtained.

| Natural Plus Incandescent Lighting | Incandescent Lighting Only |
|:---:|:---:|
| 16 | 17 |
| 18 | 13 |
| 14 | 12 |
| 17 | 14 |
| 16 | 13 |
| 19 | 15 |
| 17 | 14 |

Using $\alpha = 0.05_{2\,\text{tail}}$, what do you conclude? education

## NOTES

14.1 Most textbooks present two methods for finding $t_{\text{obt}}$ for the correlated groups design: (1) the direct-difference method and (2) a method that requires calculations of the degree of relationship (the correlation coefficient) existing between the two sets of raw scores. We have omitted the latter method because it is rarely used in practice and, in our opinion, confuses many students. The direct-difference method flows naturally and logically from the discussion of the *t* test for single samples. It is much easier to use and much more frequently employed in practice.

14.2 Occasionally, in a repeated measures experiment in which the alternative hypothesis is directional, the researcher may want to test whether the independent variable has an effect greater than some specified value other than 0. For example, assuming a directional hypothesis was justified in the present experiment, the researcher might want to test whether the average reward value of area A was greater than five bar presses per minute more than area B. In this case, the null hypothesis would be that the reward value of area A is not greater than five bar presses per minute more than area B. In this case, $\mu_D = 5$ rather than 0.

14.3 Occasionally, in an experiment involving independent groups, the alternative hypothesis is directional and specifies that the independent variable has an effect greater than some specified value other than 0. For example, in the "hormone X" experiment, assuming a directional hypothesis was legitimate, the physiologist might want to test whether hormone X has an average effect of over three matings more than the placebo. In this case, the null hypothesis would be that the average effect of the hormone X is ≤ three matings more than the placebo. We would test this hypothesis by assuming that the sample which received hormone X was a random sample from a population having a mean 3 units more than the population from which the placebo sample was taken. In this case, $\mu_{\overline{X}_1 - \overline{X}_2} = 3$, and

$$t_{\text{obt}} = \frac{(\overline{X}_1 - \overline{X}_2) - 3}{\sqrt{\left(\dfrac{SS_1 + SS_2}{n_1 + n_2 - 2}\right)\left(\dfrac{1}{n_1} + \dfrac{1}{n_2}\right)}}$$

14.4 Although we haven't previously presented the *t* equations in this form, the following can be shown:

| *t* Test for Independent Groups | | *t* Test for Correlated Groups |
|:---:|:---:|:---:|
| $t_{\text{obt}} = \dfrac{\overline{X}_1 - \overline{X}_2}{s_{\overline{X}_1 - \overline{X}_2}}$ | | $t_{\text{obt}} = \dfrac{\overline{D}}{s_D}$ |
| $= \dfrac{\overline{X}_1 - \overline{X}_2}{\sqrt{s_{\overline{X}_1}^2 + s_{\overline{X}_2}^2}}$ | | $= \dfrac{\overline{D}}{\sqrt{s_{\overline{X}_1}^2 + s_{\overline{X}_2}^2 - 2rs_{\overline{X}_1}s_{\overline{X}_2}}}$ |

Since $\overline{X}_1 - \overline{X}_2$ is equal to $\overline{D}$, the $t_{obt}$ equations for independent groups and correlated groups are identical except for the term $-2rs_{\overline{X}_1}s_{\overline{X}_2}$ in the denominator of the correlated groups equation. Thus, the higher sensitivity of the correlated groups design depends on the magnitude of $r$. The higher the value of $r$ is, the more sensitive the correlated groups design will be relative to the independent groups design. Using the data of the conservation film experiment to illustrate the use of these equations, we obtain the following:

| Independent Groups | Correlated Groups |
|---|---|

**Independent Groups**

$$t_{obt} = \frac{\overline{X}_1 - \overline{X}_2}{\sqrt{s_{\overline{X}_1}^2 + s_{\overline{X}_2}^2}}$$

where $s_{\overline{X}_1}^2 = \dfrac{s_1^2}{n_1} = \dfrac{82.083}{12} = 6.840$

and $s_{\overline{X}_2}^2 = \dfrac{s_2^2}{n_2} = \dfrac{100.364}{12} = 8.364$

Thus,

$$t_{obt} = \frac{48.917 - 46.000}{\sqrt{6.840 + 8.364}} = \frac{2.917}{\sqrt{15.204}} = 0.748$$

$$= 0.75$$

Note that these are the same values obtained previously.

**Correlated Groups**

$$t_{obt} = \frac{\overline{D}}{\sqrt{s_{\overline{X}_1}^2 + s_{\overline{X}_2}^2 - 2rs_{\overline{X}_1}s_{\overline{X}_2}}}$$

$$= \frac{2.917}{\sqrt{6.840 + 8.364 - 2(0.938)(2.615)(2.892)}}$$

$$= \frac{2.917}{\sqrt{1.017}}$$

$$= 2.91$$

## BOOK COMPANION WEBSITE

Go to www.thomsonedu.com/psychology/pagano for:

- SPSS problems and solutions
- Flash cards for review of terms
- Chapter quiz
- Statistical workshops
- And more

## WebTUTOR™

Available via WebTutor for this chapter:

- Detailed chapter outline
- *Know and Be Able To Do* section
- Drag & Drop game for review of equations, concepts, and other material
- Flash cards for review of terms
- Audio flash cards for MP3 player
- Solving problems using Excel
- Solving problems using SPSS
- More practice problems using computational equations
- Chapter quiz

# Introduction to the Analysis of Variance

CHAPTER **15**

# INTRODUCTION: THE *F* DISTRIBUTION

In Chapters 12, 13, and 14, we have been using the *mean* as the basic statistic for evaluating the null hypothesis. It's also possible to use the *variance* of the data for hypothesis testing. One of the most important tests that does this is called the *F* test, after R. A. Fisher, the statistician who developed it. In using this test, we calculate the statistic $F_{obt}$, which fundamentally is the ratio of two independent variance estimates of the same population variance $\sigma^2$. In equation form,

$$F_{obt} = \frac{\text{Variance estimate 1 of } \sigma^2}{\text{Variance estimate 2 of } \sigma^2}$$

The sampling distribution of *F* can be generated empirically by (1) taking all possible samples of size $n_1$ and $n_2$ from the same population, (2) estimating the population variance $\sigma^2$ from each of the samples using $s_1^2$ and $s_2^2$, (3) calculating $F_{obt}$ for all possible combinations of $s_1^2$ and $s_2^2$, and then (4) calculating $p(F)$ for each different value of $F_{obt}$. The resulting distribution is the *sampling distribution of F*. Thus, as with all sampling distributions,

definition  ■  *The **sampling distribution of F** gives all the possible F values along with the $p(F)$ for each value, assuming sampling is random from the population.*

Like the *t* distribution, the *F* distribution varies with *degrees of freedom*. However, the *F* distribution has two values for degrees of freedom, one for the numerator and one for the denominator. As you might guess, we lose 1 degree of freedom for each calculation of variance. Thus,

$$\text{df for the numerator} = \text{df}_1 = n_1 - 1$$
$$\text{df for the denominator} = \text{df}_2 = n_2 - 1$$

Figure 15.1 shows an *F* distribution with 3 df in the numerator and 16 df in the denominator. Several features are apparent. First, since *F* is a ratio of variance estimates, it never has a negative value ($s_1^2$ and $s_2^2$ will always be positive). Second, the *F* distribution is positively skewed. Finally, the median *F* value is approximately equal to 1.

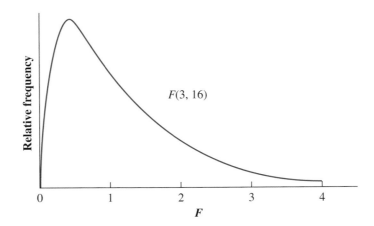

figure 15.1  *F* distribution with 3 degrees of freedom in the numerator and 16 degrees of freedom in the denominator.

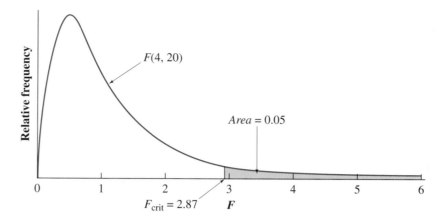

**figure 15.2** Illustration showing that $F_{crit}$ in Table F is one-tailed for the right-hand tail.

Like the *t* test, there is a family of *F* curves. With the *F* test, however, there is a different curve for each combination of $df_1$ and $df_2$. Table F in Appendix D gives the critical values of *F* for various combinations of $df_1$ and $df_2$. There are two entries for every cell. The light entry gives the critical *F* value for the 0.05 level. The dark entry gives the critical *F* value for the 0.01 level. Note that these are one-tailed values for the right-hand tail of the *F* distribution. To illustrate, Figure 15.2 shows the *F* distribution for 4 df in the numerator and 20 df in the denominator. From Table F, $F_{crit}$ at the 0.05 level equals 2.87. This means that 5% of the *F* values are equal to or greater than 2.87. The area containing these values is shown shaded in Figure 15.2.

## *F* TEST AND THE ANALYSIS OF VARIANCE (ANOVA)

The *F* test is appropriate in any experiment in which the scores can be used to form two independent estimates of the population variance. One quite frequent situation in the behavioral sciences for which the *F* test is appropriate occurs when analyzing the data from experiments that use more than two groups or conditions.

Thus far in the text, we have discussed the most fundamental experiment: the two-group study involving a control group and an experimental group. Although this design is still used frequently, it is more common to encounter experiments that involve three or more groups. A major limitation of the two-group study is that often two groups are not sufficient to allow a clear interpretation of the findings. For example, the "thalamus and pain perception" experiment (p. 337) included two groups. One received lesions in the thalamus and the other in an area "believed" to be unrelated to pain. The results showed a significantly higher pain threshold for the rats with thalamic lesions. Our conclusion was that lesions of the thalamus increased pain threshold. However, the difference between the two groups could just as well have been due to a lowering of pain threshold as a result of the other lesion rather than a raising of threshold because of the thalamic damage. This ambiguity could have been dispelled if three groups had been run rather than two. The third group would be an unlesioned control group. Comparing the pain threshold of the two lesioned groups with the unlesioned group would help resolve the issue.

Another class of experiments requiring more than two groups involves experiments in which the independent variable is varied as a factor; that is, a predetermined range of the independent variable is selected, and several values spanning the range are used in the experiment. For example, in the "hormone X and sexual behavior" problem, rather than arbitrarily picking one value of the hormone, the experimenter would probably pick several levels across the range of possible effective values. Each level would be administered to a different group of subjects, randomly sampled from the population. There would be as many groups in the experiment as there are levels of the hormone. This type of experiment has the advantage of allowing the experimenter to determine how the dependent variable changes with several different levels of the independent variable. In this example, the experimenter would find out how mating behavior varies in frequency with different levels of hormone X. Not only does using several levels allow a lawful relationship to emerge if one exists, but when the experimenter is unsure of what single level might be effective, using several levels increases the possibility of a positive result occurring from the experiment.

Given that it is frequently desirable to do experiments with more than two groups, you may wonder why these experiments aren't analyzed in the usual way. For example, if the experiment used four independent groups, why not simply compare the group means two at a time using the *t* test for independent groups? That is, why not just calculate *t* values comparing group 1 with 2, 3, and 4; 2 with 3 and 4; and 3 with 4?

The answer involves considerations of Type I error. You will recall that, when we set alpha at the 0.05 level, we are in effect saying that we are willing to risk being wrong 5% of the time when we reject $H_0$. In an experiment with two groups, there would be just one *t* calculation, and we would compare $t_{obt}$ with $t_{crit}$ to see whether $t_{obt}$ fell in the critical region for rejecting $H_0$. Let's assume alpha = 0.05. The critical value of *t* at the 0.05 level was originally determined by taking the sampling distribution of *t* for the appropriate df and locating the *t* value such that the proportion of the total number of *t* values that were equal to or more extreme than it equaled 0.05. That is, if we were randomly sampling one *t* score from the *t* distribution, the probability it would be $\geq t_{crit}$ is 0.05.

Now what happens when we do an experiment involving many *t* comparisons, say, 20 of them? We are no longer just sampling one *t* value from the *t* distribution but 20. The probability of getting *t* values equal to or greater than $t_{crit}$ obviously goes up. It is no longer equal to 0.05. The probability of making a Type I error has increased as a result of doing an experiment with many groups and analyzing the data with more than one comparison.

## OVERVIEW OF THE ONE-WAY ANALYSIS OF VARIANCE TECHNIQUE

The analysis of variance is a statistical technique used to analyze multigroup experiments. Using the *F* test allows us to make *one* overall comparison that tells whether there is a significant difference between the *means* of the groups. Thus, it avoids the problem of an increased probability of Type I error that occurs when assessing many *t* values. The analysis of variance, or ANOVA as it is frequently called, is used in both independent groups and repeated measures designs. It is also used when one or more factors (variables) are investigated in the same experiment. In this section, we shall consider the simplest of these designs: the simple randomized-group design. This design is also often referred to as the one-way analysis of variance, independent groups design. A third designation often used is the single factor experiment, independent groups design.* According to this design, subjects are randomly sampled from the population and then randomly assigned to the conditions, preferably such that there are an equal number of subjects in each condition. There are as many independent groups as there are conditions. If the study is investigating the effect of an independent variable as a factor, then the conditions would be the different levels of the independent variable used. Each group would receive a different level of the independent variable (e.g., a different concentration of hormone X). Thus, in this design, scores from several independent groups are analyzed.

The alternative hypothesis used in the analysis of variance is nondirectional. It states that one or more of the conditions have different effects from at least one of the others on the dependent variable. The null hypothesis states that the different conditions are all equally effective, in which case the scores in each group are random samples from populations having the same mean value. If there are $k$ groups, then the null hypothesis specifies that

$$\mu_1 = \mu_2 = \mu_3 = \cdots = \mu_k$$

*where*     $\mu_1$ = mean of the population from which group 1 is taken
          $\mu_2$ = mean of the population from which group 2 is taken
          $\mu_3$ = mean of the population from which group 3 is taken
          $\mu_k$ = mean of the population from which group $k$ is taken

Like the $t$ test, the analysis of variance assumes that only the mean of the scores is affected by the independent variable, not the variance. Therefore, the analysis of variance assumes that

$$\sigma_1^2 = \sigma_2^2 = \sigma_3^2 = \cdots = \sigma_k^2$$

*where*     $\sigma_1^2$ = variance of the population from which group 1 is taken
          $\sigma_2^2$ = variance of the population from which group 2 is taken
          $\sigma_3^2$ = variance of the population from which group 3 is taken
          $\sigma_k^2$ = variance of the population from which group $k$ is taken

Essentially, the analysis of variance partitions the total variability of the data ($SS_T$) into two sources: the variability that exists within each group, called the *within-groups sum of squares ($SS_W$)*, and the variability that exists between the groups, called the *between-groups sum of squares ($SS_B$)* (see Figure 15.3). Each sum of squares is used to form an independent estimate of the $H_0$ population variance. The estimate based on the within-groups variability is called the *within-groups variance estimate ($s_W^2$)*, and the estimate based on the between-groups variability is called the *between-groups variance estimate ($s_B^2$)*.[†] Finally, an $F$ ratio is calculated where

---

*The use of ANOVA with repeated measures designs is covered in B. J. Winer, D. R. Brown, and K. M. Michels, *Statistical Principles in Experimental Design*, 3rd ed., McGraw-Hill, New York, 1991.
[†]$s_B^2$ is often symbolized $MS_B$ and referred to as "mean square between." Similarly, $s_W^2$ is often symbolized as $MS_W$ and referred to as "mean square within" or "mean square error."

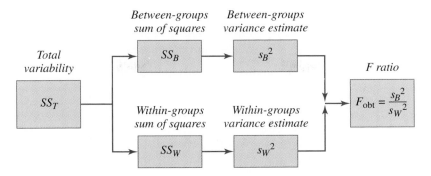

**figure 15.3** Overview of the analysis of variance technique, simple randomized-groups design.

$$F_{obt} = \frac{\text{Between-groups variance estimate } (s_B^2)}{\text{Within-groups variance estimate } (s_W^2)}$$

This process is shown in Figure 15.3. The between-groups variance estimate increases with the magnitude of the independent variable's effect, whereas the within-groups variance estimate is unaffected. Thus, the larger the $F$ ratio is, the more unreasonable the null hypothesis becomes. As with the other statistics, we evaluate $F_{obt}$ by comparing it with $F_{crit}$. If $F_{obt}$ is equal to or exceeds $F_{crit}$, we reject $H_0$. Thus, the decision rule states the following:

If $F_{obt} \geq F_{crit}$, reject $H_0$.

If $F_{obt} \leq F_{crit}$, retain $H_0$.

## Within-Groups Variance Estimate, $s_W^2$

One estimate of the $H_0$ population variance, $\sigma^2$, is based on the variability within each group. It is symbolized as $s_W^2$ and is determined in precisely the same manner as the weighted estimate $s_W^2$ used in the $t$ test for independent groups. We call it the *within-groups* variance estimate in the analysis of variance to distinguish it from the *between-groups* variance estimate discussed in the next section. You will recall that in the $t$ test for independent groups,

$$s_W^2 = \text{weighted estimate of } H_0 \text{ population variance, } \sigma^2$$
$$= \text{weighted average of } s_1^2 \text{ and } s_2^2$$
$$= \frac{SS_1 + SS_2}{(n_1 - 1) + (n_2 - 1)}$$
$$= \frac{SS_1 + SS_2}{N - 2}$$

The analysis of variance utilizes exactly the same estimate, except ordinarily we are dealing with three or more groups. Thus, for the analysis of variance,

$$s_W^2 = \text{within-groups variance estimate}$$
$$= \text{weighted estimate of } H_0 \text{ population variance, } \sigma^2$$
$$= \text{weighted average of } s_1^2, s_2^2, s_3^2, \ldots, \text{ and } s_k^2$$
$$= \frac{SS_1 + SS_2 + SS_3 + \cdots + SS_k}{(n_1 - 1) + (n_2 - 1) + (n_3 - 1) + \cdots + (n_k - 1)}$$

*where*  $k$ = number of groups

$n_k$ = number of subjects in group $k$

$SS_k$ = sum of squares of group $k$

This equation can be simplified to

$$s_W{}^2 = \frac{SS_1 + SS_2 + SS_3 + \cdots + SS_k}{N - k}$$  *conceptual equation for within-groups variance estimate*

*where*  $N = n_1 + n_2 + n_3 + \cdots + n_k$

The numerator of this equation is called the *within-groups sum of squares*. It is symbolized by $SS_W$. The denominator equals the degrees of freedom for the within-groups variance estimate. Since we lose 1 degree of freedom for each sample variance calculated and there are $k$ variances, there are $N - k$ degrees of freedom. Thus,

$$s_W{}^2 = \frac{SS_W}{df_W}$$  *within-groups variance estimate*

*where*  $SS_W = SS_1 + SS_2 + SS_3 + \cdots + SS_k$  *within-groups sum of squares*

$df_W = N - k$  *within-groups degrees of freedom*

This equation for $SS_W$ is fine conceptually, but when actually computing $SS_W$, it is better to use another equation. This equation is the algebraic equivalent of the conceptual equation, but it is easier to use and leads to fewer rounding errors. The computational equation is given here and will be discussed subsequently when we analyze the data from an experiment:

$$SS_W = \overset{\overset{\text{all}}{\text{scores}}}{\sum} X^2 - \left[\frac{(\Sigma X_1)^2}{n_1} + \frac{(\Sigma X_2)^2}{n_2} + \frac{(\Sigma X_3)^2}{n_3} + \cdots + \frac{(\Sigma X_k)^2}{n_k}\right]$$

*computational equation for $SS_W$*

## Between–Groups Variance Estimate, $s_B{}^2$

The second estimate of the variance of the null-hypothesis populations, $\sigma^2$, is based on the variability *between* the groups. It is symbolized by $s_B{}^2$. The null hypothesis states that each group is a random sample from populations where $\mu_1 = \mu_2 = \mu_3 = \cdots = \mu_k$. If the null hypothesis is correct, then we can use the variability between the means of the samples to estimate the variance of these populations, $\sigma^2$.

We know from Chapter 12 that, if we take all possible samples of size $n$ from a population and calculate their mean values, the resulting sampling distribution of means has a variance of $\sigma_{\bar{X}}{}^2 = \sigma^2/n$. Solving for $\sigma^2$, we arrive at $\sigma^2 = n\sigma_{\bar{X}}{}^2$. If $\sigma_{\bar{X}}{}^2$ can be estimated, we can substitute the estimate in the previous equation to arrive at an independent estimate of $\sigma^2$. In the actual experiment there are several sample means, so we can use the variance of these mean scores to estimate the variance of the full set of sample means, $\sigma_{\bar{X}}{}^2$. Since there are $k$ sample means, we divide by $k - 1$, just as when we have $N$ raw scores we divide by $N - 1$. Thus,

$$s_{\bar{X}}{}^2 = \frac{\Sigma(\bar{X} - \bar{X}_G)^2}{k - 1}$$  *estimate of $\sigma_{\bar{X}}{}^2$*

*where*    $\overline{X}_G$ = grand mean (overall mean of all the scores combined)
$k$ = number of groups

Using $s_{\overline{X}}^2$ for our estimate of $\sigma_{\overline{X}}^2$, we arrive at the second independent esti-mate of $\sigma^2$. This estimate is called the *between-groups variance estimate* and is symbolized by $s_B^2$. Since $\sigma^2 = n\sigma_{\overline{X}}^2$,

$$s_B^2 = \text{Estimate of } \sigma^2 = ns_{\overline{X}}^2$$

Substituting for $s_{\overline{X}}^2$,

$$s_B^2 = \frac{n \, \Sigma(\overline{X} - \overline{X}_G)^2}{k - 1}$$

Expanding the summation, we arrive at

$$s_B^2 = \frac{n \, [(\overline{X}_1 - \overline{X}_G)^2 + (\overline{X}_2 - \overline{X}_G)^2 + (\overline{X}_3 - \overline{X}_G)^2 + \cdots + (\overline{X}_k - \overline{X}_G)^2]^*}{k - 1}$$

*conceptual equation for the between-groups variance estimate*

The numerator of this equation is called the *between-groups sum of squares*. It is symbolized by $SS_B$. The denominator is the degrees of freedom for the between-groups variance estimate. It is symbolized by $df_B$. Thus,

$$s_B^2 = \frac{SS_B}{df_B} \quad \textit{between-groups variance estimate}$$

*where*    $SS_B = n[(\overline{X}_1 - \overline{X}_G)^2 + (\overline{X}_2 - \overline{X}_G)^2 + (\overline{X}_3 - \overline{X}_G)^2 + \cdots$
$+ (\overline{X}_k - \overline{X}_G)^2]$    *between-groups sum of squares*

$df_B = k - 1$    *between-groups degrees of freedom*

It should be clear that, as the effect of the independent variable increases, the differences between the sample means increase. This causes $(\overline{X}_1 - \overline{X}_G)^2$, $(\overline{X}_2 - \overline{X}_G)^2, \ldots, (\overline{X}_k - \overline{X}_G)^2$ to increase, which in turn produces an increase in $SS_B$. Since $SS_B$ is in the numerator, increases in it produce increases in $s_B^2$. Thus, the between-groups variance estimate ($s_B^2$) increases with the effect of the inde-pendent variable.

This equation for $SS_B$ is fine conceptually, but when actually computing $SS_B$, it is better to use another equation. As with $SS_W$, there is a computational equation for $SS_B$ that is the algebraic equivalent of the conceptual equation but is easier to use and leads to fewer rounding errors. The computational equation is given here and will be discussed shortly when we analyze the data from an experiment:

$$SS_B = \left[ \frac{(\Sigma X_1)^2}{n_1} + \frac{(\Sigma X_2)^2}{n_2} + \frac{(\Sigma X_3)^2}{n_3} + \cdots + \frac{(\Sigma X_k)^2}{n_k} \right]$$

$$- \frac{\left( \overset{\text{all}}{\underset{}{\overset{\text{scores}}{\sum}}} X \right)^2}{N} \quad \textit{computational equation for } SS_B$$

---

*This assumes there are $n$ subjects in each group.

## The $F$ Ratio

We noted earlier that $s_B^2$ increases with the effect of the independent variable. However, since an assumption of the analysis of variance is that the independent variable affects only the mean and not the variance of each group, the within-groups variance estimate does not change with the effect of the independent variable. Since $F = s_B^2 / s_W^2$, $F$ increases with the effect of the independent variable. Thus, the larger the $F$ ratio is, the more reasonable it is that the independent variable has had a real effect. Another way of saying this is that $s_B^2$ is really an estimate of $\sigma^2$ plus the effects of the independent variable, whereas $s_W^2$ is just an estimate of $\sigma^2$. Thus,

$$F_{\text{obt}} = \frac{s_B^2}{s_W^2} = \frac{\sigma^2 + \text{independent variable effects}}{\sigma^2}$$

The larger $F_{\text{obt}}$ becomes, the more reasonable it is that the independent variable has had a real effect. Of course, $F_{\text{obt}}$ must be equal to or exceed $F_{\text{crit}}$ before $H_0$ can be rejected. If $F_{\text{obt}}$ is less than 1, we don't even need to compare it with $F_{\text{crit}}$. It is obvious the treatment has not had a significant effect, and we can immediately conclude by retaining $H_0$.

## ANALYZING DATA WITH THE ANOVA TECHNIQUE

So far, we have been quite theoretical. Now let's do a problem to illustrate the analysis of variance technique.

an experiment

### Different Situations and Stress

Suppose you are interested in determining whether certain situations produce differing amounts of stress. You know the amount of the hormone corticosterone circulating in the blood is a good measure of how stressed a person is. You randomly assign 15 students into three groups of 5 each. The students in group 1 have their corticosterone levels measured immediately after returning from vacations (low stress). The students in group 2 have their corticosterone levels measured after they have been in class for a week (moderate stress). The students in group 3 are measured immediately before final exam week (high stress). All measurements are taken at the same time of day. You record the data shown in Table 15.1. Scores are in milligrams of corticosterone per 100 milliliters of blood.

1. What is the alternative hypothesis?
2. What is the null hypothesis?
3. What is the conclusion? Use $\alpha = 0.05$.

### SOLUTION

1. Alternative hypothesis: The alternative hypothesis states that at least one of the situations affects stress differently than at least one of the remaining situations. Therefore, at least one of the means ($\mu_1, \mu_2,$ or $\mu_3$) differs from at least one of the others.
2. Null hypothesis: The null hypothesis states that the different situations affect stress equally. Therefore, the three sample sets of scores are random samples from populations where $\mu_1 = \mu_2 = \mu_3$.

t a b l e  15.1   Stress experiment data

| Group 1, Vacation | | Group 2, Class | | Group 3, Final Exam | |
|---|---|---|---|---|---|
| $X_1$ | $X_1^2$ | $X_2$ | $X_2^2$ | $X_3$ | $X_3^2$ |
| 2 | 4 | 10 | 100 | 10 | 100 |
| 3 | 9 | 8 | 64 | 13 | 169 |
| 7 | 49 | 7 | 49 | 14 | 196 |
| 2 | 4 | 5 | 25 | 13 | 169 |
| 6 | 36 | 10 | 100 | 15 | 225 |
| 20 | 102 | 40 | 338 | 65 | 859 |

$$n_1 = 5 \qquad n_2 = 5 \qquad n_3 = 5$$

$$\overline{X}_1 = 4.00 \qquad \overline{X}_2 = 8.00 \qquad \overline{X}_3 = 13.00$$

$$\overset{\text{all}}{\underset{\text{scores}}{\sum}} X = 125 \qquad \overset{\text{all}}{\underset{\text{scores}}{\sum}} X^2 = 1299 \qquad \overline{X}_G = \dfrac{\overset{\text{all}}{\underset{\text{scores}}{\sum}} X}{N} = 8.333$$

$$N = 15$$

3. Conclusion, using $\alpha = 0.05$: The conclusion is reached in the same general way as with the other inference tests. First, we calculate the appropriate statistic, in this case $F_{\text{obt}}$, and then we evaluate $F_{\text{obt}}$ based on its sampling distribution.

**A.** Calculate $F_{\text{obt}}$.

**STEP 1: Calculate the between-groups sum of squares, $SS_B$.**   To calculate $SS_B$, we shall use the following computational equation:

$$SS_B = \left[ \frac{(\Sigma X_1)^2}{n_1} + \frac{(\Sigma X_2)^2}{n_2} + \frac{(\Sigma X_3)^2}{n_3} + \cdots + \frac{(\Sigma X_k)^2}{n_k} \right] - \frac{\left( \overset{\text{all}}{\underset{\text{scores}}{\sum}} X \right)^2}{N}$$

computational equation for $SS_B$

In this problem, since $k = 3$, this equation reduces to

$$SS_B = \left[ \frac{(\Sigma X_1)^2}{n_1} + \frac{(\Sigma X_2)^2}{n_2} + \frac{(\Sigma X_3)^2}{n_3} \right] - \frac{\left( \overset{\text{all}}{\underset{\text{scores}}{\sum}} X \right)^2}{N}$$

*where*   $\overset{\text{all}}{\underset{\text{scores}}{\sum}} X = $ sum of all the scores

Substituting the appropriate values from Table 15.1 into this equation, we obtain

$$SS_B = \left[ \frac{(20)^2}{5} + \frac{(40)^2}{5} + \frac{(65)^2}{5} \right] - \frac{(125)^2}{15} = 80 + 320 + 845 - 1041.667$$

$$= 203.333$$

**STEP 2: Calculate the within-groups sum of squares, $SS_W$.** The computational equation for $SS_W$ is as follows:

$$SS_W = \overset{\text{all scores}}{\sum} X^2 - \left[ \frac{(\Sigma X_1)^2}{n_1} + \frac{(\Sigma X_2)^2}{n_2} + \frac{(\Sigma X_3)^2}{n_3} + \cdots + \frac{(\Sigma X_k)^2}{n_k} \right]$$

*computational equation for $SS_W$*

*where* $\overset{\text{all scores}}{\sum} X^2 = $ sum of all the squared scores

Since $k = 3$, for this problem the equation reduces to

$$SS_W = \overset{\text{all scores}}{\sum} X^2 - \left[ \frac{(\Sigma X_1)^2}{n_1} + \frac{(\Sigma X_2)^2}{n_2} + \frac{(\Sigma X_3)^2}{n_3} \right]$$

Substituting the appropriate values into this equation, we obtain

$$SS_W = \overset{\text{all scores}}{\sum} X^2 - \left[ \frac{(\Sigma X_1)^2}{n_1} + \frac{(\Sigma X_2)^2}{n_2} + \frac{(\Sigma X_3)^2}{n_3} \right]$$

$$= 1299 - \left[ \frac{(20)^2}{5} + \frac{(40)^2}{5} + \frac{(65)^2}{5} \right]$$

$$= 54$$

**STEP 3: Calculate the total sum of squares, $SS_T$.** This step is just a check to be sure the calculations in steps 1 and 2 are correct. You will recall that at the beginning of the analysis of variance section, p. 362, we said this technique partitions the total variability into two parts: the within variability and the between variability. The measure of total variability is $SS_T$, the measure of within variability is $SS_W$, and the measure of between variability is $SS_B$. Thus,

$$SS_T = SS_W + SS_B$$

By independently calculating $SS_T$, we can check to see whether this relationship holds true for the calculations in steps 1 and 2:

$$SS_T = \overset{\text{all scores}}{\sum} X^2 - \frac{\left( \overset{\text{all scores}}{\sum} X \right)^2}{N}$$

You will recognize that this equation is quite similar to the sum of squares with each sample, except here we are using the scores of all the samples as a single group. Calculating $SS_T$, we obtain

$$SS_T = \overset{\text{all scores}}{\sum} X^2 - \frac{\left( \overset{\text{all scores}}{\sum} X \right)^2}{N}$$

$$= 1299 - \frac{(125)^2}{15}$$

$$= 257.333$$

Substituting the values of $SS_T$, $SS_W$, and $SS_B$ into the equation, we obtain

$$SS_T = SS_W + SS_B$$
$$257.333 = 54 + 203.333$$
$$257.333 = 257.333$$

Note that, if the within sum of squares plus the between sum of squares does not equal the total sum of squares, you've made a calculation error. Go back and check steps 1, 2, and 3 until the equation balances (within rounding error).

**STEP 4: Calculate the degrees of freedom for each estimate:**

$$df_B = k - 1 = 3 - 1 = 2$$
$$df_W = N - k = 15 - 3 = 12$$
$$df_T = N - 1 = 15 - 1 = 14$$

**STEP 5: Calculate the between-groups variance estimate, $s_B{}^2$.** The variance estimates are just the sums of squares divided by their degrees of freedom. Thus,

$$s_B{}^2 = \frac{SS_B}{df_B} = \frac{203.333}{2} = 101.667$$

**STEP 6: Calculate the within-groups variance estimate, $s_W{}^2$:**

$$s_W{}^2 = \frac{SS_W}{df_W} = \frac{54}{12} = 4.5$$

**STEP 7: Calculate $F_{obt}$.** We have calculated two independent estimates of $\sigma^2$: the between-variance estimate and the within-variance estimate. The $F$ value is the ratio of $s_B^2$ to $s_W^2$. Thus,

$$F_{obt} = \frac{s_B{}^2}{s_W{}^2} = \frac{101.667}{4.5} = 22.59$$

Note that $s_B^2$ is always put in the numerator and $s_W^2$ in the denominator.

**B.** Evaluate $F_{obt}$. Since $s_B^2$ is a measure of the effect of the independent variable as well as an estimate of $\sigma^2$, it should be larger than $s_W^2$, unless chance alone is at work. If $F_{obt} \leq 1$, it is clear that the independent variable has not had a significant effect and we conclude by retaining $H_0$ without even bothering to compare $F_{obt}$ with $F_{crit}$. If $F_{obt} > 1$, we must compare it with $F_{crit}$. If $F_{obt} \geq F_{crit}$, we reject $H_0$. From Table F in Appendix D, with $\alpha = 0.05$, $df_{numerator} = 2$, and $df_{denominator} = 12$,

$$F_{crit} = 3.88$$

Note that, in looking up $F_{crit}$ in Table F, it is important to keep the df for the numerator and denominator straight. If by mistake you had entered the table with 2 df for the denominator and 12 df for the numerator, $F_{crit}$ would equal 19.41, which is quite different from 3.88. Since $F_{obt} > 3.88$, we reject $H_0$. The three situations are not all the same in the stress levels they produce. A summary of the solution is shown in Table 15.2.

t a b l e  15.2  Summary table for ANOVA problem involving stress

| Source | $SS$ | df | $s^2$ | $F_{obt}$ |
|---|---|---|---|---|
| Between groups | 203.333 | 2 | 101.667 | 22.59* |
| Within groups | 54.000 | 12 | 4.500 | |
| Total | 257.333 | 14 | | |

*With $\alpha = 0.05$, $F_{crit} = 3.88$. Therefore, $H_0$ is rejected.

## LOGIC UNDERLYING THE ONE–WAY ANOVA

Now that we have worked through the calculations of an illustrative example, we would like to discuss in more detail the logic underlying the one-way ANOVA. Earlier, we pointed out that the one-way ANOVA partitions the total variability ($SS_T$) into two parts: the within-groups sum of squares ($SS_W$) and the between-groups sum of squares ($SS_B$). We can gain some insight into this partitioning by recognizing that it is based on the simple idea that the deviation of each score from the grand mean is made up of two parts: the deviation of the score from its own group mean and the deviation of that group mean from the grand mean. Applying this idea to the first score in group 1, we obtain

| *Deviation of each score from the grand mean* | = | *Deviation of the score from its own group mean* | + | *Deviation of that group mean from the grand mean* |
|---|---|---|---|---|
| $2 - 8.33$ | = | $2 - 4.00$ | + | $4.00 - 8.33$ |
| $X - \overline{X}_G$ | = | $X - \overline{X}_1$ | + | $\overline{X}_1 - \overline{X}_G$ |
| ↓ | | ↓ | | ↓ |
| $SS_T$ | = | $SS_W$ | + | $SS_B$ |

Note that the term on the left ($X - \overline{X}_G$) when squared and summed over all the scores becomes $SS_T$. Thus,

$$SS_T = \sum_{}^{\substack{\text{all} \\ \text{scores}}} (X - \overline{X}_G)^2$$

The term in the middle ($X - \overline{X}_1$) when squared and summed for all the scores (of course, we must subtract the appropriate group mean from each score) becomes $SS_W$. Thus,

$$SS_W = SS_1 + SS_2 + SS_3$$
$$= \Sigma(X - \overline{X}_1)^2 + \Sigma(X - \overline{X}_2)^2 + \Sigma(X - \overline{X}_3)^2$$

It is important to note that, since the subjects *within* each group receive the same level of the independent variable, variability among the scores within each group cannot be due to differences in the effect of the independent variable. Thus, the within-groups sum of squares ($SS_W$) is not a measure of the effect of the independent variable. Since $SS_W/df_W = s_W^2$, this means that the within-groups variance estimate ($s_W^2$) also is not a measure of the real effect of the independent variable. Rather, it provides us with an estimate of the inherent variability of the scores themselves. Thus, $s_W^2$ is an estimate of $\sigma^2$ that is unaffected by treatment differences.

The last term in the equation partitioning the variability of score 2 from the grand mean is $\overline{X}_1 - \overline{X}_G$. When this term is squared and summed for all the scores, it becomes $SS_B$. Thus,

$$SS_B = n(\overline{X}_1 - \overline{X}_G)^2 + n(\overline{X}_2 - \overline{X}_G)^2 + n(\overline{X}_3 - \overline{X}_G)^2$$

As discussed previously, $SS_B$ is sensitive to the effect of the independent variable, because the greater the effect of the independent variable, the more the means of each group will differ from each other and, hence, will differ from $\overline{X}_G$. Since $SS_B/df_B = s_B^2$, this means that the between-groups variance estimate ($s_B^2$) is also sensitive to the real effect of the independent variable. Thus, $s_B^2$ gives us an estimate of $\sigma^2$ plus the effects of the independent variable. Since

$$F_{obt} = \frac{s_B^2}{s_W^2} = \frac{\sigma^2 + \text{effects of the independent variable}}{\sigma^2}$$

the larger $F_{obt}$ is, the less reasonable is the null-hypothesis explanation. If the independent variable has no effect, then both $s_B^2$ and $s_W^2$ are independent estimates of $\sigma^2$ and their ratio is distributed as $F$ with df = $df_B$ (numerator) and $df_W$ (denominator). We evaluate the null hypothesis by comparing $F_{obt}$ with $F_{crit}$. If $F_{obt} \geq F_{crit}$, we reject $H_0$.

Let's try one more problem for practice.

## Practice Problem 15.1

A college professor wants to determine the best way to present an important topic to his class. He has the following three choices: (1) he can lecture, (2) he can lecture and assign supplementary reading, or (3) he can show a film and assign supplementary reading. He decides to do an experiment to evaluate the three options. He solicits 27 volunteers from his class and randomly assigns 9 to each of three conditions. In condition 1, he lectures to the students. In condition 2, he lectures plus assigns supplementary reading. In condition 3, the students see a film on the topic plus receive the same supplementary reading as the students in condition 2. The students are subsequently tested on the material. The following scores (percentage correct) were obtained:

*(continued)*

| Lecture, Condition 1 | | Lecture + Reading, Condition 2 | | Film + Reading, Condition 3 | |
|---|---|---|---|---|---|
| $X_1$ | $X_1^2$ | $X_2$ | $X_2^2$ | $X_3$ | $X_3^2$ |
| 92 | 8,464 | 86 | 7,396 | 81 | 6,561 |
| 86 | 7,396 | 93 | 8,649 | 80 | 6,400 |
| 87 | 7,569 | 97 | 9,409 | 72 | 5,184 |
| 76 | 5,776 | 81 | 6,561 | 82 | 6,724 |
| 80 | 6,400 | 94 | 8,836 | 83 | 6,889 |
| 87 | 7,569 | 89 | 7,921 | 89 | 7,921 |
| 92 | 8,464 | 98 | 9,604 | 76 | 5,776 |
| 83 | 6,889 | 90 | 8,100 | 88 | 7,744 |
| 84 | 7,056 | 91 | 8,281 | 83 | 6,889 |
| 767 | 65,583 | 819 | 74,757 | 734 | 60,088 |

$n_1 = 9$        $n_2 = 9$        $n_3 = 9$

$\overline{X}_1 = 85.222$      $\overline{X}_2 = 91$      $\overline{X}_3 = 81.556$

$\overset{\text{all scores}}{\sum} X = 2320$      $\overset{\text{all scores}}{\sum} X^2 = 200{,}428$      $\overline{X}_G = \dfrac{\overset{\text{all scores}}{\sum} X}{N} = 85.926$

$N = 27$

a. What is the overall null hypothesis?
b. What is the conclusion? Use $\alpha = 0.05$.

**SOLUTION**

a. Null hypothesis: The null hypothesis states that the different methods of presenting the material are equally effective. Therefore, $\mu_1 = \mu_2 = \mu_3$.
b. Conclusion, using $\alpha = 0.05$: To assess $H_0$, we must calculate $F_{obt}$ and then evaluate it based on its sampling distribution.

    **A.** Calculate $F_{obt}$.

        **STEP 1: Calculate $SS_B$:**

$$SS_B = \left[ \frac{(\sum X_1)^2}{n_1} + \frac{(\sum X_2)^2}{n_2} + \frac{(\sum X_3)^2}{n_3} \right] - \frac{\left( \overset{\text{all scores}}{\sum} X \right)^2}{N}$$

$$= \left[ \frac{(767)^2}{9} + \frac{(819)^2}{9} + \frac{(734)^2}{9} \right] - \frac{(2320)^2}{27}$$

$$= 408.074$$

**STEP 2: Calculate $SS_W$:**

$$SS_W = \sum_{}^{\substack{\text{all} \\ \text{scores}}} X^2 - \left[ \frac{(\Sigma X_1)^2}{n_1} + \frac{(\Sigma X_2)^2}{n_2} + \frac{(\Sigma X_3)^2}{n_3} \right]$$

$$= 200{,}428 - \left[ \frac{(767)^2}{9} + \frac{(819)^2}{9} + \frac{(734)^2}{9} \right]$$

$$= 671.778$$

**STEP 3: Calculate $SS_T$:**

$$SS_T = \sum_{}^{\substack{\text{all} \\ \text{scores}}} X^2 - \frac{\left( \sum_{}^{\substack{\text{all} \\ \text{scores}}} X \right)^2}{N}$$

$$= 200{,}428 - \frac{(2320)^2}{27}$$

$$= 1079.852$$

This step is a check to see whether $SS_B$ and $SS_W$ were correctly calculated. If so, then $SS_T = SS_B + SS_W$. This check is shown here:

$$SS_T = SS_B + SS_W$$
$$1079.852 = 408.074 + 671.778$$
$$1079.852 = 1079.852$$

**STEP 4: Calculate df:**

$$df_B = k - 1 = 3 - 1 = 2$$
$$df_W = N - k = 27 - 3 = 24$$
$$df_T = N - 1 = 27 - 1 = 26$$

**STEP 5: Calculate $s_B^2$:**

$$s_B^2 = \frac{SS_B}{df_B} = \frac{408.074}{2} = 204.037$$

**STEP 6: Calculate $s_W^2$:**

$$s_W^2 = \frac{SS_W}{df_W} = \frac{671.778}{24} = 27.991$$

**STEP 7: Calculate $F_{obt}$:**

$$F_{obt} = \frac{s_B^2}{s_W^2} = \frac{204.037}{27.991} = 7.29$$

**B.** Evaluate $F_{obt}$. With $\alpha = 0.05$, $df_{numerator} = 2$, and $df_{denominator} = 24$, from Table F,

$$F_{crit} = 3.40$$

*(continued)*

Since $F_{\text{obt}} > 3.40$, we reject $H_0$. The methods of presentation are not equally effective. The solution is summarized in Table 15.3.

**t a b l e  15.3**   Summary ANOVA table for methods of presentation experiment

| Source | SS | df | $s^2$ | $F_{\text{obt}}$ |
|---|---|---|---|---|
| Between groups | 408.074 | 2 | 204.037 | 7.29* |
| Within groups | 671.778 | 24 | 27.991 | |
| Total | 1079.852 | 26 | | |

*With $\alpha = 0.05$, $F_{\text{crit}} = 3.40$. Therefore, $H_0$ is rejected.

## THE RELATIONSHIP BETWEEN THE ANALYSIS OF VARIANCE AND THE *t* TEST

When a study involves just two independent groups and we are testing the null hypothesis that $\mu_1 = \mu_2$, we can use either the *t* test for independent groups or the analysis of variance. In such situations, it can be shown algebraically that $t^2 = F$. For a demonstration of this point, go online to the Book Companion Website for this demonstration.

## ASSUMPTIONS UNDERLYING THE ANALYSIS OF VARIANCE

The assumptions underlying the analysis of variance are similar to those of the *t* test for independent groups:

1. The populations from which the samples were taken are normally distributed.
2. The samples are drawn from populations of equal variances. As pointed out in Chapter 14 in connection with the *t* test for independent groups, this is called the homogeneity of variance assumption. The analysis of variance also assumes homogeneity of variance.*

Like the *t* test, the analysis of variance is a robust test. It is minimally affected by violations of population normality. It is also relatively insensitive to violations of homogeneity of variance provided the samples are of equal size.[†]

---

*See Chapter 14 footnote * on p. 339. Some statisticians would also limit the use of ANOVA to data that are interval or ratio in scaling. For a discussion of this point, see the references in the Chapter 2 footnote on p. 31.

[†]For an extended discussion of these points, see G. V. Glass, P. D. Peckham, and J. R. Sanders, "Consequences of Failure to Meet the Assumptions Underlying the Use of Analysis of Variance and Covariance," *Review of Educational Research, 42* (1972), 237–288.

## SIZE OF EFFECT

### Omega Squared, $\hat{\omega}^2$

In Chapter 14, we described a method for determining size of effect for the basic condition, independent groups experiment. The method involved computing a measure called omega squared ($\hat{\omega}^2$) that gave us an unbiased estimate of the proportion of the total variance of the dependent variable in the population that is accounted for by the independent variable. The larger this proportion is, the larger is the effect of the independent variable. The approach we will use here to determine size of effect with the one-way ANOVA is very similar. Again we will compute an estimate of the proportion of the total variance of the dependent variable in the population that is accounted for by the independent variable. Again the statistic used is $\hat{\omega}^2$. Conceptually, the equation is

$$\hat{\omega}^2 = \frac{\sigma_B^2}{\sigma_B^2 + \sigma_W^2} \quad \textit{Conceptual equation}$$

Since we do not know the values of these population variances, we estimate them from the sample data. The resulting equation is

$$\hat{\omega}^2 = \frac{SS_B - (k-1)s_W^2}{SS_T + s_W^2} \quad \textit{Computational equation}$$

For the data of the stress experiment (p. 361), $SS_B = 203.333$, $SS_T = 257.333$, $s_W^2 = 4.500$, and $k = 3$. The size effect for these data, using $\hat{\omega}^2$ as our measure, is

$$\hat{\omega}^2 = \frac{203.333 - (3-1)4.500}{257.333 + 4.500} = 0.7422$$

Thus, the stress situations account for 74.2% of the variance in corticosterone levels. Following Cohen's guidelines (p. 341) that for ANOVA, $\hat{\omega}^2 = 0.01$ is a small effect, $\hat{\omega}^2 = 0.06$ is a medium effect, and $\hat{\omega}^2 = 0.14$ is a large effect, this would be quite a large effect.

### Eta Squared, $\eta^2$

Eta squared is an alternative measure for determining size of effect in one-way ANOVA experiments. It is very similar to $\hat{\omega}^2$. However, instead of providing an unbiased estimate of the effect of the independent variable in the population, it gives a biased estimate that usually overestimates the true size of the effect. Nevertheless, it is quite easy to calculate, has been around longer than $\hat{\omega}^2$, and is still quite commonly used. The equation for computing eta squared ($\eta^2$) is given here.

$$\eta^2 = \frac{SS_B}{SS_T} \quad \textit{Conceptual and computational equation}$$

Again using the data of the stress experiment (p. 366), $SS_B = 203.333$, $SS_T = 257.33$, $s_W^2 = 4.500$, and $k = 3$. The size of effect for these data, using $\eta^2$ as our measure, is

$$\eta^2 = \frac{203.333}{257.333} = 0.7902$$

Based on $\eta^2$, the stress situations account for 79.0% of the variance in corticosterone levels. Note that this is a higher value than we obtained when using $\hat{\omega}^2$. Because $\hat{\omega}^2$ provides a better estimate of the size of effect in population, we recommend its use over $\eta^2$.

# POWER OF THE ANALYSIS OF VARIANCE

The power of the analysis of variance is affected by the same variables and in the same manner as was the case with the $t$ test for independent groups. You will recall that for the $t$ test for independence groups, power is affected as follows:

1. Power varies directly with $N$. Increasing $N$ increases power.
2. Power varies directly with the size of the real effect of the independent variable. The power of the $t$ test to detect a real effect is greater for large effects than for smaller ones.
3. Power varies inversely with sample variability. The greater the sample variability is, the lower the power to detect a real effect is.

Let's now look at each of these variables and how they affect the analysis of variance. This discussion is most easily understood by referring to the following equation for $F_{obt}$, for an experiment involving three groups.

$$F_{obt} = \frac{s_B^2}{s_W^2} = \frac{n[(\overline{X}_1 - \overline{X}_G)^2 + (\overline{X}_2 - \overline{X}_G)^2 + (\overline{X}_3 - \overline{X}_G)^2]/2}{(SS_1 + SS_2 + SS_3)/(N - 3)}$$

## Power and $N$

Obviously, anything that increases $F_{obt}$ also increases power. As $N$, the total number of subjects in the experiment, increases, so must $n$, the number of subjects in each group. Increases in each of these variables results in an increase in $F_{obt}$. This can be seen as follows. Referring to the $F_{obt}$ equation, as $N$ increases, since it is in the denominator of the within variance estimate $s_W^2$, $s_W^2$ decreases. Since $s_W^2$ is in the denominator of the $F_{obt}$ equation, $F_{obt}$ increases. Regarding $n$, since $n$ is in the numerator of the $F_{obt}$ equation and is a multiplier of positive values, increases in $n$ result in an increase in the between variance estimate $s_B^2$. Since $s_B^2$ is in the numerator of the $F_{obt}$ equation, increases in $s_B^2$ cause an increase in $F_{obt}$. As stated earlier, anything that increases $F_{obt}$ also increases power. *Thus, increases in N and n result in increased power.*

## Power and the Real Effect of the Independent Variable

The larger the real effect of the independent variable is, the larger will be the values of $(\overline{X}_1 - \overline{X}_G)^2$, $(\overline{X}_2 - \overline{X}_G)^2$, and $(\overline{X}_3 - \overline{X}_G)^2$. Increases in these values produce an increase in $s_B^2$. Since $s_B^2$ is in the numerator of the $F_{obt}$ equation, increases in $s_B^2$ result in an increase in $F_{obt}$. *Thus, the larger the real effect of the independent variable is, the higher is the power.*

### Power and Sample Variability

$SS_1$ (the sum of squares of group 1), $SS_2$ (the sum of squares of group 2), and $SS_3$ (the sum of squares of group 3) are measures of the variability within each group. Increases in $SS_1$, $SS_2$, and $SS_3$ result in an increase in the within variance estimate $s_w^2$. Since $s_w^2$ is in the denominator of the $F_{obt}$ equation, increases in $s_w^2$ result in a decrease in $F_{obt}$. *Thus, increases in variability result in decreases in power.*

## MULTIPLE COMPARISONS

In one-way ANOVA, a significant $F$ value indicates that all the conditions do not have the same effect on the dependent variable. For example, in the illustrative experiment presented earlier in the chapter that investigated the amount of stress produced by three situations, a significant $F$ value was obtained and we concluded that the three situations were not the same in the stress levels they produced. For pedagogical reasons, we stopped the analysis at this conclusion. However, in actual practice, the analysis does not ordinarily end at this point. Usually, we are also interested in determining which of the conditions differ from each other. A significant $F$ value tells us that at least one condition differs from at least one of the others. It is also possible that they are all different or any combination in between may be true. To determine which conditions differ, multiple comparisons between pairs of group means are usually made. In the remainder of this chapter, we shall discuss two types of comparisons that may be made: *a priori* comparisons and *a posteriori* comparisons.

### *A Priori*, or Planned, Comparisons

*A priori* comparisons are planned in advance of the experiment and often arise from predictions based on theory and prior research. With *a priori* comparisons, we do not correct for the higher probability of a Type I error that arises due to multiple comparisons, as is done with the *a posteriori* methods. This correction, which we shall cover in the next section, in effect makes it harder for the null hypothesis to be rejected. When doing *a priori* comparisons, statisticians do not agree on whether the comparisons must be orthogonal (i.e., independent).[*] We have followed the position taken by Keppel and Winer that planned comparisons need not be orthogonal as long as they flow meaningfully and logically from the experimental design and are few in number.[†]

In doing planned comparisons, the $t$ test for independent groups is used. We could calculate $t_{obt}$ in the usual way. For example, in comparing conditions 1 and 2, we could use the equation

$$t_{obt} = \frac{\overline{X}_1 - \overline{X}_2}{\sqrt{\left(\dfrac{SS_1 + SS_2}{n_1 + n_2 - 2}\right)\left(\dfrac{1}{n_1} + \dfrac{1}{n_2}\right)}}$$

---

[*]For a discussion of this point, see G. Keppel, *Design and Analysis*, Prentice Hall, Upper Saddle River, NJ, 1973, pp. 92–93.
[†]See Note 15.1 for a discussion of orthogonal comparisons.

However, remembering that $(SS_1 + SS_2)/(n_1 + n_2 - 2)$ is an estimate of $\sigma^2$ based on the within variance of the two groups, we can use a better estimate since we have three or more groups in the experiment. Instead of $(SS_1 + SS_2)/(n_1 + n_2 - 2)$, we can use the within variance estimate $s_W^2$, which is based on all of the groups. Thus,

$$t_{\text{obt}} = \frac{\overline{X}_1 - \overline{X}_2}{\sqrt{s_W^2\left(\dfrac{1}{n_1} + \dfrac{1}{n_2}\right)}} \qquad$$ t equation for a priori, or planned, comparisons, general equation

With $n_1 = n_2 = n$,

$$t_{\text{obt}} = \frac{\overline{X}_1 - \overline{X}_2}{\sqrt{2s_W^2/n}} \qquad$$ t equation for a priori, or planned, comparisons with equal n in the two groups

Let's apply this to the stress example presented earlier in the chapter. For convenience, we have shown the data and ANOVA solution in Table 15.4.

Suppose we have the *a priori* hypothesis based on theoretical grounds that the effect of condition 3 will be different from the effect of both conditions 1 and 2. Therefore, prior to collecting any data, we have planned to compare the scores

t a b l e 15.4   Stress experiment data

| Group 1 Vacation | | Group 2 Class | | Group 3 Final Exam | |
|---|---|---|---|---|---|
| $X_1$ | $X_1^2$ | $X_2$ | $X_2^2$ | $X_3$ | $X_3^2$ |
| 2 | 4 | 10 | 100 | 10 | 100 |
| 3 | 9 | 8 | 64 | 13 | 169 |
| 7 | 49 | 7 | 49 | 14 | 196 |
| 2 | 4 | 5 | 25 | 13 | 169 |
| 6 | 36 | 10 | 100 | 15 | 225 |
| 20 | 102 | 40 | 338 | 65 | 859 |

$$n_1 = 5 \qquad\qquad n_2 = 5 \qquad\qquad n_3 = 5$$
$$\overline{X}_1 = 4.00 \qquad\quad \overline{X}_2 = 8.00 \qquad\quad \overline{X}_3 = 13.00$$

$$\sum^{\substack{\text{all}\\\text{scores}}} X = 125 \qquad \sum^{\substack{\text{all}\\\text{scores}}} X^2 = 1299 \qquad \overline{X}_G = \frac{\sum^{\substack{\text{all}\\\text{scores}}} X}{N} = 8.333$$

$$N = 15$$

| Source | SS | df | $s^2$ | $F_{\text{obt}}$ |
|---|---|---|---|---|
| Between groups | 203.333 | 2 | 101.667 | 22.59[*] |
| Within groups | 54 | 12 | 4.5 | |
| Total | 257.333 | 14 | | |

[*]With $\alpha = 0.05$, $F_{\text{crit}} = 3.88$. Therefore, $H_0$ is rejected.

of group 3 with those of group 1 and group 2. To perform the planned comparisons, we first calculate the appropriate $t_{obt}$ values and then compare them with $t_{crit}$. The calculations are as follows:

*Group 1 and Group 3:*

$$t_{obt} = \frac{\overline{X}_1 - \overline{X}_3}{\sqrt{2s_W{}^2/n}} = \frac{4.00 - 13.00}{\sqrt{2(4.50)/5}} = -6.71$$

*Group 2 and Group 3:*

$$t_{obt} = \frac{\overline{X}_2 - \overline{X}_3}{\sqrt{2s_W{}^2/n}} = \frac{8.00 - 13.00}{\sqrt{2(4.50)/5}} = -3.73$$

Are any of these $t$ values significant? The value of $t_{crit}$ is found from Table D in Appendix D, using the degrees of freedom for $s_W{}^2$. Thus, with df $= N - k = 12$ and $\alpha = 0.05_{2\ tail}$,

$$t_{crit} = \pm2.18$$

Both of the obtained $t$ scores have absolute values greater than 2.18, so we conclude that condition 3 differs significantly from conditions 1 and 2.

## A *Posteriori*, or *Post Hoc*, Comparisons

When the comparisons are not planned in advance, we must use an *a posteriori* test. These comparisons usually arise after the experimenter sees the data and picks groups with mean scores that are far apart, or else they arise from doing all the comparisons possible with no theoretical *a priori* basis. Since these comparisons were not planned before the experiment, we must correct for the inflated probability values that occur when doing multiple comparisons, as mentioned in the previous section.

Many methods are available for achieving this correction.[*] The topic is fairly complex, and it is beyond the scope of this text to present all of the methods. However, we shall present two of the most commonly accepted methods: a method devised by Tukey called the HSD (Honestly Significant Difference) test and the Newman–Keuls test. Both of these tests are *post hoc* multiple comparison tests. They maintain the Type I error rate at α while making all possible comparisons between pairs of sample means.

You will recall that the problem with doing multiple $t$ test comparisons is that the critical values of $t$ were derived under the assumption that there are only two samples whose means are to be compared. This would be accomplished by performing one $t$ test. When there are many samples and hence more than one comparison, the sampling distribution of $t$ is no longer appropriate. In fact, if it were to be used, the actual probability of making a Type I error would greatly exceed alpha, particularly if many comparisons were made. Both the Tukey and Newman–Keuls method avoid this difficulty by using sampling distributions based on comparing the means of many samples

---

[*]For a detailed discussion of these methods, see R. E. Kirk, *Experimental Design*, 3rd ed., Brooks/Cole, Pacific Grove, CA, 1995, pp. 144–159.

rather than just two. These distributions, called the $Q$ or Studentized range distributions, were developed by randomly taking $k$ samples of equal $n$ from the same population (rather than just two, as with the $t$ test) and determining the difference between the highest and lowest sample means. The differences were then divided by $\sqrt{s_W^2/n}$, producing distributions that were like the $t$ distributions except that these provide the basis for making multiple comparisons, not just a single comparison as in the $t$ test. The 95th and 99th percentile points for the $Q$ distribution are given in Table G in Appendix D. These values are the critical values of $Q$ for the 0.05 and 0.01 alpha levels. As you might guess, the critical values depend on the number of sample means and the degrees of freedom associated with $s_W^2$.

In discussing the HSD and Newman–Keuls tests, it is useful to distinguish between two aspects of Type I errors: the *experiment-wise* error rate and the *comparison-wise* error rate.

definitions ■ *The* **experiment-wise** *error rate is the probability of making one or more Type I errors for the full set of possible comparisons in an experiment. The* **comparison-wise** *error rate is the probability of making a Type I error for any of the possible comparisons.*

As we shall see in the following sections, the HSD test and the Newman–Keuls test differ in which of these rates they maintain equal to alpha.

## The Tukey Honestly Significant Difference (HSD) Test

The Tukey Honestly Significant Difference test is designed to compare all possible pairs of means while maintaining the Type I error for making the complete set of comparisons at $\alpha$. Thus, the HSD test maintains the experiment-wise Type I error rate at $\alpha$. The statistic calculated for this test is $Q$. It is defined by the following equation:

$$Q_{\text{obt}} = \frac{\overline{X}_i - \overline{X}_j}{\sqrt{s_W^2/n}}$$

where
$\overline{X}_i$ = larger of the two means being compared
$\overline{X}_j$ = smaller of the two means being compared
$s_W^2$ = within-groups variance estimate
$n$ = number of subjects in each group

Note that in calculating $Q_{\text{obt}}$, the smaller mean is always subtracted from the larger mean. This always makes $Q_{\text{obt}}$ positive. Otherwise, the $Q$ statistic is very much like the $t$ statistic, except it uses the $Q$ distributions rather than the $t$ distributions. To use the statistic, we calculate $Q_{\text{obt}}$ for the desired comparisons and compare $Q_{\text{obt}}$ with $Q_{\text{crit}}$, determined from Table G. The decision rule states that if $Q_{\text{obt}} \geq Q_{\text{crit}}$, reject $H_0$. If not, then retain $H_0$.

To illustrate the use of the HSD test, we shall apply it to the data of the stress experiment. For the sake of illustration, we shall assume that all three comparisons are desired. There are two steps in using the HSD test. First, we must calculate the $Q_{obt}$ value for each comparison and then compare each value with $Q_{crit}$. The calculations for $Q_{obt}$ are as follows:

*Group 2 and Group 1:*

$$Q_{obt} = \frac{\overline{X}_2 - \overline{X}_1}{\sqrt{s_W^2/n}} = \frac{8.00 - 4.00}{\sqrt{4.50/5}} = \frac{4.00}{0.949} = 4.21$$

*Group 3 and Group 1:*

$$Q_{obt} = \frac{\overline{X}_3 - \overline{X}_1}{\sqrt{s_W^2/n}} = \frac{13.00 - 4.00}{\sqrt{4.50/5}} = \frac{9.00}{0.949} = 9.48$$

*Group 3 and Group 2:*

$$Q_{obt} = \frac{\overline{X}_3 - \overline{X}_2}{\sqrt{s_W^2/n}} = \frac{13.00 - 8.00}{\sqrt{4.50/5}} = \frac{5.00}{0.949} = 5.27$$

The next step is to compare the $Q_{obt}$ values with $Q_{crit}$. The value of $Q_{crit}$ is determined from Table G. To locate the appropriate value, we must know the df, the alpha level, and $k$. The df are the degrees of freedom associated with $s_W^2$. In this experiment, df = 12. As mentioned earlier, $k$ stands for the number of groups in the experiment. In the present experiment, $k = 3$. For this experiment, alpha was set at 0.05. From Table G, with df = 12, $k = 3$, and $\alpha = 0.05$, we obtain

$$Q_{crit} = 3.77$$

Since $Q_{obt} > 3.77$ for each comparison, we reject $H_0$ in each case and conclude that $\mu_1 \neq \mu_2 \neq \mu_3$. All three conditions differ in stress-inducing value. The solution is summarized in Table 15.5.

t a b l e 15.5 *Post hoc* individual comparisons analysis of the stress experiment using Tukey's HSD test

| | Group | | | |
|---|---|---|---|---|
| | *1* | *2* | *3* | **Calculation** |
| $\overline{X}$ | 4.00 | 8.00 | 13.00 | Groups 2 and 1: |
| $\overline{X}_i - \overline{X}_j$ | | 4.00 | 9.00 | $Q_{obt} = \dfrac{\overline{X}_2 - \overline{X}_1}{\sqrt{s_W^2/n}} = \dfrac{8.00 - 4.00}{\sqrt{4.50/5}} = 4.21$ |
| | | | 5.00 | |
| $Q_{obt}$ | | 4.21* | 9.48* | Groups 3 and 1: |
| | | | 5.27* | $Q_{obt} = \dfrac{\overline{X}_3 - \overline{X}_1}{\sqrt{s_W^2/n}} = \dfrac{13.00 - 4.00}{\sqrt{4.50/5}} = 9.48$ |
| $Q_{crit}$ | | 3.77 | 3.77 | Groups 3 and 2: |
| df = 12 | | | 3.77 | |
| $k = 3$ | | | | $Q_{obt} = \dfrac{\overline{X}_3 - \overline{X}_2}{\sqrt{s_W^2/n}} = \dfrac{13.00 - 8.00}{\sqrt{4.50/5}} = 5.27$ |
| $\alpha = 0.05$ | | | | |

*Reject $H_0$.

## The Newman–Keuls Test

The Newman–Keuls test is also a *post hoc* test that allows us to make all possible pairwise comparisons among the sample means. It is like the HSD test in that $Q_{obt}$ is calculated for each comparison and compared with $Q_{crit}$ to evaluate the null hypothesis. It differs from the HSD test in that it maintains the Type I error rate at $\alpha$ *for each comparison,* rather than for the entire set of comparisons. Thus:

*The Newman–Keuls test maintains the comparison-wise error rate at $\alpha$, whereas the HSD test maintains the experiment-wise error rate at $\alpha$.*

To keep the comparison-wise error rate at $\alpha$, the Newman–Keuls method varies the value of $Q_{crit}$ for each comparison. The value of $Q_{crit}$ used for any comparison is given by the sampling distribution of $Q$ for the number of groups having means encompassed by $\overline{X}_i$ and $\overline{X}_j$ after all the means have been rank-ordered. This number is symbolized by $r$ to distinguish it from $k$, which symbolizes the total number of groups in the experiment.

To illustrate the Newman–Keuls method, we shall use it to analyze the data from the stress experiment. The first step is to rank-order the means. This has been done in Table 15.6. Next, $Q_{obt}$ is calculated for each comparison. The calculations and $Q_{obt}$ values are also shown in Table 15.6. The next step is to determine the values of $Q_{crit}$. Note that to keep the Type I error rate for each comparison at $\alpha$, there is a different critical value for each comparison, depending on $r$. Recall that $r$ for any comparison equals the number of groups having means that are encompassed by $\overline{X}_i$ and $\overline{X}_j$, after the means have been rank-ordered. Thus, for the comparison between groups 3 and 1, $\overline{X}_i = \overline{X}_3$ and

**t a b l e  15.6** *Post hoc* individual comparisons analysis of the stress experiment using the Newman–Keuls test

| | Group | | | |
|---|---|---|---|---|
| | *1* | *2* | *3* | **Calculation** |
| $\overline{X}$ | 4.00 | 8.00 | 13.00 | Groups 3 and 1: |
| $\overline{X}_i - \overline{X}_j$ | | 4.00 | 9.00 | $Q_{obt} = \dfrac{\overline{X}_3 - \overline{X}_1}{\sqrt{s_W{}^2/n}} = \dfrac{13.00 - 4.00}{\sqrt{4.50/5}} = 9.48$ |
| | | | 5.00 | |
| $Q_{obt}$ | | 4.21* | 9.48* | Groups 3 and 2: |
| | | | 5.27* | $Q_{obt} = \dfrac{\overline{X}_3 - \overline{X}_2}{\sqrt{s_W{}^2/n}} = \dfrac{13.00 - 8.00}{\sqrt{4.50/5}} = 5.27$ |
| $Q_{crit}$ | | 3.08 | 3.77 | Groups 2 and 1: |
| df = 12 | | | 3.08 | |
| $r = 2, 3$ | | | | $Q_{obt} = \dfrac{\overline{X}_2 - \overline{X}_1}{\sqrt{s_W{}^2/n}} = \dfrac{8.00 - 4.00}{\sqrt{4.50/5}} = 4.21$ |
| $\alpha = 0.05$ | | | | |

*Reject $H_0$.

$\overline{X}_j = \overline{X}_1$. When the means are rank-ordered, there are three groups (groups 1, 2, and 3) whose means are encompassed by $\overline{X}_3$ and $\overline{X}_1$. Thus, $r = 3$ for this comparison. For the comparison between groups 3 and 2, $\overline{X}_i = \overline{X}_3$ and $\overline{X}_j = \overline{X}_2$. After rank-ordering all the means, $\overline{X}_3$ and $\overline{X}_2$ are directly adjacent, so there are only two means encompassed by $\overline{X}_3$ and $\overline{X}_2$, namely, $\overline{X}_2$ and $\overline{X}_3$. Thus, $r = 2$ for this comparison. The same holds true for the comparison between groups 2 and 1. For this comparison, $\overline{X}_i = \overline{X}_2, \overline{X}_j = \overline{X}_1$, and $r = 2$ (the two encompassed means are $\overline{X}_2$ and $\overline{X}_1$).

We are now ready to determine $Q_{\text{crit}}$ for each comparison. The value of $Q_{\text{crit}}$ is found is Table G, using the appropriate values for df, $r$, and $\alpha$. The degrees of freedom are the df for $s_W^2$, which equal 12, and we shall use the same $\alpha$ level. Thus, $\alpha = 0.05$. For the comparison between groups 1 and 3, with df = 12, $r = 3$, and $\alpha = 0.05$, $Q_{\text{crit}} = 3.77$. For the comparisons between groups 1 and 2 and groups 2 and 3, with df = 12, $r = 2$, and $\alpha = 0.05$, $Q_{\text{crit}} = 3.08$. These values are also shown in Table 15.6.

The final step is to compare $Q_{\text{obt}}$ with $Q_{\text{crit}}$. In making these comparisons, we follow the rule that we begin with the largest $Q_{\text{obt}}$ value in the table (the upper right-hand corner of the $Q_{\text{obt}}$ values) and compare it with the appropriate $Q_{\text{crit}}$. If it is significant, we proceed to the left one step and compare the next $Q_{\text{obt}}$ with the corresponding $Q_{\text{crit}}$. We continue in this manner until we finish the row or until we reach a nonsignificant $Q_{\text{obt}}$. In the latter case, all the remaining $Q_{\text{obt}}$ values left of this first nonsignificant $Q_{\text{obt}}$ are considered nonsignificant. When the row is finished or when a nonsignificant $Q_{\text{obt}}$ is reached, we drop to the next row and begin again at the rightmost $Q_{\text{obt}}$ value. We continue in this manner until all the $Q_{\text{obt}}$ values have been evaluated.

In the present example, we begin with 9.48 and compare it with 3.77. It is significant. Next, 4.21 is compared with 3.08. It is also significant. Since that comparison ends the row, we drop a row and compare 5.27 and 3.08. Again, the $Q_{\text{obt}}$ value is significant. Thus, we are able to reject $H_0$ in each comparison. Therefore, we end the analysis by concluding that $\mu_1 \neq \mu_2 \neq \mu_3$. The solution is summarized in Table 16.3.

Now let's do a practice problem.

## Practice Problem 15.2

Using the data of Practice Problem 15.1 (p. 371),

**a.** Test the planned comparisons that (1) lecture + reading and lecture have different effects and (2) that lecture + reading and film + reading have different effects. Use $\alpha = 0.05_{2\ tail}$.

**b.** Make all possible *post hoc* comparisons using the HSD test. Use $\alpha = 0.05$.

**c.** Make all possible *post hoc* comparisons using the Newman–Keuls test. Use $\alpha = 0.05$.

### SOLUTION

For convenience, the data and the ANOVA solution are shown again.

| Condition 1 Lecture | | Condition 2 Lecture + Reading | | Condition 3 Film + Reading | |
|---|---|---|---|---|---|
| $X_1$ | $X_1^2$ | $X_2$ | $X_2^2$ | $X_3$ | $X_3^2$ |
| 92 | 8,464 | 86 | 7,396 | 81 | 6,561 |
| 86 | 7,396 | 93 | 8,649 | 80 | 6,400 |
| 87 | 7,569 | 97 | 9,409 | 72 | 5,184 |
| 76 | 5,776 | 81 | 6,561 | 82 | 6,724 |
| 80 | 6,400 | 94 | 8,836 | 83 | 6,889 |
| 87 | 7,569 | 89 | 7,921 | 89 | 7,921 |
| 92 | 8,464 | 98 | 9,604 | 76 | 5,776 |
| 83 | 6,889 | 90 | 8,100 | 88 | 7,744 |
| 84 | 7,056 | 91 | 8,281 | 83 | 6,889 |
| 767 | 65,583 | 819 | 74,757 | 734 | 60,088 |

$$n_1 = 9 \qquad\qquad n_2 = 9 \qquad\qquad n_3 = 9$$
$$\overline{X}_1 = 85.222 \qquad \overline{X}_2 = 91 \qquad \overline{X}_3 = 81.556$$

$$\overset{\text{all}}{\underset{\text{scores}}{\sum}} X = 2320 \qquad \overset{\text{all}}{\underset{\text{scores}}{\sum}} X^2 = 200{,}428 \qquad \overline{X}_G = \dfrac{\overset{\text{all}}{\underset{\text{scores}}{\sum}} X}{N}$$

$$N = 27$$

$$= 85.926$$

| Source | SS | df | $s^2$ | $F_{obt}$ |
|---|---|---|---|---|
| Between groups | 408.074 | 2 | 204.037 | 7.29[*] |
| Within groups | 671.778 | 24 | 27.991 | |
| Total | 1079.852 | 26 | | |

[*]With $\alpha = 0.05$, $F_{crit} = 3.40$. Therefore, $H_0$ is rejected.

**a.** Planned comparisons: The comparisons are as follows:
Lecture + reading and Lecture (condition 2 and condition 1):

$$t_{obt} = \frac{\overline{X}_2 - \overline{X}_1}{\sqrt{2s_W^2/n}} = \frac{91 - 85.222}{\sqrt{2(27.991)/9}} = 2.32$$

Lecture + reading and Film + reading (condition 2 and condition 3):

$$t_{obt} = \frac{\overline{X}_2 - \overline{X}_3}{\sqrt{2s_W^2/n}} = \frac{91 - 81.556}{\sqrt{2(27.991)/9}} = 3.79$$

To evaluate these values of $t_{obt}$, we must determine $t_{crit}$. From Table D, with $\alpha = 0.05_{2\,tail}$ and df = 24,

$$t_{crit} = \pm 2.064$$

Since $|t_{obt}| > 2.064$ in both comparisons, we reject $H_0$ in each case and conclude that $\mu_1 \neq \mu_2$ and $\mu_2 \neq \mu_3$. By using *a priori* tests, lecture + reading appears to be the most effective method.

**b.** *Post hoc* comparisons using the HSD test: With the HSD test, $Q_{obt}$ is determined for each comparison and then evaluated against $Q_{crit}$. The value of $Q_{crit}$ is the same for each comparison and is such that the experiment-wise error rate is maintained at $\alpha$. Although it is not necessary for this test, we have first rank-ordered the means for comparison purposes with the Newman–Keuls test. They are shown in the following table. The calculations for $Q_{obt}$ are as follows:

Lecture (1) and Film + reading (3):

$$Q_{obt} = \frac{\overline{X}_1 - \overline{X}_3}{\sqrt{s_W^2/n}} = \frac{85.222 - 81.556}{\sqrt{27.991/9}} = \frac{3.666}{1.764} = 2.08$$

Lecture + reading (2) and Film + reading (3):

$$Q_{obt} = \frac{\overline{X}_2 - \overline{X}_3}{\sqrt{s_W^2/n}} = \frac{91 - 81.556}{\sqrt{27.991/9}} = \frac{9.444}{1.764} = 5.35$$

Lecture + reading (2) and Lecture (1):

$$Q_{obt} = \frac{\overline{X}_2 - \overline{X}_1}{\sqrt{s_W^2/n}} = \frac{91 - 85.222}{\sqrt{27.991/9}} = \frac{5.778}{1.764} = 3.28$$

Next, we must determine $Q_{crit}$. From Table G, with df = 24, $k = 3$, and $\alpha = 0.05$, we obtain

$$Q_{crit} = 3.53$$

Comparing the three values of $Q_{obt}$ with $Q_{crit}$, we find that only the comparison between film + reading and lecture + reading is significant. (For this comparison $Q_{obt} > 3.53$, whereas for the others $Q_{obt} < 3.53$.) Thus, on the basis of the HSD test, we may reject $H_0$ for the lecture + reading and film + reading comparison (conditions 2 and 3). Lecture + reading

*(continued)*

appears to be more effective than film + reading. However, we cannot reject $H_0$ with regard to the other comparisons. The results are summarized in the following table.

| | Condition | | | |
|---|---|---|---|---|
| | *3* | *1* | *2* | **Calculation** |
| $\overline{X}$ | 81.556 | 85.222 | 91 | Conditions 1 and 3: |
| $\overline{X}_i - \overline{X}_j$ | | 3.666 | 9.444 | $Q_{obt} = \dfrac{\overline{X}_1 - \overline{X}_3}{\sqrt{s_W^2/n}} = \dfrac{85.222 - 81.556}{\sqrt{27.991/9}} = 2.08$ |
| | | | 5.778 | |
| $Q_{obt}$ | | 2.08 | 5.35* | Conditions 2 and 3: |
| | | | 3.28 | $Q_{obt} = \dfrac{\overline{X}_2 - \overline{X}_3}{\sqrt{s_W^2/n}} = \dfrac{91 - 81.556}{\sqrt{27.991/9}} = 5.35$ |
| $Q_{crit} = 3.53$ | | 3.53 | 3.53 | |
| df = 24 | | | 3.53 | Conditions 2 and 1: |
| $k = 3$ | | | | $Q_{obt} = \dfrac{\overline{X}_2 - \overline{X}_1}{\sqrt{s_W^2/n}} = \dfrac{91 - 85.222}{\sqrt{27.991/9}} = 3.28$ |
| $\alpha = 0.05$ | | | | |

*Reject $H_0$.

c. *Post hoc* comparisons using the Newman–Keuls test: As with the HSD test, $Q_{obt}$ is calculated for each comparison and then evaluated against $Q_{crit}$. However, with the Newman–Keuls test, the value of $Q_{crit}$ changes with each comparison so as to keep the comparison-wise error rate at $\alpha$. First, the means are rank-ordered from lowest to highest. This is shown in the table that follows. Then, $Q_{obt}$ is calculated for each comparison. These calculations, as well as the $Q_{obt}$ values, have been entered in the table. Next, $Q_{crit}$ for each comparison is determined from Table G. The values of $Q_{crit}$ depend on $\alpha$, df for $s_W^2$, and *r*, where *r* equals the number of groups having means that are encompassed by $\overline{X}_i$ and $\overline{X}_j$ after the means have been rank-ordered. Thus, for the comparison between $\overline{X}_2$ and $\overline{X}_1$, $r = 2$; between $\overline{X}_2$ and $\overline{X}_3$, $r = 3$; and between $\overline{X}_1$ and $\overline{X}_3$, $r = 2$. For this experiment, df = 24 and $\alpha = 0.05$. The values of $Q_{crit}$ for each comparison have been entered in the table. Comparing $Q_{obt}$ with $Q_{crit}$, starting with the highest $Q_{obt}$ value in the first row and proceeding to the left, we find that we can reject $H_0$ for the comparison between conditions 2 and 3 but not for the comparison between conditions 1 and 3. Dropping down to the next row, since $3.28 > 2.92$, we can also reject $H_0$ for the comparison between conditions 2 and 1. Thus, based on the Newman–Keuls test, it appears that lecture + reading is superior to both lecture alone and film + reading.

| | **Condition** | | | |
|---|---|---|---|---|
| | **3** | **1** | **2** | **Calculation** |
| $\overline{X}$ | 81.556 | 85.222 | 91 | Conditions 1 and 3: |
| $\overline{X}_i - \overline{X}_j$ | | 3.666 | 9.444 | $Q_{obt} = \dfrac{\overline{X}_1 - \overline{X}_3}{\sqrt{s_W^2/n}} = \dfrac{85.222 - 81.556}{\sqrt{27.991/9}} = 2.08$ |
| | | | 5.778 | |
| $Q_{obt}$ | | 2.08 | 5.35* | Conditions 2 and 3: |
| | | | 3.28* | $Q_{obt} = \dfrac{\overline{X}_2 - \overline{X}_3}{\sqrt{s_W^2/n}} = \dfrac{91 - 81.556}{\sqrt{27.991/9}} = 5.35$ |
| $Q_{crit}$ | | 2.92 | 3.53 | |
| df = 24 | | | 2.92 | Conditions 2 and 1: |
| r = 2, 3 | | | | $Q_{obt} = \dfrac{\overline{X}_2 - \overline{X}_1}{\sqrt{s_W^2/n}} = \dfrac{91 - 85.222}{\sqrt{27.991/9}} = 3.28$ |
| $\alpha = 0.05$ | | | | |

*Reject $H_0$.

## HSD and Newman–Keuls Tests with Unequal *n*

As pointed out previously, both the HSD and the Newman–Keuls tests are appropriate when there are an equal number of subjects in each group. If the *n*s are unequal, these tests still can be used, provided the *n*s do not differ greatly. To use the HSD or the Newman–Keuls tests with unequal *n*, we calculate the harmonic mean ($\tilde{n}$) of the various *n*s and use it in the denominator of the $Q$ equation. The equation for $\tilde{n}$ is

$$\tilde{n} = \frac{k}{(1/n_1) + (1/n_2) + (1/n_3) + \cdots + (1/n_k)} \qquad \textit{harmonic mean}$$

*where*     $k$ = number of groups
$\quad\quad\quad n_k$ = number of subjects in the $k$th group

Suppose in the stress experiment that $n_1 = 5, n_2 = 7$, and $n_3 = 8$. Then

$$\tilde{n} = \frac{k}{(1/n_1) + (1/n_2) + (1/n_3)} = \frac{3}{\frac{1}{5} + \frac{1}{7} + \frac{1}{8}} = 6.41$$

## Comparison Between Planned Comparisons, Tukey's HSD, and the Newman–Keuls Tests

Since planned comparisons do not correct for an increased probability of making a Type I error, they are more powerful than either of the *post hoc* tests we have discussed. This is the method of choice when applicable. It is important to note, however, that planned comparisons should be relatively few in number and should flow meaningfully and logically from the experimental design.

Deciding between Tukey's HSD and the Newman–Keuls tests really depends on one's philosophy. Since the HSD test keeps the Type I error rate at $\alpha$ for the entire set of comparisons, whereas the Newman–Keuls test maintains the Type I error rate at $\alpha$ for each comparison, the Newman–Keuls test has a somewhat higher experiment-wise Type I error rate than the HSD test (although still considerably lower than when making no adjustment at all). Because it uses a less stringent experiment-wise $\alpha$ level than the HSD test, the Newman–Keuls test is more powerful. An example of this occurred in the last experiment we analyzed. With Newman–Keuls, we were able to reject $H_0$ for the comparisons between conditions 2 and 3 and between conditions 2 and 1. With the HSD test, we rejected $H_0$ only for the comparison between conditions 2 and 3. Thus, there is a trade-off. Newman–Keuls has a higher experiment-wise Type I error rate but a lower Type II error rate. A conservative experimenter would probably choose Tukey's HSD test, whereas a more liberal researcher would probably prefer the Newman–Keuls test. Of course, if the consequences of making a Type I error were much greater than making a Type II error, or vice versa, the researcher would choose the test that minimized the appropriate error rate.

## WHAT IS THE TRUTH?

# Much Ado About Almost Nothing

In a magazine advertisement placed by Rawlings Golf Company, Rawlings claims to have developed a new golf ball that travels a greater distance. The ball is called Tony Penna DB (DB stands for distance ball). To its credit, Rawlings not only offered terms such as *high rebound core,*

*Surlyn cover, centrifugal action,* and so forth to explain why it is reasonable to believe that its ball would travel farther but also hired a consumer testing institute to conduct an experiment to determine whether, in fact, the Tony Penna DB ball does travel farther. In this experiment, six different brands of balls were evaluated. Fifty-one golfers each hit 18 new balls (3 of each brand) off a driving tee with a driver. The

mean distance traveled for each ball was reported as follows:

1. Tony Penna DB     254.57 yd
2. Titleist Pro Trajectory    252.50 yd
3. Wilson Pro Staff     249.24 yd
4. Titleist DT     249.16 yd
5. Spalding Top-Flite     247.12 yd
6. Dunlop Blue Max     244.22 yd

Although no inference testing was reported, the ad concludes, "as you can see, while we can't promise *you* 250 yards off the tee, we can

## WHAT IS THE TRUTH?

# Much Ado About Almost Nothing *(continued)*

offer you a competitive edge, if only a yard or two. But an edge is an edge." Since you are by now thoroughly grounded in inferential statistics, how do you respond to this ad?

*Answer*    First, I think you should commend the company on conducting evaluative research that compares its product with competitors' on a very important dependent variable. It is to be further commended in engaging an impartial organization to conduct the research. Finally, it is to be commended for reporting the results and calling readers' attention to the fact that the differences between balls are quite small (although, admittedly, the wording of the ad tries to achieve a somewhat different result).

A major criticism of this ad (and an old friend by now) is that we have not been told whether

these results are statistically significant. Without establishing this point, the most reasonable explanation of the differences may be "chance." Of course, if chance is the correct explanation, then using the Tony Penna DB ball won't even give you a yard or two advantage! Before we can take the superiority claim seriously, the manufacturer must report that the differences were statistically significant. Without this statement, as a general rule, I believe we should assume the differences were tested and were not significant, in which case chance alone remains a reasonable explanation of the data. (By the way, what inference test would you have used? Did you answer ANOVA? Nice going!)

For the sake of my second point, let's say the appropriate inference testing has been done, and the data are statistically significant. We still need to ask: *"So what? Even if the results are statistically significant, is the size of the effect worth bothering about?"* Regarding the difference in yardage between the first two brands, I think the answer

is "no." Even if I were an avid golfer, I fail to see how a yard or two would make any practical difference in my golf game. In all likelihood, my 18-hole score would not change by even one stroke, regardless of which ball I used. On the other hand, if I had been using a Dunlop Blue Max ball, these results would cause me to try one of the top two brands. Regarding the third-, fourth-, and fifth-place brands, a reasonable person could go either way. If there were no difference in cost, I think I would switch to one of the first two brands, on a trial basis.

In summary, there are two points I have tried to make. The first is that *product claims of superiority based on sample data should report whether the results are statistically significant.* The second is that *"statistical significance" and "importance" are different issues.* Once statistical significance has been established, we must look at the size of the effect to see if it is large enough to warrant changing our behavior.

## SUMMARY

In this chapter, we have discussed the $F$ test and the analysis of variance. The $F$ test is fundamentally the ratio of two independent variance estimates of the same population variance, $\sigma^2$. The $F$ distribution is a family of curves that varies with degrees of freedom. Since $F_{obt}$ is a ratio, there are two values for degrees of freedom: one for the numerator and one for the denominator. The $F$ distribution (1) is positively skewed, (2) has no negative values, and (3) has a median approximately equal to 1 depending on the $n$s of the estimates.

The analysis of variance technique is used in conjunction with experiments involving more than two independent groups. Basically, it allows the means of the various groups to be compared in one overall evaluation, thus avoiding the inflated probability of making a Type I error when doing many $t$ tests. In the one-way analysis of variance, the total variability of the data ($SS_T$) is partitioned into two parts: the variability that exists within each group, called the within-groups sum of squares ($SS_W$), and the variability that exists between the groups, called the between-groups sum of squares ($SS_B$). Each sum of squares is used to form an independent estimate of the variance of the null-hypothesis populations. Finally, an $F$ ratio is calculated, where the between-groups variance estimate ($s_B^2$) is in the numerator and the within-groups variance estimate ($s_W^2$) is in the denominator. Since the between-groups variance estimate increases with the effect of the independent variable and the within-groups variance estimate remains constant, the larger the $F$ ratio, the more unreasonable the null hypothesis becomes. We evaluate $F_{obt}$ by comparing it with $F_{crit}$. If $F_{obt} \geq F_{crit}$, we reject the null hypothesis and conclude that at least one of the conditions differs significantly from at least one of the other conditions.

Next, we discussed the assumptions underlying the analysis of variance. There are two assumptions: (1) The populations from which the samples are drawn should be normal, and (2) there should be homogeneity of variance. The $F$ test is robust with regard to violations of normality and homogeneity of variance.

After discussing assumptions, we presented two methods for estimating the size of effect of the independent variable. The first is quite similar to estimating the size of effect with the $t$ test for independent groups. Again, omega squared ($\hat{\omega}^2$) is computed, although with ANOVA the equation for $\hat{\omega}^2$ is different from that with the $t$ test. The second method computes eta squared ($\eta^2$). Eta squared gives a biased estimate of the size of the effect, inflating it somewhat. Both measures estimate the percentage of the total variance in the dependent variable that is accounted for by the independent variable. The larger the percentage, the larger is the size of the effect.

Next, we presented a section on the power of the analysis of variance. As with the $t$ test, power of the ANOVA varies directly with $N$ and the size of the real effect and varies inversely with the sample variability.

Finally, we presented a section on multiple comparisons. In experiments using the ANOVA technique, a significant $F$ value indicates that the conditions are not all equal in their effects. To determine which conditions differ from each other, multiple comparisons between pairs of group means are usually performed. There are two approaches to doing multiple comparisons: *a priori*, or planned, comparisons and *a posteriori*, or *post hoc*, comparisons.

In the *a priori* approach, there are between-groups comparisons that have been planned in advance of collecting the data. These may be done in the usual way, regardless of whether the obtained $F$ value is significant, by calculating $t_{obt}$ for the two groups and evaluating $t_{obt}$ by comparing it with $t_{crit}$. In conducting the analysis, we use the within-groups variance estimate calculated in doing the analysis of variance. Since this estimate is based on more groups than the two-group estimate used in the ordinary $t$ test, it is more accurate. There is no correction necessary for multiple comparisons. However, statisticians do not agree on whether the comparisons should be orthogonal. We have followed the view that *a priori* comparisons need not be orthogonal as long as they flow meaningfully and logically from the experimental design and are few in number.

*A posteriori*, or *post hoc*, comparisons were not planned before conducting the experiment and arise after looking at the data. As a result, we must be very careful about Type I error considerations. *Post hoc* comparisons must be made with a method that corrects for the inflated Type I error probability. Many methods do this.

In this chapter, we have described Tukey's HSD test and the Newman–Keuls test. Both of these tests maintain the Type I error rate at $\alpha$ while making all possible comparisons between pairs of sample means. The HSD test keeps the experiment-wise error rate at $\alpha$, whereas the Newman–Keuls test keeps the comparison-wise error rate at $\alpha$. Both tests use the $Q$ or Studentized range statistic. As with the $t$ test, $Q_{obt}$ is calculated for each comparison and evaluated against $Q_{crit}$ determined from the sampling distribution of $Q$. If $Q_{obt} \geq Q_{crit}$, the null hypothesis is rejected.

## IMPORTANT TERMS

A *posteriori* comparisons  (p. 379)
A *priori* comparisons  (p. 377)
Analysis of variance  (p. 360)
Between-groups sum of squares
  ($SS_B$) (p. 362)
Between-groups variance estimate
  ($s_B^2$) (p. 362)
Comparison-wise error rate (p. 380)
Experiment-wise error rate  (p. 380)
Eta squared ($\eta^2$) (p. 375)
$F$ test (p. 360)

$F_{crit}$ (p. 360)
Grand mean ($\overline{X}_G$) (p. 365)
Newman–Keuls test  (p. 382)
One-way analysis of variance,
  independent groups design (p. 362)
Planned comparisons  (p. 377)
*Post hoc* comparisons  (p. 379)
$Q_{crit}$  (p. 380)
$Q_{obt}$  (p. 380)
Sampling distribution of $F$  (p. 359)

Simple randomized-group design
  (p. 362)
Single factor experiment,
  independent groups design (p. 362)
Total variability ($SS_T$) (p. 362)
Tukey's HSD test  (p. 380)
Within-groups sum of squares
  ($SS_W$) (p. 362)
Within-groups variance estimate
  ($s_W^2$) (p. 362)

## QUESTIONS AND PROBLEMS

1. Identify or define the terms in the Important Terms section.
2. What are the characteristics of the $F$ distribution?
3. What advantages are there in doing experiments with more than two groups or conditions?
4. When doing an experiment with many groups, what is the problem with doing $t$ tests between all possible groups without any correction? Why does use of the analysis of variance avoid that problem?
5. The analysis of variance technique analyzes the variability of the data. Yet a significant $F$ value indicates that there is at least one significant mean difference between the conditions. How does analyzing the variability of the data allow conclusions about the means of the conditions?
6. What are the steps in forming an $F$ ratio in using the one-way analysis of variance technique?
7. In the analysis of variance, if $F_{obt}$ is less than 1, we don't even need to compare it with $F_{crit}$. It is obvious that the independent variable has not had a significant effect. Why is this so?
8. What are the assumptions underlying the analysis of variance?
9. The analysis of variance is a nondirectional technique, yet it uses a one-tailed evaluation. Is this statement correct? Explain.
10. Find $F_{crit}$ for the following situations:
    a. df(numerator) = 2, df(denominator) = 16, $\alpha = 0.05$

    b. df(numerator) = 3, df(denominator) = 36, $\alpha = 0.05$
    c. df(numerator) = 3, df(denominator) = 36, $\alpha = 0.01$
    What happens to $F_{crit}$ as the degrees of freedom increase and alpha is held constant? What happens to $F_{crit}$ when the degrees of freedom are held constant and alpha is made more stringent?
11. In Chapter 14, Practice Problem 14.2, an independent groups experiment was conducted to investigate whether lesions of the thalamus decrease pain perception. $\alpha = 0.05_{1\ tail}$ was used in the analysis. The data are again presented here. Scores are pain threshold (milliamps) to electric shock. Higher scores indicate decreased pain perception.

| Neutral Area Lesions | Thalamic Lesions |
|---|---|
| 0.8 | 1.9 |
| 0.7 | 1.8 |
| 1.2 | 1.6 |
| 0.5 | 1.2 |
| 0.4 | 1.0 |
| 0.9 | 0.9 |
| 1.4 | 1.7 |
| 1.1 | |

Using these data, verify that $F = t^2$ when there are just two groups in the independent groups experiment.

12. What are the variables that affect the power of the one-way analysis of variance technique?

13. For each of the variables identified in Question 12, state how power is affected if the variable is increased. Use the equation for $F_{obt}$ on p. 376 to justify your answer.

14. Explain why we must correct for doing multiple comparisons when doing *post hoc* comparisons.

15. How do planned comparisons, *post hoc* comparisons using the HSD test, and *post hoc* comparisons using the Newman–Keuls test differ with regard to
    a. Power? Explain.
    b. The probability of making a Type I error? Explain.

16. What are the $Q$ or Studentized range distributions? How do they avoid the problem of inflated Type I errors that result from doing multiple comparisons with the $t$ distribution?

17. In doing planned comparisons, it is better to use $s_W^2$ from the ANOVA rather than the weighted variance estimate from the two groups being compared. Is this statement correct? Why?

18. The accompanying table is a one-way, independent groups ANOVA summary table with part of the material missing.

| Source | SS | df | $s^2$ | $F_{obt}$ |
|--------|-----|-----|-------|-----------|
| Between groups | 1253.68 | 3 | | |
| Within groups | | | | |
| Total | 5016.40 | 39 | | |

a. Fill in the missing values.
b. How many groups are there in the experiment?
c. Assuming an equal number of subjects in each group, how many subjects are there in each group?
d. What is the value of $F_{crit}$, using $\alpha = 0.05$?
e. Is there a significant effect?

19. Assume you are a nutritionist who has been asked to determine whether there is a difference in sugar content among the three leading brands of breakfast cereal (brands A, B, and C). To assess the amount of sugar in the cereals, you randomly sample six packages of each brand and chemically determine their sugar content. The following grams of sugar were found:

| **Breakfast Cereal** | | |
|-----|-----|-----|
| *A* | *B* | *C* |
| 1 | 7 | 5 |
| 4 | 5 | 4 |
| 3 | 3 | 4 |
| 3 | 6 | 5 |
| 2 | 4 | 7 |
| 5 | 7 | 8 |

a. Using the conceptual equations of the one-way ANOVA, determine whether any of the brands differ in sugar content. Use $\alpha = 0.05$.
b. Same as part **a**, except use the computational equations. Which do you prefer? Why?
c. Do a *post hoc* analysis on each pair of means using the Tukey HSD test with $\alpha = 0.05$ to determine which cereals are different in sugar content.
d. Same as part **c**, but use the Newman–Keuls test. health

20. A sleep researcher conducts an experiment to determine whether sleep loss affects the ability to maintain sustained attention. Fifteen individuals are randomly divided into the following three groups of five subjects each: group 1, which gets the normal amount of sleep (7–8 hours); group 2, which is sleep-deprived for 24 hours; and group 3, which is sleep-deprived for 48 hours. All three groups are tested on the same auditory vigilance task. Subjects are presented with half-second tones spaced at irregular intervals over a 1-hour duration. Occasionally, one of the tones is slightly shorter than the rest. The subject's task is to detect the shorter tones. The following percentages of correct detections were observed:

| Normal Sleep | Sleep-Deprived for 24 Hours | Sleep-Deprived for 48 Hours |
|-----|-----|-----|
| 85 | 60 | 60 |
| 83 | 58 | 48 |
| 76 | 76 | 38 |
| 64 | 52 | 47 |
| 75 | 63 | 50 |

a. Determine whether there is an overall effect for sleep deprivation, using the conceptual equations of the one-way ANOVA. Use $\alpha = 0.05$.

b. Same as part **a,** except use the computational equations.

c. Which do you prefer? Why?

d. Determine the size of effect, using $\hat{\omega}^2$.

e. Determine the size of effect, using $\eta^2$.

f. Explain the difference in answers between part **d** and part **e**.

g. Do a planned comparison between the means of the 48-hour sleep-deprived group and the normal sleep group to see whether these conditions differ in their effect on the ability to maintain sustained attention. Use $\alpha = 0.05_{2\text{tail}}$. What do you conclude?

h. Do *post hoc* comparisons, comparing each pair of means using the Newman–Keuls test and $\alpha = 0.05_{2\text{tail}}$. What do you conclude?

i. Same as part **h**, but use the HSD test. Compare your answers to parts **h** and **i**. Explain any difference. cognitive

21. To test whether memory changes with age, a researcher conducts an experiment in which there are four groups of six subjects each. The groups differ according to the age of subjects. In group 1, the subjects are each 30 years old; group 2, 40 years old; group 3, 50 years old; and group 4, 60 years old. Assume that the subjects are all in good health and that the groups are matched on other important variables such as years of education, IQ, gender, motivation, and so on. Each subject is shown a series of nonsense syllables (a meaningless combination of three letters such as DAF or FUM) at a rate of one syllable every 4 seconds. The series is shown twice, after which the subjects are asked to write down as many of the syllables as they can remember. The number of syllables remembered by each subject is shown here:

| 30 Years Old | 40 Years Old | 50 Years Old | 60 Years Old |
|---|---|---|---|
| 14 | 12 | 17 | 13 |
| 13 | 15 | 14 | 10 |
| 15 | 16 | 14 | 7 |
| 17 | 11 | 9 | 8 |
| 12 | 12 | 13 | 6 |
| 10 | 18 | 15 | 9 |

a. Use the analysis of variance with $\alpha = 0.05$ to determine whether age has an effect on memory.

b. If there is a significant effect in part **a**, determine the size of effect, using $\hat{\omega}^2$.

c. Determine the size of effect, using $\eta^2$.

d. Explain the difference in answers between part **b** and part **c**.

e. Using planned comparisons with $\alpha = 0.05_{2\text{ tail}}$, compare the means of the 60-year-old and the 30-year-old groups. What do you conclude?

f. Use the Newman–Keuls test with $\alpha = 0.05_{2\text{ tail}}$ to compare all possible pairs of means. What do you conclude? cognitive

22. Assume you are employed by a consumer-products rating service and your assignment is to assess car batteries. For this part of your investigation, you want to determine whether there is a difference in useful life among the top-of-the-line car batteries produced by three manufacturers (A, B, and C). To provide the database for your assessment, you randomly sample four batteries from each manufacturer and run them through laboratory tests that allow you to determine the useful life of each battery. The following are the results given in months of useful battery life:

| Battery Manufacturer | | |
|---|---|---|
| A | B | C |
| 56 | 46 | 44 |
| 57 | 52 | 53 |
| 55 | 51 | 50 |
| 59 | 50 | 51 |

a. Use the analysis of variance with $\alpha = 0.05$ to determine whether there is a difference among these three brands of batteries.

b. Suppose you are asked to make a recommendation regarding the batteries based on useful life. Use the HSD test with $\alpha = 0.05_{2\text{ tail}}$ to help you with your decision. I/O

23. In Chapter 14, an illustrative experiment involved investigating the effect of hormone X on sexual behavior. Although we presented only two concentrations in that problem, let's assume the experiment actually involved four different concentrations of the hormone. The full data

are shown here, where the concentrations are arranged in ascending order; that is, 0 concentration is where there is zero amount of hormone X (this is the placebo group), and concentration 3 represents the highest amount of the hormone:

| Concentration of Hormone X | | | |
|---|---|---|---|
| *0* | *1* | *2* | *3* |
| 5 | 4 | 8 | 13 |
| 6 | 5 | 10 | 10 |
| 3 | 6 | 12 | 9 |
| 4 | 4 | 6 | 12 |
| 7 | 5 | 6 | 12 |
| 8 | 7 | 7 | 14 |
| 6 | 7 | 9 | 9 |
| 5 | 8 | 8 | 13 |
| 4 | 4 | 7 | 10 |
| 8 | 8 | 11 | 12 |

a. Using the analysis of variance with $\alpha = 0.05$, determine whether hormone X affects sexual behavior.
b. If there is a real effect, estimate the size of the effect using $\hat{\omega}^2$.
c. Using planned comparisons with $\alpha = 0.05_{2 \text{ tail}}$, compare the mean of concentration 3 with that of concentration 0. What do you conclude?
d. Using the Newman–Keuls test with $\alpha = 0.05_{2 \text{ tail}}$, compare all possible pairs of means. What do you conclude?
e. Same as part **d**, except use the HSD test. biological

24. A clinical psychologist is interested in evaluating the effectiveness of the following three techniques for treating mild depression: cognitive restructuring, assertiveness training, and an exercise/nutrition program. Forty undergraduate students suffering from mild depression are randomly sampled from the university counseling center's waiting list and randomly assigned ten each to the three techniques previously mentioned, and the remaining ten to a placebo control group. Treatment is conducted for 10 weeks, after which depression is measured using the Beck Depression Inventory. The posttreatment depression scores are given here. Higher scores indicate greater depression.

| | Treatment | | |
|---|---|---|---|
| *Placebo* | *Cognitive restructuring* | *Assertiveness training* | *Exercise/ nutrition* |
| 27 | 10 | 16 | 26 |
| 16 | 8 | 18 | 24 |
| 18 | 14 | 12 | 17 |
| 26 | 16 | 15 | 23 |
| 18 | 18 | 9 | 25 |
| 28 | 8 | 13 | 22 |
| 25 | 12 | 17 | 16 |
| 20 | 14 | 20 | 15 |
| 24 | 9 | 21 | 18 |
| 26 | 7 | 19 | 23 |

a. What is the overall null hypothesis?
b. Using $\alpha = 0.05$, what do you conclude?
c. Do *post hoc* comparisons, using the Tukey HSD test, with $\alpha = 0.05_{2 \text{ tail}}$. What do you conclude? clinical, health

25. A university researcher knowledgeable in Chinese medicine conducted a study to determine whether acupuncture can help reduce cocaine addiction. In this experiment, 18 cocaine addicts were randomly assigned to one of three groups of 6 addicts per group. One group received 10 weeks of acupuncture treatment in which the acupuncture needles were inserted into points on the outer ear where stimulation is believed to be effective. Another group, a placebo group, had acupuncture needles inserted into points on the ear believed not to be effective. The third group received no acupuncture treatment; instead, addicts in this group received relaxation therapy. All groups also received counseling over the 10-week treatment period. The dependent variable was craving for cocaine as measured by the number of cocaine urges experienced by each addict in the last week of treatment. The following are the results.

| Acupuncture + Counseling | Placebo + Counseling | Relaxation Therapy + Counseling |
|:---:|:---:|:---:|
| 4 | 8 | 12 |
| 7 | 12 | 7 |
| 6 | 11 | 9 |
| 5 | 8 | 6 |
| 2 | 10 | 11 |
| 3 | 7 | 6 |

a. Using $\alpha = 0.05$, what do you conclude?
b. If there is a significant effect, estimate the size of effect, using $\hat{\omega}^2$.
c. This time estimate the size of the effect, using $\eta^2$.
d. Explain the difference in answers between part **b** and part **c**.  clinical, health

26. An instructor is teaching three sections of Introductory Psychology, each section covering the same material. She has made up a different final exam for each section, but she suspects that one of the versions is more difficult than the other two.

She decides to conduct an experiment to evaluate the difficulty of the exams. During the review period, just before finals, she randomly selects five volunteers from each class. Class 1 volunteers are given version 1 of the exam; class 2 volunteers get version 2, and class 3 volunteers receive version 3. Of course, all volunteers are sworn not to reveal any of the exam questions, and also, of course, all of the volunteers will receive a different final exam from the one they took in the experiment. The following are the results.

| Exam Version 1 | Exam Version 2 | Exam Version 3 |
|:---:|:---:|:---:|
| 70 | 95 | 88 |
| 92 | 75 | 76 |
| 85 | 81 | 84 |
| 83 | 83 | 93 |
| 78 | 72 | 77 |

Using $\alpha = 0.05$, what do you conclude?  education

# NOTES

15.1 *Orthogonal comparisons.* When making comparisons between the means of the groups, we can represent any comparison as a weighted sum of the means. For example, if there are four means, we can represent the comparison between any of the groups as the weighted sum of $\overline{X}_1, \overline{X}_2, \overline{X}_3,$ and $\overline{X}_4$. Thus, if we are evaluating $\overline{X}_1 - \overline{X}_2$, the weighted sum would be $(1)\overline{X}_2 + (-1)\overline{X}_2 + (0)\overline{X}_3 + (0)\overline{X}_4$, where $1, -1, 0,$ and $0$ are the weights. If we are evaluating $\overline{X}_3 - \overline{X}_4$, the weighted sum would be $(0)\overline{X}_1 + (0)\overline{X}_2 + (1)\overline{X}_3 + (-1)\overline{X}_4$, where $0, 0, 1,$ and $-1$ are the weights. *In general, two comparisons are said to be orthogonal if the sum of the products of the two weights for each mean equals zero.* Using this information, let's now determine whether the foregoing two comparisons are orthogonal. The appropriate paired weights have been multiplied and summed, as follows:

| Comparison | Weighted Sum | Weights |
|:---|:---:|:---:|
| $\overline{X}_1 - \overline{X}_2$ | $(1)\overline{X}_1 + (-1)\overline{X}_2 + (0)\overline{X}_3 + (0)\overline{X}_4$ | $1, -1, 0, 0$ |
| $\overline{X}_3 - \overline{X}_4$ | $(0)\overline{X}_1 + (0)\overline{X}_2 + (1)\overline{X}_3 + (-1)\overline{X}_4$ | $0, 0, 1, -1$ |
|  | $(1)(0) + (-1)(0) + (0)(1) + (0)(-1) = 0$ |  |

Since the sum of the products of the two weights for each mean equals zero, these two comparisons are orthogonal (i.e., independent).

In general, if there are $k$ groups in an experiment, there are $k - 1$ independent comparisons possible.*

---

*For a more detailed discussion of orthogonal comparisons, see R. E. Kirk, *Experimental Design*, 3rd ed., Brooks/Cole, Pacific Grove, CA, 1995, pp. 115–118.

**BOOK COMPANION WEBSITE**

Go to www.thomsonedu.com/psychology/pagano for:

- SPSS problems and solutions
- Flash cards for review of terms
- Chapter quiz
- Statistical workshops
- And more

**WebTUTOR**

Available via WebTutor for this chapter:

- Detailed chapter outline
- *Know and Be Able To Do* section
- Drag & Drop game for review of terms
- Flash cards for review of terms
- Audio flash cards for MP3 player
- Solving problems using Excel
- Solving problems using SPSS
- More practice problems using computational equations
- Chapter quiz

# Introduction to Two-Way Analysis of Variance

**CHAPTER 16**

## INTRODUCTION TO THE TWO-WAY ANALYSIS OF VARIANCE—QUALITATIVE PRESENTATION

In Chapter 15, we discussed the most elementary analysis of variance design. We called it the simple randomized-groups design, the one-way analysis of variance, independent groups design, or the single factor experiment, independent groups design. The characteristics of this design are that there is only one independent variable (one factor) that is being investigated, there are several levels of the independent variable (several conditions) represented, and subjects are randomly assigned to each condition.

Actually, the analysis of variance design is not limited to single factor experiments. In fact, the effect of many different factors may be investigated at the same time in one experiment. Such experiments are called factorial experiments.

**definition** ■ *A **factorial experiment** is one in which the effects of two or more factors are assessed in one experiment. In a factorial experiment, the treatments used are combinations of the levels of the factors.*

The two-way analysis of variance is a bit more complicated than the one-way design. However, we get a lot more information from the two-way design.

*Basically, the **two-way analysis of variance** allows us in one experiment to evaluate the effect of two independent variables and the interaction between them.*

To illustrate this design, suppose a professor in physical education conducts an experiment to compare the effects on nighttime sleep of different intensities of exercise and the time of day when the exercise is done. For this example, let's assume that there are two levels of exercise (light and heavy) and two times of day (morning and evening). The experiment is depicted diagrammatically in Figure 16.1. From this figure, we can see that there are two factors (or independent variables): factor A, which is *time of day,* and factor B, which is *exercise intensity*. Each factor has two levels. Thus, this design is referred to as a $2 \times 2$ (read "two by two") design where each number stands for a factor and the magnitude of the

**figure 16.1** Schematic diagram of two-way analysis of variance example involving exercise intensity and time of day.

number designates the number of levels within the factor. For example, if factor A had three levels, then the experiment would be called a 3 × 2 design. In a 2 × 4 × 3 design, there would be three factors having two, four, and three levels, respectively. In the present example, there are two factors each having two levels. This results in four cells or conditions: $a_1b_1$ (morning–light exercise), $a_1b_2$ (morning–heavy exercise), $a_2b_1$ (evening–light exercise), and $a_2b_2$ (evening–heavy exercise). Since this is an independent groups design, subjects would be randomly assigned to each of the cells so that a different group of subjects occupies each cell. Since the levels of each factor were systematically chosen by the experimenter rather than being randomly chosen, this is called a *fixed effects* design.

There are three analyses done in this design. First, we want to determine whether factor A has a significant effect, disregarding the effect of factor B. In this illustration, we are interested in determining whether "time of day" makes a difference in the effect of exercise on sleep, disregarding the effect of "exercise intensity." Second, we want to determine whether factor B has a significant effect, without considering the effect of factor A. For this experiment, we are interested in determining whether the intensity of exercise makes a difference in sleep activity, disregarding the effect of time of day. Finally, we want to determine whether there is an interaction between factors A and B. In the present experiment, we want to determine whether there is an interaction between time of day and intensity of exercise in their effect on sleep.

Figure 16.2 shows some possible outcomes of this experiment. In part (a), there are no significant effects. In part (b), there is a significant main effect for time of day but no effect for intensity of exercise and no interaction. Thus, the

| definitions | ■ | *The effect of factor A (averaged over the levels of factor B) and the effect of factor B (averaged over the levels of factor A) are called* **main effects.** *An* **interaction effect** *occurs when the effect of one factor is not the same at all levels of the other factor.* |
|---|---|---|

subjects get significantly more sleep if the exercise is done in the morning rather than in the evening. However, it doesn't seem to matter if the exercise is light or heavy. In part (c), there is a significant main effect for intensity of exercise but no effect for time of day and no interaction. In this example, heavy exercise results in significantly more sleep than light exercise, and it doesn't matter whether the exercise is done in the morning or evening—the effect appears to be the same. Part (d) shows a significant main effect for intensity of exercise and time of day, with no interaction effect.

Both parts (e) and (f) show significant interaction effects. As stated previously, the essence of an interaction is that the effect of one factor is not the same at all levels of the other factor. This means that, when an interaction occurs between factors A and B, the differences in the dependent variable due to changes in one factor are not the same for each level of the other factor. In part (e), there is a significant interaction effect between intensity of exercise and time of day. The effect of different intensities of exercise is not the same for all levels of time of day. Thus, if the exercise is done in the evening, light exercise results in significantly more sleep than heavy exercise. On the other hand, if the exercise is done in the morning, light exercise results in significantly less sleep than heavy exer-

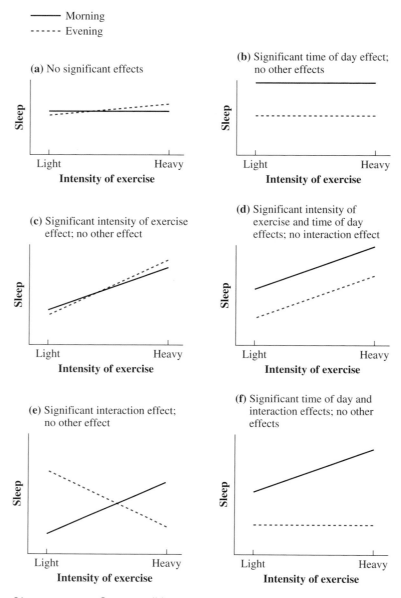

figure 16.2  Some possible outcomes of the experiment investigating the effects of intensity of exercise and time of day.

cise. In part (f), there is a significant main effect for time of day and a significant interaction effect. Thus, when the exercise is done in the morning, it results in significantly more sleep than when done in the evening, regardless of whether it is light or heavy exercise. In addition to this main effect, there is an interaction between the intensity of exercise and the time of day. Thus, there is no difference in the effect of the two intensities when the exercise is done in the evening, but when done in the morning, heavy exercise results in more sleep than light exercise.

In analyzing the data from a two-way analysis of variance design, we determine four variance estimates: $s_W^2$, $s_R^2$, $s_C^2$, and $s_{RC}^2$. The estimate $s_W^2$ is the *within-cells variance estimate* and corresponds to the within-groups variance estimate used in the one-way ANOVA. It becomes the standard against which each of the other estimates is compared. The other estimates are sensitive to the effects of the independent variables. The estimate $s_R^2$ is called the *row variance estimate*. It is based on the variability of the row means (see Figure 16.1) and, hence, is sensitive to the effects of variable A. The estimate $s_C^2$ is called the *column variance estimate*. It is based on the variability of the column means and, hence, is sensitive to the effects of variable B. The estimate $s_{RC}^2$ is the *row × column* (read "row by column") *variance estimate*. It is based on the variability of the cell means and, hence, is sensitive to the interaction effects of variables A and B. If variable A has no effect, $s_R^2$ is an independent estimate of $\sigma^2$. If variable B has no effect, then $s_C^2$ is an independent estimate of $\sigma^2$. Finally, if there is no interaction between variables A and B, $s_{RC}^2$ is also an independent estimate of $\sigma^2$. Thus, the estimates $s_R^2, s_C^2,$ and $s_{RC}^2$ are analogous to the between-groups variance estimate of the one-way design. To test for significance, three $F$ ratios are formed:

For variable A, $\qquad F_{\text{obt}} = \dfrac{s_R^2}{s_W^2}$

For variable B, $\qquad F_{\text{obt}} = \dfrac{s_C^2}{s_W^2}$

For the interaction between A and B, $\qquad F_{\text{obt}} = \dfrac{s_{RC}^2}{s_W^2}$

Each $F_{\text{obt}}$ value is evaluated against $F_{\text{crit}}$ as in the one-way analysis. For the rows comparison, if $F_{\text{obt}} \geq F_{\text{crit}}$, there is a significant main effect for factor A. If $F_{\text{obt}} \geq F_{\text{crit}}$ for the columns comparison, there is a significant main effect for factor B. Finally, if $F_{\text{obt}} \geq F_{\text{crit}}$ for the row × column comparison, there is a significant interaction effect. Thus, there are many similarities between the one-way and two-way designs. The biggest difference is that, with a two-way design, we can do essentially two one-way experiments plus we are able to evaluate the interaction between the two independent variables.

Thus far, the two-way analysis of variance, independent groups, fixed effects design has been discussed in a qualitative way. In the remainder of this chapter, we shall present a more detailed quantitative discussion of the data analysis for this design.

## QUANTITATIVE PRESENTATION OF THE TWO–WAY ANALYSIS OF VARIANCE

In the one-way analysis of variance, the total sum of squares is partitioned into two components: the within-groups sum of squares and the between-groups sum of squares. These two components are divided by the appropriate degrees of freedom to form two variance estimates: the within-groups variance estimate ($s_W^2$) and the between-groups variance estimate ($s_B^2$). If the null hypothesis is correct, then both estimates are estimates of the null-hypothesis population variance ($\sigma^2$) and the ratio $s_B^2/s_W^2$ will be distributed as $F$. If the independent variable has a real effect, then $s_B^2$ will tend to be larger than otherwise and so will the $F$ ratio. Thus, the larger the $F$ ratio is, the more unreasonable the null hypothesis becomes.

When $F_{obt} \geq F_{crit}$, we reject $H_0$ as being too unreasonable to entertain as an explanation of the data.

The situation is quite similar in the two-way analysis of variance. However, in the two-way analysis of variance, we partition the total sum of squares ($SS_T$) into four components: the within-cells sum of squares ($SS_W$), the row sum of squares ($SS_R$), the column sum of squares ($SS_C$), and the row × column sum of squares ($SS_{RC}$). This partitioning is shown in Figure 16.3. When these sums of squares are divided by the appropriate degrees of freedom, they form four variance estimates. These estimates are the within-cells variance estimate ($s_W^2$), the row variance estimate ($s_R^2$), the column variance estimate ($s_C^2$), and the row × column variance estimate ($s_{RC}^2$). In discussing each of these variance estimates, it will be useful to refer to Figure 16.4, which shows the notation and general layout of data for a two-way analysis of variance, independent groups design. We have assumed in the following discussion that the number of subjects in each cell is the same.

## Within–Cells Variance Estimate ($s_W^2$)

This estimate is derived from the variability of the scores within each cell. Since all the subjects within each cell receive the same level of variables A and B, the variability of their scores cannot be due to treatment differences. The within-cells variance estimate is analogous to the within-groups variance estimate used in the one-way analysis of variance. It is a measure of the inherent variability of the scores and, hence, gives us an estimate of the null-hypothesis population variance

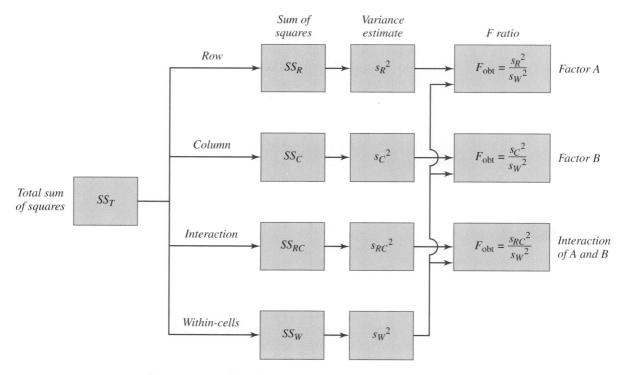

**figure 16.3**   Overview of two-way analysis of variance technique, independent groups design.

| | Levels of factor B | | | |
| | $b_1$ | $b_2$ | | $b_c$ | |
|---|---|---|---|---|---|
| $a_1$ | Cell 11 — — — — | Cell 12 — — — — | — — — — | Cell 1c — — — — | row $\overset{1}{\sum}X$ |
| $a_2$ | Cell 21 — — — | — — — — | — — — — | — — — — | row $\overset{2}{\sum}X$ |
| | — — — — — | — — — — — | — — — — — | — — — — — | |
| $a_r$ | Cell r1 — — — — | — — — — | — — — — | Cell rc — — — — | row $\overset{r}{\sum}X$ |

Levels of factor A

col. $\overset{1}{\sum}X$    col. $\overset{2}{\sum}X$    col. $\overset{c}{\sum}X$

where

$a_1$ = first level of factor $A$
$a_r$ = last level of factor $A$
$b_1$ = first level of factor $B$
$b_c$ = last level of factor $B$

$\overset{\text{row}\ 1}{\sum} X$ = sum of scores for row 1

$\overset{\text{row}\ r}{\sum} X$ = sum of scores for row $r$

$\overset{\text{col.}\ 1}{\sum} X$ = sum of scores for column 1

$\overset{\text{col.}\ c}{\sum} X$ = sum of scores for column $c$

$r$ = number of rows
$c$ = number of columns
$N$ = total number of scores
$n_{\text{cell}}$ = number of scores in each cell
$n_{\text{row}}$ = number of scores in each row
$n_{\text{col.}}$ = number of scores in each column

figure 16.4  Notation and general layout of data for a two-way analysis of variance design.

($\sigma^2$). It is the yardstick against which we compare each of the other variance estimates. In equation form,

$$s_W^2 = \frac{SS_W}{df_W} \qquad \textit{equation for within-cells variance estimate}$$

*where*    $SS_W$ = within-cells sum of squares
          $df_W$ = within-cells degrees of freedom

The within-cells sum of squares ($SS_W$) is just the sum of squares within each cell added together. Conceptually,

$$SS_W = SS_{11} + SS_{12} + \cdots + SS_{rc} \qquad \textit{conceptual equation for the within-cells sum of squares}$$

*where*    $SS_{11}$ = sum of squares for the scores in the cell defined by the intersection of row 1 and column 1
          $SS_{12}$ = sum of squares for the scores in the cell defined by the intersection of row 1 and column 2
          $SS_{rc}$ = sum of squares for the scores in the cell defined by the intersection of row $r$ and column $c$; this is the last cell in the matrix

As has been the case so often previously, the conceptual equation is not the best equation to use for computational purposes. The computational equation is given here:

$$SS_W = \overset{\text{all}}{\underset{\text{scores}}{\sum}} X^2 - \left[ \frac{\left(\overset{\text{cell}}{\underset{11}{\sum}} X\right)^2 + \left(\overset{\text{cell}}{\underset{12}{\sum}} X\right)^2 + \cdots + \left(\overset{\text{cell}}{\underset{rc}{\sum}} X\right)^2}{n_{\text{cell}}} \right]$$

*computational equation for the within-cells sum of squares*

Note the similarity of these equations to the comparable equations for the within-groups variance estimate used in the one-way ANOVA. The only difference is that in the two-way ANOVA, summation is with regard to the cells, whereas in the one-way ANOVA, summation is with regard to the groups.

In computing $SS_W$, there are $n$ deviation scores for each cell. Therefore, there are $n - 1$ degrees of freedom contributed by each cell. Since we sum over all cells in calculating $SS_W$, the within-cells degrees of freedom equal $n - 1$ times the number of cells. If we let $r$ equal the number of rows and $c$ equal the number of columns, then $rc$ equals the number of cells. Therefore, the within-cells degrees of freedom equal $rc(n - 1)$. Thus,

$$df_W = rc(n - 1) \qquad \textit{within-cells degrees of freedom}$$

*where*    $r$ = number of rows
          $c$ = number of columns

## Row Variance Estimate ($s_R^2$)

This estimate is based on the differences among the row means. It is analogous to the between-groups variance estimate ($s_B^2$) in the one-way ANOVA. You will recall that $s_B^2$ is an estimate of $\sigma^2$ plus the effect of the independent variable. Similarly, the row variance estimate ($s_R^2$) in the two-way ANOVA is an estimate of $\sigma^2$ plus the effect of factor A. If factor A has no effect, then the population row means are equal

$(\mu_{a_1} = \mu_{a_2} = \cdots = \mu_{a_r})$, and the differences among sample row means will just be due to random sampling from identical populations. In this case, $s_R^2$ becomes an estimate of just $\sigma^2$ alone. If factor A has an effect, then the differences among the row means, and hence $s_R^2$, will tend to be larger than otherwise. In equation form,

$$s_R^2 = \frac{SS_R}{df_R} \qquad \textit{equation for the row variance estimate}$$

*where*     $SS_R$ = row sum of squares
                 $df_R$ = row degrees of freedom

The row sum of squares is very similar to the between-groups sum of squares in the one-way ANOVA. The only difference is that with the row sum of squares we use the row means, whereas the between-groups sum of squares used the group means. The conceptual equation for $SS_R$ follows. Note that in computing row means, all the scores in a given row are combined and averaged. This is referred to as computing the row means "averaged over the columns" (see Figure 16.4). Thus, the row means are arrived at by averaging over the columns:

$$SS_R = n_{\text{row}}[(\overline{X}_{\text{row }1} - \overline{X}_G)^2 + (\overline{X}_{\text{row }2} - \overline{X}_G)^2 + \cdots + (\overline{X}_{\text{row }r} - \overline{X}_G)^2]$$

*conceptual equation for the
row sum of squares*

*where*     $\overline{X}_{\text{row }1} = \dfrac{\sum\limits^{\text{row}}_{1} X}{n_{\text{row }1}}$

                 $\overline{X}_{\text{row }r} = \dfrac{\sum\limits^{\text{row}}_{r} X}{n_{\text{row }r}}$

                 $\overline{X}_G$ = grand mean

From the conceptual equation, it is easy to see that $SS_R$ increases with the effect of variable A. As the effect of variable A increases, the row means become more widely separated, which in turn causes $(\overline{X}_{\text{row }1} - \overline{X}_G)^2, (\overline{X}_{\text{row }2} - \overline{X}_G)^2, \ldots,$ $(\overline{X}_{\text{row }r} - \overline{X}_G)^2$ to increase. Since these terms are in the numerator, $SS_R$ increases. Of course, if $SS_R$ increases, so does $s_R^2$.

In calculating $SS_R$, there are $r$ deviation scores. Thus, the row degrees of freedom equal $r - 1$. In equation form,

$$df_R = r - 1 \qquad \textit{row degrees of freedom}$$

Recall that the between-groups degrees of freedom $(df_B) = k - 1$ for the one-way ANOVA. The row degrees of freedom are quite similar except we are using rows rather than groups.

Again, the conceptual equation turns out not to be the best equation to use for computing $SS_R$. The computational equation is given here:

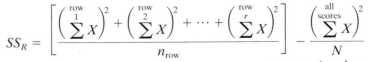

*computational equation for
the row sum of squares*

## Column Variance Estimate ($s_C^2$)

This estimate is based on the differences among the column means. It is exactly the same as $s_R^2$, except that it uses the column means rather than the row means. Since factor B affects the column means, the column variance estimate ($s_C^2$) is an estimate of $\sigma^2$ plus the effects of factor B. If the levels of factor B have no differential effect, then the population column means are equal ($\mu_{b_1} = \mu_{b_2} = \mu_{b_3} = \cdots = \mu_{b_c}$) and the differences among the sample column means are due to random sampling from identical populations. In this case, $s_C^2$ will be an estimate of $\sigma^2$ alone. If factor B has an effect, then the differences among the column means, and hence $s_C^2$, will tend to be larger than otherwise.

The equation for $s_C^2$ is

$$s_C^2 = \frac{SS_C}{df_C} \qquad \textit{column variance estimate}$$

*where*   $SS_C$ = column sum of squares
   $df_C$ = column degrees of freedom

The column sum of squares is also very similar to the row sum of squares. The only difference is that we use the column means in calculating the column sum of squares rather than the row means. The conceptual equation for $SS_C$ is shown here. Note that, in computing the column means, all the scores in a given column are combined and averaged. Thus, the column means are arrived at by averaging over the rows.

$$SS_C = n_{\text{col.}}[(\overline{X}_{\text{col. 1}} - \overline{X}_G)^2 + (\overline{X}_{\text{col. 2}} - \overline{X}_G)^2 + \cdots + (\overline{X}_{\text{col. }c} - \overline{X}_G)^2]$$

*conceptual equation for the column sum of squares*

*where*   $\overline{X}_{\text{col. 1}} = \dfrac{\overset{\text{col.}1}{\sum} X}{n_{\text{col. 1 W}}}$

   $\overline{X}_{\text{col. }c} = \dfrac{\overset{\text{col.}c}{\sum} X}{n_{\text{col. }c}}$

Again, we can see from the conceptual equation that $SS_C$ increases with the effect of variable B. As the effect of variable B increases, the column means become more widely spaced, which in turn causes $(\overline{X}_{\text{col. 1}} - \overline{X}_G)^2$, $(\overline{X}_{\text{col. 2}} - \overline{X}_G)^2$, $\ldots, (\overline{X}_{\text{col. }c} - \overline{X}_G)^2$ to increase. Since these terms are in the numerator of the equation for $SS_C$, the result is an increase in $SS_C$. Of course, an increase in $SS_C$ results in an increase in $s_C^2$.

Since there are $c$ deviation scores used in calculating $SS_C$, the column degrees of freedom equal $c - 1$. Thus,

$$df_C = c - 1 \qquad \textit{column degrees of freedom}$$

The computational equation for $SS_C$ is

*computational equation for the column sum of squares*

## Row × Column Variance Estimate ($s_{RC}{}^2$)

Earlier in this chapter, we pointed out that an interaction exists when the effect of one of the variables is not the same at all levels of the other variable. Another way of saying this is that an interaction exists when the effect of the combined action of the variables is different from that which would be predicted by the individual effects of the variables. To illustrate this point, consider Figure 16.2(f), p. 400, where there is an interaction between the time of day and the intensity of exercise. An interaction exists because the sleep score for heavy exercise done in the morning is higher than would be predicted based on the individual effects of the time of day and intensity of exercise variables. If there were no interaction, then we would expect the lines to be parallel. The intensity of exercise variable would have the same effect when done in the evening as when done in the morning.

The row × column variance estimate ($s_{RC}{}^2$) is used to evaluate the interaction of variables A and B. As such, it is based on the differences among the cell means beyond that which is predicted by the individual effects of the two variables. The row × column variance estimate is an estimate of $\sigma^2$ plus the interaction of A and B. If there is no interaction and any main effects are removed, then the population cell means are equal ($\mu_{a_1 b_1} = \mu_{a_1 b_2} = \cdots = \mu_{a_r b_c}$) and differences among cell means must be due to random sampling from identical populations. In this case, $s_{RC}{}^2$ will be an estimate of $\sigma^2$ alone. If there is an interaction between factors A and B, then the differences among the cell means and, hence $s_{RC}{}^2$, will tend to be higher than otherwise.

The equation for $s_{RC}{}^2$ is

$$s_{RC}{}^2 = \frac{SS_{RC}}{df_{RC}} \qquad \textit{row} \times \textit{column variance estimate}$$

*where*    $SS_{RC}$ = row × column sum of squares
$df_{RC}$ = row × column degrees of freedom

The row × column sum of squares is equal to the variability of the cell means when the variability due to the individual effects of factors A and B has been removed. Both the conceptual and computational equations are given here:

$$SS_{RC} = n_{\text{cell}}[(\overline{X}_{\text{cell }11} - \overline{X}_G)^2 + (\overline{X}_{\text{cell }12} - \overline{X}_G)^2 + \cdots + (\overline{X}_{\text{cell }rc} - \overline{X}_G)^2]$$
$$- SS_R - SS_C$$

*conceptual equation for the row × column sum of squares*

$$SS_{RC} = \left[ \frac{\left(\overset{\text{cell}}{\underset{11}{\sum}} X\right)^2 + \left(\overset{\text{cell}}{\underset{12}{\sum}} X\right)^2 + \cdots + \left(\overset{\text{cell}}{\underset{rc}{\sum}} X\right)^2}{n_{\text{cell}}} \right] - \frac{\left(\overset{\text{all}}{\overset{\text{scores}}{\sum}} X\right)^2}{N} - SS_R - SS_C$$

*computational equation for the row × column sum of squares*

The degrees of freedom for the row × column variance estimate equal $(r - 1)(c - 1)$. Thus,

$$df_{RC} = (r - 1)(c - 1) \qquad \textit{row} \times \textit{column degrees of freedom}$$

## Computing $F$ Ratios

Once the variance estimates have been determined, they are used in conjunction with $s_W^2$ to form $F$ ratios (see Figure 16.3) to test the main effects of the variables and their interaction. The following three $F$ ratios are computed:

*To test the main effect of variable A (row effect):*

$$F_{obt} = \frac{s_R^2}{s_W^2} = \frac{\sigma^2 + \text{effects of variable A}}{\sigma^2}$$

*To test the main effect of variable B (column effect):*

$$F_{obt} = \frac{s_C^2}{s_W^2} = \frac{\sigma^2 + \text{effects of variable B}}{\sigma^2}$$

*To test the interaction of variables A and B (row $\times$ column effect):*

$$F_{obt} = \frac{s_{RC}^2}{s_W^2} = \frac{\sigma^2 + \text{interaction effects of A and B}}{\sigma^2}$$

The ratio $s_R^2/s_W^2$ is used to test the main effect of variable A. If variable A has no main effect, $s_R^2$ is an independent estimate of $\sigma^2$ and $s_R^2/s_W^2$ is distributed as $F$ with degrees of freedom equal to $df_R$ and $df_W$. If variable A has a main effect, $s_R^2$ will be larger than otherwise and the $F_{obt}$ value for rows will increase.

The ratio $s_C^2/s_W^2$ is used to test the main effect of variable B. If this variable has no main effect, then $s_C^2$ is an independent estimate of $\sigma^2$ and $s_C^2/s_W^2$ is distributed as $F$ with degrees of freedom equal to $df_C$ and $df_W$. If variable B has a main effect, $s_C^2$ will be larger than otherwise, causing an increase in the $F_{obt}$ value for columns.

The interaction between A and B is tested using the ratio $s_{RC}^2/s_W^2$. If there is no interaction, $s_R^2$ is an independent estimate of $\sigma^2$ and $s_{RC}^2/s_W^2$ is distributed as $F$ with degrees of freedom equal to $df_{RC}$ and $df_W$. If there is an interaction, $s_{RC}^2$ will be larger than otherwise, causing an increase in the $F_{obt}$ value for interaction.

The main effect of each variable and their interaction are tested by comparing the appropriate $F_{obt}$ value with $F_{crit}$. $F_{crit}$ is found in Table F in Appendix D, using $\alpha$ and the degrees of freedom of the $F$ value being evaluated. The decision rule is the same as with the one-way ANOVA, namely,

If $F_{obt} \geq F_{crit}$, reject $H_0$.     *decision rule for evaluating $H_0$ in two-way ANOVA*

## ANALYZING AN EXPERIMENT WITH TWO-WAY ANOVA

We are now ready to analyze the data from an illustrative example.

an experiment

### Effect of Exercise on Sleep

Let's assume a professor in physical education conducts an experiment to compare the effects on nighttime sleep of different amounts of exercise and of the time of day when the exercise is done. The experiment uses a fixed effects, $3 \times 2$ factorial design with independent groups. There are three levels of exercise (light, moderate, and heavy) and two times of day (morning and evening). Thirty-six college students in good physical condition are randomly assigned to the six cells such that there are six subjects per cell.

The subjects who do heavy exercise jog for 3 miles, the subjects who do moderate exercise jog for 1 mile, and the subjects in the light exercise condition jog for only $\frac{1}{4}$ mile. Morning exercise is done at 7:30 A.M., whereas evening exercise is done at 7:00 P.M. Each subject exercises once, and the number of hours slept that night is recorded. The data are shown in Table 16.1.

1. What are the null hypotheses for this experiment?
2. Using $\alpha = 0.05$, what do you conclude?

## SOLUTION

1. Null hypotheses:
   a. *For the A variable (main effect):* The time of day when exercise is done does not affect nighttime sleep. The population row means for morning and evening exercise averaged over the different levels of exercise are equal ($\mu_{a_1} = \mu_{a_2}$).
   b. *For the B variable (main effect):* The different levels of exercise have the same effect on nighttime sleep. The population column means for light, medium, and heavy exercise averaged over time of day conditions are equal ($\mu_{b_1} = \mu_{b_2} = \mu_{b_3}$).
   c. *For the interaction between A and B:* There is no interaction between time of day and level of exercise. With any main effects removed, the population cell means are equal ($\mu_{a_1b_1} = \mu_{a_1b_2} = \mu_{a_1b_3} = \mu_{a_2b_1} = \mu_{a_2b_2} = \mu_{a_2b_3}$).
2. Conclusion, using $\alpha = 0.05$:
   a. Calculate $F_{obt}$ for each hypothesis:

**STEP 1: Calculate the row sum of squares, $SS_R$:**

$$SS_R = \left[ \frac{\left( \overset{\text{row } 1}{\sum X} \right)^2 + \left( \overset{\text{row } 2}{\sum X} \right)^2}{n_{\text{row}}} \right] - \frac{\left( \overset{\text{all scores}}{\sum X} \right)^2}{N}$$

$$= \left[ \frac{(129.2)^2 + (147.2)^2}{18} \right] - \frac{(276.4)^2}{36}$$

$$= 9.000$$

table **16.1** Data from exercise experiment

| Time of Day | Exercise | | | |
|---|---|---|---|---|
| | *Light* | *Moderate* | *Heavy* | |
| Morning | 6.5  7.4 | 7.4  7.3 | 8.0  7.6 | $\Sigma X = 129.20$ |
| | 7.3  7.2 | 6.8  7.6 | 7.7  6.6 | $\Sigma X^2 = 930.50$ |
| | 6.6  6.8 | 6.7  7.4 | 7.1  7.2 | $n = 18$ |
| | $\overline{X} = 6.97$ | $\overline{X} = 7.20$ | $\overline{X} = 7.37$ | $\overline{X} = 7.18$ |
| Evening | 7.1  7.7 | 7.4  8.0 | 8.2  8.7 | $\Sigma X = 147.20$ |
| | 7.9  7.5 | 8.1  7.6 | 8.5  9.6 | $\Sigma X^2 = 1212.68$ |
| | 8.2  7.6 | 8.2  8.0 | 9.5  9.4 | $n = 18$ |
| | $\overline{X} = 7.67$ | $\overline{X} = 7.88$ | $\overline{X} = 8.98$ | $\overline{X} = 8.18$ |
| | $\Sigma X = 87.80$ | $\Sigma X = 90.50$ | $\Sigma X = 98.10$ | $\Sigma X = 276.40$ |
| | $\Sigma X^2 = 645.30$ | $\Sigma X^2 = 685.07$ | $\Sigma X^2 = 812.81$ | $\Sigma X^2 = 2143.18$ |
| | $n = 12$ | $n = 12$ | $n = 12$ | $N = 36$ |
| | $\overline{X} = 7.32$ | $\overline{X} = 7.54$ | $\overline{X} = 8.18$ | |

**STEP 2: Calculate the column sum of squares, $SS_C$:**

$$SS_C = \left[ \frac{\left( \overset{\text{col.}}{\underset{1}{\sum}} X \right)^2 + \left( \overset{\text{col.}}{\underset{2}{\sum}} X \right)^2 + \left( \overset{\text{col.}}{\underset{3}{\sum}} X \right)^2}{n_{\text{col.}}} \right] - \frac{\left( \overset{\text{all}}{\underset{\text{scores}}{\sum}} X \right)^2}{N}$$

$$= \left[ \frac{(87.8)^2 + (90.5)^2 + (98.1)^2}{12} \right] - \frac{(276.4)^2}{36}$$

$$= 4.754$$

**STEP 3: Calculate the row $\times$ column sum of squares, $SS_{RC}$:**

$$SS_{RC} = \left[ \frac{\left( \overset{\text{cell}}{\underset{11}{\sum}} X \right)^2 + \left( \overset{\text{cell}}{\underset{12}{\sum}} X \right)^2 + \left( \overset{\text{cell}}{\underset{13}{\sum}} X \right)^2 + \left( \overset{\text{cell}}{\underset{21}{\sum}} X \right)^2 + \left( \overset{\text{cell}}{\underset{22}{\sum}} X \right)^2 + \left( \overset{\text{cell}}{\underset{23}{\sum}} X \right)^2}{n_{\text{cell}}} \right]$$

$$- \frac{\left( \overset{\text{all}}{\underset{\text{scores}}{\sum}} X \right)^2}{N} - SS_R - SS_C$$

$$= \left[ \frac{(41.8)^2 + (43.2)^2 + (44.2)^2 + (46.0)^2 + (47.3)^2 + (53.9)^2}{6} \right] - \frac{(276.4)^2}{36}$$

$$-9.000 - 4.754$$

$$= 1.712$$

**STEP 4: Calculate the within-cells sum of squares, $SS_W$:**

$$SS_W = \overset{\text{all}}{\underset{\text{scores}}{\sum}} X^2$$

$$- \left[ \frac{\left( \overset{\text{cell}}{\underset{11}{\sum}} X \right)^2 + \left( \overset{\text{cell}}{\underset{12}{\sum}} X \right)^2 + \left( \overset{\text{cell}}{\underset{13}{\sum}} X \right)^2 + \left( \overset{\text{cell}}{\underset{21}{\sum}} X \right)^2 + \left( \overset{\text{cell}}{\underset{22}{\sum}} X \right)^2 + \left( \overset{\text{cell}}{\underset{23}{\sum}} X \right)^2}{n_{\text{cell}}} \right]$$

$$= 2143.18 - \left[ \frac{(41.8)^2 + (43.2)^2 + (44.2)^2 + (46.0)^2 + (47.3)^2 + (53.9)^2}{6} \right]$$

$$= 5.577$$

**STEP 5: Calculate the total sum of squares, $SS_T$:** This step is a check to be sure the previous calculations are correct. Once we calculate $SS_T$, we can use the following equation to check the other calculations:

$$SS_T = SS_R + SS_C + SS_{RC} + SS_W$$

First, we must calculate $SS_T$:

$$SS_T = \overset{\text{all}}{\underset{\text{scores}}{\sum}} X^2 - \frac{\left( \overset{\text{all}}{\underset{\text{scores}}{\sum}} X \right)^2}{N}$$

$$= 2143.18 - \frac{(276.4)^2}{36}$$

$$= 21.042$$

Substituting the obtained values of $SS_T$, $SS_R$, $SS_C$, $SS_{RC}$, and $SS_W$ into the partitioning equation for $SS_T$, we obtain

$$SS_T = SS_R + SS_C + SS_{RC} + SS_W$$

$$21.042 = 9.000 + 4.754 + 1.712 + 5.577$$

$$21.042 = 21.043$$

The equation checks within rounding accuracy. Therefore, we can assume our calculations up to this point are correct.

**STEP 6: Calculate the degrees of freedom for each variance estimate:**

$$df_R = r - 1 = 2 - 1 = 1$$

$$df_C = c - 1 = 3 - 1 = 2$$

$$df_{RC} = (r - 1)(c - 1) = (1)2 = 2$$

$$df_W = rc(n_{cell} - 1) = 2(3)(5) = 30$$

$$df_T = N - 1 = 35$$

Note that

$$df_T = df_R + df_C + df_{RC} + df_W$$

$$35 = 1 + 2 + 2 + 30$$

$$35 = 35$$

**STEP 7: Calculate the variance estimates $s_R^2$, $s_C^2$, $s_{RC}^2$, and $s_W^2$:** Each variance estimate is equal to the sum of squares divided by the appropriate degrees of freedom. Thus,

$$\text{Row variance estimate} = s_R^2 = \frac{SS_R}{df_R} = \frac{9.000}{1} = 9.000$$

$$\text{Column variance estimate} = s_C^2 = \frac{SS_C}{df_C} = \frac{4.754}{2} = 2.377$$

$$\text{Row} \times \text{column variance estimate} = s_{RC}^2 = \frac{SS_{RC}}{df_{RC}} = \frac{1.712}{2} = 0.856$$

$$\text{Within-cells variance estimate} = s_W^2 = \frac{SS_W}{df_W} = \frac{5.577}{30} = 0.186$$

**STEP 8: Calculate the $F$ ratios:** For the row effect,

$$F_{obt} = \frac{s_R^2}{s_W^2} = \frac{9.000}{0.186} = 48.42$$

For the column effect,

$$F_{obt} = \frac{s_C^2}{s_W^2} = \frac{2.377}{0.186} = 12.78$$

For the row $\times$ column interaction effect,

$$F_{obt} = \frac{s_{RC}^2}{s_W^2} = \frac{0.856}{0.186} = 4.60$$

b. Evaluate the $F_{obt}$ values:

*For the row effect:* From Table F, with $\alpha = 0.05$, $df_{numerator} = df_R = 1$, and $df_{denominator} = df_W = 30$, $F_{crit} = 4.17$. Since $F_{obt}$ (48.42) > 4.17, we reject $H_0$ with respect to the A variable, which in this experiment is time of day. There is a significant effect for time of day.

*For the column effect:* From Table F, with $\alpha = 0.05$, $df_{numerator} = df_C = 2$, and $df_{denominator} = df_W = 30$, $F_{crit} = 3.32$. Since $F_{obt}$ (12.78) > 3.32, we reject $H_0$ with respect to the B variable, which in this experiment is amount of exercise. There is a significant main effect for amount of exercise.

*For the row × column interaction effect:* From Table F, with $\alpha = 0.05$, $df_{numerator} = df_{RC} = 2$, and $df_{denominator} = df_W = 30$, $F_{crit} = 3.32$. Since $F_{obt}$ (4.60) > 3.32, we reject $H_0$ regarding the interaction of variables A and B. There is a significant interaction between the amount of exercise and the time of day when the exercise is done.

The analysis is summarized in Table 16.2.

**t a b l e 16.2** Summary ANOVA table for exercise and time of day experiment

| Source | SS | df | $s^2$ | $F_{obt}$ | $F_{crit}$ |
|---|---|---|---|---|---|
| Rows (time of day) | 9.000 | 1 | 9.000 | 48.42[*] | 4.17 |
| Columns (exercise) | 4.754 | 2 | 2.377 | 12.79[*] | 3.32 |
| Rows × columns | 1.712 | 2 | 0.856 | 4.60[*] | 3.32 |
| Within cells | 5.577 | 30 | 0.186 | | |
| Total | 21.042 | 35 | | | |

[*]Since $F_{obt} > F_{crit}$, $H_0$ is rejected.

## Interpreting the Results

In the preceding analysis, we have rejected the null hypothesis for both the row and column effects. A significant effect for rows indicates that variable A has had a significant main effect. The differences between the row means, averaged over the columns, were too great to attribute to random sampling from populations where $\mu_{a_1} = \mu_{a_2}$. In the present experiment, the significant row effect indicates that there was a significant main effect for the time of day factor. The differences between the means for the time of day conditions averaged over the amount of exercise conditions were too great to attribute to chance. We have plotted the mean of each cell in Figure 16.5. From this figure, it can be seen that evening exercise resulted in greater sleep than morning exercise.

A significant effect for columns indicates that variable B has had a significant main effect—that the differences among the column means, computed by averaging over the rows, were too great to attribute to random sampling from the null-hypothesis population. In the present experiment, the significant effect for columns tells us that the differences between the means of the three exercise conditions computed by averaging over the time of day conditions were too great to attribute to random sampling fluctuations. From Figure 16.5, it can be seen that the effect of increasing the amount of exercise averaged over the time of day conditions was to increase the amount of sleep.

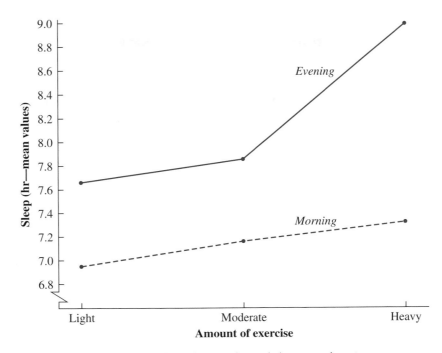

**f i g u r e  16.5**  Cell means from the exercise and sleep experiment.

The results of this experiment also showed a significant row × column interaction effect. As discussed previously, a significant interaction effect indicates that the effects of one of the factors on the dependent variable are not the same at all the levels of the other factor. Plotting the mean for each cell is particularly helpful for interpreting an interaction effect. From Figure 16.5, we can see that the increase in the amount of sleep is about the same in going from light to moderate exercise whether the exercise is done in the morning or evening. However, the difference in the amount of sleep in going from moderate to heavy exercise varies depending on whether the exercise is done in the morning or evening. Heavy exercise results in a much greater increase in the amount of sleep when the exercise is done in the evening than when done in the morning.

Let's do another problem for practice.

## Practice Problem 16.1

A statistics professor conducts an experiment to compare the effectiveness of two methods of teaching his course. Method I is the usual way he teaches the course: lectures, homework assignments, and a final exam. Method II is the same as method I, except that students receiving method II get 1 additional hour per week in which they solve illustrative problems under the guidance of the professor. The professor is also interested in how the

*(continued)*

methods affect students of differing mathematical abilities, so volunteers for the experiment are subdivided according to mathematical ability into superior, average, and poor groups. Five students from each group are randomly assigned to method I and 5 students from each group to method II. At the end of the course, all 30 students take the same final exam. The following final exam scores resulted:

| Mathematical Ability | Teaching Method | | | |
|---|---|---|---|---|
| | Method I (1) | | Method II (2) | |
| Superior (1) | 39[*] | 41 | 49 | 47 |
| | 48 | 42 | 47 | 48 |
| | 44 | | 43 | |
| Average (2) | 43 | 36 | 38 | 46 |
| | 40 | 35 | 45 | 44 |
| | 42 | | 42 | |
| Poor (3) | 30 | 33 | 37 | 41 |
| | 29 | 36 | 34 | 33 |
| | 37 | | 40 | |

[*]Scores are the number of points received out of a total of 50 possible points.

**a.** What are the null hypotheses for this experiment?
**b.** Using $\alpha = 0.05$, what do you conclude?

**SOLUTION**

**a.** Null hypotheses:
   1. *For the A variable (main effect):* The three levels of mathematical ability do not differentially affect final exam scores in this course. The population row means for the three levels of mathematical ability averaged over teaching methods are equal ($\mu_{a_1} = \mu_{a_2} = \mu_{a_3}$).
   2. *For the B variable (main effect):* Teaching methods I and II are equal in their effects on final exam scores in this course. The population column means for teaching methods I and II averaged over the three levels of mathematical ability are equal ($\mu_{b_1} = \mu_{b_2}$).
   3. *For the interaction between variables A and B:* There is no interaction effect between variables A and B. With any main effects removed, the population cell means are equal ($\mu_{a_1b_1} = \mu_{a_1b_2} = \mu_{a_2b_1} = \mu_{a_2b_2} = \mu_{a_3b_1} = \mu_{a_3b_2}$).

**b.** Conclusion, using $\alpha = 0.05$:
   1. Calculating $F_{obt}$:

   **STEP 1: Calculate $SS_R$:**

$$SS_R = \left[ \frac{\left( \overset{row.1}{\sum X} \right)^2 + \left( \overset{row.2}{\sum X} \right)^2 + \left( \overset{row.3}{\sum X} \right)^2}{n_{row}} \right] - \frac{\left( \overset{all\ scores}{\sum X} \right)^2}{N}$$

$$= \frac{(448)^2 + (411)^2 + (350)^2}{10} - \frac{(1209)^2}{30} = 489.800$$

**STEP 2: Calculate $SS_C$:**

$$SS_C = \left[ \frac{\left( \overset{\text{col.}}{\underset{1}{\sum}} X \right)^2 + \left( \overset{\text{col.}}{\underset{2}{\sum}} X \right)^2}{n_{\text{col.}}} \right] - \frac{\left( \overset{\text{all}}{\underset{\text{scores}}{\sum}} X \right)^2}{N}$$

$$= \frac{(575)^2 + (634)^2}{15} - \frac{(1209)^2}{30} = 116.033$$

**STEP 3: Calculate $SS_{RC}$:**

$$SS_{RC} = \left[ \frac{\left( \overset{\text{cell}}{\underset{11}{\sum}} X \right)^2 + \left( \overset{\text{cell}}{\underset{12}{\sum}} X \right)^2 + \left( \overset{\text{cell}}{\underset{21}{\sum}} X \right)^2 + \left( \overset{\text{cell}}{\underset{22}{\sum}} X \right)^2 + \left( \overset{\text{cell}}{\underset{31}{\sum}} X \right)^2 + \left( \overset{\text{cell}}{\underset{32}{\sum}} X \right)^2}{n_{\text{cell}}} \right]$$

$$- \frac{\left( \overset{\text{all}}{\underset{\text{scores}}{\sum}} X \right)^2}{N} - SS_R - SS_C$$

$$= \left[ \frac{(214)^2 + (234)^2 + (196)^2 + (215)^2 + (165)^2 + (185)^2}{5} \right] - \frac{(1209)^2}{30}$$

$$- 498.8 - 116.083 = 49,328.6 - 48,722.7 - 489.8 - 116.033 = 0.067$$

**STEP 4: Calculate $SS_W$:**

$$SS_W = \overset{\text{all}}{\underset{\text{scores}}{\sum}} X^2$$

$$- \left[ \frac{\left( \overset{\text{cell}}{\underset{11}{\sum}} X \right)^2 + \left( \overset{\text{cell}}{\underset{12}{\sum}} X \right)^2 + \left( \overset{\text{cell}}{\underset{21}{\sum}} X \right)^2 + \left( \overset{\text{cell}}{\underset{22}{\sum}} X \right)^2 + \left( \overset{\text{cell}}{\underset{31}{\sum}} X \right)^2 + \left( \overset{\text{cell}}{\underset{32}{\sum}} X \right)^2}{n_{\text{cell}}} \right]$$

$$= 49,587 - \left[ \frac{(214)^2 + (234)^2 + (196)^2 + (215)^2 + (165)^2 + (185)^2}{5} \right]$$

$$= 49,587 - 49,328.6 = 258.4$$

**STEP 5: Calculate $SS_T$:**   This step is to check the previous calculations:

$$SS_T = \overset{\text{all}}{\underset{\text{scores}}{\sum}} X^2 - \frac{\left( \overset{\text{all}}{\underset{\text{scores}}{\sum}} X \right)^2}{N}$$

$$= 49,587 - \frac{(1209)^2}{30}$$

$$= 864.3$$

$$SS_T = SS_R + SS_C + SS_{RC} + SS_W$$
$$864.3 = 489.8 + 116.033 + 0.067 + 258.4$$
$$864.3 = 864.3$$

*(continued)*

Since the partitioning equation checks, we can assume our calculations thus far are correct.

**STEP 6: Calculate df:**

$$df_R = r - 1 = 3 - 1 = 2$$
$$df_C = c - 1 = 2 - 1 = 1$$
$$df_{RC} = (r - 1)(c - 1) = (3 - 1)(2 - 1) = 2$$
$$df_W = rc(n_{cell} - 1) = 6(4) = 24$$
$$df_T = N - 1 = 29$$

**STEP 7: Calculate $s_R^2$, $s_C^2$, $s_{RC}^2$, and $s_W^2$:**

$$s_R^2 = \frac{SS_R}{df_R} = \frac{489.8}{2} = 244.9$$

$$s_C^2 = \frac{SS_C}{df_C} = \frac{116.033}{1} = 116.033$$

$$s_{RC}^2 = \frac{SS_{RC}}{df_{RC}} = \frac{0.067}{2} = 0.034$$

$$s_W^2 = \frac{SS_W}{df_W} = \frac{258.4}{24} = 10.767$$

**STEP 8: Calculate $F_{obt}$:** For the row effect,

$$F_{obt} = \frac{s_R^2}{s_W^2} = \frac{244.9}{10.767} = 22.75$$

For the column effect,

$$F_{obt} = \frac{s_C^2}{s_W^2} = \frac{116.033}{10.767} = 10.78$$

For the row × column effect,

$$F_{obt} = \frac{s_{RC}^2}{s_W^2} = \frac{0.034}{10.767} = 0.00$$

2. Evaluate the $F_{obt}$ values:

*For the row effect:* From Table F, with $\alpha = 0.05$, $df_{numerator} = df_R = 2$, and $df_{denominator} = df_W = 24$, $F_{crit} = 3.40$. Since $F_{obt}$ (22.75) > 3.40, we reject $H_0$ with respect to the A variable. There is a significant effect for mathematical ability.

*For the column effect:* From Table F, with $\alpha = 0.05$, $df_{numerator} = df_C = 1$, and $df_{denominator} = df_W = 24$, $F_{crit} = 4.26$. Since $F_{obt}$ (10.78) > 4.26, we reject $H_0$ with respect to the B variable. There is a significant main effect for teaching methods.

*For the row × column interaction effect:* Since $F_{obt}$ (0.00) < 1, we retain $H_0$ and conclude that the data do not support the hypothesis that there is an interaction between mathematical ability and teaching methods.

The solution to this problem is summarized in Table 16.3

table 16.3   Summary ANOVA table for teaching method and mathematical ability experiment

| Source | *SS* | df | $s^2$ | $F_{obt}$ | $F_{crit}$ |
|---|---|---|---|---|---|
| Rows (mathematical ability) | 489.800 | 2 | 244.900 | 22.75* | 3.40 |
| Columns (teaching method) | 116.033 | 1 | 116.033 | 10.78* | 4.26 |
| Rows × columns | 0.067 | 2 | 0.034 | 0.00 | 3.40 |
| Within cells | 258.400 | 24 | 10.767 | | |
| Total | 864.300 | 29 | | | |

*Since $F_{obt} > F_{crit}$, $H_0$ is rejected.

**Interpreting the results of Practice Problem 16.1**    In the preceding analysis, we rejected the null hypothesis for both the row and column effects. Rejecting $H_0$ for rows means that there was a significant main effect for variable A, mathematical ability. The differences among the means for the different levels of mathematical ability averaged over teaching methods were too great to attribute to chance. The mean of each cell has been plotted in Figure 16.6. From this figure, it can be seen that increasing the level of mathematical ability results in increased final exam scores.

Rejecting $H_0$ for columns indicates that there was a significant main effect for the B variable, teaching methods. The difference between the means for teaching method I and teaching method II averaged over mathematical ability was too great to attribute to random sampling fluctuations. From Figure 16.6, we can see that method II was superior to method I.

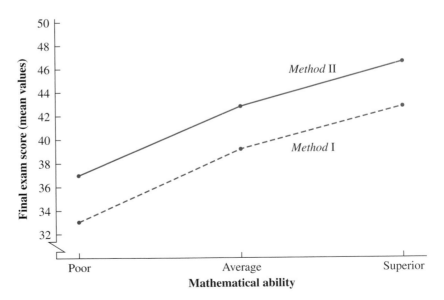

figure 16.6   Cell means from the teaching method and mathematical ability experiment.

In this experiment, there was no significant interaction effect. This means that, within the limits of sensitivity of this experiment, the effect of each variable was the same over all levels of the other variable. This can be most clearly seen by viewing Figure 16.6 with regard to variable A. The lack of a significant interaction effect indicates that the effect of different levels of mathematical ability on final exam scores was the same for teaching methods I and II. This results in parallel lines when the means of the cells are plotted (see Figure 16.6). *In fact, it is a general rule that, when the lines are parallel in a graph of the individual cell means, you can be sure there is no interaction effect.* For there to be an interaction effect, the lines must deviate significantly from parallel. In this regard, it will be useful to review Figure 16.2 to see whether you can determine which graphs show interaction effects.*

## Practice Problem 16.2

A clinical psychologist is interested in the effect that anxiety has on the ability of individuals to learn new material. She is also interested in whether the effect of anxiety depends on the difficulty of the new material. An experiment is conducted in which there are three levels of anxiety (high, medium, and low) and three levels of difficulty (high, medium, and low) for the material which is to be learned. Out of a pool of volunteers, 15 low-anxious, 15 medium-anxious, and 15 high-anxious subjects are selected and randomly assigned 5 each to the three difficulty levels. Each subject is given 30 minutes to learn the new material, after which the subjects are tested to determine the amount learned.

The following data are collected:

| Difficulty of Material | Anxiety* | | | | | |
| --- | --- | --- | --- | --- | --- | --- |
| | *Low* | | *Medium* | | *High* | |
| Low | 18 | 17 | 18 | 18 | 18 | 17 |
| | 20 | 16 | 19 | 15 | 16 | 18 |
| | 17 | | 17 | | 19 | |
| Medium | 18 | 14 | 18 | 17 | 14 | 15 |
| | 17 | 16 | 18 | 15 | 17 | 12 |
| | 14 | | 14 | | 16 | |
| High | 11 | 6 | 15 | 12 | 9 | 8 |
| | 10 | 10 | 13 | 11 | 7 | 8 |
| | 8 | | 12 | | 5 | |

*Each score is the total points obtained out of a possible 20 points.

**a.** What are the null hypotheses?
**b.** Using $\alpha = 0.05$, what do you conclude?

---

*Of course, you can't really tell whether the interaction is significant without doing a statistical analysis.

**SOLUTION**

**a.** Null hypotheses:

**1.** *For variable A (main effect):* The null hypothesis states that the difficulty of the material has no effect on the amount learned. The population row means for low, medium, and high difficulty levels averaged over anxiety levels are equal ($\mu_{a_1} = \mu_{a_2} = \mu_{a_3}$).

**2.** *For variable B (main effect):* The null hypothesis states that anxiety level has no effect on the amount learned. The population column means for low, medium, and high anxiety levels averaged over difficulty levels are equal ($\mu_{b_1} = \mu_{b_2} = \mu_{b_3}$).

**3.** *For the interaction between variables A and B:* The null hypothesis states that there is no interaction between difficulty of material and anxiety. With any main effects removed, the population cell means are equal ($\mu_{a_1b_1} = \mu_{a_1b_2} = \cdots = \mu_{a_3b_3}$).

**b.** Conclusion, using $\alpha = 0.05$:

**1.** Calculate $F_{\text{obt}}$:

**STEP 1: Calculate $SS_R$:**

$$SS_R = \left[ \frac{\left(\overset{\text{row}_1}{\sum} X\right)^2 + \left(\overset{\text{row}_2}{\sum} X\right)^2 + \left(\overset{\text{row}_3}{\sum} X\right)^2}{n_{\text{row}}} \right] - \frac{\left(\overset{\text{all scores}}{\sum} X\right)^2}{N}$$

$$= \frac{(263)^2 + (235)^2 + (145)^2}{15} - \frac{(643)^2}{45} = 506.844$$

**STEP 2: Calculate $SS_C$:**

$$SS_C = \left[ \frac{\left(\overset{\text{col.}_1}{\sum} X\right)^2 + \left(\overset{\text{col.}_2}{\sum} X\right)^2 + \left(\overset{\text{col.}_3}{\sum} X\right)^2}{n_{\text{col.}}} \right] - \frac{\left(\overset{\text{all scores}}{\sum} X\right)^2}{N}$$

$$= \frac{(212)^2 + (232)^2 + (199)^2}{15} - \frac{(643)^2}{45}$$

$$= 36.844$$

**STEP 3: Calculate $SS_{RC}$:**

$$SS_{RC} = \left[ \frac{\left(\overset{\text{cell}_{11}}{\sum} X\right)^2 + \left(\overset{\text{cell}_{12}}{\sum} X\right)^2 + \cdots + \left(\overset{\text{cell}_{33}}{\sum} X\right)^2}{n_{\text{cell}}} \right] - \frac{\left(\overset{\text{all scores}}{\sum} X\right)^2}{N} - SS_R - SS_C$$

$$= \left[ \frac{(88)^2 + (87)^2 + (88)^2 + (79)^2 + (82)^2 + (74)^2 + (45)^2 + (63)^2 + (37)^2}{5} \right]$$

$$- \frac{(643)^2}{45} - 506.844 - 36.844$$

$$= 40.756$$

*(continued)*

**STEP 4: Calculate $SS_W$:**

$$SS_W = \sum^{\substack{\text{all} \\ \text{scores}}} X^2 - \left[ \frac{\left( \sum_{11}^{\text{cell}} X \right)^2 + \left( \sum_{12}^{\text{cell}} X \right)^2 + \cdots + \left( \sum_{33}^{\text{cell}} X \right)^2}{n_{\text{cell}}} \right] = 9871$$

$$- \left[ \frac{(88)^2 + (87)^2 + (88)^2 + (79)^2 + (82)^2 + (74)^2 + (45)^2 + (63)^2 + (37)^2}{5} \right]$$

$$= 98.800$$

**STEP 5: Calculate $SS_T$:**  This step is a check on the previous calculations:

$$SS_T = \sum^{\substack{\text{all} \\ \text{scores}}} X^2 - \frac{\left( \sum^{\substack{\text{all} \\ \text{scores}}} X \right)^2}{N} = 9871 - \frac{(643)^2}{45}$$

$$= 683.244$$

$$SS_T = SS_R + SS_C + SS_{RC} + SS_W$$
$$683.244 = 506.844 + 36.844 + 40.756 + 98.800$$
$$683.244 = 683.244$$

Since the partitioning equation checks, we can assume our calculations thus far are correct.

**STEP 6: Calculate df:**

$$\text{df}_R = r - 1 = 3 - 1 = 2$$
$$\text{df}_C = c - 1 = 3 - 1 = 2$$
$$\text{df}_{RC} = (r - 1)(c - 1) = 2(2) = 4$$
$$\text{df}_W = rc(n_{\text{cell}} - 1) = 3(3)(5 - 1) = 36$$
$$\text{df}_T = N - 1 = 45 - 1 = 44$$

**STEP 7: Calculate $s_R{}^2$, $s_C{}^2$, $s_{RC}{}^2$, and $s_W{}^2$:**

$$s_R{}^2 = \frac{SS_R}{\text{df}_R} = \frac{506.844}{2} = 253.422$$

$$s_C{}^2 = \frac{SS_C}{\text{df}_C} = \frac{36.844}{2} = 18.442$$

$$s_{RC}{}^2 = \frac{SS_{RC}}{\text{df}_{RC}} = \frac{40.756}{4} = 10.189$$

$$s_W{}^2 = \frac{SS_W}{\text{df}_W} = \frac{98.800}{36} = 2.744$$

**STEP 8: Calculate $F_{\text{obt}}$:**  For the row effect,

$$F_{\text{obt}} = \frac{s_R{}^2}{s_W{}^2} = \frac{253.422}{2.744} = 92.34$$

For the column effect,

$$F_{obt} = \frac{s_C{}^2}{s_W{}^2} = \frac{18.442}{2.744} = 6.71$$

For the row $\times$ column interaction effect,

$$F_{obt} = \frac{s_{RC}{}^2}{s_W{}^2} = \frac{10.189}{2.744} = 3.71$$

**2.** Evaluate $F_{obt}$:

*For the row effect:* With $\alpha = 0.05$, $df_{numerator} = df_R = 2$, and $df_{denominator} = df_W = 36$, from Table F, $F_{crit} = 3.26$. Since $F_{obt}$ (92.34) $> 3.26$, we reject $H_0$ for the A variable. There is a significant main effect for difficulty of material.

*For the column effect:* With $\alpha = 0.05$, $df_{numerator} = df_C = 2$, and $df_{denominator} = df_W = 36$, from Table F, $F_{crit} = 3.26$. Since $F_{obt}$ (6.72) $> 3.26$, $H_0$ is rejected for the B variable. There is a significant main effect for anxiety level.

*For the row $\times$ column effect:* With $\alpha = 0.05$, $df_{numerator} = df_{RC} = 4$, and $df_{denominator} = df_W = 36$, from Table F, $F_{crit} = 2.63$. Since $F_{obt}$ (3.71) $> 2.63$, $H_0$ is rejected. There is a significant interaction between difficulty of material and anxiety level.

The solution is summarized in Table 16.4.

**table 16.4**  Summary ANOVA table for anxiety level and difficulty of material experiment

| Source | SS | df | $s^2$ | $F_{obt}$ | $F_{crit}$ |
|---|---|---|---|---|---|
| Rows (difficulty of material) | 506.844 | 2 | 253.244 | 92.35[*] | 3.26 |
| Columns (anxiety level) | 36.844 | 2 | 18.442 | 6.71[*] | 3.26 |
| Rows $\times$ columns | 40.756 | 4 | 10.189 | 3.71[*] | 2.63 |
| Within cells | 98.800 | 36 | 2.744 | | |
| Total | 683.244 | 44 | | | |

[*]Since $F_{obt} > F_{crit}$, $H_0$ is rejected.

**Interpreting the results of Practice Problem 16.2**  In the preceding analysis, there was a significant main effect for both difficulty of material and anxiety level. The significant main effect for difficulty of material indicates that the differences among the means for the three difficulty levels averaged over anxiety levels were too great to attribute to chance. The cell means have been plotted in Figure 16.7. From this figure, it can be seen that increasing the difficulty of the material results in lower mean values when the scores are averaged over anxiety levels.

The significant main effect for anxiety level is more difficult to interpret. Of course, at the operational level, this main effect tells us that the differences among the means for the three levels of anxiety when averaged over difficulty

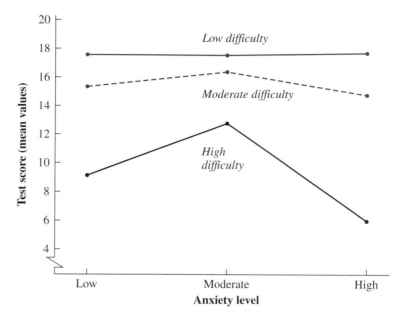

**figure 16.7**  Cell means from the difficulty of material and anxiety level experiment.

levels were too great to attribute to chance. However, beyond this, the interpretation is not clear because of the interaction between the two variables. From Figure 16.7, we can see that the effect of different anxiety levels depends on the difficulty of the material. At the low level of difficulty, differences in anxiety level seem to have no effect on the test scores. However, for the other two difficulty levels, differences in anxiety levels do affect performance. The interaction is a complicated one such that both low and high levels of anxiety seem to interfere with performance when compared with moderate anxiety. This is an example of the inverted U-shaped curve that occurs frequently in psychology when relating performance and arousal levels.

## MULTIPLE COMPARISONS

In the three examples we have just analyzed, we have ended the analyses by evaluating the $F_{obt}$ values. In actual practice, the analysis is usually carried further by doing multiple comparisons on the appropriate pairs of means. For example, in Practice Problem 16.2, there was a significant $F_{obt}$ value for difficulty of material. The next step ordinarily is to determine which difficulty levels are significantly different from each other. Conceptually, this topic is very similar to that which we presented in Chapter 15 when discussing multiple comparisons in conjunction with the one-way ANOVA. One main difference is that in the two-way ANOVA we are often evaluating pairs of *row* means or *column* means rather than pairs of group means. Further exposition of this topic is beyond the scope of this textbook.*

---

*The interested reader should consult B. J. Winer et al., *Statistical Principles in Experimental Design*, 3rd ed., McGraw-Hill, New York, 1991.

## ASSUMPTIONS UNDERLYING THE TWO-WAY ANOVA

The assumptions underlying the two-way ANOVA are the same as those for the one-way ANOVA:

1. The populations from which the samples were taken are normally distributed.
2. The population variances for each of the cells are equal. This is the *homogeneity of variance* assumption.

As with the one-way ANOVA, the two-way ANOVA is robust with regard to violations of these assumptions, provided the samples are of equal size.[*]

## SUMMARY

First, we presented a qualitative discussion of the two-way analysis of variance, independent groups design. Like the one-way design, in the two-way design, subjects are randomly assigned to the conditions. However, the two-way design allows us to investigate two independent variables and the interaction between them in one experiment. The effect of either independent variable (averaged over the levels of the other variable) is called a main effect. An interaction occurs when the effect of one of the variables is not the same at each level of the other variable.

The two-way analysis of variance is very similar to the one-way ANOVA. However, in the two-way ANOVA, the total sum of squares ($SS_T$) is partitioned into four components: the within-cells sum of squares ($SS_W$), the row sum of squares ($SS_R$), the column sum of squares ($SS_C$), and the row $\times$ column sum of squares ($SS_{RC}$). When these sums of squares are divided by the appropriate degrees of freedom, they form four variance estimates: the within-cells variance estimate ($s_W^2$), the row variance estimate ($s_R^2$), the column variance estimate ($s_C^2$), and the row $\times$ column variance estimate ($s_{RC}^2$).

The within-cells variance estimate ($s_W^2$) is the yardstick against which the other variance estimates are compared. Since all the subjects within each cell receive the same level of variables A and B, the within-cells variability cannot be due to treatment differences. Rather, it is a measure of the inherent variability of the scores and, hence, gives us an estimate of the null-hypothesis population variance ($\sigma^2$). The row variance estimate ($s_R^2$) is based on the differences among the row means. It is an estimate of $\sigma^2$ plus the effect of factor A and is used to evaluate the main effect of variable A. The column variance estimate ($s_C^2$) is based on the differences among the column means. It is an estimate of $\sigma^2$ plus the effect of factor B and is used to evaluate the main effect of variable B. The row $\times$ column variance estimate ($s_{RC}^2$) is based on the differences among the cell means beyond that which is predicted by the individual effects of the two variables. It is an estimate of $\sigma^2$ plus the interaction of A and B. As such, it is used to evaluate the interaction of variables A and B.

In addition to presenting the conceptual basis for the two-way ANOVA, equations for computing each of the four variance estimates were developed, and several illustrative examples were given for practice in using the two-way ANOVA technique. It was further pointed out that multiple comparison techniques similar to those used with the one-way ANOVA are used with the two-way ANOVA. Finally, the assumptions underlying the two-way ANOVA were presented.

---

[*]Some statisticians also require the data to be interval or ratio in scaling. For a discussion of this point, see the footnoted references in Chapter 2, p. 31.

## IMPORTANT TERMS

Column degrees of freedom ($df_C$) (p. 406)
Column sum of squares ($SS_C$) (p. 406)
Column variance estimate ($s_C^2$) (p. 406)
Factorial experiment (p. 398)
Interaction effect (p. 399)
Main effect (p. 399)

Row degrees of freedom ($df_R$) (p. 405)
Row sum of squares ($SS_R$) (p. 405)
Row × column degrees of freedom ($df_{RC}$) (p. 407)
Row × column sum of squares ($SS_{RC}$) (p. 407)
Row × column variance estimate ($s_{RC}^2$) (p. 407)
Row variance estimate ($s_R^2$) (p. 404)

Two-way analysis of variance (p. 397)
Within-cells degrees of freedom ($df_W$) (p. 404)
Within-cells sum of squares ($SS_W$) (p. 404)
Within-cells variance estimate ($s_W^2$) (p. 402)

## QUESTIONS AND PROBLEMS

1. Define or identify each of the terms in the Important Terms section.
2. What are the advantages of the two-way ANOVA compared with the one-way ANOVA?
3. What is a factorial experiment?
4. In the two-way ANOVA, what is a *main* effect? What is an *interaction*? Is it possible to have a main effect without an interaction? An interaction without a main effect? Explain.
5. In the two-way ANOVA, the total sum of squares is partitioned into four components. What are the four components?
6. Why is the within-cells variance estimate used as the yardstick against which the other variance estimates are compared?
7. The four variance estimates ($s_R^2$, $s_C^2$, $s_{RC}^2$, and $s_W^2$) are also referred to as *mean squares*. Can you explain why?
8. If the A variable's effect increased, what do you expect would happen to the differences among the row means? What would happen to $s_R^2$? Explain. Assuming there is no interaction, what would happen to the differences among the column means?
9. If the B variable's effect increased, what would happen to the differences among the column means? What would happen to $s_C^2$? Explain. Assuming there is no interaction, what would happen to the differences among the row means?
10. What are the assumptions underlying the two-way ANOVA, independent groups design?
11. It is theorized that repetition aids recall and that the learning of new material can interfere with the recall of previously learned material. A professor interested in human learning and memory conducts a 2 × 3 factorial experiment to investigate the effects of these two variables on recall. The material to be recalled consists of a list of 16 nonsense syllable pairs. The pairs are presented one at a time, for 4 seconds, cycling through the entire list, before the first pair is shown again. There are three levels of repetition: level 1, in which each pair is shown 4 times; level 2, in which each pair is shown 8 times; and level 3, in which each pair is shown 12 times. After being presented the list the requisite number of times and prior to testing for recall, each subject is required to learn some intervening material. The intervening material is of two types: type 1, which consists of number pairs, and type 2, which consists of nonsense syllable pairs. After the intervening material has been presented, the subjects are tested for recall of the original list of 16 nonsense syllable pairs. Thirty-six college freshmen serve as subjects. They are randomly assigned so that there are six per cell. The following scores are recorded; each is the number of syllable pairs from the original list correctly recalled.

| Intervening Material | Number of Repetitions | | | | | |
|---|---|---|---|---|---|---|
| | *4 times* | | *8 times* | | *12 times* | |
| Number pairs | 10 | 11 | 16 | 12 | 16 | 14 |
| | 12 | 15 | 11 | 15 | 16 | 13 |
| | 14 | 10 | 13 | 14 | 15 | 16 |
| Nonsense syllable pairs | 8 | 7 | 11 | 13 | 14 | 12 |
| | 4 | 5 | 9 | 10 | 16 | 15 |
| | 5 | 6 | 8 | 9 | 12 | 13 |

a. What are the null hypotheses for this experiment?

b. Using $\alpha = 0.05$, what do you conclude? Plot a graph of the cell means to help you interpret the results. cognitive

12. Assume you have just accepted a position as chief scientist for a leading agricultural company. Your first assignment is to make a recommendation concerning the best type of grass to grow in the Pacific Northwest and the best fertilizer for it. To provide the database for your recommendation, having just graduated *summa cum laude* in statistics, you decide to conduct an experiment involving a factorial independent groups design. Since there are three types of grass and two fertilizers under active consideration, the experiment you conduct is $2 \times 3$ factorial, where the A variable is the type of fertilizer and the B variable is the type of grass. In your field station, you duplicate the soil and the climate of the Pacific Northwest. Then you divide the soil into 30 equal areas and randomly set aside 5 for each combination of treatments. Next, you fertilize the areas with the appropriate fertilizer and plant in each area the appropriate grass seed. Thereafter, all areas are treated alike. When the grass has grown sufficiently, you determine the number of grass blades per square inch in each area. Your recommendation is based on this dependent variable. The "denser" the grass is, the better. The following scores are obtained:

| Fertilizer | Number of Grass Blades per Square Inch | | | | | |
|---|---|---|---|---|---|---|
| | *Red fescue* | | *Kentucky blue* | | *Green velvet* | |
| Type 1 | 14 | 15 | 15 | 17 | 20 | 19 |
| | 16 | 17 | 12 | 18 | 15 | 22 |
| | 10 | | 11 | | 25 | |
| Type 2 | 11 | 7 | 10 | 6 | 15 | 11 |
| | 11 | 8 | 8 | 13 | 18 | 10 |
| | 14 | | 12 | | 19 | |

a. What are the null hypotheses for this experiment?

b. Using $\alpha = 0.05$, what are your conclusions? Draw a graph of the cell means to help you interpret the results. I/O

13. A sleep researcher conducts an experiment to determine whether a hypnotic drug called Drowson, which is advertised as a remedy for insomnia, actually does promote sleep. In addition, the researcher is interested in whether a tolerance to the drug develops with chronic use. The design of the experiment is a $2 \times 2$ factorial independent groups design. One of the variables is the concentration of Drowson. There are two levels: (1) zero concentration (placebo) and (2) the manufacturer's minimum recommended dosage. The other variable concerns the previous use of Drowson. Again there are two levels: (1) subjects with no previous use and (2) chronic users. Sixteen individuals with sleep-onset insomnia (difficulty in falling asleep) who have had no previous use of Drowson are randomly assigned to the two concentration conditions such that there are eight subjects in each condition. Sixteen chronic users of Drowson are also assigned randomly to the two conditions, eight subjects per condition. All subjects take their prescribed "medication" for 3 consecutive nights, and the time to fall asleep is recorded. The scores shown in the following table are the mean times in minutes to fall asleep for each subject, averaged over the 3 days:

| Previous Use | Concentration of Drowson | | | |
|---|---|---|---|---|
| | *Placebo* | | *Minimum recommended dosage* | |
| No previous use | 45 | 53 | 30 | 47 |
| | 48 | 58 | 33 | 35 |
| | 62 | 55 | 40 | 31 |
| | 70 | 64 | 50 | 39 |
| Chronic users | 47 | 68 | 52 | 46 |
| | 52 | 64 | 60 | 49 |
| | 55 | 58 | 58 | 50 |
| | 62 | 59 | 68 | 55 |

a. What are the null hypotheses for this experiment?

b. Using $\alpha = 0.05$, what do you conclude? Plot a graph of the cell means to help you interpret the results. clinical, health

## BOOK COMPANION WEBSITE

Go to www.thomsonedu.com/psychology/pagano for:

- SPSS problems and solutions
- Flash cards for review of terms
- Chapter quiz
- Statistical workshops
- And more

## WebTUTOR

Available via WebTutor for this chapter:

- Detailed chapter outline
- *Know and Be Able To Do* section
- Drag & Drop game for review of equations, concepts, and other material
- Flash cards for review of terms
- Audio flash cards for MP3 player
- Solving problems using Excel
- Solving problems using SPSS
- More practice problems using computational equations
- Chapter quiz

# Chi-Square and Other Nonparametric Tests

## CHAPTER 17

# INTRODUCTION: DISTINCTION BETWEEN PARAMETRIC AND NONPARAMETRIC TESTS

Statistical inference tests are often classified as to whether they are parametric or nonparametric. You will recall from our discussion in Chapter 1 that a parameter is a characteristic of a population. A parametric inference test is one that depends considerably on population characteristics, or parameters, for its use. The $z$ test, $t$ test, and $F$ test are examples of parametric tests. The $z$ test, for instance, requires that we specify the mean and standard deviation of the null-hypothesis population, as well as requiring that the population scores must be normally distributed for small $N$s. The $t$ test for single samples has the same requirements, except that we don't specify $\sigma$. The $t$ tests for two samples or conditions (correlated $t$ or independent $t$) both require that the population scores be normally distributed when the samples are small. The independent $t$ test further requires that the population variances be equal. The analysis of variance has requirements quite similar to those for the independent $t$ test.

Although all inference tests depend on population characteristics to some extent, the requirements of nonparametric tests are minimal. For example, the sign test is a nonparametric test. To use the sign test, it is not necessary to know the mean, variance, or shape of the population scores. Because nonparametric tests depend little on knowing population distributions, they are often referred to as *distribution-free tests*.

Since nonparametric inference tests have fewer requirements or assumptions about population characteristics, the question arises as to why we don't use them all the time and forget about parametric tests. The answer is twofold. First, many of the parametric inference tests are robust with regard to violations of underlying assumptions. You will recall that a test is robust if violations in the assumptions do not greatly disturb the sampling distribution of its statistic. Thus, the $t$ test is robust regarding the violation of normality in the population. Even though, theoretically, normality in the population is required with small samples, it turns out empirically that unless the departures from normality are substantial, the sampling distribution of $t$ remains essentially the same. Thus, the $t$ test can be used with data even though the data violate the assumptions of normality.

The mean reasons for preferring parametric to nonparametric tests are that, in general, they are more powerful and more versatile than nonparametric tests. We saw an example of the higher power of parametric tests when we compared the $t$ test with the sign test for correlated groups. The factorial design discussed in Chapter 16 provides a good example of the versatility of parametric statistics. With this design, we can test two, three, four, or more variables and their interactions. No comparable technique exists with nonparametric statistics.

As a general rule, investigators will use parametric tests whenever possible. However, when there is an extreme violation of an assumption of the parametric test or if the investigator believes the scaling of the data makes the parametric test inappropriate, a nonparametric inference test will be employed. We have already presented one nonparametric test: the sign test. In the remaining sections of this chapter, we shall present four more: chi-square, the Wilcoxon matched-pairs signed ranks test, the Mann–Whitney $U$ test, and the Kruskal–Wallis test.*

---

*Although we cover several nonparametric tests, there are many more. The interested reader should consult S. Siegel and N. Castellan, Jr., *Nonparametric Statistics for the Behavioral Sciences,* McGraw-Hill, New York, 1988, or W. Daniel, *Applied Nonparametric Statistics,* 2nd ed., PWS-Kent, Boston, 1990.

# CHI-SQUARE ($\chi^2$)

## Single-Variable Experiments

Thus far, we have presented inference tests used primarily in conjunction with ordinal, interval, or ratio data. But what about nominal data? Experiments involving nominal data occur fairly often, particularly in social psychology. You will recall that with this type of data, observations are grouped into several discrete, mutually exclusive categories, and one counts the frequency of occurrence in each category. The inference test most often used with nominal data is a nonparametric test called *chi-square* ($\chi^2$). As has been our procedure throughout the text, we shall begin our discussion of chi-square with an experiment.

an experiment

### Preference for Different Brands of Light Beer

Suppose you are interested in determining whether there is a difference among beer drinkers living in the Puget Sound area in their preference for different brands of light beer. You decide to conduct an experiment in which you randomly sample 150 beer drinkers and let them taste the three leading brands. Assume all the precautions of good experimental design are followed, such as not disclosing the names of the brands to the subjects and so forth. The resulting data are presented in Table 17.1.

table 17.1  Preference for brands of light beer

| Brand A | Brand B | Brand C | Total |
|---------|---------|---------|-------|
| 1    45 | 2    40 | 3    65 | 150   |

### SOLUTION

The entries in each cell are the number or frequency of subjects appropriate to that cell. Thus, 45 subjects preferred brand A (cell 1); 40, brand B (cell 2); and 65, brand C (cell 3). Can we conclude from these data that there is a difference in preference in the population? The null hypothesis for this experiment states that there is no difference in preference among the brands in the population. More specifically, in the population, the proportion of individuals favoring brand A is equal to the proportion favoring brand B, which is equal to the proportion favoring brand C. Referring to the table, it is clear that in the sample the number of individuals preferring each brand is different. However, it doesn't necessarily follow that there is a difference in the population. Isn't it possible that these scores could be due to random sampling from a population of beer drinkers in which the proportion of individuals favoring each brand is equal? Of course, the answer is "yes." Chi-square allows us to evaluate this possibility.

Computation of $\chi^2_{\text{obt}}$    To calculate $\chi^2_{\text{obt}}$, we must first determine the frequency we would expect to get in each cell if sampling is random from the null-hypothesis population. These frequencies are called *expected frequencies* and are symbolized by $f_e$. The frequencies actually obtained in the experiment are called *observed frequencies* and are symbolized by $f_o$. Thus,

$$f_e = \text{expected frequency under the assumption sampling}$$
$$\text{is random from the null-hypothesis population}$$

$$f_o = \text{observed frequency in the sample}$$

It should be clear that the closer the observed frequency of each cell is to the expected frequency for that cell, the more reasonable is $H_0$. On the other hand, the greater the difference between $f_o$ and $f_e$ is, the more reasonable $H_1$ becomes.

After determining $f_e$ for each cell, we obtain the difference between $f_o$ and $f_e$, square the difference, and divide by $f_e$. In symbolic form, $(f_o - f_e)^2/f_e$ is computed for each cell. Finally, we sum the resultant values from each of the cells. In equation form,

$$\chi^2_{\text{obt}} = \Sigma \frac{(f_o - f_e)^2}{f_e} \qquad \textit{equation for calculating } \chi^2$$

*where*    $f_o$ = observed frequency in the cell
$f_e$ = expected frequency in the cell, and $\Sigma$ is over all the cells

From this equation, you can see that $\chi^2$ is basically a measure of how different the observed frequencies are from the expected frequencies.

To calculate the value of $\chi^2_{\text{obt}}$ for the present experiment, we must determine $f_e$ for each cell. The values of $f_o$ are given in the table. If the null hypothesis is true, then the proportion of beer drinkers in the population that prefers brand A is equal to the proportion that prefers brand B, which in turn is equal to the proportion that prefers brand C. This means that one-third of the population must prefer brand A; one-third, brand B; and one-third, brand C. Therefore, if the null hypothesis is true, we would expect one-third of the individuals in the population and, hence, in the sample to prefer brand A, one-third to prefer brand B, and one-third to prefer brand C. Since there are 150 subjects in the sample, $f_e$ for each cell = $\frac{1}{3}(150)$ = 50. We have redrawn the data table and entered the $f_e$ values in parentheses:

| Brand A | Brand B | Brand C | Total |
|---------|---------|---------|-------|
| 45      | 40      | 65      | **150** |
| **(50)**  | **(50)**  | **(50)**  | **(150)** |

Now that we have determined the value of $f_e$ for each cell, we can calculate $\chi^2_{\text{obt}}$. All we need do is sum the values of $(f_o - f_e)^2/f_e$ for each cell. Thus,

$$\chi^2_{\text{obt}} = \Sigma \frac{(f_o - f_e)^2}{f_e}$$

$$= \frac{(45 - 50)^2}{50} + \frac{(40 - 50)^2}{50} + \frac{(65 - 50)^2}{50}$$

$$= 0.50 + 2.00 + 4.50 = 7.00$$

**Evaluation of $\chi^2_{\text{obt}}$**  The theoretical sampling distribution of $\chi^2$ is shown in Figure 17.1. The $\chi^2$ distribution consists of a family of curves that, like the $t$ distribution, varies with degrees of freedom. For the lower degrees of freedom, the curves are positively skewed. The degrees of freedom are determined by the number of $f_o$ scores that are free to vary. In the present experiment, two of the $f_o$ scores are free to vary. Once two of the $f_o$ scores are known, the third $f_o$ score is fixed, since the sum of the three $f_o$ scores must equal $N$. Therefore, df = 2. In general, with experiments involving just one variable, there are $k - 1$ degrees of free-

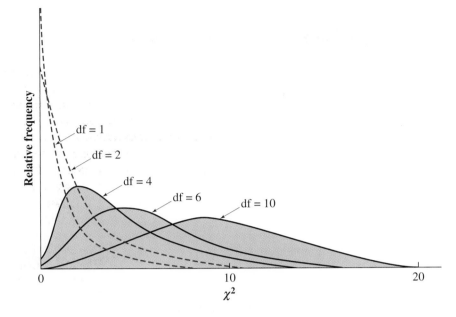

From *Design and Analysis of Experiments in Psychology and Education* by E. F. Lindquist. Copyright © 1953 Houghton Mifflin Company. Reproduced by permission.

**figure 17.1** Distribution of $\chi^2$ for various degrees of freedom.

dom, where $k$ equals the number of groups or categories. When we take up the use of $\chi^2$ with contingency tables, there will be another equation for determining degrees of freedom. We shall discuss it when the topic arises.

Table H in Appendix D gives the critical values of $\chi^2$ for different alpha levels. Since $\chi^2$ is basically a measure of the overall discrepancy between $f_o$ and $f_e$, it follows that the larger the discrepancy between the observed and expected frequencies is, the larger the value of $\chi^2_{obt}$ will be. Therefore, the larger the value of $\chi^2_{obt}$ is, the more unreasonable the null hypothesis is. As with the $t$ and $F$ tests, if $\chi^2_{obt}$ falls within the critical region for rejection, then we reject the null hypothesis. The decision rule states the following:

$$\text{If } \chi^2_{obt} \geq \chi^2_{crit}, \text{ reject } H_0.$$

It should be noted that in calculating $\chi^2_{obt}$ it doesn't matter whether $f_o$ is greater or less than $f_e$. The difference is *squared,* divided by $f_e$, and added to the other cells to obtain $\chi^2_{obt}$. Since the direction of the difference is immaterial, the $\chi^2$ test is a nondirectional test.[*] Furthermore, since each difference adds to the value of $\chi^2$, the critical region for rejection always lies under the right-hand tail of the $\chi^2$ distribution.

In the present experiment, we determined that $\chi^2_{obt} = 7.00$. To evaluate it, we must determine $\chi^2_{crit}$ to see if $\chi^2_{obt}$ falls into the critical region for rejection of $H_0$. From Table H, with df = 2 and $\alpha = 0.05$,

$$\chi^2_{crit} = 5.991$$

---

[*]Please see Note 17.1 for further discussion of this point.

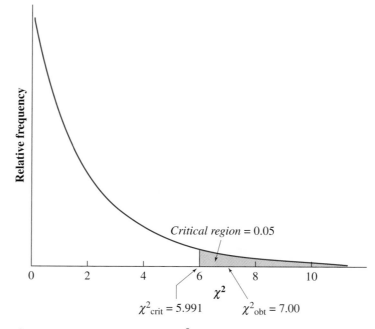

**figure 17.2** Evaluation of $\chi^2_{obt}$ for the light beer drinking problem, df = 2 and $\alpha = 0.05$.

Figure 17.2 shows the $\chi^2$ distribution with df = 2 and the critical region for $\alpha = 0.05$. Since $\chi^2_{obt} > 5.991$, it falls within the critical region and we reject $H_0$. There is a difference in the population regarding preference for the three brands of light beer tested. It appears as though brand C is the favored brand.

Let's try one more problem for practice.

## Practice Problem 17.1

A political scientist believes that, in recent years, the ethnic composition of the city in which he lives has changed. The most current figures (collected a few years ago) show that the inhabitants were 53% Norwegian, 32% Swedish, 8% Irish, 5% Hispanic, and 2% Italian. (Note that nationalities with percentages under 2% have not been included.) To test his belief, a random sample of 750 inhabitants is taken; the results are shown in the following table:

| | Norwegian | Swedish | Irish | Hispanic | Italian | Total |
|---|---|---|---|---|---|---|
| | [1] 399 | [2] 193 | [3] 63 | [4] 82 | [5] 13 | 750 |

**a.** What is the null hypothesis?

**b.** What do you conclude? Use $\alpha = 0.05$.

**SOLUTION**

**a.** Null hypothesis: The ethnic composition of the city has not changed. Therefore, the sample of 750 individuals is a random sample from a population in which 53% are Norwegian, 32% Swedish, 8% Irish, 5% Hispanic, and 2% Italian.

**b.** Conclusion, using $\alpha = 0.05$:

> **STEP 1:** **Calculate the appropriate statistic.** The appropriate statistic is $\chi^2_{\text{obt}}$. The calculations are shown here:

| Cell No. | $f_o$ | $f_e$ | $\dfrac{(f_o - f_e)^2}{f_e}$ |
|----------|-------|-------|------------------------------|
| 1 | 399 | $0.53(750) = 397.5$ | $\dfrac{(399 - 397.5)^2}{397.5} = 0.006$ |
| 2 | 193 | $0.32(750) = 240.0$ | $\dfrac{(193 - 240)^2}{240} = 9.204$ |
| 3 | 63 | $0.08(750) = 60.0$ | $\dfrac{(63 - 60)^2}{60} = 0.150$ |
| 4 | 82 | $0.05(750) = 37.5$ | $\dfrac{(82 - 37.5)^2}{37.5} = 52.807$ |
| 5 | 13 | $0.02(750) = 15.0$ | $\dfrac{(13 - 15)^2}{15} = 0.267$ |

$$\chi^2_{\text{obt}} = \sum \frac{(f_o - f_e)^2}{f_e} = 62.434$$

$$= 62.43$$

> **STEP 2:** **Evaluate the statistic.** Degrees of freedom $= 5 - 1 = 4$. With $df = 4$ and $\alpha = 0.05$, from Table H,
>
> $$\chi^2_{\text{crit}} = 9.488$$
>
> Since $\chi^2_{\text{obt}} > 9.488$, we reject $H_0$. The ethnic composition of the city appears to have changed. There has been an increase in the proportion of Hispanics and a decrease in the Swedish.

## Test of Independence Between Two Variables

One of the main uses of $\chi^2$ is in determining whether two categorical variables are independent or are related. To illustrate, let's consider the following example.

## Political Affiliation and Attitude

Suppose a bill that proposes to lower the legal age for drinking to 18 is pending before the state legislature. A political scientist living in the state is interested in determining whether there is a relationship between political affiliation and attitude toward the bill. A random sample of 200 registered Republicans and 200 registered Democrats is sent letters explaining the scientist's interest and asking the recipients whether they are in favor of the bill, are undecided, or are against the bill. Strict confidentiality is assured. A self-addressed envelope is included to facilitate responding. Answers are received from all 400 Republicans and Democrats. The results are shown in Table 17.2.

t a b l e 17.2   Political affiliation and attitude data

| | Attitude | | | Row Marginal |
|---|---|---|---|---|
| | *For* | *Undecided* | *Against* | |
| Republican | 68 | 22 | 110 | 200 |
| Democrat | 92 | 18 | 90 | 200 |
| Column Marginal | 160 | 40 | 200 | 400 |

The entries in each cell are the frequency of subjects appropriate to the cell. For example, with the Republicans, 68 are for the bill, 22 are undecided, and 110 are against. With the Democrats, 92 are for the bill, 18 are undecided, and 90 are against. This type of table is called a *contingency table.*

■   *A **contingency table** is a two-way table showing the contingency between two variables where the variables have been classified into mutually exclusive categories and the cell entries are frequencies.*

Note that in constructing a contingency table, it is essential that the categories be mutually exclusive. Thus, if an entry is appropriate for one of the cells, the categories must be such that it cannot appropriately be entered in any other cell.

   This contingency table contains the data bearing on the contingency between political affiliation and attitude toward the bill. The null hypothesis states that there is no contingency between the variables in the population. For this example, $H_0$ states that, in the population, attitude toward the bill and political affiliation are independent. If this is true, then both the Republicans and Democrats in the population should have the same proportion of individuals "for," "undecided," and "against" the bill. It is clear that in the contingency table, the frequencies in these three columns are different for Republicans and Democrats. The null hypothesis states that these frequencies are due to random sampling from a population in which the proportion of Republicans is equal to the proportion of Democrats in each of the categories. The alternative hypothesis is that Republicans and Democrats do differ in their attitudes toward the bill. If so, then in the population, the proportions would be different.

**Computation of $\chi^2_{obt}$**   To test the null hypothesis, we must calculate $\chi^2_{obt}$ and compare it with $\chi^2_{crit}$. With experiments involving two variables, the most difficult part of the process is in determining $f_e$ for each cell. As discussed, the null hypothesis states that, in the population, the proportion of Republicans for each category is the same as the proportion of Democrats. If we knew these proportions, we could just multiply them by the number of Republicans or Democrats in the sample to find $f_e$ for each cell. For example, suppose that, if $H_0$ is true, the proportion of Republicans in the population against the bill equals 0.50. To find $f_e$ for that cell, all we would have to do is multiply 0.50 by the number of Republicans in the sample. Thus, for the "Republican-against" cell, $f_e$ would equal $0.50(200) = 100$.

Since we do not know the population proportions, we estimate them from the sample. In the present experiment, 160 Republicans and Democrats out of 400 were for the bill, 40 out of 400 were undecided, and 200 out of 400 were against the bill. Since the null hypothesis assumes independence between political party and attitude, we can use these sample proportions as our estimates of the null-hypothesis population proportions. Then, we can use these estimates to calculate the expected frequencies. Our estimates for the null-hypothesis population proportions are as follows:

$$\text{Estimated } H_0 \text{ population proportion for the bill} = \frac{\text{Number of subjects for the bill}}{\text{Total number of subjects}} = \frac{160}{400}$$

$$\text{Estimated } H_0 \text{ population proportion undecided} = \frac{\text{Number of subjects undecided}}{\text{Total number of subjects}} = \frac{40}{400}$$

$$\text{Estimated } H_0 \text{ population proportion against the bill} = \frac{\text{Number of subjects against the bill}}{\text{Total number of subjects}} = \frac{200}{400}$$

Using these estimates to calculate the expected frequencies, we obtain the following values for $f_e$:

*For the Republican-for cell (cell 1 in the table on p. 436):*

$$f_e = \left(\begin{array}{c}\text{Estimated } H_0 \text{ population} \\ \text{proportion for the bill}\end{array}\right)\left(\begin{array}{c}\text{Total number of} \\ \text{Republicans}\end{array}\right) = \frac{160}{400}(200) = 80$$

*For the Republican-undecided cell (cell 2):*

$$f_e = \left(\begin{array}{c}\text{Estimated } H_0 \text{ population} \\ \text{proportion undecided}\end{array}\right)\left(\begin{array}{c}\text{Total number of} \\ \text{Republicans}\end{array}\right) = \frac{40}{400}(200) = 20$$

*For the Republican-against cell (cell 3):*

$$f_e = \left(\begin{array}{c}\text{Estimated } H_0 \text{ population} \\ \text{proportion against} \\ \text{the bill}\end{array}\right)\left(\begin{array}{c}\text{Total number of} \\ \text{Republicans}\end{array}\right) = \frac{200}{400}(200) = 100$$

*For the Democrat-for cell (cell 4):*

$$f_e = \begin{pmatrix} \text{Estimated } H_0 \text{ population} \\ \text{proportion for the bill} \end{pmatrix} \begin{pmatrix} \text{Total number of} \\ \text{Democrats} \end{pmatrix} = \frac{160}{400}(200) = 80$$

*For the Democrat-undecided cell (cell 5):*

$$f_e = \begin{pmatrix} \text{Estimated } H_0 \text{ population} \\ \text{proportion undecided} \end{pmatrix} \begin{pmatrix} \text{Total number of} \\ \text{Democrats} \end{pmatrix} = \frac{40}{400}(200) = 20$$

*For the Democrat-against cell (cell 6):*

$$f_e = \begin{pmatrix} \text{Estimated } H_0 \text{ population} \\ \text{proportion against} \\ \text{the bill} \end{pmatrix} \begin{pmatrix} \text{Total number of} \\ \text{Democrats} \end{pmatrix} = \frac{200}{400}(200) = 100$$

For convenience, the $2 \times 3$ contingency table has been redrawn here, and the $f_e$ values entered within parentheses in the appropriate cells:

| | Attitude | | | Row Marginal |
|---|---|---|---|---|
| | *For* | *Undecided* | *Against* | |
| Republican | ¹ 68 (80) | ² 22 (20) | ³ 110 (100) | 200 |
| Democrat | ⁴ 92 (80) | ⁵ 18 (20) | ⁶ 90 (100) | 200 |
| Column Marginal | 160 | 40 | 200 | 400 |

The same values for $f_e$ can also be found directly by multiplying the "marginals" for that cell and dividing by N. The marginals are the row and column totals lying outside the table. For example, the marginals for cell 1 are 160 (column total) and 200 (row total). Let's use this method to find $f_e$ for each cell. Multiplying the marginals and dividing by N, we obtain

$$f_e(\text{cell 1}) = \frac{160(200)}{400} = 80$$

$$f_e(\text{cell 2}) = \frac{40(200)}{400} = 20$$

$$f_e(\text{cell 3}) = \frac{200(200)}{400} = 100$$

$$f_e(\text{cell 4}) = \frac{160(200)}{400} = 80$$

$$f_e(\text{cell 5}) = \frac{40(200)}{400} = 20$$

$$f_e(\text{cell 6}) = \frac{200(200)}{400} = 100$$

These values are, of course, the same ones we arrived at previously. Although using the marginals doesn't give much insight into why $f_e$ should be that value, from a practical standpoint it is the best way to calculate $f_e$ for the various cells. You should note that a good check to make sure your calculations of $f_e$ are correct is to see whether the row and column totals of $f_e$ equal the row and column marginals.

Once $f_e$ for each cell has been determined, the next step is to calculate $\chi^2_{\text{obt}}$. As before, this is done by summing $(f_o - f_e)^2/f_e$ for each cell. Thus, for the present experiment,

$$\chi^2_{\text{obt}} = \Sigma \frac{(f_o - f_e)^2}{f_e}$$

$$= \frac{(68 - 80)^2}{80} + \frac{(22 - 20)^2}{20} + \frac{(110 - 100)^2}{100} + \frac{(92 - 80)^2}{80}$$

$$+ \frac{(18 - 20)^2}{20} + \frac{(90 - 100)^2}{100}$$

$$= 1.80 + 0.20 + 1.00 + 1.80 + 0.20 + 1.00 = 6.00$$

**Evaluation of $\chi^2_{\text{obt}}$**    To evaluate $\chi^2_{\text{obt}}$, we must compare it with $\chi^2_{\text{crit}}$ for the appropriate df. As discussed previously, the degrees of freedom are equal to the number of $f_o$ scores that are free to vary while keeping the totals constant. In the two-variable experiment, we must keep both the column and row marginals at the same values. Thus, the degrees of freedom for experiments involving a contingency between two variables are equal to the number of $f_o$ scores that are free to vary while at the same time keeping the column and row marginals the same. In the case of a 2 × 3 table, there are only 2 degrees of freedom. Only two $f_o$ scores are free to vary, and all the remaining $f_o$ and $f_e$ scores are fixed.

To illustrate, consider the 2 × 3 table shown here:

| | | | |
|---|---|---|---|
| 1    68 | 2    22 | 3 | **200** |
| 4 | 5 | 6 | **200** |
| 160 | 40 | 200 | 400 |

If we fill in any two $f_o$ scores, all the remaining $f_o$ scores are fully determined, provided the marginals are kept at the same values. For example, in the table, we have filled in the $f_o$ scores for cells 1 and 2. Note that all the other scores are fixed in value once two $f_o$ scores are given; for example, the $f_o$ score for cell 3 must be 110 [200 − (68 + 22)].

There is also an equation to calculate the df for contingency tables. It states

$$\text{df} = (r - 1)(c - 1)$$

*where*    $r$ = number of rows
$c$ = number of columns

Applying the equation to the present experiment, we obtain

$$\text{df} = (r - 1)(c - 1) = (2 - 1)(3 - 1) = 2$$

The $\chi^2$ test is not limited to 2 × 3 tables. It can be used with contingency tables containing any number of rows and columns. This equation is perfectly general and applies to all contingency tables. Thus, if we did an experiment involving two variables and had four rows and six columns in the table, df $= (r - 1)(c - 1) = (4 - 1)(6 - 1) = 15$.

Returning to the evaluation of the present experiment, let's assume $\alpha = 0.05$. With df $= 2$ and $\alpha = 0.05$, from Table H,

$$\chi_{crit}^2 = 5.991$$

Since $\chi_{obt}^2 > 5.991$, we reject $H_0$. Political affiliation is related to attitude toward the bill. The Democrats appear to be more favorably disposed toward the bill than the Republicans. The complete solution is shown in Table 17.3.

Let's try a problem for practice.

---

**table 17.3** Solution to political affiliation and attitude problem

---

a. Null hypothesis: Political affiliation and attitude toward the bill are independent. The frequency obtained in each cell is due to random sampling from a population where the proportions of Republicans and Democrats that are for, undecided about, and against the bill are equal.

b. Conclusion, using $\alpha = 0.05$:

STEP 1: **Calculate the appropriate statistic.** The appropriate statistic is $\chi_{obt}^2$. The data are shown on p. 434. The calculations are shown here.

STEP 2: **Evaluate the statistic.** Degrees of freedom $= (r - 1)(c - 1) = (2 - 1)(3 - 1) = 2$. With df $= 2$ and $\alpha = 0.05$, from Table H,

$$\chi_{crit}^2 = 5.991$$

Since $\chi_{obt}^2 > 5.991$, we reject $H_0$. Political affiliation and attitude toward the bill are related. Democrats appear to favor the bill more than Republicans.

| Cell No. | $f_o$ | $f_e$ | $\dfrac{(f_o - f_e)^2}{f_e}$ |
|:---:|:---:|:---:|:---:|
| 1 | 68 | $\dfrac{160(200)}{400} = 80$ | $\dfrac{(68 - 80)^2}{80} = 1.80$ |
| 2 | 22 | $\dfrac{40(200)}{400} = 20$ | $\dfrac{(22 - 20)^2}{20} = 0.20$ |
| 3 | 110 | $\dfrac{200(200)}{400} = 100$ | $\dfrac{(110 - 100)^2}{100} = 1.00$ |
| 4 | 92 | $\dfrac{160(200)}{400} = 80$ | $\dfrac{(92 - 80)^2}{80} = 1.80$ |
| 5 | 18 | $\dfrac{40(200)}{400} = 20$ | $\dfrac{(18 - 20)^2}{20} = 0.20$ |
| 6 | 90 | $\dfrac{200(200)}{400} = 100$ | $\dfrac{(90 - 100)^2}{100} = \underline{1.00}$ |

$$\chi_{obt}^2 = \Sigma\, \frac{(f_o - f_e)^2}{f_e} = 6.00$$

## Practice Problem 17.2

A university is considering implementing one of the following three grading systems: (1) All grades are pass–fail, (2) all grades are on the 4.0 system, and (3) 90% of the grades are on the 4.0 system and 10% are pass–fail. A survey is taken to determine whether there is a relationship between undergraduate major and grading system preference. A random sample of 200 students with engineering majors, 200 students with arts and sciences majors, and 100 students with fine arts majors is selected. Each student is asked which of the three grading systems he or she prefers. The results are shown in the following $3 \times 3$ contingency table:

| | Grading System | | | |
|---|---|---|---|---|
| | Pass–fail | 4.0 and Pass–fail | 4.0 | Row Marginal |
| Fine arts | 1  26 | 2  55 | 3  19 | 100 |
| Arts and sciences | 4  24 | 5  118 | 6  58 | 200 |
| Engineering | 7  20 | 8  112 | 9  68 | 200 |
| Column Marginal | 70 | 285 | 145 | 500 |

**a.** What is the null hypothesis?
**b.** What do you conclude? Use $\alpha = 0.05$.

**SOLUTION**

**a.** Null hypothesis: Undergraduate major and grading system preference are independent. The frequency obtained in each cell is due to random sampling from a population where the proportions of fine arts, arts and sciences, and engineering majors who prefer each grading system are the same.
**b.** Conclusion, using $\alpha = 0.05$:

> **STEP 1: Calculate the appropriate statistic.** The data are shown in the following table. The appropriate statistic is $\chi^2_{obt}$. Before calculating $\chi^2_{obt}$, we must first calculate $f_e$ for each cell. The values of $f_e$ were found using the marginals.

| Cell No. | $f_o$ | $f_e$ | $\dfrac{(f_o - f_e)^2}{f_e}$ |
|---|---|---|---|
| 1 | 26 | $\dfrac{70(100)}{500} = 14$ | $\dfrac{(26 - 14)^2}{14} = 10.286$ |
| 2 | 55 | $\dfrac{285(100)}{500} = 57$ | $\dfrac{(55 - 57)^2}{57} = 0.070$ |

*(continued)*

| Cell No. | $f_o$ | $f_e$ | $\dfrac{(f_o - f_e)^2}{f_e}$ |
|:---:|:---:|:---:|:---:|
| 3 | 19 | $\dfrac{145(100)}{500} = 29$ | $\dfrac{(19 - 29)^2}{29} = 3.448$ |
| 4 | 24 | $\dfrac{70(200)}{500} = 28$ | $\dfrac{(24 - 28)^2}{28} = 0.571$ |
| 5 | 118 | $\dfrac{285(200)}{500} = 114$ | $\dfrac{(118 - 114)^2}{114} = 0.140$ |
| 6 | 58 | $\dfrac{145(200)}{500} = 58$ | $\dfrac{(58 - 58)^2}{58} = 0.000$ |
| 7 | 20 | $\dfrac{70(200)}{500} = 28$ | $\dfrac{(20 - 28)^2}{28} = 2.286$ |
| 8 | 112 | $\dfrac{285(200)}{500} = 114$ | $\dfrac{(112 - 114)^2}{114} = 0.035$ |
| 9 | 68 | $\dfrac{145(200)}{500} = 58$ | $\dfrac{(68 - 58)^2}{58} = 1.724$ |

$$\chi^2_{\text{obt}} = \Sigma \frac{(f_o - f_e)^2}{f_e} = 18.561$$

$$= 18.56$$

**STEP 2:** **Evaluate the statistic.** Degrees of freedom $= (r - 1)(c - 1) = (3 - 1)(3 - 1) = 4$. With df $= 4$ and $\alpha = 0.05$, from Table H,

$$\chi^2_{\text{crit}} = 9.488$$

Since $\chi^2_{\text{obt}} > 9.488$, we reject $H_0$. Undergraduate major and grading system preference are related.

In trying to determine what the differences in preference were between the groups (since the number of subjects differ considerably for the fine arts majors), it is necessary to convert the frequency entries into proportions. These proportions are shown in Table 17.4.

table 17.4   Preferences for grading systems expressed as proportions

| | Pass–fail | 4.0 and Pass–fail | 4.0 |
|---|:---:|:---:|:---:|
| Fine arts | 0.26 | 0.55 | 0.19 |
| Arts and sciences | 0.12 | 0.59 | 0.29 |
| Engineering | 0.10 | 0.56 | 0.34 |

From this table, it appears that the differences between groups are in their preferences for the all pass–fail or all 4.0 grading systems. The fine arts students show a higher proportion favoring the pass–fail system rather than the all 4.0 system, whereas the arts and sciences and engineering students show the reverse pattern. All groups show about the same proportions favoring the system advocating a combination of 4.0 and pass–fail grades.

Let's try one more problem for practice.

## Practice Problem 17.3

A social psychologist is interested in determining whether there is a relationship between the education level of parents and the number of children they have. Accordingly, a survey is taken, and the following results are obtained:

| | No. of Children | | |
| | Two or less | More than two | Row Marginal |
|---|---|---|---|
| College education | 1   53 | 2   22 | 75 |
| High school education only | 3   37 | 4   38 | 75 |
| Column Marginal | 90 | 60 | 150 |

a. What is the null hypothesis?
b. What is the conclusion? Use $\alpha = 0.05$.

### SOLUTION

a. Null hypothesis: The educational level of parents and the number of children they have are independent. The frequency obtained in each cell is due to random sampling from a population where the proportions of college-educated and only high-school-educated parents that have (1) two or fewer and (2) more than two children are equal.

b. Conclusion, using $\alpha = 0.05$:

STEP 1: **Calculate the appropriate statistic.** The data are shown in the following table. The appropriate statistic is $\chi^2_{obt}$. The calculations follow.

(*continued*)

| Cell No. | $f_o$ | $f_e$ | $\dfrac{(f_o - f_e)^2}{f_e}$ |
|:---:|:---:|:---:|:---:|
| 1 | 53 | $\dfrac{90(75)}{150} = 45$ | $\dfrac{(53 - 45)^2}{45} = 1.422$ |
| 2 | 22 | $\dfrac{60(75)}{150} = 30$ | $\dfrac{(22 - 30)^2}{30} = 2.133$ |
| 3 | 37 | $\dfrac{90(75)}{150} = 45$ | $\dfrac{(37 - 45)^2}{45} = 1.422$ |
| 4 | 38 | $\dfrac{60(75)}{150} = 30$ | $\dfrac{(38 - 30)^2}{30} = 2.133$ |

$$\chi^2_{\text{obt}} = \Sigma \frac{(f_o - f_e)^2}{f_e} = 7.110$$

**STEP 2: Evaluate the statistic.** Degrees of freedom $= (r - 1)(c - 1) = (2 - 1)(2 - 1) = 1$. With df $= 1$ and $\alpha = 0.05$, from Table H,

$$\chi^2_{\text{crit}} = 3.841$$

Since $\chi^2_{\text{obt}} > 3.841$, we reject $H_0$. The educational level of parents and the number of children they have are related.

## Assumptions Underlying $\chi^2$

A basic assumption in using $\chi^2$ is that there is independence between each observation recorded in the contingency table. This means that each subject can have only one entry in the table. It is not permissible to take several measurements on the same subject and enter them as separate frequencies in the same or different cells. This error would produce a larger $N$ than there are independent observations.

A second assumption is that the sample size must be large enough that the *expected* frequency in each cell is at least 5 for tables where $r$ or $c$ is greater than 2. If the table is a $1 \times 2$ or $2 \times 2$ table, then each expected frequency should be at least 10. If the sample size is small enough to result in expected frequencies that violate these requirements, then the actual sampling distribution of $\chi^2$ deviates considerably from the theoretical one and the probability values given in Table H do not apply. If the experiment involves a $2 \times 2$ contingency table and the data violate this assumption, Fisher's exact probability test should be used.*

Although $\chi^2$ is used frequently when the data are only of nominal scaling, it is not limited to nominal data. Chi-square can be used with ordinal, interval, and ratio data. However, regardless of the actual scaling, the data must be reduced to mutually exclusive categories and appropriate frequencies before $\chi^2$ can be employed.

---

*This test is discussed in S. Siegel and N. Castellan, Jr., *Nonparametric Statistics for the Behavioral Sciences,* 2nd ed., McGraw-Hill, New York, 1988, pp. 103–111. It is also discussed in W. Daniel, *Applied Nonparametric Statistics,* 2nd ed., PWS-Kent, Boston, 1990, pp. 150–162.

# THE WILCOXON MATCHED-PAIRS SIGNED RANKS TEST

The Wilcoxon signed ranks test is used in conjunction with the correlated groups design with data that are at least ordinal in scaling. It is a relatively powerful test sometimes used in place of the *t* test for correlated groups when there is an extreme violation of the normality assumption or when the data are not of appropriate scaling. The Wilcoxon signed ranks test considers both the magnitude of the difference scores and their direction, which makes it more powerful than the sign test. It is, however, less powerful than the *t* test for correlated groups. To illustrate this test, let's consider the following experiment.

**an experiment**

## Promoting More Favorable Attitudes Toward Wildlife Conservation

A prominent ecological group is planning to mount an active campaign to increase wildlife conservation in their country. As part of the campaign, they plan to show a film designed to promote more favorable attitudes toward wildlife conservation. Before showing the film to the public at large, they want to evaluate its effects. A group of 10 subjects are randomly sampled and given a questionnaire that measures an individual's attitude toward wildlife conservation. Next, they are shown the film, after which they are again given the attitude questionnaire. The questionnaire has 50 possible points, and the higher the score is, the more favorable is the attitude toward wildlife conservation. The results are shown in Table 17.5.

1. What is the alternative hypothesis? Use a nondirectional hypothesis.
2. What is the null hypothesis?
3. What do you conclude? Use $\alpha = 0.05_{2\ \text{tail}}$.

### SOLUTION

1. The alternative hypothesis is usually stated without specifying any population parameters. For this example, it states that the film affects attitudes toward wildlife conservation.
2. The null hypothesis is also usually stated without specifying any population parameters. For this example, it states that the film has no effect on attitudes toward wildlife conservation.
3. Conclusion, using $\alpha = 0.05_{2\ \text{tail}}$: As with all the other inference tests, the first step is to calculate the appropriate statistic. The data have been obtained from questionnaires, so they are at least of ordinal scaling. To illustrate use of the Wilcoxon signed ranks test, we shall assume that the data meet the assumptions of this test (these will be discussed shortly). The statistic calculated by the Wilcoxon signed ranks test is $T_{\text{obt}}$. Determining $T_{\text{obt}}$ involves four steps:
   a. Calculate the difference between each pair of scores.
   b. Rank the absolute values of the difference scores from the smallest to the largest.
   c. Assign to the resulting ranks the sign of the difference score whose absolute value yielded that rank.
   d. Compute the sum of the ranks separately for the positive and negative signed ranks. The lower sum is $T_{\text{obt}}$.

These four steps have been done with the data from the attitude questionnaire, and the resultant values have been entered in Table 17.5. Thus, the difference scores have been calculated and are shown in the fourth column of Table 17.5. The ranks of the absolute values table 17.5 Data and solution for wildlife conservation problem

| Subject | Attitude Before | Attitude After | Difference | Rank of \|Difference\| | Signed Rank of Difference | Sum of Positive Ranks | Sum of Negative Ranks |
|---|---|---|---|---|---|---|---|
| 1 | 40 | 44 | 4 | 4 | 4 | 4 | |
| 2 | 33 | 40 | 7 | 6 | 6 | 6 | |
| 3 | 36 | 49 | 13 | 10 | 10 | 10 | |
| 4 | 34 | 36 | 2 | 2 | 2 | 2 | |
| 5 | 40 | 39 | −1 | 1 | −1 | | 1 |
| 6 | 31 | 40 | 9 | 8 | 8 | 8 | |
| 7 | 30 | 27 | −3 | 3 | −3 | | 3 |
| 8 | 36 | 42 | 6 | 5 | 5 | 5 | |
| 9 | 24 | 35 | 11 | 9 | 9 | 9 | |
| 10 | 20 | 28 | 8 | 7 | 7 | 7 | |
| | | | | 55 | | 51 | 4 |

$$\frac{n(n + 1)}{2} = \frac{10(11)}{2} = 55 \qquad\qquad T_{\text{obt}} = 4$$

From Table I, with $N = 10$ and $\alpha = 0.05_{2\text{ tail}}$,

$$T_{\text{crit}} = 8$$

Since $T_{\text{obt}} < 8$, $H_0$ is rejected. The film appears to promote more favorable attitudes toward wildlife conservation.

---

of the difference scores are shown in the fifth column. Note that, as a check on whether the ranking has been done correctly, the sum of the unsigned ranks should equal $n(n + 1)/2$. In the present example, this sum should equal 55 [$10(11)/2 = 55$], which it does. Step **c** asks us to give each rank the sign of the difference score whose absolute value yielded that rank. This has been done in the sixth column. Thus, the ranks of 1 and 3 are assigned minus signs, and the rest are positive. The ranks of 1 and 3 received minus signs because their associated difference scores are negative. $T_{\text{obt}}$ is determined by computing the sum of the positive ranks and the sum of the negative ranks. $T_{\text{obt}}$ is the lower of the two sums. In this example, the sum of the positive ranks equals 51, and the sum of the negative ranks equals 4. Thus,

$$T_{\text{obt}} = 4$$

Note that often it is not necessary to compute both sums. Usually it is apparent by inspection which sum will be lower. The final step is to evaluate $T_{\text{obt}}$. Table I in Appendix D contains the critical values of $T$ for various values of $N$. With $N = 10$ and $\alpha = 0.05_{2\text{ tail}}$, from Table I,

$$T_{\text{crit}} = 8$$

With the Wilcoxon signed ranks test, the decision rule is

If $T_{\text{obt}} \leq T_{\text{crit}}$, reject $H_0$.

Note that this is opposite to the rule we have been using for most of the other tests. Since $T_{\text{obt}} < 8$, we reject $H_0$ and conclude that the film does affect attitudes toward wildlife conservation. It appears to promote more favorable attitudes.

It is easy to see why the Wilcoxon signed ranks test is more powerful than the sign test but not as powerful as the *t* test for correlated groups. The Wilcoxon signed ranks test takes into account the magnitude of the difference scores, which makes it more powerful than the sign test. However, it considers only the rank order of the difference scores, not their actual magnitude, as does the *t* test. Therefore, the Wilcoxon signed ranks test is not as powerful as the *t* test.

Let's try another problem for practice.

## Practice Problem 17.4

An investigator is interested in determining whether the difficulty of the material to be learned affects the anxiety level of college students. A random sample of 12 students is each given hard and easy learning tasks. Before doing each task, they are shown a few sample examples of the material to be learned. Then their anxiety level is assessed using an anxiety questionnaire. Thus, anxiety level is assessed before each learning task. The data are shown in the following table. The higher the score is, the greater is the anxiety level. What is the conclusion, using the Wilcoxon signed ranks test and $\alpha = 0.05_{2\,\text{tail}}$?

### SOLUTION

The solution is shown in the following table. Note that there are ties in some of the difference scores. Generally, two kinds of ties are possible. First, the raw scores may be tied, yielding a difference score of 0. If this occurs, these scores are disregarded and the overall $N$ is reduced by 1 for each 0 difference score. Ties can also occur in the difference scores, as in the present example. When this happens, the ranks of these scores are given a value equal to the mean of the tied ranks. This is the same procedure we followed for the Spearman rho correlation coefficient. Thus, in this example, the two tied difference scores of 3 are assigned ranks of 2.5 [(2 + 3)/2 = 2.5], and the tied difference scores of 10 receive the rank of 9.5. Otherwise, the solution is quite similar to that of the previous example.

| Student No. | Anxiety Hard tasks | Anxiety Easy tasks | Difference | Rank of \|Difference\| | Signed Rank of Difference | Sum of Positive Ranks | Sum of Negative Ranks |
|---|---|---|---|---|---|---|---|
| 1 | 48 | 40 | 8 | 7 | 7 | 7 | |
| 2 | 33 | 27 | 6 | 5 | 5 | 5 | |
| 3 | 46 | 34 | 12 | 11 | 11 | 11 | |
| 4 | 42 | 28 | 14 | 12 | 12 | 12 | |
| 5 | 40 | 30 | 10 | 9.5 | 9.5 | 9.5 | |
| 6 | 27 | 24 | 3 | 2.5 | 2.5 | 2.5 | |

*(continued)*

| Student No. | Anxiety Hard tasks | Anxiety Easy tasks | Difference | Rank of \|Difference\| | Signed Rank of Difference | Sum of Positive Ranks | Sum of Negative Ranks |
|---|---|---|---|---|---|---|---|
| 7 | 31 | 33 | −2 | 1 | −1 | | 1 |
| 8 | 42 | 39 | 3 | 2.5 | 2.5 | 2.5 | |
| 9 | 38 | 31 | 7 | 6 | 6 | 6 | |
| 10 | 34 | 39 | −5 | 4 | −4 | | 4 |
| 11 | 38 | 29 | 9 | 8 | 8 | 8 | |
| 12 | 44 | 34 | 10 | 9.5 | 9.5 | 9.5 | |
| | | | | 78 | | 73 | 5 |

$$\frac{n(n+1)}{2} = \frac{12(13)}{2} = 78 \qquad\qquad T_{obt} = 5$$

From Table I, with $N = 12$ and $\alpha = 0.05_{2\,tail}$,

$$T_{crit} = 13$$

Since $T_{obt} < 13$, we reject $H_0$ and conclude that the difficulty of material does affect anxiety. It appears that more difficult material produces increased anxiety.

## Assumptions of the Wilcoxon Signed Ranks Test

There are two assumptions underlying the Wilcoxon signed ranks test. First, the scores within each pair must be at least of ordinal measurement. Second, the difference scores must also have at least ordinal scaling. The second requirement arises because in computing $T_{obt}$ we rank-order the difference scores. Thus, the magnitude of the difference scores must be at least ordinal so that they can be rank-ordered.

## THE MANN–WHITNEY $U$ TEST

The Mann–Whitney $U$ test is used in conjunction with the independent groups design with data that are at least ordinal in scaling. It is a powerful nonparametric test used in place of the $t$ test for independent groups when there is an extreme violation of the normality assumption or when the data are not of appropriate scaling for the $t$ test.

To illustrate this inference test, let's consider the following experiment.

an experiment

### The Effect of a High-Protein Diet on Intellectual Development

A developmental psychologist, with special competence in nutrition, believes that a high-protein diet eaten during early childhood is important for intellectual development. The diet in the geographic area where the psychologist lives is low in protein. The psychologist believes the low-protein diet eaten during the first few years of childhood is detrimental to intellectual development. If she is correct, a high-protein diet should result in higher intelligence. An experiment is conducted in which 18 children are randomly chosen from the 1-year-old children living in a nearby city. The 18 children are then randomly divided into two groups of 9 children each. The control group is fed the usual low-protein diet for 3 years, whereas the experimental group receives a diet high in protein for the same duration. At the end of the 3 years, each child is given an IQ test. The resulting data are shown in Table 17.6. One child in the experimental group moved to a different city and was not replaced.

**t a b l e   1 7 . 6**   Data from the protein and IQ experiment

| IQ Test Scores | |
| --- | --- |
| *Control group,*<br>*low protein*<br>*1* | *Experimental group,*<br>*high protein*<br>*2* |
| 102 | 110 |
| 104 | 115 |
| 105 | .117 |
| 107 | 122 |
| 108 | 125 |
| 111 | 130 |
| 113 | 135 |
| 118 | 140 |
| 120 | |

a. What is the directional alternative hypothesis?
b. What is the null hypothesis?
c. What do you conclude? Use $\alpha = 0.05_{1\ tail}$.

**SOLUTION**

1. Alternative hypothesis: As with the *t* test for independent groups, the alternative hypothesis states that a high-protein diet eaten during infancy will increase intellectual functioning relative to a low-protein diet. In the same manner as with the *t* test for independent groups, each sample is considered a random sample from its own population set of scores, with parameters $\mu_1, \sigma_1^2$, and $\mu_2, \sigma_2^2$, respectively. However, since this is a rank-order test, the Mann–Whitney *U* test does not evaluate sample mean differences and, hence, makes no prediction about the relationship of $\mu_1$ and $\mu_2$. Thus, there are no population parameters included in the statement of the alternative hypothesis.

2. Null hypothesis: The null hypothesis is also stated without any population parameters. It states that the high-protein diet, eaten during infancy, will either have no effect on intellectual functioning or it will decrease intellectual functioning.

3. Conclusion using $\alpha = 0.05_{1\ tail}$: As with the other inference tests, the conclusion involves a two-step process: Compute the appropriate statistic and then evaluate the statistic using its sampling distribution.

   **STEP 1: Compute the appropriate statistic.** The statistic calculated by the Mann–Whitney *U* test is $U_{obt}$ or $U'_{obt}$. These statistics measure the degree of separation between the two sample sets of scores. As the real effect of the independent variable increases, the samples become more separated (the scores of the two samples overlap less). As the degree of sample separation increases, $U_{obt}$ decreases and $U'_{obt}$ increases. When there is complete separation between samples (no overlap), $U_{obt} = 0$. For any experiment, $U_{obt} + U'_{obt} = n_1 n_2$. Both $U_{obt}$ and $U'_{obt}$ measure the same degree of separation. Hence, in analyzing the data from any experiment, it is necessary to compute and evaluate only $U_{obt}$ or $U'_{obt}$. $U_{obt}$ and $U'_{obt}$ are computed as follows:

a. Combine the scores from both groups, rank-order them, and assign each a rank score, using 1 for the lowest score:

| Original Score | 102 | 104 | 105 | 107 | 108 | 110 | 111 | 113 | 115 |
|---|---|---|---|---|---|---|---|---|---|
| Rank | 1 | 2 | 3 | 4 | 5 | 6 | 7 | 8 | 9 |

| Original Score | 117 | 118 | 120 | 122 | 125 | 130 | 135 | 140 |
|---|---|---|---|---|---|---|---|---|
| Rank | 10 | 11 | 12 | 13 | 14 | 15 | 16 | 17 |

b. Sum the ranks for each group; that is, determine $R_1$ and $R_2$, where $R_1 = $ sum of the ranks for group 1 and $R_2 = $ sum of the ranks for group 2.

| Control Group 1 | | Experimental Group 2 | |
|---|---|---|---|
| *Original score* | *Rank* | *Original score* | *Rank* |
| 102 | 1 | 110 | 6 |
| 104 | 2 | 115 | 9 |
| 105 | 3 | 117 | 10 |
| 107 | 4 | 122 | 13 |
| 108 | 5 | 125 | 14 |
| 111 | 7 | 130 | 15 |
| 113 | 8 | 135 | 16 |
| 118 | 11 | 140 | 17 |
| 120 | 12 | | $R_2 = 100$ |
| | $R_1 = 53$ | | $n_2 = 8$ |
| | $n_1 = 9$ | | |

c. Solve the equations for $U_{obt}$ and $U'_{obt}$. $U_{obt}$ and $U'_{obt}$ are computed by solving the following equations:

$$U_{obt} = n_1 n_2 + \frac{n_1(n_1 + 1)}{2} - R_1 \qquad \text{\textit{general equation for finding}}\ U_{obt}\ \text{\textit{or}}\ U'_{obt}$$

$$U_{obt} = n_1 n_2 + \frac{n_2(n_2 + 1)}{2} - R_2 \qquad \text{\textit{general equation for finding}}\ U_{obt}\ \text{\textit{or}}\ U'_{obt}$$

where    $n_1$ = number of scores in group 1
$n_2$ = number of scores in group 2
$R_1$ = sum of ranks for scores in group 1
$R_2$ = sum of ranks for scores in group 2

In solving these equations, we identify one of the samples as group 1 and the other as group 2. Then, we just go ahead and solve the equations. One of the equations will yield a number lower than the number from the other equation. Arbitrarily, the lower of the two numbers is assigned as $U_{\mathrm{obt}}$ and the higher of the two numbers as $U'_{\mathrm{obt}}$. It doesn't matter which sample is labeled group 1 and which is labeled group 2. If we reversed the labels, we would still obtain the same numbers from the equations. What does change with labeling is which equation yields the higher number and which yields the lower number. Since this depends on which group is labeled group 1 and which group 2, these equations are both written initially in terms of $U_{\mathrm{obt}}$. In an actual analysis, the equation that yields the lower number is the $U_{\mathrm{obt}}$ equation; the one that yields the higher number is the $U'_{\mathrm{obt}}$ equation. For the data in the present example,

$$U_{\mathrm{obt}} = n_1 n_2 + \frac{n_1(n_1 + 1)}{2} - R_1 \qquad U_{\mathrm{obt}} = n_1 n_2 + \frac{n_2(n_2 + 1)}{2} - R_2$$

$$= 9(8) + \frac{9(10)}{2} - 53 \qquad\qquad = 9(8) + \frac{8(9)}{2} - 100$$

$$= 72 + 45 - 53 \qquad\qquad\qquad = 72 + 36 - 100$$

$$= 64 \qquad\qquad\qquad\qquad\qquad = 8$$

Therefore,

$$U_{\mathrm{obt}} = 8$$

$$U'_{\mathrm{obt}} = 64$$

**STEP 2:** **Evaluate $U_{\mathrm{obt}}$ or $U'_{\mathrm{obt}}$.** Tables C.1–C.4 in Appendix D give the critical values of $U$ and $U'$. For each cell, there are two entries. The upper entry is the highest value of $U_{\mathrm{obt}}$ for various $n_1$ and $n_2$ combinations that will allow rejection of $H_0$. The lower entry is the lowest value of $U'_{\mathrm{obt}}$ that will allow rejection of $H_0$. The decision rule is as follows:

If $U_{\mathrm{obt}} \leq U_{\mathrm{crit}}$, reject $H_0$ and affirm $H_1$.
If $U'_{\mathrm{obt}} \geq U'_{\mathrm{crit}}$, reject $H_0$ and affirm $H_1$.

Since both $U_{\mathrm{obt}}$ and $U'_{\mathrm{obt}}$ measure the same degree of separation, we shall evaluate only $U_{\mathrm{obt}}$. Each of the Tables C.1–C.4 is for a different alpha level. For the data of the present experiment, Table C.4 is appropriate. With $n_1 = 9$ and $n_2 = 8$, $U_{\mathrm{crit}} = 18$ and $U'_{\mathrm{crit}} = 54$. Evaluating $U_{\mathrm{obt}}$, since $U_{\mathrm{obt}} < 18$, we reject $H_0$ and affirm $H_1$. A high-protein diet eaten during infancy appears to increase intellectual functioning relative to a low-protein diet.

**table 17.7** Data to illustrate ranking tied scores

| Group 1 | Group 2 |
|---------|---------|
| 12 | 11 |
| 14 | 12 |
| 15 | 16 |
| 17 | 17 |
| 18 | 17 |
|    | 20 |

## Tied Ranks

We've already shown how to rank-order tied scores when we discussed the Spearman rho correlation coefficient (p. 121) and the Wilcoxon signed ranks test (p. 443). To review, tied scores are handled by assigning them the average of the tied ranks. For example, consider the two sets of scores presented in Table 17.7. To rank-order the combined scores, we proceed as follows. First, the scores are arranged in ascending order. Thus,

| Raw Score | 11 | 12 | 12 | 14 | 15 | 16 | 17 | 17 | 17 | 18 | 20 |
|-----------|----|-----|-----|----|----|----|----|----|----|----|----|
| Rank | 1 | 2.5 | 2.5 | 4 | 5 | 6 | 8 | 8 | 8 | 10 | 11 |

Next, we assign each raw score its rank, beginning with 1 for the lowest score. This has been shown previously. Note that the two raw scores of 12 are tied at the ranks of 2 and 3. They are assigned the average of these tied ranks. Thus, they each get a rank of 2.5 $[(2 + 3)/2 = 2.5]$. We have already used the ranks of 2 and 3, so the next score gets a rank of 4. The raw scores of 17 are tied at the ranks of 7, 8, and 9. Therefore, they receive the rank of 8, which is the average of 7, 8, and 9 $[(7 + 8 + 9)/3 = 8]$. Note that the next rank is 10 (not 9) because we've already used ranks 7, 8, and 9 in computing the average. If the ranking is done correctly, unless there are tied ranks at the end, the last raw score should have a rank equal to $N$. In this case, $N = 11$ and so does the rank of the last score. Once the ranks have been assigned, $U_{obt}$ and $U'_{obt}$ are calculated in the usual way.

Let's do the following problem for practice.

## Practice Problem 17.5

Someone has told you that men are better in abstract reasoning than women. You are skeptical, so you decide to test this idea using a nondirectional hypothesis. You randomly select eight men and eight women from the freshman class at your university and administer an abstract reasoning test. A higher score reflects better abstract reasoning abilities. You obtain the following scores:

| Men | Women |
|-----|-------|
| 70 | 82 |
| 86 | 80 |
| 60 | 50 |
| 92 | 95 |
| 82 | 93 |
| 65 | 85 |
| 74 | 90 |
| 94 | 75 |

**a.** What is the alternative hypothesis? Assume a nondirectional hypothesis is appropriate.

**b.** What is the null hypothesis?

**c.** Using $\alpha = 0.05_{2 \text{ tail}}$, what do you conclude?

**SOLUTION**

**a.** Nondirectional alternative hypothesis: Men and women differ in abstract reasoning ability.

**b.** Null hypothesis: Men and women are equal in abstract reasoning ability.

**c.** Conclusion, using $\alpha = 0.05_{2 \text{ tail}}$:

> **STEP 1:** **Calculate $U_{\text{obt}}$ for the data:**
>
> **a.** Combine the scores, rank-order them, and assign each a rank, using 1 for the lowest score:

| Original Score | 50 | 60 | 65 | 70 | 74 | 75 | 80 | 82 |
|---|---|---|---|---|---|---|---|---|
| Rank | 1 | 2 | 3 | 4 | 5 | 6 | 7 | 8.5 |

| Original Score | 82 | 85 | 86 | 90 | 92 | 93 | 94 | 95 |
|---|---|---|---|---|---|---|---|---|
| Rank | 8.5 | 10 | 11 | 12 | 13 | 14 | 15 | 16 |

> **b.** Sum the ranks for each group; that is, determine $R_1$ and $R_2$.

| Men 1 | | Women 2 | |
|---|---|---|---|
| *Original score* | *Rank* | *Original score* | *Rank* |
| 60 | 2 | 50 | 1 |
| 65 | 3 | 75 | 6 |
| 70 | 4 | 80 | 7 |
| 74 | 5 | 82 | 8.5 |
| 82 | 8.5 | 85 | 10 |
| 86 | 11 | 90 | 12 |
| 92 | 13 | 93 | 14 |
| 94 | 15 | 95 | 16 |
| | $R_1 = 61.5$ | | $R_2 = 74.5$ |
| | $n_1 = 8$ | | $n_2 = 8$ |

> **c.** Solve the equations for $U_{\text{obt}}$ and $U'_{\text{obt}}$:

$$U_{\text{obt}} = n_1 n_2 + \frac{n_1(n_1 + 1)}{2} - R_1 \qquad U_{\text{obt}} = n_1 n_2 + \frac{n_2(n_2 + 1)}{2} - R_2$$

$$= 8(8) + \frac{8(9)}{2} - 61.5 \qquad\qquad = 8(8) + \frac{8(9)}{2} - 74.5$$

$$= 64 + 36 - 61.5 = 38.5 \qquad\quad = 64 + 36 - 74.5 = 25.5$$

(*continued*)

Thus,

$$U_{\text{obt}} = 25.5$$
$$U'_{\text{obt}} = 38.5$$

**STEP 2:** **Evaluate $U_{\text{obt}}$.** With $\alpha = 0.05_{2\text{ tail}}$, Table C.3 is appropriate. With $n_1 = n_2 = 8$, $U_{\text{crit}} = 13$ and $U'_{\text{crit}} = 51$. Since $U_{\text{obt}} > 13$, we fail to reject $H_0$, and hence, we can't affirm $H_1$. These data do not support the hypothesis that men and women differ in abstract reasoning ability.

## Assumptions Underlying the Mann–Whitney $U$ Test

Since we must be able to rank-order the data to compute $U_{\text{obt}}$ or $U'_{\text{obt}}$, the Mann–Whitney $U$ test requires that the data be at least ordinal in scaling. It does not depend on the population scores being of any particular shape (e.g., normal distributions), as does the $t$ test for independent groups. Thus, the Mann–Whitney $U$ test can be used instead of the $t$ test for independent groups when there is a serious violation of the normality assumption or when the data are not of interval or ratio scaling. The Mann–Whitney $U$ test is a powerful test. However, since it uses only the ordinal property of the scores, it is not as powerful as the $t$ test for independent groups, which uses the interval property of the scores.

## THE KRUSKAL–WALLIS TEST

The Kruskal–Wallis test is a nonparametric test that is used with an independent groups design employing $k$ samples. It is used as a substitute for the parametric one-way ANOVA discussed in Chapter 15, when the assumptions of that test are seriously violated. The Kruskal–Wallis test does not assume population normality nor homogeneity of variance, as does parametric ANOVA, and requires only ordinal scaling of the dependent variable. It is used when violations of population normality and/or homogeneity of variance are extreme or when interval or ratio scaling are required and not met by the data. To understand this test, let's begin with an experiment.

**an experiment**

### Evaluating Two Weight Reduction Programs

A health psychologist, employed by a large corporation, is interested in evaluating two weight reduction programs she is considering using with employees of her corporation. She conducts an experiment in which 18 obese employees are randomly assigned to three conditions, with 6 subjects per condition. The subjects in condition 1 are placed on a diet that reduces their daily caloric intake by 500 calories. The subjects in condition 2 receive the same restricted diet, but in addition are required to walk 2 miles each day. Condition 3 is a control condition, in which the subjects are asked to maintain their usual eating and exercise habits. The data presented in Table 17.8 are the number of pounds lost by each subject over a 6-month period. A positive number indicates weight loss and a negative number is weight gain. Assume the data show that there is a strong violation of population normality such that the psytable 17.8    Data from weight reduction experiment

| 1 Diet | | 2 Diet + Exercise | | 3 Control | |
|---|---|---|---|---|---|
| *Pounds lost* | *Rank* | *Pounds lost* | *Rank* | *Pounds lost* | *Rank* |
| 2 | 5 | 12 | 12 | 8 | 9 |
| 15 | 14 | 9 | 10 | 3 | 6 |
| 7 | 8 | 20 | 16 | −1 | 4 |
| 6 | 7 | 17 | 15 | −3 | 2 |
| 10 | 11 | 28 | 17 | −2 | 3 |
| 14 | 13 | 30 | 18 | −8 | 1 |
| $n_1 = 6$ | $R_1 = 58$ | $n_2 = 6$ | $R_2 = 88$ | $n_3 = 6$ | $R_3 = 25$ |

chologist decides to analyze the data with the Kruskal–Wallis test, rather than using parametric ANOVA.

a. What is the alternative hypothesis?
b. What is the null hypothesis?
c. What is the conclusion? Use $\alpha = 0.05$.

**SOLUTION**

a. Alternative hypothesis: As with parametric ANOVA, the alternative hypothesis states that at least one of the conditions affects weight loss differently than at least one of the other conditions. In the same manner as parametric ANOVA, each sample is considered a random sample from its own population set of scores. If there are $k$ samples, there are $k$ populations. In this example, $k = 3$. However, since this is a nonparametric test, Kruskal–Wallis makes no prediction about the population means $\mu_1, \mu_2$, or $\mu_3$. It merely asserts that at least one of the population distributions is different from at least one of the other population distributions.

b. Null hypothesis: The samples are random samples from the same or identical population distributions. There is no prediction specifically regarding $\mu_1, \mu_2$, or $\mu_3$.

c. Conclusion, using $\alpha = 0.05$: As usual, in evaluating $H_0$, we follow the two-step process: Compute the appropriate statistic and then evaluate the statistic using its sampling distribution.

**STEP 1: Compute the appropriate statistic.** The statistic we compute for the Kruskal–Wallis test is $H_{obt}$. The procedure is very much like computing $U_{obt}$ for the Mann–Whitney $U$ test. All of the scores are grouped together and rank-ordered, assigning the rank of 1 to the lowest score, 2 to the next to lowest, and $N$ to the highest. When this is done, the ranks for each condition or sample are summed. These procedures have been carried out for the data of the present example and entered in Table 17.8.

The sums of ranks for each group have been symbolized as $R_1, R_2$, and $R_3$, respectively. For these data, $R_1 = 58$, $R_2 = 88$, and $R_3 = 25$. The Kruskal–Wallis test assesses whether these sums of ranks differ so much that it is unreasonable to consider that they come from samples that were randomly selected from the same population. The larger the differences between the sums of the ranks of each sample is, the less likely it is that the samples are from the same population.

The equation for computing $H_{obt}$ is as follows:

$$H_{obt} = \left[\frac{12}{N(N+1)}\right]\left[\sum_{i=1}^{k}\frac{(R_i)^2}{n_i}\right] - 3(N+1)$$

$$= \left[\frac{12}{N(N+1)}\right]\left[\frac{R_1^2}{n_1} + \frac{R_2^2}{n_2} + \frac{R_3^2}{n_3} + \cdots + \frac{R_k^2}{n_k}\right] - 3(N+1)$$

*where* $\displaystyle\sum_{i=1}^{k}\frac{(R_i)^2}{n_i}$ tells us to square the sum of ranks for each sample, divide each squared value by the number of scores in the sample, and sum over samples

$k$ = number of samples or groups

$n_i$ = number of scores in the $i$th sample

$n_1$ = number of scores in sample 1

$n_2$ = number of scores in sample 2

$n_3$ = number of scores in sample 3

$n_k$ = number of scores in sample $k$

$N$ = number of scores in all samples combined

$R_i$ = sum of the ranks for the $i$th sample

$R_1$ = sum of the ranks for sample 1

$R_2$ = sum of the ranks for sample 2

$R_3$ = sum of the ranks for sample 3

$R_k$ = sum of the ranks for sample $k$

Substituting the appropriate values from the table into this equation, we obtain

$$H_{obt} = \left[\frac{12}{N(N+1)}\right]\left[\frac{(R_1)^2}{n_1} + \frac{(R_2)^2}{n_2} + \frac{(R_3)^2}{n_3}\right] - 3(N+1)$$

$$= \left[\frac{12}{18(18+1)}\right]\left[\frac{(58)^2}{6} + \frac{(88)^2}{6} + \frac{(25)^2}{6}\right] - 3(18+1)$$

$$= 68.61 - 57$$

$$= 11.61$$

**STEP 2: Evaluate the statistic.** It can be shown that, if the number of scores in each sample is 5 or more, the sampling distribution of the statistic $H$ is approximately the same as chi-square with df = $k - 1$. In the present experiment, df = $k - 1 = 3 - 1 = 2$. From Table H, with $\alpha = 0.05$, and df = 2,

$$H_{crit} = 5.991$$

As with parametric ANOVA, the Kruskal–Wallis test is a nondirectional test. The decision rule states that

If $H_{obt} \geq H_{crit}$, reject $H_0$.

If $H_{obt} < H_{crit}$, retain $H_0$.

Since $H_{obt} > 5.991$, we reject $H_0$. It appears that the conditions are not equal with regard to weight loss.

## Practice Problem 17.6

A business consultant is doing research in the area of management training. There are two effective managerial styles: One is people-oriented and a second is task-oriented. Well-defined, static jobs are better served by the people-oriented managers and changing, newly created jobs by the task-oriented managers. The experiment being conducted investigates whether it is better to try to train managers to have both styles or whether it is better to match managers to jobs with no attempt to train in a second style. The managers for this experiment are 24 army officers, randomly selected from a large army base. The experiment involves three conditions. In condition 1, the subjects receive training in both managerial styles. After training is completed, these subjects are randomly assigned to new jobs without matching style and job. In condition 2, the subjects receive no additional training but are assigned to jobs according to a match between their single managerial style and the job requirements. Condition 3 is a control condition in which subjects receive no additional training and are assigned to new jobs, like those in condition 1, without matching. After they are in their new job assignments for 6 months, a performance rating is obtained on each officer. The data follow. The higher the score, the better the performance. At the beginning of the experiment, there were eight subjects in each condition. However, one of the subjects in condition 2 dropped out midway into the experiment and was not replaced. Assume the data do not meet the assumptions for the parametric one-way ANOVA.

| Condition 1 Training | | Condition 2 Matching | | Condition 3 Control | |
|---|---|---|---|---|---|
| Score | Rank | Score | Rank | Score | Rank |
| 65 | 8 | 90 | 21 | 55 | 3 |
| 84 | 16 | 83 | 15 | 82 | 14 |
| 87 | 19.5 | 76 | 12 | 71 | 10 |
| 53 | 2 | 87 | 19.5 | 60 | 6 |
| 70 | 9 | 92 | 22 | 52 | 1 |
| 85 | 17 | 86 | 18 | 81 | 13 |
| 56 | 4 | 93 | 23 | 73 | 11 |
| 63 | 7 | | | 57 | 5 |
| $n_1 = 8$ | $R_1 = 82.5$ | $n_2 = 7$ | $R_2 = 130.5$ | $n_3 = 8$ | $R_3 = 63$ |

**a.** What is the alternative hypothesis?
**b.** What is the null hypothesis?
**c.** What is the conclusion? Use $\alpha = 0.05$.

(*continued*)

**SOLUTION**

a. Alternative hypothesis: At least one of the conditions has a different effect on job performance than at least one of the other conditions. Therefore, at least one of the population distributions is different from one of the others.

b. Null hypothesis: The conditions have the same effect on job performance. Therefore, the samples are random samples from the same or identical population distributions.

c. Conclusion, using $\alpha = 0.05$:

**STEP 1: Compute the appropriate statistic.**

$$H_{obt} = \left[\frac{12}{N(N+1)}\right]\left[\frac{(R_1)^2}{n_1} + \frac{(R_2)^2}{n_2} + \frac{(R_3)^2}{n_3}\right] - 3(N+1)$$

$$= \left[\frac{12}{23(23+1)}\right]\left[\frac{(82.5)^2}{8} + \frac{(130.5)^2}{7} + \frac{(63)^2}{8}\right] - 3(23+1)$$

$$= 82.17 - 72$$

$$= 10.17$$

**STEP 2: Evaluate the statistic.** In the present experiment, df $= k - 1 = 3 - 1 = 2$. From Table H, with $\alpha = 0.05$, and df $= 2$,

$$H_{crit} = 5.991$$

Since $H_{obt} > 5.991$, we reject $H_0$. It appears that the conditions are not equal with regard to their effect on job performance.

## Assumptions Underlying the Kruskal–Wallis Test

To use the Kruskal–Wallis test, the data must be of at least ordinal scaling. In addition, there must be at least five scores in each sample to use the probabilities given in the table of chi-square.*

---

*To analyze data with fewer than five scores in a sample, see S. Siegel and N. Castellan, Jr., *Nonparametric Statistics for the Behavioral Sciences,* 2nd ed., McGraw-Hill, New York, 1988, pp. 206–212.

## WHAT IS THE TRUTH?

### Statistics and Applied Social Research—Useful or "Abuseful"?

A front-page article in *The Wall Street Journal* discussed the possible misuses of social science research in connection with federally mandated changes in the U.S. welfare system. Excerpts from the article are reproduced here.

#### *Think Tanks Battle to Judge the Impact of Welfare Overhaul*

*Now that welfare overhaul is under way across the country, so is something else: an ideologically charged battle of the experts to label the various innovations as successes or failures.*

*Each side—liberal and conservative—fears the other will use early, and perhaps not totally reliable, results of surveys and studies of the impact of welfare reform to push a political agenda. And conservatives, along with other supporters of the law Congress recently passed to allow states to tinker with welfare, worry that they have the most to lose, because of the overwhelming presence of liberal scholars in the field of social science. . . .*

*Critics of the overhaul process make no bones that they intend to use research into the bill's effects to turn yesterday's angry taxpayers into tomorrow's friends of the downtrodden. . . .*

*The climate of ideological suspicions is exemplified by the California-based Kaiser Family Foundation's handling of a survey it financed of New Jersey welfare recipients. The study focused on the effect of New Jersey's controversial rule barring additional benefits for women who have children while on welfare. Last spring, shortly before Kaiser was to announce the results, it canceled a planned news conference. Some critics suspect that Kaiser didn't like some of the answers it got, such as one showing that most recipients considered the "family cap" fair. The Rutgers University researcher who conducted the survey says he has been forbidden to discuss it. Kaiser says the suspicions are unfounded and that methodological errors destroyed the survey's usefulness. . . .*

*The hopes and fears of both sides are embodied in one of the biggest private social-policy research projects ever undertaken: a five-year, $30-million study of welfare overhaul and other elements of the "New Federalism." The kick-off of the study will be announced today by the Washington-based Urban Institute.*

*The institute, founded three decades ago to examine the woes of the nation's cities, has assembled a politically balanced project staff and promises to post "nonpartisan, reliable data" on the Internet for all sides to examine. But memories are still fresh of the institute's prediction last year that the law would toss one million children into poverty, so even some of its top officials fret about how the research will be received in a political culture increasingly riven between opposing ideological camps.*

*"Everyone wants to attach a political label to everything that comes out," says Isabel Sawhill, a former Clinton administration budget official. . . . For people on both sides, "there's no such thing as unbiased information or apolitical studies anymore," she says.*

(continued)

## WHAT IS THE TRUTH?

### Statistics and Applied Social Research—Useful or "Abuseful"?

**(*continued*)**

**Playing the Numbers**

*"Hopefully, the data we produce will be unassailable," says Anna Kondratas, a one-time Reagan administration aide who is the project's co-director. Yet she recalls a decade-old admonition from a Democratic congressman who didn't like her testimony about the food-stamp program: "Everybody's entitled to his own statistics. . . ."*

*In recent years, evaluations of high-profile social programs have often found them less beneficial than many political liberals had hoped. "We are in desperate need to learn about what works," says Doug Nelson, president of the Annie E. Casey Foundation, the philanthropic organization that is the largest single backer of the Urban Institute study.*

*Assessing the crazy quilt of state welfare innovations poses an immense challenge for researchers of any ideological stripe. With so many policies changing at once, all involving potential effects on employment, childbearing and family life, figuring out which questions to ask may be as difficult as finding the answers. And the*

*swirling cross-currents over race, economics and values—the possible conflict between attempts to reduce illegitimate births and attempts to prevent increases in abortion, for example—make determinations of "success" or "failure" highly subjective.*

*That is precisely why backers of the new law, which aims to reduce welfare spending by some $54 billion over seven years, are bracing for a flood of critical studies.*

*"Social scientists want to help children and families, and they believe the way to do that is to give them more benefits," says Ron Haskins, a former developmental psychologist at the University of North Carolina who now heads the staff of a House welfare subcommittee. As a result, adds the Heritage Foundation's Robert Rector, most studies of the law's effect "will emphasize a bogus measure of material poverty" while shortchanging shifts in attitudes, values and behavior that may be hard to gauge and slower to manifest themselves. . . .*

*That contentious atmosphere has embroiled the Kaiser Foundation's $90,000 survey of New Jersey welfare recipients. Ted Goertzel, a Rutgers University sociologist not involved in the survey, notes rumors that ideology played a role in Kaiser's decision not to release the data. "The recipients said they agreed with the family cap," he says. "If you do*

*research and don't like the results, are you obligated to release it? There's an ethical question here."*

I've included this article at the end of this chapter because chi-square is one of the major inference tests used in social science research. I think you will agree that this article poses some very interesting and important questions regarding applied research in this area. For example, in applied social science research, is it really true that "there is no such thing as unbiased information"? Was the Democratic congressman correct in stating, "Everybody's entitled to his own statistics"? Is it really true that "most studies of the law's effect 'will emphasize a bogus measure of material poverty, while shortchanging shifts in attitudes, values and behavior that may be hard to gauge and slower to manifest themselves'"? If so, how will we ever find out whether this and other social programs really work? Or doesn't it matter whether we ever find out what social programs really work? Would it be better just to "pontificate" out of one's own private social values (Method of Authority), or perhaps just to cite individual case examples? Or do you agree with Doug Nelson that, "We are in desperate need to learn about what works"? If so, how can appropriate data be collected?

## WHAT IS THE TRUTH?

### Statistics and Applied Social Research—Useful or "Abuseful"?

(*continued*)

What do you think about the notion that social scientists with strong political views will go out and do research, deliberately biasing their research instruments so that the data will confirm their own political views? If it is true, does that mean we should stop funding such research? How about the ordinary layperson: How will he or she be able to intelligently interpret the results of such studies? Does this mean students should stop studying statistics, or quite the contrary, that students need to learn even more about statistics so that they will not be taken in by poor, pseudo, or biased research? Finally, what do you think about the situation where an organization conducts socially relevant research and the findings turn out to be against the interest of the organization? Does the organization have an obligation to inform the public? Is it unethical if it doesn't?

*Source:* From "Think Tanks Battle to Judge the Impact of Welfare Overhaul," by John Harwood. Reprinted by permission of *The Wall Street Journal via Copyright Clearance Center,* © 1997 Dow Jones & Company, Inc. All Rights Reserved Worldwide.

## SUMMARY

In this chapter, we have discussed nonparametric statistics. Nonparametric inference tests depend considerably less on population characteristics than do parametric tests. The $z$, $t$, and $F$ tests are examples of parametric tests; the sign test and the Mann–Whitney $U$ test are examples of nonparametric tests. Parametric tests are used when possible because they are more powerful and versatile. However, when the assumptions of the parametric tests are violated, nonparametric tests are frequently used.

One of the most frequently used inference tests for analyzing nominal data is the nonparametric test called chi-square ($\chi^2$). It is appropriate for analyzing frequency data dealing with one or two variables. Chi-square essentially measures the discrepancy between the observed frequency ($f_o$) and the expected frequency ($f_e$) for each of the cells in a one-way or two-way table. In equation form, $\chi^2_{\text{obt}} = \Sigma (f_o - f_e)^2 / f_e$, where the summation is over all the cells. In single-variable situations, the data are presented in a one-way table and the various expected frequency values are determined on an *a priori* basis. In two-variable situations, the frequency data are presented in a contingency table and we are interested in determining whether there is a relationship between the two variables. The null hypothesis states that there is no relationship—that the two variables are independent. The alternative hypothesis states that the two variables are related. The expected frequency for each cell is the frequency that would be expected if sampling is random from a population where the proportions for each category on one variable are equal for each category on the other variable. Since the population proportions are unknown, their expected values under the null hypothesis are estimated from the sample data, and the expected frequencies are calculated using these estimates.

The obtained value of $\chi^2$ is evaluated by comparing it with $\chi^2_{\text{crit}}$. If $\chi^2_{\text{obt}} \geq \chi^2_{\text{crit}}$, we reject the null hypothesis. The critical value of $\chi^2$ is determined by the sampling distribution of $\chi^2$ and the alpha level. The sampling distribution of $\chi^2$ is a family of curves that varies with the degrees of freedom. In the one-variable experiment, $df = k - 1$. In the two-variable situation, $df = (r - 1)(c - 1)$. A basic assumption of $\chi^2$ is that each subject can have only one entry in the table. A second assumption is that the expected frequency in each cell must be of a certain minimum size. The use of $\chi^2$ is not limited to nominal data, but regardless of the scaling, the data must finally be divided into mutually exclusive categories and the cell entries must be frequencies.

The Wilcoxon matched-pairs signed ranks test is a nonparametric test that is used with a correlated groups design. The statistic calculated is $T_{obt}$. Determination of $T_{obt}$ involves four steps: (1) finding the difference between each pair of scores, (2) ranking the absolute values of the difference scores, (3) assigning the appropriate sign to the ranks, and (4) separately summing the positive and negative ranks. $T_{obt}$ is the lower sum. It is evaluated by comparison with $T_{crit}$. If $T_{obt} \leq T_{crit}$, we reject $H_0$. The Wilcoxon signed ranks test requires that (1) the within-pair scores be at least of ordinal scaling and (2) the difference scores also be at least of ordinal scaling. This test serves as an alternative to the $t$ test for correlated groups when the assumptions of the $t$ test have not been met. It is more powerful than the sign test, but not as powerful as the $t$ test.

The Mann–Whitney $U$ test analyzes the degree of separation between the samples in a two-group, independent groups experiment. The less the separation, the more reasonable chance is as the underlying explanation. For any analysis, two statistics are computed. Both indicate the same degree of separation. The lower value is arbitrarily called $U_{obt}$, and the higher value is called $U'_{obt}$. Tables C.1–C.4 give the critical values of $U$ and $U'$. If $U_{obt} \leq U_{crit}$, reject $H_0$ and affirm $H_1$. If $U'_{obt} \geq U'_{crit}$, reject $H_0$ and affirm

$H_1$. Otherwise, we retain $H_0$. The Mann–Whitney $U$ test is appropriate for an independent groups design where the data are at least ordinal in scaling. It is a powerful test, often used in place of Student's $t$ test when the data do not meet the assumptions of the $t$ test.

The Kruskal–Wallis test is used as a substitute for one-way parametric ANOVA. It uses the independent groups design with $k$ samples. The null hypothesis asserts that the $k$ samples are random samples from the same or identical population distributions. No attempt is made to specifically test for population mean differences, as is the case with parametric ANOVA. The statistic computed is $H_{obt}$. If the number of scores in each sample is five or more, the sampling distribution of $H_{obt}$ is close enough to that of chi-square to use the latter in determining $H_{crit}$. If $H_{obt} \geq H_{crit}$, $H_0$ is rejected. To compute $H_{obt}$, the scores of the $k$ samples are combined and rank-ordered, assigning 1 to the lowest score. The ranks are then summed for each sample. Kruskal–Wallis tests whether it is reasonable to consider the summed ranks for each sample to be due to random sampling from a single population set of scores. The greater the differences between the sum of ranks for each sample are, the less tenable is the null hypothesis. This test assumes that the dependent variable is measured on a scale that is of at least ordinal scaling. There must also be five or more scores in each sample to validly use the chi-square sampling distribution.

## IMPORTANT TERMS

Chi-square ($\chi^2$) (p. 429)
Contingency table (p. 434)
Degree of separation (p. 449)
Expected frequency ($f_e$) (p. 429)

Kruskal–Wallis test ($H$) (p. 452)
Mann–Whitney $U$ test ($U$ or $U'$) (p. 446)
Marginals (p. 436)

Observed frequency ($f_o$) (p. 429)
Wilcoxon matched-pairs signed ranks test ($T$) (p. 443)

## QUESTIONS AND PROBLEMS

1. Briefly identify or define the terms in the Important Terms section.
2. What is the underlying rationale for the determination of $f_e$ in the two-variable experiment?
3. What are the assumptions underlying chi-square?
4. In situations involving more than 1 degree of freedom, the $\chi^2$ test is nondirectional. Is this statement correct? Explain.

5. What distinguishes parametric from nonparametric tests? Explain, giving some examples.
6. Are parametric tests preferable to nonparametric tests? Explain.
7. When might we use a nonparametric test? Give an example.
8. Under what conditions might one use the Wilcoxon signed ranks test?

9. Compare the Wilcoxon signed ranks test with the sign test and the $t$ test for correlated groups with regard to power. Explain any differences.

10. What are the assumptions of the Wilcoxon signed ranks test?

11. In a two-condition, independent groups experiment, how is the degree of separation between samples affected by the size of real effect?

12. Under what conditions might one use the Mann–Whitney $U$ test?

13. What are the assumptions underlying the Mann–Whitney $U$ test?

14. Compare the power of Student's $t$ test and the Mann–Whitney $U$ test.

15. What are the assumptions underlying the Kruskal–Wallis test?

16. A researcher is interested in whether there really is a prevailing view that overweight people are more jolly. A random sample of 80 individuals was asked the question, "Do you believe fat people are more jolly?" The following results were obtained:

| Yes | No |    |
|-----|-----|-----|
| 44  | 36  | 80  |

Using $\alpha = 0.05$, what is your conclusion? social

17. A study was conducted to determine whether big-city and small-town dwellers differed in their helpfulness to strangers. In this study, the investigators rang the doorbells of strangers living in New York City or small towns in the vicinity. They explained they had misplaced the address of a friend living in the neighborhood and asked to use the phone. The following data show the number of individuals who admitted or did not admit the strangers (the investigators) into their homes:

Helpfulness to Strangers

|  | Admitted strangers into their home | Did not admit strangers into their home |  |
|---|---|---|---|
| Big-city dweller | 60 | 90 | 150 |
| Small-town dweller | 70 | 30 | 100 |
|  | 130 | 120 | 250 |

Do big-city dwellers differ in their helpfulness to strangers? Use $\alpha = 0.05$ in making your decision. social

18. Because of rampant inflation, the government is considering imposing wage and price controls. A government economist, interested in determining whether there is a relationship between occupation and attitude toward wage and price controls, collects the following data. The data show for each occupation the number of individuals in the sample who were *for* or *against* the controls:

|  | Attitude Toward Wage and Price Controls | | |
|---|---|---|---|
|  | *For* | *Against* |  |
| Labor | 90 | 60 | 150 |
| Business | 100 | 150 | 250 |
| Professions | 110 | 90 | 200 |
|  | 300 | 300 | 600 |

Do these occupations differ regarding attitudes toward wage and price controls? Use $\alpha = 0.01$ in making your decision. I/O

19. The head of the marketing division of a leading soap manufacturer must decide among four differently styled wrappings for the soap. To provide a database for the decision, he has the soap placed in the different wrapping styles and distributed to five supermarkets. At the end of 2 weeks, he finds that the following amounts of soap were sold:

| Wrapping A | Wrapping B | Wrapping C | Wrapping D |  |
|---|---|---|---|---|
| 90 | 98 | 130 | 82 | 400 |

Is there sufficient basis for making a decision among wrappings? If so, which should he pick? Use $\alpha = 0.05$. I/O

20. A researcher believes that individuals in different occupations will show differences in their ability to be hypnotized. Six lawyers, six physicians, and six professional dancers are randomly selected for the experiment. A test of hypnotic susceptibility is administered to each. The results are shown on the following page. The higher the score, the higher the hypnotizability. Assume the data violate the assumptions required for use of the $F$ test, but are at least of ordinal scaling. Using $\alpha = 0.05$, what is your conclusion?

| Condition 1 Lawyers | Condition 2 Physicians | Condition 3 Dancers |
|---|---|---|
| 26 | 14 | 30 |
| 17 | 19 | 21 |
| 27 | 28 | 35 |
| 32 | 22 | 29 |
| 20 | 25 | 37 |
| 25 | 15 | 34 |

cognitive, social

21. A professor of religious studies is interested in finding out whether there is a relationship between church attendance and educational level. Data are collected on a sample of individuals who completed only high school and on another sample who received a college education. The following are the resultant frequency data:

Church Attendance

|  | Attend regularly | Do not attend regularly |  |
|---|---|---|---|
| High school | 88 | 112 | 200 |
| College | 56 | 104 | 160 |
|  | 144 | 216 | 360 |

What is your conclusion? Use $\alpha = 0.05$. social

22. A coffee manufacturer advertises that, in a recent experiment in which their brand (brand A) was compared with the other four leading brands of coffee, more people preferred their brand to the other four. The data from the experiment are given here:

Coffee Brand

| A | B | C | D | E |  |
|---|---|---|---|---|---|
| 60 | 45 | 52 | 43 | 50 | 250 |

Do you believe the ad to be misleading? Use $\alpha = 0.05$ in making your decision. I/O

23. A study was conducted to determine whether there is a relationship between the amount of contact white housewives have with blacks and changes in their attitudes toward blacks. In this study, the changes in attitude toward blacks were measured for white housewives who had moved into segregated public housing projects where there was little daily contact with blacks and for white housewives who had moved into fully inte-

grated public housing projects where there was a great deal of contact. The following frequency data were recorded:

Attitude Toward Blacks

|  | Less favorable | No change | More favorable |  |
|---|---|---|---|---|
| Segregated housing proj. | 9 | 42 | 24 | 75 |
| Integrated housing proj. | 7 | 46 | 72 | 125 |
|  | 16 | 88 | 96 | 200 |

Based on these data, what is your conclusion? Use $\alpha = 0.05$. social

24. A psychologist investigates the hypothesis that birth order affects assertiveness. Her subjects are 20 young adults between 20 and 25 years of age. There are seven first-born, six second-born, and seven third-born subjects. Each subject is given an assertiveness test, with the following results. High scores indicate greater assertiveness. Assume the data are so far from normally distributed that the $F$ test can't be used, but the data are at least of ordinal scaling. Use $\alpha = 0.01$ to evaluate the data. What is your conclusion?

| Condition 1 First-Born | Condition 2 Second-Born | Condition 3 Third-Born |
|---|---|---|
| 18 | 18 | 7 |
| 8 | 12 | 19 |
| 4 | 3 | 2 |
| 21 | 24 | 30 |
| 28 | 22 | 18 |
| 32 | 1 | 5 |
| 10 |  | 14 |

social

25. An investigator believes that students who rank high in certain kinds of motives will behave differently in gambling situations. To investigate this hypothesis, the investigator randomly samples 50 students high in affiliation motivation, 50 students high in achievement motivation, and 50 students high in power motivation. The students are asked to play the game of roulette, and a record is kept of the bets they make. The data are then grouped into the number of subjects with each kind of motivation who make bets involving low, medium, and high risk. Low risk means they

make bets involving low odds (even money or less), medium risk involves bets of medium odds (from 2 to 1 to 5 to 1), and high risk involves playing long shots (from 17 to 1 to 35 to 1). The following data are obtained:

Kind of Motive

|  | Affiliation | Achievement | Power |  |
|---|---|---|---|---|
| Low risk | 26 | 13 | 9 | 48 |
| Med. risk | 16 | 27 | 14 | 57 |
| High risk | 8 | 10 | 27 | 45 |
|  | 50 | 50 | 50 | 150 |

Using $\alpha = 0.05$, is there a relationship between these different kinds of motives and gambling behavior? How do the groups differ? social

26. A major oil company conducts an experiment to assess whether a film designed to tell the truth about, and also promote more favorable attitudes toward, large oil companies really does result in more favorable attitudes. Twelve individuals are run in a replicated measures design. In the "before" condition, each subject fills out a questionnaire designed to assess attitudes toward large oil companies. In the "after" condition, the subjects see the film, after which they fill out the questionnaire. The following scores were obtained. High scores indicate more favorable attitudes toward large oil companies.

| Before | After |
|---|---|
| 43 | 45 |
| 48 | 60 |
| 25 | 22 |
| 24 | 33 |
| 15 | 7 |
| 18 | 22 |
| 35 | 41 |
| 28 | 21 |
| 41 | 55 |
| 28 | 33 |
| 34 | 44 |
| 12 | 23 |

Analyze the data using the Wilcoxon signed ranks test with $\alpha = 0.05_{1\text{ tail}}$. What do you conclude? I/O

27. In Chapter 14, Problem 18, p. 352, an experiment was conducted to evaluate the effect of decreases in frontalis muscle tension on headaches. The number of headaches experienced in a 2-week baseline period was recorded in nine subjects who had been experiencing tension headaches. Then the subjects were trained to lower frontalis muscle tension using biofeedback, after which the number of headaches in another 2-week period was again recorded. The data are again shown here.

| Subject No. | No. of Headaches | |
|---|---|---|
|  | Baseline | Follow-up |
| 1 | 17 | 3 |
| 2 | 13 | 7 |
| 3 | 6 | 2 |
| 4 | 5 | 3 |
| 5 | 5 | 6 |
| 6 | 10 | 2 |
| 7 | 8 | 1 |
| 8 | 6 | 0 |
| 9 | 7 | 2 |

In that problem, the sampling distribution of $\overline{D}$ was assumed to be normally distributed, and the analysis was conducted using the $t$ test. For this problem assume the $t$ test cannot be used because of an extreme violation of its normality assumption. Use the Wilcoxon signed ranks test to analyze the data. What do you conclude, using $\alpha = 0.05_{2\text{ tail}}$? clinical, health

28. In Chapter 14, Problem 14, p. 350, an experiment was conducted to determine if an experimental birth control pill has the side effect of changing blood pressure. Ten women were randomly sampled from the city in which you live. Five of them were given a placebo for a month and then their diastolic blood pressure was measured. Then they were switched to the birth control pill for a month and again blood pressure was measured. The other five women were given the birth control pill first for a month, followed by the placebo for a month. The blood pressure readings are again shown here.

| | Diastolic Blood Pressure | |
| --- | --- | --- |
| Subject No. | *Birth control pill* | *Placebo* |
| 1 | 108 | 102 |
| 2 | 76 | 68 |
| 3 | 69 | 66 |
| 4 | 78 | 71 |
| 5 | 74 | 76 |
| 6 | 85 | 80 |
| 7 | 79 | 82 |
| 8 | 78 | 79 |
| 9 | 80 | 78 |
| 10 | 81 | 85 |

| Theology Professors | Psychology Professors |
| --- | --- |
| 36 | 13 |
| 42 | 25 |
| 22 | 40 |
| 48 | 29 |
| 31 | 10 |
| 35 | 26 |
| 47 | 43 |
| 38 | 17 |
| | 12 |
| | 32 |
| | 27 |
| | 32 |

In that problem, the sampling distribution of $\overline{D}$ was assumed to be normally distributed, and the analysis was conducted using the *t* test for correlated groups. For this problem, assume the data are so far from normally distributed as to invalidate use of the *t* test for correlated groups. Analyze the data with the Wilcoxon signed ranks test. What do you conclude, using $\alpha = 0.01_{2\ tail}$? biological, health, social

29. A social scientist believes that university theology professors are more conservative in political orientation than their colleagues in psychology. A random sample of 8 professors from the theology department and 12 professors from the psychology department at a local university are given a 50-point questionnaire that measures the degree of political conservatism. The following scores were obtained. Higher scores indicate greater conservatism.
   a. What is the alternative hypothesis? In this case, assume a nondirectional hypothesis is appropriate because there are insufficient theoretical and empirical bases to warrant a directional hypothesis.
   b. What is the null hypothesis?
   c. What is your conclusion? Use the Mann–Whitney *U* test and $\alpha = 0.05_{2\ tail}$.

social

30. An ornithologist thinks that injections of follicle-stimulating hormone (FSH) increase the singing rate of his captive male cotingas (birds). To test this hypothesis, he randomly selects 20 singing cotingas and divides them into two groups of 10 birds each. The first group receives injections of FSH and the second gets injections of saline solution, as a control for the trauma of receiving an injection. He then records the singing rate (in songs per hour) for both groups. The results are given in the following table. Note that two of the FSH birds escaped during injection and were not replaced.

| Saline | FSH |
| --- | --- |
| 17 | 10 |
| 31 | 29 |
| 14 | 37 |
| 12 | 41 |
| 29 | 16 |
| 23 | 45 |
| 7 | 34 |
| 19 | 57 |
| 28 | |
| 3 | |

a. What is the alternative hypothesis? Use a directional alternative hypothesis.
b. What is the null hypothesis?
c. Using the Mann–Whitney $U$ test and $\alpha = 0.05_{1\ tail}$, what is your conclusion? biological

31. A psychologist is interested in determining whether left-handed and right-handed people differ in spatial ability. She randomly selects 10 left-handers and 10 right-handers from the students enrolled in the university where she works and administers a test that measures spatial ability. The following are the scores (a higher score indicates better spatial ability). Note that one of the subjects did not show up for the testing.

| Left-Handers | Right-Handers |
|:---:|:---:|
| 87 | 47 |
| 94 | 68 |
| 56 | 92 |
| 74 | 73 |
| 98 | 71 |
| 83 | 82 |
| 92 | 55 |
| 84 | 61 |
| 76 | 75 |
|    | 85 |

a. What is the alternative hypothesis? Use a nondirectional hypothesis.
b. What is the null hypothesis?
c. Using the Mann–Whitney $U$ test and $\alpha = 0.05_{2\ tail}$, what do you conclude? cognitive

32. A university counselor believes that hypnosis is more effective than the standard treatment given to students who have high test anxiety. To test his belief, he randomly divides 22 students with high test anxiety into two groups. One of the groups receives the hypnosis treatment, and the other group receives the standard treatment. When the treatments are concluded, each student is given a test anxiety questionnaire. High scores on the questionnaire indicate high anxiety. Following are the results:

| Hypnosis Treatment | Standard Treatment |
|:---:|:---:|
| 20 | 42 |
| 21 | 35 |
| 33 | 30 |
| 40 | 53 |
| 24 | 57 |
| 43 | 26 |
| 48 | 37 |
| 31 | 30 |
| 22 | 51 |
| 44 | 62 |
| 30 | 59 |

a. What is the alternative hypothesis? Assume there is sufficient basis for a directional hypothesis.
b. What is the null hypothesis?
c. Using the Mann–Whitney $U$ test and $\alpha = 0.05_{1\ tail}$, what do you conclude? clinical, health

33. In Chapter 15, Problem 20, p. 392, an experiment was conducted to determine whether sleep loss affects the ability to maintain sustained attention. Fifteen individuals were randomly divided into the following three groups of five subjects each: group 1, which got the normal amount of sleep (7–8 hours); group 2, which was sleep-deprived for 24 hours; and group 3, which was sleep-deprived for 48 hours. All three groups were tested on the same auditory vigilance task. Half-second tones spaced at irregular intervals were presented over a 1-hour duration. Occasionally, one of the tones was slightly shorter than the rest. The subject's task was to detect the shorter tones. The following percentages of correct detections were observed:

| Normal Sleep | Sleep-Deprived for 24 Hours | Sleep-Deprived for 48 Hours |
|:---:|:---:|:---:|
| 85 | 60 | 60 |
| 83 | 58 | 48 |
| 76 | 76 | 38 |
| 64 | 52 | 47 |
| 75 | 63 | 50 |

In that problem, the normality assumption was assumed met, and the analysis was conducted using the $F$ test. For this problem, assume the $F$ test cannot be used because of an extreme violation of the normality assumption. Analyze the data with the Kruskal–Wallis test, using $\alpha = 0.05$. cognitive

34. A social psychologist is interested in whether there is a relationship between cohabitation before marriage and divorce. A random sample of 150 couples that were married in the past 10 years in a midwestern city were asked if they lived together before getting married and if their marriage was still intact. The following results were obtained.

|  | Divorced | Still married | |
|---|---|---|---|
| Cohabited before marriage | 58 | 42 | 100 |
| Did not cohabit before marriage | 18 | 32 | 50 |
|  | 76 | 74 | 150 |

Using $\alpha = 0.05$, what do you conclude? social

35. A political scientist conducts a study to determine whether there is a relationship between gender and attitude regarding government involvement in citizen affairs. A questionnaire is sent to a random sample of 1000 adult men and women, asking the question, "As a general policy, do you prefer the government to have a large, moderate, or small involvement in citizen affairs?" The following results were obtained.

Attitude Regarding Federal Government Involvement

|  | Large | Moderate | Small | |
|---|---|---|---|---|
| Women | 240 | 30 | 230 | 500 |
| Men | 180 | 20 | 300 | 500 |
|  | 420 | 50 | 530 | 1000 |

Using $\alpha = 0.05$, what do you conclude? I/O, social

36. Medical experts have long noticed that blacks do not receive the latest high-tech treatments. To determine whether physician bias contributed to this phenomenon, social psychologists analyzed Medicare records of 150 black and 150 white randomly selected heart attack patients who were treated either by a black or white physician. A different physician was required for each patient record used. The variable of interest is whether the patients received an angiogram. The following data were collected.

Patients Receiving Angiograms

| Physician | White | Black | |
|---|---|---|---|
| White | 72 | 48 | 120 |
| Black | 52 | 28 | 80 |
|  | 124 | 86 | 200 |

Using $\alpha = 0.05$, what do you conclude? health, social

37. A family therapist living in a large midwestern city is concerned that the proportion of single-father homes is increasing. The therapist finds that two relevant studies have been conducted. Both studies randomly surveyed 1000 families living in the city and gave information regarding single-father homes. The first was conducted in 1996; it reported there were 50 single-father homes. The second was conducted in 2002; it reported 76 such homes. If you were the therapist, what would you conclude? Use $\alpha = 0.05$ in making your decision. clinical, social

38. A public health researcher believes that smoking affects the gender of offspring. He records the gender of newborns that are delivered in local hospitals over a 1-year period. He also interviews the parents of the newborns to determine their degree of cigarette smoking. The following data are collected.

|  | Offspring | | |
|---|---|---|---|
| Cigarette Smoking | Boys | Girls | |
| Neither parent smokes at least a pack-a-day | 60 | 40 | 100 |
| One parent smokes at least a pack-a-day | 57 | 43 | 100 |
| Both parents smoke at least a pack-a-day | 18 | 32 | 50 |
|  | 135 | 115 | 250 |

What is the conclusion? Use $\alpha = 0.05$. health, social

39. The director of the athletic department of a major state university is considering adding another women's varsity team. She is trying to decide between volleyball, soccer, and softball. A survey of 750 undergraduate women revealed the following first choice preferences.

| Volleyball | Soccer | Softball | |
|---|---|---|---|
| 250 | 350 | 150 | 750 |

Does the survey reveal a reliable preference? Use $\alpha = 0.05$ in making your decision. I/O

40a. The Jones survey company conducted a national survey to see if religious sentiment in the United States changed after the terrorist attacks on the Twin Towers in New York City and the Pentagon in Washington, DC, on September 11, 2001. The survey of 1100 Americans was conducted 2 weeks after the attack; the question asked was, "Did you attend church in the past week?" Fortunately for comparison purposes, 6 months before the attack, the company had conducted a similar survey of 900 Americans, asking the same question. The data follow.

| | Yes | No | |
|---|---|---|---|
| 6-Months Preattack | 360 | 540 | 900 |
| 2-Weeks Postattack | 660 | 440 | 1100 |
| | 1020 | 980 | 2000 |

Using $\alpha = 0.05$, what do you conclude? I/O, social

40b. One year after the attacks, the Jones company conducted another national survey of 1100 Americans to determine whether the increase in religious sentiment following the attacks was still evident. To make this determination, the company used the data from their 6-month preattack and 1-year postattack surveys. The data follow.

| | Yes | No | |
|---|---|---|---|
| 6-Month Preattack | 360 | 540 | 900 |
| 1-Year Postattack | 420 | 680 | 1100 |

Using $\alpha = 0.05$, what do you conclude this time? I/O, social

## NOTES

17.1 When $df = 1$, directional alternative hypotheses can be tested with $\chi^2$. With $df = 1$, $z_{obt} = \sqrt{\chi^2_{obt}}$. Therefore, we can convert $\chi^2_{obt}$ to $z_{obt}$ and evaluate $z_{obt}$ using $z_{crit}$ for the appropriate one-tailed alpha level. Of course, the difference between $f_o$ and $f_e$ must be in the predicted direction to perform this test.

**BOOK COMPANION WEBSITE**

Go to www.thomsonedu.com/psychology/pagano for:

- Flash cards for review of terms
- Chapter quiz
- Statistical workshops
- And more

# WebTUTOR™

Available via WebTutor for this chapter:

- Detailed chapter outline
- *Know and Be Able To Do* section
- Drag & Drop game for review of equations, concepts, and other material
- Flash cards for review of terms
- Audio flash cards for MP3 player
- Solving problems using Excel
- More practice problems using computational equations
- Chapter quiz

# Review of Inferential Statistics

CHAPTER **18**

## INTRODUCTION

We have covered a lot of material since we began our discussion of hypothesis testing with the sign test. We shall begin our review of this material with the most important terms and concepts pertaining to the general process of hypothesis testing. Then we shall discuss the general process itself. From there, we shall summarize the experimental designs and the inference tests used with each design. Since this material is very logical and interconnected, I hope this review will help bring closure and greater insight to the topic of inferential statistics.

## TERMS AND CONCEPTS

**Alternative hypothesis ($H_1$)**   The alternative hypothesis states that the differences in scores between conditions are due to the action of the independent variable. The alternative hypothesis may be nondirectional or directional. A nondirectional hypothesis states that the independent variable has an effect on the dependent variable but doesn't specify the direction of the effect. A directional hypothesis states the direction of the expected effect.

**Null hypothesis ($H_0$)**   The null hypothesis is set up as the logical counterpart to the alternative hypothesis such that if the null hypothesis is false, the alternative hypothesis must be true. Conversely, if the null hypothesis is true, the alternative hypothesis must be false. The null hypothesis for a nondirectional alternative hypothesis is that the independent variable has no effect on the dependent variable. For a directional alternative hypothesis, the null hypothesis states that the independent variable does not have an effect in the direction specified.

**Null-hypothesis population(s)**   The null-hypothesis population(s) is the set or sets of scores that would result if the experiment were done on the entire population and the independent variable had no effect. In a single sample design, it is the population with known $\mu$. In a replicated measures design, it is the population of difference scores with $\mu_D = 0$ or $P = 0.50$. In an independent groups design, there are as many populations as there are groups and the samples are random samples from populations where $\mu_1 = \mu_2 = \mu_3 = \mu_k$.

**Sampling distribution**   The sampling distribution of a statistic gives all the values the statistic can take, along with the probability of getting that value if chance alone is responsible or if sampling is random from the null-hypothesis population(s). This distribution can be derived theoretically from basic probability, as we did with the sign test, or empirically, as with the $z$, $t$, and $F$ tests. Three steps are involved in constructing the sampling distribution of a statistic using the empirical approach. First, all possible different samples of size $N$ that can be formed from the population are determined. Second, the statistic for each of the samples is calculated. Finally, the probability of getting each value of the statistic is calculated under the assumption that sampling is random from the null-hypothesis population(s).

**Critical region for rejection of $H_0$**   The critical region for rejection of $H_0$ is the area under the curve that contains all the values of the statistic that will allow rejection of the null hypothesis. The critical value of a statistic is that value of the statistic that bounds the critical region. It is determined by the alpha level.

**Alpha level ($\alpha$)**   The alpha level is the threshold probability level against which the obtained probability is compared to determine the reasonableness of the null hypothesis. It also determines the critical region for rejection of the null hypothesis. Alpha is usually set at 0.05 or 0.01. The alpha level is set at the beginning of an experiment and limits the probability of making a Type I error.

**Type I error**    A Type I error occurs when the null hypothesis is rejected and it is true.

**Type II error**    A Type II error occurs when the null hypothesis is retained and it is false. Beta is equal to the probability of making a Type II error.

**Power**    The power of an experiment is equal to the probability of rejecting the null hypothesis if the independent variable has a real effect. It is useful to know the power of an experiment when designing the experiment and when interpreting nonsignificant results from an experiment that has already been conducted. Calculation of power involves two steps: (1) determining the sample outcomes that will allow rejection of the null hypothesis and (2) determining the probability of getting these outcomes under the assumed real effect of the independent variable. Power $= 1 - \beta$. Thus, as power increases, beta decreases. Power can be increased by increasing the number of subjects in the experiment, by increasing the size of real effect of the independent variable, by decreasing the variability of the data through careful experimental control and proper experimental design, and by using the most sensitive inference test possible for the design and data.

## PROCESS OF HYPOTHESIS TESTING

We have seen that in every experiment involving hypothesis testing there are two hypotheses that attempt to explain the data. They are the alternative hypothesis and the null hypothesis. In analyzing the data, we always evaluate the null hypothesis and indirectly conclude with regard to the alternative hypothesis. If $H_0$ can be rejected, then $H_1$ is accepted. If $H_0$ is not rejected, then $H_1$ is not accepted.

Two steps are involved in assessing the null hypothesis. First, we calculate the appropriate statistic, and second, we evaluate the statistic. To evaluate the statistic, we assume that the independent variable has no effect and that chance alone is responsible for the score differences between conditions. Another way of saying this is that we assume sampling is random from the null-hypothesis population(s). Then we calculate the probability of getting the obtained result or any result more extreme under the previous assumption. This probability is one- or two-tailed depending on whether the alternative hypothesis is directional or nondirectional. To calculate the obtained probability, we must know the sampling distribution of the statistic. If the obtained probability is equal to or less than the alpha level, we reject $H_0$. Alternatively, we determine whether the obtained statistic falls in the critical region for rejecting $H_0$. If it does, we reject the null hypothesis. Otherwise, $H_0$ remains a reasonable explanation, and we retain it.

If we reject $H_0$ and it is true, we have made a Type I error. The alpha level limits the probability of a Type I error. If we retain $H_0$ and it is false, we have made a Type II error. The power of the experiment determines the probability of making a Type II error. We have defined beta as the probability of making a Type II error. As power increases, beta decreases. By maintaining alpha sufficiently low and power sufficiently high, we achieve a high probability of making a correct decision when analyzing the data, no matter whether $H_0$ is true or false.

These statements apply to all experiments involving hypothesis testing. What varies from experiment to experiment is the inference test used and, consequently, the statistic calculated and evaluated. The inference test used will depend on the experimental design and the data collected.

## SINGLE SAMPLE DESIGNS

With single sample experimental designs, one or more of the null-hypothesis population parameters (the mean and/or standard deviation) must be specified. Since it is not common to have this information, the single sample experiment occurs rather infrequently. The $z$ and $t$ tests are appropriate for this design. Both tests evaluate the effect of the independent variable on the mean ($\overline{X}_{obt}$) of the sample. For these tests, the nondirectional $H_1$ states that $\overline{X}_{obt}$ is a random sample from a population having a mean $\mu$ that is not equal to the mean of the null-hypothesis population. The corresponding $H_0$ states that the $\mu$ equals the mean of the null-hypothesis population. The directional $H_1$ states that $\overline{X}_{obt}$ is a random sample from a population where $\mu$ is greater or less than the mean of the null-hypothesis population depending on the expected direction of the effect. Let's now review the $z$ and $t$ tests for single samples:

### $z$ Test for Single Samples

| Test | Statistic Calculated | Decision Rule |
|---|---|---|
| $z$ test for single samples | $z_{obt} = \dfrac{\overline{X}_{obt} - \mu}{\sigma/\sqrt{N}}$ | If $|z_{obt}| \geq |z_{crit}|$, reject $H_0$. |

General comments    The $z$ test is used in situations in which both the mean and standard deviation of the null-hypothesis population can be specified. To evaluate $H_0$, we assume $\overline{X}_{obt}$ is a random sample from a population having a mean $\mu$ and standard deviation $\sigma$ that are equal to the mean and standard deviation of the null-hypothesis population. The sampling distribution of $\overline{X}$ gives all the possible values of $\overline{X}$ for samples of size $N$ and the probability of getting each value if sampling is random from the population with a mean $\mu$ and a standard deviation $\sigma$. The sampling distribution of $\overline{X}$ has a mean $\mu_{\overline{X}} = \mu$, has a standard deviation $\sigma_{\overline{X}} = \sigma/\sqrt{N}$, and is normally shaped if the population from which the sample was drawn is normal or if $N \geq 30$, provided the population does not differ greatly from normality.

We can assess $H_0$ by (1) converting $\overline{X}_{obt}$ to its $z$-transformed value ($z_{obt}$) and determining the probability of getting a value as extreme as or more extreme than $z_{obt}$ if chance alone is operating or (2) calculating $z_{obt}$ and comparing it with $z_{crit}$. It is easier to do the latter. The equation for $z_{obt}$ is given in the preceding table. The value of $z_{obt}$ is evaluated by comparison with $z_{crit}$. The alpha level in conjunction with the sampling distribution of $z$ determines the value of $z_{crit}$. The sampling distribution of $z$ has a mean of 0 and a standard deviation of 1. If $\overline{X}_{obt}$ is normally distributed, then so is the corresponding $z$ distribution and $z_{crit}$ can be determined from Table A in Appendix D. Thus, the $z$ test requires that $N \geq 30$ or that the population of raw scores be normally distributed.

## *t* Test for Single Samples

| Test | Statistic Calculated | Decision Rule |
|------|---------------------|---------------|
| *t* test for single samples | $t_{\text{obt}} = \dfrac{\overline{X}_{\text{obt}} - \mu}{s/\sqrt{N}}$ | If $|t_{\text{obt}}| \geq |t_{\text{crit}}|$, reject $H_0$. |
| | $t_{\text{obt}} = \dfrac{\overline{X}_{\text{obt}} - \mu}{\sqrt{\dfrac{SS}{N(N-1)}}}$ | |

**General comments**   The *t* test is used in situations in which the mean of the null-hypothesis population can be specified and standard deviation is unknown. In testing $H_0$, we assume $\overline{X}_{\text{obt}}$ is a random sample from a population having a mean $\mu$ equal to the mean of the null-hypothesis population and an unknown standard deviation. The *t* test is very much like the *z* test, except that since $\sigma$ is unknown, we estimate it with *s*. When *s* is substituted for $\sigma$ in the equation for $z_{\text{obt}}$, the first equation given in the table for $t_{\text{obt}}$ results. The second equation in the table is a computational equation for $t_{\text{obt}}$, using the raw scores. To evaluate $H_0$, the value of $t_{\text{obt}}$ is compared against $t_{\text{crit}}$, using the decision rule. The value of $t_{\text{crit}}$ is determined by the alpha level and the sampling distribution of *t*. This distribution is a family of curves, shaped like the *z* distribution. The curves vary uniquely with degrees of freedom. The degrees of freedom for a statistic are equal to the number of scores that are free to vary in calculating the statistic. For the *t* test used with single samples, df = $N - 1$, because 1 degree of freedom is lost calculating *s*. The values of $t_{\text{crit}}$ are found in Table D in Appendix D, using df and $\alpha$. The *t* test has the same underlying assumptions as the *z* test. The population of raw scores should be normally distributed.

## *t* Test for Testing the Significance of Pearson *r*

| Test | Statistic Calculated | Decision Rule |
|------|---------------------|---------------|
| *t* test for testing the significance of Pearson *r* | $r_{\text{obt}}$ | If $|r_{\text{obt}}| \geq |r_{\text{crit}}|$, reject $H_0$. |

**General comments**   To determine whether a correlation exists in the population, we must test the significance of $r_{\text{obt}}$. This can be done using the *t* test. The resulting equation is

$$t_{\text{obt}} = \frac{r_{\text{obt}} - \rho}{\sqrt{\dfrac{1 - r_{\text{obt}}^2}{N - 2}}}$$

By substituting $t_{\text{crit}}$ for $t_{\text{obt}}$ in this equation, $r_{\text{crit}}$ can be determined for any df and $\alpha$ level. Once $r_{\text{crit}}$ is known, all we need to do is compare $r_{\text{obt}}$ with $r_{\text{crit}}$. The decision rule is given in the preceding table. The values of $r_{\text{crit}}$ are found in Table E in Appendix D, using df and $\alpha$. Degrees of freedom equal $N - 2$.

## TWO-CONDITION EXPERIMENTS: CORRELATED GROUPS DESIGN

The essential feature of this design is that there are paired scores between the conditions, and the differences between the paired scores are analyzed. The paired scores can result from using the same subjects in each condition, from using identical twins, or from using subjects that have been matched in some other way. The most basic form of the design employs just two conditions: an experimental condition and a control condition. The two conditions are kept as alike as possible except for values of the independent variable, which are intentionally made different. We covered three tests for analyzing data from experiments of this design: the $t$ test for correlated groups, the Wilcoxon matched-pairs signed ranks test, and the sign test.

### $t$ Test for Correlated Groups

| Test | Statistic Calculated | Decision Rule |
|------|---------------------|---------------|
| $t$ test for correlated groups | $t_{\text{obt}} = \dfrac{\overline{D}_{\text{obt}} - \mu_D}{\sqrt{\dfrac{SS_D}{N(N-1)}}}$ | If $|t_{\text{obt}}| \geq |t_{\text{crit}}|$, reject $H_0$. |

**General comments**   The $t$ test for correlated groups analyzes the effect of the independent variable on the mean of the sample difference scores $(\overline{D}_{\text{obt}})$. If the independent variable has no effect, then $\overline{D}_{\text{obt}}$ is a random sample from a population of difference scores having a mean $\mu_D = 0$ and unknown $\sigma_D$. This situation is the same as what we encountered when using the $t$ test for single samples (specifiable population mean but unknown standard deviation), except that we are dealing with difference scores rather than raw scores. Thus, the $t$ test for correlated groups is identical to the $t$ test for single samples, but it evaluates difference scores instead of raw scores.

The nondirectional $H_1$ states that the independent variable has an effect, in which case $\overline{D}_{\text{obt}}$ is due to random sampling from a population of difference scores where $\mu_D \neq 0$. The directional $H_1$ specifies that $\mu_D > 0$ (for which $H_0$ states that $\mu_D \leq 0$) or $\mu_D < 0$ (for which $H_0$ states that $\mu_D \geq 0$). $H_0$ is tested by assuming $\overline{D}_{\text{obt}}$ is a random sample from a population of difference scores where $\mu_D = 0$.

The statistic calculated is $t_{\text{obt}}$ (see the preceding table), which is evaluated by comparing it with $t_{\text{crit}}$. The sampling distribution of $t$ is the same as discussed in conjunction with the $t$ test for single samples. The degrees of freedom are equal to $N - 1$, where $N =$ the number of difference scores. The values of $t_{\text{crit}}$ are found in Table D, using df and $\alpha$. The assumptions of this test are the same as those for the $t$ test for single samples. This test is more sensitive than (1) the $t$ test for independent groups when the correlation between the paired scores is high and (2) the Wilcoxon matched-pairs signed ranks test and the sign test, which are also appropriate for the correlated groups design.

## Wilcoxon Matched–Pairs Signed Ranks Test

| Test | Statistic Calculated | Decision Rule |
|------|----------------------|---------------|
| Wilcoxon matched-pairs signed ranks test | $T_{obt}$ | If $T_{obt} \leq T_{crit}$, reject $H_0$. |

**General comments**   This is a nonparametric test that takes into account the magnitude and direction of the difference scores. It is therefore much more powerful than the sign test. Both the alternative and null hypotheses are usually stated without specifying population parameters. In analyzing the data, $T_{obt}$ is calculated by (1) obtaining the difference score for each pair of scores, (2) rank-ordering the absolute values of the difference scores, (3) assigning the appropriate signs to the ranks, and (4) separately summing the positive and negative ranks. $T_{obt}$ is the lower of the sums. $T_{obt}$ is compared with $T_{crit}$. The values of $T_{crit}$ are given in Table I in Appendix D, using $N$ and $\alpha$. The decision rule is shown in the preceding table. This test is recommended as an alternative to the $t$ test for correlated groups when the assumptions of the $t$ test are not met. The Wilcoxon signed ranks test requires that the within-pair scores be at least of ordinal scaling and that the difference scores also be at least of ordinal scaling.

## Sign Test

| Test | Statistic Calculated | Decision Rule |
|------|----------------------|---------------|
| Sign test | Number of $P$ events in a sample of size $N$ | If the one- or two-tailed $p$(number of $P$ events) $\leq \alpha$, reject $H_0$. |

**General comments**   We used the sign test to introduce hypothesis testing because it is a simple test to understand. It is not commonly used in practice because it ignores the magnitude of the difference scores and considers only their direction.

In analyzing data with the sign test, we determine the number of pluses in the sample and evaluate this statistic by using the binomial distribution. The binomial distribution is the appropriate sampling distribution when (1) there is a series of $N$ trials, (2) there are only two possible outcomes on each trial, (3) there is independence between trials, (4) the outcomes on each trial are mutually exclusive, and (5) the probability of each possible outcome on any trial stays the same from trial to trial. The binomial distribution is given by $(P + Q)^N$, where $P$ is the probability of a plus on any trial and $Q$ is the probability of a minus. If the independent variable has no effect, then $P = Q = 0.50$. The nondirectional $H_1$ states that $P \neq Q \neq 0.50$. The directional $H_1$ specifies $P > 0.50$ or $P < 0.50$, depending on the expected direction of the effect.

$H_0$ is tested by assuming that the number of $P$ events in the sample is due to random sampling from a population where $P = Q = 0.50$. The one- or two-tailed $p$(number of $P$ events) is compared with the alpha level to evaluate $H_0$. This probability is found in Table B in Appendix D, using $N$, number of $P$ events, and $P = 0.50$. Alternatively, given alpha, $N$, and the binomial distribution, we could have also determined the critical region for rejecting $H_0$ (as we did with the other statistics), in which case we would compare the obtained number of $P$ events with the critical number of $P$ events. To use the sign test, the data must be at least ordinal in scaling and ties must be excluded from the analysis.

## INDEPENDENT GROUPS DESIGN: TWO GROUPS

This design involves random sampling of subjects from the population and then random assignment of the subjects to each condition. There can be many conditions. The most basic form of the design uses two conditions, with each condition employing a different level of the independent variable. This design differs from the correlated groups design in that there is no basis for pairing scores between conditions. Analysis is performed separately on the raw scores of each sample, not on the difference scores. Both the $t$ test and the Mann–Whitney $U$ test are appropriate for this design.

### $t$ Test for Independent Groups

| Test | Statistic Calculated | Decision Rule |
|---|---|---|
| $t$ test for independent groups | $t_{\text{obt}} = \dfrac{(\overline{X}_1 - \overline{X}_2) - \mu_{\overline{X}_1 - \overline{X}_2}}{\sqrt{\left(\dfrac{SS_1 + SS_2}{n_1 + n_2 - 2}\right)\left(\dfrac{1}{n_1} + \dfrac{1}{n_2}\right)}}$ <br> When $n_1 = n_2$, <br> $t_{\text{obt}} = \dfrac{(\overline{X}_1 - \overline{X}_2) - \mu_{\overline{X}_1 - \overline{X}_2}}{\sqrt{\dfrac{SS_1 + SS_2}{n(n-1)}}}$ | If $|t_{\text{obt}}| \geq |t_{\text{crit}}|$, reject $H_0$. |

**General comments**   This test assumes that the independent variable affects the mean of the scores and not their variance. The mean of each sample is calculated, and then the difference between sample means $(\overline{X}_1 - \overline{X}_2)$ is determined. The $t$ test for independent groups analyzes the effect of the independent variable on $\overline{X}_1 - \overline{X}_2$. The sample value $\overline{X}_1$ is due to random sampling from a population having a mean $\mu_1$ and a variance $\sigma_1^2$. The sample value $\overline{X}_2$ is due to random sampling from a population having a mean $\mu_2$ and a variance $\sigma_2^2$. The variance of both populations is assumed equal ($\sigma_1^2 = \sigma_2^2 = \sigma^2$).

The sampling distribution of $\overline{X}_1 - \overline{X}_2$ has the following characteristics: (1) It has a mean $\mu_{\overline{X}_1 - \overline{X}_2} = \mu_1 - \mu_2$, (2) it has a standard deviation $\sigma_{\overline{X}_1 - \overline{X}_2} = \sqrt{\sigma^2[(1/n_1) + (1/n_2)]}$, and (3) it is normally shaped if the population from which the samples have been taken is normal. If the independent variable has no effect, then $\mu_1 = \mu_2$. The nondirectional $H_1$ states that $\mu_1 \neq \mu_2$. The directional $H_1$ states that $\mu_2 > \mu_1$ or $\mu_1 < \mu_2$, depending on the expected direction of the effect.

To assess $H_0$, we assume that the independent variable has no effect, in which case $\mu_1 = \mu_2$ and $\mu_{\overline{X}_1 - \overline{X}_2} = 0$. To test $H_0$, we could calculate $z_{\text{obt}}$, but we need to know $\sigma^2$ for this calculation. Since $\sigma^2$ is unknown, we estimate it using a weighted estimate from both samples. The resulting statistic is $t_{obt}$. Two equations for calculating $t_{obt}$ are given on p. 476. The first is a general equation, and the second can be used when the $n$s in the two samples are equal. The degrees of freedom associated with calculating $t_{obt}$ for the independent groups design is $N - 2$. We calculate two variances in determining $t_{obt}$, and we lose 1 degree of freedom for each calculation. The sampling distribution of $t$ is as described earlier. The value of $t_{obt}$ is evaluated by comparing it with $t_{crit}$ according to the decision rule given on p. 476. The values of $t_{crit}$ are found in Table D, using df and $\alpha$.

To use this test, the sampling distribution of $\mu_{\bar{X}_1 - \bar{X}_2}$ must be normally distributed. This means that the populations from which the samples were taken should be normally distributed.

In addition, to use the $t$ test for independent groups, there should be homogeneity of variance. This test is considered robust with regard to violations of the normality and homogeneity of variance assumptions, provided $n_1 = n_2 \geq 30$. If there is a severe violation of an assumption, the Mann–Whitney $U$ test serves as an alternative to the $t$ test.

## Mann–Whitney $U$ Test

| Test | Statistic Calculated | Decision Rule |
|------|----------------------|---------------|
| Mann–Whitney $U$ test | $U_{obt}$ or $U'_{obt}$, where $$U_{obt} = n_1 n_2 + \frac{n_1(n_1 + 1)}{2} - R_1$$ $$U_{obt} = n_1 n_2 + \frac{n_2(n_2 + 1)}{2} - R_2$$ | If $U_{obt} \leq U_{crit}$, reject $H_0$. |

**General comments**   The Mann–Whitney $U$ test is a nonparametric test that analyzes the degree of separation between the samples. The less the separation, the more reasonable chance is as the underlying explanation. For any analysis, there are two values that indicate the degree of separation. They both indicate the same degree of separation. The lower value is called $U_{obt}$, and the higher value is called $U'_{obt}$. The lower the $U_{obt}$ value, the greater the separation.

$U_{obt}$ and $U'_{obt}$ can be determined by using the equations given in the preceding table. Since the equations are more general, we have used them most often. For any analysis, one of the equations will yield $U$ and the other $U'$. However, which yields $U$ and which $U'$ depends on which group is labeled group 1 and which is group 2. Since both $U$ and $U'$ are measures of the same degree of separation, it is necessary to evaluate only one of them.

To evaluate $U_{obt}$, it is compared with the critical values of $U$ given in Tables C.1–C.4. Naturally, these values depend on the sampling distribution of $U$. The decision rule for rejecting $H_0$ is given in the preceding table.

The Mann–Whitney $U$ test is appropriate for an independent groups design where the data are at least ordinal in scaling. It is a powerful test, often used in place of Student's $t$ test when the data do not meet the assumptions of the $t$ test.

## MULTIGROUP EXPERIMENTS

Although a two-group design is used fairly frequently in the behavioral sciences, it is more common to encounter experiments with three or more groups. Having more than two groups has two main advantages: (1) Additional groups often clarify the interpretation of the results, and (2) additional groups allow many levels of the independent variable to be evaluated in one experiment. There is, however, one problem with doing multigroup experiments. Since many comparisons can be made, we run the risk of an inflated Type I error probability when analyzing the data. The analysis of variance technique allows us to analyze the data without incurring this risk.

### One-Way Analysis of Variance, $F$ Test

| Test | Statistic Calculated | Decision Rule |
|------|:--------------------:|:-------------:|
| Parametric one-way analysis of variance, $F$ test | $F_{obt} = \dfrac{s_B{}^2}{s_W{}^2}$ | If $F_{obt} \geq F_{crit}$, reject $H_0$. |

**General comments**    The parametric analysis of variance uses the $F$ test to evaluate the data. In using this test, we calculate $F_{obt}$, which is fundamentally the ratio of two independent variance estimates of a population variance $\sigma^2$. The sampling distribution of $F$ is composed of a family of positively skewed curves that vary with degrees of freedom. There are two values for degrees of freedom: one for the numerator and one for the denominator. The $F$ distribution (1) is positively skewed, (2) has no negative values, and (3) has a median approximately equal to 1.

The parametric analysis of variance technique can be used with both the independent groups and the correlated groups designs. We have considered only the one-way ANOVA independent groups design. The technique allows the means of all the groups to be compared in one overall evaluation, thus avoiding the inflated Type I error probability that occurs when doing many individual comparisons. Essentially, the analysis of variance partitions the total variability of the data into two parts: the variability that exists within each group (the within-groups sum of squares) and the variability that exists between the groups (the between-groups sum of squares). Each sum of squares is used to form an independent estimate of the variance of the null-hypothesis populations, $\sigma^2$. Finally, an $F$ ratio is calculated where the between-groups variance estimate is in the numerator and the within-groups variance estimate is in the denominator.

The steps and equations for calculating $F_{obt}$ are as follows:

**STEP 1: Calculate the between-groups sum of squares, $SS_B$:**

$$SS_B = \left[ \frac{(\sum X_1)^2}{n_1} + \frac{(\sum X_2)^2}{n_2} + \frac{(\sum X_3)^2}{n_3} + \cdots + \frac{(\sum X_k)^2}{n_k} \right] - \frac{\left( \overset{\text{all scores}}{\sum X} \right)^2}{N}$$

**STEP 2: Calculate the within-groups sum of squares, $SS_W$:**

$$SS_W = \overset{\overset{\text{all}}{\text{scores}}}{\sum} X^2 - \left[ \frac{(\Sigma X_1)^2}{n_1} + \frac{(\Sigma X_2)^2}{n_2} + \frac{(\Sigma X_3)^2}{n_3} + \cdots + \frac{(\Sigma X_k)^2}{n_k} \right]$$

**STEP 3: Calculate the total sum of squares, $SS_T$; check that $SS_T = SS_W + SS_B$:**

$$SS_T = \overset{\overset{\text{all}}{\text{scores}}}{\sum} X^2 - \frac{\left( \overset{\overset{\text{all}}{\text{scores}}}{\sum} X \right)^2}{N}$$

**STEP 4: Calculate the degrees of freedom for each estimate:**

$$df_B = k - 1$$
$$df_W = N - k$$
$$df_T = N - 1$$

**STEP 5: Calculate the between-groups variance estimate, $s_B{}^2$:**

$$s_B{}^2 = \frac{SS_B}{df_B}$$

**STEP 6: Calculate the within-groups variance estimate, $s_W{}^2$:**

$$s_W{}^2 = \frac{SS_W}{df_W}$$

**STEP 7: Calculate $F_{\text{obt}}$:**

$$F_{\text{obt}} = \frac{s_B{}^2}{s_W{}^2}$$

The null hypothesis for the analysis of variance assumes that the independent variable has no effect and that the samples are random samples from populations where $\mu_1 = \mu_2 = \mu_3 = \mu_k$. Since the between-groups variance estimate increases with the effect of the independent variable and the within-groups variance estimate remains constant, the larger the $F$ ratio is, the more unreasonable the null hypothesis becomes. We evaluate $F_{\text{obt}}$ by comparing it with $F_{\text{crit}}$. If $F_{\text{obt}} \geq F_{\text{crit}}$, we reject $H_0$ and conclude that at least one of the conditions differs from at least one of the other conditions. Note that the analysis of variance technique is nondirectional.

Multiple comparisons    To determine which conditions differ from each other, *a priori* or *a posteriori* comparisons between pairs of groups are performed. A priori *comparisons* (also called *planned comparisons*) are appropriate when the comparisons have been planned in advance. No adjustment for multiple comparisons is made. Planned comparisons should be relatively few in number and should arise from the logic and meaning of the experiment. In doing the planned comparisons, we usually compare the means of the specified groups using the *t* test for independent groups. The value for $t_{\text{obt}}$ is determined in the usual way, except we use $s_W{}^2$ from the analysis of variance in the denominator of the *t* equation. The $t_{obt}$ value is compared with $t_{crit}$, using $df_W$ and the alpha level and Table D to determine $t_{crit}$. The equations for calculating $t_{obt}$ are given as follows:

$$t_{obt} = \frac{\overline{X}_1 - \overline{X}_2}{\sqrt{s_W^2\left(\dfrac{1}{n_1} + \dfrac{1}{n_2}\right)}}$$

If $n_1 = n_2$,

$$t_{obt} = \frac{\overline{X}_1 - \overline{X}_2}{\sqrt{2s_W^2/n}}$$

A posteriori, or post hoc, *comparisons* were not planned before conducting the experiment. They arise either after looking at the data or from assuming the "shotgun" approach of doing all possible mean comparisons in an attempt to gain as much information from the experiment as possible. For these reasons, comparisons made *post hoc* must correct for the increase in the probability of a Type I error that arises due to multiple comparisons. There are many techniques that do this. We have described Tukey's Honestly Significant Difference (HSD) test and the Newman–Keuls test.

### Tukey's HSD test

| Test | Statistic Calculated | Decision Rule |
|------|---------------------|---------------|
| Tukey's HSD test | $Q_{obt}$, where $$Q_{obt} = \frac{\overline{X}_i - \overline{X}_j}{\sqrt{s_W^2/n}}$$ | If $Q_{obt} \geq Q_{crit}$, reject $H_0$. |

The HSD test is designed to compare all possible pairs of means while maintaining the Type I error rate for making the complete set of comparisons at $\alpha$. The $Q$ statistic is very much like the $t$ statistic, but it is always positive and uses the $Q$ distributions rather than the $t$ distributions. The $Q$ (Studentized range) distributions are derived by randomly taking $k$ samples of equal $n$ from the same population rather than just two samples as with the $t$ distributions and determining the difference between the highest and lowest sample means. To use this test, we calculate $Q_{obt}$ for the desired comparisons and compare $Q_{obt}$ with $Q_{crit}$. The values of $Q_{crit}$ are found in Table G in Appendix D, using $k$, df for $s_W^2$, and $\alpha$. The decision rule is given in the preceding table.

### Newman–Keuls test

| Test | Statistic Calculated | Decision Rule |
|------|---------------------|---------------|
| Newman–Keuls test | $Q_{obt}$, where $$Q_{obt} = \frac{\overline{X}_i - \overline{X}_j}{\sqrt{s_W^2/n}}$$ | If $Q_{obt} \geq Q_{crit}$, reject $H_0$. |

**General comments** The Newman–Keuls test is also a *post hoc* test that allows us to make all possible pairwise comparisons among the sample means. The Newman–Keuls test is like the HSD test in that $Q_{obt}$ is calculated and compared with $Q_{\text{crit}}$ to evaluate $H_0$. However, it maintains the Type I error rate at $\alpha$ for each comparison rather than for the entire set of comparisons. It does this by changing the value of $Q_{\text{crit}}$ for each comparison. The value of $Q_{\text{crit}}$ for any given comparison is given by the sampling distribution of $Q$ for the number of means that are encompassed by $\overline{X}_i$ and $\overline{X}_j$ after all the means have been rank-ordered. This number is symbolized by $r$. The specific values of $Q_{\text{crit}}$ for any analysis are found in Table G, using $r$, df for $s_W^2$, and $\alpha$.

The assumptions underlying the analysis of variance are the same as for the *t* test for independent groups. There are two assumptions: (1) The populations from which the samples were drawn should be normally distributed, and (2) there should be homogeneity of variance between the groups. The *F* test is robust with regard to violations of normality and homogeneity of variance, provided there are an equal number of subjects in each group and $n \geq 30$.

## One-Way Analysis of Variance, Kruskal–Wallis Test

| Test | Statistic Calculated | Decision Rule |
|---|---|---|
| Nonparametric one-way analysis of variance, Kruskal–Wallis test | $H_{\text{obt}} = \left[ \dfrac{12}{N(N+1)} \right] \left[ \displaystyle\sum_{i=1}^{k} \dfrac{(R_i)^2}{n_i} \right]$ $- 3(N+1)$ | If $H_{\text{obt}} > H_{\text{crit}}$, reject $H_0$. |

**General comments**   The Kruskal–Wallis test is a nonparametric test, appropriate for a *k* group, independent groups design. It is used as an alternative test to one-way parametric ANOVA, when the assumptions of that test are seriously violated. The Kruskal–Wallis test does not assume population normality and requires only ordinal scaling of the dependent variable. All the scores are grouped together and rank-ordered, assigning the rank of 1 to the lowest score, 2 to the next to lowest, and $N$ to the highest. The ranks for each condition are then summed. The Kruskal–Wallis test assesses whether these sums of ranks differ so much that it is unreasonable to consider that they come from samples that were randomly selected from the same population.

## TWO-WAY ANALYSIS OF VARIANCE, *F* TEST

The parametric two-way analysis of variance allows us to evaluate the effects of two variables and their interaction in one experiment. In the parametric two-way ANOVA, we partition the total sum of squares ($SS_T$) into four components: the within-cells sum of squares ($SS_W$), the row sum of squares ($SS_R$), the column sum of squares ($SS_C$), and the row × column sum of squares ($SS_{RC}$). When these sums of squares are divided by the appropriate degrees of freedom, they form four variance estimates: the within-cells variance estimate ($s_W^2$), the row variance estimate ($s_R^2$), the column variance estimate ($s_C^2$), and the row × column variance estimate ($s_{RC}^2$). The effect of each of the variables is determined by computing the appropriate $F_{\text{obt}}$ value and comparing it with $F_{\text{crit}}$.

## Two-Way Analysis of Variance, $F$ Test

| **Test** | **Statistic Calculated** | **Decision Rule** |
|---|---|---|
| Two-way analysis of variance, $F$ test | $F_{\text{obt}} = \dfrac{s_R^2}{s_W^2}$ <br><br> $F_{\text{obt}} = \dfrac{s_C^2}{s_W^2}$ <br><br> $F_{\text{obt}} = \dfrac{s_{RC}^2}{s_W^2}$ | If $F_{\text{obt}} > F_{\text{crit}}$, reject $H_0$. |

The steps and equations for calculating the various $F_{\text{obt}}$ values are as follows: Calculate $F_{\text{obt}}$ for the main effects and interaction:

**STEP 1: Calculate the row sum of squares, $SS_R$:**

$$SS_R = \left[ \frac{\left( \overset{\text{row}_1}{\sum} X \right)^2 + \left( \overset{\text{row}_2}{\sum} X \right)^2 + \cdots + \left( \overset{\text{row}_r}{\sum} X \right)^2}{n_{\text{row}}} \right] - \frac{\left( \overset{\text{all scores}}{\sum} X \right)^2}{N}$$

**STEP 2: Calculate the column sum of squares, $SS_C$:**

$$SS_C = \left[ \frac{\left( \overset{\text{col.}_1}{\sum} X \right)^2 + \left( \overset{\text{col.}_2}{\sum} X \right)^2 + \cdots + \left( \overset{\text{col.}_c}{\sum} X \right)^2}{n_{\text{col.}}} \right] - \frac{\left( \overset{\text{all scores}}{\sum} X \right)^2}{N}$$

**STEP 3: Calculate the row × column sum of squares, $SS_{RC}$:**

$$SS_{RC} = \left[ \frac{\left( \overset{\text{cell}_{11}}{\sum} X \right)^2 + \left( \overset{\text{cell}_{12}}{\sum} X \right)^2 + \cdots + \left( \overset{\text{cell}_{rc}}{\sum} X \right)^2}{n_{\text{cell}}} \right] - \frac{\left( \overset{\text{all scores}}{\sum} X \right)^2}{N} - SS_R - SS_C$$

**STEP 4: Calculate the within-cells sum of squares, $SS_W$:**

$$SS_W = \overset{\text{all scores}}{\sum} X^2 - \left[ \frac{\left( \overset{\text{cell}_{11}}{\sum} X \right)^2 + \left( \overset{\text{cell}_{12}}{\sum} X \right)^2 + \cdots + \left( \overset{\text{cell}_{rc}}{\sum} X \right)^2}{n_{\text{cell}}} \right]$$

**STEP 5: Calculate the total sum of squares, $SS_T$, and check that $SS_T = SS_R + SS_C + SS_{RC} + SS_W$:**

$$SS_T = \overset{\text{all scores}}{\sum} X^2 - \frac{\left( \overset{\text{all scores}}{\sum} X \right)^2}{N}$$

**STEP 6: Calculate the degrees of freedom for each variance estimate:**

$$df_R = r - 1$$
$$df_C = c - 1$$

$$\mathrm{df}_{RC} = (r - 1)(c - 1)$$
$$\mathrm{df}_W = rc\,(n_{\mathrm{cell}} - 1)$$
$$\mathrm{df}_T = N - 1$$

**STEP 7: Calculate the variance estimates:**

$$\text{Row variance estimate} = s_R{}^2 = \frac{SS_R}{\mathrm{df}_R}$$

$$\text{Column variance estimate} = s_C{}^2 = \frac{SS_C}{\mathrm{df}_C}$$

$$\text{Row} \times \text{column variance estimate} = s_{RC}{}^2 = \frac{SS_{RC}}{\mathrm{df}_{RC}}$$

$$\text{Within-cells variance estimate} = s_W{}^2 = \frac{SS_W}{\mathrm{df}_W}$$

**STEP 8: Calculate the $F$ ratios:**

For the row effect,

$$F_{\mathrm{obt}} = \frac{s_R{}^2}{s_W{}^2}$$

For the column effect,

$$F_{\mathrm{obt}} = \frac{s_C{}^2}{s_W{}^2}$$

For the row $\times$ column interaction effect,

$$F_{\mathrm{obt}} = \frac{s_{RC}{}^2}{s_W{}^2}$$

Compare the $F_{\mathrm{obt}}$ values with $F_{\mathrm{crit}}$ and conclude.

# ANALYZING NOMINAL DATA

You will recall that with nominal data, observations are grouped into several discrete, mutually exclusive categories, and one counts the frequency of occurrence in each category. The inference test most often used with nominal data is *chi-square*.

## Chi-Square Test

| Test | Statistic Calculated | Decision Rule |
|------|---------------------|---------------|
| Chi-square | $\chi^2_{\mathrm{obt}} = \Sigma \dfrac{(f_o - f_e)^2}{f_e}$ | If $\chi^2_{\mathrm{obt}} \geq \chi^2_{\mathrm{crit}}$, reject $H_0$. |

**General comments** This test is appropriate for analyzing frequency data involving one or two variables. In the two-variable situation, the frequency data are presented in a contingency table and we test to see whether there is a relationship between the two variables. The null hypothesis states that there is no relationship—that the variables are independent. The alternative hypothesis states that the two variables are related.

Chi-square measures the discrepancy between the observed frequency ($f_o$) and the expected frequency ($f_e$) for each cell in the table and then sums across cells. The equation for $\chi^2_{obt}$ is given in the table. When the data involve two variables, the expected frequency for each cell is the frequency that would be expected if sampling is random from a population where the two variables are equal in proportions for each category. Since the population proportions are unknown, their expected values under $H_0$ are estimated from the sample data, and the expected frequencies are calculated using these estimates. The simplest way to determine $f_e$ for each cell is to multiply the marginals for that cell and divide by $N$. If the data involve only one variable, the population proportions are determined on some *a priori* basis (e.g., equal population proportions for each category).

The obtained value of $\chi^2$ is evaluated by comparing it with $\chi^2_{crit}$ according to the decision rule given on p. 473. The critical value of $\chi^2$ is determined by the sampling distribution of $\chi^2$ and the alpha level. The sampling distribution of $\chi^2$ is a family of curves that varies with the degrees of freedom. In the one-variable experiment, df $= k - 1$. In the two-variable situation, df $= (r - 1)(c - 1)$. The values of $\chi^2_{crit}$ are found in Table H in Appendix D, using df and $\alpha$.

Proper use of this test assumes that (1) each subject has only one entry in the table (no repeated measures on the same subjects); (2) if $r$ or $c$ is greater than 2, $f_e$ for each cell should be at least 5; and (3) if the table is a $1 \times 2$ or $2 \times 2$ table, each $f_e$ should be at least 10.

Chi-square can also be used with ordinal, interval, and ratio data. However, regardless of the actual scaling, to use $\chi^2$, the data must be reduced to mutually exclusive categories and appropriate frequencies.

## CHOOSING THE APPROPRIATE TEST

One of the important aspects of statistical inference is choosing which test to use for any experiment or problem. Up to now, it has been easy. We just used the test that we were studying for the particular chapter. However, in this review chapter, the situation is more challenging. Since we have covered many inference tests, we now have the opportunity to choose among them in deciding which to use. This, of course, is much more like the situation we face when doing research.

In choosing an inference test, the fundamental rule that we should follow is:

*Use the most powerful test possible.*

To determine which tests are possible for a given experiment or problem, we must consider two factors: the measurement scale of the dependent variable and the design of the experiment. Referring to the flowchart of Figure 18.1, the first question we ask is, "What is the level of measurement used for the dependent variable?" If it is nominal, the only inference test we've covered that is appropriate for nominal data is $\chi^2$. Thus, if the data are nominal in scaling and the requirements of $\chi^2$ (frequency data, large enough $N$, mutually exclusive categories, and independent observations) are met, then we should choose the $\chi^2$ test. If the

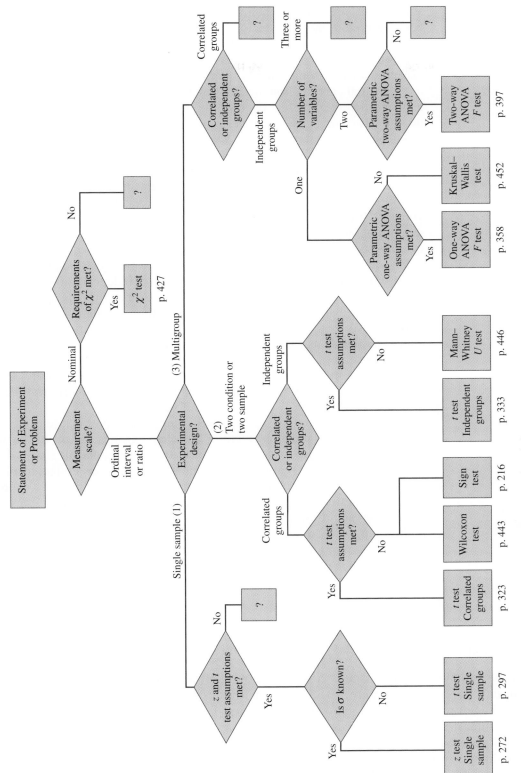

figure 18.1 Decision flowchart for choosing the appropriate inference test.

assumptions are not met, then we don't know what test to use, because it hasn't been covered in this introductory text. In the flowchart, this regrettable state of affairs is indicated by a "?". I hasten to reassure you, however, that the inference tests we've covered are the most commonly encountered ones, with the possible exception of very complicated experiments involving three or more variables.

If the data are not nominal, they must be ordinal, interval, or ratio in scaling. Having ruled out nominal data, we should next ask, "What is the experimental design?" The design used in the experiment limits the inference tests that we can use to analyze the data. We have covered three basic designs: single-sample, two-sample or two-condition, and multigroup experiments. If the design used is a single-sample design (path 1 in Figure 18.1), the two tests we have covered for this design are the $z$ test and the $t$ test for single samples. If the data meet the assumptions for these tests, to decide which to use we must ask the question, "Is $\sigma$ known?" If the answer is "yes," then the appropriate test is the $z$ test for single samples. If the answer is "no," then we must estimate $\sigma$ and use the $t$ test for single samples.

If the experimental design is a two-sample or two-condition design (path 2), we need to determine whether it is a correlated or independent groups design. If it is correlated groups and the assumptions of $t$ are met, the appropriate test is the $t$ test for correlated groups. Why? Because, if the assumptions are met, it is the most powerful test we can use for that design. If the assumptions are seriously violated, we should use an alternative test such as the Wilcoxon (if its assumptions are met) or the sign test. If it is an independent groups design and the assumptions of $t$ are met, we should use the $t$ test for independent groups. If the assumptions of $t$ are seriously violated, we should use an alternative test such as the Mann–Whitney $U$ test.

If the experimental design is a multigroup design (path 3), we need to determine whether it is an independent or correlated groups design. In this text, we have covered multigroup experiments that use the independent groups design. If the experiment is multigroup, uses an independent groups design, involves one variable, and the assumptions of parametric ANOVA are met, the appropriate test is parametric one-way ANOVA ($F$ test). If the assumptions are seriously violated, we should use its alternative, the Kruskal–Wallis test. If the design is a multigroup, independent groups design, involving two variables, and the data meet the assumptions of parametric two-way ANOVA, we would use parametric two-way ANOVA ($F$ test) to analyze the data. We have not considered the more complex designs involving three or more variables.

## QUESTIONS AND PROBLEMS

*Note to the student:* In the previous chapters covering inferential statistics, when you were asked to solve an end-of-chapter problem, there was no question about which inference test you would use—you would use the test covered in the chapter. For example, if you were doing a problem in Chapter 13, you knew you should use the $t$ test for single samples, because that was the test the chapter covered. Now you have reached the elevated position in which you know so much statistics that when solving a problem, there may be more than one inference test that could be used. Often, both a parametric and nonparametric test may be possible. This is a new challenge. The rule to follow is to use the most powerful test that the data will allow. For the problems in this chapter, always assume that the assumptions underlying the parametric test are met, unless the problem *explicitly* indicates otherwise.

1. Briefly define the following terms:
   Alternative hypothesis
   Null hypothesis
   Null-hypothesis population
   Sampling distribution
   Critical region for rejection of $H_0$
   Alpha level
   Type I error
   Type II error
   Power
2. Briefly describe the process of hypothesis testing. Be sure to include the terms listed in Question 1 in your discussion.
3. Why are sampling distributions important in hypothesis testing?
4. An educator conducts an experiment using an independent groups design to evaluate two methods of teaching third-grade spelling. The results are not significant, and the educator concludes that the two methods are equal. Is this conclusion sound? Assume that the study was properly designed and conducted; that is, proper controls were present, sample size was reasonably large, proper statistics were used, and so forth.
5. Why are parametric tests generally preferred over nonparametric tests?
6. List the factors that affect the power of an experiment and explain how they can be used to increase power.
7. What factors determine which inference test to use in analyzing the data of an experiment?
8. List the various experimental designs covered in this textbook. In addition, list the inference tests appropriate for each design in the order of their sensitivity.
9. What are the assumptions underlying each inference test?
10. What are the two steps followed in analyzing the data from any study involving hypothesis testing?
11. A new competitor in the scotch whiskey industry conducts a study to compare its scotch whiskey (called McPherson's Joy) to the other three leading brands. Two hundred scotch drinkers are randomly sampled from the scotch drinkers living in New York City. Each individual is asked to taste the four scotch whiskeys and pick the one they like the best. Of course, the whiskeys are unmarked, and the order in which they are tasted is balanced. The number of subjects that preferred each brand is shown in the following table:

| McPherson's Joy | Brand X | Brand Y | Brand Z | |
|---|---|---|---|---|
| 58 | 52 | 48 | 42 | 200 |

   a. What is the alternative hypothesis? Use a nondirectional hypothesis.
   b. What is the null hypothesis?
   c. Using $\alpha = 0.05$, what do you conclude? I/O
12. A psychologist interested in animal learning conducts an experiment to determine the effect of adrenocorticotropic hormone (ACTH) on avoidance learning. Twenty 100-day-old male rats are randomly selected from the university vivarium for the experiment. Of the 20, 10 randomly chosen rats receive injections of ACTH 30 minutes before being placed in the avoidance situation. The other 10 receive placebo injections. The number of trials for each animal to learn the task is given here:

| ACTH | Placebo |
|---|---|
| 58 | 74 |
| 73 | 92 |
| 80 | 87 |
| 78 | 84 |
| 75 | 72 |
| 74 | 82 |
| 79 | 76 |
| 72 | 90 |
| 66 | 95 |
| 77 | 85 |

   a. What is the nondirectional alternative hypothesis?
   b. What is the null hypothesis?
   c. Using $\alpha = 0.01_{2 \text{ tail}}$, what do you conclude?
   d. What error may you have made by concluding as you did in part **c**?
   e. To what population do these results apply?
   f. What is the size of the effect? biological
13. A university nutritionist wonders whether the recent emphasis on eating a healthy diet has affected freshman students at her university. Consequently, she conducts a study to determine whether the diet of freshman students currently enrolled contains less fat than that of previous freshmen. To determine their percentage of daily fat intake, 15 students in this year's freshman class keep a record of everything they eat for 7

days. The results show that for the 15 students, the mean percentage of daily fat intake is 37%, with a standard deviation of 12%. Records kept on a large number of freshman students from previous years show a mean percentage of daily fat intake of 40%, a standard deviation of 10.5%, and a normal distribution of scores.

a. Based on these data, is the daily fat intake of currently enrolled freshmen less than that of previous years? Use $\alpha = 0.05_{1 \text{ tail}}$.

b. If the actual mean daily fat intake of currently enrolled freshmen is 35%, what is the power of the experiment to detect this level of real effect?

c. If $N$ is increased to 30, what is the power to detect a real mean daily fat intake of 35%?

d. If the nutritionist wants a power of 0.9000 to detect a real effect of at least 5 mean points below the established population norms, what $N$ should she run? health, I/O

14. A physiologist conducts an experiment designed to determine the effect of exogenous thyroxin (a hormone produced by the thyroid gland) on activity. Forty male rats are randomly assigned to four groups such that there are 10 rats per group. Each of the groups is injected with a different amount of thyroxin. Group 1 gets no thyroxin and merely receives saline solution. Group 2 receives a small amount, group 3 a moderate amount, and group 4 a high amount of thyroxin. After the injections, each animal is tested in an open-field apparatus to measure its activity level. The open-field apparatus is composed of a fairly large platform with sides around it to prevent the animal from leaving the platform. A grid configuration is painted on the surface of the platform such that the entire surface is covered with squares. To measure activity, the experimenter merely counts the number of squares that the animal has crossed during a fixed period of time. In the present experiment, each rat is tested in the open-field apparatus for 10 minutes. The results are shown in the table; the scores are the number of squares crossed per minute.

a. What is the overall null hypothesis?

b. Using $\alpha = 0.05$, what do you conclude?

c. What is the size of the effect?

d. Evaluate the *a priori* hypothesis that a high amount of exogenous thyroxin produces an effect on activity different from that of saline. Use $\alpha = 0.05_{2 \text{ tail}}$.

| \multicolumn{4}{c}{**Amount of Thyroxin**} |
| *Zero,* 1 | *Low,* 2 | *Moderate,* 3 | *High,* 4 |
|---|---|---|---|
| 2 | 4 | 8 | 12 |
| 3 | 3 | 7 | 10 |
| 3 | 5 | 9 | 8 |
| 2 | 5 | 6 | 7 |
| 5 | 3 | 5 | 9 |
| 2 | 2 | 8 | 13 |
| 1 | 4 | 9 | 11 |
| 3 | 3 | 7 | 8 |
| 4 | 6 | 8 | 7 |
| 5 | 4 | 4 | 9 |

e. Use the Tukey HSD test with $\alpha = 0.05_{2 \text{ tail}}$ to compare all possible pairs of means. What do you conclude? biological

15. A study is conducted to determine whether dieting plus exercise is more effective in producing weight loss than dieting alone. Twelve pairs of matched subjects are run in the study. Subjects are matched on initial weight, initial level of exercise, age, and gender. One member of each pair is put on a diet for 3 months. The other member receives the same diet but, in addition, is put on a moderate exercise regimen. The following scores indicate the weight loss in pounds over the 3-month period for each subject:

| Pair | Diet Plus Exercise | Diet Alone |
|---|---|---|
| 1 | 24 | 16 |
| 2 | 20 | 18 |
| 3 | 22 | 19 |
| 4 | 15 | 16 |
| 5 | 23 | 18 |
| 6 | 21 | 18 |
| 7 | 16 | 17 |
| 8 | 17 | 19 |
| 9 | 19 | 13 |
| 10 | 25 | 18 |
| 11 | 24 | 19 |
| 12 | 13 | 14 |

In answering the following questions, assume the data are very nonnormal so as to preclude using the appropriate parametric test.

  a. What is the alternative hypothesis? Use a directional hypothesis.

  b. What is the null hypothesis?

  c. Using $\alpha = 0.05_{1\text{ tail}}$, what do you conclude? health

16. a. What other nonparametric test could you have used to analyze the data presented in Problem 15?

  b. Use this test to analyze the data. What do you conclude with $\alpha = 0.05_{1\text{ tail}}$?

  c. Explain the difference between your conclusions for Problems 16b and 15c.

  d. Let $P$ equal the probability for each subject that diet plus exercise will yield greater weight loss. If $P_{\text{real}} = 0.75$, using the sign test with $\alpha = 0.05_{1\text{ tail}}$, what is the power of the experiment to detect this level of effect? What is the probability of making a Type II error? health

17. A researcher in human sexuality is interested in determining whether there is a relationship between sexual gender and time-of-day preference for having intercourse. A survey is conducted, and the results are shown in the following table; entries are the number of individuals who preferred morning or evening times:

| Sexual Gender | *Morning* | *Evening* | |
|---|---|---|---|
| Male | 36 | 24 | 60 |
| Female | 28 | 32 | 60 |
| | 64 | 56 | 120 |

  a. What is the null hypothesis?

  b. Using $\alpha = 0.05$, what do you conclude? social

18. A psychologist is interested in whether the internal states of individuals affect their perceptions. Specifically, the psychologist wants to determine whether hunger influences perception. To test this hypothesis, she randomly divides 24 subjects into three groups of 8 subjects per group. The subjects are asked to describe "pictures" that they are shown on a screen. Actually, there are no pictures, just ambiguous shapes or forms. Hunger is manipulated through food deprivation. One group is shown the pictures 1 hour after eating, another group

4 hours after eating, and the last group 12 hours after eating. The number of food-related objects reported by each subject is recorded. The following data are collected:

| Food Deprivation | | |
|---|---|---|
| *1 hr,*<br>*1* | *4 hrs,*<br>*2* | *12 hrs,*<br>*3* |
| 2 | 6 | 8 |
| 5 | 7 | 10 |
| 7 | 6 | 15 |
| 2 | 10 | 19 |
| 1 | 15 | 9 |
| 8 | 12 | 14 |
| 7 | 7 | 15 |
| 6 | 6 | 12 |

  a. What is the overall null hypothesis?

  b. What is your conclusion? Use $\alpha = 0.05$.

  c. If there is a significant effect, estimate the size of the effect, using $\hat{\omega}^2$.

  d. Estimate the size of the effect, using $\eta^2$.

  e. Using the Newman–Keuls test with $\alpha = 0.05_{2\text{ tail}}$, do all possible *post hoc* comparisons between pairs of means. What is your conclusion? cognitive

19. An engineer working for a leading electronics firm claims to have invented a process for making longer-lasting TV picture tubes. Tests run on 24 picture tubes made with the new process show a mean life of 1725 hours and a standard deviation of 85 hours. Tests run over the last 3 years on a very large number of TV picture tubes made with the old process show a mean life of 1538 hours. Is the engineer correct in her claim? Use $\alpha = 0.01_{1\text{ tail}}$ in making your decision. I/O

20. In a study to determine the effect of alcohol on aggressiveness, 17 adult volunteers were randomly assigned to two groups: an experimental group and a control group. The subjects in the experimental group drank vodka disguised in orange juice, and the subjects in the control group drank only orange juice. After the drinks were finished, a test of aggressiveness was administered. The following scores were obtained. Higher scores indicate greater aggressiveness:

| Orange Juice | Vodka Plus Orange Juice |
|:---:|:---:|
| 11 | 14 |
| 9 | 13 |
| 14 | 19 |
| 15 | 16 |
| 7 | 15 |
| 10 | 17 |
| 8 | 11 |
| 10 | 18 |
| 8 | |

a. What is the alternative hypothesis? Use a nondirectional hypothesis.
b. What is the null hypothesis?
c. Using $\alpha = 0.05_{2\ tail}$, what is your conclusion? social, clinical

21. The dean of admissions at a large university wonders how strong the relationship is between high school grades and college grades. During the 2 years that he has held this position, he has weighted high school grades heavily when deciding which students to admit to the university, yet he has never seen any data relating the two variables. Having a strong experimental background, he decides to conduct a study and find out for himself. He randomly samples 15 seniors from his university and obtains their high school and college grades. The following data are obtained:

| | Grades | |
|:---:|:---:|:---:|
| Subject | High school | College |
| 1 | 2.2 | 1.5 |
| 2 | 2.6 | 1.7 |
| 3 | 2.5 | 2.0 |
| 4 | 2.2 | 2.4 |
| 5 | 3.0 | 1.7 |
| 6 | 3.0 | 2.3 |
| 7 | 3.1 | 3.0 |
| 8 | 2.6 | 2.7 |
| 9 | 2.8 | 3.2 |
| 10 | 3.2 | 3.6 |
| 11 | 3.4 | 2.5 |
| 12 | 3.5 | 2.8 |
| 13 | 4.0 | 3.2 |
| 14 | 3.6 | 3.9 |
| 15 | 3.8 | 4.0 |

a. Compute $r_{obt}$ for these data.
b. Is the correlation significant? Use $\alpha = 0.05_{2\ tail}$.
c. What proportion of the variability in college grades is accounted for by the high school grades?
d. Is the dean justified in weighting high school grades heavily when determining which students to admit to the university? education

22. An experiment is conducted to evaluate the effect of smoking on heart rate. Ten subjects who smoke cigarettes are randomly selected for the experiment. Each subject serves in two conditions. In condition 1, the subject rests for an hour, after which heart rate is measured. In condition 2, the subject rests for an hour and then smokes two cigarettes. In condition 2, heart rate is measured after the subject has finished smoking the cigarettes. The data follow.

| | Heartbeats Per Minute | |
|:---:|:---:|:---:|
| Subject | No smoking, 1 | Smoking, 2 |
| 1 | 72 | 76 |
| 2 | 80 | 84 |
| 3 | 68 | 75 |
| 4 | 74 | 73 |
| 5 | 80 | 86 |
| 6 | 85 | 88 |
| 7 | 86 | 84 |
| 8 | 78 | 80 |
| 9 | 68 | 72 |
| 10 | 67 | 70 |

a. What is the nondirectional alternative hypothesis?
b. What is the null hypothesis?
c. Using $\alpha = 0.05_{2\ tail}$, what do you conclude? biological, clinical

23. To meet the current oil crisis, the government must decide on a course of action to follow. There are two choices: (1) to allow the price of oil to rise or (2) to impose gasoline rationing. A survey is taken among individuals of various occupations to see whether there is a relationship between the occupations and the favored course of action. The results are shown in the following 3 × 2 table; cell entries are the number of individuals favoring the course of action that heads the cell:

| | Course of Action | | |
|---|---|---|---|
| Occupation | *Oil price rise* | *Gasoline rationing* | |
| Business | 180 | 120 | 300 |
| Homemaker | 135 | 165 | 300 |
| Labor | 152 | 148 | 300 |
| | 467 | 433 | 900 |

a. What is the null hypothesis?

b. Using $\alpha = 0.05$, what do you conclude? I/O

24. You are interested in testing the hypothesis that adult men and women differ in logical reasoning ability. To do so, you randomly select 16 adults from the city in which you live and administer a logical reasoning test to them. A higher score indicates better logical reasoning ability. The following scores are obtained:

| **Men** | **Women** |
|---|---|
| 70 | 80 |
| 60 | 50 |
| 82 | 81 |
| 65 | 75 |
| 83 | 95 |
| 92 | 85 |
| 85 | 93 |
| | 75 |
| | 90 |

In answering the following questions, assume that the data violate the assumptions underlying the use of the appropriate parametric test and that you must analyze the data with a nonparametric test.

a. What is the null hypothesis?

b. Using $\alpha = 0.05_{2\ tail}$, what is your conclusion? cognitive, social

25. For her doctoral thesis, a graduate student in women's studies investigated the effects of stress on the menstrual cycle. Forty-two women were randomly sampled and run in a two-condition replicated measures design. However, one of the women dropped out of the study. In the stress condition, the mean length of menstrual cycle for the remaining 41 women was 29 days, with a standard deviation of 14 days.

Based on these data, determine the 95% confidence interval for the population mean length of menstrual cycle when under stress. health, social

26. A researcher interested in social justice believes that Hispanics are underrepresented in high school teachers in the part of the country she lives. A random sample of 150 high school teachers is taken from the geographical local. The results show that there were 15 Hispanic teachers in the sample. The percentage of Hispanics living in the population of that locale equals 22%.

a. What is the null hypothesis?

b. Using $\alpha = 0.05$, what is your conclusion? social

27. A student believes that physical science professors are more authoritarian than social science professors. She conducts an experiment in which six physics, six psychology, and six sociology professors are randomly selected and given a questionnaire measuring authoritarianism. The results are shown here. The higher the score is, the more authoritarian is the individual. Assume the data seriously violate normality assumptions. What do you conclude, using $\alpha = 0.05$?

| | **Professors** | |
|---|---|---|
| *Physics* | *Psychology* | *Sociology* |
| 75 | 73 | 71 |
| 82 | 80 | 80 |
| 80 | 85 | 90 |
| 97 | 92 | 78 |
| 94 | 70 | 94 |
| 76 | 69 | 68 |

social

28. A sleep researcher is interested in determining whether taking naps can improve performance and, if so, whether it matters if the naps are taken in the afternoon or evening. Thirty undergraduates are randomly sampled and assigned to one of six conditions: napping in the afternoon or evening, resting in the afternoon or evening, or engaging in a normal activity control condition, again in the afternoon or evening. There are five subjects in each condition. Each subject per-

forms the activity appropriate for his or her assigned condition, after which a performance test is given. The higher the score is, the better is the performance. The following results were obtained. What is your conclusion? Use $\alpha = 0.05$ and assume the data are from normally distributed populations.

| Time of Day | Activity | | | | | |
|---|---|---|---|---|---|---|
| | *Napping* | | *Resting* | | *Normal* | |
| Afternoon | 8 | 9 | 7 | 8 | 3 | 4 |
| | 7 | 5 | 6 | 4 | 5 | 5 |
| | 6 | | 5 | | 6 | |
| Evening | 6 | 5 | 5 | 3 | 4 | 2 |
| | 7 | 4 | 4 | 5 | 3 | 4 |
| | 6 | | 4 | | 3 | |

cognitive

## BOOK COMPANION WEBSITE

Go to www.thomsonedu.com/psychology/pagano for:

- Statistical workshops
- And more

# APPENDIXES

# Review of Prerequisite Mathematics

APPENDIX A

Introduction
Solving Equations with One Unknown
Linear Interpolation

## INTRODUCTION

In this appendix, we shall present a review of some basic mathematical skills that we believe are important as background for an introductory course in statistics. This appendix is intended to be a review of material that you have already learned but that may be a little "rusty" from disuse. For students who have been away from mathematics for many years and who feel unsure of their mathematical background, we recommend the following books: H. M. Walker, *Mathematics Essential for Elementary Statistics* (rev. ed., Holt, New York, 1951) or A. J. Washington, *Arithmetic and Beginning Algebra* (Addison-Wesley, Reading, MA, 1984).

**Algebraic Symbols**

| Symbol | Explanation |
| --- | --- |
| $>$ | Is greater than |
| $5 > 4$ | 5 is greater than 4. |
| $X > 10$ | $X$ is greater than 10. |
| $a > b$ | $a$ is greater than $b$. |
| $<$ | Is less than |
| $7 < 9$ | 7 is less than 9. |
| $X < 12$ | $X$ is less than 12. |
| $a < b$ | $a$ is less than $b$. |
| $2 < X < 20$ | $X$ is greater than 2 and less than 20, or the value of $X$ lies between 2 and 20. |
| $X < 2$ or $X > 20$ | $X$ is less than 2 or greater than 20, or the value of $X$ lies outside the interval of 2 to 20. |
| $\geq$ | Is equal to or greater than |
| $X \geq 3$ | $X$ is equal to or greater than 3. |
| $a \geq b$ | $a$ is equal to or greater than $b$. |
| $\leq$ | Is equal to or less than |
| $X \leq 5$ | $X$ is equal to or less than 5. |
| $a \leq b$ | $a$ is equal to or less than $b$. |
| $\neq$ | Is not equal to |
| $3 \neq 5$ | 3 is not equal to 5. |
| $X \neq 8$ | $X$ is not equal to 8. |
| $a \neq b$ | $a$ is not equal to $b$. |
| $|X|$ | The absolute value of $X$; the absolute value of $X$ equals the magnitude of $X$ irrespective of its sign. |
| $|+7|$ | The absolute value of 7; $|+7| = 7$. |
| $|-5|$ | The absolute value of $-5$; $|-5| = 5$. |

**Arithmetic Operations**

| *Operation* | *Example* |
|---|---|
| 1. *Addition of two positive numbers:* To add two positive numbers, sum their absolute values and give the result a plus sign. | $2 + 8 = 10$ |
| 2. *Addition of two negative numbers:* To add two negative numbers, sum their absolute values and give the result a minus sign. | $-3 + (-4) = -7$ |
| 3. *Addition of two numbers with opposite signs:* To add two numbers with opposite signs, find the difference between their absolute values and give the number the sign of the larger absolute value. | $16 + (-10) = 6$ <br> $3 + (-14) = -11$ |
| 4. *Subtraction of one number from another:* To subtract one number from another, change the sign of the number to be subtracted and proceed as in addition (operations 1, 2, or 3). | $16 - 4 = 16 + (-4) = 12$ <br> $5 - 8 = 5 + (-8) = -3$ <br> $9 - (-6) = 9 + (+6) = 15$ <br> $-3 - 5 = -3 + (-5) = -8$ |
| 5. *Multiplying a series of numbers:* <br> a. When multiplying a series of numbers, the result is positive if there are an even number of negative values in the series. | $2(-5)(-6)(3) = 180$ <br> $-3(-7)(-2)(-1) = 42$ <br> $-a(-b) = ab$ |
| b. When multiplying a series of numbers, the result is negative if there are an odd number of negative values in the series. | $4(-5)(2) = -40$ <br> $-8(-2)(-5)(3) = -240$ <br> $-a(-b)(-c) = -abc$ |
| 6. *Dividing a series of numbers:* <br> a. When dividing a series of numbers, the result is positive if there are an even number of negative values. | $\dfrac{-4}{-8} = \dfrac{1}{2}$ <br><br> $\dfrac{-3(-4)(2)}{6} = 4$ <br><br> $\dfrac{-a}{-b} = \dfrac{a}{b}$ |
| b. When dividing a series of numbers, the result is negative if there are an odd number of negative values. | $\dfrac{-2}{5} = -0.40$ <br><br> $\dfrac{-3(-2)}{-4} = -1.5$ <br><br> $\dfrac{-a}{b} = -\dfrac{a}{b}$ |

**Rules Governing the Order of Arithmetic Operations**

| *Rule* | *Example* |
| --- | --- |
| 1. The order in which numbers are added does not change the result. | $6 + 4 + 11 = 4 + 6 + 11 = 11 + 6 + 4 = 21$ <br> $6 + (-3) + 2 = -3 + 6 + 2 = 2 + 6 + (-3) = 5$ |
| 2. The order in which numbers are multiplied does not change the result. | $3 \times 5 \times 8 = 8 \times 5 \times 3 = 5 \times 8 \times 3 = 120$ |
| 3. If both multiplication and addition or subtraction are specified, the multiplication should be performed first unless parentheses or brackets indicate otherwise. | $4 \times 5 + 2 = 20 + 2 = 22$ <br> $6 \times (14 - 12) \times 3 = 6 \times 2 \times 3 = 36$ <br> $6 \times (4 + 3) \times 2 = 6 \times 7 \times 2 = 84$ |
| 4. If both division and addition or subtraction are specified, the division should be performed first unless parentheses or brackets indicate otherwise. | $12 \div 4 + 2 = 3 + 2 = 5$ <br> $12 \div (4 + 2) = 12 \div 6 = 2$ <br> $12 \div 4 - 2 = 3 - 2 = 1$ <br> $12 \div (4 - 2) = 12 \div 2 = 6$ |

## Rules Governing Parentheses and Brackets

| *Rule* | *Example* |
|---|---|
| 1. Parentheses and brackets indicate that whatever is shown within them is to be treated as a single number. | $(2 + 8)(6 - 3 + 2) = 10(5) = 50$ |
| 2. Where there are parentheses contained within brackets, perform the operations contained within the parentheses first. | $[(4)(6 - 3 + 2) + 6][2] = [(4)(5) + 6][2]$ $= [20 + 6][2] = [26][2] = 52$ |
| 3. When it is inconvenient to reduce whatever is contained within the parentheses to a single number, the parentheses may be removed as follows: | |
|   a. If a positive sign precedes the parentheses, remove the parentheses without changing the sign of any number they contained. | $1 + (3 + 5 - 2) = 1 + 3 + 5 - 2 = 7$ |
|   b. If a negative sign precedes the parentheses, remove the parentheses and change the signs of the numbers they contained. | $4 - (6 - 2 - 1) = 4 - 6 + 2 + 1 = 1$ |
|   c. If a multiplier exists outside the parentheses, all the terms within the parentheses must be multiplied by the multiplier. | $3(2 + 3 - 4) = 6 + 9 - 12 = 3$ $a(b + c + d) = ab + ac + ad$ |
|   d. The product of two sums is found by multiplying each element of one sum by the elements of the other sum. | $(a + b)(c + d) = ac + ad + bc + bd$ |
|   e. If whatever is contained within the parentheses is operated on in any way, always do the operation first, before combining with other terms. | $5 + 4(3 + 1) + 6 = 5 + 4(4) + 6 = 5 + 16$ $+ 6 = 27$ $4 + (3 + 1)/2 = 4 + 4/2 = 4 + 2 = 6$ $1 + (3 + 2)^2 = 1 + (5)^2 = 1 + 25 = 26$ |

**Fractions**

| Operation | Example |
|---|---|
| 1. *Addition of fractions:* To add two fractions, (1) find the least common denominator, (2) express each fraction in terms of the least common denominator, and (3) add the numerators and divide the sum by the common denominator. | $\frac{1}{3} + \frac{1}{2} = \frac{2}{6} + \frac{3}{6} = \frac{5}{6}$ $\frac{a}{b} + \frac{c}{d} = \frac{ad}{bd} + \frac{cb}{bd} = \frac{ad + cb}{bd}$ |
| 2. *Multiplication of fractions:* To multiply two fractions, multiply the numerators together and divide by the product of the denominators. | $\frac{2}{5}(\frac{3}{7}) = \frac{6}{35}$ $\frac{a}{b}\left(\frac{c}{d}\right) = \frac{ac}{bd}$ |
| 3. *Changing a fraction into its decimal equivalent:* To convert a fraction into a decimal, perform the indicated division, rounding to the required number of digits (two digits in the example shown). | $\frac{3}{7} = 0.429 = 0.43$ |
| 4. *Changing a decimal into a percentage:* To convert a decimal fraction into a percentage, multiply the decimal fraction by 100. | $0.43 \times 100 = 43\%$ |
| 5. *Multiplying an integer by a fraction:* To multiply an integer by a fraction, multiply the integer by the numerator of the fraction and divide the product by the denominator. | $\frac{2}{5}(4) = \frac{8}{5} = 1.60$ |
| 6. *Cancellation:* When multiplying several fractions together, identical factors in the numerator and denominator may be canceled. | $\frac{\overset{1}{\cancel{5}}}{\underset{3}{\cancel{12}}}\left(\frac{\overset{1}{\cancel{4}}}{\underset{3}{\cancel{9}}}\right)\left(\frac{\overset{1}{\cancel{3}}}{\underset{2}{\cancel{10}}}\right) = \frac{1}{18}$ |

**Exponents**

| Operation | Example |
|---|---|
| 1. *Multiplying a number by itself 2 times* | $(4)^2 = 4(4) = 16$ <br> $a^2 = aa$ |
| 2. *Multiplying a number by itself 3 times* | $(4)^3 = 4(4)(4) = 64$ <br> $a^3 = aaa$ |
| 3. *Multiplying a number by itself N times* | $4^N = \overbrace{4(4)(4)\cdots(4)}^{N}$ |
| 4. *Multiplying two exponential quantities having the same base:* <br> The product of two exponential quantities having the same base is the base raised to the sum of the exponents. | $(2)^2(2)^4 = (2)^{2+4} = (2)^6$ <br> $a^N a^P = a^{N+P}$ |
| 5. *Dividing two exponential quantities having the same base:* <br> The quotient of two exponential quantities having the same base is the base raised to an exponent equal to the exponent of the quantity in the numerator minus the exponent of the quantity in the denominator. | $\dfrac{(2)^4}{(2)^2} = (2)^2$ <br> $\dfrac{a^N}{a^P} = a^{N-P}$ |
| 6. *Raising a base to a negative exponent:* <br> A base raised to a negative exponent is equal to 1 divided by the base raised to the positive value of the exponent. | $(2)^{-3} = \dfrac{1}{(2)^3}$ <br> $a^{-N} = \dfrac{1}{a^N}$ |

**Factoring**   When factoring an algebraic expression, we try to reduce the expression to the simplest components that when multiplied together yield the original expression.

| Example | Explanation |
|---|---|
| $ab + ac + ad = a(b + c + d)$ | We factored out $a$ from each item. |
| $abc - 2ab = ab(c - 2)$ | We factored out $ab$ from both terms. |
| $a^2 + 2ab + b^2 = (a + b)^2$ | This expression can be reduced to $a + b$ times itself. |

# SOLVING EQUATIONS WITH ONE UNKNOWN

When solving equations with one unknown, the basic idea is to isolate the unknown on one side of the equation and reduce the other side to its smallest possible value. In so doing, we make use of the principle that the equation remains an equality if whatever we do to one side of the equation, we also do the same to the other side. Thus, for example, the equation remains an equality if we add the same number to both sides. In solving the equation, we alter the equation by adding, subtracting, multiplying dividing, squaring, and so forth, so as to isolate the unknown. This is permissible as long as we do the same operation to both sides of the equation, thus maintaining the equality. The following examples illustrate many of the operations commonly used to solve equations having one unknown. In each of the examples, we shall be solving the equation for $Y$.

| Example | Explanation |
|---|---|
| $Y + 5 = 2$ <br> $Y = 2 - 5$ <br> $\quad = -3$ | To isolate $Y$, subtract 5 from both sides of the equation. |
| $Y - 4 = 6$ <br> $Y = 6 + 4$ <br> $\quad = 10$ | To isolate $Y$, add 4 to both sides of the equation. |
| $\dfrac{Y}{2} = 8$ <br> $Y = 8(2)$ <br> $\quad = 16$ | To isolate $Y$, multiply both sides of the equation by 2. |
| $3Y = 7$ <br> $Y = \frac{7}{3}$ <br> $\quad = 2.33$ | To isolate $Y$, divide both sides of the equation by 3. |
| $6 = \dfrac{Y - 3}{2}$ <br> $12 = Y - 3$ <br> $3 + 12 = Y$ <br> $15 = Y$ <br> $Y = 15$ | To isolate $Y$, <br><br> (1) multiply both sides by 2 and <br> (2) add 3 to both sides. |
| $3 = \dfrac{2}{Y}$ <br> $3Y = 2$ <br> $Y = \frac{2}{3}$ | To isolate $Y$, <br><br> (1) multiply both sides by $Y$ and <br> (2) divide both sides by 3. |
| $4(Y + 1) = 3$ <br> $Y + 1 = \frac{3}{4}$ <br> $Y = \frac{3}{4} - 1$ <br> $\quad = -\frac{1}{4}$ | To isolate $Y$, <br><br> (1) divide both sides by 4 and <br> (2) subtract 1 from both sides. |
| $\dfrac{4}{Y + 2} = 8$ <br> $\dfrac{Y + 2}{4} = \dfrac{1}{8}$ <br> $Y + 2 = \frac{4}{8}$ <br> $Y = \frac{4}{8} - 2$ <br> $\quad = -1\frac{1}{2}$ | To isolate $Y$, <br><br> (1) take the reciprocal of both sides, <br> (2) multiply both sides by 4, and <br> (3) subtract 2 from both sides. |
| $2Y + 4 = 10$ <br> $2Y = 10 - 4$ <br> $Y = \dfrac{10 - 4}{2}$ <br> $\quad = 3$ | To isolate $Y$, <br><br> (1) subtract 4 from both sides and <br><br> (2) divide both sides by 2. |

## LINEAR INTERPOLATION

Linear interpolation is often necessary when looking up values in a table. For example, suppose we wanted to find the square root of 96.5 using a table that only has the square root of 96 and 97 but not 96.5, as shown here:

| Number | Square root |
|--------|-------------|
| 96 | 9.7980 |
| 97 | 9.8489 |

Looking in the column headed by Number, we note that there is no value corresponding to 96.5. The closest values are 96 and 97. From the table, we can see that the square root of 96 is 9.7980 and that the square root of 97 is 9.8489. Obviously, the square root of 96.5 must lie between 9.7980 and 9.8489. Using *linear* interpolation, we assume there is a linear relationship between the number and its square root, and we use this linear relationship to approximate the square root of numbers not given in the table. Since 96.5 is halfway between 96 and 97, using linear interpolation, we would expect the square root of 96.5 to lie halfway between 9.7980 and 9.8489. If we let $X$ equal the square root of 96.5, then

$$X = 9.7980 + 0.5(9.8489 - 9.7980) = 9.8234$$

Although it wasn't made explicit, the computed value for $X$ was the result of setting up the following proportions and solving for $X$:

$$\frac{96.5 - 96}{97 - 96} = \frac{X - 9.7980}{9.8489 - 9.7980}$$

| Number | Square Root |
|--------|-------------|
| 96 | 9.7980 |
| 96.5 | $X$ |
| 97 | 9.8489 |

The relationship is shown graphically in Figure A.1.

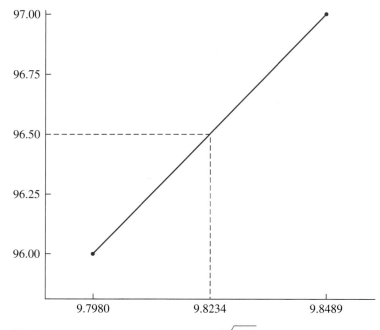

figure A.1 Linear interpolation for $\sqrt{96.5}$.

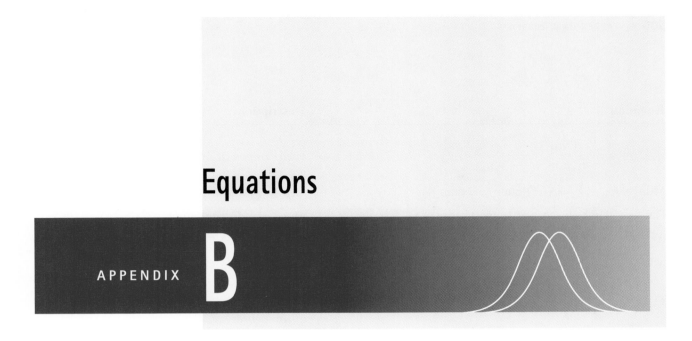

# Equations

Listed here are the computational equations used in this textbook. The page number refers to the page where the equation first appears.

| Equation | Description | Equation First Occurs on Page: |
|---|---|---|
| $\displaystyle\sum_{i=1}^{N} X_i = X_1 + X_2 + X_3 + \cdots + X_N$ | *summation* | 25 |
| $\text{cum } \% = \dfrac{\text{cum } f}{N} \times 100$ | *cumulative percentage* | 46 |
| $\text{Percentile point} = X_L + (i/f_i)(\text{cum } f_P - \text{cum } f_L)$ | *equation for computing percentile point* | 49 |
| $\text{Percentile rank} = \dfrac{\text{cum } f_L + (f_i/i)(X - X_L)}{N} \times 100$ | *equation for computing percentile rank* | 51 |
| $\overline{X} = \dfrac{\Sigma X_i}{N}$ | *mean of a sample* | 67 |
| $\mu = \dfrac{\Sigma X_i}{N}$ | *mean of a population of raw scores* | 67 |

| Equation | Description | Equation First Occurs on Page: |
|---|---|---|
| $\overline{X}_{\text{overall}} = \dfrac{n_1\overline{X}_1 + n_2\overline{X}_2 + \cdots + n_k\overline{X}_k}{n_1 + n_2 + \cdots + n_k}$ | *overall mean of several groups* | 71 |
| $\text{Mdn} = P_{50} = X_L + (i/f_i)(\text{cum } f_P - \text{cum } f_L)$ | *median of a distribution* | 72 |
| $\text{Range} = \text{Highest score} - \text{Lowest score}$ | *range of a distribution* | 76 |
| $X - \overline{X}$ | *deviation score for sample data* | 77 |
| $X - \mu$ | *deviation score for population data* | 77 |
| $s = \sqrt{\dfrac{SS}{N-1}} = \sqrt{\dfrac{\Sigma(X - \overline{X})^2}{N-1}}$ | *standard deviation of a sample of raw scores* | 78 |
| $\sigma = \sqrt{\dfrac{SS_{\text{pop}}}{N}} = \sqrt{\dfrac{\Sigma(X - \mu)^2}{N}}$ | *standard deviation of a population of raw scores* | 78 |
| $SS = \Sigma X^2 - \dfrac{(\Sigma X)^2}{N}$ | *sum of squares* | 79 |
| $s^2 = \dfrac{SS}{N-1}$ | *variance of a sample of raw scores* | 82 |
| $\sigma^2 = \dfrac{SS_{\text{pop}}}{N}$ | *variance of a population of raw scores* | 82 |
| $z = \dfrac{X - \mu}{\sigma}$ | *z score for population data* | 89 |
| $z = \dfrac{X - \overline{X}}{s}$ | *z score for sample data* | 89 |
| $X = \mu + \sigma z$ | *equation for finding a population raw score from its z score* | 97 |
| $Y = bX + a$ | *equation of a straight line* | 106 |
| $b = \text{Slope} = \dfrac{\Delta Y}{\Delta X} = \dfrac{Y_2 - Y_1}{X_2 - X_1}$ | *slope of a straight line* | 106 |
| $r = \dfrac{\Sigma z_X z_Y}{N-1}$ | *equation for Pearson r using z scores* | 115 |
| $r = \dfrac{\Sigma XY - \dfrac{(\Sigma X)(\Sigma Y)}{N}}{\sqrt{\left[\Sigma X^2 - \dfrac{(\Sigma X)^2}{N}\right]\left[\Sigma Y^2 - \dfrac{(\Sigma Y)^2}{N}\right]}}$ | *computational equation for Pearson r* | 115 |
| $r_s = 1 - \dfrac{6 \Sigma D_i^2}{N^3 - N}$ | *computational equation for Spearman rho* | 122 |
| $Y' = b_Y X + a_Y$ | *linear regression equation for predicting Y given X* | 137 |

| Equation | Description | Equation First Occurs on Page: |
|---|---|---|
| $b_Y = \dfrac{\sum XY - \dfrac{(\sum X)(\sum Y)}{N}}{\sum X^2 - \dfrac{(\sum X)^2}{N}}$ | *regression constant **b** for predicting Y given X, computational equation with raw scores* | 138 |
| $a_Y = Y - b_Y \overline{X}$ | *regression constant **a** for predicting Y given X* | 138 |
| $X' = b_X Y + a_X$ | *linear regression equation for predicting X given Y* | 144 |
| $b_X = \dfrac{\sum XY - \dfrac{(\sum X)(\sum Y)}{N}}{\sum Y^2 - \dfrac{(\sum Y)^2}{N}}$ | *regression constant **b** for predicting X given Y, computational equation with raw scores* | 145 |
| $a_X = \overline{X} - b_X \overline{Y}$ | *regression constant **a** for predicting X given Y* | 145 |
| $s_{Y|X} = \sqrt{\dfrac{SS_Y - \dfrac{[\sum XY - (\sum X)(\sum Y)/N]^2}{SS_X}}{N - 2}}$ | *computational equation for the standard error of estimate when predicting Y given X* | 147 |
| $b_Y = r\dfrac{s_Y}{s_X}$ | *equation relating r to the $b_Y$ regression constant* | 151 |
| $b_X = r\dfrac{s_X}{s_Y}$ | *equation relating r to the $b_X$ regression constant* | 151 |
| $R^2 = \dfrac{r_{YX_1}{}^2 + r_{YX_2}{}^2 - 2r_{YX_1}r_{YX_2}r_{X_1X_2}}{1 - r_{X_1X_2}{}^2}$ | *equation for computing the squared multiple correlation* | 155 |
| $p(A) = \dfrac{\text{Number of events classifiable as } A}{\text{Total number of possible events}}$ | *a priori probability* | 168 |
| $p(A) = \dfrac{\text{Number of times } A \text{ has occurred}}{\text{Total number of occurrences}}$ | *a posteriori probability* | 168 |
| $p(A \text{ or } B) = p(A) + p(B) - p(A \text{ and } B)$ | *addition rule for two events, general equation* | 170 |
| $p(A \text{ or } B) = p(A) + p(B)$ | *addition rule when A and B are mutually exclusive* | 171 |
| $p(A \text{ or } B \text{ or } C \text{ or } \ldots \text{ or } Z) = p(A) + p(B) + p(C) + \cdots + p(Z)$ | *addition rule with more than two mutually exclusive events* | 174 |
| $p(A) + p(B) + p(C) + \cdots + p(Z) = 1.00$ | *when events are exhaustive and mutually exclusive* | 174 |

| Equation | Description | Equation First Occurs on Page: |
|---|---|---|
| $P + Q = 1.00$ | *when two events are exhaustive and mutually exclusive* | 174 |
| $p(A \text{ and } B) = p(A)p(B\|A)$ | *multiplication rule with two events, general equation* | 175 |
| $p(A \text{ and } B) = 0$ | *multiplication rule with mutually exclusive events* | 175 |
| $p(A \text{ and } B) = p(A)p(B)$ | *multiplication rule with independent events* | 176 |
| $p(A \text{ and } B \text{ and } C \text{ and } \ldots \text{ and } Z) = p(A)p(B)p(C) \cdots p(Z)$ | *multiplication rule with more than two independent events* | 180 |
| $p(A \text{ and } B) = p(A)p(B\|A)$ | *multiplication rule with dependent events* | 181 |
| $p(A \text{ and } B \text{ and } C \text{ and } \ldots \text{ and } Z)$ $= p(A)p(B\|A)p(C\|AB) \cdots p(Z\|ABC \ldots)$ | *multiplication rule with more than two dependent events* | 184 |
| $p(A) = \dfrac{\text{Area under curve corresponding to } A}{\text{Total area under curve}}$ | *probability of A with a continuous variable* | 188 |
| $(P + Q)^N$ | *binomial expansion* | 203 |
| Number of $Q$ events $= N -$ Number of $P$ events | *relationship between number of Q events, number of P events, and N* | 209 |
| Beta $= 1 -$ Power | *relationship between beta and power* | 253 |
| $\mu_{\overline{X}} = \mu$ | *mean of the sampling distribution of the mean* | 274 |
| $\sigma_{\overline{X}} = \dfrac{\sigma}{\sqrt{N}}$ | *standard deviation of the sampling distribution of the mean or standard error of the mean* | 274 |
| $z_{\text{obt}} = \dfrac{\overline{X}_{\text{obt}} - \mu}{\sigma_{\overline{X}}}$ | *z transformation for $\overline{X}_{\text{obt}}$* | 281 |
| $z_{\text{obt}} = \dfrac{\overline{X}_{\text{obt}} - \mu}{\sigma/\sqrt{N}}$ | *z transformation for $\overline{X}_{\text{obt}}$* | 285 |
| $N = \left[ \dfrac{\sigma(z_{\text{crit}} - z_{\text{obt}})}{\mu_{\text{real}} - \mu_{\text{null}}} \right]^2$ | *determining N for a specified power* | 291 |
| $t_{\text{obt}} = \dfrac{\overline{X}_{\text{obt}} - \mu}{s/\sqrt{N}}$ | *equation for calculating the t statistic* | 298 |
| $t_{\text{obt}} = \dfrac{\overline{X}_{\text{obt}} - \mu}{s_{\overline{X}}}$ | *equation for calculating the t statistic* | 298 |

| **Equation** | **Description** | **Equation First Occurs on Page:** |
|---|---|---|
| $s_{\overline{X}} = \dfrac{s}{\sqrt{N}}$ | *estimated standard error of the mean* | 298 |
| $\text{df} = N - 1$ | *degrees of freedom for t test (single sample)* | 301 |
| $t_{\text{obt}} = \dfrac{\overline{X}_{\text{obt}} - \mu}{\sqrt{\dfrac{SS}{N(N-1)}}}$ | *equation for calculating the t statistic from raw scores* | 304 |
| $\mu_{\text{lower}} = \overline{X}_{\text{obt}} - s_{\overline{X}} t_{0.025}$ | *lower limit for the 95% confidence interval* | 310 |
| $\mu_{\text{upper}} = \overline{X}_{\text{obt}} + s_{\overline{X}} t_{0.025}$ | *upper limit for the 95% confidence interval* | 310 |
| $\mu_{\text{lower}} = \overline{X}_{\text{obt}} - s_{\overline{X}} t_{0.005}$ | *lower limit for the 99% confidence interval* | 311 |
| $\mu_{\text{upper}} = \overline{X}_{\text{obt}} + s_{\overline{X}} t_{0.005}$ | *upper limit for the 99% confidence interval* | 311 |
| $\mu_{\text{lower}} = \overline{X}_{\text{obt}} - s_{\overline{X}} t_{\text{crit}}$ | *general equation for the lower limit of the confidence interval* | 311 |
| $\mu_{\text{upper}} = \overline{X}_{\text{obt}} + s_{\overline{X}} t_{\text{crit}}$ | *general equation for the upper limit of the confidence interval* | 311 |
| $t_{\text{obt}} = \dfrac{r_{\text{obt}} - p}{s_r}$ | *t test for testing the significance of r* | 314 |
| $t_{\text{obt}} = \dfrac{r_{\text{obt}}}{\sqrt{\dfrac{1 - r_{\text{obt}}^2}{N-2}}}$ | *t test for testing the significance of r* | 314 |
| $t_{\text{obt}} = \dfrac{\overline{D}_{\text{obt}} - \mu_D}{s_D/\sqrt{N}}$ | *t test for correlated groups* | 324 |
| $t_{\text{obt}} = \dfrac{\overline{D}_{\text{obt}} - \mu_D}{\sqrt{\dfrac{SS_D}{N(N-1)}}}$ | *t test for correlated groups* | 324 |
| $SS_D = \Sigma D^2 - \dfrac{(\Sigma D)^2}{N}$ | *sum of squares of the difference scores* | 324 |
| $\mu_{\overline{X}_1 - \overline{X}_2} = \mu_1 - \mu_2$ | *mean of the difference between sample means* | 331 |
| $\sigma_{\overline{X}_1 - \overline{X}_2} = \sqrt{\sigma^2\left(\dfrac{1}{n_1} + \dfrac{1}{n_2}\right)}$ | *standard deviation of the difference between sample means* | 332 |

| Equation | Description | Equation First Occurs on Page: |
|---|---|---|
| $t_{obt} = \dfrac{(\overline{X}_1 - \overline{X}_2) - \mu_{\overline{X}_1 - \overline{X}_2}}{\sqrt{\left(\dfrac{SS_1 + SS_2}{n_1 + n_2 - 2}\right)\left(\dfrac{1}{n_1} + \dfrac{1}{n_2}\right)}}$ | computational equation for $t_{obt}$, independent groups design | 334 |
| $t_{obt} = \dfrac{\overline{X}_1 - \overline{X}_2}{\sqrt{\left(\dfrac{SS_1 + SS_2}{n_1 + n_2 - 2}\right)\left(\dfrac{1}{n_1} + \dfrac{1}{n_2}\right)}}$ | computational equation for $t_{obt}$ assuming the independent variable has no effect | 334 |
| $SS_1 = \Sigma\, X_1^{\,2} - \dfrac{(\Sigma\, X_1)^2}{n_1}$ | sum of squares for group 1 | 336 |
| $SS_2 = \Sigma\, X_2^{\,2} - \dfrac{(\Sigma\, X_2)^2}{n_2}$ | sum of squares for group 2 | 336 |
| $t_{obt} = \dfrac{\overline{X}_1 - \overline{X}_2}{\sqrt{\dfrac{SS_1 + SS_2}{n(n - 1)}}}$ | computational equation for $t_{obt}$ when $n_1 = n_2$ | 336 |
| $\hat{\omega}^2 = \dfrac{t_{obt}^{\,2} - 1}{t_{obt}^{\,2} + N - 1}$ | computational equation for estimating $\omega^2$ | 341 |
| $\mu_{lower} = (\overline{X}_1 - \overline{X}_2) - s_{\overline{X}_1 - \overline{X}_2} t_{0.025}$ | lower limit for the 95% confidence interval for $\mu_{\overline{X}_1 - \overline{X}_2}$ | 347 |
| $\mu_{upper} = (\overline{X}_1 + \overline{X}_2) - s_{\overline{X}_1 - \overline{X}_2} t_{0.025}$ | upper limit for the 95% confidence interval for $\mu_{\overline{X}_1 - \overline{X}_2}$ | 347 |
| $\mu_{lower} = (\overline{X}_1 - \overline{X}_2) - s_{\overline{X}_1 - \overline{X}_2} t_{0.005}$ | lower limit for the 99% confidence interval for $\mu_{\overline{X}_1 - \overline{X}_2}$ | 348 |
| $\mu_{upper} = (\overline{X}_1 - \overline{X}_2) + s_{\overline{X}_1 - \overline{X}_2} t_{0.005}$ | upper limit for the 99% confidence interval for $\mu_{\overline{X}_1 - \overline{X}_2}$ | 348 |
| $F = \dfrac{\text{Variance estimate 1 of } \sigma^2}{\text{Variance estimate 2 of } \sigma^2}$ | basic definition of F | 359 |
| $MS_B = s_B^{\,2}$ | mean square between | 362 |
| $MS_W = s_W^{\,2}$ | mean square within or mean square error | 362 |
| $F_{obt} = \dfrac{s_B^{\,2}}{s_W^{\,2}}$ | F equation for the analysis of variance | 363 |
| $s_W^{\,2} = \dfrac{SS_W}{N - k}$ | within-groups variance estimate | 364 |
| $SS_W = \displaystyle\sum^{\substack{\text{all}\\\text{scores}}} X^2 - \left[\dfrac{(\Sigma\, X_1)^2}{n_1} + \dfrac{(\Sigma\, X_2)^2}{n_2} + \dfrac{(\Sigma\, X_3)^2}{n_3} + \cdots + \dfrac{(\Sigma\, X_k)^2}{n_k}\right]$ | within-groups sum of squares, computational equation | 364 |

| Equation | Description | Equation First Occurs on Page: |
|---|---|---|
| $\mathrm{df}_W = N - k$ | degrees of freedom for the within-groups variance estimate | 364 |
| $s_B{}^2 = \dfrac{SS_B}{k - 1}$ | between-groups variance estimate | 365 |
| $SS_B = \left[ \dfrac{(\Sigma X_1)^2}{n_1} + \dfrac{(\Sigma X_2)^2}{n_2} + \dfrac{(\Sigma X_3)^2}{n_3} + \cdots + \dfrac{(\Sigma X_k)^2}{n_k} \right]$ $- \dfrac{\left( \overset{\text{all scores}}{\underset{}{\sum}} X \right)^2}{N}$ | between-groups sum of squares, computational equation | 365 |
| $\mathrm{df}_B = k - 1$ | degrees of freedom for the between-groups variance estimate | 365 |
| $SS_T = SS_W + SS_B$ | equation for checking $SS_W$ and $SS_B$ | 368 |
| $SS_T = \overset{\text{all scores}}{\sum} X^2 - \dfrac{\left( \overset{\text{all scores}}{\sum} X \right)^2}{N}$ | equation for calculating the total variability | 368 |
| $\hat{\omega}^2 = \dfrac{SS_B - (k - 1)\, s_W{}^2}{SS_T + s_W{}^2}$ | computational equation for estimating $\omega^2$ | 375 |
| $\eta^2 = \dfrac{SS_B}{SS_T}$ | Conceptual and computational equation for eta squared | 375 |
| $F_{\mathrm{obt}} = \sqrt{\dfrac{n[(\overline{X}_1 - \overline{X}_G)^2 + (\overline{X}_2 - \overline{X}_G)^2 + (\overline{X}_3 - \overline{X}_G)^2]/2}{(SS_1 + SS_2 + SS_3)/(N - 3)}}$ | F equation for three-group experiment | 376 |
| $t_{\mathrm{obt}} = \dfrac{\overline{X}_1 - \overline{X}_2}{\sqrt{s_W{}^2\left(\dfrac{1}{n_1} + \dfrac{1}{n_2}\right)}}$ | t equation for a priori comparisons, general equation | 378 |
| $t_{\mathrm{obt}} = \dfrac{\overline{X}_1 - \overline{X}_2}{\sqrt{2\, s_W{}^2/n}}$ | t equation for a priori comparisons with equal n in the two groups | 378 |
| $Q_{\mathrm{obt}} = \dfrac{\overline{X}_i - \overline{X}_j}{\sqrt{s_W{}^2/n}}$ | equation for calculating $Q_{\mathrm{obt}}$ | 380 |
| $s_W{}^2 = \dfrac{SS_W}{\mathrm{df}_W}$ | equation for within-cells variance estimate | 404 |
| $SS_W = \overset{\text{all scores}}{\sum} X^2 - \left[ \dfrac{\left( \overset{\text{cell } 11}{\sum} X \right)^2 + \left( \overset{\text{cell } 12}{\sum} X \right)^2 + \cdots + \left( \overset{\text{cell } rc}{\sum} X \right)^2}{n_{\mathrm{cell}}} \right]$ | within-cells sum of squares, computational equation | 404 |

| Equation | Description | Equation First Occurs on Page: |
|---|---|---|
| $\mathrm{df}_W = rc(n-1)$ | *within-cells degrees of freedom* | 404 |
| $s_R^2 = \dfrac{SS_R}{\mathrm{df}_R}$ | *equation for the row variance estimate* | 405 |
| $\mathrm{df}_R = r - 1$ | *row degrees of freedom* | 405 |
| $SS_R = \left[\dfrac{\left(\overset{\text{row}}{\underset{1}{\sum}} X\right)^2 + \left(\overset{\text{row}}{\underset{2}{\sum}} X\right)^2 + \cdots + \left(\overset{\text{row}}{\underset{r}{\sum}} X\right)^2}{n_{\text{row}}}\right] - \dfrac{\left(\overset{\text{all}}{\overset{\text{scores}}{\sum}} X\right)^2}{N}$ | *computational equation for the row sum of squares* | 405 |
| $s_C^2 = \dfrac{SS_C}{\mathrm{df}_C}$ | *column variance estimate* | 406 |
| $\mathrm{df}_C = c - 1$ | *column degrees of freedom* | 406 |
| $SS_C = \left[\dfrac{\left(\overset{\text{col.}}{\underset{1}{\sum}} X\right)^2 + \left(\overset{\text{col.}}{\underset{2}{\sum}} X\right)^2 + \cdots + \left(\overset{\text{col.}}{\underset{c}{\sum}} X\right)^2}{n_{\text{col.}}}\right] - \dfrac{\left(\overset{\text{all}}{\overset{\text{scores}}{\sum}} X\right)^2}{N}$ | *computational equation for the column sum of squares* | 406 |
| $s_{RC}^2 = \dfrac{SS_{RC}}{\mathrm{df}_{RC}}$ | *row × column variance estimate* | 407 |
| $SS_{RC} = \left[\dfrac{\left(\overset{\text{cell}}{\underset{11}{\sum}} X\right)^2 + \left(\overset{\text{cell}}{\underset{12}{\sum}} X\right)^2 + \cdots + \left(\overset{\text{cell}}{\underset{rc}{\sum}} X\right)^2}{n_{\text{cell.}}}\right] - \dfrac{\left(\overset{\text{all}}{\overset{\text{scores}}{\sum}} X\right)^2}{N} - SS_R - SS_C$ | *computational equation for the row × column sum of squares* | 407 |
| $\mathrm{df}_{RC} = (r-1)(c-1)$ | *row × column degrees of freedom* | 407 |
| $\chi_{\text{obt}}^2 = \sum \dfrac{(f_o - f_e)^2}{f_e}$ | *equation for calculating $\chi_{\text{obt}}^2$* | 430 |
| $U_{\text{obt}} = n_1 n_2 + \dfrac{n_1(n_1+1)}{2} - R_1$ | *general equation for calculating $U_{\text{obt}}$ or $U'_{\text{obt}}$* | 448 |
| $U_{\text{obt}} = n_1 n_2 + \dfrac{n_2(n_2+1)}{2} - R_2$ | *general equation for calculating $U_{\text{obt}}$ or $U'_{\text{obt}}$* | 448 |
| $H_{\text{obt}} = \left[\dfrac{12}{N(N+1)}\right]\left[\sum_{i=1}^{k} \dfrac{(R_i)^2}{n_i}\right] - 3(N+1)$ | *equation for computing $H_{\text{obt}}$* | 454 |

# Answers to End-of-Chapter Questions and Problems

APPENDIX **C**

## CHAPTER 1

**6. b.** (1) functioning of the hypothalamus; (2) daily food intake; (3) the 30 rats selected for the experiment; (4) all rats living in the university vivarium at the time of the experiment; (5) the daily food intake of each animal during the 2-week period after recovery; (6) the mean daily food intake of each group    **c.** (1) methods of treating depression; (2) degree or amount of depression; (3) the 60 depressed students; (4) the undergraduate body at a large university at the time of the experiment; (5) depression scores of the 60 depressed students; (6) mean of the depression scores of each treatment    **d.** (1) and (2) since this is a study and not an experiment, there is no independent variable and no dependent variable. The two variables studied are the two levels of education and the annual salaries for each educational level; (3) the 200 individuals whose annual salaries were determined; (4) all individuals living in the city at the time of the experiment, having either of the educational levels; (5) the 200 annual salaries; (6) the mean annual salary for each educational level.    **e.** (1) spacing of practice sessions; (2) number of words correctly recalled; (3) the 30 seventh graders who participated in the experiment; (4) all seventh graders enrolled at the local junior high school at the time of the experiment; (5) the retention test scores of the 30 subjects; (6) mean values for each group of the number of words correctly recalled in the test period    **f.** (1) visualization versus visualization plus appropriate self-talk; (2) foul shooting accuracy; (3) the ten players participating in the experiment; (4) all players on the college basketball team at the time of the experiment; (5) foul shooting accuracy of the ten players, before and after 1 month of practicing the techniques; (6) the mean of the difference scores of each group    **g.** (1) the arrangement of typing keys; (2) typing speed; (3) the 20 secretarial trainees who were in the experiment; (4) all secretarial trainees enrolled in the business school at the time of the experiment; (5) the typing speed scores of each trainee obtained at the end of training; (6) the mean typing speed of each group

**7. a.** constant    **b.** constant    **c.** variable
   **d.** variable    **e.** constant    **f.** variable
   **g.** variable    **h.** constant

**8. a.** descriptive statistics    **b.** descriptive statistics
   **c.** descriptive statistics    **d.** inferential statistics
   **e.** inferential statistics    **f.** descriptive statistics

**9. a.** The sample scores are the 20 scores given. The population scores are the 213 scores that would have resulted if the number of drinks during "happy hour" were measured from all of the bars. **c.** The sample scores are the 25 lengths measured. The population scores are the 600 lengths that would be obtained if all 600 blanks were measured.   **d.** The sample scores are the 30 diastolic heart rates that were recorded. The population scores are the heart rate scores that would result from recording resting, diastolic heart rate from all the female students attending Tacoma University at the time of the experiment.

## CHAPTER 2

**2. a.** continuous   **b.** discrete   **c.** discrete
   **d.** continuous   **e.** discrete   **f.** continuous
   **g.** continuous   **h.** continuous

**3. a.** ratio   **b.** nominal   **c.** interval
   **d.** ordinal   **e.** ordinal   **f.** ratio
   **g.** ratio   **h.** interval   **i.** ordinal

**4.** No, ratios are not legitimate on an interval scale. We need an absolute zero point to perform ratios. Since an ordinal scale does not have an absolute zero point, the ratio of the absolute values represented by 30 and 60 will not be $\frac{1}{2}$.

**5. a.** 18   **b.** 21.1   **d.** 590

**6. a.** 14.54   **c.** 37.84   **d.** 46.50   **e.** 52.46   **f.** 25.49

**7. a.** 9.5–10.5   **b.** 2.45–2.55   **d.** 2.005–2.015   **e.** 5.2315–5.2325

**8. a.** 25   **b.** 35   **d.** 101

**9. a.** $X_1 = 250, X_2 = 378, X_3 = 451, X_4 = 275,$ $X_5 = 225, X_6 = 430, X_7 = 325, X_8 = 334$   **b.** 2668

**10. a.** $\sum_{i=1}^{N} X_i$   **b.** $\sum_{i=1}^{3} X_i$   **c.** $\sum_{i=2}^{4} X_i$   **d.** $\sum_{i=2}^{5} X_i^2$

**11. a.** 1.4   **b.** 23.2   **c.** 100.8   **d.** 41.7   **e.** 35.3

**12.** For 5b: $\sum X^2 = 104.45$ and $(\sum X)^2 = 445.21$; for 5c: $\sum X^2 = 3434$ and $(\sum X)^2 = 21,904$

**13. a.** 34   **b.** 14   **d.** 6.5

**14. a.** 4.1, 4.15   **b.** 4.2, 4.15   **c.** 4.2, 4.16   **d.** 4.2, 4.20

## CHAPTER 3

**5. a.**

| Score | f | Score | f | Score | f | Score | f |
|---|---|---|---|---|---|---|---|
| 98 | 1 | 84 | 2 | 70 | 2 | 57 | 2 |
| 97 | 0 | 83 | 3 | 69 | 2 | 56 | 1 |
| 96 | 0 | 82 | 4 | 68 | 4 | 55 | 2 |
| 95 | 0 | 81 | 3 | 67 | 2 | 54 | 0 |
| 94 | 2 | 80 | 0 | 66 | 1 | 53 | 0 |
| 93 | 2 | 79 | 2 | 65 | 1 | 52 | 0 |
| 92 | 1 | 78 | 5 | 64 | 3 | 51 | 0 |
| 91 | 2 | 77 | 2 | 63 | 1 | 50 | 0 |
| 90 | 2 | 76 | 4 | 62 | 2 | 49 | 2 |
| 89 | 1 | 75 | 3 | 61 | 1 | 48 | 0 |
| 88 | 1 | 74 | 1 | 60 | 1 | 47 | 0 |
| 87 | 2 | 73 | 4 | 59 | 0 | 46 | 0 |
| 86 | 0 | 72 | 6 | 58 | 0 | 45 | 1 |
| 85 | 4 | 71 | 3 |  |  |  |  |

**b.**

| Class Interval | Real Limits | f |
|---|---|---|
| 96–99 | 95.5–99.5 | 1 |
| 92–95 | 91.5–95.5 | 5 |
| 88–91 | 87.5–91.5 | 6 |
| 84–87 | 83.5–87.5 | 8 |
| 80–83 | 79.5–83.5 | 10 |
| 76–79 | 75.5–79.5 | 13 |
| 72–75 | 71.5–75.5 | 14 |
| 68–71 | 67.5–71.5 | 11 |
| 64–67 | 63.5–67.5 | 7 |
| 60–63 | 59.5–63.5 | 5 |
| 56–59 | 55.5–59.5 | 3 |
| 52–55 | 51.5–55.5 | 2 |
| 48–51 | 47.5–51.5 | 2 |
| 44–47 | 43.5–47.5 | 1 |
|  |  | 88 |

**6.**

| Class Interval | f | Relative f | Cumulative f | Cumulative % |
|---|---|---|---|---|
| 96–99 | 1 | 0.01 | 88 | 100.00 |
| 92–95 | 5 | 0.06 | 87 | 98.86 |
| 88–91 | 6 | 0.07 | 82 | 93.18 |
| 84–87 | 8 | 0.09 | 76 | 86.36 |
| 80–83 | 10 | 0.11 | 68 | 77.27 |
| 76–79 | 13 | 0.15 | 58 | 65.91 |
| 72–75 | 14 | 0.16 | 45 | 51.14 |
| 68–71 | 11 | 0.12 | 31 | 35.23 |
| 64–67 | 7 | 0.08 | 20 | 22.73 |
| 60–63 | 5 | 0.06 | 13 | 14.77 |
| 56–59 | 3 | 0.03 | 8 | 9.09 |
| 52–55 | 2 | 0.02 | 5 | 5.68 |
| 48–51 | 2 | 0.02 | 3 | 3.41 |
| 44–47 | 1 | 0.01 | 1 | 1.14 |
|  | 88 | 1.00 |  |  |

**7. a.** 82.70    **b.** 72.70

**8. a.** 70.17    **c.** 85.23

**10. a.**

| Class Interval | f |
|---|---|
| 60–64 | 1 |
| 55–59 | 1 |
| 50–54 | 2 |
| 45–49 | 2 |
| 40–44 | 4 |
| 35–39 | 5 |
| 30–34 | 7 |
| 25–29 | 12 |
| 20–24 | 17 |
| 15–19 | 16 |
| 10–14 | 8 |
| 5–9 | 3 |
| | 78 |

**11.**

| Class Interval | f | Relative f | Cumulative f |
|---|---|---|---|
| 60–64 | 1 | 0.01 | 78 |
| 55–59 | 1 | 0.01 | 77 |
| 50–54 | 2 | 0.03 | 76 |
| 45–49 | 2 | 0.03 | 74 |
| 40–44 | 4 | 0.05 | 72 |
| 35–39 | 5 | 0.06 | 68 |
| 30–34 | 7 | 0.09 | 63 |
| 25–29 | 12 | 0.15 | 56 |
| 20–24 | 17 | 0.22 | 44 |
| 15–19 | 16 | 0.21 | 27 |
| 10–14 | 8 | 0.10 | 11 |
| 5–9 | 3 | 0.04 | 3 |
| | 78 | 1.00 | |

**12. a.** 23.03

**13. a.** 88.72    **b.** 67.18

**16. a.** 3.30    **b.** 2.09

**17.** 65.62

**18. a.** 34.38    **b.** 33.59    **c.** Some accuracy is lost when grouping scores because the grouped scores analysis assumes the scores are evenly distributed throughout the interval.

**20. a.**

| Class Interval | f |
|---|---|
| 360–369 | 1 |
| 350–359 | 2 |
| 340–349 | 5 |
| 330–339 | 3 |
| 320–329 | 3 |
| 310–319 | 9 |
| 300–309 | 4 |
| 290–299 | 8 |
| 280–289 | 5 |
| 270–279 | 5 |
| 260–269 | 4 |
| 250–259 | 1 |
| | 50 |

**21.**

| Class Interval | f | Relative f | Cumulative f | Cumulative % |
|---|---|---|---|---|
| 360–369 | 1 | 0.02 | 50 | 100.00 |
| 350–359 | 2 | 0.04 | 49 | 98.00 |
| 340–349 | 5 | 0.10 | 47 | 94.00 |
| 330–339 | 3 | 0.06 | 42 | 84.00 |
| 320–329 | 3 | 0.06 | 39 | 78.00 |
| 310–319 | 9 | 0.18 | 36 | 72.00 |
| 300–309 | 4 | 0.08 | 27 | 54.00 |
| 290–299 | 8 | 0.16 | 23 | 46.00 |
| 280–289 | 5 | 0.10 | 15 | 30.00 |
| 270–279 | 5 | 0.10 | 10 | 20.00 |
| 260–269 | 4 | 0.08 | 5 | 10.00 |
| 250–259 | 1 | 0.02 | 1 | 2.00 |
| | 50 | 1.00 | | |

**22. a.** 304.50    **b.** 324.50

**23. a.** 15.50    **b.** 69.30

**24. a.**

| Score | f |
|---|---|
| 12 | 1 |
| 11 | 2 |
| 10 | 4 |
| 9 | 7 |
| 8 | 9 |
| 7 | 13 |
| 6 | 15 |
| 5 | 11 |
| 4 | 10 |
| 3 | 6 |
| 2 | 5 |
| 1 | 1 |
| 0 | 1 |

**d.** 27.06, 96.47

## CHAPTER 4

**13.** All the scores must have the same value.

**16. a.** $\overline{X} = 3.56$, Mdn = 3, mode = 2
**c.** $\overline{X} = 3.03$, Mdn = 2.70, no mode

**17. a.** $\overline{X}_{orig.} = 4.00$, $\overline{X}_{new} = 6.00$, $\overline{X}_{new} = \overline{X}_{orig.} + a$
**b.** $\overline{X}_{orig.} = 4.00$, $\overline{X}_{new} = 2.00$, $\overline{X}_{new} = \overline{X}_{orig.} - a$
**c.** $\overline{X}_{orig.} = 4.00$, $\overline{X}_{new} = 8.00$, $\overline{X}_{new} = a\overline{X}_{orig.}$
**d.** $\overline{X}_{orig.} = 4.00$, $\overline{X}_{new} = 2.00$, $\overline{X}_{new} = \overline{X}_{orig.}/a$

**18. a.** 72.00 **b.** 72

**19. a.** 68.83 **b.** 64.5

**20. a.** 2.93 **b.** 2.8

**21. a.** the mean, because there are no extreme scores **b.** the mean, again because there are no extreme scores **c.** the median, because the distribution contains an extreme score (25)

**22. a.** positively skewed **b.** negatively skewed **c.** symmetrical

**23. a.** $\overline{X} = 2.54$ hours per day
**b.** Mdn = 2.7 hours per day
**c.** mode = 0 hours per day

**25. a.** $\overline{X} = 15.44$ **b.** Mdn = 14 **c.** There is no mode.

**26.** 197.44

**27. a.** range = 6, $s = 2.04$, $s^2 = 4.14$
**c.** range = 9.1, $s = 3.64$, $s^2 = 13.24$

**29.** 4.00 minutes

**30.** 7.17 months

**31. a.** $s_{orig.} = 2.12$, $s_{new} = 2.12$, $s_{new} = s_{orig.}$
**b.** $s_{orig.} = 2.12$, $s_{new} = 2.12$, $s_{new} = s_{orig.}$
**c.** $s_{orig.} = 2.12$, $s_{new} = 4.24$, $s_{new} = as_{orig.}$
**d.** $s_{orig.} = 2.12$, $s_{new} = 1.06$, $s_{new} = s_{orig.}/a$

**32. a.** 4.50 **b.** 5 **c.** 7 **d.** 7 **e.** 2.67 **f.** 7.14

**33.** Distribution *b* is most variable, followed by distribution *a* and then distribution *c*. For distribution *b*, $s = 11.37$; for distribution *a*, $s = 3.16$; and for distribution *c*, $s = 0$.

**34. a.** $s = 1.86$ **b.** 11.96, Because the standard deviation is sensitive to extreme scores and 35 is an extreme score

**35. a.** $\overline{X} = 7.90$ **b.** 8 **c.** 8 **d.** 15 **e.** 4.89 **f.** 23.88

**36. a.** 347.50 **b.** 335 **c.** There is no mode. **d.** 220 **e.** 87.28 **f.** 7617.50

**37. a.** 22.67 **b.** 21.50 **c.** There is no mode. **d.** 22 **e.** 7.80 **f.** 60.78

**38. a.** $\overline{X} + a$ **b.** $\overline{X} - a$ **c.** $a\overline{X}$ **d.** $\overline{X}/a$

**39. a.** *s* stays the same. **b.** *s* stays the same. **c.** *s* is multiplied by *a*. **d.** *s* is divided by *a*.

**40. a.** 2.67, 3.33, 6.33, 4.67, 6.67, 4.67, 3.00, 4.00, 7.67, 6.67 **b.** 3.00, 2.00, 8.00, 6.00, 6.00, 4.00, 2.00, 3.00, 8.00, 7.00 **c.** Expect more variability in the medians. **d.** *s*(medians) = 2.38, *s*(means) = 1.76

## CHAPTER 5

**8. a.**

| Raw Score | z Score |
|-----------|---------|
| 10 | −1.41 |
| 12 | −0.94 |
| 16 | 0.00 |
| 18 | 0.47 |
| 19 | 0.71 |
| 21 | 1.18 |

**b.** mean = 0.00, standard deviation = 1.00

**9. a.**

| Raw Score | z Score |
|-----------|---------|
| 10 | −1.55 |
| 12 | −1.03 |
| 16 | 0.00 |
| 18 | 0.52 |
| 19 | 0.77 |
| 21 | 1.29 |

**b.** mean = 0.00, standard deviation = 1.00

**10. a.** 1.14 **b.** −0.86 **c.** 1.86 **d.** 0.00 **e.** 1.00 **f.** −1.00

**11. a.** 50.00% **b.** 15.87% **c.** 6.18% **d.** 2.02% **e.** 0.07% **f.** 32.64%

**12. a.** 34.13% **b.** 34.13% **c.** 49.04% **d.** 49.87% **e.** 0.00% **f.** 25.17% **g.** 26.73%

**13. a.** 0.00 **b.** 1.96 **c.** 1.64 **d.** 0.52 **e.** −0.84 **f.** −1.28

**15. a.** statistics **b.** 92.07

**16. a.** 3.75% **b.** 99.81% **c.** 98.54% **d.** 12.97% **e.** 3.95 kilograms **f.** 3.64 **g.** 13,623

**17. a.** 95.99% **b.** 99.45% **c.** 15.87% **d.** 4.36% **e.** 50.00%

**18. a.** 16.85% **b.** 0.99% **c.** 59.87% **d.** 97.50% **e.** 50.00%

**19. a.** 51.57% **b.** 34.71% **c.** 23.28%

**20. a.**

| Distance | z Score |
|----------|---------|
| 30 | −1.88 |
| 31 | −1.50 |
| 32 | −1.13 |
| 33 | −0.75 |
| 34 | −0.38 |
| 35 | 0.00 |
| 36 | 0.38 |
| 37 | 0.75 |
| 38 | 1.13 |

**b.** and **c.**

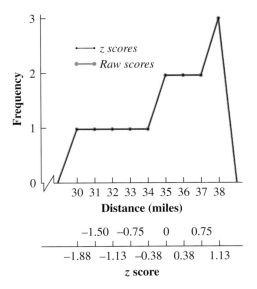

**d.** The $z$ distribution is not normally shaped. The $z$ distribution takes the same shape as the distribution of raw scores. In this problem, the raw scores are not normally shaped. Therefore, the $z$ distribution will not be normally shaped either. **e.** mean = 0.00, standard deviation = 1.00

**21. a.** 92.36%   **b.** 55.04%   **c.** 96.78%   **d.** $99.04

**22.** business

**23.** Rebecca did better on exam 2. Maurice did better on exam 1.

**24.** 93.64

## CHAPTER 6

**3. a.** linear, perfect positive   **b.** curvilinear, perfect   **c.** linear, imperfect negative   **d.** curvilinear, imperfect   **e.** linear, perfect negative   **f.** linear, imperfect positive

**14. a.** For set A, $r = 1.00$; for set B, $r = 0.11$; for set C, $r = -1.00$.   **b.** same value as in part **a.**   **c.** The $r$ values are the same.   **d.** The $r$ values remain the same.   **e.** The $r$ values do not change if a constant is subtracted from the raw scores or if the raw scores are divided by a constant. The value of $r$ does not change when the scale is altered by adding or subtracting a constant to it, nor does $r$ change if the scale is transformed by multiplying or dividing by a constant.

**16. b.** $r = 0.79$

**17. b.** $r = 0.68$   **c.** 0.03. Decreasing the range produced a decrease in $r$.   **d.** $r^2 = 0.46$. If illness is causally related to smoking, $r^2$ allows us to evaluate how important a factor smoking is in producing illness.

**18. b.** $r = 0.98$.   **c.** Yes, this is a reliable test because $r^2 = 0.95$. Almost all of the variability of the scores on the second administration can be accounted for by the scores on the first administration.

**19. a.** $r = 0.85$   **b.** $r_s = 0.86$

**20. b.** $r = -0.06$   **e.** $r = 0.93$

**21. b.** $r = 0.95$

**22. a.** negative   **b.** $r = -0.56$

**23. a.** $r_s = 0.85$   **b.** For the paper and pencil test and psychiatrist A, $r_s = 0.73$; for the paper and pencil test and psychiatrist B, $r_s = 0.79$.

**24. b.** $r = 0.59$   **d.** $r = 0.91$   **e.** Yes, test 2, because $r^2$ accounts for 82.4% of the variability in work performance. Although there are no doubt other factors operating, this test appears to offer a good adjunct to the interview. Test 1 does not do nearly as well.

## CHAPTER 7

**10. b.** The relationship is negative, imperfect, and linear.   **c.** $r = -0.56$   **d.** $Y' = -0.513X + 24.964$; negative, because the relationship is negative   **f.** 13.16

**11.** No. A scatter plot of the paired scores reveals that there is a perfect relationship between length of left index finger and weight. Thus, Mr. Clairvoyant can exactly predict my weight having measured the length of my left index finger.   **b.** $Y' = 7.5X + 37$   **c.** 79.75

**12. b.** The relationship is negative, imperfect, and linear. **c.** $r = -0.69$ **d.** $Y' = -1.429X + 125.883$; negative, because the relationship is negative **f.** 71.60 **g.** 10.87

**13. a.** $Y' = 10.828X + 11.660$ **b.** $196,000 **c.** Technically, the relationship holds only within the range of the base data. It may be that if a lot more money is spent, the relationship would change such that no additional profit or even loss is the result. Of course, the manager could experiment by "testing the waters" (e.g., by spending $25,000 on advertising to see whether the relationship still holds at that level).

**14. a.** Yes, $r = 0.85$ **b.** % games won = 5.557(tenure) + 34.592 **c.** 73.49%

**15. a.** $Y' = -1.212X + 131.77$ **b.** $130.96 **c.** 17.31

**16. a.** $Y' = 4.213X + 91.652$ **b.** 123.25

**17. a.** $Y' = 0.857X + 17.894$ **b.** 32.46

**18. a.** $Y' = -0.075X + 6.489$ **b.** 3.28

**19.** $R^2 = 85.3\%$, $r^2 = 82.4\%$; using test 1 doesn't seem worth the extra work.

## CHAPTER 8

**9.** a, c, e

**10.** a, c, d, e

**11.** a, c

**12. a.** 2 to 3 **b.** 0.6000 **c.** 0.4000

**13. a.** 0.0192 **b.** 0.0769 **c.** 0.3077 **d.** 0.5385

**15. a.** 0.4000 **b.** 0.0640 **c.** 0.0350 **d.** 0.2818

**16. a.** 0.4000 **b.** 0.0491 **c.** 0.0409 **d.** 0.2702

**17. a.** 0.0029 **b.** 0.0087 **c.** 0.0554

**18.** 0.0001

**19.** 0.0238

**20. a.** 0.0687 **b.** 0.5581 **c.** 0.2005

**21.** 0.1479

**22.** 0.00000001

**23. a.** 0.1429 **b.** 0.1648 **c.** 0.0116

**25. a.** 0.0301 **b.** 0.6268 **c.** 0.0301

**26. a.** 0.0192 **b.** 0.9525 **c.** 0.1949

**28. a.** 0.0146 **b.** 0.9233 **c.** 0.0344

**29. a.** 0.0764 **b.** 0.4983 **c.** 0.0021

**30. a.** 0.0400 **b.** 0.1200 **c.** 0.0400

## CHAPTER 9

**3.** 0.90

**4. a.** 0.0369 **b.** $6P^5Q$ **c.** 0.0369 (The answers are the same.)

**5. a.** 0.0161 **b.** 0.0031 **c.** 0.0192 **d.** 0.0384

**6. a.** 0.0407 **b.** 0.0475 **c.** 0.0475

**7. a.** 0.1369 **b.** 0.2060 **c.** 0.2060

**8. a.** 0.0020 **b.** 0.0899 **c.** 0.1798

**10.** 0.3487

**11.** 0.0037

**13.** 0.0039

**14. a.** 0.0001 **b.** 0.0113

**15. a.** 32 **b.** 37

**16. a.** 0.0001 **b.** 0.4437 **c.** 0.1382 **d.** 0.5563

**17. a.** 0.0039 **b.** 0.3164 **c.** 0.6836

**18. a.** 0.0576 **b.** 0.0001 **c.** 0.0100 **d.** 0.8059

**19. a.** 0.0000 **b.** 0.0013

**20. a.** 0.0098 **b.** 1

## CHAPTER 10

**10. a.** The alternative hypothesis states that the new teaching method increases the amount learned. **b.** The null hypothesis states that the two methods are equal in the amount of material learned or the old method does better. **c.** $p$(14 or more pluses) = 0.0577. Since $0.0577 > 0.05$, you retain $H_0$. You cannot conclude that the new method is better. **d.** You may be making a Type II error, retaining $H_0$ if it is false. **e.** The results apply to the eighth-grade students in the school district at the time of the experiment.

**11. a.** The alternative hypothesis states that increases in the level of angiotensin II will produce change in thirst level. **b.** The null hypothesis states that increases in the level of angiotensin II will not have any effect on thirst. **c.** $p$(0, 1, 2, 14, 15, or 16 pluses) = 0.0040. Since $0.0040 < 0.05$, you reject $H_0$. Increases in the level of angiotensin II appear to increase thirst. **d.** You may be making a Type I error, rejecting $H_0$ if it is true. **e.** The results apply to the rats living in the vivarium of the drug company at the time of the experiment.

**12. a.** The alternative hypothesis states that using Very Bright toothpaste instead of Brand X results in brighter teeth.    **b.** The null hypothesis states that Very Bright and Brand X toothpastes are equal in their brightening effects or Brand X is better.    **c.** $p$(7 or more pluses) = 0.1719. Since 0.1719 > 0.05, you retain $H_0$. You cannot conclude that Very Bright is better.    **d.** You may be making a Type II error, retaining $H_0$ if it is false.    **e.** The results apply to the employees of the Pasadena plant at the time of the experiment.

**13. a.** The alternative hypothesis states that acupuncture affects pain tolerance.    **b.** The null hypothesis states that acupuncture has no effect on pain tolerance.    **c.** $p$(0, 1, 2, 3, 12, 13, 14, or 15 pluses) = 0.0352. Since 0.0352 < 0.05, you reject $H_0$ and conclude that acupuncture affects pain tolerance. It appears to increase pain tolerance.    **d.** You may have made a Type I error, rejecting $H_0$ if it is true.    **e.** The conclusion applies to the large pool of university undergraduate volunteers.

## CHAPTER 11

**8.** For $P_{real}$ = 0.80, power = 0.8042, and beta = 0.1958.

**9.** power = 0.8417, beta = 0.1583

**10.** power = 0.1493

**11.** Power = 0.0955, and beta = 0.9045. No, it is not legitimate to conclude that stimulus isolation had no effect on depression. That conclusion is the same thing as concluding that $H_0$ is true. Of course, we cannot prove $H_0$ is true from the data of an experiment. Particularly, in this case, the preceding analysis shows that this experiment has a low probability of detecting a real but weak effect (power = 0.0955). This experiment is insensitive to weak effects, and therefore, we cannot conclude stimulus isolation has no effect just because the results of the experiment were not significant.

**12.** Power = 0.1268, and beta = 0.8732. No, we cannot conclude that the TV program has no effect on violence in teenagers. We cannot prove $H_0$ is true. In this experiment, the power to detect a moderate effect was quite low (0.1268). It could very well be true that the program really does increase violence, but due to lack of sufficient power, we failed to detect it.

## CHAPTER 12

**17. a.** The sampling distribution of the mean is given here:

| $(\overline{X})$ | $p(\overline{X})$ |
| --- | --- |
| 7.0 | 0.04 |
| 6.5 | 0.08 |
| 6.0 | 0.12 |
| 5.5 | 0.16 |
| 5.0 | 0.20 |
| 4.5 | 0.16 |
| 4.0 | 0.12 |
| 3.5 | 0.08 |
| 3.0 | 0.04 |

**b.** From the population raw scores, $\mu$ = 5.00, and from the 25 sample means, $\mu_{\overline{X}}$ = 5.00. Therefore, $\mu_{\overline{X}} = \mu$.    **c.** From the 25 sample means, $\sigma_{\overline{X}}$ = 1.00. From the population raw scores, $\sigma$ = 1.41. Thus, $\sigma_{\overline{X}} = \sigma/\sqrt{N} = 1.41/\sqrt{2} = 1.41/1.41 = 1.00$.

**18. a.** The distribution is normally shaped; $\mu_{\overline{X}}$ = 80, $\sigma_{\overline{X}}$ = 2.00.    **b.** The distribution is normally shaped; $\mu_{\overline{X}}$ = 80, $\sigma_{\overline{X}}$ = 1.35.    **c.** The distribution is normally shaped; $\mu_{\overline{X}}$ = 80, $\sigma_{\overline{X}}$ = 1.13.    **d.** As $N$ increases, $\mu_{\overline{X}}$ stays the same but $\sigma_{\overline{X}}$ decreases.

**19.** $z_{obt}$ = 3.16, and $z_{crit}$ = ±1.96. Since $|z_{obt}|$ > 1.96, we reject $H_0$. It is not reasonable to consider the sample a random sample from a population with $\mu$ = 60 and $\sigma$ = 10.

**20. a.** $z_{obt}$ = −2.05, and $z_{crit}$ = −2.33. Since $|z_{obt}|$ < 2.33, we can't reject the hypothesis that the sample is a random sample from a population with $\mu$ = 22 and $\sigma$ = 8.    **b.** power = 0.1685    **c.** power = 0.5675    **d.** $N$ = 161 (actually gives a power = 0.7995)

**22.** $z_{obt}$ = 4.03, and $z_{crit}$ = 1.645. Since $|z_{obt}|$ > 1.645, reject $H_0$ and conclude that this year's class is superior to the previous ones.

**23.** $z_{obt}$ = 1.56, and $z_{crit}$ = 1.645. Since $|z_{obt}|$ < 1.645, retain $H_0$. We cannot conclude that the new engine saves gas.

**24. a.** power = 0.5871    **b.** power = 0.9750    **c.** $N$ = 91 (rounded to nearest integer)

**25.** $z_{obt}$ = 4.35, and $z_{crit}$ = 1.645. Since $|z_{obt}|$ > 1.645, reject $H_0$ and conclude that exercise appears to slow down the "aging" process, at least as measured by maximum oxygen consumption.

## CHAPTER 13

11. $t_{obt} = -1.37$, and $t_{crit}$ with 29 df $= \pm 2.756$. Since $|t_{obt}| < 2.756$, we retain $H_0$. It is reasonable to consider the sample a random sample from a population with $\mu = 85$.

12. $t_{obt} = 3.08$, and $t_{crit}$ with 28 df $= 2.467$. Since $t_{obt} > 2.467$, we can reject $H_0$, which specifies that the sample is a random sample from a population with a mean $\leq 72$. Therefore, we can accept the hypothesis that the sample is a random sample from a population with a mean $> 72$.

13. $t_{obt} = 2.08$, and $t_{crit}$ with 21 df $= 1.721$. Since $|t_{obt}| > 1.721$, we reject $H_0$. It is not reasonable to consider the sample a random sample from a normal population with $\mu = 38$.

14.

| | 95% | 99% |
|---|---|---|
| **a.** | 21.68–28.32 | 20.39–29.61 |
| **c.** | 28.28–32.92 | 27.45–33.75 |
| **d.** | 22.76–27.24 | 21.98–28.02 |

Increasing $N$ decreases the width of confidence interval.

15. $t_{obt} = -1.57$, and $t_{crit} = \pm 2.093$. Since $|t_{obt}| < 2.093$, you fail to reject $H_0$ and therefore cannot conclude that the student's technique shortens the duration of stay. The difference in conclusions is due to the greater sensitivity of the $z$ test.

17. **a.** 18.34–21.66      **b.** 17.79–22.21

18. **a.** $z_{obt} = 3.96$, and $z_{crit} = 1.645$. Since $|z_{obt}| > 1.645$, we reject $H_0$ and conclude that the amount of smoking in women appears to have increased in recent years. The professor was correct.      **b.** $t_{obt} = 3.67$, and $t_{crit} = 1.658$. Reject $H_0$; same conclusion as in part **a**.

19. $t_{obt} = 4.32$, and $t_{crit}$ with 7 df $= \pm 2.365$. Since $|t_{obt}| > 2.365$, we reject $H_0$ and conclude that the drug affects short-term memory. It appears to improve it.

20. $t_{obt} = 1.65$, and $t_{crit} = 1.796$. Since $|t_{obt}| < 1.796$, we retain $H_0$. We cannot conclude that middle-age men employed by the corporation have become fatter.

21. $t_{obt} = 0.98$, and $t_{crit} = \pm 2.262$. Since $|t_{obt}| < 2.262$, we retain $H_0$. From these data, we cannot con-

clude that the graduates of the local business school get higher salaries for their first jobs than the national average.

22. **a.** 109.09–140.91      **b.** 103.14–146.86

23. **b.** $r = 0.63$.
    **c.** Yes, reject $H_0$ since $r_{crit} = 0.5760$.

24. **a.** $r = 0.98$.
    **b.** Yes, reject $H_0$ since $r_{crit} = 0.6319$.

25. **a.** $r_{obt} = 0.630$      **b.** $r_{crit} = 0.7067$. Retain $H_0$; correlation is not significant. No, $\rho$ may actually differ from 0, and power may be too low to detect it.      **c.** $r_{crit} = 0.4438$. Reject $H_0$; correlation is significant. Power is greater with $N = 20$.

26. $r_{crit} = 0.5139$. Reject $H_0$; correlation is significant.

## CHAPTER 14

15. **a.** The alternative hypothesis states that memory for pictures is superior to memory for words. $\mu_1 > \mu_2$.      **b.** The null hypothesis states that memory for pictures is not superior to memory for words. $\mu_1 \leq \mu_2$.      **c.** $t_{obt} = 1.86$, and $t_{crit} = 1.761$. Since $|t_{obt}| > 1.761$, you reject $H_0$ and conclude that memory for pictures is superior to memory for words.      **d.** $\hat{\omega}^2 = 0.134$, accounting for 13.4% of the variance. No, using Cohen's criterion, the effect is a medium one.

17. $t_{obt} = 4.10$, and $t_{crit} = \pm 2.145$. Since $|t_{obt}| > 2.145$, you reject $H_0$ and conclude that newspaper advertising really does make a difference. It appears to increase cosmetics sales.

18. **a.** $t_{obt} = 4.09$, and $t_{crit} = \pm 2.306$. Since $|t_{obt}| > 2.306$, you reject $H_0$ and conclude that biofeedback training reduces tension headaches.      **b.** If the sampling distribution of $D$ is not normally distributed, you cannot use the $t$ test. However, you can use the sign test, because it does not assume anything about the shape of the scores. By using the sign test, $p(0, 1, 8, \text{or } 9 \text{ pluses}) = 0.0392$. Since $0.0392 < 0.05$, you reject $H_0$, as before.

19. $t_{obt} = 3.50$, and $t_{crit} = \pm 2.306$. Since $|t_{obt}| > 2.306$, we reject $H_0$ and conclude that other factors, such as attention, have an effect on tension headaches. They appear to decrease them.

20. $t_{obt} = 2.83$, and $t_{crit} = \pm 2.120$. Since $|t_{obt}| > 2.120$, you reject $H_0$ and conclude that the decrease obtained with biofeedback training cannot be attributed solely to other factors, such as attention. The biofeedback training itself has an effect on tension headaches. It appears to decrease them.

21. $t_{obt} = 0.60$, and $t_{crit} = \pm 2.228$. Since $|t_{obt}| < 2.228$, we retain $H_0$. Based on these data, we cannot conclude that hiring part-time workers instead of full-time workers will affect productivity.

22. **a.** $t_{obt} = -2.83$, and $t_{crit} = \pm 2.131$. Since $|t_{obt}| > 2.131$, you reject $H_0$ and conclude that the clinician was right. Depression interferes with sleep. **b.** $\hat{\omega}^2 = 0.219$, accounting for 21.9% of the variance. Yes, the effect is a large one.

23. $t_{obt} = 2.11$ and $t_{crit} = \pm 2.201$. Since $|t_{obt}| < 2.201$, you retain $H_0$. You cannot conclude that early exposure to schooling affects IQ.

24. **a.** $t_{obt} = 2.23$, and $t_{crit} = \pm 2.074$. Since $|t_{obt}| > 2.074$, you reject $H_0$ and conclude that sleep has an effect on memory. It appears to improve it. **b.** 95% confidence interval = 0.13–3.70. Reject $H_0$. Size of effect = 0.13–3.70 more objects. **c.** 99% confidence interval = $-0.51$–4.34. We are 99% confident that the interval $-0.51$–4.34 contains the real effect. Since 0 is one of those values, we conclude by failing to reject $H_0$. We cannot affirm $H_1$. The results of the experiment are not significant at $\alpha = 0.01$. Check it out for yourself, using the null-hypothesis approach and $\alpha = 0.01$.

25. $t_{obt} = 5.36$, and $t_{crit} = \pm 3.106$. Since $|t_{obt}| > 3.106$, you reject $H_0$ and conclude that high levels of curiosity in childhood appears to effect IQ. It seems to increase it.

26. $t_{obt} = 1.98$, and $t_{crit} = \pm 2.160$. Since $|t_{obt}| < 2.160$, you retain $H_0$ and conclude that the data do not allow the conclusion that women and men differ in recalling emotional events. However, you also note that $t_{obt}$ is very close to $t_{crit}$. With only 15 subjects, power is probably low and it may be premature to give up on $H_1$.

27. $t_{obt} = 3.28$, and $t_{crit} = \pm 2.101$. Since $|t_{obt}| > 2.101$, you reject $H_0$ and conclude that women and men differ in recalling emotional events. Women appear to recall emotional events better than men. Increasing the power of the experiment allowed $H_0$ to be rejected.

28. $t_{obt} = 3.14$, and $t_{crit} = \pm 2.179$. Since $|t_{obt}| > 2.179$, you reject $H_0$ and conclude that natural lighting affects student learning. It appears to improve it.

## CHAPTER 15

10. **a.** $F_{crit} = 3.63$ **b.** $F_{crit} = 2.86$ **c.** $F_{crit} = 4.38$

11. $F_{obt} = 8.64$, and $t_{obt}$ from Practice Problem 14.2 $= -2.94$. Therefore, $F = t^2$.

18. **a.**

| Source | SS | df | $s^2$ | $F_{obt}$ |
|---|---|---|---|---|
| Between | 1253.68 | 3 | 417.89 | 4.00 |
| Within | 3762.72 | 36 | 104.52 | |
| Total | 5016.40 | 39 | | |

**b.** 4 **c.** 10 **d.** 2.86 **e.** Yes, the effect is significant.

19. **a.** and **b.**

| Source | SS | df | $s^2$ | $F_{obt}$ |
|---|---|---|---|---|
| Between | 23.444 | 2 | 11.722 | 4.77 |
| Within | 36.833 | 15 | 2.456 | |
| Total | 60.278 | 17 | | |

$F_{crit} = 3.68$. Since $F_{obt} > 3.68$, you reject $H_0$ and conclude that at least one of the cereals differs in sugar content.

**c.**

| | Breakfast Cereal | | |
|---|---|---|---|
| Condition | A | B | C |
| $\overline{X}$ | 3.000 | 5.333 | 5.500 |
| $\overline{X}_i - \overline{X}_j$ | | 2.333 | 2.500 |
| | | | 0.167 |
| $Q_{obt}$ | | 3.65 | 3.91 |
| | | | 0.26 |
| $Q_{crit} = 3.67$ | | | |

Reject $H_0$ for the comparison between cereals A and C. Cereal A is significantly lower in sugar content than cereal C. Retain $H_0$ for all other comparisons.

**d.**

| | Breakfast Cereal | | |
|---|---|---|---|
| Condition | A | B | C |
| $\overline{X}$ | 3.000 | 5.333 | 5.500 |
| $\overline{X}_i - \overline{X}_j$ | | 2.333 | 2.500 |
| | | | 0.167 |
| $Q_{obt}$ | | 3.65 | 3.91 |
| | | | 0.26 |
| $Q_{crit}$ | | 3.01 | 3.67 |
| | | | 3.01 |

Reject $H_0$ for the comparison of cereals B and C. Cereal A is significantly lower in sugar content than cereals B and C. Retain $H_0$ for the comparison between cereals B and C. We cannot conclude that they differ in sugar content.

**21. a.**

| Source | SS | df | $s^2$ | $F_{obt}$ |
|---|---|---|---|---|
| Between | 108.333 | 3 | 36.111 | 5.40 |
| Within | 133.667 | 20 | 6.683 | |
| Total | 242.000 | 23 | | |

$F_{crit} = 3.10$. Since $F_{obt} > 3.10$, we reject $H_0$ and conclude that age affects memory.
**b.** $\hat{\omega}^2 = 0.355$ accounting for 35.5% of the variance.
**c.** $\eta^2 = 0.448$, accounting for 44.8% of the variance.
**e.** $t_{obt} = 3.13$, and $t_{crit} = \pm 2.086$. Reject $H_0$ and conclude that the 60-year-old group is significantly different from the 30-year-old group.

**f.**

| Condition | 60 yr | 30 yr | 50 yr | 40 yr |
|---|---|---|---|---|
| $\overline{X}$ | 8.833 | 13.500 | 13.667 | 14.000 |
| $\overline{X}_i - \overline{X}_j$ | | 4.667 | 4.834 | 5.167 |
| | | | 0.167 | 0.500 |
| | | | | 0.333 |
| $Q_{obt}$ | | 4.42 | 4.58 | 4.90 |
| | | | 0.16 | 0.47 |
| | | | | 0.32 |
| $Q_{crit}$ | | 2.95 | 3.58 | 3.96 |
| | | | 2.95 | 3.58 |
| | | | | 2.95 |

Reject $H_0$ for all comparisons involving the 60-year-old group. This age group is significantly different from each of the other age groups. Retain $H_0$ for all other comparisons. It appears that memory begins to deteriorate somewhere between the ages of 50 and 60.

**22. a.**

| Source | SS | df | $s^2$ | $F_{obt}$ |
|---|---|---|---|---|
| Between | 100.167 | 2 | 50.084 | 4.87 |
| Within | 92.500 | 9 | 10.278 | |
| Total | 192.667 | 11 | | |

$F_{crit} = 4.26$. Since $F_{obt} > 4.26$, we reject $H_0$ and conclude that the batteries of at least one manufacturer differ regarding useful life.

**b.**

| Condition | Battery | | |
|---|---|---|---|
| | C | B | A |
| $\overline{X}$ | 49.5 | 49.75 | 56.75 |
| $\overline{X}_i - \overline{X}_j$ | | 0.25 | 7.25 |
| | | | 7.00 |
| $Q_{obt}$ | | 0.17 | 5.04 |
| | | | 4.87 |
| $Q_{crit} = 3.95$ | | | |

Reject $H_0$ for the comparisons between the batteries of manufacturer A and the other two manufacturers. Retain $H_0$ for the comparison between the batteries of manufacturers B and C. The batteries of manufacturer A have significantly longer life. On this basis, you recommend them over the batteries made by manufacturers B and C.

**23. a.**

| Source | SS | df | $s^2$ | $F_{obt}$ |
|---|---|---|---|---|
| Between | 221.6 | 3 | 73.867 | 22.77 |
| Within | 116.8 | 36 | 3.244 | |
| Total | 338.4 | 39 | | |

$F_{crit} = 2.86$. Since $F_{obt} > 2.86$, we reject $H_0$ and conclude that hormone X affects sexual behavior.
**b.** $\hat{\omega}^2 = 0.620$, accounting for 62.0% of the variance.
**c.** $t_{obt} = 7.20$, and $t_{crit} = \pm 2.029$. Reject $H_0$ and conclude that concentration 3 of hormone X significantly increases the number of matings.

**d.**

| Condition | Concentration of Hormone X | | | |
|---|---|---|---|---|
| | 0 | 1 | 2 | 3 |
| $\overline{X}$ | 5.6 | 5.8 | 8.4 | 11.4 |
| $\overline{X}_i - \overline{X}_j$ | | 0.2 | 2.8 | 5.8 |
| | | | 2.6 | 5.6 |
| | | | | 3.0 |
| $Q_{obt}$ | | 0.35 | 4.92 | 10.18 |
| | | | 4.56 | 9.83 |
| | | | | 5.27 |
| $Q_{crit}$ | | 2.87 | 3.46 | 3.81 |
| | | | 2.87 | 3.46 |
| | | | | 2.87 |

Reject $H_0$ for all comparisons except between the placebo and concentration 1. Thus, increasing the concentration of hormone X increases the number of matings. The failure to find a significant effect for concentration 1 was probably due to low power to detect a difference for this low level of concentration. Alternatively, there may be a threshold that must be exceeded before the hormone becomes effective.

**e.**

| Condition | Concentration of Hormone X | | | |
|---|---|---|---|---|
| | *0* | *1* | *2* | *3* |
| $\overline{X}$ | 5.6 | 5.8 | 8.4 | 11.4 |
| $\overline{X}_i - \overline{X}_j$ | | 0.2 | 2.8 | 5.8 |
| | | | 2.6 | 5.6 |
| | | | | 3.0 |
| $Q_{obt}$ | | 0.35 | 4.92 | 10.18 |
| | | | 4.56 | 9.83 |
| | | | | 5.27 |
| $Q_{crit} = 3.81$ | | | | |

Same conclusion as in part **d.**

**24. a.** The treatments are equally effective; $\mu_1 = \mu_2 = \mu_3 = \mu_4$

**b.**

| Source | SS | df | $s^2$ | $F_{obt}$ |
|---|---|---|---|---|
| Between | 762.88 | 3 | 254.29 | 15.92 |
| Within | 574.90 | 36 | 15.97 | |
| Total | 1337.78 | | | |

$F_{obt} = 15.92$, $F_{crit} = 2.86$; reject $H_0$, affirm $H_1$.

**c.**

| Condition | Treatments | | | |
|---|---|---|---|---|
| | *1* | *2* | *3* | *4* |
| $\overline{X}$ | 22.80 | 11.60 | 16.00 | 20.90 |
| $\overline{X}_i - \overline{X}_j$ | | 11.20 | 6.80 | 1.90 |
| | | | 4.40 | 9.30 |
| | | | | 4.90 |
| $Q_{obt}$ | | 8.86 | 5.38 | 1.50 |
| | | | 3.48 | 7.36 |
| | | | | 3.88 |
| $Q_{crit} = 3.79$ | | | | |

Reject $H_0$ for cognitive restructuring (2) and assertiveness training (3) versus the placebo control group (1). Retain $H_0$ for exercise/nutrition (4) versus the placebo group (1). Reject $H_0$ for cognitive restructuring (2) and assertiveness training (3) versus exercise/nutrition (4). Retain $H_0$ for cognitive restructuring (2) versus assertiveness training (3).

**25. a.**

| Source | SS | df | $s^2$ | $F_{obt}$ |
|---|---|---|---|---|
| Between | 80.11 | 2 | 40.06 | 8.54 |
| Within | 70.33 | 15 | 4.69 | |
| Total | 150.44 | 17 | | |

**a.** $F_{obt} = 8.54$, $F_{crit} = 3.68$, reject $H_0$ and conclude that acupuncture in combination with counseling affects cocaine addition. They appear to help reduce cocaine addiction.

**b.** $\hat{\omega}^2 = 0.46$

**c.** $\eta^2 = 0.53$

**26. a.**

| Source | SS | df | $s^2$ | $F_{obt}$ |
|---|---|---|---|---|
| Between | 16.53 | 2 | 8.27 | 0.12 |
| Within | 795.20 | 12 | 66.27 | |
| Total | 811.73 | 14 | | |

$F_{obt} = 0.12$, $F_{crit} = 3.88$, retain $H_0$ and conclude that the data do not support the hypothesis that any of the tests are different in difficulty. Note, since $F_{obt} < 1.00$, you could have concluded to retain $H_0$ without determining $F_{crit}$.

## CHAPTER 16

**11. a.** The different types of intervening material have the same effect on recall. $\mu_{a_1} = \mu_{a_2}$. The different amounts of repetition have the same effect on recall. $\mu_{b_1} = \mu_{b_2} = \mu_{b_3}$. There is no interaction between the number of repetitions and the type of intervening material in their effects on recall. With any main effects removed, $\mu_{a_1b_1} = \mu_{a_1b_2} = \mu_{a_1b_3} = \mu_{a_2b_1} = \mu_{a_2b_2} = \mu_{a_2b_3}$.

**b.**

| Source | SS | df | $s^2$ | $F_{obt}$ | $F_{crit}$ |
|---|---|---|---|---|---|
| Rows (intervening material) | 121.000 | 1 | 121.000 | 41.41 | 4.17 |
| Columns (number of repetitions) | 176.167 | 2 | 88.084 | 30.14 | 3.32 |
| Rows × columns | 35.166 | 2 | 17.583 | 6.02 | 3.32 |
| Within-cells | 87.667 | 30 | 2.922 | | |
| Total | 420.000 | 35 | | | |

Since in all cases $F_{obt} > F_{crit}$, $H_0$ is rejected for both main effects and the interaction effect. From the pattern of cell means, it is apparent that (1) increasing the number of repetitions increases recall; (2) using nonsense syllable pairs for intervening material decreases recall; and (3) there is an interaction such that the lower the number of repetitions, the greater the difference in effect between the two types of material.

13. **a.** For the concentrations administered, previous use of Drowson has no effect on its effectiveness. $\mu_{a_1} = \mu_{a_2}$. There is no difference between the placebo and the minimum recommended dosage of Drowson in their effects on insomnia. $\mu_{b_1} = \mu_{b_2}$. There is no interaction between the previous use of Drowson and the effect on insomnia of the two concentrations of Drowson. With any main effects removed, $\mu_{a_1b_1} = \mu_{a_1b_2} = \mu_{a_2b_1} = \mu_{a_2b_2}$.

**b.**

| Source | SS | df | $s^2$ | $F_{obt}$ | $F_{crit}$ |
|---|---|---|---|---|---|
| Rows (previous use) | 639.031 | 1 | 639.031 | 11.63 | 4.20 |
| Columns (concentration) | 979.031 | 1 | 979.031 | 17.82 | 4.20 |
| Rows × columns | 472.782 | 1 | 472.782 | 8.61 | 4.20 |
| Within-cells | 1538.125 | 28 | 54.933 | | |
| Total | 3628.969 | 31 | | | |

Since $F_{obt} > F_{crit}$ for each comparison, $H_0$ is rejected for both main effects and the interaction effect. From the pattern of cell means, it is apparent that Drowson promotes faster sleep onset in subjects who have had no previous use of the drug. However, the effect, if any, is much lower in chronic users, indicating that a tolerance to Drowson develops with chronic use.

## CHAPTER 17

16. $\chi^2_{obt} = 0.80$. Since $\chi^2_{crit} = 3.841$, we retain $H_0$. These data do not support the hypothesis that the prevailing view is fat people are more jolly.

17. $\chi^2_{obt} = 21.63$. Since $\chi^2_{crit} = 3.841$, we reject $H_0$ and conclude that big-city and small-town dwellers differ in their helpfulness to strangers. Converting the frequencies to proportions, we can see that the small-town dwellers were more helpful.

19. $\chi^2_{obt} = 13.28$, and $\chi^2_{crit} = 7.815$. Since $\chi^2_{obt} > 7.815$, we reject $H_0$ and conclude that the wrappings differ in their effect on sales. The manager should choose wrapping C.

20. $H_{obt} = 7.34$. Since $H_{crit} = 5.991$, we reject $H_0$ and conclude that at least one of the occupations differs from at least one of the others.

21. $\chi^2_{obt} = 3.00$. Since $\chi^2_{crit} = 3.841$, we retain $H_0$. Based on these data, we cannot conclude that church attendance and educational level are related.

22. $\chi^2_{obt} = 3.56$, and $\chi^2_{crit} = 9.488$. Since $\chi^2_{obt} < 9.488$, we retain $H_0$. Yes, the advertising is misleading because the data do not show a significant difference among brands.

23. $\chi^2_{obt} = 12.73$, and $\chi^2_{crit} = 5.991$. Since $\chi^2_{obt} > 5.991$, we reject $H_0$ and conclude that there is a relationship between the amount of contact white housewives have with blacks and changes in their attitudes toward blacks. The contact in the integrated housing projects appears to have had a positive effect on the attitude of the white housewives.

24. $H_{obt} = 0.69$. Since $H_{crit} = 9.210$, we must retain $H_0$. We cannot conclude that birth order affects assertiveness.

25. $\chi^2_{obt} = 29.57$, and $\chi^2_{crit} = 9.488$. Since $\chi^2_{obt} > 9.488$, we reject $H_0$. There is a relationship between gambling behavior and the different

motives. Those high in power motivation appear to take the high risks more often. Most of the subjects with high power motivation placed high-risk bets, whereas the majority of those high in achievement motivation opted for medium-risk bets and the majority of those high in affiliation motivation chose the low-risk bets. These results are consistent with the views that (1) people with high power motivation will take high risks to achieve the attention and status that accompany such risk, (2) people high in achievement motivation will take medium risks to maximize the probability of having a sense of personal accomplishment, and (3) people with high affiliation motivation will take low risks to avoid competition and maximize the sense of belongingness.

**26.** $T_{obt} = 15$, and $T_{crit} = 17$. Since $T_{obt} < 17$, you reject $H_0$ and conclude that the film promotes more favorable attitudes toward major oil companies.

**27.** $T_{obt} = 1$, and $T_{crit} = 5$. Since $T_{obt} < 5$, you reject $H_0$ and conclude that biofeedback to relax frontalis muscle affects tension headaches. It appears to decrease them.

**28.** $T_{obt} = 14$, and $T_{crit} = 3$. Since $T_{obt} > 3$, you retain $H_0$. You cannot conclude that the pill affects blood pressure.

**30. a.** The alternative hypothesis states that FSH increases the singing rate in captive male cotingas.    **b.** The null hypothesis states that FSH does not increase the singing rate of captive male cotingas.    **c.** $U_{obt} = 15.5$, $U'_{obt} = 64.5$. Since $U_{obt} < 20$, you reject $H_0$ and conclude that FSH appears to increase the singing rate of male cotingas.

**31. a.** The alternative hypothesis states that right-handed and left-handed people differ in spatial ability.    **b.** The null hypothesis states that right-handed people and left-handed people are equal in spatial ability.    **c.** $U_{obt} = 20.5$, $U'_{obt} = 69.5$. Since $U_{obt} > 20$, you retain $H_0$. You cannot conclude that right-handed and left-handed people differ in spatial ability.

**32. a.** The alternative hypothesis states that hypnosis is more effective than the standard treatment in reducing test anxiety.    **b.** The null hypothesis states that hypnosis is not more effective than the standard treatment in reducing test anxiety.    **c.** $U_{obt} = 31$, $U'_{obt} = 90$. Since $U_{obt} < 34$, you reject $H_0$ and conclude that hypnosis is more effective than the standard treatment in reducing test anxiety.

**33.** $H_{obt} = 10.16$, $H_{crit} = 5.991$. Reject $H_0$; affirm $H_1$. Sleep deprivation has an effect on the ability to maintain sustained attention.

**34.** $\chi^2_{obt} = 6.454$, $\chi^2_{crit} = 3.841$. Reject $H_0$; affirm $H_1$. There is a relationship between cohabitation and divorce. There is a significantly higher proportion of divorced couples among those that cohabited before marriage than among those that did not cohabit before marriage.

**35.** $\chi^2_{obt} = 19.82$. Since $\chi^2_{crit} = 5.991$, you reject $H_0$ and conclude that there is a relationship between gender and attitude regarding government involvement in citizen affairs. Men appear to favor a small role, whereas women seem to favor a large one.

**36.** $\chi^2_{obt} = 0.51$. Since $\chi^2_{crit} = 3.841$, retain $H_0$ and conclude that even though overall, black patients received fewer angiograms than white patients, physician racial bias does not appear to have contributed to this phenomenon.

**37.** $\chi^2_{obt} = 5.00$. Since $\chi^2_{crit} = 3.841$, you reject $H_0$ and conclude that the number of single-father homes has changed. It appears to have increased.

**38.** $\chi^2_{obt} = 8.333$. Since $\chi^2_{crit} = 5.991$, reject $H_0$ and conclude that cigarette smoking affects gender of offspring. It appears that when both parents smoke at least one pack of cigarettes a day, their offspring are more likely to be girls.

**39.** $\chi^2_{obt} = 80.00$. Since $\chi^2_{crit} = 5.991$, reject $H_0$ and conclude that the survey does reveal a reliable preference. Women undergraduates at the university seem to prefer soccer.

**40. a.** $\chi^2_{obt} = 79.23$. Since $\chi^2_{crit} = 3.841$, reject $H_0$ and conclude that the September 11, 2001, attacks affected religious sentiment. They appeared to increase it.    **b.** $\chi^2_{obt} = 0.69$. Since $\chi^2_{crit} = 3.841$, retain $H_0$; the data do not support the hypothesis that increased religious sentiment was still evident 1-year after the attacks. It appears that religious sentiment has returned to preattack levels.

## CHAPTER 18

**11. a.** The alternative hypothesis states that the four brands of scotch whiskey are not equal in preference among the scotch drinkers in New York City. **b.** The null hypothesis states that the four brands of scotch whiskey are equal in preference among the scotch drinkers in New York City.

**c.** $\chi^2_{obt} = 2.72$, $\chi^2_{crit} = 7.815$. Since $\chi^2_{obt} < 7.815$, retain $H_0$. You cannot conclude that the scotch drinkers in New York City differ in their preference for the four brands of scotch whiskey.

12. **a.** The alternative hypothesis states that ACTH affects avoidance learning. $\mu_1 \neq \mu_2$. **b.** The null hypothesis states that ACTH has no effect on avoidance learning. $\mu_1 = \mu_2$. **c.** $t_{obt} = -3.24$, $t_{crit} = \pm 2.878$. Since $|t_{obt}| > 2.878$, reject $H_0$ and conclude that ACTH has an effect on avoidance learning. It appears to facilitate avoidance learning. **d.** You may be making a Type I error. The null hypothesis may be true and it has been rejected. **e.** These results apply to the 100-day-old male rats living in the university vivarium at the time the sample was selected. **f.** $\hat{\omega}^2 = 0.321$, accounting for 32.1% of the variability.

14. **a.** Exogenous thyroxin has no effect on activity. Therefore, $\mu_1 = \mu_2 = \mu_3 = \mu_4$.

**b.**

| Source | SS | df | $s^2$ | $F_{obt}$ |
|---|---|---|---|---|
| Between | 260.9 | 3 | 86.967 | 33.96 |
| Within | 92.2 | 36 | 2.561 | |
| Total | 353.1 | 39 | | |

$F_{crit} = 2.86$. Since $F_{obt} > 2.86$, you reject $H_0$ and conclude that exogenous thyroxin affects activity level. **c.** $\hat{\omega}^2 = 0.712$, accounting for 71.2% of the variability. **d.** $t_{obt} = 8.94$, and $t_{crit} = \pm 2.029$. Reject $H_0$ and conclude that there is a significant difference between high amounts of exogenous thyroxin and saline on activity level. Exogenous thyroxin appears to increase activity level.

**e.**

| | Amount of Thyroxin | | | |
|---|---|---|---|---|
| Condition | Zero, 1 | Low, 2 | Moderate, 3 | High, 4 |
| $\overline{X}$ | 3.0 | 3.9 | 7.1 | 9.4 |
| $\overline{X}_i - \overline{X}_j$ | | 0.9 | 4.1 | 6.4 |
| | | | 3.2 | 5.5 |
| $Q_{obt}$ | | 1.78 | 8.10 | 12.65 |
| | | | 6.32 | 10.87 |
| | | | | 4.54 |

$Q_{crit} = 3.81$

Reject $H_0$ for all comparisons except between groups 1 and 2. Increases in the amount of exogenous thyroxin produce significantly higher levels of activity. The failure to find a significant difference between groups 1 and 2 is probably due to low power. Alternatively, there may be a threshold that must be exceeded before exogenous thyroxin becomes effective.

15. **a.** The alternative hypothesis states that dieting plus exercise is more effective in producing weight loss than dieting alone. **b.** The null hypothesis states that dieting plus exercise is not more effective in producing weight loss than dieting alone. **c.** Since it is not valid to use the $t$ test for correlated groups, the next most sensitive test is the Wilcoxon signed ranks test. $T_{obt} = 10.5$, and $T_{crit} = 17$. Since $T_{obt} < 17$, reject $H_0$ and conclude that dieting plus exercise is more effective than dieting alone in producing weight loss.

16. **a.** sign test **b.** $p(8, 9, 10, 11, $ or $12$ pluses$) = 0.1937$. Since the obtained probability is greater than alpha, you retain $H_0$. **c.** The Wilcoxon signed ranks test is more powerful than the sign test. **d.** Power $= 0.3907$, beta $= 0.6093$

17. **a.** The null hypothesis states that there is no relationship between gender and time-of-day preference for having intercourse. **b.** $\chi^2_{obt} = 2.14$, $\chi^2_{crit} = 3.841$. Since $\chi^2_{obt} < 3.841$, retain $H_0$. You cannot conclude that there is a relationship between gender and time-of-day preference for having intercourse.

18. **a.** The null hypothesis states that food deprivation (hunger) has no effect on the number of food-related objects reported. Therefore, $\mu_1 = \mu_2 = \mu_3$.

**b.**

| Source | SS | df | $s^2$ | $F_{obt}$ |
|---|---|---|---|---|
| Between | 256.083 | 2 | 128.042 | 11.85 |
| Within | 226.875 | 21 | 10.804 | |
| Total | 482.958 | 23 | | |

$F_{crit} = 3.47$. Since $F_{obt} > 3.47$, reject $H_0$ and conclude that food deprivation has an effect on the number of food-related objects reported.

**c.** $\hat{\omega}^2 = 0.47$

**d.** $\eta^2 = 0.53$

**e.**

| Condition | Food Deprivation | | |
|---|---|---|---|
| | *1 hr,*<br>*1* | *4 hrs,*<br>*2* | *12 hrs,*<br>*3* |
| $\overline{X}$ | 4.750 | 8.625 | 12.750 |
| $\overline{X}_i - \overline{X}_j$ | | 3.875 | 8.000 |
| | | | 4.125 |
| $Q_{obt}$ | | 3.33 | 6.88 |
| | | | 3.55 |
| $Q_{crit}$ | | 2.94 | 3.57 |
| | | | 2.94 |

Reject $H_0$ for all comparisons. All three conditions differ significantly from each other. Increasing the number of hours from eating results in an increase in the number of food-related objects reported.

**19.** $t_{obt} = 10.78$, and $t_{crit} = 2.500$. Since $|t_{obt}| > 2.500$, reject $H_0$. Yes, the engineer is correct in her opinion. The new process results in significantly longer life for TV picture tubes.

**20. a.** The alternative hypothesis states that alcohol has an effect on aggressiveness, $\mu_1 \neq \mu_2$. **b.** The null hypothesis states that alcohol has no effect on aggressiveness. $\mu_1 = \mu_2$. **c.** $t_{obt} = -3.93$, and $t_{crit} = \pm 2.131$. Since $|t_{obt}| > 2.131$, reject $H_0$ and conclude that alcohol has an effect on aggressiveness. It appears to increase aggressiveness.

**21. a.** $r_{obt} = 0.70$. **b.** $r_{crit} = 0.5139$. Since $|r_{obt}| > 0.5139$, reject $H_0$. The correlation is significant. **c.** $r^2 = 0.48$. **d.** Yes, although it is clear that there is still a lot of variability unaccounted for.

**22. a.** The alternative hypothesis states that smoking affects heart rate. $\mu_D \neq 0$. **b.** The null hypothesis states that smoking has no effect on heart rate. $\mu_D = 0$. **c.** $t_{obt} = -3.40$, and $t_{crit} = \pm 2.262$. Since $|t_{obt}| > 2.262$, reject $H_0$ and conclude that smoking affects heart rate. It appears to increase heart rate.

**23. a.** The null hypothesis states that there is no relationship between the occupations and the course of action that is favored. **b.** $\chi^2_{obt} = 13.79$, and $\chi^2_{crit} = 5.991$. Since $\chi^2_{obt} > 5.991$, reject $H_0$ and conclude that there is a relationship between the occupations and the course of action that is favored. From the proportions shown in the sample, business is in favor of letting the oil price rise, the homemakers favor gasoline rationing, and labor is fairly evenly divided.

**24. a.** The null hypothesis states that men and women do not differ in logical reasoning ability. **b.** $U_{obt} = 25.5$, $U'_{obt} = 37.5$, and $U_{crit} = 12$. Since $U_{obt} > 12$, retain $H_0$. You cannot conclude that men and women differ in logical reasoning ability. **c.** You may be making a Type II error. The null hypothesis may be false and you retained it.

**25.** 24.58–33.42

**26. a.** The null hypothesis states that Hispanics are not underrepresented in high school teachers in the part of the country the researcher lives. Therefore, the sample is a random sample from a population of high school teachers where the percentage of Hispanic teachers equals 22%. **b.** $\chi^2_{obt} = 12.59$, and $\chi^2_{crit} = 3.841$. Since $\chi^2_{obt} > 3.841$, reject $H_0$. It appears that high school teachers are underrepresented in the geographical locale studied.

**27.** $H_{obt} = 1.46$. Since $H_{crit} = 5.991$, we must retain $H_0$. We cannot conclude that physical science professors are more authoritarian than social science professors.

**28.**

| Source | SS | df | $s^2$ | $F_{obt}$ | $F_{crit}$ |
|---|---|---|---|---|---|
| Rows (time) | 17.633 | 1 | 17.633 | 11.76[*] | 4.26 |
| Columns (activity) | 28.800 | 2 | 14.400 | 9.60[*] | 3.40 |
| Rows × columns | 0.267 | 2 | 0.133 | 0.09 | 3.40 |
| Within-cells | 36.000 | 24 | 1.500 | | |
| Total | 82.700 | 29 | | | |

[*]Since $F_{obt} > F_{crit}$ for the rows and columns effects, we reject $H_0$ for the main effects. We must retain $H_0$ for the interaction effect. It appears that performance is affected differently by at least one of the activity conditions and by the time of day when it is conducted. It appears that napping and afternoon produce superior performance.

# Tables

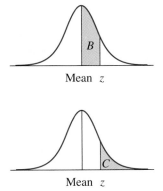

Mean  $z$

Mean  $z$

*Column A* gives the positive $z$ score.

*Column B* gives the area between the mean and $z$. Since the curve is symmetrical, areas for negative $z$ scores are the same as for positive ones.

*Column C* gives the area that is beyond $z$.

**t a b l e  A**  Areas under the normal curve

| $z$ A | Area Between Mean and $z$ B | Area Beyond $z$ C | $z$ A | Area Between Mean and $z$ B | Area Beyond $z$ C |
|---|---|---|---|---|---|
| 0.00 | .0000 | .5000 | 0.45 | .1736 | .3264 |
| 0.01 | .0040 | .4960 | 0.46 | .1772 | .3228 |
| 0.02 | .0080 | .4920 | 0.47 | .1808 | .3192 |
| 0.03 | .0120 | .4880 | 0.48 | .1844 | .3156 |
| 0.04 | .0160 | .4840 | 0.49 | .1879 | .3121 |
| 0.05 | .0199 | .4801 | 0.50 | .1915 | .3085 |
| 0.06 | .0239 | .4761 | 0.51 | .1950 | .3050 |
| 0.07 | .0279 | .4721 | 0.52 | .1985 | .3015 |
| 0.08 | .0319 | .4681 | 0.53 | .2019 | .2981 |
| 0.09 | .0359 | .4641 | 0.54 | .2054 | .2946 |
| 0.10 | .0398 | .4602 | 0.55 | .2088 | .2912 |
| 0.11 | .0438 | .4562 | 0.56 | .2123 | .2877 |
| 0.12 | .0478 | .4522 | 0.57 | .2157 | .2843 |
| 0.13 | .0517 | .4483 | 0.58 | .2190 | .2810 |
| 0.14 | .0557 | .4443 | 0.59 | .2224 | .2776 |
| 0.15 | .0596 | .4404 | 0.60 | .2257 | .2743 |
| 0.16 | .0636 | .4364 | 0.61 | .2291 | .2709 |
| 0.17 | .0675 | .4325 | 0.62 | .2324 | .2676 |
| 0.18 | .0714 | .4286 | 0.63 | .2357 | .2643 |
| 0.19 | .0753 | .4247 | 0.64 | .2389 | .2611 |
| 0.20 | .0793 | .4207 | 0.65 | .2422 | .2578 |
| 0.21 | .0832 | .4168 | 0.66 | .2454 | .2546 |
| 0.22 | .0871 | .4129 | 0.67 | .2486 | .2514 |
| 0.23 | .0910 | .4090 | 0.68 | .2517 | .2483 |
| 0.24 | .0948 | .4052 | 0.69 | .2549 | .2451 |
| 0.25 | .0987 | .4013 | 0.70 | .2580 | .2420 |
| 0.26 | .1026 | .3974 | 0.71 | .2611 | .2389 |
| 0.27 | .1064 | .3936 | 0.72 | .2642 | .2358 |
| 0.28 | .1103 | .3897 | 0.73 | .2673 | .2327 |
| 0.29 | .1141 | .3859 | 0.74 | .2704 | .2296 |
| 0.30 | .1179 | .3821 | 0.75 | .2734 | .2266 |
| 0.31 | .1217 | .3783 | 0.76 | .2764 | .2236 |
| 0.32 | .1255 | .3745 | 0.77 | .2794 | .2206 |
| 0.33 | .1293 | .3707 | 0.78 | .2823 | .2177 |
| 0.34 | .1331 | .3669 | 0.79 | .2852 | .2148 |
| 0.35 | .1368 | .3632 | 0.80 | .2881 | .2119 |
| 0.36 | .1406 | .3594 | 0.81 | .2910 | .2090 |
| 0.37 | .1443 | .3557 | 0.82 | .2939 | .2061 |
| 0.38 | .1480 | .3520 | 0.83 | .2967 | .2033 |
| 0.39 | .1517 | .3483 | 0.84 | .2995 | .2005 |
| 0.40 | .1554 | .3446 | 0.85 | .3023 | .1977 |
| 0.41 | .1591 | .3409 | 0.86 | .3051 | .1949 |
| 0.42 | .1628 | .3372 | 0.87 | .3078 | .1922 |
| 0.43 | .1664 | .3336 | 0.88 | .3106 | .1894 |
| 0.44 | .1700 | .3300 | 0.89 | .3133 | .1867 |

(*continued*)

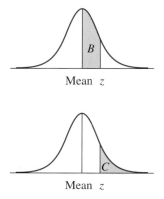

Mean   z

Mean   z

*Column A* gives the positive *z* score.

*Column B* gives the area between the mean and *z*. Since the curve is symmetrical, areas for negative *z* scores are the same as for positive ones.

*Column C* gives the area that is beyond *z*.

**table A**   (*continued*)

| z A | Area Between Mean and z B | Area Beyond z C | z A | Area Between Mean and z B | Area Beyond z C |
|---|---|---|---|---|---|
| 0.90 | .3159 | .1841 | 1.35 | .4115 | .0885 |
| 0.91 | .3186 | .1814 | 1.36 | .4131 | .0869 |
| 0.92 | .3212 | .1788 | 1.37 | .4147 | .0853 |
| 0.93 | .3238 | .1762 | 1.38 | .4162 | .0838 |
| 0.94 | .3264 | .1736 | 1.39 | .4177 | .0823 |
| 0.95 | .3289 | .1711 | 1.40 | .4192 | .0808 |
| 0.96 | .3315 | .1685 | 1.41 | .4207 | .0793 |
| 0.97 | .3340 | .1660 | 1.42 | .4222 | .0778 |
| 0.98 | .3365 | .1635 | 1.43 | .4236 | .0764 |
| 0.99 | .3389 | .1611 | 1.44 | .4251 | .0749 |
| 1.00 | .3413 | .1587 | 1.45 | .4265 | .0735 |
| 1.01 | .3438 | .1562 | 1.46 | .4279 | .0721 |
| 1.02 | .3461 | .1539 | 1.47 | .4292 | .0708 |
| 1.03 | .3485 | .1515 | 1.48 | .4306 | .0694 |
| 1.04 | .3508 | .1492 | 1.49 | .4319 | .0681 |
| 1.05 | .3531 | .1469 | 1.50 | .4332 | .0668 |
| 1.06 | .3554 | .1446 | 1.51 | .4345 | .0655 |
| 1.07 | .3577 | .1423 | 1.52 | .4357 | .0643 |
| 1.08 | .3599 | .1401 | 1.53 | .4370 | .0630 |
| 1.09 | .3621 | .1379 | 1.54 | .4382 | .0618 |
| 1.10 | .3643 | .1357 | 1.55 | .4394 | .0606 |
| 1.11 | .3665 | .1335 | 1.56 | .4406 | .0594 |
| 1.12 | .3686 | .1314 | 1.57 | .4418 | .0582 |
| 1.13 | .3708 | .1292 | 1.58 | .4429 | .0571 |
| 1.14 | .3729 | .1271 | 1.59 | .4441 | .0559 |
| 1.15 | .3749 | .1251 | 1.60 | .4452 | .0548 |
| 1.16 | .3770 | .1230 | 1.61 | .4463 | .0537 |
| 1.17 | .3790 | .1210 | 1.62 | .4474 | .0526 |
| 1.18 | .3810 | .1190 | 1.63 | .4484 | .0516 |
| 1.19 | .3830 | .1170 | 1.64 | .4495 | .0505 |
| 1.20 | .3849 | .1151 | 1.65 | .4505 | .0495 |
| 1.21 | .3869 | .1131 | 1.66 | .4515 | .0485 |
| 1.22 | .3888 | .1112 | 1.67 | .4525 | .0475 |
| 1.23 | .3907 | .1093 | 1.68 | .4535 | .0465 |
| 1.24 | .3925 | .1075 | 1.69 | .4545 | .0455 |
| 1.25 | .3944 | .1056 | 1.70 | .4554 | .0446 |
| 1.26 | .3962 | .1038 | 1.71 | .4564 | .0436 |
| 1.27 | .3980 | .1020 | 1.72 | .4573 | .0427 |
| 1.28 | .3997 | .1003 | 1.73 | .4582 | .0418 |
| 1.29 | .4015 | .0985 | 1.74 | .4591 | .0409 |
| 1.30 | .4032 | .0968 | 1.75 | .4599 | .0401 |
| 1.31 | .4049 | .0951 | 1.76 | .4608 | .0392 |
| 1.32 | .4066 | .0934 | 1.77 | .4616 | .0384 |
| 1.33 | .4082 | .0918 | 1.78 | .4625 | .0375 |
| 1.34 | .4099 | .0901 | 1.79 | .4633 | .0367 |

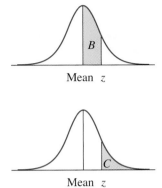

Mean  *z*

Mean  *z*

*Column A* gives the positive *z* score.

*Column B* gives the area between the mean and *z*. Since the curve is symmetrical, areas for negative *z* scores are the same as for positive ones.

*Column C* gives the area that is beyond *z*.

**t a b l e  A**  Areas under the normal curve  (*continued*)

| *z* A | Area Between Mean and *z* B | Area Beyond *z* C | *z* A | Area Between Mean and *z* B | Area Beyond *z* C |
|---|---|---|---|---|---|
| 1.80 | .4641 | .0359 | 2.25 | .4878 | .0122 |
| 1.81 | .4649 | .0351 | 2.26 | .4881 | .0119 |
| 1.82 | .4656 | .0344 | 2.27 | .4884 | .0116 |
| 1.83 | .4664 | .0336 | 2.28 | .4887 | .0113 |
| 1.84 | .4671 | .0329 | 2.29 | .4890 | .0110 |
| 1.85 | .4678 | .0322 | 2.30 | .4893 | .0107 |
| 1.86 | .4686 | .0314 | 2.31 | .4896 | .0104 |
| 1.87 | .4693 | .0307 | 2.32 | .4898 | .0102 |
| 1.88 | .4699 | .0301 | 2.33 | .4901 | .0099 |
| 1.89 | .4706 | .0294 | 2.34 | .4904 | .0096 |
| 1.90 | .4713 | .0287 | 2.35 | .4906 | .0094 |
| 1.91 | .4719 | .0281 | 2.36 | .4909 | .0091 |
| 1.92 | .4726 | .0274 | 2.37 | .4911 | .0089 |
| 1.93 | .4732 | .0268 | 2.38 | .4913 | .0087 |
| 1.94 | .4738 | .0262 | 2.39 | .4916 | .0084 |
| 1.95 | .4744 | .0256 | 2.40 | .4918 | .0082 |
| 1.96 | .4750 | .0250 | 2.41 | .4920 | .0080 |
| 1.97 | .4756 | .0244 | 2.42 | .4922 | .0078 |
| 1.98 | .4761 | .0239 | 2.43 | .4925 | .0075 |
| 1.99 | .4767 | .0233 | 2.44 | .4927 | .0073 |
| 2.00 | .4772 | .0228 | 2.45 | .4929 | .0071 |
| 2.01 | .4778 | .0222 | 2.46 | .4931 | .0069 |
| 2.02 | .4783 | .0217 | 2.47 | .4932 | .0068 |
| 2.03 | .4788 | .0212 | 2.48 | .4934 | .0066 |
| 2.04 | .4793 | .0207 | 2.49 | .4936 | .0064 |
| 2.05 | .4798 | .0202 | 2.50 | .4938 | .0062 |
| 2.06 | .4803 | .0197 | 2.51 | .4940 | .0060 |
| 2.07 | .4808 | .0192 | 2.52 | .4941 | .0059 |
| 2.08 | .4812 | .0188 | 2.53 | .4943 | .0057 |
| 2.09 | .4817 | .0183 | 2.54 | .4945 | .0055 |
| 2.10 | .4821 | .0179 | 2.55 | .4946 | .0054 |
| 2.11 | .4826 | .0174 | 2.56 | .4948 | .0052 |
| 2.12 | .4830 | .0170 | 2.57 | .4949 | .0051 |
| 2.13 | .4834 | .0166 | 2.58 | .4951 | .0049 |
| 2.14 | .4838 | .0162 | 2.59 | .4952 | .0048 |
| 2.15 | .4842 | .0158 | 2.60 | .4953 | .0047 |
| 2.16 | .4846 | .0154 | 2.61 | .4955 | .0045 |
| 2.17 | .4850 | .0150 | 2.62 | .4956 | .0044 |
| 2.18 | .4854 | .0146 | 2.63 | .4957 | .0043 |
| 2.19 | .4857 | .0143 | 2.64 | .4959 | .0041 |
| 2.20 | .4861 | .0139 | 2.65 | .4960 | .0040 |
| 2.21 | .4864 | .0136 | 2.66 | .4961 | .0039 |
| 2.22 | .4868 | .0132 | 2.67 | .4962 | .0038 |
| 2.23 | .4871 | .0129 | 2.68 | .4963 | .0037 |
| 2.24 | .4875 | .0125 | 2.69 | .4964 | .0036 |

(*continued*)

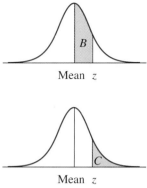

Mean *z*

Mean *z*

*Column A* gives the positive *z* score.

*Column B* gives the area between the mean and *z*. Since the curve is symmetrical, areas for negative *z* scores are the same as for positive ones.

*Column C* gives the area that is beyond *z*.

**t a b l e  A**  (*continued*)

| z A | Area Between Mean and z B | Area Beyond z C | z A | Area Between Mean and z B | Area Beyond z C |
|---|---|---|---|---|---|
| 2.70 | .4965 | .0035 | 3.00 | .4987 | .0013 |
| 2.71 | .4966 | .0034 | 3.01 | .4987 | .0013 |
| 2.72 | .4967 | .0033 | 3.02 | .4987 | .0013 |
| 2.73 | .4968 | .0032 | 3.03 | .4988 | .0012 |
| 2.74 | .4969 | .0031 | 3.04 | .4988 | .0012 |
| 2.75 | .4970 | .0030 | 3.05 | .4989 | .0011 |
| 2.76 | .4971 | .0029 | 3.06 | .4989 | .0011 |
| 2.77 | .4972 | .0028 | 3.07 | .4989 | .0011 |
| 2.78 | .4973 | .0027 | 3.08 | .4990 | .0010 |
| 2.79 | .4974 | .0026 | 3.09 | .4990 | .0010 |
| 2.80 | .4974 | .0026 | 3.10 | .4990 | .0010 |
| 2.81 | .4975 | .0025 | 3.11 | .4991 | .0009 |
| 2.82 | .4976 | .0024 | 3.12 | .4991 | .0009 |
| 2.83 | .4977 | .0023 | 3.13 | .4991 | .0009 |
| 2.84 | .4977 | .0023 | 3.14 | .4992 | .0008 |
| 2.85 | .4978 | .0022 | 3.15 | .4992 | .0008 |
| 2.86 | .4979 | .0021 | 3.16 | .4992 | .0008 |
| 2.87 | .4979 | .0021 | 3.17 | .4992 | .0008 |
| 2.88 | .4980 | .0020 | 3.18 | .4993 | .0007 |
| 2.89 | .4981 | .0019 | 3.19 | .4993 | .0007 |
| 2.90 | .4981 | .0019 | 3.20 | .4993 | .0007 |
| 2.91 | .4982 | .0018 | 3.21 | .4993 | .0007 |
| 2.92 | .4982 | .0018 | 3.22 | .4994 | .0006 |
| 2.93 | .4983 | .0017 | 3.23 | .4994 | .0006 |
| 2.94 | .4984 | .0016 | 3.24 | .4994 | .0006 |
| 2.95 | .4984 | .0016 | 3.30 | .4995 | .0005 |
| 2.96 | .4985 | .0015 | 3.40 | .4997 | .0003 |
| 2.97 | .4985 | .0015 | 3.50 | .4998 | .0002 |
| 2.98 | .4986 | .0014 | 3.60 | .4998 | .0002 |
| 2.99 | .4986 | .0014 | 3.70 | .4999 | .0001 |

t a b l e   B    Binomial distribution

| N | No. of P or Q Events | .05 | .10 | .15 | .20 | .25 | .30 | .35 | .40 | .45 | .50 |
|---|---|---|---|---|---|---|---|---|---|---|---|
| 1 | 0 | .9500 | .9000 | .8500 | .8000 | .7500 | .7000 | .6500 | .6000 | .5500 | .5000 |
|   | 1 | .0500 | .1000 | .1500 | .2000 | .2500 | .3000 | .3500 | .4000 | .4500 | .5000 |
| 2 | 0 | .9025 | .8100 | .7225 | .6400 | .5625 | .4900 | .4225 | .3600 | .3025 | .2500 |
|   | 1 | .0950 | .1800 | .2550 | .3200 | .3750 | .4200 | .4550 | .4800 | .4950 | .5000 |
|   | 2 | .0025 | .0100 | .0225 | .0400 | .0625 | .0900 | .1225 | .1600 | .2025 | .2500 |
| 3 | 0 | .8574 | .7290 | .6141 | .5120 | .4219 | .3430 | .2746 | .2160 | .1664 | .1250 |
|   | 1 | .1354 | .2430 | .3251 | .3840 | .4219 | .4410 | .4436 | .4320 | .4084 | .3750 |
|   | 2 | .0071 | .0270 | .0574 | .0960 | .1406 | .1890 | .2389 | .2880 | .3341 | .3750 |
|   | 3 | .0001 | .0010 | .0034 | .0080 | .0156 | .0270 | .0429 | .0640 | .0911 | .1250 |
| 4 | 0 | .8145 | .6561 | .5220 | .4096 | .3164 | .2401 | .1785 | .1296 | .0915 | .0625 |
|   | 1 | .1715 | .2916 | .3685 | .4096 | .4219 | .4116 | .3845 | .3456 | .2995 | .2500 |
|   | 2 | .0135 | .0486 | .0975 | .1536 | .2109 | .2646 | .3105 | .3456 | .3675 | .3750 |
|   | 3 | .0005 | .0036 | .0115 | .0256 | .0469 | .0756 | .1115 | .1536 | .2005 | .2500 |
|   | 4 | .0000 | .0001 | .0005 | .0016 | .0039 | .0081 | .0150 | .0256 | .0410 | .0625 |
| 5 | 0 | .7738 | .5905 | .4437 | .3277 | .2373 | .1681 | .1160 | .0778 | .0503 | .0312 |
|   | 1 | .2036 | .3280 | .3915 | .4096 | .3955 | .3602 | .3124 | .2592 | .2059 | .1562 |
|   | 2 | .0214 | .0729 | .1382 | .2048 | .2637 | .3087 | .3364 | .3456 | .3369 | .3125 |
|   | 3 | .0011 | .0081 | .0244 | .0512 | .0879 | .1323 | .1811 | .2304 | .2757 | .3125 |
|   | 4 | .0000 | .0004 | .0022 | .0064 | .0146 | .0284 | .0488 | .0768 | .1128 | .1562 |
|   | 5 | .0000 | .0000 | .0001 | .0003 | .0010 | .0024 | .0053 | .0102 | .0185 | .0312 |
| 6 | 0 | .7351 | .5314 | .3771 | .2621 | .1780 | .1176 | .0754 | .0467 | .0277 | .0156 |
|   | 1 | .2321 | .3543 | .3993 | .3932 | .3560 | .3025 | .2437 | .1866 | .1359 | .0938 |
|   | 2 | .0305 | .0984 | .1762 | .2458 | .2966 | .3241 | .3280 | .3110 | .2780 | .2344 |
|   | 3 | .0021 | .0146 | .0415 | .0819 | .1318 | .1852 | .2355 | .2765 | .3032 | .3125 |
|   | 4 | .0001 | .0012 | .0055 | .0154 | .0330 | .0595 | .0951 | .1382 | .1861 | .2344 |
|   | 5 | .0000 | .0001 | .0004 | .0015 | .0044 | .0102 | .0205 | .0369 | .0609 | .0938 |
|   | 6 | .0000 | .0000 | .0000 | .0001 | .0002 | .0007 | .0018 | .0041 | .0083 | .0156 |
| 7 | 0 | .6983 | .4783 | .3206 | .2097 | .1335 | .0824 | .0490 | .0280 | .0152 | .0078 |
|   | 1 | .2573 | .3720 | .3960 | .3670 | .3115 | .2471 | .1848 | .1306 | .0872 | .0547 |
|   | 2 | .0406 | .1240 | .2097 | .2753 | .3115 | .3177 | .2985 | .2613 | .2140 | .1641 |
|   | 3 | .0036 | .0230 | .0617 | .1147 | .1730 | .2269 | .2679 | .2903 | .2918 | .2734 |
|   | 4 | .0002 | .0026 | .0109 | .0287 | .0577 | .0972 | .1442 | .1935 | .2388 | .2734 |
|   | 5 | .0000 | .0002 | .0012 | .0043 | .0115 | .0250 | .0466 | .0774 | .1172 | .1641 |
|   | 6 | .0000 | .0000 | .0001 | .0004 | .0013 | .0036 | .0084 | .0172 | .0320 | .0547 |
|   | 7 | .0000 | .0000 | .0000 | .0000 | .0001 | .0002 | .0006 | .0016 | .0037 | .0078 |
| 8 | 0 | .6634 | .4305 | .2725 | .1678 | .1001 | .0576 | .0319 | .0168 | .0084 | .0039 |
|   | 1 | .2793 | .3826 | .3847 | .3355 | .2670 | .1977 | .1373 | .0896 | .0548 | .0312 |
|   | 2 | .0515 | .1488 | .2376 | .2936 | .3115 | .2965 | .2587 | .2090 | .1569 | .1094 |
|   | 3 | .0054 | .0331 | .0839 | .1468 | .2076 | .2541 | .2786 | .2787 | .2568 | .2188 |
|   | 4 | .0004 | .0046 | .0185 | .0459 | .0865 | .1361 | .1875 | .2322 | .2627 | .2734 |
|   | 5 | .0000 | .0004 | .0026 | .0092 | .0231 | .0467 | .0808 | .1239 | .1719 | .2188 |
|   | 6 | .0000 | .0000 | .0002 | .0011 | .0038 | .0100 | .0217 | .0413 | .0703 | .1094 |
|   | 7 | .0000 | .0000 | .0000 | .0001 | .0004 | .0012 | .0033 | .0079 | .0164 | .0312 |
|   | 8 | .0000 | .0000 | .0000 | .0000 | .0000 | .0001 | .0002 | .0007 | .0017 | .0039 |

(*continued*)

table B  (continued)

| N | No. of P or Q Events | .05 | .10 | .15 | .20 | .25 | .30 | .35 | .40 | .45 | .50 |
|---|---|---|---|---|---|---|---|---|---|---|---|
| 9 | 0 | .6302 | .3874 | .2316 | .1342 | .0751 | .0404 | .0277 | .0101 | .0046 | .0020 |
|   | 1 | .2985 | .3874 | .3679 | .3020 | .2253 | .1556 | .1004 | .0605 | .0339 | .0176 |
|   | 2 | .0629 | .1722 | .2597 | .3020 | .3003 | .2668 | .2162 | .1612 | .1110 | .0703 |
|   | 3 | .0077 | .0446 | .1069 | .1762 | .2336 | .2668 | .2716 | .2508 | .2119 | .1641 |
|   | 4 | .0006 | .0074 | .0283 | .0661 | .1168 | .1715 | .2194 | .2508 | .2600 | .2461 |
|   | 5 | .0000 | .0008 | .0050 | .0165 | .0389 | .0735 | .1181 | .1672 | .2128 | .2461 |
|   | 6 | .0000 | .0001 | .0006 | .0028 | .0087 | .0210 | .0424 | .0743 | .1160 | .1641 |
|   | 7 | .0000 | .0000 | .0000 | .0003 | .0012 | .0039 | .0098 | .0212 | .0407 | .0703 |
|   | 8 | .0000 | .0000 | .0000 | .0000 | .0001 | .0004 | .0013 | .0035 | .0083 | .0176 |
|   | 9 | .0000 | .0000 | .0000 | .0000 | .0000 | .0000 | .0001 | .0003 | .0008 | .0020 |
| 10 | 0 | .5987 | .3487 | .1969 | .1074 | .0563 | .0282 | .0135 | .0060 | .0025 | .0010 |
|   | 1 | .3151 | .3874 | .3474 | .2684 | .1877 | .1211 | .0725 | .0403 | .0207 | .0098 |
|   | 2 | .0746 | .1937 | .2759 | .3020 | .2816 | .2335 | .1757 | .1209 | .0763 | .0439 |
|   | 3 | .0105 | .0574 | .1298 | .2013 | .2503 | .2668 | .2522 | .2150 | .1665 | .1172 |
|   | 4 | .0010 | .0112 | .0401 | .0881 | .1460 | .2001 | .2377 | .2508 | .2384 | .2051 |
|   | 5 | .0001 | .0015 | .0085 | .0264 | .0584 | .1029 | .1536 | .2007 | .2340 | .2461 |
|   | 6 | .0000 | .0001 | .0012 | .0055 | .0162 | .0368 | .0689 | .1115 | .1596 | .2051 |
|   | 7 | .0000 | .0000 | .0001 | .0008 | .0031 | .0090 | .0212 | .0425 | .0746 | .1172 |
|   | 8 | .0000 | .0000 | .0000 | .0001 | .0004 | .0014 | .0043 | .0106 | .0229 | .0439 |
|   | 9 | .0000 | .0000 | .0000 | .0000 | .0000 | .0001 | .0005 | .0016 | .0042 | .0098 |
|   | 10 | .0000 | .0000 | .0000 | .0000 | .0000 | .0000 | .0000 | .0001 | .0003 | .0010 |
| 11 | 0 | .5688 | .3138 | .1673 | .0859 | .0422 | .0198 | .0088 | .0036 | .0014 | .0005 |
|   | 1 | .3293 | .3835 | .3248 | .2362 | .1549 | .0932 | .0518 | .0266 | .0125 | .0054 |
|   | 2 | .0867 | .2131 | .2866 | .2953 | .2581 | .1998 | .1395 | .0887 | .0513 | .0269 |
|   | 3 | .0137 | .0710 | .1517 | .2215 | .2581 | .2568 | .2254 | .1774 | .1259 | .0806 |
|   | 4 | .0014 | .0158 | .0536 | .1107 | .1721 | .2201 | .2428 | .2365 | .2060 | .1611 |
|   | 5 | .0001 | .0025 | .0132 | .0388 | .0803 | .1231 | .1830 | .2207 | .2360 | .2256 |
|   | 6 | .0000 | .0003 | .0023 | .0097 | .0268 | .0566 | .0985 | .1471 | .1931 | .2256 |
|   | 7 | .0000 | .0000 | .0003 | .0017 | .0064 | .0173 | .0379 | .0701 | .1128 | .1611 |
|   | 8 | .0000 | .0000 | .0000 | .0002 | .0011 | .0037 | .0102 | .0234 | .0462 | .0806 |
|   | 9 | .0000 | .0000 | .0000 | .0000 | .0001 | .0005 | .0018 | .0052 | .0126 | .0269 |
|   | 10 | .0000 | .0000 | .0000 | .0000 | .0000 | .0000 | .0002 | .0007 | .0021 | .0054 |
|   | 11 | .0000 | .0000 | .0000 | .0000 | .0000 | .0000 | .0000 | .0000 | .0002 | .0005 |
| 12 | 0 | .5404 | .2824 | .1422 | .0687 | .0317 | .0138 | .0057 | .0022 | .0008 | .0002 |
|   | 1 | .3413 | .3766 | .3012 | .2062 | .1267 | .0712 | .0368 | .0174 | .0075 | .0029 |
|   | 2 | .0988 | .2301 | .2924 | .2835 | .2323 | .1678 | .1088 | .0639 | .0339 | .0161 |
|   | 3 | .0173 | .0852 | .1720 | .2362 | .2581 | .2397 | .1954 | .1419 | .0923 | .0537 |
|   | 4 | .0021 | .0213 | .0683 | .1329 | .1936 | .2311 | .2367 | .2128 | .1700 | .1208 |
|   | 5 | .0002 | .0038 | .0193 | .0532 | .1032 | .1585 | .2039 | .2270 | .2225 | .1934 |
|   | 6 | .0000 | .0005 | .0040 | .0155 | .0401 | .0792 | .1281 | .1766 | .2124 | .2256 |
|   | 7 | .0000 | .0000 | .0006 | .0033 | .0115 | .0291 | .0591 | .1009 | .1489 | .1934 |
|   | 8 | .0000 | .0000 | .0001 | .0005 | .0024 | .0078 | .0199 | .0420 | .0762 | .1208 |
|   | 9 | .0000 | .0000 | .0000 | .0001 | .0004 | .0015 | .0048 | .0125 | .0277 | .0537 |
|   | 10 | .0000 | .0000 | .0000 | .0000 | .0000 | .0002 | .0008 | .0025 | .0068 | .0161 |
|   | 11 | .0000 | .0000 | .0000 | .0000 | .0000 | .0000 | .0001 | .0003 | .0010 | .0029 |
|   | 12 | .0000 | .0000 | .0000 | .0000 | .0000 | .0000 | .0000 | .0000 | .0001 | .0002 |

**P or Q**

t a b l e  B   Binomial distribution   (*continued*)

| N | No. of P or Q Events | .05 | .10 | .15 | .20 | .25 | .30 | .35 | .40 | .45 | .50 |
|---|---|---|---|---|---|---|---|---|---|---|---|
| 13 | 0 | .5133 | .2542 | .1209 | .0550 | .0238 | .0097 | .0037 | .0013 | .0004 | .0001 |
| | 1 | .3512 | .3672 | .2774 | .1787 | .1029 | .0540 | .0259 | .0113 | .0045 | .0016 |
| | 2 | .1109 | .2448 | .2937 | .2680 | .2059 | .1388 | .0836 | .0453 | .0220 | .0095 |
| | 3 | .0214 | .0997 | .1900 | .2457 | .2517 | .2181 | .1651 | .1107 | .0660 | .0349 |
| | 4 | .0028 | .0277 | .0838 | .1535 | .2097 | .2337 | .2222 | .1845 | .1350 | .0873 |
| | 5 | .0003 | .0055 | .0266 | .0691 | .1258 | .1803 | .2154 | .2214 | .1989 | .1571 |
| | 6 | .0000 | .0008 | .0063 | .0230 | .0559 | .1030 | .1546 | .1968 | .2169 | .2095 |
| | 7 | .0000 | .0001 | .0011 | .0058 | .0186 | .0442 | .0833 | .1312 | .1775 | .2095 |
| | 8 | .0000 | .0000 | .0001 | .0011 | .0047 | .0142 | .0336 | .0656 | .1089 | .1571 |
| | 9 | .0000 | .0000 | .0000 | .0001 | .0009 | .0034 | .0101 | .0243 | .0495 | .0873 |
| | 10 | .0000 | .0000 | .0000 | .0000 | .0001 | .0006 | .0022 | .0065 | .0162 | .0349 |
| | 11 | .0000 | .0000 | .0000 | .0000 | .0000 | .0001 | .0003 | .0012 | .0036 | .0095 |
| | 12 | .0000 | .0000 | .0000 | .0000 | .0000 | .0000 | .0000 | .0001 | .0005 | .0016 |
| | 13 | .0000 | .0000 | .0000 | .0000 | .0000 | .0000 | .0000 | .0000 | .0000 | .0001 |
| 14 | 0 | .4877 | .2288 | .1028 | .0440 | .0178 | .0068 | .0024 | .0008 | .0002 | .0001 |
| | 1 | .3593 | .3559 | .2539 | .1539 | .0832 | .0407 | .0181 | .0073 | .0027 | .0009 |
| | 2 | .1229 | .2570 | .2912 | .2501 | .1802 | .1134 | .0634 | .0317 | .0141 | .0056 |
| | 3 | .0259 | .1142 | .2056 | .2501 | .2402 | .1943 | .1366 | .0845 | .0462 | .0222 |
| | 4 | .0037 | .0349 | .0998 | .1720 | .2202 | .2290 | .2022 | .1549 | .1040 | .0611 |
| | 5 | .0004 | .0078 | .0352 | .0860 | .1468 | .1963 | .2178 | .2066 | .1701 | .1222 |
| | 6 | .0000 | .0013 | .0093 | .0322 | .0734 | .1262 | .1759 | .2066 | .2088 | .1833 |
| | 7 | .0000 | .0002 | .0019 | .0092 | .0280 | .0618 | .1082 | .1574 | .1952 | .2095 |
| | 8 | .0000 | .0000 | .0003 | .0020 | .0082 | .0232 | .0510 | .0918 | .1398 | .1833 |
| | 9 | .0000 | .0000 | .0000 | .0003 | .0018 | .0066 | .0183 | .0408 | .0762 | .1222 |
| | 10 | .0000 | .0000 | .0000 | .0000 | .0003 | .0014 | .0049 | .0136 | .0312 | .0611 |
| | 11 | .0000 | .0000 | .0000 | .0000 | .0000 | .0002 | .0010 | .0033 | .0093 | .0222 |
| | 12 | .0000 | .0000 | .0000 | .0000 | .0000 | .0000 | .0001 | .0005 | .0019 | .0056 |
| | 13 | .0000 | .0000 | .0000 | .0000 | .0000 | .0000 | .0000 | .0001 | .0002 | .0009 |
| | 14 | .0000 | .0000 | .0000 | .0000 | .0000 | .0000 | .0000 | .0000 | .0000 | .0001 |
| 15 | 0 | .4633 | .2059 | .0874 | .0352 | .0134 | .0047 | .0016 | .0005 | .0001 | .0000 |
| | 1 | .3658 | .3432 | .2312 | .1319 | .0668 | .0305 | .0126 | .0047 | .0016 | .0005 |
| | 2 | .1348 | .2669 | .2856 | .2309 | .1559 | .0916 | .0476 | .0219 | .0090 | .0032 |
| | 3 | .0307 | .1285 | .2184 | .2501 | .2252 | .1700 | .1110 | .0634 | .0318 | .0139 |
| | 4 | .0049 | .0428 | .1156 | .1876 | .2252 | .2186 | .1792 | .1268 | .0780 | .0417 |
| | 5 | .0006 | .0105 | .0449 | .1032 | .1651 | .2061 | .2123 | .1859 | .1404 | .0916 |
| | 6 | .0000 | .0019 | .0132 | .0430 | .0917 | .1472 | .1906 | .2066 | .1914 | .1527 |
| | 7 | .0000 | .0003 | .0030 | .0138 | .0393 | .0811 | .1319 | .1771 | .2013 | .1964 |
| | 8 | .0000 | .0000 | .0005 | .0035 | .0131 | .0348 | .0710 | .1181 | .1647 | .1964 |
| | 9 | .0000 | .0000 | .0001 | .0007 | .0034 | .0116 | .0298 | .0612 | .1048 | .1527 |
| | 10 | .0000 | .0000 | .0000 | .0001 | .0007 | .0030 | .0096 | .0245 | .0515 | .0916 |
| | 11 | .0000 | .0000 | .0000 | .0000 | .0001 | .0006 | .0024 | .0074 | .0191 | .0417 |
| | 12 | .0000 | .0000 | .0000 | .0000 | .0000 | .0001 | .0004 | .0016 | .0052 | .0139 |
| | 13 | .0000 | .0000 | .0000 | .0000 | .0000 | .0000 | .0001 | .0003 | .0010 | .0032 |
| | 14 | .0000 | .0000 | .0000 | .0000 | .0000 | .0000 | .0000 | .0000 | .0001 | .0005 |
| | 15 | .0000 | .0000 | .0000 | .0000 | .0000 | .0000 | .0000 | .0000 | .0000 | .0000 |

*P or Q* (column header spanning .05–.50)

(*continued*)

t a b l e  B  (*continued*)

| N | No. of P or Q Events | P or Q |  |  |  |  |  |  |  |  |  |
|---|---|---|---|---|---|---|---|---|---|---|---|
|  |  | .05 | .10 | .15 | .20 | .25 | .30 | .35 | .40 | .45 | .50 |
| 16 | 0 | .4401 | .1853 | .0743 | .0281 | .0100 | .0033 | .0010 | .0003 | .0001 | .0000 |
|  | 1 | .3706 | .3294 | .2097 | .1126 | .0535 | .0228 | .0087 | .0030 | .0009 | .0002 |
|  | 2 | .1463 | .2745 | .2775 | .2111 | .1336 | .0732 | .0353 | .0150 | .0056 | .0018 |
|  | 3 | .0359 | .1423 | .2285 | .2463 | .2079 | .1465 | .0888 | .0468 | .0215 | .0085 |
|  | 4 | .0061 | .0514 | .1311 | .2001 | .2252 | .2040 | .1553 | .1014 | .0572 | .0278 |
|  | 5 | .0008 | .0137 | .0555 | .1201 | .1802 | .2099 | .2008 | .1623 | .1123 | .0667 |
|  | 6 | .0001 | .0028 | .0180 | .0550 | .1101 | .1649 | .1982 | .1983 | .1684 | .1222 |
|  | 7 | .0000 | .0004 | .0045 | .0197 | .0524 | .1010 | .1524 | .1889 | .1969 | .1746 |
|  | 8 | .0000 | .0001 | .0009 | .0055 | .0197 | .0487 | .0923 | .1417 | .1812 | .1964 |
|  | 9 | .0000 | .0000 | .0001 | .0012 | .0058 | .0185 | .0442 | .0840 | .1318 | .1746 |
|  | 10 | .0000 | .0000 | .0000 | .0002 | .0014 | .0056 | .0167 | .0392 | .0755 | .1222 |
|  | 11 | .0000 | .0000 | .0000 | .0000 | .0002 | .0013 | .0049 | .0142 | .0337 | .0667 |
|  | 12 | .0000 | .0000 | .0000 | .0000 | .0000 | .0002 | .0011 | .0040 | .0115 | .0278 |
|  | 13 | .0000 | .0000 | .0000 | .0000 | .0000 | .0000 | .0002 | .0008 | .0029 | .0085 |
|  | 14 | .0000 | .0000 | .0000 | .0000 | .0000 | .0000 | .0000 | .0001 | .0005 | .0018 |
|  | 15 | .0000 | .0000 | .0000 | .0000 | .0000 | .0000 | .0000 | .0000 | .0001 | .0002 |
|  | 16 | .0000 | .0000 | .0000 | .0000 | .0000 | .0000 | .0000 | .0000 | .0000 | .0000 |
| 17 | 0 | .4181 | .1668 | .0631 | .0225 | .0075 | .0023 | .0007 | .0002 | .0000 | .0000 |
|  | 1 | .3741 | .3150 | .1893 | .0957 | .0426 | .0169 | .0060 | .0019 | .0005 | .0001 |
|  | 2 | .1575 | .2800 | .2673 | .1914 | .1136 | .0581 | .0260 | .0102 | .0035 | .0010 |
|  | 3 | .0415 | .1556 | .2359 | .2393 | .1893 | .1245 | .0701 | .0341 | .0144 | .0052 |
|  | 4 | .0076 | .0605 | .1457 | .2093 | .2209 | .1868 | .1320 | .0796 | .0411 | .0182 |
|  | 5 | .0010 | .0175 | .0668 | .1361 | .1914 | .2081 | .1849 | .1379 | .0875 | .0472 |
|  | 6 | .0001 | .0039 | .0236 | .0680 | .1276 | .1784 | .1991 | .1839 | .1432 | .0944 |
|  | 7 | .0000 | .0007 | .0065 | .0267 | .0668 | .1201 | .1685 | .1927 | .1841 | .1484 |
|  | 8 | .0000 | .0001 | .0014 | .0084 | .0279 | .0644 | .1143 | .1606 | .1883 | .1855 |
|  | 9 | .0000 | .0000 | .0003 | .0021 | .0093 | .0276 | .0611 | .1070 | .1540 | .1855 |
|  | 10 | .0000 | .0000 | .0000 | .0004 | .0025 | .0095 | .0263 | .0571 | .1008 | .1484 |
|  | 11 | .0000 | .0000 | .0000 | .0001 | .0005 | .0026 | .0090 | .0242 | .0525 | .0944 |
|  | 12 | .0000 | .0000 | .0000 | .0000 | .0001 | .0006 | .0024 | .0081 | .0215 | .0472 |
|  | 13 | .0000 | .0000 | .0000 | .0000 | .0000 | .0001 | .0005 | .0021 | .0068 | .0182 |
|  | 14 | .0000 | .0000 | .0000 | .0000 | .0000 | .0000 | .0001 | .0004 | .0016 | .0052 |
|  | 15 | .0000 | .0000 | .0000 | .0000 | .0000 | .0000 | .0000 | .0001 | .0003 | .0010 |
|  | 16 | .0000 | .0000 | .0000 | .0000 | .0000 | .0000 | .0000 | .0000 | .0000 | .0001 |
|  | 17 | .0000 | .0000 | .0000 | .0000 | .0000 | .0000 | .0000 | .0000 | .0000 | .0000 |
| 18 | 0 | .3972 | .1501 | .0536 | .0180 | .0056 | .0016 | .0004 | .0001 | .0000 | .0000 |
|  | 1 | .3763 | .3002 | .1704 | .0811 | .0338 | .0126 | .0042 | .0012 | .0003 | .0001 |
|  | 2 | .1683 | .2835 | .2556 | .1723 | .0958 | .0458 | .0190 | .0069 | .0022 | .0006 |
|  | 3 | .0473 | .1680 | .2406 | .2297 | .1704 | .1046 | .0547 | .0246 | .0095 | .0031 |
|  | 4 | .0093 | .0070 | .1592 | .2153 | .2130 | .1681 | .1104 | .0614 | .0291 | .0117 |
|  | 5 | .0014 | .0218 | .0787 | .1507 | .1988 | .2017 | .1664 | .1146 | .0666 | .0327 |
|  | 6 | .0002 | .0052 | .0310 | .0816 | .1436 | .1873 | .1941 | .1655 | .1181 | .0708 |
|  | 7 | .0000 | .0010 | .0091 | .0350 | .0820 | .1376 | .1792 | .1892 | .1657 | .1214 |
|  | 8 | .0000 | .0002 | .0022 | .0120 | .0376 | .0811 | .1327 | .1734 | .1864 | .1669 |
|  | 9 | .0000 | .0000 | .0004 | .0033 | .0139 | .0386 | .0794 | .1284 | .1694 | .1855 |
|  | 10 | .0000 | .0000 | .0001 | .0008 | .0042 | .0149 | .0385 | .0771 | .1248 | .1669 |
|  | 11 | .0000 | .0000 | .0000 | .0001 | .0010 | .0046 | .0151 | .0374 | .0742 | .1214 |

t a b l e  B    Binomial distribution    (*continued*)

| N | No. of P or Q Events | P or Q | | | | | | | | | |
|---|---|---|---|---|---|---|---|---|---|---|---|
| | | .05 | .10 | .15 | .20 | .25 | .30 | .35 | .40 | .45 | .50 |
| 18 | 12 | .0000 | .0000 | .0000 | .0000 | .0002 | .0012 | .0047 | .0145 | .0354 | .0708 |
| | 13 | .0000 | .0000 | .0000 | .0000 | .0000 | .0002 | .0012 | .0045 | .0134 | .0327 |
| | 14 | .0000 | .0000 | .0000 | .0000 | .0000 | .0000 | .0002 | .0011 | .0039 | .0117 |
| | 15 | .0000 | .0000 | .0000 | .0000 | .0000 | .0000 | .0000 | .0002 | .0009 | .0031 |
| | 16 | .0000 | .0000 | .0000 | .0000 | .0000 | .0000 | .0000 | .0000 | .0001 | .0006 |
| | 17 | .0000 | .0000 | .0000 | .0000 | .0000 | .0000 | .0000 | .0000 | .0000 | .0001 |
| | 18 | .0000 | .0000 | .0000 | .0000 | .0000 | .0000 | .0000 | .0000 | .0000 | .0000 |
| 19 | 0 | .3774 | .1351 | .0456 | .0144 | .0042 | .0011 | .0003 | .0001 | .0000 | .0000 |
| | 1 | .3774 | .2852 | .1529 | .0685 | .0268 | .0093 | .0029 | .0008 | .0002 | .0000 |
| | 2 | .1787 | .2852 | .2428 | .1540 | .0803 | .0358 | .0138 | .0046 | .0013 | .0003 |
| | 3 | .0533 | .1796 | .2428 | .2182 | .1517 | .0869 | .0422 | .0175 | .0062 | .0018 |
| | 4 | .0112 | .0798 | .1714 | .2182 | .2023 | .1491 | .0909 | .0467 | .0203 | .0074 |
| | 5 | .0018 | .0266 | .0907 | .1636 | .2023 | .1916 | .1468 | .0933 | .0497 | .0222 |
| | 6 | .0002 | .0069 | .0374 | .0955 | .1574 | .1916 | .1844 | .1451 | .0949 | .0518 |
| | 7 | .0000 | .0014 | .0122 | .0443 | .0974 | .1525 | .1844 | .1797 | .1443 | .0961 |
| | 8 | .0000 | .0002 | .0032 | .0166 | .0487 | .0981 | .1489 | .1797 | .1771 | .1442 |
| | 9 | .0000 | .0000 | .0007 | .0051 | .0198 | .0514 | .0980 | .1464 | .1771 | .1762 |
| | 10 | .0000 | .0000 | .0001 | .0013 | .0066 | .0220 | .0528 | .0976 | .1449 | .1762 |
| | 11 | .0000 | .0000 | .0000 | .0003 | .0018 | .0077 | .0233 | .0532 | .0970 | .1442 |
| | 12 | .0000 | .0000 | .0000 | .0000 | .0004 | .0022 | .0083 | .0237 | .0529 | .0961 |
| | 13 | .0000 | .0000 | .0000 | .0000 | .0001 | .0005 | .0024 | .0085 | .0233 | .0518 |
| | 14 | .0000 | .0000 | .0000 | .0000 | .0000 | .0001 | .0006 | .0024 | .0082 | .0222 |
| | 15 | .0000 | .0000 | .0000 | .0000 | .0000 | .0000 | .0001 | .0005 | .0022 | .0074 |
| | 16 | .0000 | .0000 | .0000 | .0000 | .0000 | .0000 | .0000 | .0001 | .0005 | .0018 |
| | 17 | .0000 | .0000 | .0000 | .0000 | .0000 | .0000 | .0000 | .0000 | .0001 | .0003 |
| | 18 | .0000 | .0000 | .0000 | .0000 | .0000 | .0000 | .0000 | .0000 | .0000 | .0000 |
| | 19 | .0000 | .0000 | .0000 | .0000 | .0000 | .0000 | .0000 | .0000 | .0000 | .0000 |
| 20 | 0 | .3585 | .1216 | .0388 | .0115 | .0032 | .0008 | .0002 | .0000 | .0000 | .0000 |
| | 1 | .3774 | .2702 | .1368 | .0576 | .0211 | .0068 | .0020 | .0005 | .0001 | .0000 |
| | 2 | .1887 | .2852 | .2293 | .1369 | .0669 | .0278 | .0100 | .0031 | .0008 | .0002 |
| | 3 | .0596 | .1901 | .2428 | .2054 | .1339 | .0716 | .0323 | .0123 | .0040 | .0011 |
| | 4 | .0133 | .0898 | .1821 | .2182 | .1897 | .1304 | .0738 | .0350 | .0139 | .0046 |
| | 5 | .0022 | .0319 | .1028 | .1746 | .2023 | .1789 | .1272 | .0746 | .0365 | .0148 |
| | 6 | .0003 | .0089 | .0454 | .1091 | .1686 | .1916 | .1712 | .1244 | .0746 | .0370 |
| | 7 | .0000 | .0020 | .0160 | .0545 | .1124 | .1643 | .1844 | .1659 | .1221 | .0739 |
| | 8 | .0000 | .0004 | .0046 | .0222 | .0609 | .1144 | .1614 | .1797 | .1623 | .1201 |
| | 9 | .0000 | .0001 | .0011 | .0074 | .0271 | .0654 | .1158 | .1597 | .1771 | .1602 |
| | 10 | .0000 | .0000 | .0002 | .0020 | .0099 | .0308 | .0686 | .1171 | .1593 | .1762 |
| | 11 | .0000 | .0000 | .0000 | .0005 | .0030 | .0120 | .0336 | .0710 | .1185 | .1602 |
| | 12 | .0000 | .0000 | .0000 | .0001 | .0008 | .0039 | .0136 | .0355 | .0727 | .1201 |
| | 13 | .0000 | .0000 | .0000 | .0000 | .0002 | .0010 | .0045 | .0146 | .0366 | .0739 |
| | 14 | .0000 | .0000 | .0000 | .0000 | .0000 | .0002 | .0012 | .0049 | .0150 | .0370 |
| | 15 | .0000 | .0000 | .0000 | .0000 | .0000 | .0000 | .0003 | .0013 | .0049 | .0148 |
| | 16 | .0000 | .0000 | .0000 | .0000 | .0000 | .0000 | .0000 | .0003 | .0013 | .0046 |
| | 17 | .0000 | .0000 | .0000 | .0000 | .0000 | .0000 | .0000 | .0000 | .0002 | .0011 |
| | 18 | .0000 | .0000 | .0000 | .0000 | .0000 | .0000 | .0000 | .0000 | .0000 | .0002 |
| | 19 | .0000 | .0000 | .0000 | .0000 | .0000 | .0000 | .0000 | .0000 | .0000 | .0000 |
| | 20 | .0000 | .0000 | .0000 | .0000 | .0000 | .0000 | .0000 | .0000 | .0000 | .0000 |

**t a b l e  C.1**   Critical values of $U$ and $U'$ for a one-tailed test at $\alpha = 0.005$ or a two-tailed test at $\alpha = 0.01$

*To be significant for any given $n_1$ and $n_2$: $U_{\text{obt}}$ must be equal to or **less than** the value shown in the table. $U'_{\text{obt}}$ must be equal to or **greater than** the value shown in the table.*

Each cell shows the $U$ value (top) and the $U'$ value (bottom, underlined).

| $n_2$ \ $n_1$ | 1 | 2 | 3 | 4 | 5 | 6 | 7 | 8 | 9 | 10 | 11 | 12 | 13 | 14 | 15 | 16 | 17 | 18 | 19 | 20 |
|---|---|---|---|---|---|---|---|---|---|---|---|---|---|---|---|---|---|---|---|---|
| 1 | — | — | — | — | — | — | — | — | — | — | — | — | — | — | — | — | — | — | — | — |
| 2 | — | — | — | — | — | — | — | — | — | — | — | — | — | — | — | — | — | — | 0 / 38 | 0 / 40 |
| 3 | — | — | — | — | — | — | — | — | 0 / 27 | 0 / 30 | 0 / 33 | 1 / 35 | 1 / 38 | 1 / 41 | 2 / 43 | 2 / 46 | 2 / 49 | 2 / 52 | 3 / 54 | 3 / 57 |
| 4 | — | — | — | — | — | 0 / 24 | 0 / 28 | 1 / 31 | 1 / 35 | 2 / 38 | 2 / 42 | 3 / 45 | 3 / 49 | 4 / 52 | 5 / 55 | 5 / 59 | 6 / 62 | 6 / 66 | 7 / 69 | 8 / 72 |
| 5 | — | — | — | — | 0 / 25 | 1 / 29 | 1 / 34 | 2 / 38 | 3 / 42 | 4 / 46 | 5 / 50 | 6 / 54 | 7 / 58 | 7 / 63 | 8 / 67 | 9 / 71 | 10 / 75 | 11 / 79 | 12 / 83 | 13 / 87 |
| 6 | — | — | — | 0 / 24 | 1 / 29 | 2 / 34 | 3 / 39 | 4 / 44 | 5 / 49 | 6 / 54 | 7 / 59 | 9 / 63 | 10 / 68 | 11 / 73 | 12 / 78 | 13 / 83 | 15 / 87 | 16 / 92 | 17 / 97 | 18 / 102 |
| 7 | — | — | — | 0 / 28 | 1 / 34 | 3 / 39 | 4 / 45 | 6 / 50 | 7 / 56 | 9 / 61 | 10 / 67 | 12 / 72 | 13 / 78 | 15 / 83 | 16 / 89 | 18 / 94 | 19 / 100 | 21 / 105 | 22 / 111 | 24 / 116 |
| 8 | — | — | — | 1 / 31 | 2 / 38 | 4 / 44 | 6 / 50 | 7 / 57 | 9 / 63 | 11 / 69 | 13 / 75 | 15 / 81 | 17 / 87 | 18 / 94 | 20 / 100 | 22 / 106 | 24 / 112 | 26 / 118 | 28 / 124 | 30 / 130 |
| 9 | — | — | 0 / 27 | 1 / 35 | 3 / 42 | 5 / 49 | 7 / 56 | 9 / 63 | 11 / 70 | 13 / 77 | 16 / 83 | 18 / 90 | 20 / 97 | 22 / 104 | 24 / 111 | 27 / 117 | 29 / 124 | 31 / 131 | 33 / 138 | 36 / 144 |
| 10 | — | — | 0 / 30 | 2 / 38 | 4 / 46 | 6 / 54 | 9 / 61 | 11 / 69 | 13 / 77 | 16 / 84 | 18 / 92 | 21 / 99 | 24 / 106 | 26 / 114 | 29 / 121 | 31 / 129 | 34 / 136 | 37 / 143 | 39 / 151 | 42 / 158 |
| 11 | — | — | 0 / 33 | 2 / 42 | 5 / 50 | 7 / 59 | 10 / 67 | 13 / 75 | 16 / 83 | 18 / 92 | 21 / 100 | 24 / 108 | 27 / 116 | 30 / 124 | 33 / 132 | 36 / 140 | 39 / 148 | 42 / 156 | 45 / 164 | 48 / 172 |
| 12 | — | — | 1 / 35 | 3 / 45 | 6 / 54 | 9 / 63 | 12 / 72 | 15 / 81 | 18 / 90 | 21 / 99 | 24 / 108 | 27 / 117 | 31 / 125 | 34 / 134 | 37 / 143 | 41 / 151 | 44 / 160 | 47 / 169 | 51 / 177 | 54 / 186 |
| 13 | — | — | 1 / 38 | 3 / 49 | 7 / 58 | 10 / 68 | 13 / 78 | 17 / 87 | 20 / 97 | 24 / 106 | 27 / 116 | 31 / 125 | 34 / 125 | 38 / 144 | 42 / 153 | 45 / 163 | 49 / 172 | 53 / 181 | 56 / 191 | 60 / 200 |
| 14 | — | — | 1 / 41 | 4 / 52 | 7 / 63 | 11 / 73 | 15 / 83 | 18 / 94 | 22 / 104 | 26 / 114 | 30 / 124 | 34 / 134 | 38 / 144 | 42 / 154 | 46 / 164 | 50 / 174 | 54 / 184 | 58 / 194 | 63 / 203 | 67 / 213 |
| 15 | — | — | 2 / 43 | 5 / 55 | 8 / 67 | 12 / 78 | 16 / 89 | 20 / 100 | 24 / 111 | 29 / 121 | 33 / 132 | 37 / 143 | 42 / 153 | 46 / 164 | 51 / 174 | 55 / 185 | 60 / 195 | 64 / 206 | 69 / 216 | 73 / 227 |
| 16 | — | — | 2 / 46 | 5 / 59 | 9 / 71 | 13 / 83 | 18 / 94 | 22 / 106 | 27 / 117 | 31 / 129 | 36 / 140 | 41 / 151 | 45 / 163 | 50 / 174 | 55 / 185 | 60 / 196 | 65 / 207 | 70 / 218 | 74 / 230 | 79 / 241 |
| 17 | — | — | 2 / 49 | 6 / 62 | 10 / 75 | 15 / 87 | 19 / 100 | 24 / 112 | 29 / 124 | 34 / 148 | 39 / 148 | 44 / 160 | 49 / 172 | 54 / 184 | 60 / 195 | 65 / 207 | 70 / 219 | 75 / 231 | 81 / 242 | 86 / 254 |
| 18 | — | — | 2 / 52 | 6 / 66 | 11 / 79 | 16 / 92 | 21 / 105 | 26 / 118 | 31 / 131 | 37 / 143 | 42 / 156 | 47 / 169 | 53 / 181 | 58 / 194 | 64 / 206 | 70 / 218 | 75 / 231 | 81 / 243 | 87 / 255 | 92 / 268 |
| 19 | — | 0 / 38 | 3 / 54 | 7 / 69 | 12 / 83 | 17 / 97 | 22 / 111 | 28 / 124 | 33 / 138 | 39 / 151 | 45 / 164 | 51 / 177 | 56 / 191 | 63 / 203 | 69 / 216 | 74 / 230 | 81 / 242 | 87 / 255 | 93 / 268 | 99 / 281 |
| 20 | — | 0 / 40 | 3 / 57 | 8 / 72 | 13 / 87 | 18 / 102 | 24 / 116 | 30 / 130 | 36 / 144 | 42 / 158 | 48 / 172 | 54 / 186 | 60 / 200 | 67 / 213 | 73 / 227 | 79 / 241 | 86 / 254 | 92 / 268 | 99 / 281 | 105 / 295 |

Dashes in the body of the table indicate that no decision is possible at the stated level of significance.

t a b l e  **C.2**   Critical values of $U$ and $U'$ for a one-tailed test at $\alpha = 0.01$ or a two-tailed test at $\alpha = 0.02$

*To be significant for any given $n_1$ and $n_2$: $U_{obt}$ must be equal to or **less than** the value shown in the table. $U'_{obt}$ must be equal to or **greater than** the value shown in the table.*

Each cell shows $U$ (upper) over $U'$ (lower).

| $n_2$ \ $n_1$ | 1 | 2 | 3 | 4 | 5 | 6 | 7 | 8 | 9 | 10 | 11 | 12 | 13 | 14 | 15 | 16 | 17 | 18 | 19 | 20 |
|---|---|---|---|---|---|---|---|---|---|---|---|---|---|---|---|---|---|---|---|---|
| 1 | — | — | — | — | — | — | — | — | — | — | — | — | — | — | — | — | — | — | — | — |
| 2 | — | — | — | — | — | — | — | — | — | — | — | — | 0/26 | 0/28 | 0/30 | 0/32 | 0/34 | 0/36 | 1/37 | 1/39 |
| 3 | — | — | — | — | — | — | 0/21 | 0/24 | 1/26 | 1/29 | 1/32 | 2/34 | 2/37 | 2/40 | 3/42 | 3/45 | 4/47 | 4/50 | 4/52 | 5/55 |
| 4 | — | — | — | — | 0/20 | 1/23 | 1/27 | 2/30 | 3/33 | 3/37 | 4/40 | 5/43 | 5/47 | 6/50 | 7/53 | 7/57 | 8/60 | 9/63 | 9/67 | 10/70 |
| 5 | — | — | — | 0/20 | 1/24 | 2/28 | 3/32 | 4/36 | 5/40 | 6/44 | 7/48 | 8/52 | 9/56 | 10/60 | 11/64 | 12/68 | 13/72 | 14/76 | 15/80 | 16/84 |
| 6 | — | — | — | 1/23 | 2/28 | 3/33 | 4/38 | 6/42 | 7/47 | 8/52 | 9/57 | 11/61 | 12/66 | 13/71 | 15/75 | 16/80 | 18/84 | 19/89 | 20/94 | 22/98 |
| 7 | — | — | 0/21 | 1/27 | 3/32 | 4/38 | 6/43 | 7/49 | 9/54 | 11/59 | 12/65 | 14/70 | 16/75 | 17/81 | 19/86 | 21/91 | 23/96 | 24/102 | 26/107 | 28/112 |
| 8 | — | — | 0/24 | 2/30 | 4/36 | 6/42 | 7/49 | 9/55 | 11/61 | 13/67 | 15/73 | 17/79 | 20/84 | 22/90 | 24/96 | 26/102 | 28/108 | 30/114 | 32/120 | 34/126 |
| 9 | — | — | 1/26 | 3/33 | 5/40 | 7/47 | 9/54 | 11/61 | 14/67 | 16/74 | 18/81 | 21/87 | 23/94 | 26/100 | 28/107 | 31/113 | 33/120 | 36/126 | 38/133 | 40/140 |
| 10 | — | — | 1/29 | 3/37 | 6/44 | 8/52 | 11/59 | 13/67 | 16/74 | 19/81 | 22/88 | 24/96 | 27/103 | 30/110 | 33/117 | 36/124 | 38/132 | 41/139 | 44/146 | 47/153 |
| 11 | — | — | 1/32 | 4/40 | 7/48 | 9/57 | 12/65 | 15/73 | 18/81 | 22/88 | 25/96 | 28/104 | 31/112 | 34/120 | 37/128 | 41/135 | 44/143 | 47/151 | 50/159 | 53/167 |
| 12 | — | — | 2/34 | 5/43 | 8/52 | 11/61 | 14/70 | 17/79 | 21/87 | 24/96 | 28/104 | 31/113 | 35/121 | 38/130 | 42/138 | 46/146 | 49/155 | 53/163 | 56/172 | 60/180 |
| 13 | — | 0/26 | 2/37 | 5/47 | 9/56 | 12/66 | 16/75 | 20/84 | 23/94 | 27/103 | 31/112 | 35/121 | 39/130 | 43/139 | 47/148 | 51/157 | 55/166 | 59/175 | 63/184 | 67/193 |
| 14 | — | 0/28 | 2/40 | 6/50 | 10/60 | 13/71 | 17/81 | 22/90 | 26/100 | 30/110 | 34/120 | 38/130 | 43/139 | 47/149 | 51/159 | 56/168 | 60/178 | 65/187 | 69/197 | 73/207 |
| 15 | — | 0/30 | 3/42 | 7/53 | 11/64 | 15/75 | 19/86 | 24/96 | 28/107 | 33/117 | 37/128 | 42/138 | 47/148 | 51/159 | 56/169 | 61/179 | 66/189 | 70/200 | 75/210 | 80/220 |
| 16 | — | 0/32 | 3/45 | 7/57 | 12/68 | 16/80 | 21/91 | 26/102 | 31/113 | 36/124 | 41/135 | 46/146 | 51/157 | 56/168 | 61/179 | 66/190 | 71/201 | 76/212 | 82/222 | 87/233 |
| 17 | — | 0/34 | 4/47 | 8/60 | 13/72 | 18/84 | 23/96 | 28/108 | 33/120 | 38/132 | 44/143 | 49/155 | 55/166 | 60/178 | 66/189 | 71/201 | 77/212 | 82/224 | 88/235 | 93/247 |
| 18 | — | 0/36 | 4/50 | 9/63 | 14/76 | 19/89 | 24/102 | 30/114 | 36/126 | 41/139 | 47/151 | 53/163 | 59/175 | 65/187 | 70/200 | 76/212 | 82/224 | 88/236 | 94/248 | 100/260 |
| 19 | — | 1/37 | 4/53 | 9/67 | 15/80 | 20/94 | 26/107 | 32/120 | 38/133 | 44/146 | 50/159 | 56/172 | 63/184 | 69/197 | 75/210 | 82/222 | 88/235 | 94/248 | 101/260 | 107/273 |
| 20 | — | 1/39 | 5/55 | 10/70 | 16/84 | 22/98 | 28/112 | 34/126 | 40/140 | 47/153 | 53/167 | 60/180 | 67/193 | 73/207 | 80/220 | 87/233 | 93/247 | 100/260 | 107/273 | 114/286 |

Dashes in the body of the table indicate that no decision is possible at the stated level of significance.

**t a b l e  C.3**  Critical values of $U$ and $U'$ for a one-tailed test at $\alpha = 0.025$ or a two-tailed test at $\alpha = 0.05$

*To be significant for any given $n_1$ and $n_2$: $U_{obt}$ must be equal to or **less than** the value shown in the table. $U'_{obt}$ must be equal to or **greater than** the value shown in the table.*

Each cell shows $U$ (top) / $U'$ (underlined, bottom).

| $n_2$ \\ $n_1$ | 1 | 2 | 3 | 4 | 5 | 6 | 7 | 8 | 9 | 10 | 11 | 12 | 13 | 14 | 15 | 16 | 17 | 18 | 19 | 20 |
|---|---|---|---|---|---|---|---|---|---|---|---|---|---|---|---|---|---|---|---|---|
| 1 | — | — | — | — | — | — | — | — | — | — | — | — | — | — | — | — | — | — | — | — |
| 2 | — | — | — | — | — | — | — | 0/16 | 0/18 | 0/20 | 0/22 | 1/23 | 1/25 | 1/27 | 1/29 | 1/31 | 2/32 | 2/34 | 2/36 | 2/38 |
| 3 | — | — | — | — | 0/15 | 1/17 | 1/20 | 2/22 | 2/25 | 3/27 | 3/30 | 4/32 | 4/35 | 5/37 | 5/40 | 6/42 | 6/45 | 7/47 | 7/50 | 8/52 |
| 4 | — | — | — | 0/16 | 1/19 | 2/22 | 3/25 | 4/28 | 4/32 | 5/35 | 6/38 | 7/41 | 8/44 | 9/47 | 10/50 | 11/53 | 11/57 | 12/60 | 13/63 | 13/67 |
| 5 | — | — | 0/15 | 1/19 | 2/23 | 3/27 | 5/30 | 6/34 | 7/38 | 8/42 | 9/46 | 11/49 | 12/53 | 13/57 | 14/61 | 15/65 | 17/68 | 18/72 | 19/76 | 20/80 |
| 6 | — | — | 1/17 | 2/22 | 3/27 | 5/31 | 6/36 | 8/40 | 10/44 | 11/49 | 13/53 | 14/58 | 16/62 | 17/67 | 19/71 | 21/75 | 22/80 | 24/84 | 25/89 | 27/93 |
| 7 | — | — | 1/20 | 3/25 | 5/30 | 6/36 | 8/41 | 10/46 | 12/51 | 14/56 | 16/61 | 18/66 | 20/71 | 22/76 | 24/81 | 26/86 | 28/91 | 30/96 | 32/101 | 34/106 |
| 8 | — | 0/16 | 2/22 | 4/28 | 6/34 | 8/40 | 10/46 | 13/51 | 15/57 | 17/63 | 19/69 | 22/74 | 24/80 | 26/86 | 29/91 | 31/97 | 34/102 | 36/108 | 38/111 | 41/119 |
| 9 | — | 0/18 | 2/25 | 4/32 | 7/38 | 10/44 | 12/51 | 15/57 | 17/64 | 20/70 | 23/76 | 26/82 | 28/89 | 31/95 | 34/101 | 37/107 | 39/114 | 42/120 | 45/126 | 48/132 |
| 10 | — | 0/20 | 3/27 | 5/35 | 8/42 | 11/49 | 14/56 | 17/63 | 20/70 | 23/77 | 26/84 | 29/91 | 33/97 | 36/104 | 39/111 | 42/118 | 45/125 | 48/132 | 52/138 | 55/145 |
| 11 | — | 0/22 | 3/30 | 6/38 | 9/46 | 13/53 | 16/61 | 19/69 | 23/76 | 26/84 | 30/91 | 33/99 | 37/106 | 40/114 | 44/121 | 47/129 | 51/136 | 55/143 | 58/151 | 62/158 |
| 12 | — | 1/23 | 4/32 | 7/41 | 11/49 | 14/58 | 18/66 | 22/74 | 26/82 | 29/91 | 33/99 | 37/107 | 41/115 | 45/123 | 49/131 | 53/139 | 57/147 | 61/155 | 65/163 | 69/171 |
| 13 | — | 1/25 | 4/35 | 8/44 | 12/53 | 16/62 | 20/71 | 24/80 | 28/89 | 33/97 | 37/106 | 41/115 | 45/124 | 50/132 | 54/141 | 59/149 | 63/158 | 67/167 | 72/175 | 76/184 |
| 14 | — | 1/27 | 5/37 | 9/47 | 13/51 | 17/67 | 22/76 | 26/86 | 31/95 | 36/104 | 40/114 | 45/123 | 50/132 | 55/141 | 59/151 | 64/160 | 67/171 | 74/178 | 78/188 | 83/197 |
| 15 | — | 1/29 | 5/40 | 10/50 | 14/61 | 19/71 | 24/81 | 29/91 | 34/101 | 39/111 | 44/121 | 49/131 | 54/141 | 59/151 | 64/161 | 70/170 | 75/180 | 80/190 | 85/200 | 90/210 |
| 16 | — | 1/31 | 6/42 | 11/53 | 15/65 | 21/75 | 26/86 | 31/97 | 37/107 | 42/118 | 47/129 | 53/139 | 59/149 | 64/160 | 70/170 | 75/181 | 81/191 | 86/202 | 92/212 | 98/222 |
| 17 | — | 2/32 | 6/45 | 11/57 | 17/68 | 22/80 | 28/91 | 34/102 | 39/114 | 45/125 | 51/136 | 57/147 | 63/158 | 67/171 | 75/180 | 81/191 | 87/202 | 93/213 | 99/224 | 105/235 |
| 18 | — | 2/34 | 7/47 | 12/60 | 18/72 | 24/84 | 30/96 | 36/108 | 42/120 | 48/132 | 55/143 | 61/155 | 67/167 | 74/168 | 80/190 | 86/202 | 93/213 | 99/225 | 106/236 | 112/248 |
| 19 | — | 2/36 | 7/50 | 13/63 | 19/76 | 25/89 | 32/101 | 38/114 | 45/126 | 52/138 | 58/151 | 65/163 | 72/175 | 78/188 | 85/200 | 92/212 | 99/224 | 106/236 | 113/248 | 119/261 |
| 20 | — | 2/38 | 8/52 | 13/67 | 20/80 | 27/93 | 34/106 | 41/119 | 48/132 | 55/145 | 62/158 | 69/171 | 76/184 | 83/197 | 90/210 | 98/222 | 105/235 | 112/248 | 119/261 | 127/273 |

Dashes in the body of the table indicate that no decision is possible at the stated level of significance.

**t a b l e   C.4**   Critical values of $U$ and $U'$ for a one-tailed test at $\alpha = 0.05$ or a two-tailed test at $\alpha = 0.10$

*To be significant for any given $n_1$ and $n_2$: $U_{obt}$ must be equal to or **less than** the value shown in the table. $U'_{obt}$ must be equal to or **greater than** the value shown in the table.*

Each cell shows $U$ (upper) / $U'$ (lower, underlined). Dashes indicate no decision is possible.

| $n_2$ \ $n_1$ | 1 | 2 | 3 | 4 | 5 | 6 | 7 | 8 | 9 | 10 | 11 | 12 | 13 | 14 | 15 | 16 | 17 | 18 | 19 | 20 |
|---|---|---|---|---|---|---|---|---|---|---|---|---|---|---|---|---|---|---|---|---|
| **1** | — | — | — | — | — | — | — | — | — | — | — | — | — | — | — | — | — | — | 0/19 | 0/20 |
| **2** | — | — | — | — | 0/10 | 0/12 | 0/14 | 1/15 | 1/17 | 1/19 | 1/21 | 2/22 | 2/24 | 2/26 | 3/27 | 3/29 | 3/31 | 4/32 | 4/34 | 4/36 |
| **3** | — | — | 0/9 | 0/12 | 1/14 | 2/16 | 2/19 | 3/21 | 3/24 | 4/26 | 5/28 | 5/31 | 6/33 | 7/35 | 7/38 | 8/40 | 9/42 | 9/45 | 10/47 | 11/49 |
| **4** | — | — | 0/12 | 1/15 | 2/18 | 3/21 | 4/24 | 5/27 | 6/30 | 7/33 | 8/36 | 9/39 | 10/42 | 11/45 | 12/48 | 14/50 | 15/53 | 16/56 | 17/59 | 18/62 |
| **5** | — | 0/10 | 1/14 | 2/18 | 4/21 | 5/25 | 6/29 | 8/32 | 9/36 | 11/39 | 12/43 | 13/47 | 15/50 | 16/54 | 18/57 | 19/61 | 20/65 | 22/68 | 23/72 | 25/75 |
| **6** | — | 0/12 | 2/16 | 3/21 | 5/25 | 7/29 | 8/34 | 10/38 | 12/42 | 14/46 | 16/50 | 17/55 | 19/59 | 21/63 | 23/67 | 25/71 | 26/76 | 28/80 | 30/84 | 32/88 |
| **7** | — | 0/14 | 2/19 | 4/24 | 6/29 | 8/34 | 11/38 | 13/43 | 15/48 | 17/53 | 19/58 | 21/63 | 24/67 | 26/72 | 28/77 | 30/82 | 33/86 | 35/91 | 37/96 | 39/101 |
| **8** | — | 1/15 | 3/21 | 5/27 | 8/32 | 10/38 | 13/43 | 15/49 | 18/54 | 20/60 | 23/65 | 26/70 | 28/76 | 31/81 | 33/87 | 36/92 | 39/97 | 41/103 | 44/108 | 47/113 |
| **9** | — | 1/17 | 3/24 | 6/30 | 9/36 | 12/42 | 15/48 | 18/54 | 21/60 | 24/66 | 27/72 | 30/78 | 33/84 | 36/90 | 39/96 | 42/102 | 45/108 | 48/114 | 51/120 | 54/126 |
| **10** | — | 1/19 | 4/26 | 7/33 | 11/39 | 14/46 | 17/53 | 20/60 | 24/66 | 27/73 | 31/79 | 34/86 | 37/93 | 41/99 | 44/106 | 48/112 | 51/119 | 55/125 | 58/132 | 62/138 |
| **11** | — | 1/21 | 5/28 | 8/36 | 12/43 | 16/50 | 19/58 | 23/65 | 27/72 | 31/79 | 34/87 | 38/94 | 42/101 | 46/108 | 50/115 | 54/122 | 57/130 | 61/137 | 65/144 | 69/151 |
| **12** | — | 2/22 | 5/31 | 9/39 | 13/47 | 17/55 | 21/63 | 26/70 | 30/78 | 34/86 | 38/94 | 42/102 | 47/109 | 51/117 | 55/125 | 60/132 | 64/140 | 68/148 | 72/156 | 77/163 |
| **13** | — | 2/24 | 6/33 | 10/42 | 15/50 | 19/59 | 24/67 | 28/76 | 33/84 | 37/93 | 42/101 | 47/109 | 51/118 | 56/126 | 61/134 | 65/143 | 70/151 | 75/159 | 80/167 | 84/176 |
| **14** | — | 2/26 | 7/35 | 11/45 | 16/54 | 21/63 | 26/72 | 31/81 | 36/90 | 41/99 | 46/108 | 51/117 | 56/126 | 61/135 | 66/144 | 71/153 | 77/161 | 82/170 | 87/179 | 92/188 |
| **15** | — | 3/27 | 7/38 | 12/48 | 18/57 | 23/67 | 28/77 | 33/87 | 39/96 | 44/106 | 50/115 | 55/125 | 61/134 | 66/144 | 72/153 | 77/163 | 83/172 | 88/182 | 94/191 | 100/200 |
| **16** | — | 3/29 | 8/40 | 14/50 | 19/61 | 25/71 | 30/82 | 36/92 | 42/102 | 48/112 | 54/122 | 60/132 | 65/143 | 71/153 | 77/163 | 83/173 | 89/183 | 95/193 | 101/203 | 107/213 |
| **17** | — | 3/31 | 9/42 | 15/53 | 20/65 | 26/76 | 33/86 | 39/97 | 45/108 | 51/119 | 57/130 | 64/140 | 70/151 | 77/161 | 83/172 | 89/183 | 96/193 | 102/204 | 109/214 | 115/225 |
| **18** | — | 4/32 | 9/45 | 16/56 | 22/68 | 28/80 | 35/91 | 41/103 | 48/114 | 55/123 | 61/137 | 68/148 | 75/159 | 82/170 | 88/182 | 95/193 | 102/204 | 109/215 | 116/226 | 123/237 |
| **19** | 0/19 | 4/34 | 10/47 | 17/59 | 23/72 | 30/84 | 37/96 | 44/108 | 51/120 | 58/132 | 65/144 | 72/156 | 80/167 | 87/179 | 94/191 | 101/203 | 109/214 | 116/226 | 123/238 | 130/250 |
| **20** | 0/20 | 4/36 | 11/49 | 18/62 | 25/75 | 32/88 | 39/101 | 47/113 | 54/126 | 62/138 | 69/151 | 77/163 | 84/176 | 92/188 | 100/200 | 107/213 | 115/225 | 123/237 | 130/250 | 138/262 |

Dashes in the body of the table indicate that no decision is possible at the stated level of significance.

**t a b l e  D**  Critical values of Student's *t* distribution

*The values listed in the table are the critical values of t for the specified degrees of freedom (left column) and the alpha level (column heading). For two-tailed alpha levels, $t_{crit}$ is both + and −. To be significant, $|t_{obt}| \geq |t_{crit}|$.*

| df | Level of Significance for One-Tailed Test | | | | | |
|---|---|---|---|---|---|---|
| | **.10** | **.05** | **.025** | **.01** | **.005** | **.0005** |
| | Level of Significance for Two-Tailed Test | | | | | |
| | **.20** | **.10** | **.05** | **.02** | **.01** | **.001** |
| 1 | 3.078 | 6.314 | 12.706 | 31.821 | 63.657 | 636.619 |
| 2 | 1.886 | 2.920 | 4.303 | 6.965 | 9.925 | 31.598 |
| 3 | 1.638 | 2.353 | 3.182 | 4.541 | 5.841 | 12.941 |
| 4 | 1.533 | 2.132 | 2.776 | 3.747 | 4.604 | 8.610 |
| 5 | 1.476 | 2.015 | 2.571 | 3.365 | 4.032 | 6.859 |
| 6 | 1.440 | 1.943 | 2.447 | 3.143 | 3.707 | 5.959 |
| 7 | 1.415 | 1.895 | 2.365 | 2.998 | 3.499 | 5.405 |
| 8 | 1.397 | 1.860 | 2.306 | 2.986 | 3.355 | 5.041 |
| 9 | 1.383 | 1.833 | 2.262 | 2.821 | 3.250 | 4.781 |
| 10 | 1.372 | 1.812 | 2.228 | 2.764 | 3.169 | 4.587 |
| 11 | 1.363 | 1.796 | 2.201 | 2.718 | 3.106 | 4.437 |
| 12 | 1.356 | 1.782 | 2.179 | 2.681 | 3.055 | 4.318 |
| 13 | 1.350 | 1.771 | 2.160 | 2.650 | 3.012 | 4.221 |
| 14 | 1.345 | 1.761 | 2.145 | 2.624 | 2.977 | 4.140 |
| 15 | 1.341 | 1.753 | 2.131 | 2.602 | 2.947 | 4.073 |
| 16 | 1.337 | 1.746 | 2.120 | 2.583 | 2.921 | 4.015 |
| 17 | 1.333 | 1.740 | 2.110 | 2.567 | 2.898 | 3.965 |
| 18 | 1.330 | 1.734 | 2.101 | 2.552 | 2.878 | 3.922 |
| 19 | 1.328 | 1.729 | 2.093 | 2.539 | 2.861 | 3.883 |
| 20 | 1.325 | 1.725 | 2.086 | 2.528 | 2.845 | 3.850 |
| 21 | 1.323 | 1.721 | 2.080 | 2.518 | 2.831 | 3.819 |
| 22 | 1.321 | 1.717 | 2.074 | 2.508 | 2.819 | 3.792 |
| 23 | 1.319 | 1.714 | 2.069 | 2.500 | 2.807 | 3.767 |
| 24 | 1.318 | 1.711 | 2.064 | 2.492 | 2.797 | 3.745 |
| 25 | 1.316 | 1.708 | 2.060 | 2.485 | 2.787 | 3.725 |
| 26 | 1.315 | 1.706 | 2.056 | 2.479 | 2.779 | 3.707 |
| 27 | 1.314 | 1.703 | 2.052 | 2.473 | 2.771 | 3.690 |
| 28 | 1.313 | 1.701 | 2.048 | 2.467 | 2.763 | 3.674 |
| 29 | 1.311 | 1.699 | 2.045 | 2.462 | 2.756 | 3.659 |
| 30 | 1.310 | 1.697 | 2.042 | 2.457 | 2.750 | 3.646 |
| 40 | 1.303 | 1.684 | 2.021 | 2.423 | 2.704 | 3.551 |
| 60 | 1.296 | 1.671 | 2.000 | 2.390 | 2.660 | 3.460 |
| 120 | 1.289 | 1.658 | 1.980 | 2.358 | 2.617 | 3.373 |
| ∞ | 1.282 | 1.645 | 1.960 | 2.326 | 2.576 | 3.291 |

t a b l e  E   Critical values of Pearson *r*

*The values listed in the table are the critical values of r for the specified degrees of freedom (left column) and the alpha level (column heading). For two-tailed alpha levels, $r_{crit}$ is both + and −. To be significant, $|r_{obt}| \geq |r_{crit}|$.*

| df = N − 2 | Level of Significance for One-Tailed Test | | | | |
| --- | --- | --- | --- | --- | --- |
| | **.05** | **.025** | **.01** | **.005** | **.0005** |
| | Level of Significance for Two-Tailed Test | | | | |
| | **.10** | **.05** | **.02** | **.01** | **.001** |
| 1 | .9877 | .9969 | .9995 | .9999 | 1.0000 |
| 2 | .9000 | .9500 | .9800 | .9900 | .9990 |
| 3 | .8054 | .8783 | .9343 | .9587 | .9912 |
| 4 | .7293 | .8114 | .8822 | .9172 | .9741 |
| 5 | .6694 | .7545 | .8329 | .8745 | .9507 |
| 6 | .6215 | .7067 | .7887 | .8343 | .9249 |
| 7 | .5822 | .6664 | .7498 | .7977 | .8982 |
| 8 | .5494 | .6319 | .7155 | .7646 | .8721 |
| 9 | .5214 | .6021 | .6851 | .7348 | .8471 |
| 10 | .4973 | .5760 | .6581 | .7079 | .8233 |
| 11 | .4762 | .5529 | .6339 | .6835 | .8010 |
| 12 | .4575 | .5324 | .6120 | .6614 | .7800 |
| 13 | .4409 | .5139 | .5923 | .6411 | .7603 |
| 14 | .4259 | .4973 | .5742 | .6226 | .7420 |
| 15 | .4124 | .4821 | .5577 | .6055 | .7246 |
| 16 | .4000 | .4683 | .5425 | .5897 | .7084 |
| 17 | .3887 | .4555 | .5285 | .5751 | .6932 |
| 18 | .3783 | .4438 | .5155 | .5614 | .6787 |
| 19 | .3687 | .4329 | .5034 | .5487 | .6652 |
| 20 | .3598 | .4227 | .4921 | .5368 | .6524 |
| 25 | .3233 | .3809 | .4451 | .4869 | .5974 |
| 30 | .2960 | .3494 | .4093 | .4487 | .5541 |
| 35 | .2746 | .3246 | .3810 | .4182 | .5189 |
| 40 | .2573 | .3044 | .3578 | .3932 | .4896 |
| 45 | .2428 | .2875 | .3384 | .3721 | .4648 |
| 50 | .2306 | .2732 | .3218 | .3541 | .4433 |
| 60 | .2108 | .2500 | .2948 | .3248 | .4078 |
| 70 | .1954 | .2319 | .2737 | .3017 | .3799 |
| 80 | .1829 | .2172 | .2565 | .2830 | .3568 |
| 90 | .1726 | .2050 | .2422 | .2673 | .3375 |
| 100 | .1638 | .1946 | .2301 | .2540 | .3211 |

**t a b l e  F**  Critical values of the *F* distribution for α = 0.05 (Roman type) and α = 0.01 (boldface type)

*The values listed in the table are the critical values of F for the degrees of freedom of the numerator of the F ratio (column headings) and the degrees of freedom of the denominator of the F ratio (row headings). To be significant, $F_{obt} \geq F_{crit}$.*

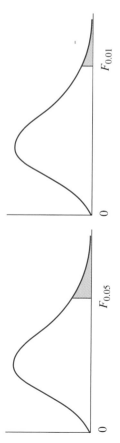

**Degrees of Freedom: Numerator**

| Degrees of Freedom: Denominator | 1 | 2 | 3 | 4 | 5 | 6 | 7 | 8 | 9 | 10 | 11 | 12 | 14 | 16 | 20 | 24 | 30 | 40 | 50 | 75 | 100 | 200 | 500 | ∞ |
|---|---|---|---|---|---|---|---|---|---|---|---|---|---|---|---|---|---|---|---|---|---|---|---|---|
| 1 | 161 | 200 | 216 | 225 | 230 | 234 | 237 | 239 | 241 | 242 | 243 | 244 | 245 | 246 | 248 | 249 | 250 | 251 | 252 | 253 | 253 | 254 | 254 | 254 |
|  | **4,052** | **4,999** | **5,403** | **5,625** | **5,764** | **5,859** | **5,928** | **5,981** | **6,022** | **6,056** | **6,082** | **6,106** | **6,142** | **6,169** | **6,208** | **6,234** | **6,258** | **6,286** | **6,302** | **6,323** | **6,334** | **6,352** | **6,361** | **6,366** |
| 2 | 18.51 | 19.00 | 19.16 | 19.25 | 19.30 | 19.33 | 19.36 | 19.37 | 19.38 | 19.39 | 19.40 | 19.41 | 19.42 | 19.43 | 19.44 | 19.45 | 19.46 | 19.47 | 19.47 | 19.48 | 19.49 | 19.49 | 19.50 | 19.50 |
|  | **98.49** | **99.00** | **99.17** | **99.25** | **99.30** | **99.33** | **99.34** | **99.36** | **99.38** | **99.40** | **99.41** | **99.42** | **99.43** | **99.44** | **99.45** | **99.46** | **99.47** | **99.48** | **99.48** | **99.49** | **99.49** | **99.49** | **99.50** | **99.50** |
| 3 | 10.13 | 9.55 | 9.28 | 9.12 | 9.01 | 8.94 | 8.88 | 8.84 | 8.81 | 8.78 | 8.76 | 8.74 | 8.71 | 8.69 | 8.66 | 8.64 | 8.62 | 8.60 | 8.58 | 8.57 | 8.56 | 8.54 | 8.54 | 8.53 |
|  | **34.12** | **30.82** | **29.46** | **28.71** | **28.24** | **27.91** | **27.67** | **27.49** | **27.34** | **27.23** | **27.13** | **27.05** | **26.92** | **26.83** | **26.69** | **26.60** | **26.50** | **26.41** | **26.35** | **26.27** | **26.23** | **26.18** | **26.14** | **26.12** |
| 4 | 7.71 | 6.94 | 6.59 | 6.39 | 6.26 | 6.16 | 6.09 | 6.04 | 6.00 | 5.96 | 5.93 | 5.91 | 5.87 | 5.84 | 5.80 | 5.77 | 5.74 | 5.71 | 5.70 | 5.68 | 5.66 | 5.65 | 5.64 | 5.63 |
|  | **21.20** | **18.00** | **16.69** | **15.98** | **15.52** | **15.21** | **14.98** | **14.80** | **14.66** | **14.54** | **14.45** | **14.37** | **14.24** | **14.15** | **14.02** | **13.93** | **13.83** | **13.74** | **13.69** | **13.61** | **13.57** | **13.52** | **13.48** | **13.46** |
| 5 | 6.61 | 5.79 | 5.41 | 5.19 | 5.05 | 4.95 | 4.88 | 4.82 | 4.78 | 4.74 | 4.70 | 4.68 | 4.64 | 4.60 | 4.56 | 4.53 | 4.50 | 4.46 | 4.44 | 4.42 | 4.40 | 4.38 | 4.37 | 4.36 |
|  | **16.26** | **13.27** | **12.06** | **11.39** | **10.97** | **10.67** | **10.45** | **10.27** | **10.15** | **10.05** | **9.96** | **9.89** | **9.77** | **9.68** | **9.55** | **9.47** | **9.38** | **9.29** | **9.24** | **9.17** | **9.13** | **9.07** | **9.04** | **9.02** |
| 6 | 5.99 | 5.14 | 4.76 | 4.53 | 4.39 | 4.28 | 4.21 | 4.15 | 4.10 | 4.06 | 4.03 | 4.00 | 3.96 | 3.92 | 3.87 | 3.84 | 3.81 | 3.77 | 3.75 | 3.72 | 3.71 | 3.69 | 3.68 | 3.67 |
|  | **13.74** | **10.92** | **9.78** | **9.15** | **8.75** | **8.47** | **8.26** | **8.10** | **7.98** | **7.87** | **7.79** | **7.72** | **7.60** | **7.52** | **7.39** | **7.31** | **7.23** | **7.14** | **7.09** | **7.02** | **6.99** | **6.94** | **6.90** | **6.88** |
| 7 | 5.59 | 4.47 | 4.35 | 4.12 | 3.97 | 3.87 | 3.79 | 3.73 | 3.68 | 3.63 | 3.60 | 3.57 | 3.52 | 3.49 | 3.44 | 3.41 | 3.38 | 3.34 | 3.32 | 3.29 | 3.28 | 3.25 | 3.24 | 3.23 |
|  | **12.25** | **9.55** | **8.45** | **7.85** | **7.46** | **7.19** | **7.00** | **6.84** | **6.71** | **6.62** | **6.54** | **6.47** | **6.35** | **6.27** | **6.15** | **6.07** | **5.98** | **5.90** | **5.85** | **5.78** | **5.75** | **5.70** | **5.67** | **5.65** |
| 8 | 5.32 | 4.46 | 4.07 | 3.84 | 3.69 | 3.58 | 3.50 | 3.44 | 3.39 | 3.34 | 3.31 | 3.28 | 3.23 | 3.20 | 3.15 | 3.12 | 3.08 | 3.05 | 3.03 | 3.00 | 2.98 | 2.96 | 2.94 | 2.93 |
|  | **11.26** | **8.65** | **7.59** | **7.01** | **6.63** | **6.37** | **6.19** | **6.03** | **5.91** | **5.82** | **5.74** | **5.67** | **5.56** | **5.48** | **5.36** | **5.28** | **5.20** | **5.11** | **5.06** | **5.00** | **4.96** | **4.91** | **4.88** | **4.86** |
| 9 | 5.12 | 4.26 | 3.86 | 3.63 | 3.48 | 3.37 | 3.29 | 3.23 | 3.18 | 3.13 | 3.10 | 3.07 | 3.02 | 2.98 | 2.93 | 2.90 | 2.86 | 2.82 | 2.80 | 2.77 | 2.76 | 2.73 | 2.72 | 2.71 |
|  | **10.56** | **8.02** | **6.99** | **6.42** | **6.06** | **5.80** | **5.62** | **5.47** | **5.35** | **5.26** | **5.18** | **5.11** | **5.00** | **4.92** | **4.80** | **4.73** | **4.64** | **4.56** | **4.51** | **4.45** | **4.41** | **4.36** | **4.33** | **4.31** |
| 10 | 4.96 | 4.10 | 3.71 | 3.48 | 3.33 | 3.22 | 3.14 | 3.07 | 3.02 | 2.97 | 2.94 | 2.91 | 2.86 | 2.82 | 2.77 | 2.74 | 2.70 | 2.67 | 2.64 | 2.61 | 2.59 | 2.56 | 2.55 | 2.54 |
|  | **10.04** | **7.56** | **6.55** | **5.99** | **5.64** | **5.39** | **5.21** | **5.06** | **4.95** | **4.85** | **4.78** | **4.71** | **4.60** | **4.52** | **4.41** | **4.33** | **4.25** | **4.17** | **4.12** | **4.05** | **4.01** | **3.96** | **3.93** | **3.91** |
| 11 | 4.84 | 3.98 | 3.59 | 3.36 | 3.20 | 3.09 | 3.01 | 2.95 | 2.90 | 2.86 | 2.82 | 2.79 | 2.74 | 2.70 | 2.65 | 2.61 | 2.57 | 2.53 | 2.50 | 2.47 | 2.45 | 2.42 | 2.41 | 2.40 |
|  | **9.65** | **7.20** | **6.22** | **5.67** | **5.32** | **5.07** | **4.88** | **4.74** | **4.63** | **4.54** | **4.46** | **4.40** | **4.29** | **4.21** | **4.10** | **4.02** | **3.94** | **3.86** | **3.80** | **3.74** | **3.70** | **3.66** | **3.62** | **3.60** |
| 12 | 4.75 | 3.88 | 3.49 | 3.26 | 3.11 | 3.00 | 2.92 | 2.85 | 2.80 | 2.76 | 2.72 | 2.69 | 2.64 | 2.60 | 2.54 | 2.50 | 2.46 | 2.42 | 2.40 | 2.36 | 2.35 | 2.32 | 2.31 | 2.30 |
|  | **9.33** | **6.93** | **5.95** | **5.41** | **5.06** | **4.82** | **4.65** | **4.50** | **4.39** | **4.30** | **4.22** | **4.16** | **4.05** | **3.98** | **3.86** | **3.78** | **3.70** | **3.61** | **3.56** | **3.49** | **3.46** | **3.41** | **3.38** | **3.36** |
| 13 | 4.67 | 3.80 | 3.41 | 3.18 | 3.02 | 2.92 | 2.84 | 2.77 | 2.72 | 2.67 | 2.63 | 2.60 | 2.55 | 2.51 | 2.46 | 2.42 | 2.38 | 2.34 | 2.32 | 2.28 | 2.26 | 2.24 | 2.22 | 2.21 |
|  | **9.07** | **6.70** | **5.74** | **5.20** | **4.86** | **4.62** | **4.44** | **4.30** | **4.19** | **4.10** | **4.02** | **3.96** | **3.85** | **3.78** | **3.67** | **3.59** | **3.51** | **3.42** | **3.37** | **3.30** | **3.27** | **3.21** | **3.18** | **3.16** |
| 14 | 4.60 | 3.74 | 3.34 | 3.11 | 2.96 | 2.85 | 2.77 | 2.70 | 2.65 | 2.60 | 2.56 | 2.53 | 2.48 | 2.44 | 2.39 | 2.35 | 2.31 | 2.27 | 2.24 | 2.21 | 2.19 | 2.16 | 2.14 | 2.13 |
|  | **8.86** | **6.51** | **5.56** | **5.03** | **4.69** | **4.46** | **4.28** | **4.14** | **4.03** | **3.94** | **3.86** | **3.80** | **3.70** | **3.62** | **3.51** | **3.43** | **3.34** | **3.26** | **3.21** | **3.14** | **3.11** | **3.06** | **3.02** | **3.00** |

**Degrees of Freedom: Numerator**

| Degrees of Freedom: Denominator | 1 | 2 | 3 | 4 | 5 | 6 | 7 | 8 | 9 | 10 | 11 | 12 | 14 | 16 | 20 | 24 | 30 | 40 | 50 | 75 | 100 | 200 | 500 | ∞ |
|---|---|---|---|---|---|---|---|---|---|---|---|---|---|---|---|---|---|---|---|---|---|---|---|---|
| 15 | 4.54 **8.68** | 3.68 **6.36** | 3.29 **5.42** | 3.06 **4.89** | 2.90 **4.56** | 2.79 **4.32** | 2.70 **4.14** | 2.64 **4.00** | 2.59 **3.89** | 2.55 **3.80** | 2.51 **3.73** | 2.48 **3.67** | 2.43 **3.56** | 2.39 **3.48** | 2.33 **3.36** | 2.29 **3.29** | 2.25 **3.20** | 2.21 **3.12** | 2.18 **3.07** | 2.15 **3.00** | 2.12 **2.97** | 2.10 **2.92** | 2.08 **2.89** | 2.07 **2.87** |
| 16 | 4.49 **8.53** | 3.63 **6.23** | 3.24 **5.29** | 3.01 **4.77** | 2.85 **4.44** | 2.74 **4.20** | 2.66 **4.03** | 2.59 **3.89** | 2.54 **3.78** | 2.49 **3.69** | 2.45 **3.61** | 2.42 **3.55** | 2.37 **3.45** | 2.33 **3.37** | 2.28 **3.25** | 2.24 **3.18** | 2.20 **3.10** | 2.16 **3.01** | 2.13 **2.96** | 2.09 **2.89** | 2.07 **2.86** | 2.04 **2.80** | 2.02 **2.77** | 2.01 **2.75** |
| 17 | 4.45 **8.40** | 3.59 **6.11** | 3.20 **5.18** | 2.96 **4.67** | 2.81 **4.34** | 2.70 **4.10** | 2.62 **3.93** | 2.55 **3.79** | 2.50 **3.68** | 2.45 **3.59** | 2.41 **3.52** | 2.38 **3.45** | 2.33 **3.35** | 2.29 **3.27** | 2.23 **3.16** | 2.19 **3.08** | 2.15 **3.00** | 2.11 **2.92** | 2.08 **2.86** | 2.04 **2.79** | 2.02 **2.76** | 1.99 **2.70** | 1.97 **2.67** | 1.96 **2.65** |
| 18 | 4.41 **8.28** | 3.55 **6.01** | 3.16 **5.09** | 2.93 **4.58** | 2.77 **4.25** | 2.66 **4.01** | 2.58 **3.85** | 2.51 **3.71** | 2.46 **3.60** | 2.41 **3.51** | 2.37 **3.44** | 2.34 **3.37** | 2.29 **3.27** | 2.25 **3.19** | 2.19 **3.07** | 2.15 **3.00** | 2.11 **2.91** | 2.07 **2.83** | 2.04 **2.78** | 2.00 **2.71** | 1.98 **2.68** | 1.95 **2.62** | 1.93 **2.59** | 1.92 **2.57** |
| 19 | 4.38 **8.18** | 3.52 **5.93** | 3.13 **5.01** | 2.90 **4.50** | 2.74 **4.17** | 2.63 **3.94** | 2.55 **3.77** | 2.48 **3.63** | 2.43 **3.52** | 2.38 **3.43** | 2.34 **3.36** | 2.31 **3.30** | 2.26 **3.19** | 2.21 **3.12** | 2.15 **3.00** | 2.11 **2.92** | 2.07 **2.84** | 2.02 **2.76** | 2.00 **2.70** | 1.96 **2.63** | 1.94 **2.60** | 1.91 **2.54** | 1.90 **2.51** | 1.88 **2.49** |
| 20 | 4.35 **8.10** | 3.49 **5.85** | 3.10 **4.94** | 2.87 **4.43** | 2.71 **4.10** | 2.60 **3.87** | 2.52 **3.71** | 2.45 **3.56** | 2.40 **3.45** | 2.35 **3.37** | 2.31 **3.30** | 2.28 **3.23** | 2.23 **3.13** | 2.18 **3.05** | 2.12 **2.94** | 2.08 **2.86** | 2.04 **2.77** | 1.99 **2.69** | 1.96 **2.63** | 1.92 **2.56** | 1.90 **2.53** | 1.87 **2.47** | 1.85 **2.44** | 1.84 **2.42** |
| 21 | 4.32 **8.02** | 3.47 **5.78** | 3.07 **4.87** | 2.84 **4.37** | 2.68 **4.04** | 2.57 **3.81** | 2.49 **3.65** | 2.42 **3.51** | 2.37 **3.40** | 2.32 **3.31** | 2.28 **3.24** | 2.25 **3.17** | 2.20 **3.07** | 2.15 **2.99** | 2.09 **2.88** | 2.05 **2.80** | 2.00 **2.72** | 1.96 **2.63** | 1.93 **2.58** | 1.89 **2.51** | 1.87 **2.47** | 1.84 **2.42** | 1.82 **2.38** | 1.81 **2.36** |
| 22 | 4.30 **7.94** | 3.44 **5.72** | 3.05 **4.82** | 2.82 **4.31** | 2.66 **3.99** | 2.55 **3.76** | 2.47 **3.59** | 2.40 **3.45** | 2.35 **3.35** | 2.30 **3.26** | 2.26 **3.18** | 2.23 **3.12** | 2.18 **3.02** | 2.13 **2.94** | 2.07 **2.83** | 2.03 **2.75** | 1.98 **2.67** | 1.93 **2.58** | 1.91 **2.53** | 1.87 **2.46** | 1.84 **2.42** | 1.81 **2.37** | 1.80 **2.33** | 1.78 **2.31** |
| 23 | 4.28 **7.88** | 3.42 **5.66** | 3.03 **4.76** | 2.80 **4.26** | 2.64 **3.94** | 2.53 **3.71** | 2.45 **3.54** | 2.38 **3.41** | 2.32 **3.30** | 2.28 **3.21** | 2.24 **3.14** | 2.20 **3.07** | 2.14 **2.97** | 2.10 **2.89** | 2.04 **2.78** | 2.00 **2.70** | 1.96 **2.62** | 1.91 **2.53** | 1.88 **2.48** | 1.84 **2.41** | 1.82 **2.37** | 1.79 **2.32** | 1.77 **2.28** | 1.76 **2.26** |
| 24 | 4.26 **7.82** | 3.40 **5.61** | 3.01 **4.72** | 2.78 **4.22** | 2.62 **3.90** | 2.51 **3.67** | 2.43 **3.50** | 2.36 **3.36** | 2.30 **3.25** | 2.26 **3.17** | 2.22 **3.09** | 2.18 **3.03** | 2.13 **2.93** | 2.09 **2.85** | 2.02 **2.74** | 1.98 **2.66** | 1.94 **2.58** | 1.89 **2.49** | 1.86 **2.44** | 1.82 **2.36** | 1.80 **2.33** | 1.76 **2.27** | 1.74 **2.23** | 1.73 **2.21** |
| 25 | 4.24 **7.77** | 3.38 **5.57** | 2.99 **4.68** | 2.76 **4.18** | 2.60 **3.86** | 2.49 **3.63** | 2.41 **3.46** | 2.34 **3.32** | 2.28 **3.21** | 2.24 **3.13** | 2.20 **3.05** | 2.16 **2.99** | 2.11 **2.89** | 2.06 **2.81** | 2.00 **2.70** | 1.96 **2.62** | 1.92 **2.54** | 1.87 **2.45** | 1.84 **2.40** | 1.80 **2.32** | 1.77 **2.29** | 1.74 **2.23** | 1.72 **2.19** | 1.71 **2.17** |
| 26 | 4.22 **7.72** | 3.37 **5.53** | 2.98 **4.64** | 2.74 **4.14** | 2.59 **3.82** | 2.47 **3.59** | 2.39 **3.42** | 2.32 **3.29** | 2.27 **3.17** | 2.22 **3.09** | 2.18 **3.02** | 2.15 **2.96** | 2.10 **2.86** | 2.05 **2.77** | 1.99 **2.66** | 1.95 **2.58** | 1.90 **2.50** | 1.85 **2.41** | 1.82 **2.36** | 1.78 **2.28** | 1.76 **2.25** | 1.72 **2.19** | 1.70 **2.15** | 1.69 **2.13** |
| 27 | 4.21 **7.68** | 3.35 **5.49** | 2.96 **4.60** | 2.73 **4.11** | 2.57 **3.79** | 2.46 **3.56** | 2.37 **3.39** | 2.30 **3.26** | 2.25 **3.14** | 2.20 **3.06** | 2.16 **2.98** | 2.13 **2.93** | 2.08 **2.83** | 2.03 **2.74** | 1.97 **2.63** | 1.93 **2.55** | 1.88 **2.47** | 1.84 **2.38** | 1.80 **2.33** | 1.76 **2.25** | 1.74 **2.21** | 1.71 **2.16** | 1.68 **2.12** | 1.67 **2.10** |
| 28 | 4.20 **7.64** | 3.34 **5.45** | 2.95 **4.57** | 2.71 **4.07** | 2.56 **3.76** | 2.44 **3.53** | 2.36 **3.36** | 2.29 **3.23** | 2.24 **3.11** | 2.19 **3.03** | 2.15 **2.95** | 2.12 **2.90** | 2.06 **2.80** | 2.02 **2.71** | 1.96 **2.60** | 1.91 **2.52** | 1.87 **2.44** | 1.81 **2.35** | 1.78 **2.30** | 1.75 **2.22** | 1.72 **2.18** | 1.69 **2.13** | 1.67 **2.09** | 1.65 **2.06** |
| 29 | 4.18 **7.60** | 3.33 **5.42** | 2.93 **4.54** | 2.70 **4.04** | 2.54 **3.73** | 2.43 **3.50** | 2.35 **3.33** | 2.28 **3.20** | 2.22 **3.08** | 2.18 **3.00** | 2.14 **2.92** | 2.10 **2.87** | 2.05 **2.77** | 2.00 **2.68** | 1.94 **2.57** | 1.90 **2.49** | 1.85 **2.41** | 1.80 **2.32** | 1.77 **2.27** | 1.73 **2.19** | 1.71 **2.15** | 1.68 **2.10** | 1.65 **2.06** | 1.64 **2.03** |
| 30 | 4.17 **7.56** | 3.32 **5.39** | 2.92 **4.51** | 2.69 **4.02** | 2.53 **3.70** | 2.42 **3.47** | 2.34 **3.30** | 2.27 **3.17** | 2.21 **3.06** | 2.16 **2.98** | 2.12 **2.90** | 2.09 **2.84** | 2.04 **2.74** | 1.99 **2.66** | 1.93 **2.55** | 1.89 **2.47** | 1.84 **2.38** | 1.79 **2.29** | 1.76 **2.24** | 1.72 **2.16** | 1.69 **2.13** | 1.66 **2.07** | 1.64 **2.03** | 1.62 **2.01** |
| 32 | 4.15 **7.50** | 3.30 **5.34** | 2.90 **4.46** | 2.67 **3.97** | 2.51 **3.66** | 2.40 **3.42** | 2.32 **3.25** | 2.25 **3.12** | 2.19 **3.01** | 2.14 **2.94** | 2.10 **2.86** | 2.07 **2.80** | 2.02 **2.70** | 1.97 **2.62** | 1.91 **2.51** | 1.86 **2.42** | 1.82 **2.34** | 1.76 **2.25** | 1.74 **2.20** | 1.69 **2.12** | 1.67 **2.08** | 1.64 **2.02** | 1.61 **1.98** | 1.59 **1.96** |
| 34 | 4.13 **7.44** | 3.28 **5.29** | 2.88 **4.42** | 2.65 **3.93** | 2.49 **3.61** | 2.38 **3.38** | 2.30 **3.21** | 2.23 **3.08** | 2.17 **2.97** | 2.12 **2.89** | 2.08 **2.82** | 2.05 **2.76** | 2.00 **2.66** | 1.95 **2.58** | 1.89 **2.47** | 1.84 **2.38** | 1.80 **2.30** | 1.74 **2.21** | 1.71 **2.15** | 1.67 **2.08** | 1.64 **2.04** | 1.61 **1.98** | 1.59 **1.94** | 1.57 **1.91** |
| 36 | 4.11 **7.39** | 3.26 **5.25** | 2.86 **4.38** | 2.63 **3.89** | 2.48 **3.58** | 2.36 **3.35** | 2.28 **3.18** | 2.21 **3.04** | 2.15 **2.94** | 2.10 **2.86** | 2.06 **2.78** | 2.03 **2.72** | 1.98 **2.62** | 1.93 **2.54** | 1.87 **2.43** | 1.82 **2.35** | 1.78 **2.26** | 1.72 **2.17** | 1.69 **2.12** | 1.65 **2.04** | 1.62 **2.00** | 1.59 **1.94** | 1.56 **1.90** | 1.55 **1.87** |

*(continued)*

table F (continued)

*The values listed in the table are the critical values of F for the degrees of freedom of the numerator of the F ratio (column headings) and the degrees of freedom of the denominator of the F ratio (row headings). To be significant, $F_{obt} \geq F_{crit}$.*

Degrees of Freedom: Numerator

(Each cell lists the roman value (top) and the bold value (bottom), shown here as roman / **bold**.)

| Denominator | 1 | 2 | 3 | 4 | 5 | 6 | 7 | 8 | 9 | 10 | 11 | 12 | 14 | 16 | 20 | 24 | 30 | 40 | 50 | 75 | 100 | 200 | 500 | ∞ |
|---|---|---|---|---|---|---|---|---|---|---|---|---|---|---|---|---|---|---|---|---|---|---|---|---|
| 38 | 4.10/**7.35** | 3.25/**5.21** | 2.85/**4.34** | 2.62/**3.86** | 2.46/**3.54** | 2.35/**3.32** | 2.26/**3.15** | 2.19/**3.02** | 2.14/**2.91** | 2.09/**2.82** | 2.05/**2.75** | 2.02/**2.69** | 1.96/**2.59** | 1.92/**2.51** | 1.85/**2.40** | 1.80/**2.32** | 1.76/**2.22** | 1.71/**2.14** | 1.67/**2.08** | 1.63/**2.00** | 1.60/**1.97** | 1.57/**1.90** | 1.54/**1.86** | 1.53/**1.84** |
| 40 | 4.08/**7.31** | 3.23/**5.18** | 2.84/**4.31** | 2.61/**3.83** | 2.45/**3.51** | 2.34/**3.29** | 2.25/**3.12** | 2.18/**2.99** | 2.12/**2.88** | 2.07/**2.80** | 2.04/**2.73** | 2.00/**2.66** | 1.95/**2.56** | 1.90/**2.49** | 1.84/**2.37** | 1.79/**2.29** | 1.74/**2.20** | 1.69/**2.11** | 1.66/**2.05** | 1.61/**1.97** | 1.59/**1.94** | 1.55/**1.88** | 1.53/**1.84** | 1.51/**1.81** |
| 42 | 4.07/**7.27** | 3.22/**5.15** | 2.83/**4.29** | 2.59/**3.80** | 2.44/**3.49** | 2.32/**3.26** | 2.24/**3.10** | 2.17/**2.96** | 2.11/**2.86** | 2.06/**2.77** | 2.02/**2.70** | 1.99/**2.64** | 1.94/**2.54** | 1.89/**2.46** | 1.82/**2.35** | 1.78/**2.26** | 1.73/**2.17** | 1.68/**2.08** | 1.64/**2.02** | 1.60/**1.94** | 1.57/**1.91** | 1.54/**1.85** | 1.51/**1.80** | 1.49/**1.78** |
| 44 | 4.06/**7.24** | 3.21/**5.12** | 2.82/**4.26** | 2.58/**3.78** | 2.43/**3.46** | 2.31/**3.24** | 2.23/**3.07** | 2.16/**2.94** | 2.10/**2.84** | 2.05/**2.75** | 2.01/**2.68** | 1.98/**2.62** | 1.92/**2.52** | 1.88/**2.44** | 1.81/**2.32** | 1.76/**2.24** | 1.72/**2.15** | 1.66/**2.06** | 1.63/**2.00** | 1.58/**1.92** | 1.56/**1.88** | 1.52/**1.82** | 1.50/**1.78** | 1.48/**1.75** |
| 46 | 4.05/**7.21** | 3.20/**5.10** | 2.81/**4.24** | 2.57/**3.76** | 2.42/**3.44** | 2.30/**3.22** | 2.22/**3.05** | 2.14/**2.92** | 2.09/**2.82** | 2.04/**2.73** | 2.00/**2.66** | 1.97/**2.60** | 1.91/**2.50** | 1.87/**2.42** | 1.80/**2.30** | 1.75/**2.22** | 1.71/**2.13** | 1.65/**2.04** | 1.62/**1.98** | 1.57/**1.90** | 1.54/**1.86** | 1.51/**1.80** | 1.48/**1.76** | 1.46/**1.72** |
| 48 | 4.04/**7.19** | 3.19/**5.08** | 2.80/**4.22** | 2.56/**3.74** | 2.41/**3.42** | 2.30/**3.20** | 2.21/**3.04** | 2.14/**2.90** | 2.08/**2.80** | 2.03/**2.71** | 1.99/**2.64** | 1.96/**2.58** | 1.90/**2.48** | 1.86/**2.40** | 1.79/**2.28** | 1.74/**2.20** | 1.70/**2.11** | 1.64/**2.02** | 1.61/**1.96** | 1.56/**1.88** | 1.53/**1.84** | 1.50/**1.78** | 1.47/**1.73** | 1.45/**1.70** |
| 50 | 4.03/**7.17** | 3.18/**5.06** | 2.79/**4.20** | 2.56/**3.72** | 2.40/**3.41** | 2.29/**3.18** | 2.20/**3.02** | 2.13/**2.88** | 2.07/**2.78** | 2.02/**2.70** | 1.98/**2.62** | 1.95/**2.56** | 1.90/**2.46** | 1.85/**2.39** | 1.78/**2.26** | 1.74/**2.18** | 1.69/**2.10** | 1.63/**2.00** | 1.60/**1.94** | 1.55/**1.86** | 1.52/**1.82** | 1.48/**1.76** | 1.46/**1.71** | 1.44/**1.68** |
| 55 | 4.02/**7.12** | 3.17/**5.01** | 2.78/**4.16** | 2.54/**3.68** | 2.38/**3.37** | 2.27/**3.15** | 2.18/**2.98** | 2.11/**2.85** | 2.05/**2.75** | 2.00/**2.66** | 1.97/**2.59** | 1.93/**2.53** | 1.88/**2.43** | 1.83/**2.35** | 1.76/**2.23** | 1.72/**2.15** | 1.67/**2.06** | 1.61/**1.96** | 1.58/**1.90** | 1.52/**1.82** | 1.50/**1.78** | 1.46/**1.71** | 1.43/**1.66** | 1.41/**1.64** |
| 60 | 4.00/**7.08** | 3.15/**4.98** | 2.76/**4.13** | 2.52/**3.65** | 2.37/**3.34** | 2.25/**3.12** | 2.17/**2.95** | 2.10/**2.82** | 2.04/**2.72** | 1.99/**2.63** | 1.95/**2.56** | 1.92/**2.50** | 1.86/**2.40** | 1.81/**2.32** | 1.75/**2.20** | 1.70/**2.12** | 1.65/**2.03** | 1.59/**1.93** | 1.56/**1.87** | 1.50/**1.79** | 1.48/**1.74** | 1.44/**1.68** | 1.41/**1.63** | 1.39/**1.60** |
| 65 | 3.99/**7.04** | 3.14/**4.95** | 2.75/**4.10** | 2.51/**3.62** | 2.36/**3.31** | 2.24/**3.09** | 2.15/**2.93** | 2.08/**2.79** | 2.02/**2.70** | 1.98/**2.61** | 1.94/**2.54** | 1.90/**2.47** | 1.85/**2.37** | 1.80/**2.30** | 1.73/**2.18** | 1.68/**2.09** | 1.63/**2.00** | 1.57/**1.90** | 1.54/**1.84** | 1.49/**1.76** | 1.46/**1.71** | 1.42/**1.64** | 1.39/**1.60** | 1.37/**1.56** |
| 70 | 3.98/**7.01** | 3.13/**4.92** | 2.74/**4.08** | 2.50/**3.60** | 2.35/**3.29** | 2.23/**3.07** | 2.14/**2.91** | 2.07/**2.77** | 2.01/**2.67** | 1.97/**2.59** | 1.93/**2.51** | 1.89/**2.45** | 1.84/**2.35** | 1.79/**2.28** | 1.72/**2.15** | 1.67/**2.07** | 1.62/**1.98** | 1.56/**1.88** | 1.53/**1.82** | 1.47/**1.74** | 1.45/**1.69** | 1.40/**1.62** | 1.37/**1.56** | 1.35/**1.53** |
| 80 | 3.96/**6.96** | 3.11/**4.88** | 2.72/**4.04** | 2.48/**3.56** | 2.33/**3.25** | 2.21/**3.04** | 2.12/**2.87** | 2.05/**2.74** | 1.99/**2.64** | 1.95/**2.55** | 1.91/**2.48** | 1.88/**2.41** | 1.82/**2.32** | 1.77/**2.24** | 1.70/**2.11** | 1.65/**2.03** | 1.60/**1.94** | 1.54/**1.84** | 1.51/**1.78** | 1.45/**1.70** | 1.42/**1.65** | 1.38/**1.57** | 1.35/**1.52** | 1.32/**1.49** |
| 100 | 3.94/**6.90** | 3.09/**4.82** | 2.70/**3.98** | 2.46/**3.51** | 2.30/**3.20** | 2.19/**2.99** | 2.10/**2.82** | 2.03/**2.69** | 1.97/**2.59** | 1.92/**2.51** | 1.88/**2.43** | 1.85/**2.36** | 1.79/**2.26** | 1.75/**2.19** | 1.68/**2.06** | 1.63/**1.98** | 1.57/**1.89** | 1.51/**1.79** | 1.48/**1.73** | 1.42/**1.64** | 1.39/**1.59** | 1.34/**1.51** | 1.30/**1.46** | 1.28/**1.43** |
| 125 | 3.92/**6.84** | 3.07/**4.78** | 2.68/**3.94** | 2.44/**3.47** | 2.29/**3.17** | 2.17/**2.95** | 2.08/**2.79** | 2.01/**2.65** | 1.95/**2.56** | 1.90/**2.47** | 1.86/**2.40** | 1.83/**2.33** | 1.77/**2.23** | 1.72/**2.15** | 1.65/**2.03** | 1.60/**1.94** | 1.55/**1.85** | 1.49/**1.75** | 1.45/**1.68** | 1.39/**1.59** | 1.36/**1.54** | 1.31/**1.46** | 1.27/**1.40** | 1.25/**1.37** |
| 150 | 3.91/**6.81** | 3.06/**4.75** | 2.67/**3.91** | 2.43/**3.44** | 2.27/**3.14** | 2.16/**2.92** | 2.07/**2.76** | 2.00/**2.62** | 1.94/**2.53** | 1.89/**2.44** | 1.85/**2.37** | 1.82/**2.30** | 1.76/**2.20** | 1.71/**2.12** | 1.64/**2.00** | 1.59/**1.91** | 1.54/**1.83** | 1.47/**1.72** | 1.44/**1.66** | 1.37/**1.56** | 1.34/**1.51** | 1.29/**1.43** | 1.25/**1.37** | 1.22/**1.33** |
| 200 | 3.89/**6.76** | 3.04/**4.71** | 2.65/**3.88** | 2.41/**3.41** | 2.26/**3.11** | 2.14/**2.90** | 2.05/**2.73** | 1.98/**2.60** | 1.92/**2.50** | 1.87/**2.41** | 1.83/**2.34** | 1.80/**2.28** | 1.74/**2.17** | 1.69/**2.09** | 1.62/**1.97** | 1.57/**1.88** | 1.52/**1.79** | 1.45/**1.69** | 1.42/**1.62** | 1.35/**1.53** | 1.32/**1.48** | 1.26/**1.39** | 1.22/**1.33** | 1.19/**1.28** |
| 400 | 3.86/**6.70** | 3.02/**4.66** | 2.62/**3.83** | 2.39/**3.36** | 2.23/**3.06** | 2.12/**2.85** | 2.03/**2.69** | 1.96/**2.55** | 1.90/**2.46** | 1.85/**2.37** | 1.81/**2.29** | 1.78/**2.23** | 1.72/**2.12** | 1.67/**2.04** | 1.60/**1.92** | 1.54/**1.84** | 1.49/**1.74** | 1.42/**1.64** | 1.38/**1.57** | 1.32/**1.47** | 1.28/**1.42** | 1.22/**1.32** | 1.16/**1.24** | 1.13/**1.19** |
| 1000 | 3.85/**6.66** | 3.00/**4.62** | 2.61/**3.80** | 2.38/**3.34** | 2.22/**3.04** | 2.10/**2.82** | 2.02/**2.66** | 1.95/**2.53** | 1.89/**2.43** | 1.84/**2.34** | 1.80/**2.26** | 1.76/**2.20** | 1.70/**2.09** | 1.65/**2.01** | 1.58/**1.89** | 1.53/**1.81** | 1.47/**1.71** | 1.41/**1.61** | 1.36/**1.54** | 1.30/**1.44** | 1.26/**1.38** | 1.19/**1.28** | 1.13/**1.19** | 1.08/**1.11** |
| ∞ | 3.84/**6.64** | 2.99/**4.60** | 2.60/**3.78** | 2.37/**3.32** | 2.21/**3.02** | 2.09/**2.80** | 2.01/**2.64** | 1.94/**2.51** | 1.88/**2.41** | 1.83/**2.32** | 1.79/**2.24** | 1.75/**2.18** | 1.69/**2.07** | 1.64/**1.99** | 1.57/**1.87** | 1.52/**1.79** | 1.46/**1.69** | 1.40/**1.59** | 1.35/**1.52** | 1.28/**1.41** | 1.24/**1.36** | 1.17/**1.25** | 1.11/**1.15** | 1.00/**1.00** |

t a b l e  G    Critical values of the studentized range (Q) distribution

*The values listed in the table are the critical values of Q for α = 0.05 and 0.01, as a function of degrees of freedom of $s_W^2$ and k (the number of means) or r (the number of means encompassed by $\overline{X}_i$ and $\overline{X}_j$, after the means have been rank-ordered). To be significant, $Q_{obt} \geq Q_{crit}$.*

| $s_W^2$ df | α | k (Number of Means) or r (Number of Means Encompassed by $\overline{X}_i$ and $\overline{X}_j$) | | | | | | | | | |
|---|---|---|---|---|---|---|---|---|---|---|---|
| | | 2 | 3 | 4 | 5 | 6 | 7 | 8 | 9 | 10 | 11 |
| 5 | .05 | 3.64 | 4.60 | 5.22 | 5.67 | 6.03 | 6.33 | 6.58 | 6.80 | 6.99 | 7.17 |
| | .01 | 5.70 | 6.98 | 7.80 | 8.42 | 8.91 | 9.32 | 9.67 | 9.97 | 10.24 | 10.48 |
| 6 | .05 | 3.46 | 4.34 | 4.90 | 5.30 | 5.63 | 5.90 | 6.12 | 6.32 | 6.49 | 6.65 |
| | .01 | 5.24 | 6.33 | 7.03 | 7.56 | 7.97 | 8.32 | 8.61 | 8.87 | 9.10 | 9.30 |
| 7 | .05 | 3.34 | 4.16 | 4.68 | 5.06 | 5.36 | 5.61 | 5.82 | 6.00 | 6.16 | 6.30 |
| | .01 | 4.95 | 5.92 | 6.54 | 7.01 | 7.37 | 7.68 | 7.94 | 8.17 | 8.37 | 8.55 |
| 8 | .05 | 3.26 | 4.04 | 4.53 | 4.89 | 5.17 | 5.40 | 5.60 | 5.77 | 5.92 | 6.05 |
| | .01 | 4.75 | 5.64 | 6.20 | 6.62 | 6.96 | 7.24 | 7.47 | 7.68 | 7.86 | 8.03 |
| 9 | .05 | 3.20 | 3.95 | 4.41 | 4.76 | 5.02 | 5.24 | 5.43 | 5.59 | 5.74 | 5.87 |
| | .01 | 4.60 | 5.43 | 5.96 | 6.35 | 6.66 | 6.91 | 7.13 | 7.33 | 7.49 | 7.65 |
| 10 | .05 | 3.15 | 3.88 | 4.33 | 4.65 | 4.91 | 5.12 | 5.30 | 5.46 | 5.60 | 5.72 |
| | .01 | 4.48 | 5.27 | 5.77 | 6.14 | 6.43 | 6.67 | 6.87 | 7.05 | 7.21 | 7.36 |
| 11 | .05 | 3.11 | 3.82 | 4.26 | 4.57 | 4.82 | 5.03 | 5.20 | 5.35 | 5.49 | 5.61 |
| | .01 | 4.39 | 5.15 | 5.62 | 5.97 | 6.25 | 6.48 | 6.67 | 6.84 | 6.99 | 7.13 |
| 12 | .05 | 3.08 | 3.77 | 4.20 | 4.51 | 4.75 | 4.95 | 5.12 | 5.27 | 5.39 | 5.51 |
| | .01 | 4.32 | 5.05 | 5.50 | 5.84 | 6.10 | 6.32 | 6.51 | 6.67 | 6.81 | 6.94 |
| 13 | .05 | 3.06 | 3.73 | 4.15 | 4.45 | 4.69 | 4.88 | 5.05 | 5.19 | 5.32 | 5.43 |
| | .01 | 4.26 | 4.96 | 5.40 | 5.73 | 5.98 | 6.19 | 6.37 | 6.53 | 6.67 | 6.79 |
| 14 | .05 | 3.03 | 3.70 | 4.11 | 4.41 | 4.64 | 4.83 | 4.99 | 5.13 | 5.25 | 5.36 |
| | .01 | 4.21 | 4.89 | 5.32 | 5.63 | 5.88 | 6.08 | 6.26 | 6.41 | 6.54 | 6.66 |
| 15 | .05 | 3.01 | 3.67 | 4.08 | 4.37 | 4.59 | 4.78 | 4.94 | 5.08 | 5.20 | 5.31 |
| | .01 | 4.17 | 4.84 | 5.25 | 5.56 | 5.80 | 5.99 | 6.16 | 6.31 | 6.44 | 6.55 |
| 16 | .05 | 3.00 | 3.65 | 4.05 | 4.33 | 4.56 | 4.74 | 4.90 | 5.03 | 5.15 | 5.26 |
| | .01 | 4.13 | 4.79 | 5.19 | 5.49 | 5.72 | 5.92 | 6.08 | 6.22 | 6.35 | 6.46 |
| 17 | .05 | 2.98 | 3.63 | 4.02 | 4.30 | 4.52 | 4.70 | 4.86 | 4.99 | 5.11 | 5.21 |
| | .01 | 4.10 | 4.74 | 5.14 | 5.43 | 5.66 | 5.85 | 6.01 | 6.15 | 6.27 | 6.38 |
| 18 | .05 | 2.97 | 3.61 | 4.00 | 4.28 | 4.49 | 4.67 | 4.82 | 4.96 | 5.07 | 5.17 |
| | .01 | 4.07 | 4.70 | 5.09 | 5.38 | 5.60 | 5.79 | 5.94 | 6.08 | 6.20 | 6.31 |
| 19 | .05 | 2.96 | 3.59 | 3.98 | 4.25 | 4.47 | 4.65 | 4.79 | 4.92 | 5.04 | 5.14 |
| | .01 | 4.05 | 4.67 | 5.05 | 5.33 | 5.55 | 5.73 | 4.89 | 6.02 | 6.14 | 6.25 |
| 20 | .05 | 2.95 | 3.58 | 3.96 | 4.23 | 4.45 | 4.62 | 4.77 | 4.90 | 5.01 | 5.11 |
| | .01 | 4.02 | 4.64 | 5.02 | 5.29 | 5.51 | 5.69 | 5.84 | 5.97 | 6.09 | 6.19 |
| 24 | .05 | 2.92 | 3.53 | 3.90 | 4.17 | 4.37 | 4.54 | 4.68 | 4.81 | 4.92 | 5.01 |
| | .01 | 3.96 | 4.55 | 4.91 | 5.17 | 5.37 | 5.54 | 5.69 | 5.81 | 5.92 | 6.02 |
| 30 | .05 | 2.89 | 3.49 | 3.85 | 4.10 | 4.30 | 4.46 | 4.60 | 4.72 | 4.82 | 4.92 |
| | .01 | 3.89 | 4.45 | 4.80 | 5.05 | 5.24 | 5.40 | 5.54 | 5.65 | 5.76 | 5.85 |
| 40 | .05 | 2.86 | 3.44 | 3.79 | 4.04 | 4.23 | 4.39 | 4.52 | 4.63 | 4.73 | 4.82 |
| | .01 | 3.82 | 4.37 | 4.70 | 4.93 | 5.11 | 5.26 | 5.39 | 5.50 | 5.60 | 5.69 |
| 60 | .05 | 2.83 | 3.40 | 3.74 | 3.98 | 4.16 | 4.31 | 4.44 | 4.55 | 4.65 | 4.73 |
| | .01 | 3.76 | 4.28 | 4.59 | 4.82 | 4.99 | 5.13 | 5.25 | 5.36 | 5.45 | 5.53 |
| 120 | .05 | 2.80 | 3.36 | 3.68 | 3.92 | 4.10 | 4.24 | 4.36 | 4.47 | 4.56 | 4.64 |
| | .01 | 3.70 | 4.20 | 4.50 | 4.71 | 4.87 | 5.01 | 5.12 | 5.21 | 5.30 | 5.37 |
| ∞ | .05 | 2.77 | 3.31 | 3.63 | 3.86 | 4.03 | 4.17 | 4.29 | 4.39 | 4.47 | 4.55 |
| | .01 | 3.64 | 4.12 | 4.40 | 4.60 | 4.76 | 4.88 | 4.99 | 5.08 | 5.16 | 5.23 |

table H  Chi-square ($\chi^2$) distribution

*The first column (df) locates each $\chi^2$ distribution. The other columns give the proportion of area under the $\chi^2$ distribution that is above the tabled value of $\chi^2$. The $\chi^2$ values under the column headings of .05 and .01 are the critical values of $\chi^2$ for $\alpha = 0.05$ and 0.01. To be significant, $\chi^2_{obt} \geq \chi^2_{crit}$.*

| Degrees of freedom df | P = .99 | .98 | .95 | .90 | .80 | .70 | .50 | .30 | .20 | .10 | .05 | .02 | .01 |
|---|---|---|---|---|---|---|---|---|---|---|---|---|---|
| 1 | .000157 | .000628 | .00393 | .0158 | .0642 | .148 | .455 | 1.074 | 1.642 | 2.706 | 3.841 | 5.412 | 6.635 |
| 2 | .0201 | .0404 | .103 | .211 | .446 | .713 | 1.386 | 2.408 | 3.219 | 4.605 | 5.991 | 7.824 | 9.210 |
| 3 | .115 | .185 | .352 | .584 | 1.005 | 1.424 | 2.366 | 3.665 | 4.642 | 6.251 | 7.815 | 9.837 | 11.341 |
| 4 | .297 | .429 | .711 | 1.064 | 1.649 | 2.195 | 3.357 | 4.878 | 5.989 | 7.779 | 9.488 | 11.668 | 13.277 |
| 5 | .554 | .752 | 1.145 | 1.610 | 2.343 | 3.000 | 4.351 | 6.064 | 7.289 | 9.236 | 11.070 | 13.388 | 15.086 |
| 6 | .872 | 1.134 | 1.635 | 2.204 | 3.070 | 3.828 | 5.348 | 7.231 | 8.558 | 10.645 | 12.592 | 15.033 | 16.812 |
| 7 | 1.239 | 1.564 | 2.167 | 2.833 | 3.822 | 4.671 | 6.346 | 8.383 | 9.803 | 12.017 | 14.067 | 16.622 | 18.475 |
| 8 | 1.646 | 2.032 | 2.733 | 3.490 | 4.594 | 5.527 | 7.344 | 9.524 | 11.030 | 13.362 | 15.507 | 18.168 | 20.090 |
| 9 | 2.088 | 2.532 | 3.325 | 4.168 | 5.380 | 6.393 | 8.343 | 10.656 | 12.242 | 14.684 | 16.919 | 19.679 | 21.666 |
| 10 | 2.558 | 3.059 | 3.940 | 4.865 | 6.179 | 7.267 | 9.342 | 11.781 | 13.442 | 15.987 | 18.307 | 21.161 | 23.209 |
| 11 | 3.053 | 3.609 | 4.575 | 5.578 | 6.989 | 8.148 | 10.341 | 12.899 | 14.631 | 17.275 | 19.675 | 22.618 | 24.725 |
| 12 | 3.571 | 4.178 | 5.226 | 6.304 | 7.807 | 9.034 | 11.340 | 14.011 | 15.812 | 18.549 | 21.026 | 24.054 | 26.217 |
| 13 | 4.107 | 4.765 | 5.892 | 7.042 | 8.634 | 9.926 | 12.340 | 15.119 | 16.985 | 19.812 | 22.362 | 25.472 | 27.688 |
| 14 | 4.660 | 5.368 | 6.571 | 7.790 | 9.467 | 10.821 | 13.339 | 16.222 | 18.151 | 21.064 | 23.685 | 26.873 | 29.141 |
| 15 | 5.229 | 5.985 | 7.261 | 8.547 | 10.307 | 11.721 | 14.339 | 17.322 | 19.311 | 22.307 | 24.996 | 28.259 | 30.578 |
| 16 | 5.812 | 6.614 | 7.962 | 9.312 | 11.152 | 12.624 | 15.338 | 18.418 | 20.465 | 23.542 | 26.296 | 29.633 | 32.000 |
| 17 | 6.408 | 7.255 | 8.672 | 10.085 | 12.002 | 13.531 | 16.338 | 19.511 | 21.615 | 24.769 | 27.587 | 30.995 | 33.409 |
| 18 | 7.015 | 7.906 | 9.390 | 10.865 | 12.857 | 14.440 | 17.338 | 20.601 | 22.760 | 25.989 | 28.869 | 32.346 | 34.805 |
| 19 | 7.633 | 8.567 | 10.117 | 11.651 | 13.716 | 15.352 | 18.338 | 21.689 | 23.900 | 27.204 | 30.144 | 33.687 | 36.191 |
| 20 | 8.260 | 9.237 | 10.851 | 12.443 | 14.578 | 16.266 | 19.337 | 22.775 | 25.038 | 28.412 | 31.410 | 35.020 | 37.566 |
| 21 | 8.897 | 9.915 | 11.591 | 13.240 | 15.445 | 17.182 | 20.337 | 23.858 | 26.171 | 29.615 | 32.671 | 36.343 | 38.932 |
| 22 | 9.542 | 10.600 | 12.338 | 14.041 | 16.314 | 18.101 | 21.337 | 24.939 | 27.301 | 30.813 | 33.924 | 37.659 | 40.289 |
| 23 | 10.196 | 11.293 | 13.091 | 14.848 | 17.187 | 19.021 | 22.337 | 26.018 | 28.429 | 32.007 | 35.172 | 38.968 | 41.638 |
| 24 | 10.856 | 11.992 | 13.848 | 15.659 | 18.062 | 19.943 | 23.337 | 27.096 | 29.553 | 33.196 | 36.415 | 40.270 | 42.980 |
| 25 | 11.524 | 12.697 | 14.611 | 16.473 | 18.940 | 20.867 | 24.337 | 28.172 | 30.675 | 34.382 | 37.652 | 41.566 | 44.314 |
| 26 | 12.198 | 13.409 | 15.379 | 17.292 | 19.820 | 21.792 | 25.336 | 29.246 | 31.795 | 35.563 | 38.885 | 42.856 | 45.642 |
| 27 | 12.879 | 14.125 | 16.151 | 18.114 | 20.703 | 22.719 | 26.336 | 30.319 | 32.912 | 36.741 | 40.113 | 44.140 | 46.963 |
| 28 | 13.565 | 14.847 | 16.928 | 18.939 | 21.588 | 23.647 | 27.336 | 31.391 | 34.027 | 37.916 | 41.337 | 45.419 | 48.278 |
| 29 | 14.256 | 15.574 | 17.708 | 19.768 | 22.475 | 24.577 | 28.336 | 32.461 | 35.139 | 39.087 | 42.557 | 46.693 | 49.588 |
| 30 | 14.953 | 16.306 | 18.493 | 20.599 | 23.364 | 25.508 | 29.336 | 33.530 | 36.250 | 40.256 | 43.773 | 47.962 | 50.892 |

Area

0  $\chi^2$

table I   Critical values of *T* for Wilcoxon signed ranks test

*The values listed in the table are the critical values of T for the specified N (left column) and alpha level (column heading).*
*To be significant, $T_{obt} \leq T_{crit}$.*

| | Level of Significance for One-Tailed Test | | | |
|---|---|---|---|---|
| | **.05** | **.025** | **.01** | **.005** |
| | Level of Significance for Two-Tailed Test | | | |
| **N** | **.10** | **.05** | **.02** | **.01** |
| 5 | 0 | — | — | — |
| 6 | 2 | 0 | — | — |
| 7 | 3 | 2 | 0 | — |
| 8 | 5 | 3 | 1 | 0 |
| 9 | 8 | 5 | 3 | 1 |
| 10 | 10 | 8 | 5 | 3 |
| 11 | 13 | 10 | 7 | 5 |
| 12 | 17 | 13 | 9 | 7 |
| 13 | 21 | 17 | 12 | 9 |
| 14 | 25 | 21 | 15 | 12 |
| 15 | 30 | 25 | 19 | 15 |
| 16 | 35 | 29 | 23 | 19 |
| 17 | 41 | 34 | 27 | 23 |
| 18 | 47 | 40 | 32 | 27 |
| 19 | 53 | 46 | 37 | 32 |
| 20 | 60 | 52 | 43 | 37 |
| 21 | 67 | 58 | 49 | 42 |
| 22 | 75 | 65 | 55 | 48 |
| 23 | 83 | 73 | 62 | 54 |
| 24 | 91 | 81 | 69 | 61 |
| 25 | 100 | 89 | 76 | 68 |
| 26 | 110 | 98 | 84 | 75 |
| 27 | 119 | 107 | 92 | 83 |

| | Level of Significance for One-Tailed Test | | | |
|---|---|---|---|---|
| | **.05** | **.025** | **.01** | **.005** |
| | Level of Significance for Two-Tailed Test | | | |
| **N** | **.10** | **.05** | **.02** | **.01** |
| 28 | 130 | 116 | 101 | 91 |
| 29 | 140 | 126 | 110 | 100 |
| 30 | 151 | 137 | 120 | 109 |
| 31 | 163 | 147 | 130 | 118 |
| 32 | 175 | 159 | 140 | 128 |
| 33 | 187 | 170 | 151 | 138 |
| 34 | 200 | 182 | 162 | 148 |
| 35 | 213 | 195 | 173 | 159 |
| 36 | 227 | 208 | 185 | 171 |
| 37 | 241 | 221 | 198 | 182 |
| 38 | 256 | 235 | 211 | 194 |
| 39 | 271 | 249 | 224 | 207 |
| 40 | 286 | 264 | 238 | 220 |
| 41 | 302 | 279 | 252 | 233 |
| 42 | 319 | 294 | 266 | 247 |
| 43 | 336 | 310 | 281 | 261 |
| 44 | 353 | 327 | 296 | 276 |
| 45 | 371 | 343 | 312 | 291 |
| 46 | 389 | 361 | 328 | 307 |
| 47 | 407 | 378 | 345 | 322 |
| 48 | 426 | 396 | 362 | 339 |
| 49 | 446 | 415 | 379 | 355 |
| 50 | 466 | 434 | 397 | 373 |

table J  Random numbers

| | 1 | 2 | 3 | 4 | 5 | 6 | 7 | 8 | 9 |
|---|---|---|---|---|---|---|---|---|---|
| 1 | 32942 | 95416 | 42339 | 59045 | 26693 | 49057 | 87496 | 20624 | 14819 |
| 2 | 07410 | 99859 | 83828 | 21409 | 29094 | 65114 | 36701 | 25762 | 12827 |
| 3 | 59981 | 68155 | 45673 | 76210 | 58219 | 45738 | 29550 | 24736 | 09574 |
| 4 | 46251 | 25437 | 69654 | 99716 | 11563 | 08803 | 86027 | 51867 | 12116 |
| 5 | 65558 | 51904 | 93123 | 27887 | 53138 | 21488 | 09095 | 78777 | 71240 |
| 6 | 99187 | 19258 | 86421 | 16401 | 19397 | 83297 | 40111 | 49326 | 81686 |
| 7 | 35641 | 00301 | 16096 | 34775 | 21562 | 97983 | 45040 | 19200 | 16383 |
| 8 | 14031 | 00936 | 81518 | 48440 | 02218 | 04756 | 19506 | 60695 | 88494 |
| 9 | 60677 | 15076 | 92554 | 26042 | 23472 | 69869 | 62877 | 19584 | 39576 |
| 10 | 66314 | 05212 | 67859 | 89356 | 20056 | 30648 | 87349 | 20389 | 53805 |
| 11 | 20416 | 87410 | 75646 | 64176 | 82752 | 63606 | 37011 | 57346 | 69512 |
| 12 | 28701 | 56992 | 70423 | 62415 | 40807 | 98086 | 58850 | 28968 | 45297 |
| 13 | 74579 | 33844 | 33426 | 07570 | 00728 | 07079 | 19322 | 56325 | 84819 |
| 14 | 62615 | 52342 | 82968 | 75540 | 80045 | 53069 | 20665 | 21282 | 07768 |
| 15 | 93945 | 06293 | 22879 | 08161 | 01442 | 75071 | 21427 | 94842 | 26210 |
| 16 | 75689 | 76131 | 96837 | 67450 | 44511 | 50424 | 82848 | 41975 | 71663 |
| 17 | 02921 | 16919 | 35424 | 93209 | 52133 | 87327 | 95897 | 65171 | 20376 |
| 18 | 14295 | 34969 | 14216 | 03191 | 61647 | 30296 | 66667 | 10101 | 63203 |
| 19 | 05303 | 91109 | 82403 | 40312 | 62191 | 67023 | 90073 | 83205 | 71344 |
| 20 | 57071 | 90357 | 12901 | 08899 | 91039 | 67251 | 28701 | 03846 | 94589 |
| 21 | 78471 | 57741 | 13599 | 84390 | 32146 | 00871 | 09354 | 22745 | 65806 |
| 22 | 89242 | 79337 | 59293 | 47481 | 07740 | 43345 | 25716 | 70020 | 54005 |
| 23 | 14955 | 59592 | 97035 | 80430 | 87220 | 06392 | 79028 | 57123 | 52872 |
| 24 | 42446 | 41880 | 37415 | 47472 | 04513 | 49494 | 08860 | 08038 | 43624 |
| 25 | 18534 | 22346 | 54556 | 17558 | 73689 | 14894 | 05030 | 19561 | 56517 |
| 26 | 39284 | 33737 | 42512 | 86411 | 23753 | 29690 | 26096 | 81361 | 93099 |
| 27 | 33922 | 37329 | 89911 | 55876 | 28379 | 81031 | 22058 | 21487 | 54613 |
| 28 | 78355 | 54013 | 50774 | 30666 | 61205 | 42574 | 47773 | 36027 | 27174 |
| 29 | 08845 | 99145 | 94316 | 88974 | 29828 | 97069 | 90327 | 61842 | 29604 |
| 30 | 01769 | 71825 | 55957 | 98271 | 02784 | 66731 | 40311 | 88495 | 18821 |
| 31 | 17639 | 38284 | 59478 | 90409 | 21997 | 56199 | 30068 | 82800 | 69692 |
| 32 | 05851 | 58653 | 99949 | 63505 | 40409 | 85551 | 90729 | 64938 | 52403 |
| 33 | 42396 | 40112 | 11469 | 03476 | 03328 | 84238 | 26570 | 51790 | 42122 |
| 34 | 13318 | 14192 | 98167 | 75631 | 74141 | 22369 | 36757 | 89117 | 54998 |
| 35 | 60571 | 54786 | 26281 | 01855 | 30706 | 66578 | 32019 | 65884 | 58485 |
| 36 | 09531 | 81853 | 59334 | 70929 | 03544 | 18510 | 89541 | 13555 | 21168 |
| 37 | 72865 | 16829 | 86542 | 00396 | 20363 | 13010 | 69645 | 49608 | 54738 |
| 38 | 56324 | 31093 | 77924 | 28622 | 83543 | 28912 | 15059 | 80192 | 83964 |
| 39 | 78192 | 21626 | 91399 | 07235 | 07104 | 73652 | 64425 | 85149 | 75409 |
| 40 | 64666 | 34767 | 97298 | 92708 | 01994 | 53188 | 78476 | 07804 | 62404 |
| 41 | 82201 | 75694 | 02808 | 65983 | 74373 | 66693 | 13094 | 74183 | 73020 |
| 42 | 15360 | 73776 | 40914 | 85190 | 54278 | 99054 | 62944 | 47351 | 89098 |
| 43 | 68142 | 67957 | 70896 | 37983 | 20487 | 95350 | 16371 | 03426 | 13895 |
| 44 | 19138 | 31200 | 30616 | 14639 | 44406 | 44236 | 57360 | 81644 | 94761 |
| 45 | 28155 | 03521 | 36415 | 78452 | 92359 | 81091 | 56513 | 88321 | 97910 |
| 46 | 87971 | 29031 | 51780 | 27376 | 81056 | 86155 | 55488 | 50590 | 74514 |
| 47 | 58147 | 68841 | 53625 | 02059 | 75223 | 16783 | 19272 | 61994 | 71090 |
| 48 | 18875 | 52809 | 70594 | 41649 | 32935 | 26430 | 82096 | 01605 | 65846 |
| 49 | 75109 | 56474 | 74111 | 31966 | 29969 | 70093 | 98901 | 84550 | 25769 |
| 50 | 35983 | 03742 | 76822 | 12073 | 59463 | 84420 | 15868 | 99505 | 11426 |

**t a b l e   J**    Random numbers    (*continued*)

|     | 1 | 2 | 3 | 4 | 5 | 6 | 7 | 8 | 9 |
|-----|-------|-------|-------|-------|-------|-------|-------|-------|-------|
| 51  | 12651 | 61646 | 11769 | 75109 | 86996 | 97669 | 25757 | 32535 | 07122 |
| 52  | 81769 | 74436 | 02630 | 72310 | 45049 | 18029 | 07469 | 42341 | 98173 |
| 53  | 36737 | 98863 | 77240 | 76251 | 00654 | 64688 | 09343 | 70278 | 67331 |
| 54  | 82861 | 54371 | 76610 | 94934 | 72748 | 44124 | 05610 | 53750 | 95938 |
| 55  | 21325 | 15732 | 24127 | 37431 | 09723 | 63529 | 73977 | 95218 | 96074 |
| 56  | 74146 | 47887 | 62463 | 23045 | 41490 | 07954 | 22597 | 60012 | 98866 |
| 57  | 90759 | 64410 | 54179 | 66075 | 61051 | 75385 | 51378 | 08360 | 95946 |
| 58  | 55683 | 98078 | 02238 | 91540 | 21219 | 17720 | 87817 | 41705 | 95785 |
| 59  | 79686 | 17969 | 76061 | 83748 | 55920 | 83612 | 41540 | 86492 | 06447 |
| 60  | 70333 | 00201 | 86201 | 69716 | 78185 | 62154 | 77930 | 67663 | 29529 |
| 61  | 14042 | 53536 | 07779 | 04157 | 41172 | 36473 | 42123 | 43929 | 50533 |
| 62  | 59911 | 08256 | 06596 | 48416 | 69770 | 68797 | 56080 | 14223 | 59199 |
| 63  | 62368 | 62623 | 62742 | 14891 | 39247 | 52242 | 98832 | 69533 | 91174 |
| 64  | 57529 | 97751 | 54976 | 48957 | 74599 | 08759 | 78494 | 52785 | 68526 |
| 65  | 15469 | 90574 | 78033 | 66885 | 13936 | 42117 | 71831 | 22961 | 94225 |
| 66  | 18625 | 23674 | 53850 | 32827 | 81647 | 80820 | 00420 | 63555 | 74489 |
| 67  | 74626 | 68394 | 88562 | 70745 | 23701 | 45630 | 65891 | 58220 | 35442 |
| 68  | 11119 | 16519 | 27384 | 90199 | 79210 | 76965 | 99546 | 30323 | 31664 |
| 69  | 41101 | 17336 | 48951 | 53674 | 17880 | 45260 | 08575 | 49321 | 36191 |
| 70  | 32123 | 91576 | 84221 | 78902 | 82010 | 30847 | 62329 | 63898 | 23268 |
| 71  | 26091 | 68409 | 69704 | 82267 | 14751 | 13151 | 93115 | 01437 | 56945 |
| 72  | 67680 | 79790 | 48462 | 59278 | 44185 | 29616 | 76531 | 19589 | 83139 |
| 73  | 15184 | 19260 | 14073 | 07026 | 25264 | 08388 | 27182 | 22557 | 61501 |
| 74  | 58010 | 45039 | 57181 | 10238 | 36874 | 28546 | 37444 | 80824 | 63981 |
| 75  | 56425 | 53996 | 86245 | 32623 | 78858 | 08143 | 60377 | 42925 | 42815 |
| 76  | 82630 | 84066 | 13592 | 60642 | 17904 | 99718 | 63432 | 88642 | 37858 |
| 77  | 14927 | 40909 | 23900 | 48761 | 44860 | 92467 | 31742 | 87142 | 03607 |
| 78  | 23740 | 22505 | 07489 | 85986 | 74420 | 21744 | 97711 | 36648 | 35620 |
| 79  | 32990 | 97446 | 03711 | 63824 | 07953 | 85965 | 87089 | 11687 | 92414 |
| 80  | 05310 | 24058 | 91946 | 78437 | 34365 | 82469 | 12430 | 84754 | 19354 |
| 81  | 21839 | 39937 | 27534 | 88913 | 49055 | 19218 | 47712 | 67677 | 51889 |
| 82  | 08833 | 42549 | 93981 | 94051 | 28382 | 83725 | 72643 | 64233 | 97252 |
| 83  | 58336 | 11139 | 47479 | 00931 | 91560 | 95372 | 97642 | 33856 | 54825 |
| 84  | 62032 | 91144 | 75478 | 47431 | 52726 | 30289 | 42411 | 91886 | 51818 |
| 85  | 45171 | 30557 | 53116 | 04118 | 58301 | 24375 | 65609 | 85810 | 18620 |
| 86  | 91611 | 62656 | 60128 | 35609 | 63698 | 78356 | 50682 | 22505 | 01692 |
| 87  | 55472 | 63819 | 86314 | 49174 | 93582 | 73604 | 78614 | 78849 | 23096 |
| 88  | 18573 | 09729 | 74091 | 53994 | 10970 | 86557 | 65661 | 41854 | 26037 |
| 89  | 60866 | 02955 | 90288 | 82136 | 83644 | 94455 | 06560 | 78029 | 98768 |
| 90  | 45043 | 55608 | 82767 | 60890 | 74646 | 79485 | 13619 | 98868 | 40857 |
| 91  | 17831 | 09737 | 79473 | 75945 | 28394 | 79334 | 70577 | 38048 | 03607 |
| 92  | 40137 | 03981 | 07585 | 18128 | 11178 | 32601 | 27994 | 05641 | 22600 |
| 93  | 77776 | 31343 | 14576 | 97706 | 16039 | 47517 | 43300 | 59080 | 80392 |
| 94  | 69605 | 44104 | 40103 | 95635 | 05635 | 81673 | 68657 | 09559 | 23510 |
| 95  | 19916 | 52934 | 26499 | 09821 | 87331 | 80993 | 61299 | 36979 | 73599 |
| 96  | 02606 | 58552 | 07678 | 56619 | 65325 | 30705 | 99582 | 53390 | 46357 |
| 97  | 65183 | 73160 | 87131 | 35530 | 47946 | 09854 | 18080 | 02321 | 05809 |
| 98  | 10740 | 98914 | 44916 | 11322 | 89717 | 88189 | 30143 | 52687 | 19420 |
| 99  | 98642 | 89822 | 71691 | 51573 | 83666 | 61642 | 46683 | 33761 | 47542 |
| 100 | 60139 | 25601 | 93663 | 25547 | 02654 | 94829 | 48672 | 28736 | 84994 |

# ACKNOWLEDGMENTS

The tables contained in this appendix have been adapted with permission from the following sources:

**Table A**  R. Clarke, A. Coladarch, and J. Caffrey, *Statistical Reasoning and Procedures*, Charles E. Merrill Publishers, Columbus, Ohio, 1965, Appendix 2.

**Table B**  R. S. Burington and D. C. May, *Handbook of Probability and Statistics with Tables*, 2nd ed., McGraw-Hill Book Company, New York, 1970.

**Table C**  H. B. Mann and D. R. Whitney, "On a Test of Whether One of Two Random Variables Is Stochastically Larger Than the Other," *Annals of Mathematical Statistics*, 18 (1947), 50–60, and D. Auble, "Extended Tables for the Mann–Whitney Statistic," *Bulletin of the Institute of Educational Research at Indiana University, 1*, No. 2 (1953), as used in Runyon and Haber, *Fundamentals of Behavioral Statistics*, 3rd ed., Addison-Wesley Publishing Company, Inc., Reading, Mass., 1976.

**Table D**  Fisher and Yates, *Statistical Tables for Biological, Agricultural, and Medical Research*, Longman Group Ltd., London (previously published by Oliver & Boyd Ltd., Edinburgh), 1974, Table III.

**Table E**  Fisher and Yates, *Statistical Tables for Biological, Agricultural, and Medical Research*, Longman Group Ltd., London (previously published by Oliver & Boyd Ltd., Edinburgh), 1974, Table VII.

**Table F**  G. W. Snedecor, *Statistical Methods*, 5th ed., Iowa State University Press, Ames, 1956.

**Table G**  E. S. Pearson and H. O. Hartley, eds., *Biometrika Tables for Statisticians*, Vol. 1, 3rd ed., Cambridge University Press, New York, 1966, Table 29.

**Table H**  Fisher and Yates, *Statistical Tables for Biological, Agricultural, and Medical Research*, Longman Group Ltd., London (previously published by Oliver & Boyd Ltd., Edinburgh), 1974, Table IV.

**Table I**  F. Wilcoxon, S. Katte, and R. A. Wilcox, *Critical Values and Probability Levels for the Wilcoxon Rank Sum Test and the Wilcoxon Signed Ranks Test*, American Cyanamid Co., New York, 1963, and F. Wilcoxon and R. A. Wilcox, *Some Rapid Approximate Statistical Procedures*, Lederle Laboratories, New York, 1964, as used in Runyon and Haber, *Fundamentals of Behavioral Statistics*, 3rd ed., Addison-Wesley Publishing Company, Inc., Reading, Mass., 1976.

**Table J**  RAND Corporation, *A Million Random Digits*, Free Press of Glencoe, Glencoe, Ill., 1955.

# GLOSSARY

**Alpha level** A probability level set by an investigator at the beginning of an experiment to limit the probability of making a Type I error. *(pp. 220, 224)*

**Arithmetic mean** The sum of the scores divided by the number of scores. In equation form,

$$\overline{X} = \frac{\sum X_i}{N} = \frac{X_1 + X_2 + X_3 + \cdots + X_N}{N}$$

*mean of a sample*

or $\quad \mu = \frac{\sum X_i}{N} = \frac{X_1 + X_2 + X_3 + \cdots + X_N}{N}$

*mean of a population set of scores*

where $\quad X_1, \ldots, X_N$ = raw scores
$\overline{X}$ (read "X bar") = mean of a sample set of scores
$\mu$ (read "mew") = mean of a population set of scores
$\sum$ (read "sigma") = summation sign
$N$ = number of scores

*(p. 67)*

**Beta** The probability of making a Type II error. *(p. 223)*

**Binomial distribution** A probability distribution that results when five conditions are met: (1) There is a series of $N$ trials; (2) on each trial there are only two possible outcomes; (3) on each trial, the two possible outcomes are mutually exclusive; (4) there is independence between the outcomes of each trial; and (5) the probability of each possible outcome on any trial stays the same from trial to trial. The binomial distribution gives each possible outcome of the $N$ trials and the probability of getting each of these outcomes. *(p. 200)*

**Comparison-wise error rate** The probability of making a Type I error for any of the possible comparisons in an experiment. *(p. 380)*

**Confidence interval** A range of values that probably contains the population value. *(p. 309)*

**Confidence limits** The values that state the boundaries of the confidence interval. *(p. 309)*

**Contingency table** A two-way table showing the contingency between two variables where the variables have been classified into mutually exclusive categories and the cell entries are frequencies. *(p. 434)*

**Continuous variable** A variable that theoretically can have an infinite number of values between adjacent units on the scale. *(p. 32)*

**Correlation coefficient** A quantitative expression of the magnitude and direction of a relationship. *(p. 111)*

**Critical region for rejection of the null hypothesis** The area under the curve that contains all the values of the statistic that allow rejection of the null hypothesis. *(p. 281)*

**Critical value of a statistic** The value of the statistic that bounds the critical region. *(p. 281)*

**Cumulative frequency distribution** The number of scores that fall below the upper real limit of each interval. *(p. 45)*

**Cumulative percentage distribution** The percentage of scores that fall below the upper real limit of each interval. *(p. 45)*

**Data** The measurements that are made on the subjects of an experiment. *(p. 7)*

**Degrees of freedom (df)** The number of scores that are free to vary in calculating a statistic. *(p. 299)*

**Dependent variable** The variable in an experiment that an investigator measures to determine the effect of the independent variable. *(p. 7)*

**Descriptive statistics** Techniques that are used to describe or characterize the obtained sample data. *(p. 10)*

**Deviation score** The distance of the raw score from the mean of its distribution. *(p. 77)*

**Discrete variable** A variable for which no values are possible between adjacent units on the scale. *(p. 32)*

**Eta squared** Biased estimate of the size of effect of the independent variable. *(p. 375)*

**Exhaustive set of events** A set that includes all of the possible events. *(p. 174)*

**Experiment-wise error rate** The probability of making one or more Type I errors for the full set of possible comparisons in an experiment. *(p. 380)*

**Factorial experiment** An experiment in which the effects of two or more factors are assessed and the treatments used are combinations of the levels of the factors. *(p. 398)*

**Frequency distribution** A listing of score values and their frequency of occurrence. *(p. 39)*

**Imperfect relationship** A positive or negative relationship for which all of the points do not fall on the line. *(p. 108)*

**Independence of two events** The occurrence of one event has no effect on the probability of occurrence of the other. *(p. 175)*

**Independent variable** The variable in an experiment that is systematically manipulated by an investigator. *(p. 6)*

**Inferential statistics** Techniques that use the obtained sample data to infer to populations. *(p. 10)*

**Interaction effect** The result observed when the effect of one factor is not the same at all levels of the other factor. *(p. 399)*

**Least-squares regression line** The prediction line that minimizes $\sum (Y - Y')^2$. *(p. 137)*

**Linear relationship** A relationship between two variables that can be most accurately represented by a straight line. *(p. 105)*

**Main effects** The effect of factor $A$ (averaged over the levels of factor $B$) and the effect of factor $B$ (averaged over the levels of factor $A$). *(p. 399)*

**Median (Mdn)** The scale value below which 50% of the scores fall. *(p. 72)*

**Mode** The most frequent score in the distribution. *(p. 74)*

**Mutually exclusive events** Two events that cannot occur together; that is, the occurrence of one precludes the occurrence of the other. *(p. 170)*

**Negative relationship** An inverse relationship between two variables. *(p. 107)*

**Negatively skewed curve** A curve on which most of the scores occur at the higher values, and the curve tails off toward the lower end of the horizontal axis. *(p. 58)*

**Null-hypothesis population** An actual or theoretical set of population scores that would result if the experiment were done on the entire population and the independent variable had no effect; it is used to test the validity of the null hypothesis. *(p. 269)*

**Omega squared** Unbiased estimate of the size of the effect of teh independent variable. *(p. 341)*

**$P_{null}$** The probability of getting a plus with any subject in the sample of the experiment when the independent variable has no effect (appropriate for sign test). *(p. 246)*

**$P_{real}$** The probability of getting a plus with any subject in the sample of the experiment when the independent variable has a real effect; the proportion of pluses in the population if the experiment were done on the entire population and the independent variable has a real effect (appropriate for sign test). *(p. 246)*

**Parameter** A number calculated on population data that quantifies a characteristic of the population. *(p. 7)*

**Pearson $r$** A measure of the extent to which paired scores occupy the same or opposite positions within their own distributions. *(p. 113)*

**Percentile** The value on the measurement scale below which a specified percentage of the scores in the distribution fall. *(p. 46)*

**Percentile point** *See* Percentile.

**Percentile rank (of a score)** The percentage of scores with values lower than the score in question. *(p. 50)*

**Perfect relationship** A positive or negative relationship for which all of the points fall on the line. *(p. 108)*

**Population** The complete set of individuals, objects, or scores that an investigator is interested in studying. *(p. 6)*

**Positive relationship** A direct relationship between two variables. *(p. 107)*

**Positively skewed curve** A curve on which most of the scores occur at the lower values, and the curve tails off toward the higher end of the horizontal axis. *(p. 58)*

**Power** The probability that the results of an experiment will allow rejection of the null hypothesis if the independent variable has a real effect. *(p. 246)*

**Probability of occurrence of $A$ or $B$** The probability of occurrence of $A$ plus the probability of occurrence of $B$ minus the probability of occurrence of both $A$ and $B$. *(p. 170)*

**Probability of occurrence of both $A$ and $B$** The probability of occurrence of $A$ times the probability of occurrence of $B$ given that $A$ has occurred. *(p. 175)*

**Random sample** A sample selected from the population by a process that ensures that (1) each possible sample of a given size has an equal chance of being selected and (2) all the members of the population have an equal chance of being selected into the sample. *(p. 164)*

**Range** The difference between the highest and lowest scores in the distribution. *(p. 76)*

**Real limits of a continuous variable** Those values that are above and below the recorded value by one-half of the smallest measuring unit of the scale. *(p. 33)*

**Regression** A topic that considers using the relationship between two or more variables for prediction. *(p. 135)*

**Relative frequency distribution** The proportion of the total number of scores that occur in each interval. *(p. 45)*

**Sample** A subset of the population. *(p. 6)*

**Sampling distribution of $F$** Gives all the possible $F$ values along with the $p(F)$ for each value, assuming sampling is random from the population. *(p. 359)*

**Sampling distribution of $t$** A probability distribution of the $t$ values that would occur if all possible different samples of a fixed size $N$ were drawn from the null-hypothesis population. It gives (1) all the possible different $t$ values for samples of size $N$ and (2) the probability of getting each value if sampling is random from the null-hypothesis population. *(p. 299)*

**Sampling distribution of the mean** A listing of all the values the mean can take, along with the proba-

bility of getting each value if sampling is random from the null-hypothesis population. *(p. 273)*

**Sampling distribution of a statistic** A listing of (1) all the values that the statistic can take and (2) the probability of getting each value under the assumption that it results from chance alone, or if sampling is random from the null-hypothesis population. *(pp. 268, 272)*

**Sampling with replacement** A method of sampling in which each member of the population selected for the sample is returned to the population before the next member is selected. *(p. 167)*

**Sampling without replacement** A method of sampling in which the members of the sample are not returned to the population before selecting subsequent members. *(p. 167)*

**Scatter plot** A graph of paired $X$ and $Y$ values. *(p. 104)*

**Skewed curve** A curve whose two sides do not coincide if the curve is folded in half; that is, a curve that is not symmetrical. *(p. 57)*

**Statistic** A number calculated on sample data that quantifies a characteristic of the sample. *(p. 7)*

**Symmetrical curve** A curve whose two sides coincide if the curve is folded in half. *(p. 57)*

**Type I error** A decision to reject the null hypothesis when the null hypothesis is true. *(p. 222)*

**Type II error** A decision to retain the null hypothesis when the null hypothesis is false. *(p. 222)*

**Variable** Any property or characteristic of some event, object, or person that may have different values at different times depending on the conditions. *(p. 6)*

**$z$ score** A transformed score that designates how many standard deviation units the corresponding raw score is above or below the mean. *(p. 89)*

# INDEX

Page numbers followed by "n" refer to notes at the bottom of the page or at the end of the chapter.

## TO THE OWNER OF THIS BOOK:

I hope that you have found *Understanding Statistics in the Behavioral Sciences, Eighth Edition*, useful. So that this book can be improved in a future edition, would you take the time to complete this sheet and return it? Thank you.

School and address: _____

_____

Department: _____

Instructor's name: _____

1. What I like most about this book is: _____

_____

_____

2. What I like least about this book is: _____

_____

_____

3. My general reaction to this book is: _____

_____

_____

4. The name of the course in which I used this book is: _____

_____

5. Were all of the chapters of the book assigned for you to read? _____

   If not, which ones weren't? _____

6. In the space below, or on a separate sheet of paper, please write specific suggestions for improving this book and anything else you'd care to share about your experience in using this book.

_____

_____

_____

_____

_____

OPTIONAL:

Your name: _____ Date: _____

May we quote you, either in promotion for *Understanding Statistics in the Behavioral Sciences, Eighth Edition*, or in future publishing ventures?

Yes: _____ No: _____

Sincerely yours,

Robert Pagano

FOLD HERE

------------------------------------------------------------------------------------------    ----------------------------

FOLD HERE

| Symbols | Meaning | Symbol First Occurs on Page: |
|---------|---------|------------------------------|
| $a_X$ | $X$-axis intercept for the least-squares regression line predicting $X$ given $Y$ | 144 |
| $a_Y$ | $Y$-axis intercept for the least-squares regression line predicting $Y$ given $X$ | 137 |
| $b_X$ | slope of the least-squares regression line for predicting $X$ given $Y$ | 144 |
| $b_Y$ | slope of the least-squares regression line for predicting $Y$ given $X$ | 137 |
| $c$ | number of columns in a contingency table | 437 |
|  | number of columns in a two-way ANOVA data table | 403 |
| cum $f$ | cumulative frequency | 46 |
| cum $f_L$ | frequency of scores below the lower real limit of the interval containing the percentile point | 48 |
| cum $f_P$ | frequency of scores below the percentile point | 47 |
| cum % | cumulative percentage | 46 |
| $D$ | difference between paired scores | 325 |
| $\bar{D}_{obt}$ | mean of the differences between paired scores | 325 |
| df | degrees of freedom | 300 |
| $df_B$ | between-group degrees of freedom | 365 |
| $df_C$ | column degrees of freedom | 406 |
| $df_R$ | row degrees of freedom | 405 |
| $df_{RC}$ | row $\times$ column degrees of freedom | 407 |
| $df_W$ | within-cells degrees of freedom | 404 |
|  | within-groups degrees of freedom | 364 |
| $F$ | ratio of two variance estimates | 359 |
| $f$ | frequency | 39 |
| $f_e$ | expected frequency | 429 |
| $f_i$ | frequency of the interval containing the percentile point | 49 |
| $f_o$ | observed frequency | 429 |
| $H_0$ | null hypothesis | 220 |
| $H_1$ | alternative hypothesis | 220 |
| $H_{obt}$ | statistic calculated with Kruskal–Wallis | 454 |
| $i$ | width of the interval | 44 |
| $k$ | number of groups or means | 364 |

*(continued)*

| Symbols | Meaning | Symbol First Occurs on Page: |
|---|---|---|
| Mdn | median | 72 |
| $N$ | total number of scores | 25 |
| | number of paired scores | 137 |
| $n_k$ | number of scores in the $k$th group | 70 |
| $P$ | in a two-event situation, the probability of one of the events | 174 |
| $p$ | probability | 168 |
| $p(A)$ | probability of event $A$ | 168 |
| $p(B \mid A)$ | probability of $B$ given $A$ has occurred | 175 |
| $P_{null}$ | the proportion of pluses in the population if the independent variable has no effect | 246 |
| $P_{real}$ | the proportion of pluses in the population if the independent variable has a real effect | 246 |
| $Q$ | in a two-event situation, the probability of one of the events | 174 |
| | Studentized range statistic | 385 |
| $r$ | Pearson product moment correlation coefficient | 112 |
| | number of means encompassed by $\bar{X}_i$ and $\bar{X}_j$ | 386 |
| | number of rows in a contingency table | 437 |
| | number of rows in a two-way ANOVA data table | 403 |
| $r^2$ | coefficient of determination | 120 |
| $R^2$ | multiple coefficient of determination | 155 |
| | squared multiple correlation | 155 |
| $r_b$ | biserial correlation coefficient | 121 |
| $r_s$ | Spearman rank order correlation coefficient, rho | 121 |
| $s$ | standard deviation of a sample | 78 |
| | estimate of a population standard deviation | 78 |
| $s_D$ | standard deviation of sample difference scores | 324 |
| $s_X$ | standard deviation of the $X$ variable | 151 |
| $s_Y$ | standard deviation of the $Y$ variable | 151 |
| $s_{Y \mid X}$ | standard error of estimate when predicting $Y$ given $X$ | 147 |
| $s_{\bar{X}}$ | estimated standard error of the mean | 298 |
| $s_{\bar{X}_1 - \bar{X}_2}$ | estimated standard error of the difference between sample means | 333 |
| $s^2$ | variance of a sample | 82 |
| $s_B{}^2$ | between-groups variance estimate | 364 |
| $s_C{}^2$ | column variance estimate | 400 |
| $s_R{}^2$ | row variance estimate | 400 |

# SYMBOLS

Listed below are the symbols we have used in this textbook. The meaning of each symbol is given to the right of the symbol. The last column gives the page number where the symbol first appears.

| Greek Letters | Meaning | Symbol First Occurs on Page: |
|---|---|---|
| $\alpha$ | threshold probability level for rejecting $H_0$; with a continuous variable, the probability of a Type I error | 220 |
| $\beta$ | probability of a Type II error | 245 |
| $\chi^2$ | chi-square | 429 |
| $\phi$ | correlation coefficient for dichotomous variables | 121 |
| $\eta$ | curvilinear correlation coefficient | 121 |
| $\eta^2$ | estimate of size of effect | 375 |
| $\mu$ | mean of a population | 67 |
| $\mu_D$ | mean of the population of difference scores | 324 |
| $\mu_{\text{null}}$ | mean of the null-hypothesis population | 288 |
| $\mu_{\text{real}}$ | mean of population when there is a real effect | 288 |
| $\mu_{\bar{X}}$ | mean of the sampling distribution of the mean | 274 |
| $\mu_{\bar{X}_1 - \bar{X}_2}$ | mean of the sampling distribution of the difference between sample means | 331 |
| $\rho$ | population linear correlation coefficient | 313 |
| $\Sigma$ | the sum of | 25 |
| $\sigma$ | standard deviation of a population | 78 |
| $\sigma^2$ | variance of a population | 82 |
| $\sigma_{\bar{X}}$ | standard error of the mean | 274 |
| $\sigma_{\bar{X}}^2$ | variance of the sampling distribution of the mean | 275 |
| $\sigma_{\bar{X}_1 - \bar{X}_2}$ | standard error of the difference beween sample means | 331 |
| $\hat{\omega}^2$ | estimate of size of effect | 341 |